Handbook of Behavioral Finance

Edited by

Brian Bruce

Founding Director, The Center for Investment Research
CEO and Chief Investment Officer, Hillcrest Asset Management

Edward Elgar
Cheltenham, UK • Northampton, MA, USA

Published by
Edward Elgar Publishing Limited
The Lypiatts
15 Lansdown Road
Cheltenham
Glos GL50 2JA
UK

Edward Elgar Publishing, Inc.
William Pratt House
9 Dewey Court
Northampton
Massachusetts 01060
USA

A catalogue record for this book is available from the British Library

Library of Congress Control Number: 2010925945

MIX
Paper from responsible sources
FSC® C018575

ISBN 978 1 84844 651 9 (cased)

Typeset by Servis Filmsetting Ltd, Stockport, Cheshire
Printed and bound by MPG Books Group, UK

Contents

Contributors

Lucy F. Ackert, Michael J. Coles College of Business, Kennesaw State University and Research Department, Federal Reserve Bank of Atlanta, USA

Julie Agnew, Assistant Professor of Finance & Economics, The College of William & Mary, VA, USA

Kremena Bachmann, University of Zurich, Swiss Banking Institute, Switzerland

Thomas Berry, Department of Finance, DePaul University, IL, USA

Natividad Blasco, Department of Accounting and Finance, Faculty of Economics, University of Zaragoza, Spain

Pablo Calafiore, Department of Economics and Finance, College of Business Administration, The University of Texas-Pan American, USA

Lee-Lee Chong, Multimedia University, Faculty of Management, Malaysia

Bryan K. Church, College of Management, Georgia Tech, USA

Anna M. Cianci, Department of Accounting, LeBow College of Business, Drexel University, PA, USA

Pilar Corredor, Department of Business Administration, Public University of Navarre, Spain

Satoris S. Culbertson, Department of Psychology, College of Arts and Sciences, Kansas State University, USA

Sinclair Davidson, School of Economics, Finance and Marketing, RMIT University, Melbourne, Australia

Kirsten Ely, School of Business and Economics, Sonoma State University, CA, USA

Tom Evans, Associate Professor, Department of Geography, Indiana University, USA

Dimas Mateus Fazio, University of Brasilia

Sandra Ferreruela, Department of Accounting and Finance, University School of Business Studies of Zaragoza, Spain

Suzanne O'Curry Fogel, Department of Marketing, DePaul University, IL, USA

Gavin Francis, Managing Director of Pareto Investment Management Limited, London

Ryan Garvey, Duquesne University, PA, USA

Christoph Gort, Harcourt Investment Consulting AG

Thorsten Hens, University of Zurich, Swiss Banking Institute, Switzerland

Daniel C. Indro, Associate Professor of Finance, Penn State University – Great Valley, USA

H. Joel Jeffrey, Department of Computer Science, Northern Illinois University, USA

Hugh Kelley, Associate Professor, Department of Economics, National University of Ireland, Galway

Erich Kirchler, Professor of Psychology at the University of Vienna, Austria

Ming-Ming Lai, Multimedia University, Faculty of Management, Malaysia

Byunghwan Lee, Assistant Professor of Accounting Department, School of Business Administration, California State Polytechnic University, Pomona, USA

Mirjam Lehenkari, Postdoctoral Researcher, University of Oulu, Finland

Boris Maciejovsky, Assistant Professor in Marketing at Imperial College, London

Jeff Madura, SunTrust Bank Professor of Finance, Florida Atlantic University, USA

Anthony Murphy, Hartford College, CT, USA

John O'Brien, Associate Professor of Accounting and Experimental Economics, Tepper School of Business, Carnegie Mellon University, PA, USA

Noriyuki Okuyama, Managing Director of Pareto Investment Management Limited, London

Jukka Perttunen, Professor of Finance, University of Oulu, Finland

Vikash Ramiah, School of Economics, Finance and Marketing, RMIT University, Melbourne, Australia

Nivine Richie, Assistant Professor of Finance, Sigmund Weis School of Business, Susquehanna University, PA, USA

K. Sivaramakrishnan, Professor & Bauer Endowed Chair of Accounting, Department of Accountancy & Taxation, C.T. Bauer College of Business, University of Houston, TX, USA

Gökçe Soydemir, Department of Economics and Finance, College of Business Administration, University of Texas-Pan American, USA

Lisa Szykman, Associate Professor of Marketing, The College of William & Mary, VA, USA

Benjamin Miranda Tabak, Banco Central do Brasil and Catholic University of Brasilia

Siow-Hooi Tan, Multimedia University, Faculty of Management, Malaysia

Rahul Verma, Department of Finance, Accounting and CIS, College of Business, University of Houston – Downtown, TX, USA

Mei Wang, Assistant Professor of Finance and Financial Markets, Swiss Banking Institute, University of Zurich, Switzerland

Martin Weber, Chair of Business Administration and Finance at the University of Mannheim, Germany

Jiawen Yang, Professor of International Business, George Washington University, Washington, DC, USA

Lili Zhu, Assistant Professor of Finance, Shenandoah University, VA, USA

Preface

The journey to produce this book began in 1998 when The Institute of Psychology and Markets was founded to study the impact of psychology on investor decision making. As the new century approached, the understanding of markets was moving beyond the perception that financial market participants are perfectly rational. The Institute was founded on the belief that new research would explore important dynamic processes previously ignored by traditional finance.

The Institute was interested in studying ways in which psychology played a role in understanding how financial markets function. The goal was to address issues surrounding the integration of many disciplines into the field of investing including social psychology, group psychology, psychiatry, organizational behavior, accounting, marketing, sociology, anthropology, behavioral economics, finance and decision making.

This initial meeting, held in Aspen, Colorado in December 1998, was limited to 25 participants and included some of the most important minds in the study of behavioral finance.

The Advisory Board of the Institute consisted of a diverse group of psychiatrists, psychologists, economists and market practitioners. They included:

Professor Brian Bruce, Department of Finance, Southern Methodist University
Mr David Dreman, Chairman of Dreman Value Advisors
Dr Richard A. Geist, affiliated with the Harvard Medical School
Dr Peter Neubauer, Clinical Professor of Psychiatry, New York University and Chairman Emeritus, Columbia University, Center for Psychoanalytic Training and Research
Professor Robert Olson, Department of Finance, California State University, Chico
Professor Fred Renwick, Department of Finance, New York University
Dr John W. Schott, affiliated with the Harvard Medical School
Professor Paul Slovic, President of Decision Research, Eugene, Oregon
Professor Vernon Smith, Director of Research and Education, University of Arizona
Professor Albert Solnit, Pediatrics and Psychiatry, Yale University
Mr Arnold Wood, President, Martingale Asset Management

As a result of this group's efforts came the launching of the Journal of Psychology and Markets (currently known as The Journal of Behavioral Finance) in January 1999. The journal aimed to be a source for sophisticated analysis of developments in the rapidly expanding new area of behavioral finance. The journal brought together leaders in many fields to address the implications of current work on individual and group emotion, cognition and behavior in markets. These included specialists in personality, social, cognitive and clinical psychology; psychiatry; organizational behavior; accounting; marketing; sociology; anthropology; behavioral economics; finance and the multidisciplinary study of judgment and decision making.

This book takes the foundations created by the *Journal of Behavioral Finance* and strives to bring to readers new interdisciplinary research and theory to build a body of knowledge about psychological influences on market fluctuations and contribute to a new understanding of markets that can improve investment decision making. Offering penetrating insights into the performance of today's financial markets, the book is an indispensable resource for academics and practitioners who want to utilize behavioral concepts to understand the 'how, what, when and where' of investing. We hope you enjoy the results of this effort.

Brian Bruce

Abbreviations

AAII	American Association of Individual Investors
AMEX	American Stock Exchange
ANOVA	analysis of variance
APT	arbitrage pricing theory
BAPM	behavioural asset pricing model
BSA	buy-side analyst
CAPM	capital asset pricing model
CFO	chief finance officer
CRA	conditional risk attribution
CRRA	constant relative risk aversion
DMA	direct market access
EMH	efficient markets hypothesis
EPS	earnings per share
ETF	exchange-traded funds
FDI	foreign direct investment
FGM	first-generation model
GCRA	generalized conditional risk attribution
GDP	gross domestic product
II	Investor Intelligence
IMF	International Monetary Fund
IPO	initial public offering
IRF	impulse response function
IRS	Internal Revenue Service (USA)
KLSE	Kuala Lumpur Stock Exchange
KLSEB	Kuala Lumpur Stock Exchange Berhad
MCA	market contribution to asymmetry
MIS	management information systems
NAV	net asset value
NYSE	New York Stock Exchange
OLS	ordinary least squares
PGR	proportion of gains realized
PLR	proportion of losses realized
PPP	purchasing power parity
RM	ringgit Malaysia
ROA	return on assets
ROC	receiver operating characteristic
SD	standard deviation (std dev.)
SES	Singapore Stock Exchange
SEU	subjective expected utility

SGM	second-generation model
SSA	sell-side analyst
VAR	vector auto regression
WTI	West Texas Intermediate (oil)

Introduction

Brian Bruce

The following paragraphs outline the structure of the handbook.

In Chapter 1, the results of an asset market experiment, in which 64 subjects trade two assets on eight markets in a computerized continuous double auction, indicate that objectively irrelevant information influences trading behavior. It was found that positively and negatively framed information leads to a particular trading pattern, but leaves trading prices and volume unaffected. The experiment also provided support for the disposition effect. Participants who experience a gain sell their assets more rapidly than participants who experience a loss, and positively framed subjects generally sell their assets later than negatively framed subjects.

Chapter 2 examines whether information overload might partially explain why defined contribution plan participants tend to limit their information search and use simple heuristics. The results of the experiments performed suggest that the success of certain plan features depends strongly on the financial background of the participant. We find that low-knowledge individuals opt for the default allocation more often than high-knowledge individuals. The results emphasize the importance of plan design, especially the selection of plan defaults, and the need to improve the financial literacy of participants.

The third chapter examines investment decisions using the fundamental investment decision matrix to define investment success and investment error. The framework is effective in describing passive investment. Conditional risk attribution (CRA) is a tool for identifying the asymmetric returns available to passive investors. The geometric interpretation is expanded into generalized conditional risk attribution (GCRA) to measure the effectiveness of active decision-making processes.

Recent studies have documented a strong tendency for individual investors to delay realizing capital losses, while realizing gains prematurely. This tendency has been termed the 'disposition effect.' In the fourth chapter individual investors were surveyed and it was found that more respondents reported regret about holding on to a losing stock too long than about selling a winning stock too soon. This finding suggests that individual investors are consistently engaging in behavior that they have been warned can cost them money and that they might regret later.

Chapter 5 presents a study of overreaction, motivated by the unique characteristics of exchange-traded funds (ETFs), which should contribute to market efficiency. Since ETFs represent portfolios of stocks, they may not be as susceptible to short-term overreaction as individual stocks. In addition, they can be traded throughout the day and can be sold short, which might further limit potential overreaction. Yet the tradability of ETFs may allow unusual pressure on ETF prices that is not initiated by price movements of all the component stocks.

Chapter 6 examines the intentional herd behavior of market participants within different international markets using a new approach that permits the detection of even moderate herding over the whole range of market return. This approach compares the cross-sectional deviation of returns of each of the selected markets with the cross-sectional deviation of returns of an 'artificially created' market free of herding effects. It is suggested that intentional herding is likely to be better revealed when we analyze familiar stocks.

Chapter 7 synthesizes the financial crisis contagion literature through the gravity model from physics and tests the hypothesis that the severity of contagion relates positively to trade and financial linkages but negatively to psychic distance between countries, when macroeconomic fundamentals and institutional factors are controlled for. The psychic distance variable, a behavioral predictor constructed along four dimensions, including geographic distance, common language, development level and common membership, is of key interest in this study.

Chapter 8 examines how commissions influence trading behavior by analyzing a unique data set of the equity trades of both individual and institutional active traders. Individual traders pay higher trading costs than institutional traders. As a result, they engage in more risky trading behaviors in order to cover these costs. Individual traders also trade significantly less because of their higher costs of trading. Individual traders tend to trade higher-priced stocks, hold their trades longer, and they experience much larger price swings than institutional traders. This leads individual traders to realize more dramatic gains and losses on their round trips.

Economic simulations typically focus almost exclusively on economic variables. If non-economic factors are included at all, it is usually in some form of utility function calculation. Chapter 9 presents a model that allows formal specification of a much broader range of factors, processes and quantities involved in human communities. The phenomena include the hierarchically structured social practices of the group, the principles that underlie choices in the community, and the recognizable positions or statuses in the community. This allows one to model intrinsic or expressive behavior, capturing the concept of multi-aspect identity and the impact of the principles of the group on individual behaviors, all in formal and quantitative form. Having these factors represented formally enables the creation of significantly more realistic simulations incorporating a much wider range of variables, particularly when the economic facts and quantities of interest are affected by and affect several other kinds of factors that are not, on the face of it, economic.

Chapter 10 examines the relationship between net aggregate equity fund flow and investor sentiment using weekly flow data. Using sentiment indicators from the American Association of Individual Investors and Investor Intelligence, it was found that net aggregate equity fund flow in the current week is higher when individual investors became more bullish in the previous and current weeks. Moreover, higher net aggregate equity fund flow in the current week induces newsletter writers to become more bullish in the subsequent week. The relationship between net aggregate equity fund flow and investor sentiment remains strong even after accounting for the effects of risk premium and inflation. Overall, the evidence suggests that the behavior of equity fund investors is influenced not only by economic fundamentals, but also by investor sentiment.

Chapter 11 provides experimental evidence about the differences between buy-side analyst (BSA) and sell-side analyst (SSA) earnings forecasts, and investigates both motivational and cognitive determinants of these differences. The results indicate that, as expected, SSAs make more favorable earnings forecast revisions than BSAs, and, consistent with prior research, analyst forecasts are greater as forecast horizon increases. In addition, while information variability does not contribute to optimism, differences in trend and recency do. Specifically, analysts act as if they discount both past earnings information with a decreasing trend and negative recent information when revising their forecasts. Directions for additional research on motivational and cognitive determinants of analyst forecasts are offered.

Empirical studies show that people tend to be overconfident about the precision of their knowledge, leading to miscalibration. Chapter 12 discusses this miscalibration, highlighting the decision makers of Swiss pension plans. These decision makers provided too narrow confidence intervals when asked to estimate past returns of various assets. Their confidence intervals are also very narrow in their forecasts of future returns. They are less miscalibrated, however, than the laypeople sample. Individual differences between the participants' degree of overconfidence are large and stable across those two different tasks. In a linear regression model the evidence shows that the size of participants' confidence intervals is linked to individual characteristics. In the sample, younger people with a degree from university and with more experience in finance provide larger intervals than older people without such an education and with less experience.

Chapter 13 reviews the hypotheses from a recent paper on rational versus bounded rationality, and discusses the results of stronger tests conducted using data from two complete business cycles to examine whether they can be validated beyond one business cycle. The original study tested two contrasting theoretical approaches, rational versus boundedly rational, to understanding the growth forecasting behavior of financial analysts as well as related decision making by managers.

Chapter 14 focuses on a model of forecasting behavior in which analysts do not always make forecasts that are consistent with their private information. Using this model to provide theoretical direction, the authors conducted experimental sessions to investigate individual forecasting behavior. The results were further examined to provide a less disperse distribution.

Chapter 15 argues that behavioural finance not only provides a theoretical foundation for financial advising, but also has highly practical relevance. To support this claim, this chapter reviews the main paradigms of traditional finance, expected utility theory and mean–variance analysis, and showed that mean–variance analysis does not serve well as a rational benchmark for investment decision making. This is followed by a short overview of the main insights of behavioral finance, which showed which aspects of the observed investor's behavior should be accepted as part of his preferences and which aspects should be corrected because they lead to irrational decisions.

Chapter 16 investigates whether traders' state-dependent expectations biases can account for anomalous country fund discount movements. A multiple-agent asset pricing model that includes both rational traders and traders who display biases in expectations formation following market states with large amounts of price variance or CNN financial news is provided. Importantly, traders' biased behavior is based on evidence of state-dependent over- or underreaction biases observed in asset price forecasting experiments. Closed-form solutions from a multi-agent pricing model predict a multiple-driver property of fund prices. Empirical tests for these drivers' influence in field data finds that up to 21 percent of the out-of-sample country fund discount variance can be explained by dummies representing the occurrence of behavioral bias trigger states.

Recent literature reports evidence on investor behavior that is inconsistent with traditional finance theory. One currently being debated is behavioral irrationality, the tendency of investors to hold losing investments too long and sell winning investments too soon, a phenomenon known as the disposition effect. Chapter 17 analyzes the trading records of all individual investors in the Finnish stock market and documents that capital losses reduce the selling propensity of investors. There is, however, no opposite effect identifiable with respect to capital gains. The results also showed, somewhat surprisingly, that both positive and negative historical returns significantly reinforce the negative association between the selling propensity of investors and capital losses. While these findings offer no direct support for the disposition effect, they do suggest that investors are loss averse.

Chapter 18 analyzes the effect of business and consumer confidence indexes on the returns of the Brazilian stock market using a model that accounts for fundamentals (rational) and noise components (irrational) of confidence indexes on the São Paulo leading index Bovespa. Consistent with previous studies for the US markets, statistically significant impacts of rational components of the indexes on Bovespa were found. In particular, there are immediate positive responses of the stock market returns to rational feedback, but negative responses of stock market returns to irrational feedback corrected by positive responses in the upcoming periods. There are positive effects of past stock market returns on rational but not on irrational feedback. The results support the economic-fundamentals-based arguments of stock returns.

Chapter 19 describes the interaction between noise traders and information traders. It is not assumed that information traders are error-free. Instead information traders make mistakes, leading to underreaction and overreaction. Information traders may even add to pricing errors in the market. These interactions are captured in an information-adjusted noise model. The model is tested using data from the Australian Stock Exchange. This market has a continuous information disclosure regime that allows a determination of when information is released to the market. Evidence is presented that is consistent with the notion that the market is often informationally inefficient.

Chapter 20 investigates behavioral effects known as illusion of control and ambiguity aversion using an experiment with business and economics students in Brazil. Empirical results suggest that people present both ambiguity aversion and illusion of control. Nonetheless, most agents are not willing to pay a premium to reduce or eliminate ambiguity aversion and to gain 'control.' These results share some similarities with results for developed markets, but it seems that cultural differences may play a role in these results.

Chapter 21 examines the investment practices of Malaysian institutional investors during bullish and bearish periods. The factors and forces that drive the Malaysian stock market are also identified. The investors used a great deal of information within and outside the firm before making any stock selection. The analysis of fundamentals appears to be the most popular method for share appraisal. The survey findings demonstrated that Malaysian investors appeared to be rational and prudent in making financial decisions.

PART I

BEHAVIORAL BIASES

1 Framing effects, selective information and market behavior: an experimental analysis

Erich Kirchler, Boris Maciejovsky and Martin Weber

INTRODUCTION

Communication about asset return distribution is a central issue in finance. Investment advisors are legally obligated to inform clients about potential investment risks, which are usually expressed as the variance or standard deviation of the underlying distribution of the investment's future returns. Investors are implicitly assumed to accurately perceive and interpret statistical information, irrespective of how that information is presented.

In recent years, many new ways of acquiring financial information have become available, with the main source, of course, being the Internet. Yahoo!Finance, for instance, offers free market information, business news and personal finance plans, while BigCharts allows investors to create personalized interactive charts. Market data provider eSignal even assumes a positive relationship between information quantity and investment success by promising 'You'll make more, because you'll know more.'

Evidence suggests that investors generally benefit from the provision of information. Empirical studies, however, indicate that more information does not necessarily lead to more knowledge. In the psychological literature, this is referred to as the illusion of knowledge, and is confirmed empirically for many decision domains. For example, Park (2001) shows that even when news media recipients are socially involved with issues covered in the media, they are prone to the illusion of knowledge. The tendency increases the more recipients use the media.

In the finance domain, Barber and Odean (2001) investigate the performance of investors who switched from phone-based trading to internet trading. While these traders initially beat the market by about 3 percent prior to going online, their performance decreased afterward, resulting in a performance of 2 percent below the market. Similarly, Choi et al. (2002) report evidence of underperformance in the market timing of online traders in 401(k) plans. Access to vast quantities of investment data on the Internet, therefore, does not necessarily imply better performance.

Information plays an important role not only in individual investment decisions, but also in market environments. Market efficiency requires that aggregate market prices will not be affected by either objectively irrelevant information, or by selectively distributed information. For example, if some traders receive a positive signal about an asset's likely returns, and an equal number receive the opposite signal, this information, because it is completely revealed, should not affect aggregate market prices. Thus, while individual investors may be prone to biases like the illusion of knowledge, aggregate market prices are considered unbiased.

This chapter focuses on the communication and the quality of information in the context of a competitive asset market. We investigate the impact of objectively irrelevant information on trading behavior by drawing upon a novel type of framing. Traders are confronted with randomly distributed selective information about the performance of potential investments. The information is provided in either a positive or a negative frame, and is essentially irrelevant to the decision. Since we symmetrically distribute the additional information among traders, aggregate market behavior is expected to remain unaffected. In addition, we also investigate the robustness of the disposition effect in a competitive market environment with available real-time data.

Our results indicate that objectively irrelevant information does influence trading behavior. Moreover, positively and negatively framed information leads to a particular trading pattern, but leaves trading prices and trading volume unaffected. Our findings also support the disposition effect. Participants who experience a gain sell their assets more rapidly than those who experience a loss. This effect is further moderated by framing: positively framed market participants generally sell their assets later than negatively framed participants.

The next section discusses framing effects and the disposition effect. We introduce the experimental design and the procedure in the section that follows it. The third section covers the results, and the final section discusses our findings.

FRAMING EFFECTS

Expected utility theory assumes descriptive invariance, which implies that different representations of the same choice problem should yield the same preference. However, several empirical studies indicate that this axiom is frequently violated in individual decision making. McNeil et al. (1982), for example, show that the same medical statistics, framed either in terms of mortality rates or in terms of survival rates, lead to different preferences. Framing effects are also observed in decisions involving risky lotteries and monetary payoffs (Kahneman and Tversky, 1983; Tversky and Kahneman, 1981). More recently, Statman (1995) and Kahneman and Riepe (1998) have applied the concept of framing to financial decisions, such as dollar-cost averaging.

Weber et al. (2000) investigated the impact of endowment framing on market prices in an experimental asset market. Participants were given either (1) cash plus a certain amount of positively valued risky assets (long position, positive framing), or (2) a larger amount of cash and certain state-contingent liabilities (short position, negative framing). In terms of final wealth, the endowments were identical. In line with the predictions of prospect theory, Weber et al. (2000) found that overpricing[1] was observed more often for negatively framed market participants than for positively framed participants.

In contrast to the Weber et al. (2000) study, where participants' actual initial endowments were altered, we investigate whether framing effects are also robust under weaker conditions, for example, when participants only obtain different and more importantly irrelevant information.

Our experimental procedure differs from the way framing effects were originally studied by Tversky and Kahneman (1981). Their subjects were presented with scenarios in which a hypothetical decision problem was semantically framed in terms of 'gains' or 'losses.' However, the concept of framing in studies emphasizing the role of language in the decision problem lacks conclusive empirical evidence. Kühberger (1995) found that a variation of missing items of information in the decision problem produced markedly different framing effects. Moreover, with fully described decision problems, no framing effects emerged at all.

However, the results of a meta-analysis of 136 empirical studies indicate that the framing effect is a generally reliable phenomenon (Kühberger, 1998). A further meta-analysis, which focused particularly on Asian disease-like studies, indicates that risk preference depends on the size of the payoff, the probability level, and the type of goods at stake (Kühberger et al., 1999).

In our experimental procedure, we use a novel type of framing that is not based on semantic variations of a decision problem. Instead, participants are informed that dividends are randomly determined and drawn from a normal distribution with a commonly known fixed μ and fixed σ, where we assume that μ is the aspirational reference payoff. For a given probability p, p between 0 and 0.5, we let $\underline{Xp}$ and $\overline{Xp}$ denote the $100p$ and $100(1 - p)$ percentiles, respectively. For a given p, subjects are told that dividends will be less than $\underline{Xp}$ with probability p (negative framing), or that dividends will exceed $\overline{Xp}$ with probability p (positive framing). We distinguish between two independent markets, A and B, in which percentile information follows two different probabilities. The framed information on market A deviates more extremely from μ than the framed information on market B ($p_A < p_B$).

Our experimental approach is also related to the 'anchoring and adjustment' bias (Tversky and Kahneman, 1974), a sequential decision situation in which initial information serves as an anchor from which adjustments in the decision process are made insufficiently.[2] In our design, the positively and negatively deviating dividend information represents the initial information, the anchor. If subjects respond to this additional percentile information, we expect trading behavior to be influenced systematically. This is because positive information should increase traders' dividend expectations and negative information should lower them, leading to a particular trading pattern. Positively framed buyers are expected to purchase assets from negatively framed sellers, and negatively framed sellers are expected to sell their assets to positively framed buyers.

If the framed information does have a systematic impact on traders' dividend expectations, we hypothesize that there will be differential trading activity on markets A and B. Because the additional irrelevant information deviates more strongly from the aspirational reference payoff μ on market A, we expect that the more extreme information on this market will create more diverging dividend expectations on the part of the traders. We assume this will increase the likelihood that pairs of participants willing to trade will actually meet on the market.

The experimental design also allows us to investigate whether framing effects vanish if the decision problem is fully described, as suggested by Kühberger (1995). The market possesses complete information in our experiment, as positively and negatively framed information is symmetrically distributed among traders.

One might argue that the percentile information in our approach serves two different roles: an informational role, and a framing role. From a normative perspective, the additional percentile information is logically redundant. Nevertheless, knowledge of the mean and the standard deviation of the normal distribution may be perceived as useful in the decision-making process, for example, to learn about the shape of the distribution.

Assuming that information dissemination takes place,[3] however, rules out the informational role, since the redundant percentile information was symmetrically distributed to market participants with prior statistical training. Any behavioral regularities observed are therefore likely to be due only to the framing role.

DISPOSITION EFFECT

The disposition effect is one implication of prospect theory (Kahneman and Tversky, 1979, Tversky and Kahneman, 1992). In contrast to the utility function implied by expected utility theory, the value function *v* postulated by prospect theory is defined in terms of gains and losses relative to a reference point, not in terms of absolute levels of final wealth. Prospect theory assumes that the value function is concave for gains and convex for losses. In a financial context, therefore, we expect that winner assets will be sold more readily than loser assets in order to collect the gain and 'repair' the loss, respectively (Shefrin and Statman, 1985).

This hypothesis has been supported empirically for field data (Heisler, 1994; Odean, 1998), and in experimental asset markets (Heilmann et al., 2000; Weber and Camerer, 1998). Odean (1998) analyzed trading records for 10 000 accounts at a large discount brokerage house and found that investors held losing stocks for a median of 124 days, while winners were held for only 104 days. Using an experimental call market, Heilmann et al. (2000) showed that the number of assets offered and sold was higher during periods of rising trading prices than during periods of falling trading prices.

In contrast to Heilmann et al. (2000), who used the price of the previous trading period as the reference point, we focus on individual behavior. We define the reference point, as Weber and Camerer (1998) did, as the subject's purchase price. But unlike the experimental procedure of Weber and Camerer (1998), which determined prices by a random process, our market prices are determined solely by the market participants themselves on a computerized experimental asset market.

We contribute to the existing literature by studying the disposition effect in the context of a competitive market environment using available real-time data. We expect that purchase prices that are lower than the previous trading price will imply a gain and lead to more rapid selling, while purchase prices that are higher than the previous trading price will imply a loss and lead to less rapid selling.

THE EXPERIMENT

Participants

Our experiment consisted of eight sessions of an experimental asset market. There were 64 participants, all students at either Vienna University or the Vienna University of Economics and Business Administration. Forty-nine were economics students; the remaining 15 were enrolled in other social science disciplines. All participants had taken at least introductory courses in statistics.

There were 22 females and 42 males, aged 19 to 31 (M = 22.52, SD = 2.90). On

Table 1.1 Positive and negative dividend information for all periods – markets A and B

	Market and (Period)	$\sigma_1 = 20$ $\underline{Xp} - \overline{Xp}$	Market and (Period)	$\sigma_2 = 30$ $\underline{Xp} - \overline{Xp}$	Market and (Period)	$\sigma_3 = 40$ $\underline{Xp} - \overline{Xp}$
$\mu_1 = 95$	*A*(1)	56–134	*A*(2)	36–154	*A*(3)	17–174
	B(9)	92–98	*B*(8)	91–99	*B*(7)	90–100
$\mu_2 = 135$	*A*(4)	96–174	*A*(5)	76–194	*A*(6)	57–214
	B(6)	132–138	*B*(5)	131–139	*B*(4)	130–140
$\mu_3 = 105$	*A*(7)	66–144	*A*(8)	46–164	*A*(9)	27–184
	B(3)	102–108	*B*(2)	101–109	*B*(1)	100–110

average, participants earned €19.14, with a standard deviation of €14.94. The experiment took about 2 hours and 15 minutes.

Experimental Design

The experiment was conducted in a 2 × 2 factorial design in order to study the interaction of differently framed participants within one market. The independent variables were (1) the framing of dividend information (positively versus negatively) as a between-subjects factor, and (2) the probability of the framed information as a within-subjects factor (low versus high probability; $p_A = 0.05$ and $p_B = 0.45$). Participants were randomly assigned to one of the two framing conditions. All were informed that dividends would be randomly drawn from a normal distribution with a μ of 95, 105 or 135 and a σ of 20, 30 or 40. See Table 1.1 for the combination and sequence of μ and σ. In order to keep subjects' attention levels high, we balanced μ and σ across trading periods.

Prior to the trading periods, participants were given the actual μ and σ as well as additional irrelevant percentile information, $\underline{Xp}$ (negative framing) and $\overline{Xp}$ (positive framing). Figure 1.1 shows what information was available to subjects at the beginning of the trading periods.

Experimental Procedure

The experiment consisted of four phases:

1. We measured subjective propensity toward risk by using certainty equivalents and binary lottery choices to control for possible differences in individual risk attitude.
2. We opened the experimental asset market and assets were traded.
3. Participants were asked to complete a short questionnaire.
4. We repeated the procedure to control for risk attitude. The exact sequence of events in the experiment is shown in Figure 1.2.

Phase 1

After brief instructions, participants were asked to reveal their certainty equivalent for a lottery that offers a payoff of 100 experimental currency units (ECUs)[4] with a probability of $p = 0.50$ and zero otherwise. They were also asked to make seven decisions

In this period, dividends are randomly drawn from a normal distribution with a mean of 95 ECU and a standard deviation of 20 ECU. With a probability of 5 percent the next dividend will be larger (smaller) or equal to 134 ECU (56 ECU). This means that on average in five out of 100 cases the observed dividend will be larger (smaller) or equal to 134 ECU (56 ECU).

Note: The information provided to subjects in the negative framing condition is displayed in parentheses.

Figure 1.1 Available information at the beginning of the first trading period of market A for positively and negatively framed subjects

among risky lotteries.[5] The payoffs of the lotteries are listed in Table 1.2. As a control for position effects, the lotteries were systematically varied with respect to $a1$ (the highest possible payoff), $a2$ (the lowest possible payoff), A (certain payoff), and the sequence of $a1/a2$ (risky payoff).

The certainty equivalent allows us to infer participants' attitudes toward risk. More precisely, it allows us to discriminate between risk aversion, risk neutrality and risk-seeking behavior. A certainty equivalent that is lower than the expected value of the lottery, which is 50 ECUs, indicates risk aversion; a certainty equivalent equal to 50 ECUs indicates risk neutrality; and a certainty equivalent above 50 ECUs indicates risk-seeking behavior.

The seven lottery decisions can also be used to infer risk attitude. However, since each lottery has the same expected value, we can discriminate only between risk aversion (if the certain payoff is chosen) and risk neutrality (if the risky payoff is chosen).

We randomly selected one of the seven decisions to determine the individual payoff. This payoff from the lotteries was then added to the total payoff from the market. Phase 1 took 15 to 20 minutes.

Phase 2

After receiving instructions about the experimental asset market[6] and a short questionnaire to check their understanding of the instructions, subjects participated in two trial periods of six minutes each to become familiar with the market's selling and buying procedures. After the trial periods, we opened the asset market. Overall, we ran eight sessions with eight subjects each on a computerized asset market using the software z-Tree (the Zurich Toolbox for Readymade Economic Experiments, Fischbacher, 2007).

The computer screen for the auction is shown in Figure 1.3. Each market participant was entitled to (1) submit bids and asks, (2) accept standing bids and asks, where only better offers, i.e. higher bids and lower asks, were allowed, or (3) remain passive. Bids and asks were automatically ranked to indicate the most favorable offer. Information about the trading history, provided as a chronological list of contracts, was displayed throughout the trading periods.

The market was performed as a continuous anonymous double auction. Participants were endowed with 1000 ECUs (100 ECUs equals €0.18), plus five risky assets A and five risky assets B (these assets were traded separately on markets A and B). To ensure comparability, the sequence of the two markets was chosen in advance and applied to all

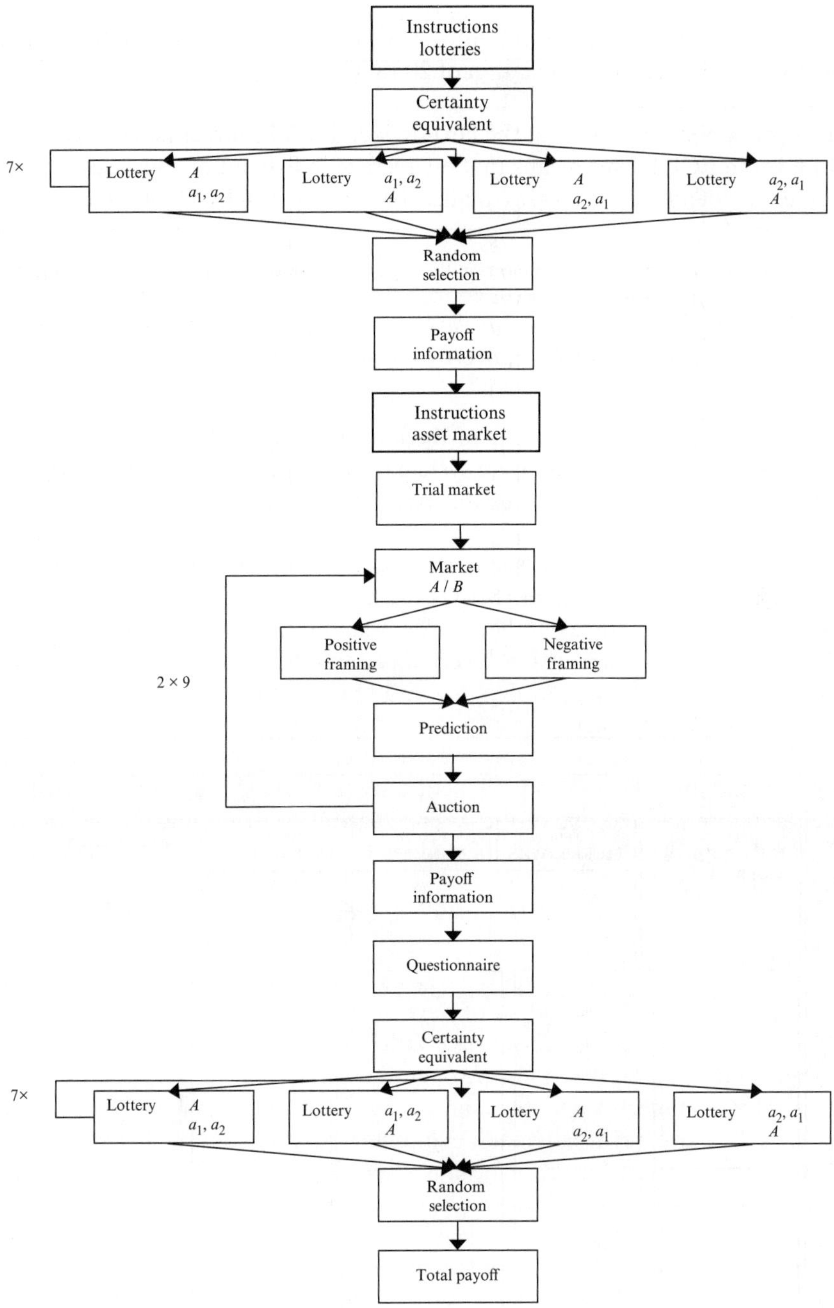

Figure 1.2 Sequence of events in the experiments

Table 1.2 Lottery payoffs in experimental currency units

Lottery		Payoff	p	Expected value
1	*a*1	160	0.20	88
	*a*2	70	0.80	
	A	88	1.00	88
2	*a*1	150	0.32	99
	*a*2	75	0.68	
	A	99	1.00	99
3	*a*1	178	0.28	106
	*a*2	78	0.72	
	A	106	1.00	106
4	*a*1	140	0.35	101
	*a*2	80	0.65	
	A	101	1.00	101
5	*a*1	135	0.40	105
	*a*2	85	0.60	
	A	105	1.00	105
6	*a*1	188	0.25	98
	*a*2	68	0.75	
	A	98	1.00	98
7	*a*1	130	0.30	102
	*a*2	90	0.70	
	A	102	1.00	102

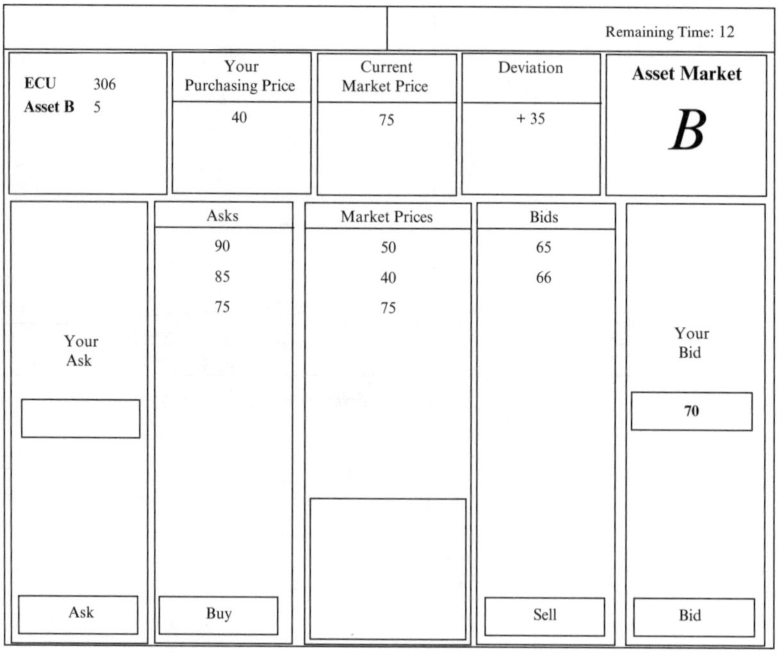

Figure 1.3 Auction computer screen

eight sessions. Dividends were randomly determined and drawn from a normal distribution (see Table 1.1).

We informed participants that the markets would be open for at least eight periods, and at most 12 periods. The probability that the markets would end after the eighth, ninth, tenth, or eleventh period was 25 percent. At the end of the final market period, the liquidation value of the asset would be zero. Again to ensure comparability, we randomly chose the last market period once for all eight sessions. According to this random selection, we determined that each market ended after the ninth period. Each trading period lasted for 180 seconds.

Before the market opened, participants were told which market (*A* or *B*) and which trading period (1 to 9) were open, and the last average market price and closing price of the asset traded. They were also given either positively or negatively framed dividend information, and asked to predict the next average trading price of the assets. Phase 2 took about 80 to 90 minutes.

Phase 3

Participants were asked to fill out a computerized post-experimental questionnaire with items designed to measure how well they had understood the experiment and how much effort they had put into arriving at accurate decisions. Phase 3 took about 15 to 20 minutes.

Phase 4

Participants again had to reveal their certainty equivalent for a lottery offering a payoff of 100 ECUs with a probability of $p = 0.50$ and zero otherwise, and to make seven decisions among lotteries (100 ECUs equals €0.73). The payoffs were identical to those used in phase 1 (see Table 1.2). Phase 4 took about 15 to 20 minutes.

EXPERIMENTAL RESULTS

Data Analysis

Over the eight sessions, with two times nine trading periods each, participants submitted 6983 offers, of which 3168 contracts were concluded. Thus the participants concluded an average of 22 contracts per period (SD = 9.19), ranging from a minimum of four to a maximum of 68 contracts. The average market price was 368.15 ECUs (SD = 390.71).

Figures 1.4 and 1.5 indicate that, over the trading periods, the number of concluded contracts decreased in both markets, *A* ($\chi^2(1) = 112.91, p < 0.001$) and *B* ($\chi^2(1) = 73.83, p < 0.001$), while the number of offers not accepted increased in both markets, *A* ($\chi^2(1) = 75.02, p < 0.001$) and *B* ($\chi^2(1) = 20.16, p < 0.05$). We posit that prices may have increased over trading periods, and this conjecture was confirmed. Average trading prices were statistically significantly higher in the last period of both markets, *A* ($M_{A,9} = 235.77$, $SD_{A,9} = 216.29$) and *B* ($M_{B,9} = 354.34$, $SD_{B,9} = 425.30$), compared to the first period ($M_{A,1} = 150.06$, $SD_{A,1} = 83.73$; $F(1; 649) = 40.52, p < 0.001$; $M_{B,1} = 163.94$, $SD_{B,1} = 82.45$; $F(1; 625) = 50.74, p < 0.001$).

However, Figure 1.6 indicates that average trading prices on both markets sharply

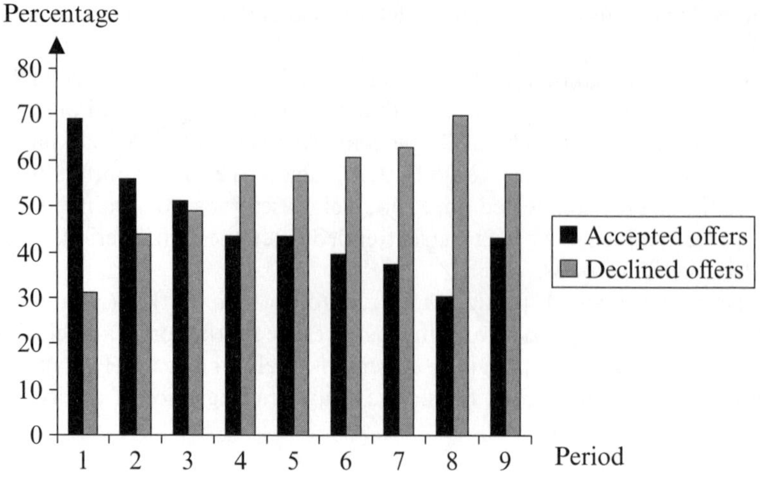

Figure 1.4 Percentage of accepted and declined offers for market A

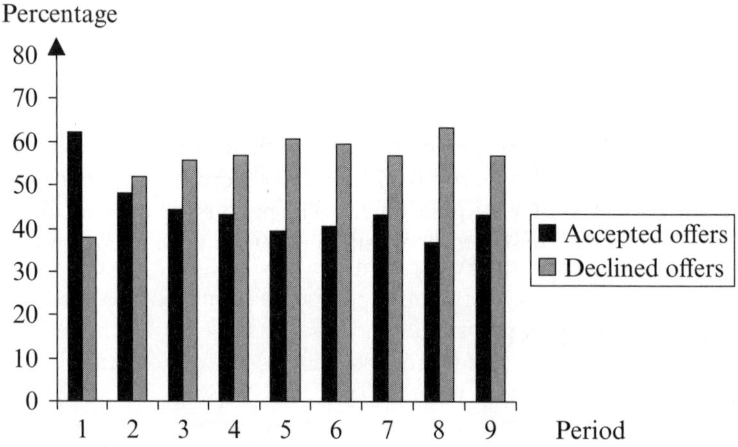

Figure 1.5 Percentage of accepted and declined offers for market B

declined in late trading periods, when uncertainty about market duration was important. This uncertainty about market termination depressed average trading prices, although they were still higher in the last period than in the first. Figure 1.6 also indicates that during highly uncertain times, especially in late trading periods, the variance of market prices increased.

To control for possible differences in individual risk attitude, we investigated whether risk attitude differed between sessions and between experimental conditions, with respect to elicited certainty equivalents and binary lottery decisions. The average certainty equivalent revealed by the subjects was 44.23 (SD = 31.20), indicating a slight degree of risk aversion. Certainty equivalents did not differ significantly between the eight sessions ($F(7; 56) = 0.48$, $p = 0.84$).

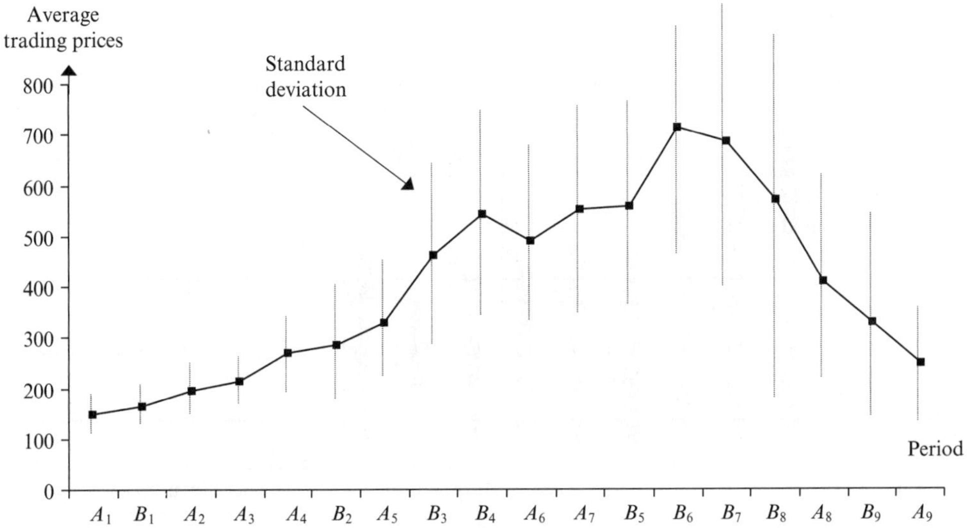

Figure 1.6 Average trading prices and standard deviations for markets A *and* B *across periods*

We computed a risk attitude index from the seven decisions among lotteries ranging from 0 = risk neutrality to 7 = risk aversion. The average risk attitude was 3.66 (SD = 2.15). Again, we observed no statistically significant difference between the eight sessions ($F(7; 56) = 0.95$, $p = 0.47$). Nor was there any statistically significant difference between positively and negatively framed subjects with respect to the certainty equivalent ($F(1; 62) = 0.09$, $p = 0.76$) and the lottery decisions ($F(1; 62) = 0.05$, $p = 0.82$). Thus any differences in observed behavior between experimental conditions are not likely to be caused by different underlying risk attitudes. There was also no difference in risk attitude between the first measurement (before the market was performed) and the second measurement for either the certainty equivalents ($M_I = 44.23$, $SD_I = 31.20$; $M_{II} = 45.58$, $SD_{II} = 31.91$; $F(1; 62) = 0.15$, $p = 0.70$) or the lottery decisions ($M_I = 3.34$, $SD_I = 2.10$; $M_{II} = 3.67$, $SD_{II} = 2.44$; $F(1; 62) = 1.22$, $p = 0.27$). The results indicate that market behavior did not have a recursive impact on individual risk attitude.

The results from the questionnaire reveal that the instructions were clear and easy to understand (M = 7.16, SD = 2.00), and confirmed that the participants carefully considered their buying orders (M = 6.13, SD = 1.91) and selling orders (M = 6.09, SD = 2.08). Subjects also emphasized that they had tried to maximize their earnings (M = 6.83, SD = 1.94). All questions were formulated as statements that subjects could disagree or agree with (ranging from 1 = do not agree to 9 = fully agree).

Framing Effects

The results confirm our hypothesis that positively framed buyers purchase assets from negatively rather than from positively framed sellers ($\chi^2(1) = 6.61$, $p < 0.01$), and that negatively framed sellers sell their assets to positively rather than to negatively framed

Table 1.3 *Observed and expected trading volume between positively framed buyers and positively and negatively framed sellers*

	Positively framed buyers	
	Observed trading volume	Expected trading volume
Positively framed sellers	634	683.6
Negatively framed sellers	870	820.4
	1504	

Table 1.4 *Observed and expected trading volume between negatively framed sellers and positively and negatively framed buyers*

	Negatively framed sellers	
	Observed trading volume	Expected trading volume
Positively framed buyers	905	839.5
Negatively framed buyers	634	699.5
	1539	

buyers ($\chi^2(1) = 11.26, p < 0.001$). Tables 1.3 and 1.4 show the observed and the expected trading volume between positively and negatively framed subjects.

We also expected that varying the probabilities of the framed information would shape individual price expectations. Since the framed dividend information on market *A* was more extreme than on market *B*, we expected trading volume on market *A* to be higher due to more diverging dividend expectations.

The results at least weakly support our conjecture. The total number of concluded contracts was higher on market *A* (1636) than on market *B* (1532) ($\chi^2(1) = 3.41, p = 0.07$). However, the total number of offers not accepted did not differ between the two ($\chi^2(1) = 0.12, p = 0.73$). On market *A*, the number was 1918; on market *B* it was 1897.

Figure 1.6 indicates that participants did not seem to distinguish between the two asset markets, so the observed higher trading volume on market *A* may be attributable to the unbalanced sequence of periods of the two markets. Figure 1.6 indicates that prices followed an upward trend on both markets up to the sixth period of market *B*, and then sharply decreased in later trading periods. Note that at the beginning of the experiment, when participants were still highly inexperienced, market *A* was opened more often than market *B*, while in later trading periods this pattern was reversed. Thus the higher number of concluded contracts may be a result of this sequence of trading periods.

We also investigated whether the observed matching of unequally informed subjects led to different trading prices. For this analysis we distinguished between: (1) trades with negatively framed sellers and buyers, (2) trades with positively framed sellers and buyers, and (3) trades with mixed pairs of sellers and buyers. We ran a repeated ANOVA (analysis of variance) with the trading pattern as a between-subjects factor and the market (*A* or *B*) as a within-subjects factor. We aggregated the data by replacing the nine periods of the two markets by the overall mean of each market. The

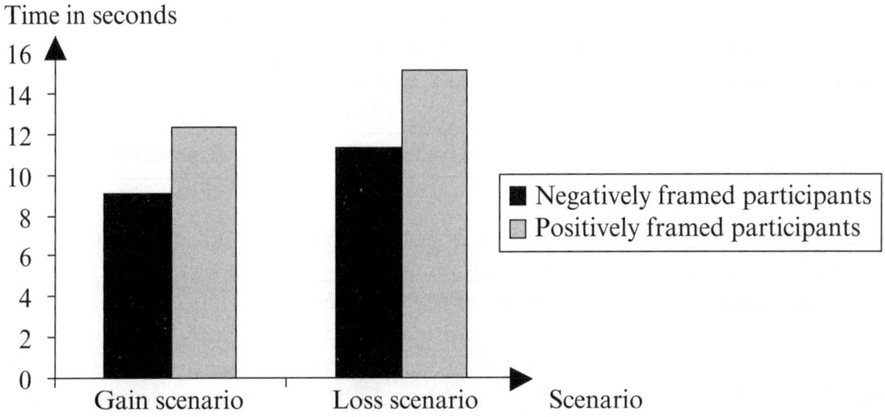

Figure 1.7 Average time difference between buying action and the next selling action for positively and negatively framed participants in gain and loss scenarios

results indicate that trading prices were not statistically significantly different between trading patterns ($F(2; 21) = 0.07$, $p = 0.93$), but did differ across the two markets ($F(2; 21) = 28.71$, $p < 0.001$).

Our findings indicate that objectively irrelevant information influences trading behavior: positively framed buyers purchase assets from negatively rather than from positively framed sellers, and negatively framed sellers sell their assets to positively rather than to negatively framed buyers. The matching of unequally informed subjects, however, does not lead to different trading prices. We also find that a probability variation of the framed information impacts trading volume. We believe that this is attributable primarily to the unbalanced sequence of trading periods across markets.

Disposition Effect

Based on the predictions of prospect theory, we expect that a purchase price lower than the previous market price implies a gain situation that leads to more rapid selling. In turn, a purchase price higher than the previous trading price implies a loss situation that leads to less rapid selling.

To test this conjecture, we defined two scenarios, one for a gain where the purchase price is below the previous market price, and the other for a loss, where the purchase price is higher than the previous market price. The software z-Tree used in the experiment (Fischbacher, 2007) enabled us to calculate the exact time in seconds between a subject's buying and selling, so we are able to show that market participants who experienced a gain sold their assets significantly earlier ($M_G = 10.12$, $SD_G = 23.30$) than market participants who experienced a loss ($M_L = 13.66$, $SD_L = 26.90$; $F(2; 1306) = 3.01$, $p < 0.05$).

This effect was moderated by framing (see Figure 1.7). Positively framed market participants generally sold their assets later than negatively framed market participants ($M_P = 13.90$, $SD_P = 27.62$; $M_N = 10.32$, $SD_N = 23.72$; $F(1; 1307) = 6.34$, $p < 0.05$). Thus we assume that framing shapes individual expectations, and thereby influences market behavior. Positively framed participants seemed to be more optimistic about the likely performance and profit of their assets. They were thus also more patient, in both gain and in loss situations.

CONCLUSIONS

This chapter investigates the impact of objectively irrelevant information on trading behavior. We draw upon a novel type of framing that is not based on semantic variations of a decision problem. Participants are given complete information about a distribution, and receive additional percentile information that either positively or negatively deviates from an aspirational reference payoff. Normative decision theories such as expected utility theory require that this additional information be neglected in the decision process, so it is not expected to influence behavior in a market environment. From a behavioral perspective, however, we expect that the additional information will serve as an anchor in the decision process, and systematically influence individual behavior even in market environments.

We also investigated the impact of a probability variation of the framed information and the robustness of the disposition effect in a competitive market environment with real-time data. Our results indicate:

1. Objectively irrelevant information does influence individual trading behavior. Moreover, positively and negatively framed information leads to a particular trading pattern: positively framed buyers purchase assets from negatively framed sellers, and negatively framed sellers sell their assets to positively framed buyers. The observed matching of unequally informed subjects, however, does not lead to different trading prices.
2. There is weak support for the conjecture that a probability variation of the framed information impacts trading volume. However, we believe that this effect is attributable to the unbalanced sequence of trading periods in the two asset markets, not to the available information.
3. The disposition effect was confirmed. Participants sold their assets more readily in gain situations than in loss situations. The effect was further moderated by framing: positively framed market participants generally sold their assets later than negatively framed participants. The framing of dividend information influenced individual expectations, and therefore market behavior as well.

Since objectively irrelevant information influenced market behavior, our findings violate expected utility theory and the invariance axiom. They are also inconsistent with refinements of the expected utility theory that do not account for framing effects, such as rank-dependent utility theories (Quiggin, 1982). Such theories are similar to cumulative prospect theory (see, e.g., Weber and Camerer, 1987 for a more in-depth discussion). The results reported in this chapter stress the importance of the subjective perception of information, which is not captured by expected utility theory or by rank-dependent utility theories because they focus on the processing of objective, and thus invariant, information.

Our results may have important implications for financial decision making. A huge amount of investment information is available to an increasing number of investors all around the world. Standard finance theory assumes that markets filter out irrelevant information, allowing individuals to arrive at unbiased decisions. In particular, it assumes that even if irrelevant information helps nothing, it does not harm anything either. But our findings cast doubt on this assertion. Additional irrelevant information does not leave the decision problem unchanged. It can systematically influence trading behavior even in competitive market environments.

ACKNOWLEDGMENTS

The authors acknowledge financial support from the Austrian National Bank (Jubiläumsfonds 8382). We are grateful for valuable comments from Jordi Brandts, Werner Güth, Hans Haumer, Christian Helmenstein, Manfred Königstein, Christian Schade, Erik Theissen and Anthony Ziegelmeyer. We also benefited from comments by seminar participants at the Humboldt University of Berlin, the ENDEAR workshop in Amsterdam, the ESA meeting in Barcelona, the IAREP conference in Bath, and the public-choice meeting in San Diego. Thanks also go to Tarek El-Sehity, Eva Hofmann and Herbert Schwarzenberger, who helped run the experiment at the University of Vienna. The order of authorship is alphabetical.

NOTES

1. Overpricing refers to market prices that exceed the total value of the lotteries traded (Rietz, 1993).
2. Tversky and Kahneman (1974) asked subjects to estimate the percentage of African countries in the United Nations after a number between 0 and 100 had been drawn by spinning a wheel of fortune. Estimates were dependent on the initially drawn number. The authors found that when a high number was drawn, the subjects tended to estimate a higher median percentage of countries than when a low number was drawn.
3. There is indeed strong experimental evidence that asset markets are highly informationally efficient (for a survey on the literature, see Sunder, 1995).
4. One hundred ECUs equal €0.73.
5. Correspondence between the two measures of certainty equivalents and lottery choices is investigated by, e.g., El-Sehity et al. (2002) and Fellner and Maciejovsky (2007).
6. See the appendix for an English translation of the instructions.

REFERENCES

Barber, B.M. and T. Odean (2001), 'The Internet and the investor,' *Journal of Economic Perspectives*, **15**, 41–54.

Choi, J.J., D. Laibson and A. Metrick (2002), 'How does the Internet affect trading? Evidence from investor behavior in 401(k) plans,' *Journal of Financial Economics*, **64**, 397–421.

El-Sehity, T., H. Haumer, C. Helmenstein, E. Kirchler and B. Maciejovsky (2002), 'Hindsight bias and individual risk attitude within the context of experimental asset markets,' *Journal of Psychology and Financial Markets*, **3**, 227–35.

Fellner, G. and B. Maciejovsky (2007), 'Risk attitude and market behavior: evidence from experimental asset markets,' *Journal of Economic Psychology*, **28**, 338–50.

Fischbacher, U. (2007), 'z-tree: Zurich Toolbox for Ready-made Economic Experiments: experimenter's manual,' *Experimental Economics*, **10**, 171–89.

Heilmann, K., V. Läger and A. Oehler (2000), 'The disposition effect: evidence about investors' aversion to realize losses: a contribution to behavioral finance through the use of experimental call markets,' University of Bamberg.
Heisler, J. (1994), 'Loss aversion in a futures market: an empirical test,' *Review of Futures Markets*, **13**, 793–822.
Kahneman, D. and M.W. Riepe (1998), 'Aspects of investor psychology,' *Journal of Portfolio Management*, **24**, 52–65.
Kahneman, D. and A. Tversky (1979), 'Prospect theory: an analysis of choice under risk,' *Econometrica*, **47**, 263–91.
Kahneman, D. and A. Tversky (1983), 'Choices, values, and frames,' *American Psychologist*, **39**, 341–50.
Kühberger, A. (1995), 'The framing of decisions: a new look at old problems,' *Organizational Behavior and Human Decision Processes*, **62**, 230–40.
Kühberger, A. (1998), 'The influence of framing on risky decisions: a meta-analysis,' *Organizational Behavior and Human Decision Processes*, **75**, 23–55.
Kühberger, A., M. Schulte-Mecklenbeck and J. Perner (1999), 'The effects of framing, reflection, probability, and payoff on risk preference in choice tasks,' *Organizational Behavior and Human Decision Processes*, **78**, 204–31.
McNeil, B.J., S.G. Pauker, H.C. Sox and A. Tversky (1982), 'On the elicitation of preferences for alternative therapies,' *New England Journal of Medicine*, **306**, 1259–62.
Odean, T. (1998), 'Are investors reluctant to realize their losses?,' *Journal of Finance*, **53**, 1775–98.
Park, C.Y. (2001), 'News media exposure and self-perceived knowledge: the illusion of knowing,' *International Journal of Public Opinion Research*, **13**, 419–25.
Quiggin, J. (1982), 'A theory of anticipated utility,' *Journal of Economic Behavior and Organization*, **3**, 323–43.
Rietz, T.A. (1993), 'Arbitrage asset prices and risk allocation in experimental markets,' Working Paper 109, Department of Finance, Kellogg Graduate School of Management, Northwestern University.
Shefrin, H. and M. Statman (1985), 'The disposition to sell winners too early and ride losers too long,' *Journal of Finance*, **40**, 777–90.
Statman, M. (1995), 'A behavioral framework for dollar-cost averaging,' *Journal of Portfolio Management*, **22**, 70–78.
Sunder, S. (1995), 'Experimental asset markets,' in J.H. Kagel and A.E. Roth (eds), *Handbook of Experimental Economics*, Princeton, NJ: Princeton University Press, pp. 445–500.
Tversky, A. and D. Kahneman (1974), 'Judgment under uncertainty: heuristics and biases,' *Science*, **185**, 1124–31.
Tversky, A. and D. Kahneman (1981), 'The framing effect of decisions and the psychology of choice,' *Science*, **211**, 453–8.
Tversky, A. and D. Kahneman (1992), 'Advances in prospect theory: cumulative representation of uncertainty,' *Journal of Risk and Uncertainty*, **5**, 297–324.
Weber, M. and C. Camerer (1987), 'Recent developments in modelling preferences under risk,' *OR Spektrum*, **9**, 129–51.
Weber, M. and C. Camerer (1998), 'The disposition effect in securities trading: an experimental analysis,' *Journal of Economic Behavior and Organization*, **33**, 167–84.
Weber, M., H.J. Keppe and G. Meyer-Delius (2000), 'The impact of endowment framing on market prices: an experimental analysis,' *Journal of Economic Behavior and Organization*, **41**, 159–76.

APPENDIX

Instructions about the Market

Thank you for participating in our experiment. The experiment will last for about 2 hours and 15 minutes. You will trade assets on a market, and your payoff will be contingent on your decisions.

The following explains the trading mechanism in detail. You will learn how to place buy and sell offers and how to accept offers by other market participants. When you have read the instructions, there will be time to ask questions. Afterwards there will be a short test to check whether you have understood the trading rules. The experiment will not begin until all participants have correctly answered all the questions in the test. You will then participate in a trial market lasting two periods, where you will have the opportunity to try out the buying and selling procedures without affecting your payoffs. The two trial periods will last for six minutes each. After the trial market, the real asset market will be opened.

Let us now explain how the asset market works. Generally, there are two ways to buy and two ways to sell assets.

Let us start with buying. You can either (1) submit a bid to the market, or (2) accept a standing ask made by another market participant. If you want to submit a bid, you must type your maximum buying price in the input box marked 'your bid,' and press the button marked 'bid.' If you want to accept a standing ask made by another market participant, simply press the button 'buy.' Standing asks for the assets are ranked according to prices and listed in columns. Of course, the best offer for you, and all other potential buyers, is the lowest ask, which is listed at the bottom of the column.

Let us now explain selling. You can either (1) submit an ask to the market, or (2) accept a standing bid made by another market participant. To submit an ask, type your minimum selling price in the input box marked 'your ask,' and press the button marked 'ask.' To accept a standing bid made by another market participant, press the button marked 'sell.' Standing bids for the assets are ranked according to prices and listed in columns. Of course, the best offer for you, and all other potential sellers, is the highest bid, again listed at the bottom of the column.

Note that you can engage simultaneously in buying and selling. However, you cannot buy more assets than your cash holdings allow, and you cannot sell more assets than you own. If you have submitted a bid to the market, your available money for further activities is reduced by this amount. If you have submitted an ask to the market, your available asset holdings are reduced by this one offer. We do not grant any credit or allow short-selling.

Only improving offers, i.e., higher bids and lower asks, are allowed on the market. During a trading period, you can buy assets, sell assets, or remain passive.

You can also engage in more than one activity at all times. In fact, you can simultaneously submit buy offers, submit sell offers, and accept standing offers made by other market participants.

You will be informed about the remaining trading time, the current period number, and the previous trades and their trading prices. All trades are chronologically listed in the column marked 'previous trades.'

You will now have the opportunity to try out the buying and selling procedures without affecting your payoffs. The trial market will consist of two periods, each lasting for six minutes.

Now the 'real' markets will be opened. You will trade assets on two separate markets, *A* and *B*. At the beginning of each trading period, you will be reminded whether market *A* or *B* is being opened. The sequence of the market was determined randomly. Each trading period lasts for 180 seconds.

At the beginning of the market, you will be endowed with 1000 experimental currency units (100 ECUs equals E0.18), plus five assets on market *A* and five assets on market *B*. Note that the monetary endowment is carried forward on both markets, but type *A* assets can only be traded on market *A* and type *B* assets can only be traded on market *B*.

The minimum number of trading periods for each of the two markets is eight; the maximum is 12. The probability that the market will end after the eighth, ninth, tenth, or eleventh period is 25 percent. This means there is a 75 percent probability that the market will continue after period 8. Similarly, once each period has been reached, there is an equal chance that the market will continue. Only when period 12 is reached is it certain that this will be the final market period.

Dividends are randomly drawn from a normal distribution with a certain mean and standard deviation. At the beginning of each period, you will be informed about the mean and the standard deviation of the distribution. At the end of the final market period, the liquidation value of the asset is zero. This means that once the final market period is reached, the assets carry no intrinsic value; they will be worth zero ECUs.

2 Information overload and information presentation in financial decision making

Julie Agnew and Lisa Szykman

INTRODUCTION

Information overload is a condition that exists because of the limited cognitive capacity humans have to process information. It is a topic that has been widely studied across a number of different disciplines such as management, marketing, accounting and management information systems (MIS). Eppler and Mengis (2004) provide a comprehensive interdisciplinary review of this literature. Information overload can have serious consequences in the context of financial decision making. When individuals experience information overload, it can impair their judgment by causing them to limit their information search and use simple heuristics instead. Given the well-documented use of heuristics in retirement plan investing, as well as the prevalence of biases such as the default bias and inertia, it is very possible that information overload is a contributing factor (see Agnew, forthcoming, for an overview). This chapter will highlight two recent experimental studies we have conducted that support this assertion. Our results suggest that finding ways to reduce information overload (through changes to plan design, financial education and information presentation) may help individuals make more informed financial decisions.

This chapter is laid out as follows. We begin with a brief discussion of what information overload is and how it relates to financial decision making. We then discuss our first paper in this area, Agnew and Szykman (2005). In this paper, we examine how the presentation of investment information and the number of investment choices offered relate to information overload. We find that financial literacy plays an important role in how changes to these plan features influence a participant's feelings of overload. We then turn to a new study that examines the influence of message framing on a common decision retiree's face: whether to annuitize their wealth or invest it on their own. Similar to our earlier study, we find financial literacy is related to information overload. In addition, we find that individuals are more likely to choose an option that requires less effort as they experience more information overload.

WHAT IS INFORMATION OVERLOAD AND HOW MIGHT IT RELATE TO FINANCIAL DECISIONS?

Information overload occurs when the amount of information available to process exceeds a human's processing capacity. When this happens, stress and anxiety may occur, making the excessive information more harmful than helpful. Therefore public policy makers and consumer researchers have long been interested in how to effectively communicate to the public. A central question is: what causes information overload? Eppler and Mengis (2004) enumerate five factors that can cause information overload at both the organizational and interpersonal levels. These factors are the information itself, the person receiving the information, the tasks that need to be completed, the organizational design or structure and the information technology that is used. In this chapter, we focus specifically on two that directly relate to financial decision making – the information itself and the characteristics of the person receiving the information.

The amount of information that is presented to a decision maker is a critical factor contributing to information overload. Financial providers face a constant dilemma regarding this issue when they are developing information for their investors. On the one hand, financial decisions are often complicated, so providing a fine level of detail to investors seems prudent. On the other hand, all this additional information may serve only to overwhelm investors, which may lead them to use heuristics (or shortcuts) instead of a deliberate and thoughtful decision-making process.

The economics of information literature suggests that consumers tend to use information more extensively if it costs less in time and/or money to acquire (Stigler, 1961; Nelson, 1970, 1974). These findings suggest that when information is easier to obtain and evaluate, consumers are more likely to use it when making decisions or choices. For example, in the nutritional labeling literature, it has been shown that as dependable information becomes easier to utilize (such as information presented in a standardized format), consumers use the information more to determine food quality, acquire more nutrition information prior to purchase, and improve their overall decision quality (Roe et al., 1999; Ippolito and Mathios, 1990, 1994; Moorman, 1990, 1996; Muller, 1985). This suggests that if the information about investment options is presented in a way that is easier to use, then investors should experience less information overload and be more likely to use more information when making their asset allocation decisions.

Another potential source of information overload is the number of investment options offered in the plan. Research has shown that too many choices may hamper decision making. A study conducted by Iyengar and Lepper (2000) compared consumers' reactions to two displays of jam – one with six flavors, the other with 24. While more consumers showed an interest in the larger display, it was the smaller display that elicited more purchases. Their experiment demonstrates that consumers not only reduce the amount of processing when a task becomes overwhelming, but that they may, in fact, decide to withdraw from the task entirely. This might be one of the reasons why so many retirement investors procrastinate and/or succumb to the default bias.

Third, the complexity of the choice may also lead to information overload. Individuals who are overwhelmed by their choices may select the option that requires minimal effort to execute. There is already substantial empirical evidence supporting a default bias in retirement plan investing (Choi et al., 2002). The success of automatic enrollment in substantially increasing participation rates over voluntary enrollment plans is a clear example of this fact. One reason the default may influence behavior so much is that it requires the least effort; in other words it is the 'path of least resistance.'

Another information characteristic that may be a potential source of overload is the similarity of the options offered. As the number of funds that are offered grows, it is possible that the funds will become perceived to be more alike. For example, when participants must choose from multiple vendors (e.g. many university 403(b) plans), it is not unrealistic that the vendors will offer similar types of funds. Most likely a great deal of overlap will exist among the most popular fund types (e.g. index funds). As similarity in the funds increases, overload may also increase because funds are harder to differentiate from each other. If so, this would indicate that more distinct choice offerings are better.

Finally, turning to a person-related characteristic, the last factor we consider is a person's own financial knowledge. Consumer researchers have found that there exists an inverted U-shaped relationship between information search and knowledge – consumers with a moderate level of knowledge search the most before making a product choice (Bettman and Park, 1980). Experts have no need to do an extensive search because they already know a great deal, and an extensive search would be redundant. People with moderate knowledge search the most because they have a basic understanding that allows them to interpret the information, but also to realize the benefits associated with a more extensive search. Novices, who have very little knowledge, become overwhelmed by a choice task very quickly, so despite the fact that they would benefit the most from doing an extensive information search, they do not do it. Lacking the knowledge and experience to compare the available investment alternatives can make the whole process even more intimidating, making it even more likely for investors to look for an easy way out. In the case of defined contribution plans, the easy way out may be choosing the default or using some other choice heuristic.[1] Thus knowledge may be a critical individual difference that profoundly impacts a person's investment choices and their feelings of information overload.

EXPERIMENTAL TESTS OF THE INFLUENCE OF INFORMATION PRESENTATION, NUMBER OF CHOICES AND FINANCIAL KNOWLEDGE ON INFORMATION OVERLOAD

Our interest in information overload as it relates to retirement decision making began with intriguing empirical evidence suggesting that adding additional investment choices to retirement plan menus reduced participation rates. Sethi-Iyengar et al. (2004) found that for every ten funds added to an investment menu, the probability of participation in the plan decreased by 1.5 to 2 percent. While it may seem surprising that individuals would procrastinate on financial decisions that are directly associated with their financial well-being, it is the very high stakes of the decisions and the associated complexities that are most likely the reasons they delay. In fact, O'Donoghue and Rabin's (2001) model predicts that an individual's tendency to procrastinate increases as the goal becomes more important and as the number of available options increases.

International evidence also supports a choice overload hypothesis. Although this hypothesis is not formally tested, the high number of choices (over 500) offered to participants in Sweden's public pension private accounts might also explain the tendency for participants to opt for the investment default. In that plan, with the exception of the first year, over 80 percent of the eligible new participants invested according to the default option (Weaver, 2002). While the number of choices in the Swedish system may seem extreme, at the time we conducted our 2005 study the authors' 403(b) plan offered over 285 investment choices across several vendors. One vendor alone offered 146 choices.[2]

These findings motivated us to study experimentally how the number of investment

Table 2.1 Investment types and reported financial attributes

(a) Investment types
1. Money market funds
2. Bond index funds
3. Equity index funds
4. Equity growth funds
5. Equity blended funds
6. Equity value funds

(b) Reported financial attributes
1. Investment type
2. Year-to-date return (%)
3. One-year return (%)
4. Three-year return(%)
5. Five-year return
6. Expense ratio (%)
7. Net assets ($ millions)
8. Risk (standard deviation of one-year returns)
9. Analyst risk description (relative to other funds in investment type: low, below average, average, above average, high)
10. Manager tenure (years)
11. 7-day yield (%) (only reported for money market funds)

choices related to information overload. We also wanted to explore how the similarity of the options, the format of the information and financial knowledge might play a role. Therefore, in our 2005 paper (Agnew and Szykman, 2005), we conducted two laboratory experiments where four variables were studied (display of information (low versus high search costs), number of choices (low versus high), similarity among choices (low versus high) and individual financial knowledge).

For both experiments, we asked participants to allocate a fictitious $1000 in retirement savings among several mutual funds. They also were given the option to put the entire $1000 in a conservative default option (money market fund). To facilitate their decision making, they were given information regarding the performance of the asset choices based on 11 commonly reported attributes, including returns over various time periods, the standard deviation of the one-year returns and the investment type. The reported statistics given to participants were actual performance measures from real funds and were obtained from Morningstar's website. The funds were divided into five fictitious fund families. Each fund family offered at least one investment fund in each investment type. Table 2.1 summarizes the investment types and the reported statistics. The real names of the funds were changed to avoid biasing the results. Pretests were done on the fund family names to ensure that they did not have overly positive or negative attitudes associated with them.

We randomly assigned participants to the two experiments. Based on the demographics of each sample, the randomization was successful. Both samples were predominantly

Table 2.2 Summary of test questions

	Test question	Percentage answering correctly[a]
1.	Which of the following types of investments are typically found in a money market fund? Stocks, bonds or short-term securities	13
2.	When is the best time to transfer money into a long-term bond fund? When interest rates are expected to: increase, remain stable, decrease, interest rate doesn't matter, don't know	32
3.	If you were to invest $1000 in a STOCK FUND, would it be possible to have less than $1000 when you decide to withdraw or move it to another fund?	84
4.	If you were to invest $1000 in a BOND FUND, would it be possible to have less than $1000 when you decide to withdraw or move it to another fund?	43
5.	If you were to invest $1000 in a MONEY MARKET FUND, would it be possible to have less than $1000 when you decide to withdraw or move it to another fund?	45
6.	A stock fund's beta rating can best be described as: (a) a measure of relative volatility of the fund versus the S&P 500 index, (b) a measure of relative growth versus the S&P 500 index, (c) a measure of the relative capital outflow of the fund versus the S&P 500 index?	22
7.	A money market mutual fund is guaranteed by the US government against principal loss. True or false?	45
8.	High-yield bond funds are invested in bonds with strong credit ratings. True or false?	37
9.	If you invest in a bond mutual fund with an average maturity of five years, this means that you cannot withdraw your money from the fund within a five-year period without incurring a penalty. True or false?	29
10.	A stock market index fund is actively managed by a fund portfolio manager. True or false?	24

Note: [a] The percentage answering correctly refers to participants in both experiments.

female, with a majority of the individuals more than 30 years old. There was a broad representation of occupations, including professional administrators, professors, secretarial staff and maintenance workers. Salary and education levels were also well distributed.

Recognizing that financial knowledge may play a role, each participant was given a ten-question financial literacy exam during the experiment. The questions in the exam were taken directly from or adapted from questions asked in the John Hancock Financial Services Defined Contribution Plan Survey (2002) and financial literacy exams used by Wilcox (2003) and Dwyer et al. (2002).

Our overall financial knowledge results support prior findings that many investors lack even a basic understanding of financial concepts (John Hancock Financial Services Eighth Defined Contribution Survey, 2002). Each question in the ten-point exam was worth one point. Table 2.2 reports the results of the exam. In both samples, the mean and

Table 2.3 Composition of overload and satisfaction measures

Overload measure	
1. There were too many different options to consider (Scale 1 to 6, Strongly Disagree to Strongly Agree)	
2. This decision required a great deal of thought (Scale 1 to 6, Strong Disagree to Strongly Agree)	
3. This was a difficult decision (Scale 1 to 6, Strong Disagree to Strongly Agree)	
4. I found this decision to be overwhelming (Scale 1 to 6, Strong Disagree to Strongly Agree)	
5. It was difficult to comprehend all of the information available to me (Scale 1 to 6, Strong Disagree to Strongly Agree)	
6. This task was stressful (Scale 1 to 6, Strong Disagree to Strongly Agree)	
7. It was a relief to make a decision (Scale 1 to 6, Strong Disagree to Strongly Agree)	Standardized item alpha 0.8007

median test scores are below 50 percent. In fact, more than one-third of all participants answered two or fewer questions correctly.

Experiment One: Information Display, Number of Choices and Financial Knowledge

In the first experiment, we used a 2 (display) × 2 (number of choices) × 2 (financial knowledge) between-subjects design. To manipulate the display of the information, fund choices were presented in either a table (low search cost) or booklet (high search cost) format. For both conditions, existing 403(b) plan information was used to develop the stimulus. For the low search cost condition (table), the asset choices were presented on one page in a standard spreadsheet format and organized by investment type. For the high search condition (booklet), the same exact information was presented for each asset but the fund options were presented in a booklet organized by fund family. Each page of the booklet was dedicated to one fund family and was not organized by investment type. This format produced higher search costs because participants were forced to sort through multiple booklet pages in order to compare options within one investment type. This is similar to what a participant in a 403(b) would have to do when comparing offerings from different fund vendors.

The number of fund choices was also manipulated. Participants were given either six funds (low number of choices) or 60 funds (high number of choices).[3] Finally, as described in the previous section, individuals were divided into 'high knowledge' and 'low knowledge' categories based on their financial knowledge test scores.

Once the allocation decision was made, participants were asked to complete measures on their information overload. Table 2.3 reports the questions used in this measure and its reliability.

Results

Table 2.4, Panel (a) reports the cell means for the overload measure. Using a three-factor analysis of variance, we found two significant main effects. As expected, there was a significant difference in measured overload between the two knowledge categories ($F(1,186) = 20.54$, $p < 0.01$).[4] Individuals with less than average knowledge were significantly more

Table 2.4 Experiment one-cell means

(a) Mean of overload measure

	Table		Booklet		Knowledge type mean:
	Low number of choices	High number of choices	Low number of choices	High number of choices	
Low knowledge	27.10 (30)	28.83 (23)	26.52 (27)	25.96 (26)	27.05*** (106)
High knowledge	19.09 (22)	23.12 (26)	22.78 (18)	26.18 (22)	22.81*** (88)
All	23.71 (52)	25.80 (49)	25.02 (45)	26.06 (48)	
Display type mean:	24.72 (101)		25.56 (93)		
Low number of choices mean:			24.32** (97)		
High number of choices mean:			25.93** (97)		

(b) Mean of default measure

	Table		Booklet		Knowledge type mean:
	Low number of choices	High number of choices	Low number of choices	High number of choices	
Low knowledge	0.31 (32)	0.09 (23)	0.25 (28)	0.12 (26)	0.20*** (109)
High knowledge	0.00 (22)	0.04 (26)	0.00 (18)	0.04 (23)	0.02*** (89)
All	0.19 (54)	0.06 (49)	0.15 (46)	0.08 (49)	
Display Type Mean:	0.13 (103)		0.12 (95)		
Low number of choices mean:			0.17 (100)		
High number of choices mean:			0.07 (98)		

Notes: The cell means are shown for the display experiment. The number of participants in each cell is in parentheses. *** indicates significance at the 1% level; ** indicates significance at the 5% level; * indicates significance at the 10% level.

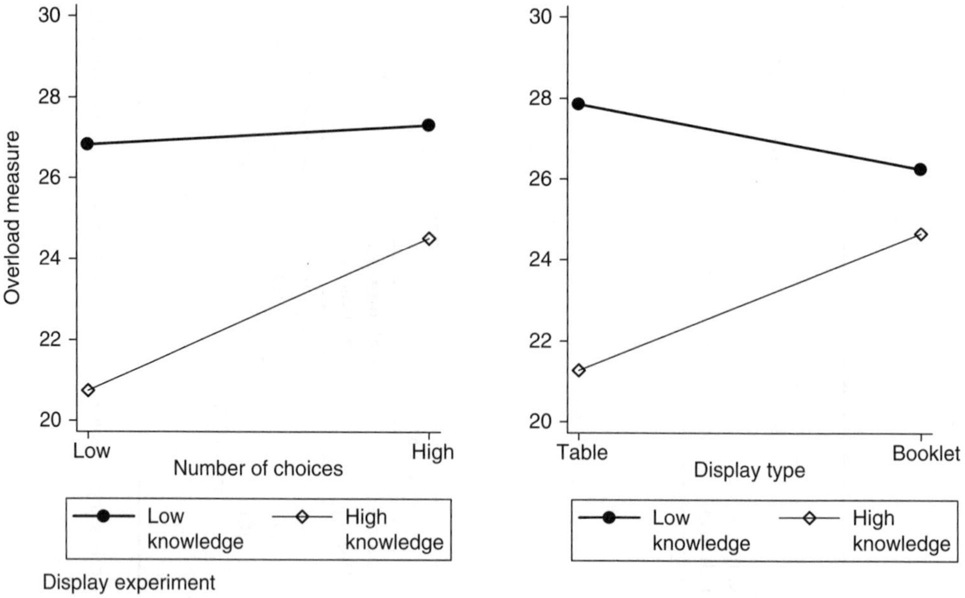

Figure 2.1 Experiment one – interaction effects for overload

overwhelmed than those with above average knowledge. In addition, individuals presented with more choices experienced greater overload ($F(1,186) = 5.11$, $p < 0.05$). This supports the notion that as the number of alternatives increases, participants begin to experience information overload. A main effect related to the display condition (booklet versus table) was not found.

Two significant interaction effects were also found, suggesting that how individuals react to changes in the number of options or how the information is displayed depends on their relative knowledge. Figure 2.1 displays the results graphically. In the leftmost graph, individuals with below average knowledge are overwhelmed regardless of the number of choices they are given. This is confirmed statistically with Scheffe multiple-comparison tests. A statistical difference in experienced overload is not found between the high choice and low choice conditions for individuals with below average knowledge. Interestingly, the number of choices does have an impact on the reported overload for individuals with above average knowledge. These individuals experience statistically greater feelings of overload with more choices ($p < 0.10$).[5] This is an important finding because it indicates that while a change in plan design, such as reducing the number of choices, may reduce information overload, it may only be effective for some participants. In this case, it only helps those with above average knowledge and does nothing for a very vulnerable group, those with below average knowledge. Another striking result is that individuals with above average knowledge and few investment options are significantly less overloaded than below average knowledge participants in either context ($p < 0.01$ in both cases).

The second significant interaction effect is between knowledge and the display condition. Individuals with above average knowledge who were given the table format

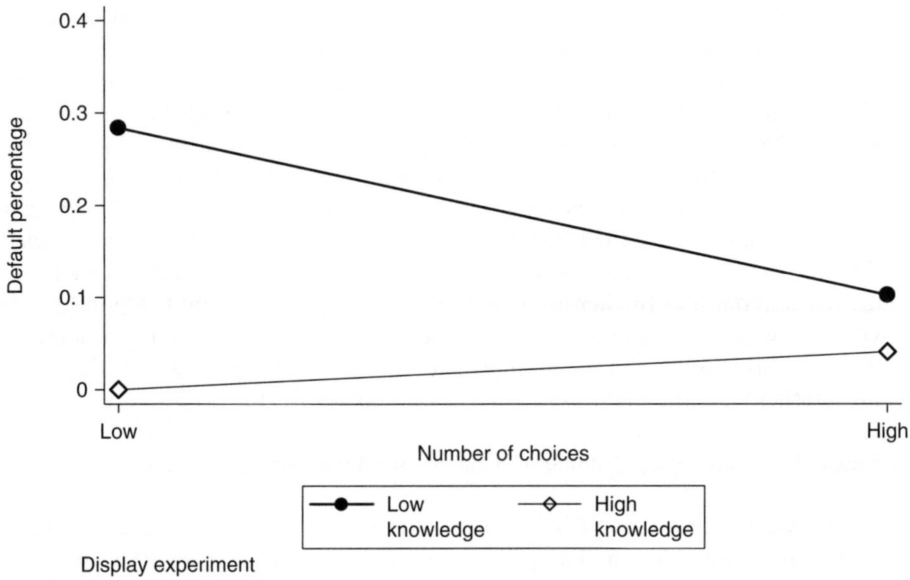

Figure 2.2 Experiment one – interaction effects for default

were significantly less overloaded than the below average knowledge individuals given either format ($p < 0.01$ in both cases). However, there are no differences in the overload measure of the high knowledge participants in the booklet condition and the low knowledge participants in either format. In addition, manipulating the display does nothing to attenuate the low knowledge or high knowledge participants' feelings of overload.

In addition to measuring overload, we wanted to test whether actual allocation choices were affected. We were interested in whether information overload or financial knowledge may relate to how much influence the default has on allocations. To test this in our experiments, we coded an indicator variable that was set equal to one if the participant chose the default option and zero if they chose a non-default allocation. The cell means of this variable equate to the percentage of individuals in each cell that opted for the default.

The results are reported in Table 2.4, panel (b). Once again the influence of knowledge is significant. Twenty percent of the low knowledge individuals chose the default option compared to 2 percent of the high knowledge individuals ($F(1,190) = 14.41$, $p < 0.01$). There were no other significant main effects.

In addition, a significant interaction is found between knowledge and the number of choices (see Figure 2.2). High knowledge individuals do show an increase in the mean default rate when the number of choices increases, but the increase is not significant. Contrary to our expectations, low knowledge individuals chose the default more often when given a low number of choices as opposed to a high number of choices. According to the Scheffe multiple-comparison tests, the difference is significant ($p < 0.05$). Given that the low knowledge individuals experienced an insignificant difference in overload, we expected that the same insignificant difference in default would be found.

Together these results suggest a strong mediating effect of knowledge. Feelings of information overload experienced by individuals with below average knowledge are unaffected by changes in the number of options offered or the display type. These individuals are simply overwhelmed by the investment decision in general. For these individuals, changing the format of information does nothing to relieve their overload. On the other hand, reducing the number of options does significantly reduce information overload for individuals with above average knowledge. Turning to the actual asset allocation decision, significantly fewer individuals with high knowledge chose the default option compared to their below average counterparts. However, low knowledge participants were less likely to choose the default when given more choice. This result is inconclusive and requires further investigation. While these participants reported feeling overwhelmed, we expect that they would 'shut down' their decision making in some way. Obviously they are not doing this through selection of the default. However, they may be utilizing another heuristic that has not been captured in this study.

Experiment Two: Similarity, Number of Choices and Financial Knowledge

The second experiment used a 2 (similarity) × 2 (number of choices) × 2 (financial knowledge) between-subjects design. The procedure for this experiment was the same as for the previous one. All of the investment information was presented in the low search cost table format.

Participants were given options that were either highly similar or very distinct. Similar options were found by choosing funds that were listed under the same Morningstar category, had comparable investment strategies and similar performance.[6] For example, the high information/low similarity condition included 60 fund options that included five money market funds, five bond funds and 50 equity funds. The 50 equity funds included five different equity index funds, 15 different growth funds, 15 different blended funds and 15 different value funds. In contrast, the high information/high similarity option included the same number of fund choices, but only one money market fund and one bond index fund were offered. The remaining choices were made from 58 equity index funds. This is admittedly extreme. Even in the case where multiple vendors might offer similar funds, it is unlikely that this many index funds would be offered. However, the advantage of this design is that if similarity is not a significant factor in this extreme case, we can conclude that it will not be a factor in less extreme and more realistic cases.

Results

As in the first experiment, knowledge plays a large role in the individuals' level of overload. Table 2.5 reports the cell means. Using a three-factor analysis of variance, we find that information overload is significantly higher for individuals with low knowledge ($F(1,190) = 37.54, p < 0.01$). In addition, information overload increases with the number of choices offered ($F(1,190) = 13.93$, $p < 0.001$). There are no significant interaction effects in this experiment.

As in experiment one, individuals with above average knowledge chose the default option less often ($F(1,192) = 19.34, p < 0.01$). However, in this case, there is also a three-way interaction between similarity, information and knowledge. Figure 2.3 displays the results. It appears that for high knowledge individuals, the default option is chosen more frequently when more funds are offered and the funds are more similar. This supports the

Table 2.5 Experiment two-cell means

(a) Mean of overload measure

	Low Similarity		High Similarity		Knowledge type mean:
	Low number of choices	High number of choices	Low number of choices	High number of choices	
Low knowledge	27.10 (30)	28.83 (23)	24.50 (24)	29.00 (21)	27.28*** (98)
High knowledge	19.09 (22)	23.12 (26)	19.83 (24)	23.89 (28)	21.66*** (100)
All	23.71 (52)	25.80 (49)	22.17 (48)	26.08 (49)	
Similarity Mean:	24.72 (101)		24.14 (97)		
Low number of choices mean:			22.97*** (100)		
High number of choices mean:			25.94*** (98)		

(b) Mean of default measure

	Low Similarity		High Similarity		Knowledge type mean:
	Low number of choices	High number of choices	Low number of choices	High number of choices	
Low knowledge	0.31 (32)	0.09 (23)	0.21 (24)	0.38 (21)	0.25*** (100)
High knowledge	0.00 (22)	0.04 (26)	0.04 (24)	0.07 (28)	0.04*** (100)
All	0.19 (54)	0.06 (49)	0.13 (48)	0.20 (49)	
Similarity Mean:	0.13 (103)		0.16 (97)		
Low number of choices mean:			0.16 (102)		
High number of choices mean:			0.13 (98)		

Notes: The cell means are shown for the similarity experiment. The number of participants in each cell is in parentheses. *** indicates significance at the 1% level; ** indicates significance at the 5% level; * indicates significance at the 10% level.

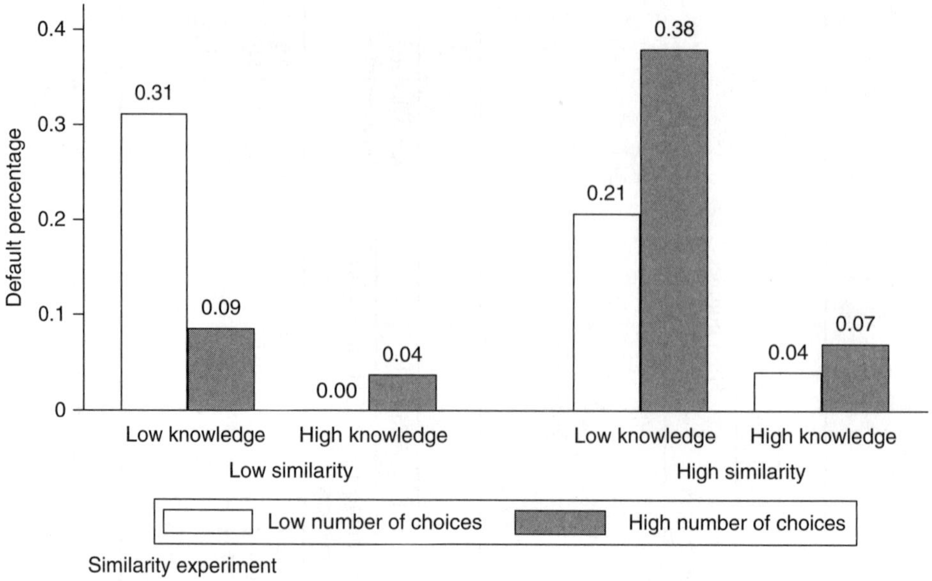

Figure 2.3 Experiment two – interaction effects for default

notion that people become more overloaded as alternatives are harder to differentiate. For the low knowledge individuals, the reaction to the number of choices depends on the similarity of the options. When the choices are large, increasing similarity does increase the number who default. However, when the choices are small, increasing the similarity has the opposite effect.

Supporting the results from experiment one, relative investor knowledge played a key role in reported overload and default choice. While the similarity of the options did not contribute to reported feelings of overload, the options similarity did have some influence on asset allocation. Once again, the investment patterns of the individuals with low knowledge were unusual and unexpected. The lack of predictability in their investment choices may be a result of their high level of overload. This again highlights the importance of investors' knowledge.

Experiment Three: Information Framing and Financial Knowledge

The results from Agnew and Szykman (2005) strongly suggest that information presentation can influence feelings of information overload and that these feelings can be related to financial knowledge. These findings prompted us to further investigate the role of information presentation. To do this, we focused on the decision whether to purchase an annuity or not. Specifically, we focused on a fixed, lifetime, immediate annuity. The decision to purchase this type of security is most often associated with the decumulation phase of retirement savings. This is the time period after the individual retires and begins to draw down on their accumulated savings. Decisions in the decumulation phase have been a recent focus of behavioral finance researchers.

For years, researchers have wondered why individuals do not purchase more annuities for their portfolios. Theoretically, the size of the annuity market should be much larger than observed. This fact is commonly referred to as the 'annuity puzzle.' Models designed to predict the size of the annuity market have assumed that individuals act rationally, and do not fully explain the small size of the market. Brown (2008) provides an excellent review of this past literature. Brown suggests that researchers turn to behavioral finance to explain this phenomenon, since rational models fall short. In a later study by Brown et al. (2008), they find that individuals are more likely to prefer an annuity when it is presented in a consumption frame versus an investment frame. This suggests that the low demand for annuities could be because individuals are making their decision from an investment frame.

Our interest is also in the influence of framing, but in a different type of frame called negative message framing. In a 2008 study, we hypothesized that we could make one option look more attractive by negatively framing the other option. Specifically, in order to make the annuity option seem more attractive, we highlighted the potential negatives associated with an investment option and vice versa. In Agnew et al. (2008), we tested this and found evidence that negative message framing can influence behavior. In the experiment, participants had to choose between an investment option and an annuity option in a simulated 'retirement game.' The investment and annuity options were 'framed' in a short five-minute presentation made to participants prior to when they had to decide how to invest their experimental money.

The framing technique we used in the study has already been shown to be effective in improving preventative health behaviors by highlighting negative consequences of not performing the behavior. Past researchers have effectively used negative message framing to increase health behaviors related to such diseases as breast cancer, sexually transmitted diseases and skin cancer (Block and Keller, 1995, Meyerowitz and Chaiken, 1987; Rothman et al., 1993).

While our presentations in the experiments to participants were purposefully biased, we have no evidence to suggest that financial advisors in the real world intentionally highlight the negative consequences related to annuities in order to encourage consumers to invest in stock funds. However, it may be that individuals prefer investments to annuities because the potential negative consequences related to investing in annuities are more salient to them than the potential negative consequences related to the stock market.[7] This then interferes with their rationality when making their choice.

To test whether the information effects can influence the annuity decision, our experiment was designed to highlight the potential financial losses or costs associated with the annuity choice and the investment choice. We used a series of pretests to develop three different slide show presentations that favored one option over the other. For example, one slide show highlighted the negative features of the investment option (such as the potential for losing a substantial amount of money in a market downturn or outliving resources) and provided the annuity as the solution to avoid the drawbacks ('annuity bias'). The second slide show highlighted the negative features of an annuity (such as dying soon after purchasing an annuity and not being able to provide an inheritance) and provided the investment option as the solution to overcome the drawbacks ('investment bias'). The third slide show was a neutral condition, in which neither option was favored.

Since defaults have also been shown to be effective in influencing financial decisions, we added defaults as our second independent variable. Participants were either exposed to an annuity default, an investment default or no default.

In this chapter, we present some new results from these experiments that have not been previously reported. As a follow-up on our earlier studies, we wanted to test how information overload related to the choice and measured financial literacy. Applying the same overload measure used by Agnew and Szykman (2005) and using the same sample from Agnew et al. (2008), we measured participants' feelings of overload after they made their choice and played the game ($\alpha = 0.827$). The mean was calculated for the overload measure and it was used to form a high and low overload group. A ten-question financial literacy test was also used to measure participants' financial knowledge. We split participants into three equal groups based on their financial literacy scores: low financial literacy, medium financial literacy and high financial literacy. The financial literacy test was slightly different than the one used in Agnew and Szykman (2005) and the questions can be found in Table 2.6.

Our basic experimental design for this new experiment was a 3 (annuity bias, investment bias, no bias) × 3 (annuity default, investment default, no default) between-subject design. More detailed information about the experimental procedure can be found in Agnew et al. (2008); however, a general overview of the methodology follows.

In the experiment, participants first completed a financial literacy quiz and a lottery choice experiment to determine their risk preferences. Then they were shown one of the presentations that was either neutral or favored one of the options. Once the 5-minute slide show presentation was over, participants were led through detailed instructions and examples on how to play the 'retirement game.' Once this was complete, participants were told they had $60 in an 'account' to begin the game. The first step of the game was for each participant to decide whether to 'purchase an annuity' that would give them a fixed payment or to invest the money in our simulated 'market.'[8] If participants chose the annuity, they received $16.77 for every period they 'survived' in the game, which was determined by a die roll. If the investment choice was selected, several decisions had to be made in each round. First, they needed to decide how much to withdraw (to simulate living expenses), and then they had to decide how much to invest in the 'market.' Once these decisions were made, dice were rolled to determine the market return or loss. After a new remaining balance was calculated, another die roll was done to determine whether the participant survived to continue playing the game.

In addition to the information presentation, the very thorough directions and demonstrated examples made it obvious that the annuity choice was the easier choice – the participant had to make only one choice at the beginning of the game. With the investment option, the participant would have to revisit the amount of money to invest and withdraw for each round. While annuities may not be the less complicated choice in reality, for the purposes of our game the annuity decision was a simpler option.[9] In other words, if someone was overwhelmed, or overloaded, during this task, we would have expected the annuity option to be chosen.

Results

We created a variable that equals one if the person picked an annuity and zero if they picked the investment. We report the cell means for this variable in Table 2.7. An ANOVA was used to determine whether the cell means were different from one another.

Table 2.6 Summary of test questions used in experiment three

Test question

1. If you are saving for a future goal, it's better to start early. That way your money earns more and builds up faster over time.
   (a) True
   (b) False
   (c) Not sure
2. Keeping a balance on your credit card is okay as long as you can make the minimum payment each month.
   (a) True
   (b) False
   (c) Not sure
3. If you take out an adjustable rate mortgage to buy a house, and interest rates go up, your monthly payments will also go up.
   (a) True
   (b) False
   (c) Not sure
4. If you were to invest $1000 in a stock mutual fund, it is possible to have less than $1000 if you withdraw the money.
   (a) True
   (b) False
   (c) Not sure
5. Historically, which option provides the highest long-term growth?
   (a) Savings account
   (b) Certificate of deposit
   (c) Insurance policy
   (d) Stock mutual fund
   (e) Not sure
6. Which of the following types of investments are typically found in a money market fund?
   (a) Stocks
   (b) Bonds
   (c) Short-term debt securities
   (d) Not sure
7. When an investor diversifies his investments, does the risk of losing money increase or decrease?
   (a) Decrease
   (b) Increase
   (c) Not Sure
8. A money market fund is riskier than a stock fund.
   (a) True
   (b) False
   (c) Not sure
9. A stock fund's beta rating can best be described as:
   (a) A measure of relative volatility of the fund versus the S&P 500 index
   (b) A measure of relative growth versus the S&P 500 index
   (c) A measure of relative capital outflow of the fund versus the S&P 500 index
   (d) Not sure
10. If interest rates go up, then bond prices generally:
   (a) Increase
   (b) Decrease
   (c) Not sure

Table 2.7 *Cell means for the variable pick annuity for experiment three*

	Annuity frame			Neutral frame			Investment frame			Total
	Annuity default	No default	Investment default	Annuity default	No default	Investment default	Annuity default	No default	Investment default	
Low overload	0.33(36)	0.54(46)	0.39(61)	0.25(44)	0.25(32)	0.28(50)	0.22(36)	0.14(77)	0.21(52)	0.28(439)***
High overload	0.65(34)	0.48(52)	0.43(35)	0.40(35)	0.40(35)	0.33(49)	0.25(32)	0.29(42)	0.25(28)	0.39(350)***
Total	0.47(264)***			0.31(245)***			0.21(267)***			

Notes: The number of participants in each cell is in parentheses. *** indicates significance at the 1% level; ** indicates significance at the 5% level; * indicates significance at the 10% level.

Table 2.8 Cell means for overload for experiment three

	Low financial literacy	Medium financial literacy	High financial literacy
Overload	18.173(168)***	16.652(256)***	14.466(337)***

Notes: The number of participants in each cell is in parentheses. *** indicates significance at the 1% level; ** indicates significance at the 5% level; * indicates significance at the 10% level.

As shown in the table, two main effects were found. Consistent with the finding of Agnew et al. (2008), participants in the annuity bias were more likely to choose the annuity option and those in the investment frame were the least likely ($F(2,775) = 17.807$, $p < 0.0001$). In addition, participants who experienced a higher level of information overload were more likely to choose the annuity option than the participants who experienced low levels of information overload ($F(1,775) = 7.568$, $p < 0.01$). This finding is consistent with the hypothesis that individuals who are overwhelmed are more likely to choose the option that demands the least effort.

We then investigated the relationship between financial knowledge and information overload. The cell means are reported in Table 2.8. Using an ANOVA, we found that people with different levels of financial literacy reported higher levels of information overload ($F(2,760) = 27.452$, $p < 0.0001$)

These findings in this preliminary study suggest once again that consumer choices can be impacted by how information is presented. In addition, we find evidence that when consumers experience information overload, they are more likely to choose a less complicated option versus one that would require more thought. Moreover, we find that consumers who are less financially literate experience greater feelings of information overload. These preliminary findings are consistent with the first two experiments and provide further evidence that information overload and financial knowledge may influence financial decision making and should be taken into account.

CONCLUSIONS

This chapter describes three recent experiments focused on the relationship between information presentation, financial literacy and information overload. Our experimental findings suggest that individuals with below average knowledge are more overwhelmed by the investment decisions and the information presented than those with more knowledge. In one experiment, altering the plan by offering investment information in a more easily comparable format and by reducing the choices offered did not attenuate the low knowledge individuals' feelings of overload. On the other hand, reducing the number of choices did lessen the reported overload of individuals with above average knowledge. These results have powerful implications for plan design. Mainly, it suggests that plan sponsors must think beyond simple changes in plan design in order to help all types of participants. In particular, attention must be paid to educating participants with below average financial knowledge in addition to simplifying plan design. Without improving the financial knowledge of the below average individuals, changes in plan design may not have their intended effect.

The importance of financial education has not gone unnoticed by policy makers. In 2002, Alan Greenspan stated that 'education can play a critical role by equipping consumers with the knowledge required to make wise decisions when choosing among the myriad of financial products and providers.' Our results show that financial knowledge plays a large role in who opts for the default. We find that low knowledge individuals are opting for the default allocation more often than high knowledge individuals. In experiment one, 20 percent of the low knowledge participants chose the default compared to 2 percent of the high knowledge individuals. The results were even more striking in experiment two (25 percent versus 4 percent). These findings are consistent with individuals opting for the 'path of least resistance' when they are less financially knowledgeable. As a result, more research into new and innovative ways to educate these participants is needed. Towards this end, Lusardi (2009) outlines the many challenges facing financial educators and provides suggestions for increasing the effectiveness of these programs.

The tendency towards the path of least resistance was also apparent in the new results from our final experiment. Although the choice between annuities and investments was fair, individuals who reported higher feelings of information overload were more likely to select the option that was perceived to require the least effort. Individuals experiencing the most overload were also the least financially literate, consistent with the other experiments.

Finally, the last experiment demonstrated that negative message framing can influence financial decision making. This has implications for consumers, financial firms and regulators. Consumers should be careful to watch for potentially biased information from financial advisors, the media and marketing information, while financial firms should train employees to make balanced and fair presentations. It is very possible that employees may be unintentionally framing information in a way that favors one option simply based on their background. Regulators should also realize that the information presented in this experiment was all factual. Therefore, even without resorting to inaccurate claims, individuals can be significantly swayed by negative message framing.

In closing, we note that plan sponsors and financial firms should be careful how they present information to investors. They should heed lessons learned from the efforts to improve nutritional labeling. Furthermore, plan sponsors should consider their plan's design and recognize what choices represent the path of least resistance. Until we can formally test whether improving financial knowledge and/or feelings of information overload improves thoughtful decision making, careful plan design will be key.

ACKNOWLEDGEMENT

The Agnew and Szykman (2005) research reported herein was made possible by a grant from the U.S. Social Security Administration (SSA) funded as part of the Retirement Research Consortium (RRC). The opinions and conclusions expressed are solely those of the authors and do not represent the opinions of SSA, any agency of the federal government, the RRC, or Boston College. The authors are grateful for the generous funding that supported the research discussed in this chapter. Annuity findings were generated from research funding from the FINRA Investor Education Foundation.

NOTES

1. For example, participants following the $1/n$ heuristic opt to divide their contribution allocations evenly among the fund options offered. While this strategy can result in a well-diversified portfolio, Benartzi and Thaler (2001) have shown that it can also lead to large *ex ante* welfare losses. Agnew (2006) finds that those with relatively low salaries are most likely to follow the $1/n$ heuristic. In this case, salary may be proxying for financial knowledge.
2. The authors note that their current investment plans have undergone a change and the number of choices available decreased dramatically.
3. Pretests were done to determine the number of funds that were considered 'low' versus 'high.'
4. Consistent with the marketing literature, we report the F statistic estimated from the ANOVA analysis related to the variable being discussed. Degrees of freedom are reported within parentheses. In this example, the F-statistic is 20.54 for the knowledge variable. The $p < 0.01$ indicates that the significance level is less than 0.01.
5. The p-values reported in all of the discussions of the interaction variables are based on the Scheffe-adjusted significance levels. In this case, the Scheffe-adjusted significance level is less than 0.10.
6. Similarity between funds was confirmed through pretests.
7. Note that this experiment was conducted prior to the recent market downturn. It would be interesting to test whether the actual market events have made annuities more attractive.
8. Unfair annuity pricing and adverse selection were avoided by making the annuity price actuarially fair and making subjects aware of their identical survival probabilities over the six-period game up front.
9. In reality, the number of different types of fixed and variable annuity choices in the market could easily overwhelm an investor, especially somebody who is unfamiliar with these products.

REFERENCES

Agnew, J. (2006), 'Do behavioral biases vary across individuals?: Evidence from individual level 401(k) data,' *The Journal of Financial and Quantitative Analysis*, **41** (4), 939–61.

Agnew, J. (forthcoming), 'Pension plan behavior,' in H. Baker and J. Nofsinger (eds), *Behavioral Finance*, Hoboken, NJ: John Wiley & Sons, Inc.

Agnew, J. and L. Szykman (2005), 'Asset allocation and information overload: the influence of information display, asset choice, and investor experience,' *The Journal of Behavioral Finance*, **6** (2), 57–70.

Agnew, J., L. Anderson, J. Gerlach and L. Szykman (2008), 'Who chooses annuities? An experimental investigation of the role of gender, framing, and defaults,' *American Economic Review: Papers and Proceedings*, **98** (1), 418–22.

Benartzi, S. and R. Thaler (2001), 'Naive diversification strategies in retirement saving plans,' *American Economic Review*, **91** (1), 79–98.

Bettman, J. and C.W. Park (1980), 'Effects of prior knowledge and experience and phase of the choice process on consumer decision processes: a protocol analysis,' *Journal of Consumer Research*, **7** (December), 234–48.

Block, L. and P.A. Keller (1995), 'When to accentuate the negative: the effects of perceived efficacy and message framing on intentions to perform a health-related behavior,' *Journal of Marketing Research*, **32** (May), 192–203.

Brown, J. (2008), 'Understanding the role of annuities in retirement planning,' in Annamaria Lusardi (ed.), *Overcoming the Saving Slump: How to Increase the Effectiveness of Financial Education and Savings Programs*, Chicago, IL: University of Chicago Press, pp. 178–208.

Brown, J., J. Kling, S. Mullainathan and M. Wrobel (2008), 'Why don't people insure late-life consumption? A framing explanation of the under-annuitization puzzle,' *American Economic Review*, **98** (2), 304–9.

Choi, James, David Laibson, Brigitte Madrian and Andrew Metrick (2002), 'Defined contribution pensions: plan rules, participant decisions, and the path of least resistance,' in James M. Poterba (ed.), *Tax Policy and the Economy*, Cambridge, MA: MIT Press, Vol. 16, pp. 67–113.

Dwyer, P., J. Gilkeson and J. List (2002), 'Gender differences in revealed risk taking: evidence from mutual fund investors,' *Economic Letters*, **76** (2), 151–9.

Eppler, M. and J. Mengis (2004), 'The concept of information overload: a review of literature from organizational science, accounting, marketing, MIS, and related disciplines,' *The Information Society*, **20**, 325–44.

Greenspan, A. (2002) 'Prepared statement,' *Hearings on the State of Financial Literacy and Education in America*, US Senate Committee on Banking, Housing and Urban Affairs, 6 February.

Ippolito, P. and A. Mathios (1990), 'Information, advertising and health choice: a study of the cereal market,' *RAND Journal of Economics*, **21** (3), 459–80.

Ippolito, P. and A. Mathios (1994), 'Information, policy, and the sources of fat and cholesterol in the U.S. diet,' *Journal of Public Policy and Marketing*, **13** (2), 200–217.

Iyengar, S. and M. Lepper (2000), 'When choice is demotivating: can one desire too much of a good thing?,' *Journal of Personality and Social Psychology*, **76**, 995–1006.

John Hancock Financial Services (2002), 'Insight into participant investment, knowledge and behavior,' Eighth Defined Contribution Survey.

Lusardi, A. (ed.) (2009), *Overcoming the Saving Slump: How to Increase the Effectiveness of Financial Education and Savings Programs*, Chicago, IL: University of Chicago Press.

Meyerowitz, B. and S. Chaiken (1987), 'The effects of message framing on breast self-examination attitudes, intentions and behavior,' *Journal of Personality and Social Psychology*, **52** (3), 500–510.

Moorman, C. (1990), 'The effects of stimulus and consumer characteristics on the utilization of nutrition information,' *Journal of Consumer Research*, **17** (December), 362–74.

Moorman, C. (1996), 'A quasi experiment to assess the consumer and informational determinants of nutrition information processing activities: the case of the Nutrition Labeling and Education Act,' *Journal of Public Policy and Marketing*, **15** (1), 28–44.

Muller, T. (1985), 'Structural information factors which stimulate the use of nutrition information: a field experiment,' *Journal of Marketing Research*, **22** (May), 143–57.

Nelson, P. (1970), 'Information and consumer behavior,' *Journal of Political Economy*, **78** (March/April), 311–29.

Nelson, P. (1974), 'Advertising as information,' *Journal of Political Economy*, **83** (July/August), 729–54.

O'Donoghue, T. and M. Rabin (2001), 'Choice and procrastination,' *Quarterly Journal of Economics*, **116** (1), 121–60.

Roe, B., A. Levy and B. Derby (1999), 'The impact of health claims on consumer search and product evaluation outcomes: results from FDA experimental data,' *Journal of Public Policy and Marketing*, **18** (Spring), 89–105.

Rothman, A., P. Salovey, C. Antone, K. Keough and C. Martin (1993), 'The influence of message framing on intentions to perform health behaviors,' *Journal of Experimental Social Psychology*, **29**, 408–33.

Sethi-Iyengar, S., G. Huberman and W. Jiang (2004), 'How much choice is too much? Contributions to 401(k) retirement plans,' in O. Mitchell and S. Utkus (eds), *Pension Design and Structure: New Lessons from Behavioral Finance*, Oxford: Oxford University Press, pp. 83–95.

Stigler, G. (1961), 'The economics of information,' *Journal of Political Economy*, **69** (June), 213–55.

Weaver, K. (2002), 'Reforming social security: lessons from abroad,' Conference Proceeding from Retirement Research Consortium's Fourth Annual Conference, 30–31 May.

Wilcox, R. (2003), 'Bargain hunting or star gazing? Investors' preferences for stock mutual funds,' *Journal of Business*, **76** (4), 645–55.

3 Revealing the information content of investment decisions

Noriyuki Okuyama and Gavin Francis

INTRODUCTION

Conventional performance measurement methods concentrate on investment outcomes rather than the underlying investment process. This chapter examines the effectiveness of the investment process by considering the essential part of any investment strategy: the investment decision. As recognized by Kahneman and Tversky (1979), the essential first step is to decompose returns into gains and losses.

We introduce tools to indentify the asymmetries in investment returns available to passive and active investors. The approach fits naturally into an enhanced risk budgeting framework for more effective portfolio construction.

INVESTMENT DECISIONS

An investment decision results in a change of exposure in an underlying portfolio, exchanging one stream of returns for another. Since this must be based on an assessment of relative performance, we define an investment exposure as a zero size long/short portfolio, holding a position in a risky asset against an equal and opposing position in a risk-free asset. A risk-free asset earns the risk-free rate, but cannot suffer a loss. This is the numeraire against which all other returns are measured. Each currency's cash rate is considered as the risk-free rate for the assets denominated in that currency. We can broaden the scope for a long/short position created by two assets denominated in different currencies, each considered as a risk exposure against the local cash rate. This approach incorporates the difference of the two currencies' cash rates: the interest rate differential.

It is widely recognized in the field of behavioral finance that the basis of an investment decision is an assessment of the trade-off between gain and loss. Ultimately, all investment decisions are binary: to act or not to act, that is the question. Having implemented the decision, the outcome can be success or error. These outcomes are summarized in Figure 3.1.

The four quadrants of the matrix represent the principal outcomes of an investment decision. Investment success can be either the capture of gains, a true positive, or the avoidance of loss, a true negative. Investment error occurs either by incurring a loss, a false positive or 'type I error' or as a result of missing out on a gain, a false negative or 'type II error.' See Luce and Raiffa (1989) for a general discussion of decision theory.

This simple matrix demonstrates that there are two sides to investment error: holding

		Actual outcome (*ex post*)	
		Gain	Loss
Investment decision (*ex ante*)	Take exposure (visible)	Capture gains (true positive) success	Incur losses (false positive) type I error
	Avoid exposure (invisible)	Give up gains (false negative) type II error	Avoid losses (true negative) success

Figure 3.1 Fundamental investment decision matrix

an asset when it falls in value or holding cash when the asset is rising. Investment error is defined as any uncertainty that contributes negatively to an investor's potential wealth. This decomposition of risk demonstrates that a full evaluation of investment error must include both false positives and false negatives. Following this line of reasoning, an investment success is any uncertainty that contributes positively to returns. There are two ways to improve returns: by capturing gains through true positives or by avoiding losses through true negatives. Making a 5 percent gain and avoiding a 5 percent loss both have an equal effect on an investor's wealth.

This chapter proposes that active investment skill lies in the ability to maximize investment success relative to investment error. When making an assessment of the historic performance of an investment decision maker, this is superior to measuring return versus volatility.

However, one should ask why traditional approaches to risk management, such as mean-variance analysis and value at risk, focus on only one of the two sources of investment error: the risk of incurring losses. The answer lies in the fact that captured gains and incurred losses are both 'visible': they are the returns observed in the portfolio, whereas the losses one avoids and the gains given up are both 'invisible'. This means that it is normally hard to evaluate the costs of false negatives and true negatives. We can define this visibility as the degree to which the investor sees *ex post* gains and losses in the portfolio. Any investment decision contains a trade-off between visibility and invisibility of its investment outcome, which is determined by the size of the risk exposure.

Investment Error versus Volatility

Several consequences ensue from equating investment risk with investment errors (both false positives and false negatives). It becomes highly questionable to consider volatility as a proper measure of investment risk, since it simply looks at a degree of deviation from an achieved return on both negative and positive sides. In other words, the traditional mean-variance framework assumes that any uncertainty in possible outcomes should be considered as risk. This is a typical heuristic approach in many of the performance metrics that have emerged from the framework of modern portfolio theory that fails to

		Actual outcome (*ex post*)	
		Gain	Loss
Investment decision (*ex ante*)	Take exposure (visible)	Higher volatility (true positive) success	Higher volatility (false positive) type I error
	Avoid exposure (invisible)	Lower volatility (false negative) type II error	Lower volatility (true negative) success

Figure 3.2 Shortcomings in the use of volatility

distinguish between loss and gain. It ranks different returns according to their degrees of uncertainty without disentangling constituent factors behind: losses and gains are mixed together.

Consider the Sharpe ratio, described by Sharpe (1994). Losses and gains are mixed to obtain an average return. This is divided by the volatility of returns, which would only be a useful measure of loss if the returns were described by a normal distribution with a mean of zero. The Sharpe ratio, like the information ratio, measures a signal-to-noise ratio, but it does not measure the balance between investment success and investment error. Noise contains both gains and losses. A signal-to-noise ratio can be meaningful only if perpetually matching a target outcome is the top priority. But in investment, exceeding the target is a benefit. A positive outcome (even if due to luck) is always welcome and should not be penalized. This asymmetry in investment utility cannot be captured by return and volatility alone.

From the perspective of the decision matrix, the uncertainty of an achieved return should be decomposed into the uncertainty of positive returns and the uncertainty of negative returns. This suggests that a larger negative return and a smaller positive return both represent real investment errors to the same extent. However, while larger uncertainties in negative returns will increase overall volatility, smaller uncertainties in positive returns reduce overall volatility. Even though both cases are investment errors, the impact on volatility is opposite.

In contrast, the chances of smaller negative returns or larger positive returns both constitute investment success. Yet these also have opposite effects on volatility. This means that volatility can properly represent neither investment errors nor investment success.

Figure 3.2 shows that volatility makes an incorrect assessment of realized gains. In order to analyze investment error/success appropriately, one needs to go to the trouble of decomposing returns into negatives (losses relative to the risk-free portfolio) and positives (or gains). Unlike the mean-variance 'two-tails-combined' approach, this risk decomposition approach enables us to reveal to what extent either skill in reducing losses or skill in capturing gains has contributed to a total return.

Aware of the shortcomings in the use of volatility, Markowitz (1959) proposed the use of a downside risk measure. The Sortino ratio (Sortino and Price Lee, 1994) looks at negative observations rather than volatility, but the numerator of the ratio remains a mixture of losses and gains. Although this is an improvement on volatility, because it does not penalize gains, it is not an effective measure of investment error because it still ignores false negatives. The weakness in the conventional approach is its focus on the final outcome, not on the decision-making process that generates it.

Passive and Active Management

A passive investment management strategy results from a single investment decision to match a pre-defined benchmark payoff. For example, a static buy-and-hold approach makes no attempt to change exposures over time. Since no further investment decisions are required, this is a matter of implementation rather than management. It is almost a tautology to say that a pure passive strategy has no expected return relative to its benchmark (before costs).

An active manager, however, makes decisions to change the risk exposure through time, so exposures are not held statically. The key distinction is that a successful active manager uses information to enhance the balance between losses and gains, whereas a passive manager does not enhance this balance. Biglova et al. (2004) describe the Rachev ratio, which compares the probabilities of extreme gains against extreme losses by defining an upper and a lower threshold. When both of these thresholds are aligned to zero return, we move closer to a useful measure of loss versus gain.

In the long term, however, the return on an investment is the difference, not the ratio, between gain and loss. Utility theory has been used to attempt to disentangle the impacts of losses and gains from inputs that mix them, such as return, volatility and correlation. Superior portfolios would be available to investors who could directly measure the loss and gain of investment processes. Fishburn (1977) defined the lower partial moments of a distribution relative to a threshold. This chapter extends that approach by measuring the upper partial moments of a distribution and comparing these against the lower partial moments. This is called conditional risk attribution (CRA).

FORMAL DEFINITIONS OF PARTIAL MOMENTS

The starting point is to measure the log returns[1] of the outcomes of the investment process relative to the appropriate risk-free rate.[2] This determines a set of n outcomes, x_i. CRA segments the set of observations into losses (the negative returns) and gains (the positive returns). As a result, rather than analyzing a single distribution of outcomes, CRA analyses it in two parts: the distribution of losses and the distribution of gains (see Figure 3.3).

Clearly neither losses (L) nor gains (G) are distributed according to a Gaussian curve. Both distributions are bounded at zero and their modes would normally lie close to the origin. The frequency distribution of losses may be characterized by the lower partial moments: the averages of L, L^2, L^3, L^4 etc., and similarly for the distribution of gains. Recognizing that these distributions were originally derived from a single distribution of n outcomes, the moments are scaled according to the total number of original observations, n.

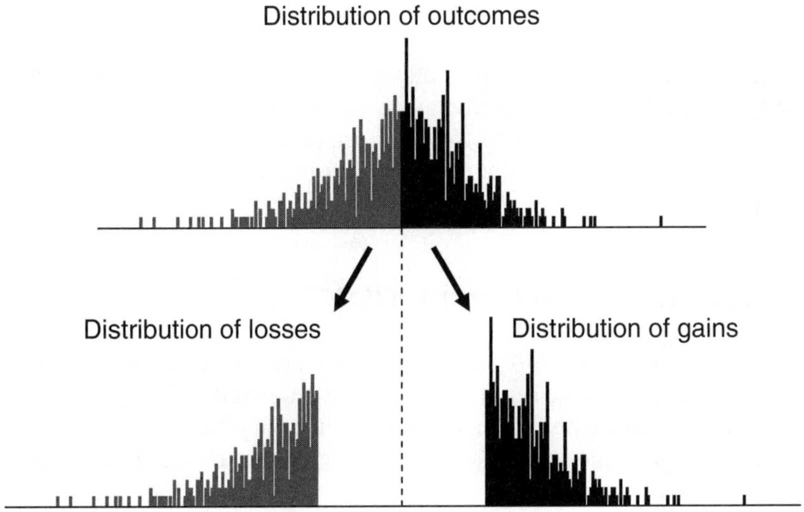

Figure 3.3 Disentangling gains from losses

	Lower partial moment	Upper partial moment
First	$\overline{L} = \frac{1}{n}\sum_{x_i<0} x_i$	$\overline{G} = \frac{1}{n}\sum_{x_i \geq 0} x_i$
Second	$\overline{L^2} = \frac{1}{n}\sum_{x_i<0} x_i^{\,2}$	$\overline{G^2} = \frac{1}{n}\sum_{x_i \geq 0} x_i^{\,2}$
Kth	$\overline{L^k} = \frac{1}{n}\sum_{x_i<0} x_i^{\,k}$	$\overline{G^k} = \frac{1}{n}\sum_{x_i \geq 0} x_i^{\,k}$

Figure 3.4 Definitions of partial moments

This leads to the formal definitions of partial moments[3] (see Figure 3.4). The general definition allows any (integer or non-integer) partial moment to be calculated. The 'zeroeth' moments define the fractions of observations that were losses or gains: the proportions of so-called 'down months' and 'up months', for a monthly track record. The first partial moments represents average loss and gain, while the second partial moments represents dispersion of loss and gain, with the third partial moments being more strongly influenced by the tails. If the distribution is asymmetric, the segregation of losses and gains extracts more information from the frequency distribution than simply taking the average.

The second moment, $\overline{L^2}$, is a measure of the dispersion of losses. Here we start to diverge more significantly from the traditional approach of calculating the variance of the returns. The variance is a measure of the average squared deviation from the mean observation. But since CRA is concerned with losses and gains, the second partial moment is based on the average squared deviation from zero (i.e. from the risk-free return).

Higher moments are more strongly influenced by the extreme observations. This higher moment effect can be a disadvantage when attempting to forecast the future. However, from the perspective of historic performance analysis, these are precisely the observations that are the most important in assessing the investment decision-making process.

CONDITIONAL RISK ATTRIBUTION

Conditional risk attribution (CRA) is a tool for comparing investments that are held passively. A passive strategy is the result of a single investment decision, made at inception. No attempt is made to change the exposure through time. It is not widely recognized that this assumption of passivity is implicit in the output of standard mean–variance optimizers.

Taking Risk Passively in a Symmetric World

We begin by applying the fundamental investment decision matrix (Figure 3.1) to a simplified, constrained scenario. If we relax the constraints, the scenario becomes more representative of the real world. This leads to the concept of CRA.

Consider a world in which there is a risk-free asset and a single risky asset that generates symmetric returns with 50 percent gains and 50 percent losses. The passive investor has the choice of statically holding one asset or the other.

We would normally expect the investor to begin with the risk-free asset. In this case, the decision to switch to the risky asset would be a risk-taking decision. This approach successfully captures all gains, but the portfolio incurs the full impact of losses.

Figure 3.5 shows that false positives are expected to occur 50 percent of the time, i.e. type I errors are maximized. Note that when the risky asset is held, losses and gains are fully visible as portfolio returns.

Compare this with holding the risk-free asset, shown in Figure 3.6, where the decision threshold has shifted. This successfully avoids all losses, but the portfolio is deprived of ever making a gain. As a result, false negatives, i.e. type II errors, are maximized. The effect is to incur type II error rather than type I error.

This fact is not obvious to investors who consider only the volatility of observed outcomes, because both the missed gains and losses are invisible, in the sense that they do not show up as portfolio returns. Behavioral bias tends to prefer visibility.

We now relax one of the constraints and allow the investor to be partially invested in the risky asset. Clearly, this is simply an intermediate between the two extremes. For example, with a 50 percent exposure position to the risky asset, one would expect to see a quarter of observations in each quadrant, resulting in 25 percent of type I error and 25 percent of type II error. Note from Figure 3.7 that the passive approach trades off type I errors for type II errors on a one-for-one basis, so total investment error remains at 50 percent.

The level of a passive exposure determines the horizontal decision threshold between

		Actual outcome (*ex post*)	
		Gain	Loss
Investment decision (*ex ante*) 100%	Take exposure 100% visible	Capture gains (true positive) 50% success	Incur losses (false positive) 50% type I error
	Avoid exposure 0% invisible		

Figure 3.5 *Passively holding a risk exposure*

		Actual outcome (*ex post*)	
		Gain	Loss
Investment decision (*ex ante*) 100%	Take exposure 0% visible		
	Avoid exposure 100% invisible	Give up gains (false negative) 50% type II error	Avoid losses (true negative) 50% success

Figure 3.6 *Passively holding a risk-free exposure*

		Actual outcome (*ex post*)	
		Gain	Loss
Investment decision (*ex ante*) 100%	Take exposure 50% visible	Capture gains (true positive) 25% success	Incur losses (false positive) 25% type I error
	Avoid exposure 50% invisible	Give up gains (false negative) 25% type II error	Avoid losses (true negative) 25% success

Figure 3.7 *Passively holding a partial risk exposure*

visibility and invisibility. The threshold in the box simply slides up or down in parallel, depending on the choice of benchmark static exposure.

Any reduction of incurred losses is accompanied by a reduction of captured gains. Incurring a loss (type I error) and missing a gain (type II error) have exactly the same negative impact on expected return. In the simplified case, where risk exposures that have an equal chance of rising or falling, we conclude that:

(a) all passive exposures have the same expected return;
(b) different passive benchmark selections represent different utilities on visibility of outcomes (different preference/aversion to regret);
(c) all passive exposures incur exactly the same amount of investment error!

Reducing Risk Passively in a Symmetric World

In the above, it was assumed that the investor started with the risk-free asset. If, however, an investor is already 100 percent invested in the risky asset, it is possible to take a risk-reducing decision. This can be achieved most simply by cutting back exposure in exchange for the risk-free asset. Alternatively, risk can be reduced by hedging. This is done by adding a risk exposure that acts as an offset, by reliably generating returns opposite to the risky asset held in the portfolio. In order to be effective, a hedge must have a correlation reliably close to −1, in all market environments. The magnitude of the hedge will determine whether it partially or fully offsets the other risk exposure. The degree of offset is called the hedge ratio, which, by definition, can lie only between zero and one. Hedges can be managed either passively or actively. A hedge has the special property of reducing the size of the maximum potential loss of the portfolio. So hedging is a risk-reducing activity.

As an example, we assume that an investor has currency exposure in a portfolio of international assets. A passive currency hedging strategy consistently maintains a predetermined benchmark hedge ratio throughout an investment horizon, regardless of any subsequent subjective views. There is no attempt to distinguish dynamically between currency gain environments and currency loss environments over time. As we concluded earlier, for a risky asset with symmetric returns, any level of passive hedge results in 50 percent investment error.

Identifying Asymmetry in Passive Investments

Most market participants recognize that financial assets exhibit asymmetric returns. An investment return is mathematically equivalent to the excess of gains over losses. The entire rationale for passive investment therefore relies on finding risky assets with asymmetric returns. In this way, investors can benefit from investment success of more than 50 percent (and investment error of less than 50 percent) without making any active investment decisions. In fact the active decisions are delegated. For example, a passive investment in the S&P 500 index delegates active decisions to the managers of the largest 500 US companies and to the set of rules used to construct the index.

CRA is designed to measure the asymmetries or 'market bias' between the partial moments of a distribution of returns. Often a positive asymmetry in the first moment (a positive return) is associated with negative asymmetries in the higher moments (a large negative tail).

In order to create the fundamental investment decision matrix (Figure 3.1), it was necessary to decompose returns into losses and gains. This matrix can be used to analyze

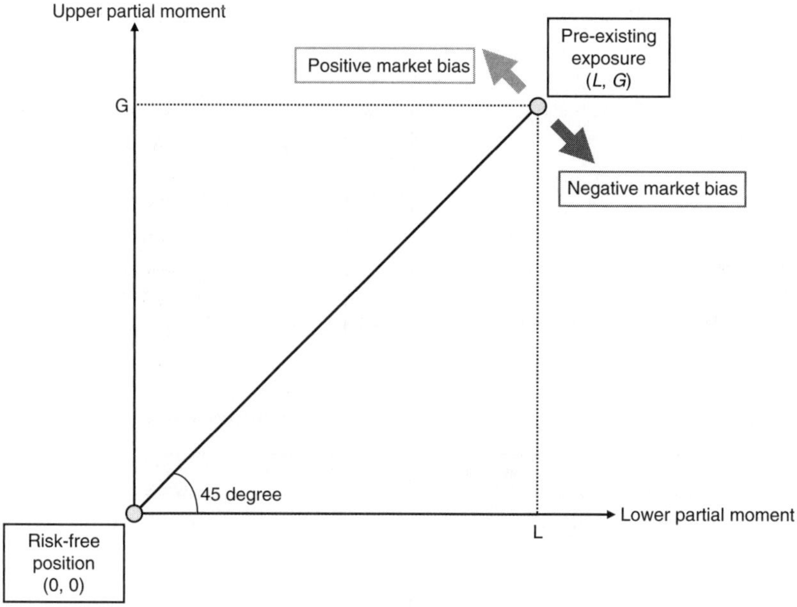

Figure 3.8 Conditional risk attribution

binary decisions, such as the success or failure of a medical test. However, investment outcomes can be quantified in numerical terms. So we must move from a discrete framework to a continuum. The underlying principle of CRA is to compare the result of passive management against a set of perfectly symmetric outcomes. Having calculated the upper and lower partial moments, conditional upon the time period of the observations, we plot each pair in a CRA diagram. It is convenient to rescale each moment to the same dimension, i.e. to plot $(\overline{G^k})^{1/k}$ versus $(\overline{L^k})^{1/k}$, for $k > 0$. The vertical axis represents the upper partial moment, while horizontal axis represents the corresponding lower partial moment (see Figure 3.8).

Now, if the evolution of the underlying risk exposure were determined by the toss of a coin, it would follow a random walk. In this case, we would expect that in the short term the upper partial moment of a pre-existing exposure G would deviate from the lower partial moment L. However, the long-run expectation would be for G to match L, so that the CRA diagram becomes square.

Holding a partial exposure statically (or passively hedging) reduces risk by avoiding both losses and gains, without employing any active information to discriminate between them. Therefore the impact on the upper and lower partial moments is identical. This one-for-one ratio gives the slope of a diagonal line between the pre-existing exposure (L, G) and the risk-free position (0, 0). Under the random walk assumption, the slope would be 45 degrees. Any deviations from the 45 degree passive line indicate either positive or negative market bias.

When investing in financial assets, we hope to identify clues from the higher moments of the distribution to give us confidence that a positive deviation in the first moment (i.e. positive return) is sustainable and not just a short-term trend in a random walk.

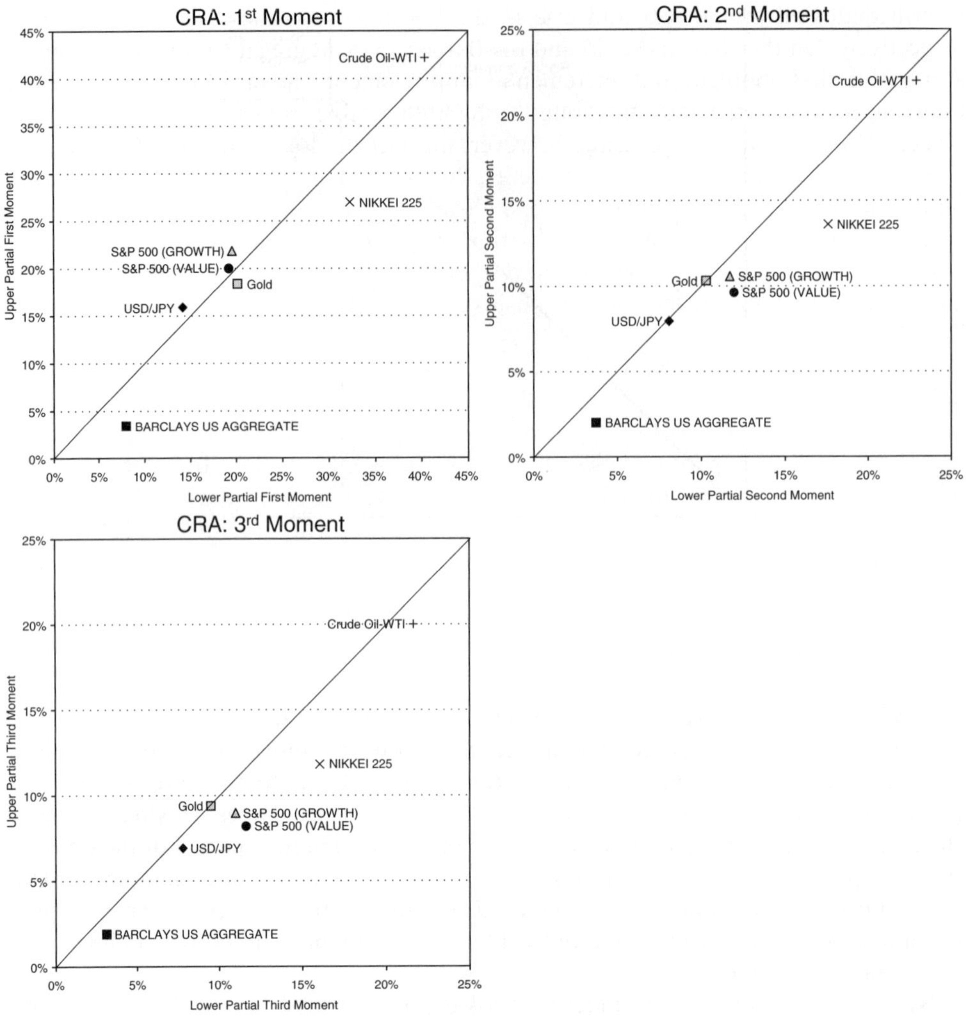

Source: DataStream.

Figure 3.9 CRA examples of different moments

Empirical Examples

With historical price data from January 1988 to July 2009, we calculated both upper and lower partial moments (first, second and third moments) for various investments (see Figure 3.9).[4] Looking at the S&P 500 composite data, both growth and value sectors showed a positive first moment but an incremental deterioration towards higher moments, implying episodic large losses over the long-term investment horizon. This is consistent with an overall distribution of outcomes possessing a positive mean, but a pronounced negative tail. The same observation was identified in the WTI (West Texas

Intermediate) oil price index and also in the US dollar–Japanese yen exchange rate respectively. On the contrary, gold and the Barclays US Aggregate bond index showed a negative first moment but incremental improvements towards higher moments, implying episodic large gains in a long-lasting unfavorable environment. The Japanese Nikkei 225 stock index represents, however, an unorthodox example. It consistently showed negatives through higher moments, due to the fall-out from the stock market bubble in the late 1980s in Japan. It burst abruptly in early 1990, sinking the Japanese economy into ten years of asset depreciation. The significant impact of the initial fall dominates through higher moments. Nevertheless, it is rare to see in a passive exposure any consistent significant bias, either positive or negative, throughout all moments in the CRA.

These considerations are very important when searching for risk exposures to buy and hold in a portfolio, for example, in determining a strategic portfolio allocation, selecting a private equity investment or when hiring an investment manager. There are also significant implications for diversification in portfolio construction. Investors who rely on volatility as a risk measure fail to differentiate between positive and negative tail risk. This makes them dependent upon diversification to control losses. More enlightened investors can control losses directly by constructing portfolios from risk exposures that are less prone to negative tail risk.

GENERALIZED CONDITIONAL RISK ATTRIBUTION

Generalized conditional risk attribution (GCRA) is a tool to indentify active investment decision-making skill. We have argued that successful investment decisions achieve greater investment success than investment error. It is possible to achieve this passively if the underlying investments consistently exhibit asymmetry between gain and loss. Active management involves taking decisions through time. A skillful active manager should be able to introduce additional positive asymmetry into a distribution of returns, over and above that available to a passive investment.

Maximum Permitted Active Risk Exposure

We now turn our attention to the assessment of active investment processes. We show that a skillful active manager is able to vary the size (visibility) of a risk exposure through time in order to improve the trade-off of gain versus loss. While the purpose of CRA was to compare passive investments against a symmetric random walk, the objective of GCRA is to compare the result of active management against passive management. This requires a definition of the range of outcomes that could have been available from a static exposure, determined by the maximum permitted active risk exposure. In the context of unleveraged, long-only investment, this is well defined as the size of the initial amount of capital.

The concept of a maximum permitted active risk exposure is crucial to the analysis. This is what defines the potential passive returns, against which the active returns should be compared. The maximum permitted exposure determines the 'size of the box' in the CRA diagram (Figure 3.8). In the case of a hedging mandate, the maximum exposure equals the underlying exposure. Many active mandates fail to specify maximum permitted exposures, relying on less precise concepts, such as *ex ante* volatility and notional portfolio sizes. This omission makes it very difficult to assess the decision-making skill of the manager.

Normalization of Market Contribution to Asymmetry

The first step is to eliminate any deviations from the 45 degree line that were available to passive management. These deviations, which make G no longer equal to L, do not contain any active information; they simply represent market bias over the time period of observation that creates episodic asymmetry in gains and losses. Clearly, in assessing the skill of an active manager, this market bias needs to be removed. This process is called 'normalization'.

We first calculate the degree of market bias by taking the ratio of the upper and lower partial moments.

$$\text{Market bias} = \frac{G}{L}$$

This ratio represents the market-biased slope of the passive line, which can be replicated by holding a static exposure. Normalization is a process to reset to zero any incremental deviations caused by market bias. This adjustment is a perpendicular shift from the market-biased passive line to the 45 degree market-neutral passive line. Although the 'market bias' ratio is indifferent to any exposure level, the degree of asymmetry is different at each exposure level. The perpendicular distance from the 45-degree line is a quantity to be normalized. It is called 'market contribution to asymmetry' (MCA) (see Figure 3.10).

The MCA is determined for all passive benchmark exposure levels, but not for the outcomes of active management. The appropriate shift for active outcomes should always refer to the MCA normalization corresponding to the benchmark exposure against which the active manager is measured. This preserves the displacement of the active manager's outcome relative to the benchmark.[5] Normalization removes the market bias, revealing a genuine active skill that is the remaining perpendicular distance from the 45-degree normalized passive line.

After normalization, the CRA diagram becomes a square and therefore symmetric. However, the side of the square will be equal to the average of the upper and lower partial moments of the maximum permitted risk exposure. The outcome of the actively managed portfolio must lie within this square. We take one further step to generalize the approach by rescaling the axes to one unit. This is achieved by taking the coordinates of every point on the diagram and dividing them by the length of the side of the square. Finally we arrive at a unit square that permits a comparison between different managers managing different investment exposures over different time periods. We call this active information diagram the generalized conditional risk attribution (GCRA) (see Figure 3.11).

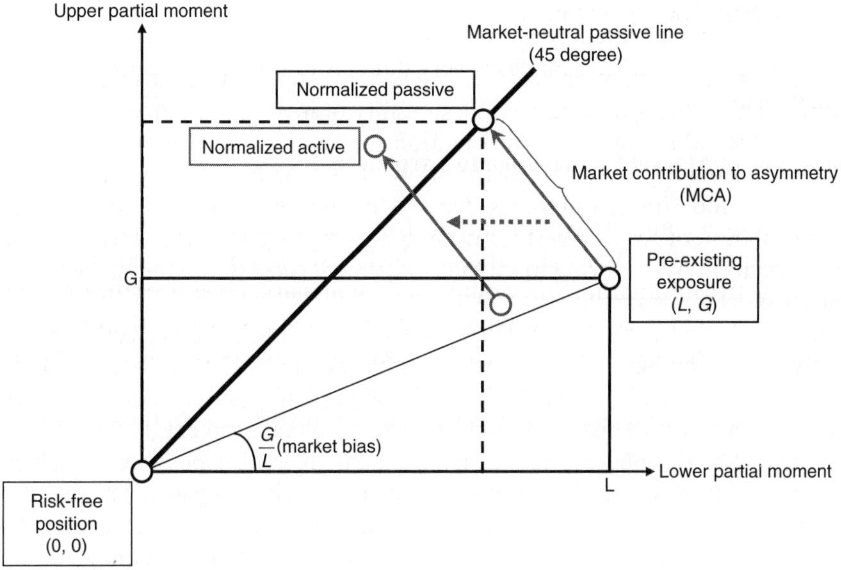

Figure 3.10 *Normalizing market contribution to asymmetry*

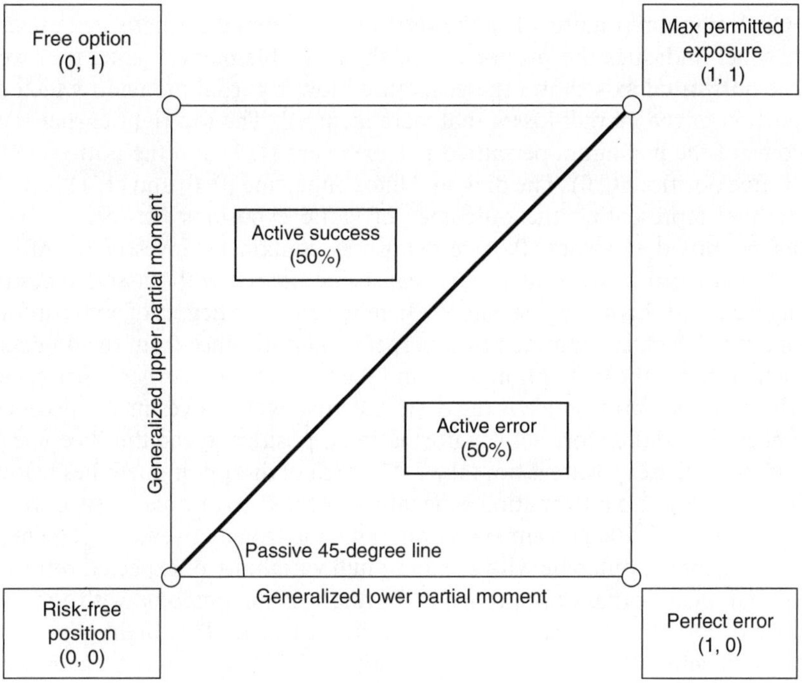

Figure 3.11 *Generalized conditional risk attribution*

Perfect Foresight – the Free Option

We define 'active information' as the level of investment success relative to investment error. This reflects the degree of desirability of investment outcomes in respect of economic values. Positive active information means positive economic values, which introduces 'optionality' into the distribution of outcomes. Negative active information results in undesirable outcomes. On this definition, all passive approaches have active information of zero. The objective of active management is to introduce positive active information by achieving more than 50 percent success and therefore less than 50 percent error.

If one had perfect foresight, both gains and losses could be perfectly predicted in advance without any kind of error. All available gains would therefore be guaranteed, with no losses. This case is known as a free-option pay-off (a perfect outcome) where type I and II errors are zero. This constitutes perfect active management.

Note that with the poorest active management, it is also possible to achieve 100 percent error. All losses would therefore be incurred, with no gains. This would result in 50 percent false positives and 50 percent false negatives (perfect error). Because perfect foresight and error are the two most extreme cases of active management, active information ('optionality') should be constrained by these two cases.

Optionality and Visibility

In the GCRA diagram (Figure 3.11), the vertical axis shows the generalized upper partial moment, which indicates the proportion of the available market gains that were captured. The horizontal axis shows the generalized lower partial moment, which displays the proportion of the market losses that were incurred. The top right corner represents the outcome of the maximum permitted risk exposure (1, 1) and the bottom left corner is the risk-free position (0, 0). The diagonal line connecting (0, 0) and (1, 1) is the passive 45-degree line, representing the outcomes of static exposures between zero and the maximum permitted exposure. Passive exposures contain no investment information. An actively managed investment process can be compared with passive investment by measuring it against this 45 degree line. We hereby define the degree of active information as 'optionality', which is quantified by a perpendicular distance from the 45-degree line. The top left corner is the free option (0, 1) and the bottom right corner is perfect error (1, 0). Clearly the upper left triangle is the desirable area, where investment success exceeds investment error and therefore active information is positive. It can thus become the area of regret if any active exposure is not taken. The area of disappointment lies below the 45 degree line, where active information is negative, because error exceeds success.

Note that the ideal, 100 percent successful outcome from active management is a free option. This is not the outcome with the minimum variability of expected return, sought by traditional mean–variance approaches. In fact it is the outcome with the minimum uncertainty of loss and the *maximum* uncertainty of gain! This highlights once again our strong conviction that it is essential to distinguish between loss and gain in order to assess the performance of an active manager.

It is no coincidence that Figure 3.11 resembles the receiver operating characteristic (ROC) diagrams used in decision theory (see Marques de Sa, 2001). An ROC diagram

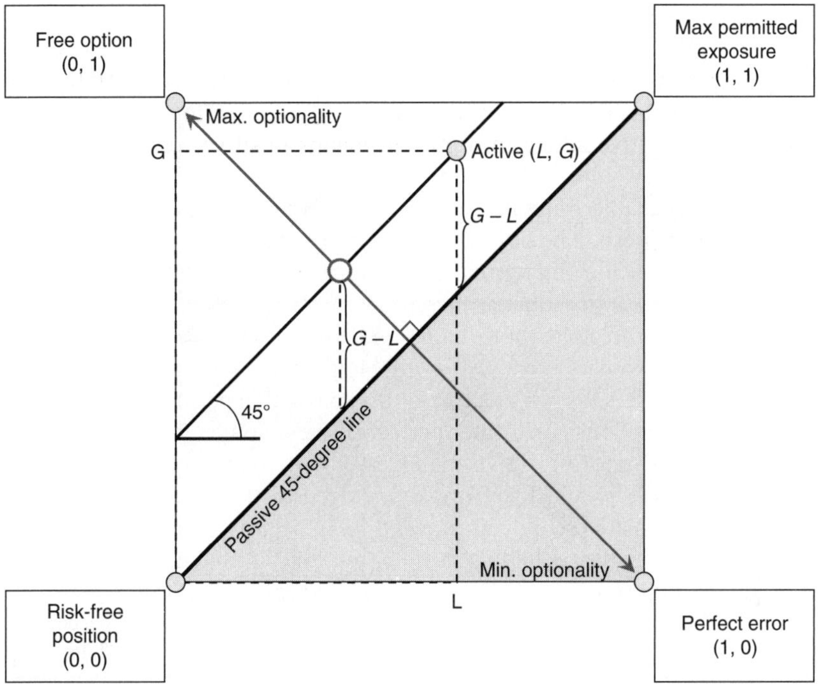

Figure 3.12 Definition of optionality

displays the trade-off between the proportions of false positives and false negatives. The 'zeroeth' generalized partial moments show exactly this information for an investment process. But GCRA goes beyond this, by plotting the higher moments. This allows the investor to measure not just the percentage of investment errors, but also the significance of their impact.

Optionality

Figure 3.12 shows that the free option represents the maximum optionality. We use the term 'optionality' because the ideal objective of an active manager is to capture all available gains and avoid all potential losses. Such outcomes are offered by option contracts, at a price determined by the market. Genuine investment skill lies in using insights or private information to create option-like outcomes more cheaply than the market. All points on the same line running parallel with the passive 45-degree line have the same degree of active information, i.e. given that the generalized upper partial moment of a specific outcome is *G* and the generalized lower partial moment of the same outcome is *L*, a vertical distance (G – L) is constant for all points on the line. This quantity defines the optionality demonstrated by active management.

Visibility

The degree to which the investor sees the impact of the actively managed exposure in the partial moments of the portfolio returns is called 'visibility', defined as the sum of

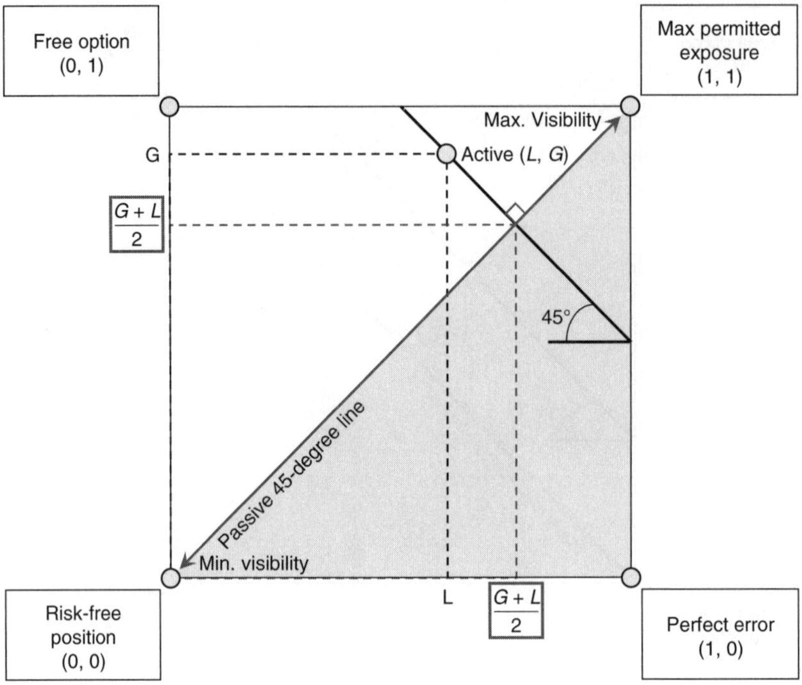

Figure 3.13 Definition of visibility

exposures to both the upper and lower generalized partial moments ($G + L$). Visibility is zero at the risk-free position and the distance from the risk-free position to each line running perpendicular to the passive 45 degree line represents incremental visibility. Figure 3.13 shows that the generalized maximum permitted exposure in the top right corner represents the maximum visibility. Visibility itself does not represent active information, as it is always measured on the passive 45-degree line, where no active information is deployed. All decision making on visibility is therefore a passive judgment.

The investor's utility on visibility pre-determined by an initial benchmark selection should distinguish investment outcomes which contain the same economic value (see Figure 3.14).

Outcome A would therefore be appropriate for an investor who is cautious about incurring loss and therefore willing to be exposed to potentially large regret of missing out on gains. This type of regret-tolerant investor is an invisibility seeker, trying to reduce regret through active manager's skill rather than a passive judgment.

Outcome B would suit an investor who is keen to capture the full extent of potential gains and minimize regret at the expense of being exposed to potentially large losses. This type of regret-averse investor is a visibility seeker, limiting regret by a passive judgment while trying to reduce losses through active manager's skill.

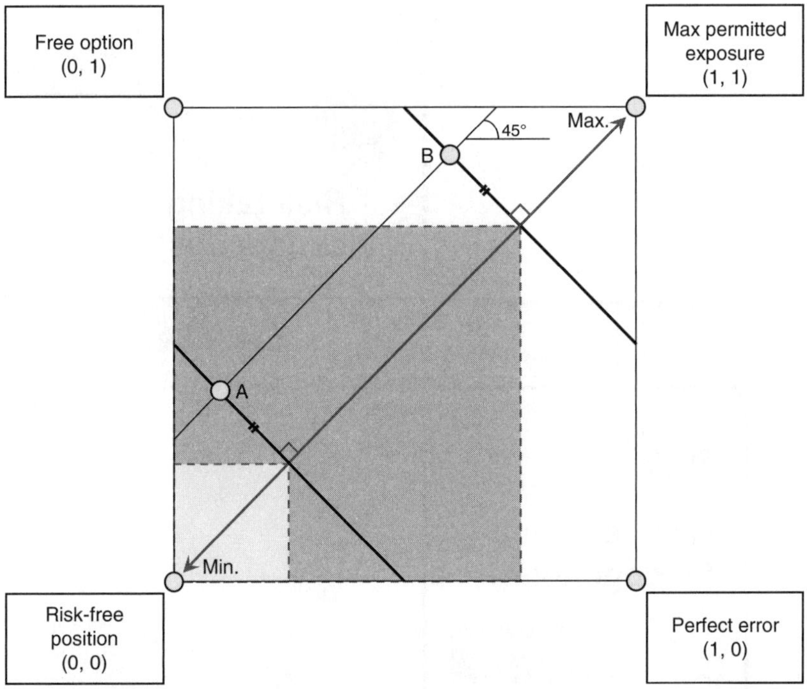

Figure 3.14 Invisibility seeker versus visibility seeker

RISK BUDGETING

Risk-reducing decisions and risk-taking decisions are different choices about different outcomes. Risk reduction considers only the exposures already held in the portfolio, whereas risk taking considers only exposures that are not held in the portfolio (see Figure 3.15).

The initial portfolio construction phase is a risk-taking activity, investing risk-free assets, such as cash, in simple long-only strategies in conventional asset classes, such as equities and bonds. This can be achieved either passively or actively within a pre-determined risk budget. Since a risk budget is always finite, the only way to achieve better risk-adjusted returns is to reduce risk where it is poorly rewarded. The role of risk-reducing decisions is therefore of fundamental importance to successful investment strategies. This risk-reducing activity can also be achieved either passively or actively.

The effect of reducing risk is to free up part of the risk budget so that an investor can reallocate it to better rewarded risk-taking activities. An investment process should always follow a route from risk taking through risk reducing to further risk taking. In other words, a risk-reducing activity is considered as a bridge from an initial long-only investment portfolio to a more efficient portfolio where long-only strategies, hedging and long-short strategies coexist.

The framework developed here proposes enhancing the wealth of the investor by

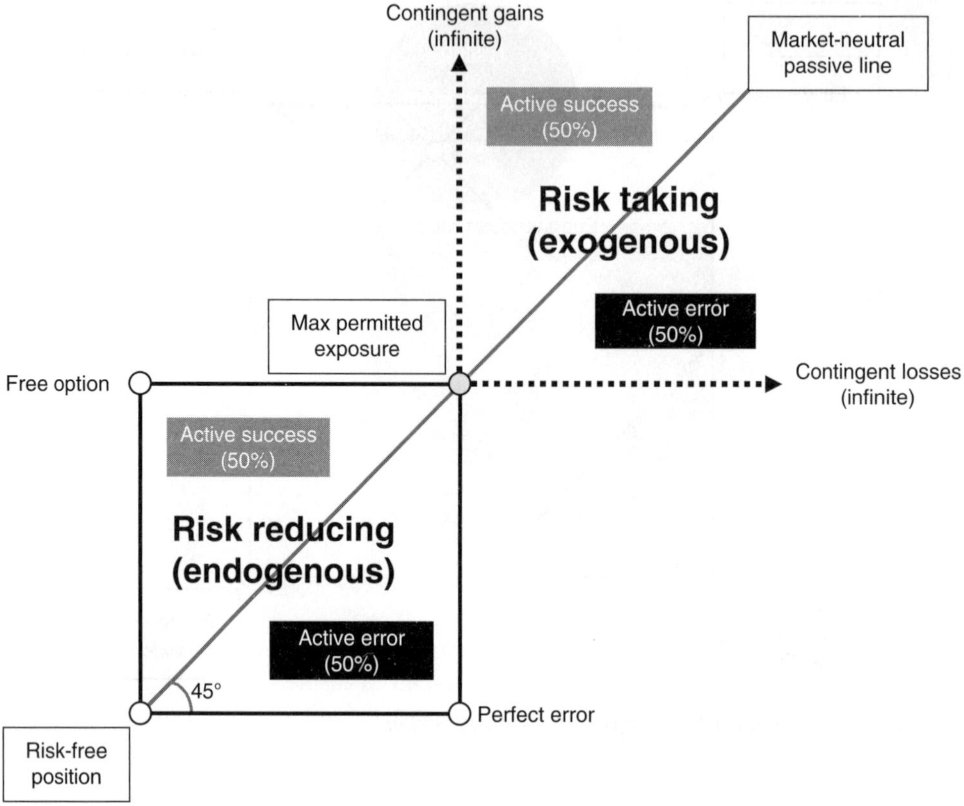

Figure 3.15 Geometric representation of risk reducing and risk taking

improving the balance of investment success to investment error. Whether an investor is reducing risk or increasing risk, the objective is the same: to exploit active information (optionality) in order to increase investment success. See Figure 3.16 for a clear depiction of the repeating cycle of risk re-budgeting.

The risk re-budgeting approach described above highlights the significant importance of distinguishing risk reducing from risk taking, so that one can achieve a better risk-adjusted return within a pre-determined risk budget. Without making a clear strategic distinction, neither the first process (a creation of budget) nor the second process (an enhancement of returns) will be implemented efficiently. Both will be achieved through increasing investment successes.

CONCLUSION

This chapter examined investment decisions using the fundamental investment decision matrix to define investment success and investment error. The framework was effective in describing passive investment. CRA is a tool for identifying the asymmetric

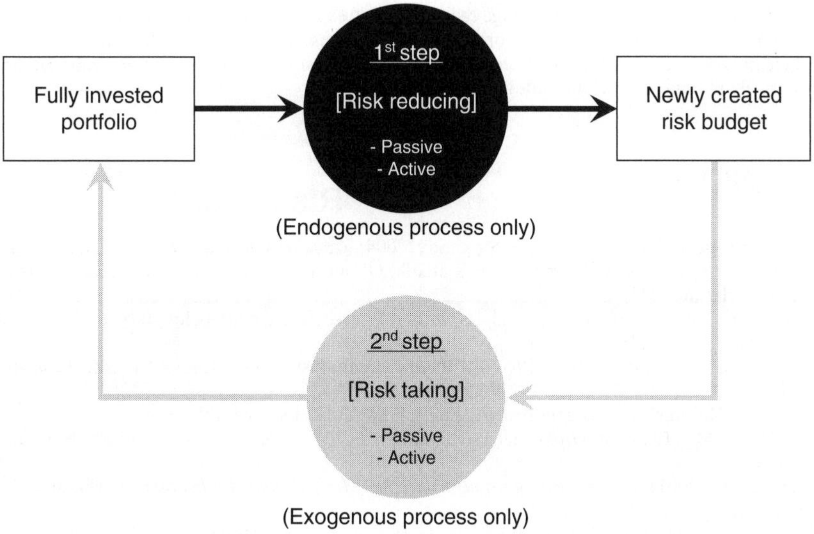

Figure 3.16 Risk re-budgeting framework

returns available to passive investors. We expanded this geometric interpretation into generalized conditional risk attribution (GCRA) to measure the effectiveness of active decision-making processes. Manager skill is associated with active information that is exploited by the investment process. GCRA avoids cognitive confusion between impacts from active and passive decision making, and conducts a heuristic approach to identify genuine investment contributions from active skill.

Modern portfolio theory assumes, as an axiom, that financial returns are symmetric. The tools presented in this chapter are designed to measure the degree of asymmetry (market bias and optionality) in investment returns. The skill of passive management is to find naturally occurring forms of market bias. The role of active managers is to create optionality.

This led to a clear distinction between risk-reducing and risk-taking decisions. By disentangling the cognitive bias inherent in the conventional mean–variance approach, risk budgeting in a GCRA framework allows the portfolio construction process to reflect a better assessment of investment decisions.

NOTES

1. Since our objective is to distinguish asymmetry from symmetry, it is important to avoid performance metrics that contain asymmetric properties, such as geometric returns, where a 25 percent gain is offset by a 20 percent loss.
2. Risk-free rate in the general sense defined by Sharpe (1994) is the risk-free benchmark portfolio against which the investment is evaluated.
3. For convenience, we adopt the convention that a zero return is considered a gain.
4. The risk-free rate used for the US dollar denominated investments (S&P 500 Value & Growth, Barclays US Aggregate bond index, WTI, gold) was JPMorgan US dollar cash 1 month rate, while the rate for the Japanese yen denominated investments (Nikkei 225) was the JPMorgan Japanese yen cash 1 month rate.

For the US dollar–Japanese yen exchange rate, the risk-free rate adjustment was made by the interest rate differential between US dollar cash 1 month rate and Japanese yen cash 1 month rate.

5. If the benchmark is the risk-free position, there is no market contribution to asymmetry, so there is no shift in the actively managed portfolio outcome.

REFERENCES

Biglova, A., S. Ortobelli, S.T. Rachev and S. Stoyanov (2004), *Comparison among Different Approaches for Risk Estimation in Portfolio Theory*, Lehrstuhl für Statistik, Ökonometrie und Mathematische Finanzwirtschaft, Universität Karlsruhe (TH).

Fishburn, Peter C. (1977), 'Mean-risk analysis with risk associated with below-target returns,' *American Economic Review*, **67**(2), 116–26.

Kahneman, D. and A. Tversky (1979), 'Prospect theory: an analysis of decision under risk,' *Econometrica*, **47** (2), 263–92.

Luce R.D. and H. Raiffa (1989), *Games and Decisions*, New York: Dover Publications.

Markowitz, Harry M. (1959), *Portfolio Selection: Efficient Diversification of Investments*, New York: John Wiley and Sons.

Marques de Sa, J.P. (2001), *Pattern Recognition: Concepts, Methods and Applications*, Berlin and Heidelberg: Springer-Verlag, pp. 116–21.

Sharpe, William F. (1994), 'The Sharpe ratio,' *The Journal of Portfolio Management*, **3** (3), 49–58.

Sortino, Frank A. and Lee N. Price (1994), 'Performance measurement in a downside risk framework,' *The Journal of Investing*, **3** (3), 59–64.

4 The disposition effect and individual investor decisions: the roles of regret and counterfactual alternatives

Suzanne O'Curry Fogel and Thomas Berry

Investors are frequently cautioned to resist attachments to particular stocks in order to avoid holding losers too long (e.g. Sease and Prestbo, 1993). Although this advice seems obvious, a number of recent studies have documented a strong tendency for individual investors to delay realizing capital losses, while realizing gains prematurely (Odean, 1998; Shefrin and Statman, 1985; Weber and Camerer, 1998). This tendency has been termed the 'disposition effect.' The disposition effect is inconsistent with normative approaches to stock sales, such as those based on tax losses (see, e.g., Constantinides, 1983). We found when we surveyed individual investors that many more respondents reported feeling regret about holding on to a losing stock too long than for selling a winning stock too soon. This finding suggests that individual investors understand, at least in hindsight, the repercussions of an investment style that they are warned against.

This chapter reports some of the results of our survey of individual investors as well as the findings of two experiments that probe some of the factors underlying investor satisfaction and regret, in the context of the disposition effect. We focus on the disposition effect because it is a pervasive phenomenon that is contrary to normative approaches to individual investing and reliably leads to consequences that evoke regret. First, we briefly review the literature on the disposition effect and relevant findings from the study of regret. We follow with our studies, and conclude with suggestions for future research.

THE DISPOSITION EFFECT

Shefrin and Statman (1985) first put the decision to realize capital gains and losses into a behavioral context. They cited numerous accounts of both professional traders and individual investors failing to cut losses in an effort to break even with the purchase price of a stock. They documented the greater tendency of investors to sell stocks that have appreciated and to hold those that have declined in value, and coined the term 'disposition effect'. They also noted that greater activity in December could be the result of December acting as an impetus to self-control due to tax considerations. Their evidence was inconsistent with normative approaches to stock sales. They attributed their findings to a descriptive theory based on loss aversion (Kahneman and Tversky, 1979), self-control (Thaler and Shefrin, 1981), mental accounting, and the desire to avoid regret (Thaler, 1980).

Lakonishok and Smidt (1986) examined aggregate market volume data and found that volume movements were positively correlated to past price movements, consistent with the disposition effect. Ferris et al. (1988) also used volume to study the disposition effect. They first determined an expected normal level of volume and then looked at actual volume relative to the expected after-price changes. Price declines led to negative relative volume and price increases led to greater than normal volume, confirming the disposition effect. This effect was pervasive, even in December, despite the tax benefits of selling losers at that time. Weber and Camerer (1998) used an experimental setting to study the disposition effect. They found that the original purchase price served as a reference point to assess a particular outcome, and that a desire to avoid losses relative to the reference point leads to holding on to losers too long. They not only confirm the disposition effect, but found that winners are sold too soon and that losers are held too long, compounding the negative impact of the effect.

In an analysis of trading records of 10000 individual investors, Odean (1998) showed that losing stocks were held longer than winning stocks, and that the proportion of realized gains was about 50 percent higher than realized losses, except for tax-motivated selling in December. Odean also compared subsequent stock prices of sold winners, held winners, sold losers and held losers at 16 weeks and one year. He found that the average return of sold winners was over twice that of held losers at both time periods, demonstrating the impact on longer-run portfolio performance of holding losers and selling winners. Odean's data came from a discount brokerage, thus reflecting the decisions of individual investors who did not feel the need for a retail broker's services.

These explanations rely primarily on loss aversion to explain investor decisions to realize gains and losses. Emotional aspects of decision making are also likely to play a significant role in choosing to realize gains and losses. The sale of a losing stock results in an immediate tangible loss while holding it leaves the option that it may reverse direction. In addition, the investor may be in a state of denial about a bad decision, and forgoing the sale allows this denial to continue. Another aspect is the regret associated with the loss. The desire to avoid regret was cited by Shefrin and Statman as one factor behind the disposition effect. We turn now to a brief review of the literature on regret and decision making.

REGRET

Regret has been studied in a number of different contexts and is commonly defined as a negative emotion evoked by the knowledge that a different choice would have led to a better outcome than the one obtained. Thus regret can only be experienced fully after the fact, although it can be anticipated before an action. Shefrin and Statman mentioned regret as a factor in the disposition effect because the pain associated with realizing a loss was assumed to be greater than the pride associated with realizing a gain. There are, however, other aspects of regret that are relevant to the decision to realize gains or losses. These include the forgone alternatives to actual outcomes, and whether outcomes were obtained through acts of omission or commission. Also, the degree of regret may be affected by whether a decision was made by an individual or an agent. Connolly and Zeelenberg (2002) suggested that regret comprises two components, an evaluation of the realized outcome compared to some alternative and a feeling of self-blame for having made a bad choice.

The degree of regret experienced appears to co-vary with the 'closeness' of the forgone or counterfactual alternative (Kahneman and Miller, 1986). For example, the holder of a lottery ticket with five of six winning numbers is likely to feel more regret about his or her choice of numbers than the holder of a ticket with four of six winning numbers. Similarly, an investor who comes close to selling a loser but continues to hold the stock will experience more regret than the investor who only briefly considered the same trade.

Another aspect of regret is whether an outcome is obtained through an act of omission or commission. Typically, subjects report feeling more regret for actions they took that led to a bad outcome, rather than bad outcomes that occurred as a result of a failure to act (Kahneman and Tversky, 1982; Ritov and Baron, 1995). However, Gilovich and Medvec (1995) showed that long-run regret is often linked to things not done, rather than actions taken. The conflicting results are most likely attributable to the length of time between the regret-evoking event and the evaluation of the event. Gilovich and Medvec's results were based on a study that asked older subjects to reflect on their lives. The studies in which acts of commission produced more regret were based on scenarios, and subjects evaluated the degree of regret immediately after reading the scenarios. A longer time span may produce more opportunity to reflect on alternative courses of action, leading to more regret for actions not taken. Investors may be reluctant to realize losses because anticipated regret is more salient for the action of selling compared to the inaction of continuing to hold. However, in the long run, regret may be greater for not cutting a loss, because the cost of the outcome is made more apparent over time. Ritov and Baron (1995) showed that anticipated regret was greater when people knew that they would have complete information about outcomes, compared to situations in which information was available only about the chosen alternative. In the case of investments, one will always have information about forgone alternatives. The power of anticipated regret was shown by Cooke et al. (2001), who demonstrated that experimental subjects preferred to minimize future regret even at the cost of maximizing earnings.

A possible factor in regret related to omission–commission differences is whether regret is alleviated through the actions of an agent. When negative outcomes occur, the agent can be blamed, while one can take the credit oneself for positive outcomes (or at least take the credit for selecting a good agent). This is consistent with self-serving attributions, in which people are more likely to take credit for successes than blame for failures (Miller and Ross, 1975). However, Connolly et al. (1997) demonstrated that outcome valence is more important than responsibility in overall ratings of happiness and regret.

STUDIES

Study 1: Preliminary Survey

We conducted a survey of individual investors in order to gain insight into a number of issues related to investor decision making, including influences on decisions to sell, preferences for income form, and regret about past investment decisions. The findings of the survey were used to refine our experimental hypotheses.

Method

We developed a brief questionnaire of closed-ended questions relating to the issues mentioned above, as well as demographic and portfolio information. The questionnaire was mailed to a random sample of 500 members of the American Association of Individual Investors.

Results

We received 176 responses for a response rate of 35 percent. The respondents were predominantly male (82 percent), well educated (89 percent college graduate or graduate degree), with a mean age of 59.5 years. Mean annual income was $99 000, with 23.9 percent derived from investments. The majority of respondents were still working, with only 30 percent retired. Approximate portfolio size averaged $588 000.

Investment questions

The question most relevant to this chapter was the following:

Thinking back to investment decisions that you now regret, do you feel more regret for:

- *Selling a 'winning' stock too soon?*
- *Not selling a 'losing' stock soon enough?*

Only one respondent had no regret for any investment decision. Of the less fortunate balance, 59 percent reported more regret for not selling a loser soon enough, while 41 percent reported more regret for selling a winning stock too soon.

The other directly relevant question asked respondents to rate the importance of different factors in their decisions to sell. Table 4.1 reports the percentage of respondents who answered '1' or 'most important' for each factor. The strongest influence on selling appears to be broker recommendation, followed closely by stock price reaching a predetermined target and need for liquidity. The desire to cut losses and the desire to take profits appear to be less influential, followed only by the anticipated direction of the market.

Two other survey questions were related to the disposition effect. One asked whether respondents spent more time on decisions to buy or sell; the other asked whether the decision to buy or to sell was more difficult. The majority of respondents (62 percent)

Table 4.1 Percentage of 'most important' ratings for influences on selling

Broker recommendation	52.2
Stock price has reached a predetermined target	47.7
Need for liquidity	46.6
Desire to purchase a different stock or other investment	41.5
Desire to cut losses	39
Desire to take profits	33.1
Anticipated direction of the market	32

$N = 177$

spent more time on decisions to buy, while 8.5 percent spent more time on decisions to sell and 29.5 percent said they spent about the same amount of time on each decision. Interestingly, 51 percent of respondents said that decisions to sell were more difficult, 32 percent said both were about the same, and 17 percent said that decisions to buy were more difficult.

The reported difficulty associated with decisions to sell, in conjunction with the reliance on brokers and predetermined target prices, suggests that issues of anticipated regret and self-control may play an important role in the disposition effect.

EXPERIMENTS

Study 2

The goal of our first experiment was to explore three questions about investor regret. First, we wanted to examine the role of omission versus commission with respect to holding losers and selling winners. In the survey, we found that more respondents felt regret for holding losers, which is an act of omission. This is in line with the Gilovich and Medvec finding, but at odds with earlier work. We had not measured regret in the survey, given that each respondent had different circumstances. We did not have a clear directional hypothesis for this question, because previous work is not consistent in predicting whether omission or commission leads to greater regret.

Second, we wanted to compare the impact of counterfactual outcomes with real outcomes on degree of regret. How would the regret associated with a missed gain compare with the regret associated with a loss? A missed gain is an opportunity cost, yet prior research indicates that opportunity costs tend to be underweighted (Kahneman and Tversky, 1982). From this perspective, greater regret should be associated with an actual loss than with an opportunity cost. In addition, missed losses evoke feelings of relief (Loomes and Sugden, 1982). Is the satisfaction experienced from a missed loss similar to that associated with an actual gain, where the financial outcome is better; or to that associated with a missed gain, where the financial outcome is identical?

Finally, we wanted to explore whether a broker's involvement alleviated regret and how credit and blame were allocated between broker and investor for different outcomes. Attribution theory (Ross, 1977) suggests that brokers are likely to be blamed for bad outcomes more than they will be given credit for good outcomes.

Hypotheses

H1A: Rated satisfaction/regret for a missed loss will be closer to rated satisfaction/regret associated with a real gain than that for a missed gain.

H1B: Rated satisfaction/regret for a missed gain will be closer to rated satisfaction/regret associated with a real loss than that for a missed loss.

H2: More responsibility will be attributed to brokers for negative outcomes than for positive outcomes.

Method

Independent variables were Action (Hold versus Sell), Outcome (Positive versus Negative), and Actor (Self versus Broker). Dependent variables were degree of satisfaction/regret and, for problems involving a broker, allocation of responsibility between self and broker. Each subject read two problems of the following form, one version of which involved a broker.

> Imagine that last year you purchased some stock in 'Company A' at $15.00 a share. After it fell in value to $11.00 a share you *decided to sell/thought about selling, but decided to hold.* You found out this morning that the current price is *$27.00 / $6.00* a share.

The version with the broker began, 'Imagine that last year, based on your broker's advice,' but was otherwise identical, except that Company A became Company B.

Subjects were asked to rate their satisfaction with the decision using an 11-point scale anchored by 'Regret very much' at the low end and 'Very satisfied' on the high end. Responsibility for outcome was allocated by dividing 100 points between the broker and self.

The experiment was conducted in a classroom setting with adult undergraduate and MBA students at a large Midwestern business school. All subjects had taken at least one course in finance. One hundred twenty five students participated in exchange for course credit.

Results

Satisfaction / regret A three-way analysis of variance was conducted on the satisfaction/regret measure. The main effects of action (sell/hold) and outcome (positive/negative) as well as the two-way interaction between action and outcome were all significant at $p < 0.01$ or less. The three-way interaction was not significant. In order to understand the nature of the effects, a more detailed analysis was undertaken, following Keppel (1982). Figure 4.1 reports the cell means. ANOVA results are reported in Table 4.2. Missed losses were rated much closer to real gains than to missed gains, while missed gains were rated as negatively as real losses. Thus H1A and H1B were supported.

The interaction between action and actor was significant in the 'self' condition ($F(1\,120) = 25.43$, $p < 0.001$ for self, $F(1\,120) = 1.71$, n.s. for broker). Degree of satisfaction was greater for independently made decisions when the action was holding rather than selling. There was no difference in satisfaction between holding and selling when a broker's advice was used. This result is consistent with the disposition effect in that holding a stock reaffirms that one has made a good choice.

The interaction between action and outcome was significant when the outcome was positive, but not when the outcome was negative ($F(1\,120) = 38.02$, $p < 0.001$ for positive outcomes, $F(1\,120) < 1$, n.s. for negative outcomes). Holding yielded higher satisfaction than selling when the outcome was positive. Again, holding a stock reaffirms the good choice one made originally. While we had not made a prediction with respect to omission and commission, we did not see any difference in regret ratings for holding (omission) and selling (commission).

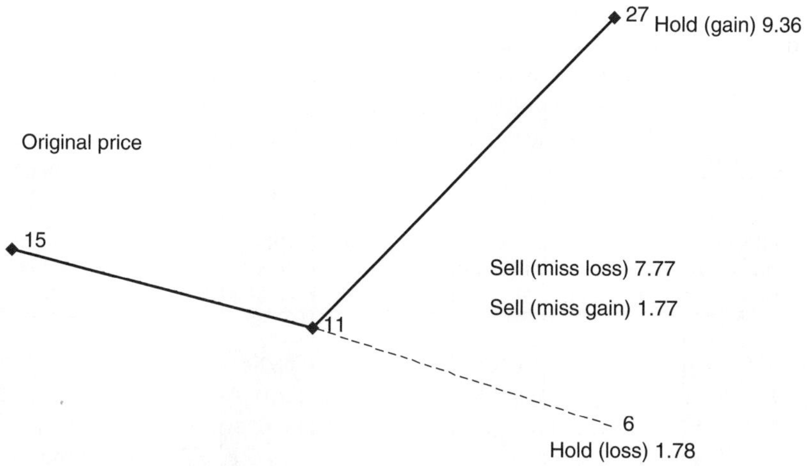

Figure 4.1 *Regret satisfaction ratings for outcomes, study 2*

Table 4.2 *ANOVA results, study 2*

Source	SS	df	MS	F	
Action	319.7	1	319.7	20.28	$p < 0.001$
Outcome	2387.7	1	2387.7	151.51	$p < 0.001$
Actor	168.33	1	168.33	10.68	$p < 0.01$
Action × outcome	283.84	1	283.84	18.01	$p < 0.001$
Action × actor	110.71	1	110.71	7.02	$p < 0.01$
Actor × outcome	113.45	1	113.45	7.19	$p < 0.01$
Action × outcome × actor	55.1	1	55.1	3.49	n.s.

Allocation of responsibility We had hypothesized that brokers would be blamed more for bad outcomes than they would be given credit for good outcomes. While the mean allocations of responsibility are in the right direction to support this idea, they are not statistically significant. The mean allocations are listed in Figure 4.2. Interestingly, the data indicate that the greatest responsibility is attributed to self for missed losses, followed by gains, losses and missed losses.

Discussion The first issue addressed by the experiment was whether counterfactual alternatives affected rated satisfaction/regret in a way consistent with the disposition effect. Our original survey results showed that more respondents associated regret with holding losers than with selling winners too soon, demonstrating an *ex post* awareness of the long-term consequences of the disposition effect. Interestingly, there appeared to be no difference between holding and selling when outcome was negative, even though the financial outcome for holding was significantly worse than for selling. The significant difference for positive results may be attributed to the difference in absolute financial outcomes.

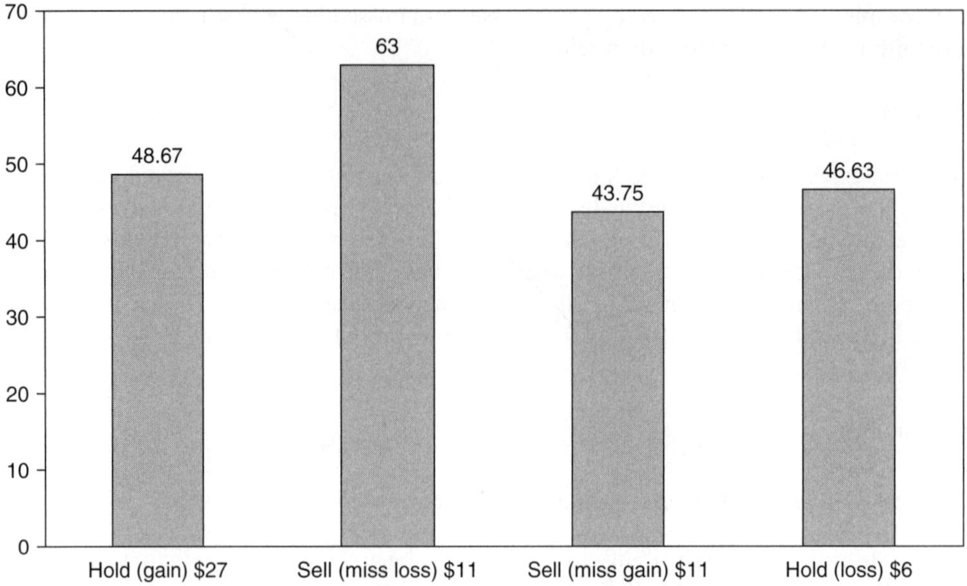

Figure 4.2 Allocation of responsibility to self by outcome, study 2

The positive and negative outcomes in our experiment were of four types: real gain, missed loss (both positive), missed gain and real loss (both negative). The financial outcomes for the missed loss and missed gain conditions were identical; the stock was sold at $11.00 in both conditions. What distinguished the conditions from each other were the counterfactual alternatives in each condition. The missed loss could have been a real loss; the missed gain could have been a real gain. The rated satisfaction/regret for the identical financial outcomes in these conditions demonstrates the power of counterfactual alternatives to influence evaluations of outcomes. The regret ratings for the missed gains are as low as for actual losses, even though the financial outcome was much better with missed gains. Individual investors may anticipate a great deal of regret for selling too soon and missing a gain. Indeed, the original purchase is prompted by a belief that the stock price will rise, and selling in the face of a loss points to a poor decision in the first place. Unlike the individual investor, the market does not recognize what could have been. Successful investors must learn from experience and go forward, cutting their losses when necessary.

Finally, transactions involving brokers produced no more regret than those with no broker when outcome was negative, across both holding and selling. The significant difference for positive outcomes appears to have been driven by higher satisfaction with a missed loss when a broker advised a sale than when the decision was made independently. In addition to advising and facilitating transactions, the role of a broker may be to bear some of the weight of responsibility for decisions. Recall that the investor survey showed that most respondents considered decisions to sell more difficult than decisions to buy. Placing some of the burden on a broker could lead to higher satisfaction with the decision. Interestingly, the data indicate that the greatest responsibility is attributed to self for missed losses, followed by gains, losses and missed losses. Note that the extremes are both for holding, rather than selling.

Study 3

The first experiment presented a decision as a *fait accompli*, and then asked subjects to assess their satisfaction with the decision and to allocate responsibility for the outcome. The second experiment was designed to allow subjects to make a decision themselves and learn the result, then assess their satisfaction and allocate responsibility for the outcome. The point of this was to make the situation somewhat less artificial. The second experiment included the possibility of allocating responsibility to the market, as well as to self and the broker.

Hypotheses

H3: Ratings of satisfaction/regret will be more extreme for subjects who do not take advice.
H4: Allocation of responsibility to a broker will be greater for losses than gains.
H5: Allocation of responsibility to oneself will be greater for decisions to hold, compared to decisions to sell.
H6: Allocation of responsibility to the market will be greater for losses than for gains.

Method

Independent variables were Broker's Advice (hold versus sell) and Outcome (positive versus negative). Subjects read the following scenario in a classroom setting:

About six months ago, you purchased 100 shares of stock in a food product company that has been having a few problems, but seems basically sound. The market has been fairly stable, with mild random fluctuations. The current share price is $20.00.
You are not sure whether or not you should continue to hold this stock.

You now have the opportunity to ask a broker you met at a party for advice.
BROKER: *Sell! (Hold!)*

Subjects then chose whether to take the broker's advice. At this point, the current stock price was revealed as either $25.00 or $15.00, and subjects learned whether they had won or lost. There were four possible outcomes: gain ($25 per share), missed loss ($20 per share), missed gain ($20 per share), and loss ($15 per share). Both the gain and missed loss were coded as positive outcomes and both the missed gain and loss were coded as negative outcomes. Subjects then rated their satisfaction with their decision on a 1–7 scale and allocated responsibility for the outcome between themselves, the broker, and the market by dividing 100 points.

Subjects were 106 adult MBA students in finance classes at a large Midwestern university.

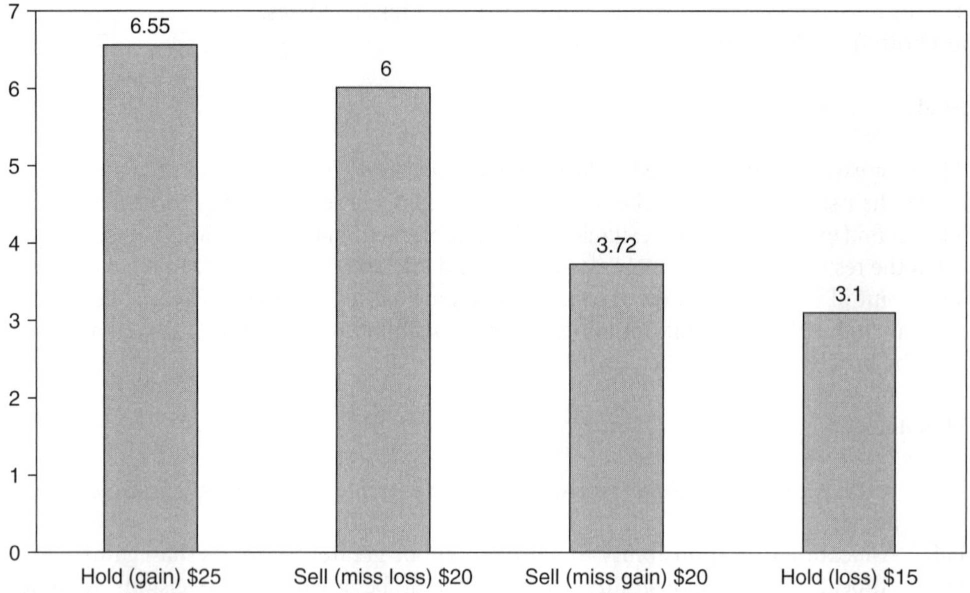

Figure 4.3 Overall satisfaction regret ratings, study 3

Results

The dependent variables were the choice to follow the broker's advice or not, degree of satisfaction or regret with the decision, and allocation of responsibility for the outcome to self, the broker and the market.

Taking the broker's advice The ratio of subjects who did not take the broker's advice to those who did was almost 3:1. Eighty did not take the advice, while 26 did. There was no significant difference of whether the broker's advice was to sell or hold, χ^2 (1) = 1.13, n.s. When the advice was 'sell,' 11 took the advice and 45 did not. When the advice was 'hold,' 15 took the advice and 35 did not.

Satisfaction/regret The first examination of degree of satisfaction/regret was a two-way analysis of variance (broker advice × outcome). The effect of broker advice (sell versus hold) was marginally significant, $F(1\ 100) = 3.34$, $p = 0.07$. The advice to hold was somewhat more likely to lead to higher satisfaction, supporting H3. Not surprisingly, the effect of 'outcome' was highly significant, $F(1\ 100) = 160.49$, $p < 0.0001$. The interaction between broker advice and outcome was not significant, $F(1\ 100) = 1.29$, n.s. Figures 4.3 and 4.4 list mean satisfaction/regret scores for the different conditions. Table 4.3 reports ANOVA results for Study 3.

As in the first experiment, we were interested in whether satisfaction/regret for identical actual outcomes but different counterfactual outcomes varied. In this case, the outcomes for missed loss and missed gain were $20, but the counterfactual outcomes were $25 and $15, respectively. The mean satisfaction/regret score for the missed gain was 3.71, while for the missed loss it was 6.00. A *t*-test on the mean satisfaction/regret scores

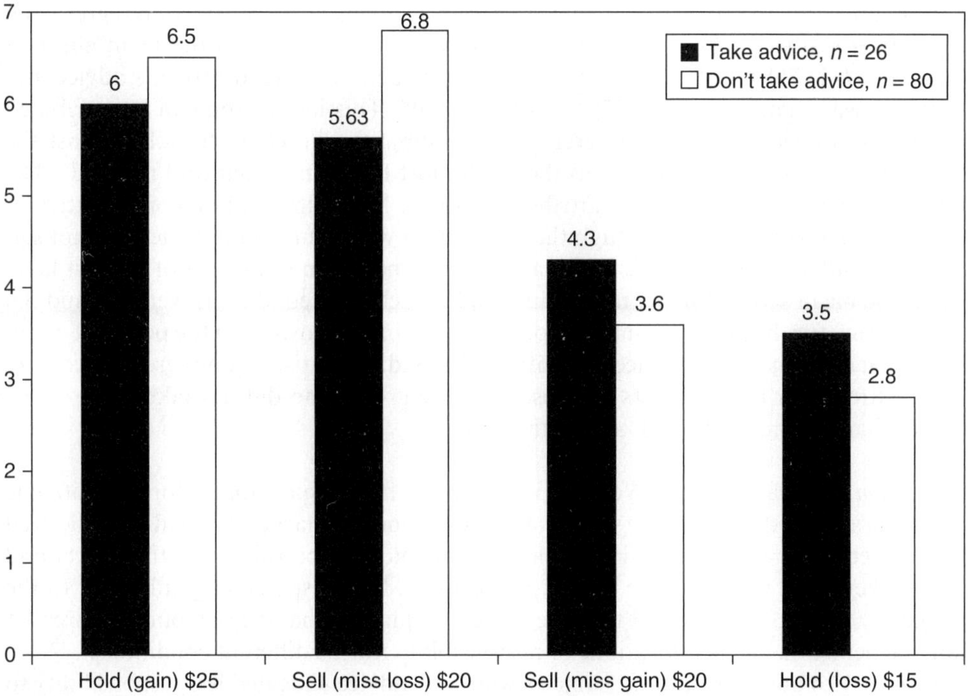

Figure 4.4 Satisfaction regret ratings by advice taken or not, study 3

Table 4.3 ANOVA results, study 3

Source	SS	df	MS	F	
Broker advice	4.54	1	4.54	3.34	$p = 0.07$
Outcome	218.05	1	218.05	160.49	$p < 0.0001$
Broker advice × outcome	1.76	1	1.76	1.30	n.s.

showed that despite the identical financial outcome, the evaluation of the choice was significantly different, $t\ (44) = -6.08, p < 0.0001$.

Some of the questions we were investigating required a more detailed analysis based on whether or not subjects chose to take the broker's advice, as well as whether the advice was to sell or hold and the ultimate outcome of the situation. Rather than deal with the unbalanced effects inherent in an analysis in which there is a 75 percent/25 percent split on a factor, we conducted separate analyses for subjects who did and did not take the broker's advice. For subjects who took the broker's advice, both the nature of the advice (sell versus hold) and the outcome (positive versus negative) had significant effects on satisfaction/regret, $F(1, 21) = 4.36, p < 0.05$ and $F(1, 21) = 12.23, p < 0.005$, respectively. The interaction was not significant, however. Advice to hold was more likely to lead to higher satisfaction than advice to sell, and naturally, a positive outcome was more likely to lead to higher satisfaction than a negative outcome.

For subjects who did not take advice, there was no effect on satisfaction/regret from the broker's advice, $F(1, 75) = 0.65$, n.s. However, in addition to the main effect of outcome ($F(1, 75) = 188.22$, $p < 0.0001$), the interaction between broker's advice and outcome was significant, $F(1, 75) = 5.43$, $p < 0.05$. This interaction can be attributed to the much lower satisfaction/regret score for subjects who chose to hold against the 'sell' advice, then lost, compared to those who lost by selling when told to 'hold'. The lower score here is also partially attributable to the lower financial outcome relative to the missed gain condition, although the satisfaction with winning outcomes was not significantly different despite different financial outcomes. Two points are of interest here. First, the mean scores for the missed loss and missed gain conditions were 6.8 and 3.6 respectively, for the identical financial outcome, again demonstrating the power of counterfactual outcomes to influence evaluations. Second, the satisfaction/regret scores were more extreme for both winners and losers for the group who did not take the broker's advice than for those who did, supporting H3.

Allocation of responsibility We were interested in how responsibility for the outcome would be allocated between the subject, the broker and the market. We had hypothesized that subjects who took the advice would attribute more responsibility to the broker and the market when they lost. We also expected to see little responsibility allocated to the broker by subjects who did not take the advice, no matter what the outcome. Figures 4.5 and 4.6 depict the mean allocations of responsibility for the different conditions.

Contrary to our expectations, subjects who took advice allocated less responsibility to themselves for wins than for losses (40 percent for wins versus 64.29 percent for losses). For these subjects, the market received credit for wins, but little blame for losses (46.25 percent for wins versus 17.14 percent for losses). The broker received more blame for losses than credit for wins (13.75 percent for wins versus 18.57 percent for losses).

For subjects who did not take advice, there were no major differences in allocation of responsibility across wins and losses, although about 9 percent of responsibility was attributed to the broker in both cases.

Interestingly, for all subjects the greatest allocation of responsibility to self occurred in the missed gain condition. Taking the broker's advice or not had no effect (63 percent versus 67 percent). This may be because the loss in this case is through actively going against one's previous choice: selling a stock that had been purchased in the hope of positive return. The missed gain condition was also the highest allocation of responsibility to the broker, even for those who did not take the advice (25 percent for advice takers, 13.5 percent for non-takers).

CONCLUSIONS AND FUTURE RESEARCH

Our results show that satisfaction with investment decisions is not simply a function of outcome. Instead, alternative outcomes affect evaluations of decisions. Anticipation of regret may lead investors into the trap of continuing to hold losing stocks rather than risk selling just before a hoped-for upturn in the market. A survey of active individual investors showed that while less than 10 percent spent more time on sell decisions than buy, less than 20 percent felt that buy decisions were more difficult. Virtually all survey

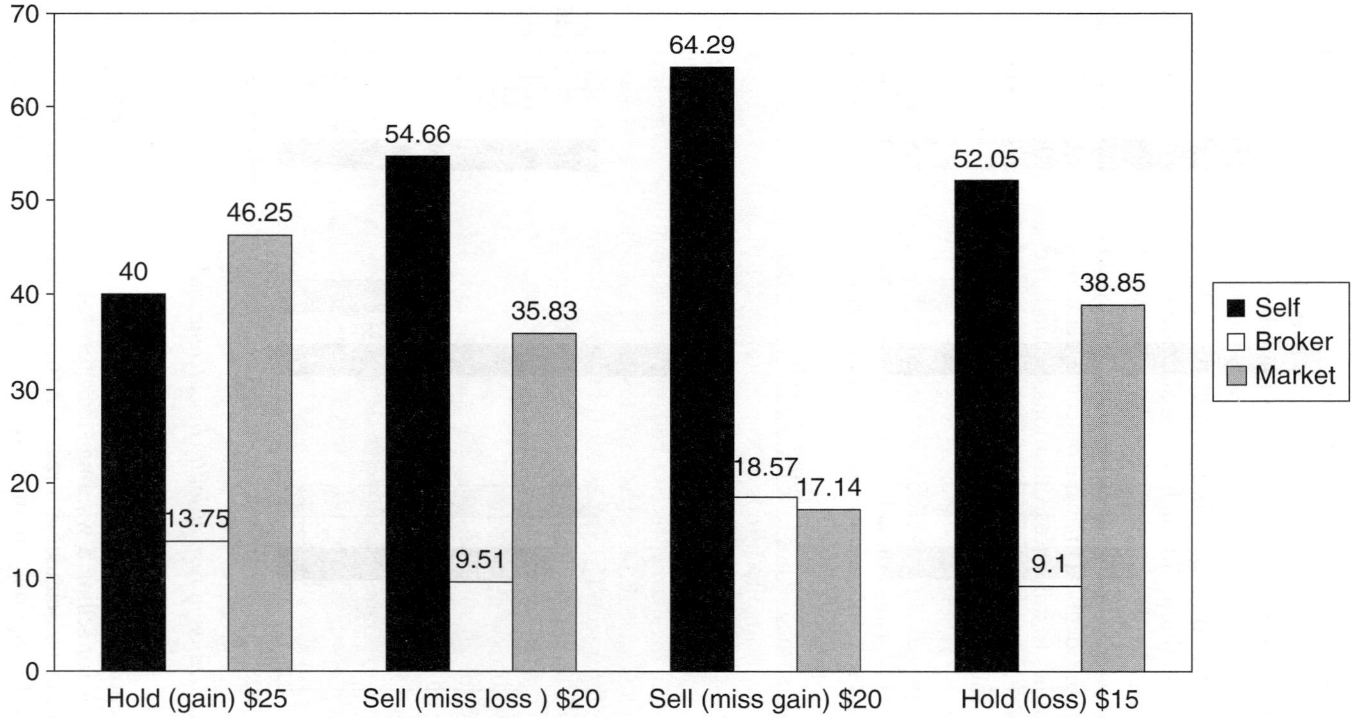

Figure 4.5 Overall allocation of responsibility by outcome, study 3

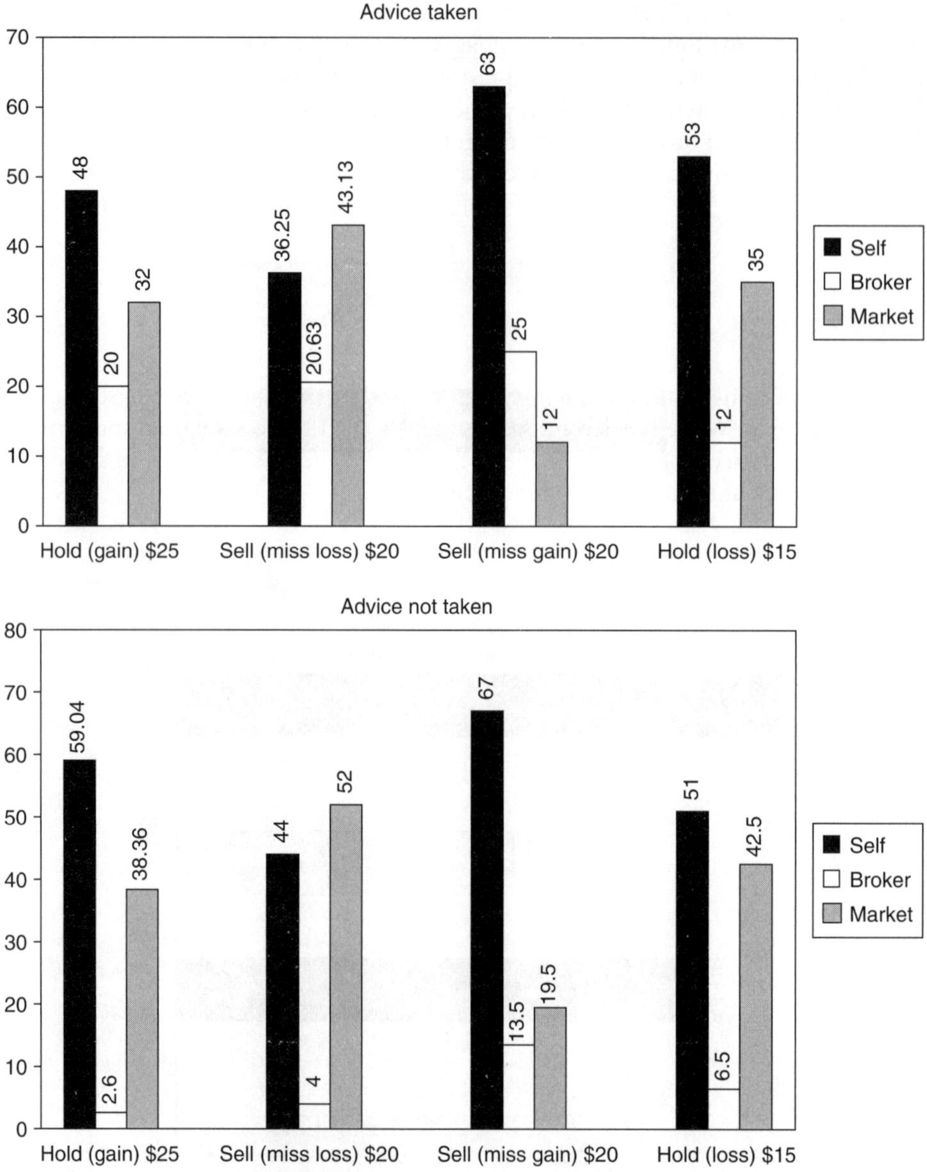

Figure 4.6 Allocation of responsibility by outcome and reaction to advice, study 3

respondents reported regret for investment decisions, either for not selling a losing stock soon enough or for selling a winning stock too soon. Our experiments were designed to assess if factors associated with regret in the psychological literature (counterfactual alternatives and omission/commission) would affect investor satisfaction. The results indicate that investor satisfaction is more complicated than the absolute financial outcome. In both experiments, an identical financial outcome led to wide differences in satisfaction/regret, depending on the counterfactual alternative. Initial results to see if losses were attributed to broker advice were negative, but our second experiment showed a potentially more complicated result. It may be since there was relatively little additional information that the broker advice served as an anchor – whether that advice was directly followed or not. Apparently, for those who did follow the broker's advice the extremes of satisfaction and regret were mitigated. Further tests are warranted to better determine the nature of the relationship between advice and outcomes and satisfaction.

LIMITATIONS

The most significant limitation of our studies is that the experiments were based on hypothetical situations. While the second study was designed to be somewhat more realistic by imposing a choice situation on subjects before the outcome was known, subjects did not have any real financial stake in the outcome.

REFERENCES

Connolly, T. and M. Zeelenberg (2002), 'Regret in decision making,' *Current Directions in Psychological Science*, **11**, 212–30.

Connolly, T., L. Ordonez and R. Coughlan (1997), 'Regret and responsibility in the evaluation of decision outcomes,' *Organizational Behavior and Human Decision Processes*, **10**, 73–85.

Constantinides, G. (1983), 'Capital market equilibrium with personal tax,' *Econometrica*, **51**, 611–36.

Cooke, A., T. Meyvis and A. Schwartz (2001), 'Avoiding future regret in purchase-timing decisions,' *Journal of Consumer Research*, **27**, 447–57.

Ferris, S., R. Haugen and A. Makhija (1988), 'Predicting contemporary volume with historical volume at differential price levels: evidence supporting the disposition effect,' *Journal of Finance*, **43**, 677–97.

Gilovich, T. and V. Medvec (1995), 'The experience of regret: what, when and why,' *Psychological Review*, **102**, 379–95.

Kahneman, D. and D.T. Miller (1986), 'Norm theory: comparing reality to its alternatives,' *Psychological Review*, **93**, 136–53.

Kahneman, D. and A. Tversky (1979), 'Prospect theory: an analysis of decisions under risk,' *Econometrica*, **47**, 263–91.

Kahneman, D. and A. Tversky (1982), 'The psychology of preferences,' *Scientific American*, **246**, 167–73.

Keppel, G. (1982), *Design and Analysis: A Researcher's Handbook*, Englewood Cliffs, NJ: Prentice-Hall.

Lakonishok, J. and S. Smidt (1986), 'Capital gain taxation and volume of trading,' *Journal of Finance*, **41**, 951–74.

Loomes, G. and R. Sugden (1982), 'Regret theory: an alternative theory of rational choice under uncertainty,' *Economic Journal*, **92**, 805–24.

Miller, D. and M. Ross (1975), 'Self-serving biases in the attribution of causality: fact or fiction?,' *Psychological Bulletin*, **82**, 213–25.

Odean, T. (1998), 'Are investors reluctant to realize their losses?,' *Journal of Finance*, **53**, 1775–98.

Ritov, I. and J. Baron (1995), 'Outcome knowledge, regret, and omission bias,' *Organizational Behavior and Human Decision Processes*, **64**, 119–27.

Ross, L. (1977), 'The intuitive psychologist and his shortcomings,' in L. Berkowitz (ed.), *Advances in Experimental Social Psychology*, Vol. 10, New York: Academic.

Sease, D. and J. Prestbo (1993), *Barron's Guide to Making Investment Decisions*, Englewood Cliffs, NJ: Prentice-Hall.

Shefrin, H. and M. Statman (1985), 'The disposition to sell winners too early and ride losers too long: theory and evidence,' *Journal of Finance*, **40**, 777–90.

Thaler, R. (1980), 'Toward a positive theory of consumer choice,' *Journal of Economic Behavior and Organization*, **1**, 39–60.

Thaler, R. and H. Shefrin (1981), 'An economic theory of self-control,' *Journal of Political Economy*, **89**, 392–410.
Weber, M. and C. Camerer (1998), 'The disposition effect in securities trading,' *Journal of Economic Behavior & Organization*, **33**, 167–84.

5 Overreaction of exchange-traded funds during the bubble of 1998–2002

Jeff Madura and Nivine Richie

INTRODUCTION

The phenomenon of under/overreaction cuts directly at the heart of market efficiency. If markets are truly efficient, all relevant information should be immediately and fully reflected in the stock price. Underreaction indicates this is not the case; information is instead incorporated over a period of time. Overreaction, on the other hand, suggests that stock prices consistently overshoot, and their reversals can be predicted from past price movements.

A study of broad market indices by Richards (1997) finds evidence of overreaction. In the past, such inefficiencies were not exploitable because indices were not actively traded. Today, however, the advent of exchange-traded funds (ETFs) makes further study appropriate. In contrast with stock market indices of the past, ETFs offer investors the opportunity to actively trade the market. In the past, investors who sought to invest in the 'market' could choose mutual funds that mirrored their index of choice. However, mutual funds investors can only transact once per day at the closing net asset value (NAV) set by the fund manager. Unlike mutual funds, ETFs are traded on exchanges throughout the day at prices set by the market. They also allow investors to sell securities short without the constraint of the 'uptick' rule. ETFs should be properly priced by the market since they are not subject to constraints on intraday trading and short sales.

This chapter attempts to determine whether ETFs are subject to particular forms of overreaction. We also assess whether the pricing behavior of ETFs during normal hours differs from after hours. Most of the after-hours trading occurs in a 90-minute night session just after the normal trading hours, and a 90-minute early morning session preceding the next day's normal trading hours. The normal and after-hours periods, distinguished by their respective levels of liquidity and trading behavior, may experience different degrees of overreaction.

We do find substantial overreaction of ETFs during the normal and after-hours trading periods. Furthermore, much of the reversal (correction) occurs in the trading period immediately following the ETFs' extreme stock price movements, which are more prevalent after hours. However, the after-hours reversals of extreme price movements during normal trading hours are more pronounced than the normal period reversals that occurred in the previous after-hours period. This implies that the extreme stock price movements during the day reflect a greater degree of overreaction than those in the after-hours period. In addition, the degree of overreaction is more pronounced for international ETFs. These results hold even after controlling for other factors.

The remainder of the chapter is organized as follows: the second section discusses the literature related to overreaction. The third section presents our hypotheses, and the fourth section provides the research design. The fifth section presents the results and the final section offers conclusions.

LITERATURE REVIEW

Our theories about the pricing of ETFs are based on (1) theoretical studies that explain mispricing, and (2) empirical research on under- or overreaction.

Theory of Over- or Underreaction

Poterba and Summers (1988) suggest that transition periods may exist when stock prices deviate from their fundamental values in illogical ways. Some research explains the deviations, such as Griffin and Tversky (1992), who suggest that people tend to place too much emphasis on the strength of new information. When applied to the stock valuation, this theory may explain why investors overreact to rumors or to facts.

Daniel et al. (1998) present a version of the investor overconfidence theory, which suggests that individuals overestimate the value of information they generate privately and underestimate publicly available information. Tversky and Kahneman (1974) show that the heuristics used by individuals to make decisions under uncertainty may result in 'systematic errors' (p. 1124). In violation of Bayes's rule, individuals do not consider prior probabilities when making their assessments, but rather arrive at subjective probabilities of occurrence based on how similar, or 'representative', the event is to their preconceived notions. This representativeness heuristic can lead investors to drive values beyond their correct valuations, resulting in the empirical phenomenon of overreaction documented here.

Possible under- or overreaction attracts feedback traders who may attempt to arbitrage the mispricing. Cutler et al. (1990) suggest that stock price behavior may be influenced by feedback traders who trade based on recent price movements rather than fundamental factors. If stock market pricing can't be explained by fundamentals, feedback traders can capitalize on price movements that deviate from the fundamental values, providing support for studies finding evidence of overreaction.

Barberis et al. (1998) acknowledge the possibility of feedback traders. But they believe that investors who attempt to correct mispricing risk the possibility that it will not be corrected, at least in the short run. That is, even if a price has deviated from its fundamental value, it may stray further until there is sufficient force from feedback traders to correct it.

Empirical Research on Over- and Underreaction

Overreaction has been researched in the context of individual stocks as well as market indices, with mixed results. Most overreaction studies identify stocks as winners and losers on the basis of past price performance, and then track subsequent abnormal gains to the winner and loser portfolios. Positive (negative) cumulative abnormal returns following large positive (negative) price movements indicate underreaction, while reversals of returns indicate overreaction. DeBondt and Thaler (1985) find that, 36 months after portfolio formation, loser portfolios outperform the market on average, while winner portfolios underperform on average. Most of the overreaction is in the second and third year following portfolio formation.

Jegadeesh (1990) examines market efficiency and the serial correlation of returns. He finds significant negative first-order serial correlation in monthly stock returns and significant positive serial correlation in 12-month returns, suggesting overreaction in the short term and underreaction in the long term. Similarly, Chan (2003) cites many studies that document a long-term drift following specific events, which he attributes to underreaction.

A related issue is how the degree of overreaction may depend on the market of concern. Da Costa (1994) finds that Brazilian stocks experience price reversals over two-year periods. Bremer et al. (1997) find a small degree of overreaction for Japanese loser stocks, but conclude that economic profits are not possible. Richards (1997) documents overreaction of stock market indices when using horizons beyond one year to measure performance, but finds that the degree of overreaction varies among markets.

More recently, a study by Baytas and Cakici (1999) assessed stock market overreaction in seven industrialized markets including the USA. They find evidence of long-term overreaction for all countries except the USA. They also find that the degree of overreaction and the characteristics to which it is related vary among countries. In some countries, overreaction is tied to the stock's price level. In others, it is tied to firm size. This study sheds new light on the topic because it suggests that results can vary among markets even when controlling for time period, the model used to identify winners and losers, and the model used to estimate abnormal returns in the subsequent holding period. Results may be partially dependent on the characteristics of a particular market and on the investors who trade there.

Previous research does not offer direct implications for ETFs because, as tradable composites of stocks, they exhibit unique characteristics. This tradability allows for potential arbitrage to eliminate mispricing, and therefore overcomes market imperfections that prevailed when stock indexes were not tradable. Furthermore, none of the previous research assesses the pricing dynamics of ETFs (or stock indexes in general) during the normal versus after-hours trading periods. This study builds on the existing work by testing for overreaction of ETFs and by comparing overreaction during normal hours versus after hours.

HYPOTHESES

Our hypotheses focus on (1) whether ETFs are subject to overreaction, (2) whether the overreaction is conditional on the trading period, and (3) how the degree of overreaction is conditional on ETF-specific characteristics.

Overreaction of ETFs

Because an ETF represents a portfolio of stocks, it may be less susceptible to unusual share price jumps that reflect overreaction. The ease of trading ETFs in an open market allows for quick correction if the price strays from its proper value. Access to intraday trading without short-sale constraints should allow investors to take advantage of predictable mispricing in the market. Thus ETF prices should reflect all available information. Our null hypothesis is that ETFs will not experience overreaction.

We also consider a counter-hypothesis. ETFs enable investors to easily take positions in stock composites, which could allow for more rapid and volatile price movements of those composites. The ease of trading may increase participation by uninformed or 'noise' traders. Kyle (1985) describes a scenario where the presence of uninformed traders provides depth to the market and allows informed traders to 'hide'. Extending his work to the overreaction hypothesis, we suggest that informed traders will benefit at the expense of uninformed traders' mispricings, causing the overreaction of noise traders to be systematically corrected by informed traders.

DeLong et al. (1990) describe the market as a contest between noise traders driven by market sentiment and arbitrageurs with rational expectations. Consequently, the price of an asset may deviate from its fundamental value. This theory may also explain the behavior of a single tradable asset that reflects a sector or a market. That is, the pricing of an asset like an ETF that represents a sector or a market is also subject to the dynamics between noise traders and arbitrageurs, causing the price to stray from its fundamental valuation. Accordingly, our alternate hypothesis is that ETFs will experience overreaction and subsequent reversals (corrections). We test this hypothesis by identifying large stock price movements in ETFs and measuring abnormal returns after those movements.

Overreaction During Normal Trading Hours versus After Hours

Our null hypothesis is that a large stock price movement of an ETF during normal trading hours will not elicit a market response after hours. In addition, a large stock price movement of an ETF in an after-hours period will not elicit a market response in the following normal trading period. The null hypothesis is based on the premise that trading behavior during normal hours is similar to trading behavior after hours. If the same types of traders trade during normal hours and after hours, any price discrepancy occurring during one period should be corrected within that period. Under these conditions, large stock price movements of ETFs in one period should not be followed by a predictable adjustment in the next period.

If, however, trading behavior during normal hours is distinctly different from that after hours, an ETF with an extreme stock price movement in one period may experience a reversal the next. This theory does not require that all informed traders participate strictly during normal hours or after hours. Instead, it suggests that noise traders and feedback traders may trade in either period. However, extreme stock price movements that reflect price discrepancies may occur in one period, but not be corrected in that period. Consequently, a different set of feedback traders transacting in the following period may be able to capitalize on (and therefore correct for) those price discrepancies. In essence, feedback traders trading after hours may exploit price discrepancies caused earlier by noise traders that have not yet been corrected. Similarly, feedback traders may exploit price discrepancies during normal trading hours that were caused by noise traders in the previous after-hours period that have not been corrected.

Normal and after-hours periods may rightfully be considered as two separate markets because of differences in liquidity and types of market participants.[1] The liquidity of a security can change within the day in a given market (see Stoll and Whaley, 1990; Foster and Viswanathan, 1993), and can vary among markets. The average trading volume per after-hours period is 70 million shares, versus 1.2 billion shares traded each day on the New York Stock Exchange.[2]

Barclay and Hendershott (2004) suggest that the after-hours market is characterized by less volume than regular trading sessions. They estimate the implied bid–ask spread using Roll's (1984) measure, and find that after-hours trades are more costly than those made during the regular trading sessions. By assuming that liquidity-motivated traders will choose to trade during the less expensive day session, they conclude that the after-hours market has a higher proportion of informed traders to uninformed traders than the normal day market.[3]

Cox and Peterson (1994) show how overreaction can vary among US stock exchanges due to liquidity differences. Richards (1997) shows how overreaction can vary among country markets, which he attributes to differences in liquidity and stock volatility. Baytas and Cakici (1999) document how overreaction can vary among markets when each country's stocks are traded on a separate market.

We extend the definition of markets from stock exchanges within the USA or across national borders to different trading sessions within a 24-hour period. ETFs may be subject to different trading behavior and liquidity during normal trading hours versus after hours. Thus after-hours trading may correct for unusually large price movements of ETFs that occurred during normal trading hours, and trading during normal hours may correct for unusually large price movements of ETFs that occurred in the previous after-hours period. This is because an extreme stock price movement of an ETF during normal hours may be viewed as excessive by feedback traders who trade after hours, and vice versa. We investigate separately the market efficiency of ETFs during normal trading hours and after hours.

ETF-specific Characteristics that may Affect the Degree of Overreaction

We expect the degree of overreaction of an ETF to be conditional on the following characteristics specific to the ETF.

Size of trigger

According to Daniel et al. (1998), investors place more weight on recent information than on prior information, and overemphasize recent stock price movements, causing overreaction. Thus a more extreme stock price movement may represent a greater degree of overreaction and lead to a larger reversal.

Trading volume

More liquid ETFs should be less susceptible to mispricing because a sufficient number of investors are involved. Conversely, less liquid ETFs may be more susceptible to mispricing, since there may be fewer informed traders who maintain prices at or near their fundamental values.

Cox and Peterson (1994) identify liquidity as a significant factor in explaining reversals of returns. After controlling for the bid–ask bounce and market liquidity, they find no evidence of overreaction. If our findings of overreaction are primarily driven by the effects of market liquidity, we would expect liquidity to be the dominant force in explaining the cross-sectional variation in the degree of overreaction among ETFs.

Volatility

More volatile stocks are more likely to overreact. Richards (1997) makes a similar argument for stock indexes over a long-term period, but more volatile stocks may also be more susceptible to mispricing in the short run.

Type

ETFs are classified as international, sector or broad-based. Broad-based ETFs may be less susceptible to temporary mispricing (and therefore to overreaction) because they represent widely diversified portfolios of US stocks. International ETFs may be more susceptible to mispricing because they may exhibit more price sensitivity to other systematic factors such as foreign country or currency, for which information is less readily available.

RESEARCH DESIGN

Our tests of overreaction require the following elements of a research design:

1. *The type of securities assessed* Related studies vary substantially in terms of the types of securities assessed. Atkins and Dyl (1990) focus on large stocks traded on the New York Stock Exchange; Bremer and Sweeney (1991) assess Fortune 500 stocks. Cox and Peterson (1994) include smaller stocks traded on the Nasdaq market within their study. Foreign stocks have also been assessed: Da Costa (1994) focuses on Brazilian stocks, and Bremer et al. (1997) on Japanese stocks.

   The overreaction of stock indexes has also been tested. Richards (1997) focuses on extreme stock price movements of stock indexes. Our focus on a sample of ETFs is closely related to studies on stock indexes, but is different in that the tradability of ETFs allows investors to capitalize on any pricing discrepancies.
2. *The time horizon used to measure the extreme stock price movement* The horizon has ranged from one day (Atkins and Dyl, 1990; Bremer and Sweeney, 1991) to three years (DeBondt and Thaler, 1985) and Richards (1997). We use two separate time horizons: normal trading hours and the after-hours period. The day period represents normal trading hours (9.30 a.m. to 4 p.m.); after-hours reflects the period from the close of normal trading hours (4 p.m.) to the open of normal trading hours the next day (9.30 a.m.). Thus the two periods together encompass a total of 24 hours.
3. *The size of the stock price movement (also called the 'trigger')* For a one-day horizon, the typical minimum trigger to qualify for a sample in other studies is 10 percent for individual stocks. We use a minimum trigger of 5 percent, since ETFs represent stock composites and should not be as volatile as individual stocks.
4. *The time horizon used to test for a correction* This horizon is usually matched with the time horizon in which the extreme stock price movement is measured to qualify

for the sample. For our sample, the time horizon is either the after-hours period following earlier extreme price movements during normal trading hours, or the normal hours following extreme price movements during the previous after-hours period.

5. *The method of measuring abnormal stock price movement* Most studies testing short-term overreaction of stocks use the market model (Atkins and Dyl, 1990), the market-adjusted returns model (Da Costa, 1994), the mean-adjusted returns model (Cox and Peterson, 1994), or all three models to derive abnormal returns. Since ETFs represent stock composites, they sometimes represent an entire market, and so the market model is not applicable. Consequently, we apply the mean-adjusted returns model to measure abnormal stock price movements in the period after the trigger is identified.

Data

Exchange-traded funds gained popularity during the bubble of 1998–2002. Although the SPDR, Standard & Poor's depository receipt (ticker symbol SPY) has been in existence since 1993, more focused ETFs, such as sector funds and international funds, have only recently been introduced.

ETFs in general are passively managed mutual funds designed to mirror indices. They trade around the clock on exchanges such as the American Stock Exchange (AMEX). Regular mutual funds investors can only transact once daily at the 4 p.m. closing net asset value (NAV). Furthermore, ETFs are unique in that investors have access to an arbitrage mechanism where, in the event of market mispricing or supply and demand imbalances, units of 50 000 shares of the ETF can be exchanged for the underlying assets and vice versa.

Our sample includes observations of daily opening and closing prices for AMEX-traded ETFs between August 1998 and August 2002. This period encompasses most of the trading of ETFs. The entire sample consists of 1989 extreme ETF price changes that satisfy the minimum 5 percent trigger level. The numbers of extreme price increases (winners) and decreases (losers) across normal and after-hours periods by different types of ETFs shown in panel (a) of Table 5.1. As Panel B shows, of the entire sample, 1035 (52 percent) are winners, and the remaining 954 (48 percent) are losers. A total of 268 observations (13 percent) qualify during the normal day period versus 1721 (87 percent) after hours.

The sample is further segmented by ETF type. Again, these are classified as broad-based, sector or international, and allow investors to add exposure to various segments of the market. Broad-based funds like the SPDR or the Nasdaq-100 Index Tracking Stock (ticker symbol QQQ) allow investors to allocate portions of their portfolios to diversified equities with minimal transaction costs. Sector funds such as the iShares Dow Jones US Financial Sector fund (ticker symbol IYF) or the Select Sector SPDR Technology fund (ticker symbol XLK) allow investors to shift asset allocation to specific sectors of the equity market and yet remain diversified. Finally, international ETFs like the iShares MSCI EAFE fund (ticker symbol EFA) or the iShares MSCI Japan fund (ticker symbol EWJ) allow investors to gain exposure to international markets on a broad scale (EFA) or on a more focused scale (EWJ).

Table 5.1 Distribution of sample that satisfies the 5 percent trigger

(a) Distribution of winners and losers across days and after hours. Percentage' of total extreme price movements from far right column in italics

	Winners		Losers		Total
	Day	After hours	Day	After hours	
International ETFs	91	346	46	315	798
	11%	*43%*	*6%*	*39%*	*100%*
Sector ETFs	61	382	55	391	889
	7%	*43%*	*6%*	*44%*	*100%*
Broad-based ETFs	7	148	8	139	302
	2%	*49%*	*3%*	*46%*	*100%*
Entire sample	159	876	109	845	1989
	8%	*44%*	*5%*	*42%*	*100%*

(b) Distribution of subsamples across type of ETF. Percentages of entire sample from bottom row in italics

	Total day	Total after hours	Total winners	Total losers
International ETFs	137	661	437	361
	51%	*38%*	*42%*	*38%*
Sector ETFs	116	773	443	446
	43%	*45%*	*43%*	*47%*
Broad-based ETFs	15	287	155	147
	6%	*17%*	*15%*	*15%*
Entire sample	268	1721	1035	954
	100%	*100%*	*100%*	*100%*

Note: The sample of ETF returns over the day and after hours periods is screened for a gain of at least 5% (winners) lower than −5% (losers). Italicized numbers are the percentages of the total extreme price movements in the far right column.

By definition, sector funds and international funds are more focused and less diversified than their broad-based counterparts. Our data show that the majority of extreme price movements are concentrated among the sector ETFs and the international ETFs. Panel (b) of Table 5.1 shows that 51 percent of the 268 extreme price movements during the day are attributed to international ETFs, and 43 percent are attributed to sector ETFs. Similarly, 38 percent and 45 percent of the 1721 after-hours observations are attributed to international and sector ETFs, respectively. Of the 798 international ETF observations in the sample, 55 percent are winners and 45 percent are losers.

The specific proportion of normal hours observations versus after-hours observations varies by ETF type, but the after-hours observations dominate for each type. One explanation for this is that the underlying stocks in the international ETFs are traded on foreign stock exchanges after normal US trading hours. Thus large price movements of international ETFs after hours in the USA may reflect large price changes of the underlying foreign stocks that are being traded on foreign stock exchanges at that time. But this phenomenon would not explain the dominance of after-hours observations in the subsamples of US broad-based and sector ETFs.

The high frequency of after-hours observations that qualify for the sample suggests that more pronounced movements in ETF prices occur at after hours. Whether such a difference implies a greater degree of overreaction in one period versus the other can only be determined empirically.

Methodology

To identify the existence of overreaction following a large price movement, we first identify the expected reaction following such a move. We use a mean-adjusted expected return and a time-series standard deviation test following Brown and Warner (1980).[4] Expected returns ($\bar{R}$) are calculated using a 255-day estimation period ending 15 days prior to the event, and are required to have at least 90 useable returns in the estimation period.

Expected returns for ETFs during normal trading hours are based on returns that occur during normal trading hours over the estimation period, while expected returns of ETFs after hours are based on returns after hours over the estimation period. This allows for possible differences between average returns during the day period versus after hours. The abnormal return in the 24-hour period following each trigger is the mean-adjusted return using close-to-close prices following a trigger during normal trading hours and open-to-open prices following a trigger after hours. Therefore the 24-hour period following normal trading hours (in which a winner or a loser ETF is identified) represents the following after-hours period and subsequent normal trading period; the 24-hour period following a trigger after hours represents the following day and after-hours periods. The test statistic for abnormal returns is measured based on the 'crude dependence adjustment' of Brown and Warner (1980).

Cross-sectional Analysis

The abnormal returns following extreme price movements are conditional on the following characteristics: (1) the period assessed (normal versus after hours), (2) the size of the extreme return (the trigger) of the ETF, (3) the type of ETF, (4) the volatility of the ETF, and (5) volume of the ETF. An extreme stock price movement is classified according to whether it occurred in the day or after hours with a dummy variable. The trigger is measured as the return that allowed the ETF to qualify for the sample based on the +5 percent or –5 percent threshold levels. Each ETF is classified as international, sector or broad-based. The three types are separately coded using dummy variables representing international ETFs and sector ETFs. ETF volatility is measured as the standard deviation of returns over the past 90 days. An ETF's liquidity is measured as the average daily trading volume in the period in which the trigger occurred.

We apply the following multivariate model to all winners and losers to test for the significance of the trading period (normal versus after hours) while controlling for the other variables.

$$AR_j = \beta_0 + \beta_1 AFTERHOURS + \beta_2 TRIGGER + \beta_3 INTLDUM + \beta_4 SECTDUM + \beta_5 VOLAT + \beta_6 VOLUME + \varepsilon$$

where:

AR = abnormal return during the period following the extreme return,
AFTERHOURS = the dummy variable, with a value of 1 if the extreme stock price movement occurs after hours and 0 otherwise,
TRIGGER = return of the ETF; must be > +5 percent or < −5 percent in a normal or after-hours period,
INTLDUM = the dummy variable, with a value of 1 if the ETF is an international fund and 0 otherwise,
SECTDUM = the dummy variable, with a value of 1 if the ETF is a sector fund and 0 otherwise,
VOLAT = the standard deviation of returns over the past 90 days for the ETF, and
VOLUME = the natural logarithm of the volume of shares traded for the ETF.

The model is tested for heteroskedasticity and corrected using White's (1980) test.

We also adapt the multivariate model above to assess the cross-sectional variation in abnormal returns of the normal (day) and after-hours sample separately. In this case, the after-hours dummy variable does not apply and is excluded from the model. Since this particular analysis includes winners and losers in the same sample, a dummy variable, *LOSDUM*, is included to distinguish losers from winners. It is assigned a value of 1 if the extreme price movement represents a loss and 0 otherwise.

The coefficients in the analysis are restricted to be the same regardless of the ETF type. To obtain estimates of coefficients for each type, we repeat the analysis separately for each subsample of ETFs by type. The dummy variables representing the type of ETF are not applicable for this analysis since all ETFs in each subsample are classified as the same.

RESULTS

We first report the results for the estimation of abnormal returns following the extreme price movements of ETFs, and then for the cross-sectional analyses of the abnormal returns.

Abnormal Returns for the Entire Sample

Column 1 of Table 5.2 shows the abnormal returns associated with the extreme stock price changes of ETFs that occurred during the day for the entire sample of winners and losers and the various subsamples. The abnormal returns following day triggers are shown in the third, fourth and fifth columns, according to whether the extreme stock price change reflects a gain (winner) in panel (a) or a loss (loser) in panel (b). For winners and losers, the results are shown for trigger levels of at least 5 percent, at least 6 percent

Table 5.2 Full sample abnormal returns following day triggers

	Day (Period 0)	After hours (Period 1)	Day (Period 2)	24 hour (Periods 1 – 2)	Proportion of the overreaction reversed in the following period
(a) Winners					Pd 1 AR / Pd 0 AR
Trigger > 5%	6.75	−3.69	−0.7	−4.28	54.67%
(N = 159)	(24.710) ****	(−6.865) ****	(−2.547) ***	(−10.113) ****	
	100%:0%	*25%:75%*	*38%:62%*	*14%:86%*	
Trigger > 6%	8.2	−4.21	−0.93	−5.09	51.34%
(N = 77)	(18.854) ****	(−5.340) ****	(−2.143) **	(−8.277) ****	
	100%:0%	*21%:79%*	*37%:63%*	*16%:84%*	
Trigger > 7%	9.52	−4.99	−1.15	−6.13	52.42%
(N = 45)	(18.222) ****	(−5.559) ****	(−2.203) **	(−8.108) ****	
	100%:0%	*18%:82%*	*30%:70%*	*15%:85%*	
(b) Losers					
Trigger < −5%	−6.61	6.59	0.16	6.82	99.70%
(N = 109)	(−18.645) ****	(9.189) ****	(0.439)	(12.213) ****	
	0%:100%	*94%:6%*	*60%:40%*	*96%:4%*	
Trigger < −6%	−7.8	8.28	−0.22	8.02	106.15%
(N = 53)	(−14.663) ****	(8.383) ****	(−0.417)	(10.341) ****	
	0%:100%	*94%:6%*	*49%:51%*	*96%:4%*	
Trigger < −7%	−8.93	8.47	0.34	8.75	94.85%
(N = 27)	(−13.780) ****	(6.811) ****	(0.519)	(9.131) ****	
	0%:100%	*93%:7%*	*62%:38%*	*96%:4%*	

Notes: Comparison period-adjusted abnormal returns are reported using a 255-day estimation period which ends 15 days prior to the large price move and requires 90 days of usable returns. The *t*-statistics in parentheses are adjusted using the crude dependence adjustment. Proportion of positive observations:proportion of negative observations shown in italics.
*, **, ***, and **** indicate significance at the 10%, 5%, 1%, and 0.1% levels, respectively, using a 1-tailed test for significance.

and at least 7 percent. The sample size is reduced when the minimum trigger level is higher.

Abnormal Returns After Hours following Day Winners

Table 5.2 shows the abnormal returns of ETFs for the after-hours period (third column) following the day in which extreme stock price movement occurred, and column 4 shows the returns for the following day period. These two periods comprise the 24-hour period following the day when the extreme changes occurred, and results for this 24-hour period are shown in the fifth column. The sixth column shows the proportion of the extreme stock price movement that is reversed in the subsequent period.

As shown in panel (a) of Table 5.2, the day period winners experience a significant negative abnormal return after hours, regardless of the trigger level. At least 75 percent experienced negative abnormal returns after hours. Thus the general results here are not due to outliers. The reversal after hours suggests that the extreme stock price movements during the day reflect an overreaction.

Notice in the sixth column that more than 50 percent of the mean extreme stock price movement of winners is reversed for the subsamples partitioned by different minimum trigger levels. Overall, a strong response follows an extreme stock price movement during the day. Apparently, some investors behave as feedback traders after hours and capitalize on the overreaction of ETFs that occurred earlier in the day.

One could argue that the correction after hours is wrong, and therefore does not verify that the earlier extreme price movement was an overreaction. Yet abnormal returns continue to be negative and significant during the following day. More than 80 percent of the corrections over the 24-hours following the extreme movement during the day occur after hours.

Comparison of After-hours Reversals among Trigger Levels

The size of the reversal after hours during the following normal day period, and over the combination of those two periods, is more pronounced when a larger trigger level is used. For example, the ETFs that qualify for a +5 percent trigger experience a mean abnormal return of –3.69 percent after hours, while the ETFs that qualify for a +7 percent trigger experience a mean abnormal return of –4.99 percent. Similar results hold for the 24-hour period following the day when the extreme stock price movement occurred.

Abnormal Returns After Hours following Day Losers

As shown in panel (b) of Table 5.2, the normal day period losers experience a significant positive abnormal return after hours, regardless of the trigger level. While results vary with the minimum trigger level used, at least 93 percent experienced positive abnormal returns after hours. These findings confirm market overreaction by the day loser ETFs. The abnormal returns during the following day are not significant.

For ETFs that qualify for the –5 percent trigger level, the mean abnormal return after hours is about equal to the mean extreme stock price movement that occurred earlier in the day. For the ETFs that qualify for the –6 percent or –7 percent trigger levels, the abnormal return after hours exceeds the extreme movement, on average. Thus, on average, the gain after hours completely offsets the loss during normal trading hours.

As with winners, the size of the reversal for losers after hours is more pronounced when the losers qualify for the higher trigger (larger loss) level. Notice from the sixth column that at least 90 percent of the extreme stock price movements of losers is reversed for the subsamples partitioned by different trigger levels.

Abnormal Returns During the Day following After-hours Winners

Table 5.3 shows the abnormal returns following extreme stock price changes of ETFs that occur after hours are shown for the overall sample. Results are segmented according

Table 5.3 Full sample abnormal returns following after-hours triggers

	After hours (Period 0)	Day (Period 1)	After hours (Period 2)	24 hour (Periods 1–2)	Proportion of the overreaction reversed in the following period.
(a) Winners					Pd 1 AR / Pd 0 AR
Trigger > 5%	7.02	−1.93	1.82	−0.19	27.49%
(*N* = 876)	(21.954) ****	(−12.688) ****	(5.68) ****	(−0.706)	
	100%:0%	*18%:82%*	*70%:30%*	*45%:55%*	
Trigger > 6%	8.33	−2.29	2.21	−0.19	27.49%
(*N* = 474)	(20.715) ****	(−11.804) ****	(5.497) ****	(−0.573)	
	100%:0%	*17%:83%*	*71%:29%*	*46%:54%*	
Trigger > 7%	9.5	−2.75	2.61	−0.32	28.95%
(*N* = 288)	(18.673) ****	(−11.065) ****	(5.128) ****	(−0.746)	
	100%:0%	*18%:82%*	*71%:29%*	*44%:56%*	
(b) Losers					
Trigger < −5%	−6.97	2.74	−1.51	1.16	39.31%
(*N* = 835)	(−24.114) ****	(19.855) ****	(−5.232) ****	(4.734) ****	
	0%:100%	*89%:11%*	*39%:61%*	*62%:38%*	
Trigger < −6%	−8.12	3.36	−1.51	1.73	41.38%
(*N* = 488)	(−20.648) ****	(17.442) ****	(−3.854) ****	(5.211) ****	
	0%:100%	*92%:8%*	*42%:58%*	*67%:33%*	
Trigger < −7%	−9.42	4.09	−1.45	2.49	43.42%
(*N* = 281)	(−18.002) ****	(15.811) ****	(−2.779) ***	(5.734) ****	
	0%:100%	*93%:7%*	*47%:53%*	*72%:28%*	

Notes: As for Table 5.2.

to whether the extreme change reflects a gain (winner) in Panel (a) or a loss (loser) in panel (b), and are also segmented according to trigger level. The abnormal returns of ETFs are shown for the day period (third column) following the after-hours period in which extreme the stock price movement occurred, and are shown for the following after-hours period (fourth column) as well. These two periods comprise a 24-hour period following the after-hours period in which the extreme changes occurred, and results for this period are shown in the fifth column. The sixth column shows the mean proportion of the extreme movement after hours that is reversed during normal hours the following day.

As shown in panel (a) of Table 5.3, after-hours winners experience a significant negative abnormal return the next day, regardless of the trigger level. For the 5 percent trigger, 82 percent of after-hours winners experienced negative abnormal returns the following day.

Table 5.4 Test of difference in mean abnormal returns

Trigger	AR following day trigger (%)	AR following after-hours trigger (%)	Mean difference(%)	T-statistic
5% winner	−3.69	−1.93	−1.76	−4.194****
6% winner	−4.21	−2.29	−1.92	−2.703***
7% winner	−5.00	−2.75	−2.25	−2.056**
5% loser	6.59	2.74	3.85	8.764****
6% loser	8.28	3.36	4.92	7.738****
7% loser	8.47	4.09	4.38	3.946****

Notes: *T*-test for difference in means of two samples assuming unequal variance using a two-tailed test for significance. The mean difference is calculated as AR following a day trigger less AR following an after hours trigger.
*, **, ***, and **** indicate significance at the 10%, 5%, 1%, and 0.1% levels, respectively, using a 2-tailed test for significance.

Abnormal Returns During the Day following After-hours Losers

As shown in panel (b) of Table 5.3, after-hours losers experience a significant positive abnormal return the following day, regardless of the trigger level. As the sixth column shows, for ETFs that qualify for the –5 percent trigger level, the abnormal return represents about a 39 percent reversal on average.

Comparison of Abnormal Returns between Day and After-hours Winners

A comparison of the magnitude of reversal between the normal day and after-hours periods is shown in Table 5.4. For day winners that qualify for the 5 percent minimum trigger, the mean reversal after hours is −3.69 percent; for after-hours winners, the following day reversal is −1.93 percent on average. The mean difference between two types of reversals is −1.76 percent, with a *t*-statistic of −4.194 and significant at the 0.001 level.

Thus the degree of overreaction of ETF winners during the day is more pronounced than the degree of overreaction of ETF winners after hours. In other words, the after-hours correction of ETFs that experience extreme stock price gains during the day is more pronounced than the day correction of ETFs that experienced extreme gains during the previous after-hours period. For the 6 percent trigger level, the *t*-statistic from testing the difference in day and after-hours reversals is −2.703, which is significant at the 0.01 level. For the 7 percent trigger level, it is −2.056, significant at the 0.05 level.

Comparison of Abnormal Returns between Day and After-hours Losers

A comparison of the magnitude of the reversal between the day and after-hours periods is also conducted for losers. For day losers that qualify for the 5 percent trigger, the reversal after hours is 6.59 percent, while for after-hours losers the reversal is 2.74 percent. The mean after-hours reversal of the extreme stock movements of ETFs during the day is about 2.4 times the mean day reversal of extreme stock movements of ETFs after hours. The mean difference between the two types of reversals is 3.85 percent, with a t-statistic of 8.764 and significant at the 0.001 level. Thus the degree of overreaction of ETF losers during the day is more pronounced than the degree of overreaction of ETF losers after hours. As with winners, the after-hours correction of ETFs that experience extreme stock price losses during the day is more pronounced than the day correction of ETFs that experience extreme losses in the previous after-hours period.

For losers that qualify for the −6 percent trigger level, the t-statistic from testing the difference in reversals of day and after-hours periods is 7.738, significant at the 0.001 level. For losers that qualify for the −7 percent trigger level, the t-statistic is 3.946, significant at the 0.001 level. These comparisons offer further support of more pronounced reversals after hours, which implies more pronounced overreaction during the day.

Comparison of Abnormal Returns among Types of ETFs

Since results may vary by ETF type, the analysis is repeated separately for each type in Table 5.5. Notice that international ETFs experience significant reversals. The 5 percent trigger is used again here, but the analysis is also applied to 6 percent and 7 percent triggers. The results are qualitatively similar but not reported.

Panel A shows the results for winners and losers during the day, while Panel B shows after-hours results. The mean reversal following day winners and losers is significant. The reversal following after-hours winners and losers is also significant, but less pronounced. These results are consistent with those found for the entire sample.

Sector ETFs experience a significant reversal. Panel A shows that the reversal of day winners is less pronounced than the reversal of day losers. The reversal following day losers is more pronounced than the reversal following after-hours losers found in Panel B. These results are also consistent with those found for the entire sample.

Broad-based ETF day winners do not experience a significant reversal after hours, but do experience a significant reversal the following day. Broad-based day losers experience a significant reversal after hours, and both experience significant reversals the following day. Yet the reversal following after-hours losers is less pronounced on average than the reversal following day losers.

A comparison among ETFs types is also conducted to determine if the degree of overreaction is more noticeable for a particular type. Table 5.6 compares the reversals by type within the separate subsamples of day winners, day losers, after-hours winners, and after-hours losers. The 5 percent trigger level is again used here to determine the ETFs that qualify for each sample. The results for the broad-based winner ETFs should be interpreted with caution, however, since only seven qualify as day winners while 148 qualify as after-hours winners.

Panel (a) of Table 5.6 summarizes the reversals (as measured by abnormal returns), while panel (b) shows two-way comparisons. Panel B shows that the mean reversal of day winners is significantly more pronounced for international ETF day winners than for sector or broad-based ETF winners. For day losers, the mean reversal is significantly larger for international and sector ETFs than for broad-based ETFs.

For after-hours winners, the reversal of the international ETFs is significantly more pronounced than for other types, and the reversal of sector ETFs is significantly more pronounced than for broad-based ETFs. For after-hours losers, the reversal is

Table 5.5 Abnormal returns following extreme stock price movements for ETF subsamples

	Day (Period 0)	After hours (Period 1)	Day (Period 2)	24-Hour (Periods 1 – 2)
(a) Extreme price changes during the day				
Winners				
International ETFs	7.11	−5.14	0.12	−4.98
(N = 91)	(26.853) ****	(−11.202) ****	(0.468)	(−14.366) ****
	100%:0%	*10%:90%*	*47%:53%*	*10%:90%*
Sector ETFs	6.32	−1.87	−1.68	−3.51
(N = 61)	(13.880)	(−2.04) **	(−3.684) ****	(−4.786) ****
	100%:0%	*43%:57%*	*29%:71%*	*20%:80%*
Broad-based ETFs	6.04	−0.62	−2.51	−2.21
(N = 7)	(6.045) ****	(−0.291)	(−2.517) ***	(−1.274)
	100%:0%	*57%:43%*	*13%:87%*	*13%:87%*
Losers				
International ETFs	−6.89	6.02	0.20	6.20
(N = 46)	(−18.963) ****	(9.159) ****	(0.543)	(12.430) ****
	0%:100%	*96%:4%*	*55%:45%*	*96%:4%*
Sector ETFs	−6.53	7.09	0.08	7.32
(N = 55)	(−10.766) ****	(5.792) ****	(0.138)	(7.712) ****
	0%:100%	*93%:7%*	*62%:38%*	*96%:4%*
Broad-based ETFs	−5.63	6.45	0.42	6.89
(N = 8)	(−10.704) ****	(4.829) ****	(0.798)	(6.006) ****
	0%:100%	*100%:0%*	*78%:22%*	*100%:0%*
(b) Extreme price changes after hours				
Winners				
International ETFs	6.74	−2.45	2.28	−0.26
(N = 346)	25.095) ****	(−15.995) ****	(8.491) ****	(−1.341) *
	100%:0%	*10%:90%*	*74%:26%*	*40%:60%*
Sector ETFs	7.51	−1.89	1.79	−0.09
(N = 382)	(16.301) ****	(−8.092) ****	(3.88) ****	(−0.229)
	100%:0%	*19%:81%*	*68%:32%*	*49%:51%*
Broad-based ETFs	6.39	−1.07	0.85	−0.29
(N = 148)	(12.640) ****	(−4.764) ****	(1.687) **	(−0.643)
	100%:0%	*28%:72%*	*68%:32%*	*48%:52%*
Losers				
International ETFs	−7.13	3.25	−2.17	1.00
(N = 315)	(−24.377) ****	(19.810) ****	(−7.418) ****	(4.736) ****
	0%:100%	*91%:9%*	*30%:70%*	*63%:37%*
Sector ETFs	−6.97	2.41	−1.65	0.71
(N = 391)	(−18.089) ****	(13.257) ****	(−4.293) ****	(2.106) **
	0%:100%	*86%:14%*	*38%:63%*	*57%:43%*
Broad-based ETFs	−6.58	2.51	0.36	2.74
(N = 139)	(−13.132) ****	(11.734) ****	(0.713)	(6.038) ****
	0%:100%	*91%:9%*	*60%:40%*	*73%:27%*

Table 5.5 (continued)

Notes: Comparison period-adjusted abnormal returns are reported (in %) using a 255 day estimation period which ends 15 days prior to the large price move of + and − 5% for winners and losers, respectively, and requires 90 days of usable returns. The *t*-statistics in parentheses are adjusted using the crude dependence adjustment. Proportion of positive observations:proportion of negative observations shown in italics.
*, **, ***, and **** indicate significance at the 10%, 5%, 1%, and 0.1% levels, respectively using a 1-tailed test for significance.

Table 5.6 Comparison of abnormal returns by type of ETF

(a) Summary of abnormal returns by type following a 5% trigger

	International ETF(%)	Sector ETF(%)	Broad-based ETF(%)
Day Winners	−5.14	−1.87	−0.62
Day Losers	6.02	7.09	2.51
After hours Winners	−2.45	−2.04	−1.08
After hours Losers	3.25	2.41	2.51

(b) Difference in abnormal returns (*t*-statistic in parentheses)

	AR intl – AR sector	AR intl – AR broad	AR sector – AR broad
Day winners	−3.27%	−4.52%	−1.25%
	(−3.80)****	(−4.65)****	(−1.14)
Day losers	−1.07%	3.51%	4.58%
	(−1.16)	(4.66)****	(8.03)****
After-hours winners	−0.41%	−1.37%	−0.96%
	(−2.60)***	(−7.62)****	(−5.85)****
After-hours losers	0.84%	0.74%	−0.10%
	(3.93)****	(3.21)***	(−0.51)

Notes: For each of the four categories defined in the first column, the abnormal returns are displayed in the period following the extreme stock price movement based on a 5% trigger.
*, **, ***, and **** indicate significance at the 10%, 5%, 1%, and 0.1% levels, respectively using a 2-tailed test for significance.

significantly higher for international ETFs than for other types. Overall, the results suggest that international ETFs tend to experience a greater degree of overreaction, leading to a more pronounced correction in the following period.

Multivariate Analysis of ETF Winners and Losers

Results of the multivariate analyses of ETF winners and losers are shown in Tables 5.7 and 5.8. Table 5.7 shows results for the entire sample. For winner ETFs, the *AFTERHOURS* dummy variable is positive and significant, indicating that the reversal following an after-hours winner is more favorable (less unfavorable) than the reversal following a day winner. That is, the subsequent correction of after-hours winners is less pronounced than that of day winners. This finding corroborates the earlier comparisons of reversals following extreme gains during the day versus after hours. In addition, the trigger variable is negative and significant.

The coefficient of −0.412 indicates that the reversal (loss) is 41 percent of the preceding extreme price movement on average, after controlling for other factors. The *INTLDUM* variable is negative and significant, which suggests that the reversal is more pronounced for international ETF winners. This finding corroborates the earlier comparisons of reversals among the three ETF types.

A similar multivariate model is used to assess the entire sample of losers. The *AFTERHOURS* dummy variable is negative and significant, which suggests that the reversal following an after-hours loser is less pronounced than the reversal following a day winner. This finding is consistent with the earlier comparisons of abnormal returns for losers during the day versus after hours. The *TRIGGER* variable is negative and significant with a coefficient of −0.248, suggesting that the reversal (gain) is approximately 25 percent of the preceding extreme price movement.

Multivariate Analysis of Extreme Price Movements

Table 5.7 shows the results from applying the multivariate model to all the observations where the extreme price movement happened during the day. The *TRIGGER* variable is negative and significant with a coefficient of −0.66, which indicates that 66 percent of the extreme price movement of an ETF during the day is reversed after hours. The same model is estimated for all observations where the extreme price movement happened after hours. While the number of observations is much higher ($N = 1721$ versus $N = 268$), the degree of reversal is lower. The *TRIGGER* coefficient is still negative and significant but the coefficient is −0.26, indicating a 26 percent reversal.

Cross-sectional Results by Type of ETF

Since the sensitivity of abnormal returns to factors may vary with the ETF type, additional cross-sectional analyses are conducted for each type, with results displayed in Table 5.8. For the sample of international ETF winners (panel (a)), the *AFTERHOURS* dummy variable is positive and significant, which implies that the reversal (loss) is less pronounced for after-hours winners than day winners. The trigger variable is negative and significant, but the other variables are not significant.

For the sample of international ETF losers, the *AFTERHOURS* dummy is negative and significant, which implies that the reversal (gain) following after-hours losers is less pronounced than for day losers. The *TRIGGER* variable is negative and significant, but the other variables are not significant.

For the sector ETF winners (panel (b)), the *AFTERHOURS* dummy variable is not significant. The *TRIGGER* variable is negative and significant, which implies larger reversals in response to larger triggers. The *VOLAT* variable is negative and significant, which implies a larger reversal following an extreme stock price movement when the ETF is more volatile. For sector ETF losers, *AFTERHOURS* is negative and significant, implying less reversal for after-hours losers than day losers.

For the broad-based ETF winners (panel (c)), the model is not significant and this

Table 5.7 Cross-sectional regression of abnormal returns following extreme price movements for full sample of ETFs

Sample	*Intercept*	*AFTER-HOURS*	*LOSDUM*	*TRIGGER*	*INTLDUM*	*SECTDUM*	*VOLAT*	*VOLUME*	*Adj.* R^2
Winners	0.001	0.013		−0.412	−0.013	−0.001	−0.137	0.000	0.2069
(*N* = 1035)	(0.13)	(3.49)****		(−5.83)****	(−5.96)****	(−0.41)	(−0.88)	(0.93)	
Losers	0.056	−0.042		−0.248	0.004	−0.002	−0.097	0.000	0.2193
(*N* = 954)	(6.15)****	(−7.98)****		(−2.20)**	(1.65)*	(−0.77)	(−0.74)	(−0.83)	
Day	0.012		0.012	−0.660	−0.019	0.007	−0.285	0.001	0.5963
(*N* = 268)	(0.53)		(0.76)	(−5.22)****	(−1.76)*	(0.61)	(−1.18)	(1.07)	
After hours	0.008		0.010	−0.260	−0.002	−0.002	−0.298	0.000	0.5355
(*N* = 1721)	(1.27)		(0.88)	(−3.10)**	(−1.62)	(−1.54)	(−3.75)****	(−0.76)	

Notes: The next-period AR is regressed on the explanatory variables according to the following model. *T*-statistics in parentheses using standard errors adjusted for heteroskedasticity with White's (1980) adjustment. The *AFTERHOURS* variable is replaced with *LOSDUM* variable for the day and after-hours subsamples.
See page 000 for the equation.
*, **, ****, and **** indicate significance at the 10%, 5%, 1%, and 0% levels, respectively using a 1-tailed test for significance.

Table 5.8 *Cross-sectional regressions of abnormal returns following extreme price movements*

Sample	*Intercept*	*AFTER-HOURS*	*LOSDUM*	*TRIGGER*	*VOLAT*	*VOLUME*	*Adj. R^2*
(a) International ETFs							
Winners	−0.015	0.022		−0.533	−0.242	0.000	0.3115
(*N* = 437)	(−1.28)	(4.48)****		(−5.81)****	(−1.26)	(1.09)	
Losers	0.008	−0.035		−0.667	−0.251	0.002	0.2785
(*N* = 361)	(0.41)	(−4.34)****		(−3.69)****	(−0.80)	(1.41)	
Day	−0.025		0.037	−0.546	−0.361	0.002	0.6062
(*N* = 137)	(−0.81)		(1.72)*	(−3.48)****	(−0.78)	(0.76)	
After hours	0.011		−0.029	−0.612	−0.195	0.000	0.6487
(*N* = 661)	(1.19)		(−1.88)*	(−5.21)****	(−0.94)	(1.98)	
(b) Sector ETFs							
Winners	0.020.	−0.006		−0.259	−0.433	0.000	0.0801
(*N* = 443)	(1.66)*	(−0.97)		(−2.90)**	(−2.17)**	(−0.57)	
Losers	0.070	−0.050		−0.097	−0.097	0.000	0.2808
(*N* = 446)	(6.05)****	(−7.63)****		(−1.35)	(−0.68)	(−0.10)	
Day	0.046		−0.045	−1.062	−0.288	0.002	0.5213
(*N* = 116)	(1.64)		(−1.25)	(−3.63)****	(−0.99)	(0.86)	
After hours	0.001		0.025	−0.116	−0.302	0.000	0.4862
(*N* = 773)	(0.10)		(2.76)**	(−1.77)*	(−2.99)**	(−1.02)	
(c) Broad-based ETFs							
Winners	0.005	−0.008		−0.091	−0.353	0.000	−0.0015
(*N* = 155)	(0.35)	(−0.86)		(−0.77)	(−1.10)	(0.61)	
Losers	0.069	−0.066)		−0.734	−0.438	−0.001	0.4447
(*N* = 147)	(2.65)**	(−3.22)**		(−6.34)****	(−0.86)	(−4.13)****	
Day	−0.059		0.019	−0.076	1.479	0.002	0.5476
(*N* = 15)	(−1.68)		(0.31)	(−0.19)	(1.17)	(1.01)	
After hours	0.019		0.005	−0.222	−0.842	0.000	0.6002
(*N* = 287)	(2.85)***		(0.47)	(−2.22)**	(−3.79)****	(−1.57)	

Notes: As for Table 5.7

is the only subsample for which this is true. For the broad-based losers, *TRIGGER* is negative and significant, consistent with the results found for other subsamples of loser ETFs. In addition, *AFTERHOURS* is negative and significant, which is consistent with the results found for other loser ETFs.

While the sensitivity of abnormal returns to cross-sectional characteristics varies by ETF type, we offer two generalizations. First, the reversal is usually conditioned on the size of the trigger, which implies greater overreaction for specific ETFs with more extreme stock price movements. Second, the reversal is more pronounced in response to the extreme price movements that occur during the day than those that occur after hours.

CONCLUSIONS

Exchange-traded funds (ETFs) differ from individual stocks because they represent composites of stocks. They differ from stock indexes in that they can be traded continuously in an open market and can even be sold short. The accessibility and ease of trading ETFs allow uninformed investors to take positions in stock composites, which could allow for more rapid and volatile price movements of those composites. Our analysis is based on extreme changes in the share price of ETFs that occur within either normal trading hours or after hours (more than 5 percent in either direction). Based on an assessment of 1989 extreme stock price movements of ETFs, we find substantial reversals on average, which implies a correction to investor overreaction.

Based on the multivariate analyses, the reversals are consistently more pronounced for ETFs that experience more extreme stock price movement. Second, the reversal is generally more pronounced for international ETFs. Third, there is a less pronounced reversal of extreme price movements that occurred after hours. Our findings support the proposition that informed traders in both the normal day and after-hours periods benefit at the expense of uninformed traders and systematically correct for their overreactions, particularly those that occurred during the day sessions.

ACKNOWLEDGEMENTS

Jeff Madura acknowledges research support from the Lynn Chair International Business Grant at Florida Atlantic University. Nivine Richie acknowledges research support from a grant provided by the Sigmund Weis School of Business at Susquehanna University. A version of this chapter appeared in *The Journal of Behavioral Finance*, **5** (2), 91–104 (2004).

NOTES

1. Our definition of night includes any trading after the close of the normal trading day and before the open of the next day's normal trading hours. Therefore our definition of night includes the early morning trading session.

2. See 'The market's closed – wake up', *Business Week*, 3 March 2002, p. 132.
3. 'The market's closed – wake up', pp. 132–3, quotes Brooks McFeely, the president of Midnight Trader, an online service that collects market information: 'the day-trading cowboys of the Internet era are no longer in the market. The dumb money is gone, and the more sophisticated investors are in charge.'
4. A nonparametric bootstrapped version of the time-series standard deviation test was performed with no change to the level of significance and, therefore, results are not reported.

REFERENCES

Atkins, A. and E. Dyl (1990), 'Price reversals, bid–ask spreads, and market efficiency', *Journal of Financial and Quantitative Analysis*, **25**, 535–47.

Barberis, N.C., A. Shleifer and R.Vishny (1998), 'A model of investor sentiment', *Journal of Financial Economics*, **49**, 307–43.

Barclay, M. and T. Hendershott (2004), 'Liquidity externalities and adverse selection: evidence from trading after hours', *Journal of Finance*, **58**, 681–710.

Baytas, A. and N. Cakici (1999), 'Do markets overreact? International evidence', *Journal of Banking and Finance*, 1121–44.

Bremer, M. and R. Sweeney (1991), 'The reversal of large stock price decreases', *Journal of Finance*, **46**, 747–54.

Bremer, M., T.R. Hiraki and R.J. Sweeney (1997), 'Predictable patterns after large stock price changes in the Tokyo Stock Exchange', *Journal of Financial and Quantitative Analysis*, **32**, 345–65.

Brown, S.J. and J.B. Warner (1980), 'Measuring security price performance', *Journal of Financial Economics*, **8** (3), 205–58.

Chan, W.S. (2003), 'Stock price reaction to news and no-news: drift and reversal after headlines', *Journal of Financial Economics*, **70**, 223–60.

Cox, D.R. and D.R. Peterson (1994), 'Stock returns following large one-day declines: evidence on short-term reversals and longer-term performance', *Journal of Finance*, **40**, 255–67.

Cutler, D.M., J.M. Poterba and L.H. Summers (1990), 'Speculative dynamics and the role of feedback traders', *American Economic Review*, **80**, 63–8.

Da Costa, N.C.A. (1994), 'Overreaction in the Brazilian stock market', *Journal of Banking and Finance*, **18**, 633–42.

Daniel, K., D. Hirshleifer and A. Subrahmanyam (1998), 'Investor psychology and security market under- and overreactions', *Journal of Finance*, **53**, 1839–85.

DeBondt, W.F.M. and R.H. Thaler (1985), 'Does the stock market overreact?', *Journal of Finance*, **40**, 793–805.

DeLong, J.B., A. Shleifer, L. Summers and R.J. Waldmann (1990), 'Noise trader risk in financial markets', *Journal of Political Economy*, **98**, 703–38.

Foster, F.D. and S. Viswanathan (1993), 'Variations in trading volume, return volatility, and trading costs: evidence on recent price formation models', *Journal of Finance*, **48**, 187–211.

Griffin, D. and A. Tversky (1992), 'The weighing of evidence and the determinants of confidence', *Cognitive Psychology*, **24**, 411–35.

Jegadeesh, N. (1990), 'Evidence of predictable behavior of security returns', *Journal of Finance*, **45**, 881–98.

Kyle, A. (1985), 'Continuous auctions and insider trading', *Econometrica*, **53**, 1315–35.

Poterba, J.M. and L.H. Summers (1988), 'Mean reversion in stock prices: evidence and implications', *Journal of Financial Economics*, **22**, 27–59.

Richards, A.J. (1997), 'Winner–loser reversals in national stock market indices: can they be explained?', *Journal of Finance*, **52**, 2129–44.

Roll, R. (1984), 'A simple implicit measure of the effective bid–ask spread in an efficient market', *Journal of Finance*, **39**, 1127–39.

Stoll, H. and R. Whaley (1990), 'Stock market structure and volatility', *Review of Financial Studies*, **3**, 37–71.

Tversky, A. and D. Kahneman (1974), 'Judgment under uncertainty: heuristics and biases', *Science*, **185**, 1124–31.

White, H. (1980), 'A heteroskedasticity-consistent covariance matrix estimator and a direct test for heteroskedasticity', *Econometrica*, **48**, 817–38.

6 Intentional herding in stock markets: an alternative approach in an international context

Natividad Blasco, Pilar Corredor and Sandra Ferreruela

INTRODUCTION

One of the issues of greatest concern in the world of finance is trying to understand how investors make decisions. The classic theoretical explanations are based on conditions of investor rationality and the perfection of markets, and the use of information available in the market as a decisive tool. In recent years the branch of behavioural finance has emerged strongly in the field to try to expand this vision of investor behaviour. Factors associated with the psychological and sociological behaviour of individuals have been introduced as significant elements that go some way to explain investor decisions. Thaler (1991) and Shefrin (2000), among others, have incorporated an emotional component into the classic models considering both visions as compatible and complementary. A survey of the history and contributions in this field of finance in recent years can be found in Sewell (2007).

Within this context arises the concept of herding, which provides an additional explanation of investor behaviour. Bikhchandani and Sharma (2000) define herding as a decision of agents to intentionally copy the behaviour of other investors. However, there are a number of points of terminology than can lead to misunderstandings. So-called spurious herding or unintentional herding, as defined by Bikhchandani and Sharma (2000), refers to similar actions being observed among investors who respond in a similar manner to a similar information set, which is to say that it is the response of agents to movements of fundamental variables. This does not mean that investors are imitating each other, but are simply reacting in a similar manner as a result of independent individual decisions. This type of herding is not of real concern as part of investor behaviour, so we shall concentrate on non-spurious herding. Here we can distinguish between rational herding and irrational herding. Devenow and Welch (1996) argue that irrational herding is based on the phenomenon of investors ignoring their own beliefs and blindly following others. On the other hand, Avery and Zemsky (1998) state that rational herding is the phenomenon of investors imitating each other, taking maximum advantage because they believe others to be better informed than themselves, or because there is a degree of uncertainty about the information at their disposal. Herding in the market probably includes a combination of these various factors and therefore their inclusion in rational models could lead to a better understanding of the behaviour of capital markets. Avery and Zemsky (1998) provide a detailed explanation of the theoretical relationship between herding and market information efficiency.

The theory of herding, both rational and irrational, contributes various explanations for the phenomenon. Bikhchandani et al. (1992) suggest that investors infer information when observing the transactions of others, and this leads to the creation of information cascades. The agency relationship between principal and agent in which managers imitate the actions of others, ignoring their own information in order to preserve their reputation, is one of the most widespread explanations. Scharfstein and Stein (1990), Roll (1992), Brennan (1993), Rajan (1994), Trueman (1994) and Maug and Naik (1996) are some of the authors who have made such a case. Gompers and Metrick (2001) suggest that herding can arise when investors are attracted by assets with similar characteristics. From a less theoretical point of view, other explanations include the degree of institutional participation (Lakonishok et al., 1992, Grinblatt et al., 1995, Wermers, 1999, Nofsinger and Sias, 1999 and Sias, 2004), the quality of published information, the spread of opinions, the market sector or the volume of trading, among others (Patterson and Sharma, 2006; Demirer and Kutan, 2006; and Henker et al., 2006). Hirshleifer and Teoh (2003) provide an exhaustive survey of the various explanations offered in the literature.

Although from a theoretical standpoint the arguments in favour of herding are clear, empirical results are not so conclusive (Bikhchandani and Sharma, 2000). The main reason for this is a lack of consistency owing to the great difficulty of measuring the herding effect.

Various proposals for such measurement have been offered in the literature. Lakonishok et al. (1992) contributed a method for measuring herding among institutional investors, considering that these represent a noticeable part of the market. Other proposals for measuring have considered all market participants together. Christie and Huang (1995) and Chang et al. (2000) consider herding as a leader–follower relationship which they describe statistically by means of calculating the deviations between the returns of stocks and the returns of the market. Both measurements assume that herding occurs, and that it will be especially intense at moments of high stress in the market. These are the most commonly used measurements in the literature. More recently Hwang and Salmon (2004) proposed an improvement in these measurements by also using cross-sectional deviations, comparing the sensitivity of stocks in the CAPM (capital asset pricing model). Patterson and Sharma (2006) present a study of herding following the information cascade proposal of Bikhchandani et al. (1992), obtaining a herding statistic based on checking the length of trade sequences for each stock listed in the market. However, as stated earlier, the results of the majority of studies using these measurements have not found many indicators supporting the existence of herding. This suggests that the assumptions on which the measurements are based are too stringent, so that herding in the market is not detected.

Given these circumstances, the objective of this work is to analyse the presence of herding in different international markets over a time scale that includes periods of crisis and of calm in the markets. The herding measure is calculated initially following the methodology proposed by Blasco and Ferreruela (2008). This proposal is based on the idea of trying to recreate a 'herding-free' market and using the information provided by cross-sectional deviations of stocks compared to their corresponding market index, thus observing whether the cross-sectional deviations of the markets analysed deviate significantly from those of the 'herding-free' market. This idea is not new given that the underlying basis in all the previously described measurement models is a comparison between the real market and a reference situation. The main difficulty is to establish this reference situation in which there is no intentional herding.

The contribution of this work to the literature is that it represents an advance in the study of imitative behaviour using a more innovative herding measurement that tries to overcome some of the assumptions involved in more traditional measurements. This method attempts to verify whether there is collective behaviour in the market not only at moments of stress but also during calmer periods. We analyse several international markets in order to provide a more globalized vision of the phenomenon under study. In each of these markets we use 'familiar stocks' – those stocks that are better known in the market and therefore subject to greater capitalization or trading volume. Ganzach (2000) has shown that familiarity also affects preferences in the analysis of financial data. Furthermore, some studies have revealed that herding occurs to a greater extent with this type of stock and to a much smaller degree in stocks subject to fewer market transactions (Blasco and Ferreruela, 2007; Blasco et al., 2009). If herding is observed with these stocks, this would be an argument favouring rational and intentional herding. Information about such stocks is easily available to investors so that if imitation is observed, this cannot be due to lack of information but is rather an intentional decision by investors to follow others. Finally, another positive contribution of the work is that it uses a sufficiently wide database to be able to include both relevant crisis periods and periods of calm in the markets. This in turn aids understanding of the phenomenon and its possible variation in changing market conditions.

The work is organized as follows. The next section describes the database and then a section explains the methodology. The section after that is devoted to a discussion of the results obtained, and the conclusions to be drawn from the study are set out in the final section.

DATABASE

Our empirical study is based on the possible presence of herding in several international markets. The database comprises daily prices during the period from 1 June 1999 to 1 June 2009. The analysis has been carried out with two data subsets with different uses.

On the one hand, we have the daily prices for the most important companies in the countries under study, and which are therefore considered as familiar stocks in these countries. For each country, ten companies have been selected among those considered to be the most prominent or familiar.[1] Using familiar stocks in the analysis is important given that, as previously explained, those dealing in familiar stocks have direct access to relevant information so that any imitative behaviour that is detected can be attributed to intentional herding. The Appendix lists the companies included in the analysis. The markets in which the possible presence of herding is investigated are: Germany, the UK, France, Spain, Mexico, the USA and China. The choice of these markets was made with the intention of analysing a representative sample at an international level, with different individual procedures and dynamics in functioning and in information.

On the other hand, 28 international indexes have been used. These indexes are used in the calculation of an artificially recreated market which we consider to be 'herding-free'. The 28 international indexes for which we have daily prices are the following: CAC40 (France), SMI (Switzerland), AEX AMSTERDAM (Holland), MERVAL (Argentina), JSE (South Africa), DOW JONES (the USA), SET BANGKOK (Thailand), IBEX35

(Spain), ST SINGAPORE (Singapore), IGBVL LIMA (Peru), RTS MOSCOW (Russia), MIB30 (Italy), IPC MEXICO (Mexico), KUALA LUMPUR (Malaysia), NIKKEI (Japan), TEL-AVIV 100 (Israel), JAKARTA (Indonesia), HELSINKI ALL (Finland), DAX (Germany), CMA EL CAIRO (Egypt), KOSPI SEUL (South Korea), FTSE100 (the UK), HANG SENG (China), IGPA (Chile), IBOVESPA (Brazil), KFX COPENHAGEN (Denmark), SYDNEY (Australia) and ATHENS GRAL (Greece). It can be appreciated that this set represents a wide range of markets whose diversity is essential for the purposes of this study.

METHODOLOGY

Traditional Methodology

As already explained, various methods have evolved over time for measuring herding. However, the underlying idea in most cases is that in the presence of herding, investors forget their own beliefs and follow the market consensus.

Christie and Huang (1995) (hereafter referred to as CH(95)) suggest that, empirically, this means observing how the return on stocks deviates from the market return, the latter being considered as the market consensus. As these differences remain small, the presence of herding can be inferred because the movement of the stocks reflects that of the market overall. These authors suggest that such evidence should be especially marked during periods of substantial price changes. The measurements of Chang et al. (2000) and Hwang and Salmon (2004) also share this idea.

The methodology proposed by CH(95) consists of calculating the standard deviation in stock returns with respect to the market, in cross-section (CSSD) for each period t, and observing their behaviour at periods of extreme market movements. The CSSD are calculated as follows:

$$CSSD_t = \sqrt{\frac{\sum_{i=1}^{n}(R_{i,t} - R_{m,t})^2}{n-1}} \tag{6.1}$$

where $R_{i,t}$ is the observed stock return on company i at the time t, $R_{m,t}$ is the aggregate return of the market portfolio at the time t and thus represents the market consensus, and n is the number of stocks being observed. The test of the existence of herding is carried out using the following regression model:

$$CSSD_t = \alpha + \beta_D D_t^L + \beta_U D_t^U + \varepsilon_t \tag{6.2}$$

where $D_t^L = 1$ if the market return on day t is in the lower tail of the distribution and equal to 0 otherwise, and $D_t^U = 1$ if the market return on day t is in the upper tail of the distribution and equal to 0 otherwise. The dummy variables enable the presence of herding behaviour to be identified among market participants. Although in this work herding will not be measured directly with the CH(95) measurement, the CSSD calculation is used as described in (6.1).

Alternative Methodology

Theoretical justification

Although it seems obvious that herding behaviour would be most likely to occur at times of significant price changes, as CH(95) claim, this does not mean that such behaviour cannot appear at any other time. Investors can adopt strategies that mimic the general movement of the market independently of market volatility or the arrival of information. It therefore appears essential to fill this gap in the literature by trying to use less stringent measures that enable herding behaviour to be detected at other times, and thus less intense herding levels to be identified.

Following Blasco and Ferreruela (2008), the fundamental basis of the proposal is to compare the market under study with an 'ideal' market in which managers respect their own private information and do not intentionally mimic the actions of others. Moreover, the possible existence of imperfections other than herding behaviour would have to be respected as well as the different circumstances experienced by stock markets at each moment. The key to this proposal is to find this 'ideal' market or at least an approximation at each moment. As the market under study deviates from this intentional herding-clean market, we can speak of the existence of herding behaviour.

Our approach starts from the premise that the detection of a herding effect in a particular market can be done only in relative terms. Incentives to mimic and the intensity of imitative behaviour might not be the same at moments of worldwide economic crisis (e.g. the crash of September 2008 and the subsequent months) in which there is a contagious effect among stock exchanges and inexplicable overreactions occur that are not necessarily attributable to intentional herding, and periods of greater international financial calm where each market is more inclined to process its own information. In other words, we need to know how a herding-free market behaves at moments of crisis and at moments of calm in order to be able to observe the differences that in such circumstances can be attributable to rational herding.

At the same time, other stock market characteristics that are usually identified with deviations from the normal distribution of returns and that are not directly related to intentional imitation should not obscure the results of investigations into herding. For example, there are references in the literature to the fact that the existence of fat tails in market return probability distributions could be related to mimicking behaviour by agents (Eguiluz and Zimmermann, 2000). However, the herding effect is not the only cause of the thickness of the tails, and therefore a herding-free market could have fatter than normal tails in its distribution of returns. For this reason the comparison in relative terms with a herding-free market, although such a market might exhibit other 'imperfections', remains an attractive approach.

With this aim it is proposed to make use of the information extracted from the cross-sectional standard deviation of returns (CSSD), given that we believe this adequately represents the spirit of imitative behaviour. The distribution of the CSSD statistics should be calculated for each one of the markets under study and for the artificially recreated market. This market should reasonably be identified as 'herding-clean' in order to establish the possible differences.

The key issue for this methodology lies in the search for ideal characteristics in the recreated market. To achieve this, it is important to work with real data and not with artificially generated (usually by computational simulation) data. In other words, we consider it of interest to use data from real market transactions. This enables us to rely on characteristics inherent in markets both in terms of the transactions themselves and of the imperfections and anomalies present in real transactions. Moreover, real data will include a component of herding difficult to extract, such as spurious herding. As the markets under study deviate from the recreated market, we can attribute the possible herding observed to an intentional decision of investors to mimic others.

However, it is important to note at this point that although the intention is for the fictitious market to be identified with the characteristics of a market free of intentional herding, in no way is it the intention to deliberately incorporate characteristics that can be related to optimum levels of information processing, or corrective elements of risk levels, or indicators of efficiency in the taking of decisions. That is, what is being constructed is not a 'theoretically perfect and efficient' market, but a market with reasonable limits that enables us to distinguish exclusively the existence of rationally intentional herding behaviour.

Methodological stages

The description of the methodological stages leading up to the comparison of the CSSD distribution for the herding-free market and that of the other international markets follows that set out in Blasco and Ferreruela (2008).

Stage 1 A stock index is compiled that we call NMI_t. This fictitious index is made up of the average weighted return of 28 real international indexes. The data from these indexes are used to calculate the daily return corresponding to the notional market index (NMI_t), constructed as the daily average return of the 28 international indexes listed in the database section. International indexes have been used because the correlations between international markets are generally lower than between domestic markets. This implies, by construction, that the herding levels in this recreated market will be lower, although there may be parallels between markets for different reasons.

The idea, therefore, is to identify each of the indexes of the 28 countries with one individual stock with its own particular characteristics, which could be the level of information, the quality, the importance of institutional or individual investors, the volume of trading or the level of risk among others. By considering in this way a broad spectrum of countries, we can ensure diversity among the stocks employed and consequently the diversity of factors and characteristics that can appear in the global market. Thus the NMI_t includes *a priori* many different forms of individual behaviour that respond to very different circumstances and characteristics, a necessary condition for our purpose. Bikhchandani and Sharma (2000) support this argument in affirming that imitative behaviour will be greater in proportion to the homogeneity of the group.

Stage 2 Once the market index is calculated, the next step is to select the financial assets that will be analysed individually. Here we choose the international indexes least correlated among each other and that are identified as having non-imitative individual behaviour. In other words, these indexes are considered to be representative of herding-free behaviour within the world market artificially created and represented by NMI_t. Specifically, the correlation is evaluated between each international index with each of the other 27 indexes by means of a correlation matrix, and for each index we then select the ten indexes least correlated with it. In a second selection, we choose the ten indexes least correlated with the others that we call LCI_j, with j = AEX AMSTERDAM, MERVAL, IBEX35, RTS MOSCOW, TEL-AVIV 100, HANG-SENG, IBOVESPA, IGBVL LIMA, KUALA LUMPUR and JAKARTA. These ten indexes are considered as individual assets that, having a weak correlation with the others, would be expected to produce returns independently and therefore able to simulate what can be understood as intentional herding-free assets.

Stage 3 Now that we have the recreated market index and the assets to be traded in this fictitious market, we need a deviation measure of these LCI_j assets in relation to the weighted NMI_t for each day t of the time period considered. The calculation is made according to equation (6.1), following the structure of CH(95). In this equation the return R_{it} corresponds to the daily return of the LCI_j on day t, that is to say what we have called LCI_{jt}. The market return, R_{mt} in equation (6.1), corresponds to the return of the weighted NMI_t on day t. We call the time series obtained from the cross-sectional deviations calculated in the fictitious market $CSSD_{NH}$, considering that these correspond to a herding-free market due to its construction.

Stage 4 The three preceding stages are necessary for calculating the data relating to the CSSD probability distribution of the market that we shall use as a reference in the comparison. We now need data relating to each of the markets being analysed: Germany, the UK, France, Spain, Mexico, the USA and China. In this case, the CSSD time series and their corresponding probability distributions are calculated for each of these markets, using the assets chosen as being familiar in each country and the reference index of each of the markets.

Stage 5 Finally, having calculated both the CSSD distribution of the herding-free market and the CSSD distribution of each of the seven countries under analysis, the next step consists of comparing the distributions. The idea is that if in each market analysed herding does not exist, the CSSD distribution of the said market will not differ empirically from the $CSSD_{NH}$ distribution in the recreated market, especially in the probability of finding low CSSD values. A concentration of probability around small deviation values would show a greater tendency of market stocks towards moving together and therefore towards herding behaviour. In other words, displacement towards the left of the probability distribution of the CSSD statistic for a specific market compared to the herding-free market should be interpreted as evidence in favour of rational mimetic behaviour.

The next question is how to carry out this comparison. Given the difficulty of knowing the type of distribution of the CSSD, it has been considered appropriate to use a bootstrap analysis for the comparison. The bootstrap-based procedure applied in this chapter is very simple, although computer-intensive, and follows Chou (2004). According to the nature of significance tests, in order to calculate the significance of the differences in probability under the null hypothesis of absence of intentional herding effect, we must resample with replacement from $CSSD_{NH}$ the same number of observations as in our raw data set for each market under study. We construct 5000 bootstrapped data sets to guarantee the accuracy of the analysis. The null hypothesis of absence of intentional herding effect is identified with the absence of significant differences between the CSSD distribution in the herding-clean market and the CSSD distributions in each of the markets analysed for low values of the CSSD statistic.

If we denote $FCSSD_{NH}^{booti}$ with $i = 1, \ldots, 5000$, the bootstrapped data set i from $CSSD_{NH}$, the differences in the probability of landing in the same interval between every bootstrapped distribution and the $CSSD_{NH}$ distribution ($FCSSD_{NH}$) corresponding to the null hypothesis and between the raw distribution and $FCSSD_{NH}$ are computed for 156 intervals in which we divide the whole range of CSSD values. For each interval $j = 1 \ldots 156$, with lower and upper limits l_j and l_{j+1}, respectively, the differences in the probability can be expressed as follows:

$$\Pr(l_j \leq x < l_{j+1} | FCSSD_{NH}^{booti}) - \Pr(l_j \leq x < l_{j+1} | FCSSD_{NH}) = Dj_{NH}^{booti}$$

$$\Pr(l_j \leq x < l_{j+1} | FCSSD^{raw}) - \Pr(l_j \leq x < l_{j+1} | FCSSD_{NH}) = Dj^{raw} \quad (6.3)$$

for $i = 1, \ldots 5000$, and $l_1 = 0.0025$, $l_{156} = 0.08$, with $FCSSD^{raw}$ being the raw distribution of the CSSD for each market under study. The computed differences Dj_{NH}^{booti} with $i = 1, \ldots, 5000$ are used to generate the bootstrap p-values for interval j as

$$p_j^{boot} = \Pr(Dj_{NH}^{boot} \geq Dj^{raw}) \text{ when } Dj^{raw} > 0 \quad (6.4)$$

or

$$p_j^{boot} = \Pr(Dj_{NH}^{boot} \leq Dj^{raw}) \text{ when } Dj^{raw} < 0$$

However, in our case it is only the significance of the positive probability for low CSSD values that are of interest. We identify the presence of a herding effect with a higher significant probability of finding low deviation values, suggesting a coordinated movement of all the representative market stocks. This coordinated movement suggests the joint evolution of the stocks independently of the specific information issued in the market about each one of them or characteristics associated with their activity sector. In other words, we identify the presence of a herding effect with a significant displacement towards the left in the probability distributions of the CSSD statistics. This significance is given by:

$$p_j^{boot} = \Pr(Dj_{NH}^{boot} \geq Dj^{raw}) \text{ when } Dj^{raw} > 0 \text{ and } j \text{ takes low values}$$

The above equations calculate the p-value for finding the same or higher bootstrapped differences in probability without implying the true presence of a herding effect compared to the difference between any raw CSSD distribution and the distribution corresponding to the null hypothesis.

It is not possible to establish precise conclusions if the distribution of the CSSD statistics of each of the markets indicates a displacement towards the right in relation to the corresponding distribution of the herding-free market and/or if the probability differences are significant for high deviation values, given that the fictitious market is not constructed based on a hypothesis establishing limiting characteristics for large CSSD values.

EMPIRICAL RESULTS

Figure 6.1 (a)–(h) shows the CSSD data of the herding-free market and the seven markets analysed in relation to return levels. In all cases it can be seen that for extreme returns, both positive and negative, there is an increase in the values of the cross-sectional deviations.[2] This would appear to indicate that there is no evidence of herding according to the approach of CH(95). Moreover, such an interpretation would be consistent with the results of Chang et al. (2000) in the USA and Hong Kong markets, and Demirer and Kutan (2006) in Chinese markets, among others. However, it can be observed that even for the artificially recreated market, the graph is very similar. If it is true that, in agreement with the approach of these authors, the reduction in deviations at moments of high volatility is indicative of herding behaviour, it is nevertheless difficult to find such a particular situation in the market. However, professionals recognize that mimetic behaviour occurs more frequently than these very particular situations.

Given this discrepancy between the professional beliefs and the empirical findings, it seems appropriate to propose less restrictive herding measures in order to detect such imitative behaviour. Following this idea and applying our methodological tool, the results relating to the comparison between the herding-free market and the seven markets analysed are shown in Table 6.1.

Given that the interest lies in the low CSSD statistical values, the table is structured showing information about the probabilities, the differences in probability with respect to the herding-free market and significance *p*-values of the differences for the lowest 10 per cent of CSSD values. Because the intervals are defined from values lower than 0.0025 to values beyond 0.08, we have set an upper limit to the information shown in the table (0.1*0.08 = 0.008) to make the table easier to read. We show the significant probabilities up to 10 per cent for the positive probability differences. As can be seen, the Spanish market is the one that most clearly provides results favourable to the herding effect. Nine of the 12 intervals analysed show significant differences. The other three intervals continue to show higher probabilities of finding low values for cross-sectional deviations, even though they are not statistically significant in terms of usual significance levels. Spain is the only country analysed with positive probability differences over the whole range studied. It should be noted that in 10 per cent of the lower values of the statistics there is a concentration of a 23.09 per cent probability, marking a clear difference with the other distributions.

Although to a lesser degree, results favourable to herding are also revealed in the US market, indicating that in certain circumstances participating agents in the market intensify their tendency towards imitative behaviour. In this case the accumulated probability up to a CSSD value of 0.008 decreases to 18 per cent. Although we also find some significantly positive differences in probability for the French, UK and Mexican markets, both the cumulative probability and the sequence of positive and negative differences of probability discourage the interpretation of such results as evidence of intentional herding.

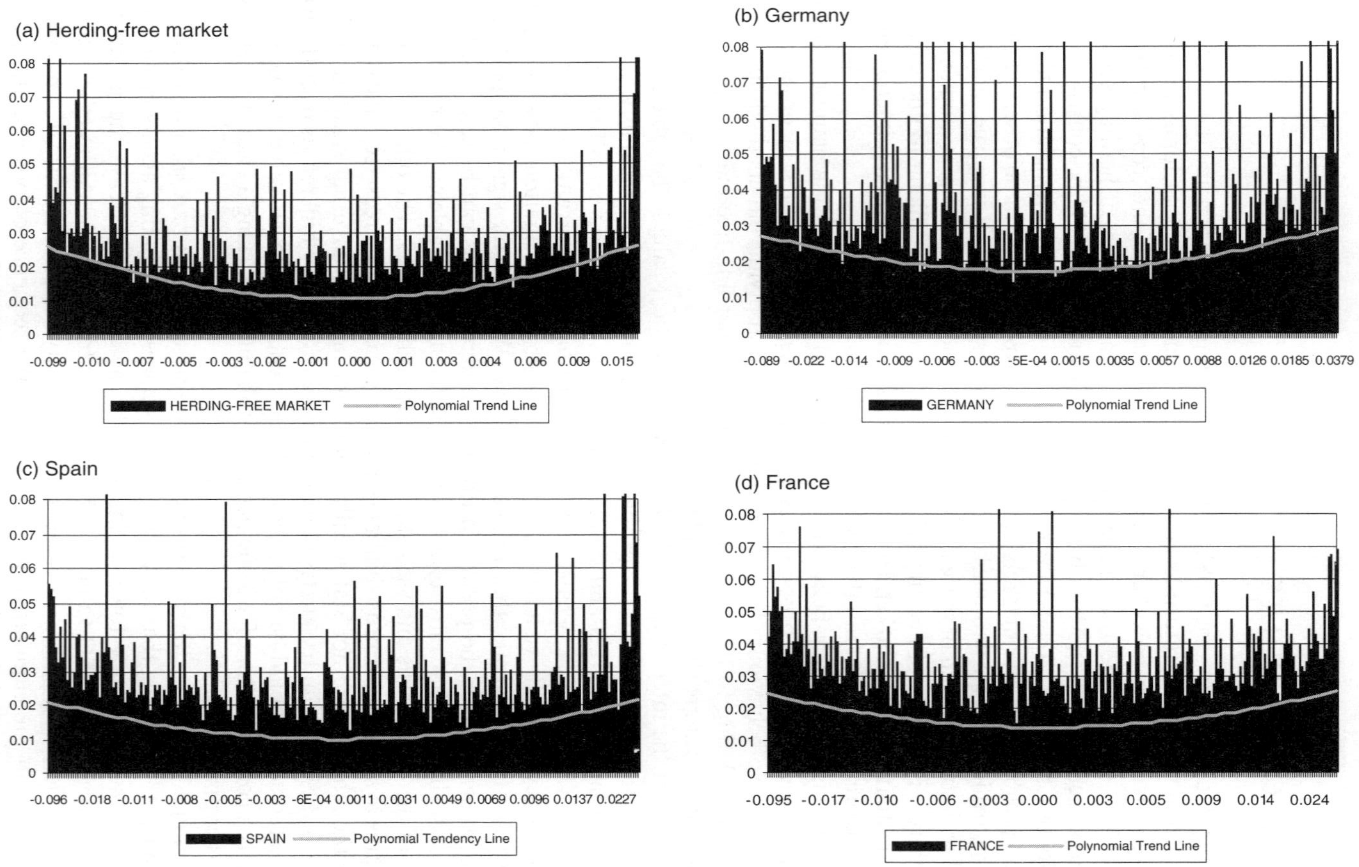
(a) Herding-free market
0.08
0.07
0.06
0.05
0.04
0.03
0.02
0.01
0
-0.099 -0.010 -0.007 -0.005 -0.003 -0.002 -0.001 0.000 0.001 0.003 0.004 0.006 0.009 0.015
HERDING-FREE MARKET
Polynomial Trend Line
(b) Germany
-0.089 -0.022 -0.014 -0.009 -0.006 -0.003 -5E-04 0.0015 0.0035 0.0057 0.0088 0.0126 0.0185 0.0379
GERMANY
Polynomial Trend Line
(c) Spain
-0.096 -0.018 -0.011 -0.008 -0.005 -0.003 -6E-04 0.0011 0.0031 0.0049 0.0069 0.0096 0.0137 0.0227
SPAIN
Polynomial Tendency Line
(d) France
-0.095 -0.017 -0.010 -0.006 -0.003 0.000 0.003 0.005 0.009 0.014 0.024
FRANCE
Polynomial Trend Line

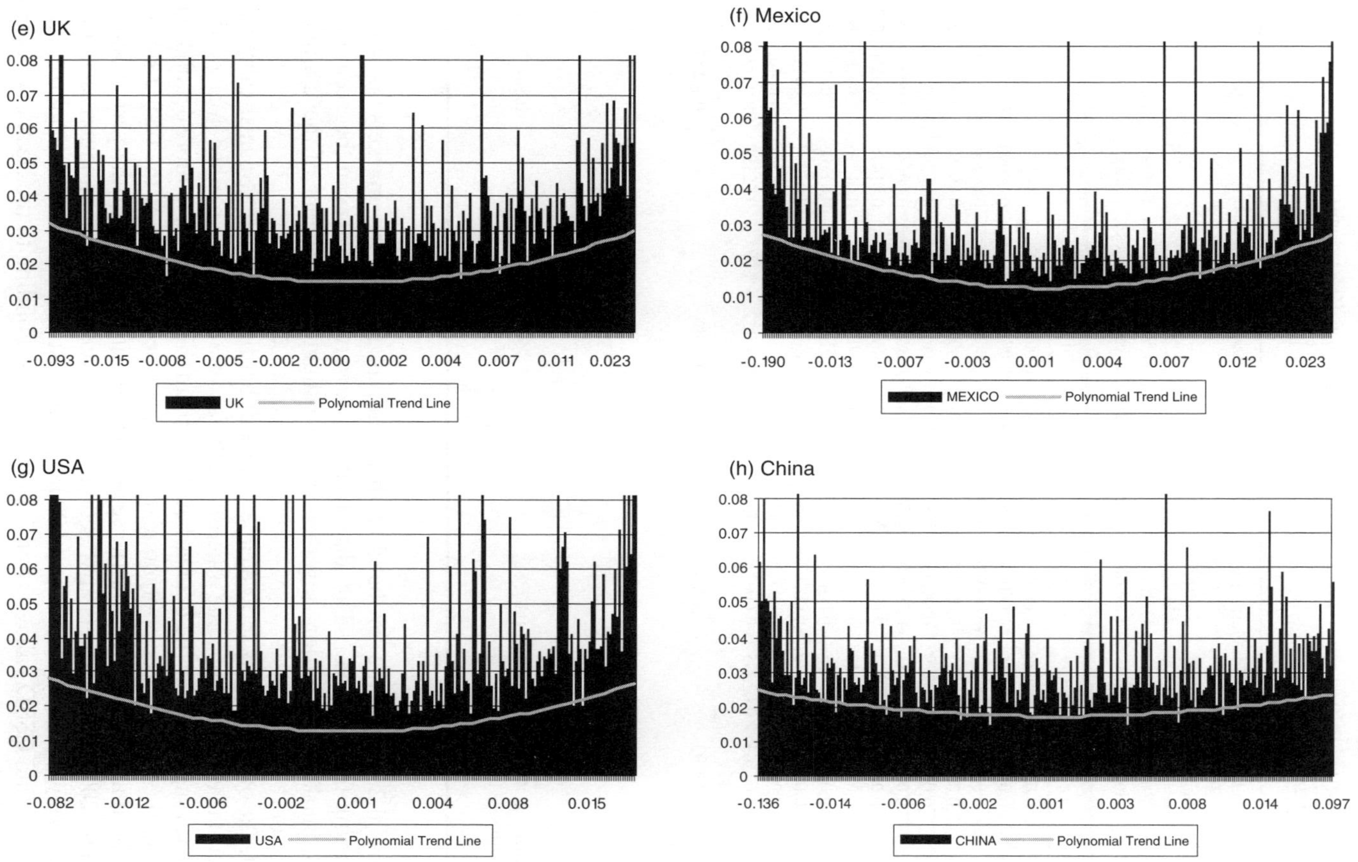

Figure 6.1 *CSSD values over the whole return range and second-order polynomial fit*

Table 6.1 Comparison between the herding-free market and the seven markets analysed. Probabilities, differences in probability with respect to the herding-free market and significance p-*values of the differences for 10 per cent of the lowest CSSD values*

Stock market	Herding-free market	Germany			Spain			France		
Interval limit	Probability	Probability	Difference of probability	*p*-values	Probability	Difference of probability	*p*-values	Probability	Difference of probability	*p*-values
0.0025	0.00111	0.00038	−0.00073	NS	0.00197	0.00086	NS	0.00197	0.00079	NS
0.003	0.00037	0.00076	0.00039	NS	0.00345	0.00308	0.005	0.00098	0.00058	NS
0.0035	0.00297	0.00227	−0.00070	NS	0.00369	0.00073	NS	0.00131	−0.00170	NS
0.004	0.00111	0.00303	0.00192	NS	0.00813	0.00702	0	0.00361	0.00238	NS
0.0045	0.00260	0.00379	0.00119	NS	0.01059	0.00800	0.015	0.00361	0.00090	NS
0.005	0.00742	0.00681	−0.00060	NS	0.01528	0.00787	0.035	0.00787	0.00021	NS
0.0055	0.00890	0.01022	0.00132	NS	0.01774	0.00885	0.040	0.01476	0.00540	0.065
0.006	0.01706	0.01817	0.00111	NS	0.02514	0.00809	NS	0.01575	−0.00181	NS
0.0065	0.01520	0.01665	0.00145	NS	0.02908	0.01388	0	0.01706	0.00132	NS
0.007	0.02076	0.01779	−0.00297	NS	0.03327	0.01251	0.035	0.02297	0.00147	NS
0.0075	0.02781	0.02271	−0.00510	NS	0.04042	0.01262	0.060	0.02395	−0.00462	NS
0.008	0.03263	0.02385	−0.00878	NS	0.04214	0.00952	0.095	0.02198	−0.01135	NS
Accumulated probability up to a CSSD value of 0.008	0.13793		0.12642			0.2309			0.13583	
Accumulated probability thereafter	0.86207		0.87358			0.7690			0.86417	

Figure 6.2 shows the probability distributions for all the markets as well as the herding-free market.[3] The displacement towards the left can be seen in the Spanish market distribution, together with the slight displacement of the US market distribution.

While the overall results show clear evidence of herding only in the Spanish market, we consider it feasible to find some other partially favourable results in other stock markets, as has been suggested for the US market. To explain this argument in more detail, Figure 6.3 shows the second-order polynomial fit of the time evolution of the CSSD statistics for the herding-free market and the seven markets under study in the period January 2002–June 2009. The markets analysed had their moments of minimum cross-sectional deviation between the years 2004 and 2006, and almost all the countries seem to exhibit a tendency to find CSSD values lower than those corresponding to the clean market from the end of 2003.

This fact leads us to make a partial analysis of the period 2003–07. These results are

Table 6.1 Comparison between the herding-free market and the seven markets analysed. Probabilities, differences in probability with respect to the herding-free market and significance p-*values of the differences for 10 per cent of the lowest CSSD values* (cont.)

UK			Mexico			USA			China		
Probability	Difference of probability	*p*-values	Probability	Difference of probability	*p*-values	Probability	Difference of probability	*p*-values	Probability	Difference of probability	*p*-values
0.00128	0.00017	NS	0.00000	−0.00111	NS	0.00033	−0.00079	NS	0.00000	−0.00111	NS
0.00096	0.00059	NS	0.00000	−0.00037	NS	0.00098	0.00061	NS	0.00000	−0.00037	NS
0.00128	−0.00168	NS	0.00096	−0.00201	NS	0.00229	−0.00067	NS	0.00000	−0.00297	NS
0.00192	0.00081	0.08	0.00287	0.00175	0.08	0.00556	0.00445	0.005	0.00062	−0.00049	NS
0.00224	−0.00035	NS	0.00191	−0.00068	NS	0.00917	0.00657	0.04	0.00187	−0.00072	NS
0.00449	−0.00293	NS	0.00287	−0.00455	NS	0.01113	0.00371	NS	0.00312	−0.00430	NS
0.01250	0.00360	NS	0.00717	−0.00173	NS	0.01506	0.00616	0.08	0.00187	−0.00703	NS
0.00929	−0.00776	NS	0.00669	−0.01037	NS	0.02455	0.00749	0.105	0.00187	−0.01518	NS
0.01282	−0.00238	NS	0.00956	−0.00565	NS	0.02586	0.01066	0.01	0.00437	−0.01084	NS
0.01474	−0.00602	NS	0.01147	−0.00930	NS	0.02553	0.00477	NS	0.00437	−0.01640	NS
0.02051	−0.00730	NS	0.01816	−0.00965	NS	0.02946	0.00165	NS	0.00561	−0.02219	NS
0.02404	−0.00859	NS	0.01863	−0.01400	NS	0.03077	−0.00186	NS	0.00998	−0.02265	NS
	0.10609			0.08027			0.18069			0.03369	
	0.89391			0.91973			0.81931			0.96631	

summarized in Table 6.2. Additionally to the significant results of the Spanish market, we find significant differences in probability for small CSSD values in the US market and the French market if the analysis is carried out only during 2003–07. It is worth noting that this period can be considered a calm period between the final period of the Asian and Russian crisis in 1999, the bursting of the high-tech bubble in 2000–02 and the outbreak of the international financial crisis in 2008.

Similarly, almost all the countries increased their cross-sectional deviations as from the second half of 2007, these increases being especially high in the second half of 2008, coinciding with the outbreak of the world financial crisis. Possibly this phenomenon occurred because of the big differences in trading in companies especially badly affected by the deterioration of specific productive sectors or the repercussions of international trading relations.[4] These findings agree with those reported by Hwang and Salmon (2006), who find evidence of herding when investors believe that they know where the market is heading rather than when the market is in crisis.

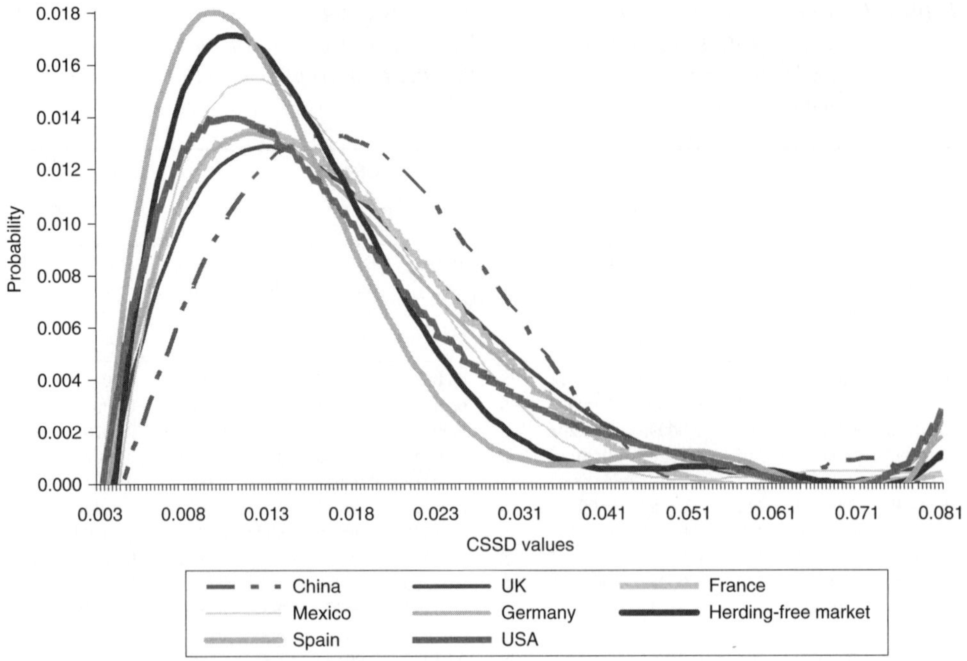

Figure 6.2 CSSD probability distribution (fifth-order polynomial fit)

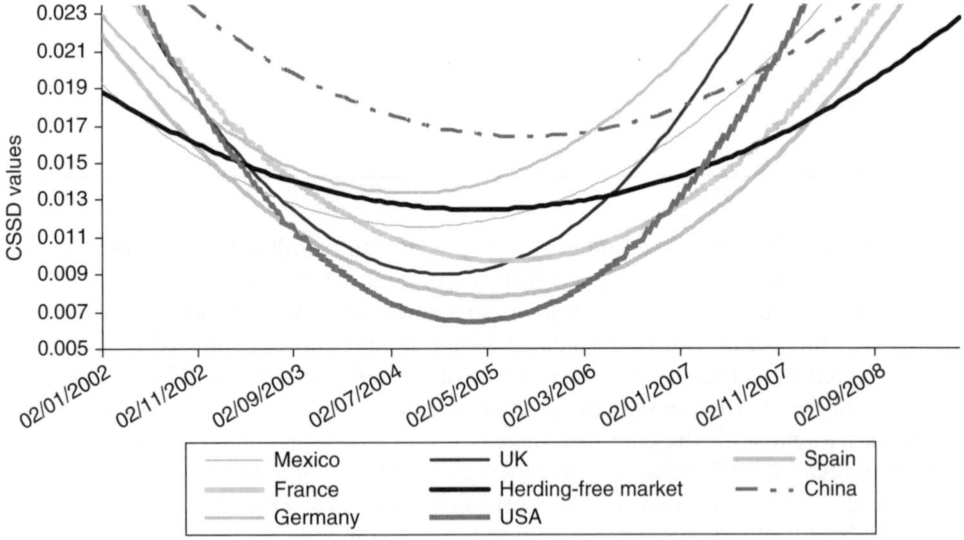

Figure 6.3 CSSD evolution (second-order polynomial fit)

As a consequence of the previous results, it can be noted that there are differences between the markets studied during the time frame considered. While CSSD statistics oscillated in the case of the French, US and UK markets, other markets such as the Spanish and Chinese maintained a more stable level of deviation. This result shows that the concept of herding is relative. The sensitivity to the choice of the analysis period can only be corrected with a comparison with a herding-free market that, in other respects, is subject to the same influences of the international environment and shares the particularities of each period under analysis.[5]

CONCLUSIONS

This study has attempted to extend our knowledge of the behaviour of decision-making agents. Specifically, an analysis has been carried out of seven international markets in which the possible presence of a herding effect has been studied. For this purpose a fictitious market has been constructed that, by its own construction, has no intentional herding, although it does have other characteristics and imperfections implicit in the dynamics of trading. This construction is based on real data of market transactions to ensure that the intrinsic characteristics of financial market trading are retained. A bootstrap technique has been used for the comparison between the distributions of the ideal market and the different markets analysed. Only familiar stocks have been considered in the markets analysed, with the aim of associating possible results in favour of the presence of herding with rational intentional herding. The analysis period was 1 June 1999 to 1 June 2009, ensuring the inclusion of periods of calm and of stress in the market. This is of interest in order to determine the presence of herding outside the specific crisis periods in the market, which are the periods usually studied.

The results reveal differences between the countries analysed. Whereas in the Spanish market favourable evidence was discovered of the presence of herding (as already demonstrated by means of alternative methodologies by Blasco and Ferreruela, 2007, 2008), and certain favourable indicators were shown in the US market, the other countries did not reveal clear results indicative of an intentional herding effect. Nevertheless, our methodological approach leads us to conclude that herding is a relative concept that changes over time. Some of the stock markets analysed exhibit evidence of intentional herding behaviour when specific shorter time intervals are considered, even if these periods are periods of calm.

According to the suggestions in Colander et al. (2009), much of the financial literature shows that human decisions act in a way that bears no resemblance to the rational expectations paradigm. Since economic activity is of an essentially interactive nature, great efforts should be made to propose more flexible market models that allow for interaction, leaving room for imperfect knowledge, adaptative adjustments and heterogeneity of agents with differences in information, motives, knowledge and capabilities. Our purpose is to contribute to the understanding of investors' behaviour by using data-driven methods leading to the definition of new herding measures that are flexible enough to fit the reality of stock market data.

Table 6.2 Comparison between the herding-free market and the seven markets analysed, period 2003–07. Probabilities, differences in probability with respect to the herding-free market and significance p-*values of the differences for 10 per cent of the lowest CSSD values*

Stock market	Herding-free market	Germany			Spain			France		
Interval limit	Probability	Probability	Difference of probability	*p*-values	Probability	Difference of probability	*p*-values	Probability	Difference of probability	*p*-values
0.0025	0.00000	0.00078	0.00078	NS	0.00633	0.00633	NS	0.00235	0.00235	NS
0.008	0.20879	0.21664	0.00785	NS	0.38242	0.17363	0.000	0.27237	0.06358	0.0437
Accumulated probability up to a CSSD value of 0.008	0.20879		0.21743			0.38876			0.27473	
Accumulated probability thereafter	0.79121		0.78257			0.61124			0.72527	

ACKNOWLEDGEMENTS

Natividad Blasco and Sandra Ferreruela wish to acknowledge the financial support of the Spanish Ministry of Education and Science (SEJ2006-C03-03/ECON), the Spanish Ministry of Science and Innovation (ECO2009-12819-C03-02), ERDF funds, the Caja de Ahorros de la Inmaculada (Europe XXI Programme) and the Government of Aragon. Pilar Corrredor is grateful for the financial support of the Spanish Ministry of Education and Science (SEJ2006-14809-C03), the Spanish Ministry of Science and Innovation (ECO2009-12819-C03-01), ERDF funds and the Government of Navarra.

NOTES

1. Eleven individual stocks in those cases where there were no significant differences in trading volume or when the absence of trading makes the consideration of an additional financial asset useful.
2. The polynomial fit enables a fast and easy visualization of the results.
3. A degree 5 polynomial fit has been done to soften the lines and assist in the viewing of the distributions.
4. Nevertheless, Blasco et al. (2010), using intraday data and a different herding measure, find that herding was more intense in the most heavily traded stocks in the Spanish market during the outbreak of the Asian crisis and the following months (from October 1997 to September 1998).
5. The remaining question is the interpretation of the results of the deviations greater than those in the herding-free market. In principle, as with other tests in the literature (e.g. non-linear causality), the statistical test is interpreted in only one sense, that of deviations smaller than that in the herding-free market. Deviation values higher than that specified in the herding-free market should, in principle, be interpreted as substantial differences of interpretation and information processing, whether for specialization, differences in information diffusion, differences in broker rewards or differences in risk levels in the market.

Table 6.2 Comparison between the herding-free market and the seven markets analysed, period 2003–07. Probabilities, differences in probability with respect to the herding-free market and significance p-*values of the differences for 10 per cent of the lowest CSSD values* (cont.)

UK			Mexico			USA			China		
Probability	Difference of probability	*p*-values	Probability	Difference of probability	*p*-values	Probability	Difference of probability	*p*-values	Probability	Difference of probability	*p*-values
0.00157	0.00157	NS	0.00000	0.00000	NS	0.00000	0.00000	NS	0.00000	0.00000	NS
0.20079	−0.00800	NS	0.09660	−0.11220	NS	0.36638	0.15758	0.0000	0.03476	−0.17403	NS
	0.20236			0.09660			0.36638			0.03476	
	0.79764			0.90340			0.63362			0.96524	

REFERENCES

Avery, C. and P. Zemsky (1998), 'Multidimensional uncertainty and herd behavior in financial markets', *American Economic Review*, **88**, 724–48.

Bikhchandani, S. and S. Sharma (2000), 'Herd behavior in financial markets: a review', IMF Working Paper WP/00/48 (International Monetary Fund, Washington).

Bikhchandani, S., D. Hirshleifer and I. Welch (1992), 'A theory of fads, fashion, custom, and cultural change as informational cascades', *Journal of Political Economy*, **100**, 992–1026.

Blasco, N. and S. Ferreruela (2007), 'Comportamiento imitador en el Mercado bursátil español: evidencia intradiaria', *Revista de Economía Financiera*, **13**, 56–75.

Blasco, N. and S. Ferreruela (2008), 'Testing intentional *herding* in familiar stocks: an experiment in an international context', *The Journal of Behavioral Finance*, **9** (2), 72–84.

Blasco, N., P. Corredor and S. Ferreruela (2009), 'Generadores de comportamiento imitador en el mercado de valores español', *Revista Española de Financiación y Contabilidad*, **38** (142), 197–249.

Blasco, N., P. Corredor and S. Ferreruela (2010), '¿Influyen los tigres asiáticos en el comportamiento gregario español?', *Trimestre Económico*, **77** (2) 306, 423–54.

Brennan, M. (1993), 'Agency and asset prices', Finance Working Paper No. 6–93, UCLA.

Chang, E.C., J.W. Cheng and A. Khorana (2000), 'An examination of herd behavior in equity markets: an international perspective', *Journal of Banking and Finance*, **24**, 1651–79.

Chou, P.H. (2004), 'Bootstrap tests for multivariate event studies', *Review of Quantitative Finance and Accounting*, **23** (3), 275–90.

Christie, W.G. and R.D. Huang (1995), 'Following the pied piper: do individual returns herd around the market?', *Financial Analysts Journal*, July–August, 31–7.

Colander, D., D.H. Föllmer, A. Haas, M. Goldberg, K. Juselius, A. Kirman, T. Lux and B. Sloth (2009), 'The financial crisis and the systemic failure of academic economics', The Dahlem Report, 98th Dahlem Workshop 2008, University of Copenhagen Department of Economics Discussion Paper No. 09–03. Available at SSRN: http://ssrn.com/abstract=1355882.

Demirer, R. and A. Kutan (2006), 'Does herding behavior exist in Chinese stock markets?', *Journal of International Financial Markets, Institutions and Money*, **16** (2), 123–42.

Devenow, A. and I. Welch (1996), 'Rational herding in financial economics', *European Economic Review*, **40**, 603–15.

Eguiluz, V.M. and M.G. Zimmermann (2000), 'Transmission of information and herd behavior: an application to financial markets', *Physical Review Letters*, **85**, 5659–62.

Ganzach, Y. (2000), 'Judging risk and return of financial assets', *Organizational Behavior and Human Decision Processes*, **83**, 353–70.

Gompers, P.A. and A. Metrick (2001), 'Institutional investors and equity prices', *Quarterly Journal of Economics*, **116** (1), 229–59.

Grinblatt, M., S. Titman and R. Wermers (1995), 'Momentum investment strategies, portfolio performance and herding: a study of mutual fund behaviour', *American Economic Review*, **85**, 1088–105.

Henker J., T. Henker and A. Mitsios (2006), 'An intraday analysis of herding behaviour in the Australian equities market', *International Journal of Managerial Finance*, **2** (3), 196–219.

Hirshleifer, D. and S.H. Teoh (2003), 'Herd behaviour and cascading in capital markets: a review and synthesis', *European Financial Management*, **9** (1), 25–66.

Hwang, S. and M. Salmon (2004), 'Market stress and herding', *Journal of Empirical Finance*, **11**, 585–616.

Hwang, S. and M. Salmon (2006), 'Sentiment and beta herding in financial markets', Invited plenary address to the Australian Conference of Economists, Perth.

Lakonishok, J., A. Shleifer and R.W. Vishny (1992), 'The impact of institutional trading on stock prices', *Journal of Financial Economics*, **32**, 23–43.

Maug, E. and N. Naik (1996), 'Herding and delegated portfolio management', mimeo, London Business School.

Nofsinger, J.R. and R.W. Sias (1999), 'Herding and feedback trading by institutional investors', *Journal of Finance*, **54**, 2263–316.

Patterson, D.M. and V. Sharma (2006), 'Do traders follow each other at the NYSE?', Working Paper, http://ssrn.com/abstract=712401.

Rajan, R.G. (1994), 'Why credit policies fluctuate: a theory and some evidence', *Quarterly Journal of Economics*, **436**, 399–442.

Roll, R. (1992), 'A mean/variance analysis of tracking error', *Journal of Portfolio Management*, Summer, 13–22.

Scharfstein, D.S. and J.C. Stein (1990), 'Herd behavior and investment', *American Economic Review*, **80**, 465–79.

Sewell, M. (2007) 'Behavioural finance', http://www.behaviouralfinance.net.

Shefrin, H. (2000), *Beyond Greed and Fear: Understanding Behavioral Finance and the Psychology of Investing*, Cambridge: HBS Press.

Sias, R.W. (2004), 'Institutional herding', *Review of Financial Studies*, **17** (1), 165–206.

Thaler, R. (1991), *Quasi-rational Economics*, New York: Russell Sage Foundation.

Trueman, B. (1994), 'Analyst forecasts and herding behaviour', *Review of Financial Studies*, **7**, 97–124.

Wermers, R. (1999), 'Mutual fund herding and the impact on stock prices', *Journal of Finance*, **54**, 581–622.

APPENDIX: INDEX AND INDIVIDUAL STOCKS SELECTED FOR EACH MARKET

Market	Germany	Spain	France	UK	Mexico	USA	China
Market index	*DAX*	*IBEX*	*CAC 40*	*FTSE 100*	*IPC MEXICO*	*DOW JONES*	*HANG SENG*
Individual stocks	*VOLKSWAGEN*	*ACERINOX*	*PEUGEOT*	*CADBURY SCHW*	*WALMEX*	*PROCTER GAMB*	*SINOPEC CORP.*
	SCHERING	*BANKINTER*	*MICHELIN*	*BOOTS GROUP*	*TLEVISA CPO*	*MICROSOFT*	*BOC HONG KONG*
	SAP	*BBVA*	*L'OREAL*	*BARCLAYS*	*TELMEX*	*JP MORGAN*	*COSCO PACIFIC.*
	HENKEL	*CORP.MAPFRE*	*DANONE*	*TESCO*	*KIMBER*	*IBM INT*	*CHALCO*
	BMW	*METROVACESA*	*CARREFOUR*	*SHELL TRANSP*	*GFNORTE*	*GEN MOTO*	*CHINA LIFE*
	BAYER	*REPSOL YPF*	*CAP GEMINI*	*SMITHS GROUP*	*GFINBUR*	*GEN. ELECTRIC*	*CHINA MOBILE*
	BASF	*TELEFONICA*	*BNP PARIBAS*	*MARKS&SPENC*	*COMERCI UBC*	*EXXON MOBIL*	*CHINA OVERSEAS*
	ALLIANZ	*ENDESA*	*AXA UAP*	*BRIT.AIRWAYS*	*CEMEX CPO*	*CITIGROUP*	*CHINA UNICOM*
	ADIDAS	*IBERDROLA*	*AVENTIS*	*VODAFONE GRP*	*BIMBO*	*COCA-COLA*	*HSBC HOLDING*
	SIEMENS	*FCC*	*SOCIETE GRAL*	*ROYAL & SUN*	*ALFA*	*AT&T CORP.*	*PETROCHINA*
	DT.BANK		*FRANCE TELEC*		*AMX L*		

7 Psychic distance in the eight-year crisis: an empirical study

Lili Zhu and Jiawen Yang

INTRODUCTION

The international financial system went through an unusual period between 1994 and 2002. During the eight-year period, the world witnessed a series of financial crises in emerging markets such as the Latin American tequila crises in 1994–95, the Asian financial crisis in 1997–98, the Russian debt crisis in 1998, the Brazilian currency devaluation in 1999, and eventually the financial turmoil occurred in Turkey, Argentina and Uruguay between 2000 and 2002. Some consider 1994–2002 a period of 'eight-year crisis' and the above-mentioned episodes are just different stages of a mega-crisis (Taylor, 2007).

One focal point in economic and financial research on the eight years of crises is the transmission of the financial turmoil across countries/economies – a phenomenon called 'contagion.' However, there is no consensus on the definition of contagion, the channels through which shocks are accentuated and transmitted, or what determines the degree of contagion. For the definition of contagion, Masson (1998) first distinguishes between 'fundamentals-based contagion' and 'true contagion' or 'pure contagion.' As for the channels of contagion, there are financial channels related with the activities of banks, mutual funds, pension funds and insurance companies, and so on, and trade channels (Kaminsky and Reinhart, 2000; Rijckeghem and Weder, 2001). Other causes of contagion are macroeconomic similarities, financial interdependence, common shocks and shifts in investor sentiment (alternatively, market psychology, herd behavior, 'rush for the exits' and so on) (see Caramazza et al., 2000; Pesenti and Tille, 2000). Even neighborhood effects were investigated by some studies (Hernandez and Valdes, 2001). Empirical studies of financial crisis contagion have been conducted along different directions. Initially weaknesses in macroeconomic fundamentals were considered as the most important.[1] Later trade and financial linkages attracted more attention. Among them, financial linkages were found to be more relevant. Then there were studies that focus on the role of visible similarities among emerging markets in explaining financial contagion (e.g. Ahluwalia, 2000). While these studies have contributed to the understanding of financial crisis contagion in various important respects, there seems to be a lack of a common thread to provide a unified framework for the analyses.

The purpose of this chapter is first to integrate the empirical work into a coherent structure, and second, to add a behavioral dimension to the investigation of financial contagion effects. We follow Sachs et al. (1996) (hereafter referred to as the STV model) in combining the various explanatory variables in one linear regression framework, but differ from them in two respects. First, we introduce a psychic distance variable to the analysis. The STV model advocates three intuitively reasonable fundamentals for financial crisis contagion: real exchange rate overvaluation; weakness in the banking system;

and low international reserves (relative to broad money). In this chapter, we specify a model with the same dependent variable as that of the STV model – the crisis index – but employ four categories of independent variables: the monsoonal effects; the spillover effects, institutional factors; and psychic distance. Each category represents the explanation of one type of contagion discussed in the literature. The psychic distance variable is composed of various dimensions including geographic distance, cultural distance, development level and membership and/or neighborhood effects. This variable is designated to account for the occurrence of the so-called 'true contagion' – a cross-market herding behavior in the format of speculation, mimic or rush for exit that is not related to a country's macroeconomic fundamentals, but due to changes in expectations based on incomplete information or on psychological perceptions.

Second, we adopt a gravity model to synthesize the explanatory variables used in the current literature. The gravity model from physics is widely used in the social sciences. Various works use gravitational forces to help explain the flows of migration and trade between different regions or countries (see Askari et al., 2003; Wall, 1999; Hufbauer et al., 1997). Such models have the advantage of classifying explanatory variables into 'pull' and 'push' factors for interactions between two regions or countries. We believe that the gravitational forces of interaction can also help explain the transfer of financial crisis among different regions or countries. The pull factors are international economic linkages, namely trade linkages and financial linkages. The push factor is the psychic distance between countries, rather than geographic distance, although intuitively geographic distance can be considered as part of psychic distance. Our hypothesis is that the severity of financial contagion is in direct proportion to the trade and financial linkages and inversely proportional to the psychic distance between the originating country and the country affected, when macroeconomic fundamentals and institutional factors are controlled for.

The remainder of the chapter is organized as follows. We first review the theoretical and empirical literature on financial crisis and contagion. We also survey the concept of psychic distance to provide a basis for inclusion of this variable in the current study. Next we present the empirical strategy and data sources. The gravity model and the construction of the psychic distance variable are described in this section. The results of the statistical analysis are then reported and analyzed. The final section summarizes and highlights our empirical findings.

LITERATURE REVIEW

The literature on financial contagion is an integral part of that on financial crisis. In this section, we survey the fundamental models of financial crisis and the different theories of financial contagion from which we derive our empirical model used in the study.

Models of Financial Crisis

Different terminologies have been used to refer to financial crises of different nature, such as economic crises, currency crises or even banking crises.[2] The economic literature focusing on currency crises has gone through at least two generations. The first-generation models (FGMs), also referred to as the exogenous-policy models or models of speculative attacks, were pioneered by Krugman (1979) and refined by Flood and Garber (1984). The essence of these models is that currency crises are an unavoidable outcome of a deterioration of the fundamentals, typically due to inconsistency of economic policies. Domestic credit expansion, chronic structural imbalances such as persistent current account deficit, domestic fiscal imbalances or combinations of these cause excess demand for foreign currency and deplete the country's international reserves. When the reserves are exhausted, the country will have no choice but to let go of the fixed exchange rate regime; hence currency crises occur.

The second-generation models (SGMs), exemplified by Obstfeld (1994, 1997), use a game-theoretic approach. These models focus on government optimization and view devaluation decision as a result of choosing between conflicting policy targets, such as achieving low unemployment, supporting sound financial system, stimulating economic growth or even maintaining political integration with its 'neighbors.' After balancing the costs and the benefits of a fixed exchange rate policy, devaluation can be a trade-off decision in response to self-fulfilling speculative attacks. The models that center on the government's optimizing decisions were also called the 'new crisis model' (as in Krugman, 1996).

Models of Financial Crisis Contagion

Both FGMs and SGMs emphasize macroeconomic and financial fundamentals, which are essential in analyzing the spread of crises across countries. According to Pesenti and Tille (2000), there have been two basic approaches to the study of the simultaneity or contagion of currency crises across countries. The first approach views currency crises as the unavoidable result of unsustainable policies or fundamental imbalances. Contagion occurs when different countries encounter common shocks, have trade linkages, or have common creditors. The second approach highlights the possibility of self-fulfilling exchange rate crises. Information frictions in capital markets can cause herding behavior, which in turn fulfills expectation of a crisis. These models, as reviewed below, are not mutually exclusive.

'Monsoonal Effects' of Financial Crises

In Masson (1998), the term 'monsoonal effects' is used to refer to the impact of policies undertaken by industrial countries on emerging markets. The emerging markets are vulnerable to shocks or major policy changes in industrial countries due to fixed exchange rate regimes, foreign currency borrowing and dependence on exports to industrial countries. The debt crisis in the early 1980s was to a substantial extent a common response to the sharp increase in interest rate in the USA relative to their very low levels (in real terms) of the late 1970s (Masson, 1998). Wysocki (1995) points out that US interest rates profoundly affect capital inflows and outflows in emerging markets. In a study of US interest rates and portfolio investments in Latin America, Yang (1997) finds a statistically significant negative relationship for Mexico, Brazil and Argentina. When US rates drop, they encourage US investors to seek higher rates abroad. But when US rates rise, the investments tend to flow back home. That is what occurred in 1994, in the sell-off of stocks and bonds in many emerging countries (Wysocki, 1995). Wysocki believes that the outflow was a fundamental cause of the financial crisis in Mexico in December 1994. If multiple emerging countries get hit by this type of common shock, simultaneity of financial crises across countries occurs.

The essential presumption of the monsoonal effects is the susceptibility of economies to these shocks. In this regard, small or weak and open economies are akin to financial crises ignited by policy shifts in industrial countries. According to Reisen (2008), the monsoon effects hit small open economies easily through merchandise trade precisely because they are both small and open to trade. Low-income countries will be mostly hit through the monsoon channel as recession in OECD countries deepens. Reisen believes that financial crises that are caused by the monsoon effect or by financial contagion can in principle be predicted through the monitoring of macroeconomic variables.

Spillover Models of Contagion

In the absence of common shocks, a currency crisis can be transmitted from one country to another if structural links and international spillovers make the economies of the two countries interdependent (Pesenti and Tille, 2000). According to Drazen (2000), trade linkages have been at the center of spillover models of financial contagion. On the one hand, a devaluation forced by speculative attacks in one country will enhance its price competitiveness, and thus may result in trade deficits and declining reserves for its trading partners. Meanwhile, a decrease in demand in the crisis country may also hurt its trade partners. Hence financial crisis can transmit from a crisis country to its trade partners directly. On the other hand, however, multilateral linkages or third-party trade are found to be more relevant than bilateral trade linkages. Consider the Asian crisis again. Asian countries have significant exports to Japan and the USA, while the bilateral trade volumes between crisis-affected countries were not very large. Asian countries compete with each other for the same markets and, in most cases, in the same product segments. It is possible that competitive devaluation expedited the contagion of crisis. Many empirical studies have demonstrated the role of trade linkages, especially the third-party trade linkage, in explaining the occurrence of financial contagion (Glick and Rose, 1999; Kaminsky and Reinhart, 2000; Caramazza et al., 2000).

We see more attention being given to financial linkages in recent studies. Theoretically, Hernandez and Valdes (2001) summarize four ways that financial linkages can explain contagion. First, direct financial linkages, which refer to foreign direct investments (FDIs), connect corporate and financial sector returns across countries. Thailand's devaluation can drive down the stock prices in Malaysia because it imposes losses on Malaysian corporations investing in Thailand. Second, many fund managers treat assets of different countries as complementary. Contagion occurs when fund managers rebalance their portfolios following a negative shock from one country to maintain fixed weights of assets in these countries. Third, after suffering a shock, financial institutions facing liquidity problems in one market could be forced to adjust positions in other markets, resulting in cross-market contagion. Fourth, information asymmetries and herding behavior produce co-movement across countries, as discussed in the information cascade models.

Except for FDI, the aforementioned explanations emphasize the financial linkages due to banking activities and the behavior of hedge funds, mutual funds and other institutional investors. The discussion of banking activities concentrates on the 'common creditor' or 'competition for funds' argument (Rijckeghem and Weder, 2001; Caramazza et al., 2000). If a bank is highly exposed to a crisis country, its adjustments to restore capital adequacy, meet margin calls or rebalance its portfolios can reduce the credit line to a second country, which has been in competition with the crisis country for funds from the bank. According to Caramazza et al. (2000), if the common creditor is the major lender to a crisis country, countries sharing the common lender may experience capital outflows irrespective of their macroeconomic fundamentals simply because their assets are viewed as risky as well. This is more related with the 'wake-up call' argument and herding behavior. In Kaminsky and Reinhart (2000)'s work, international bank lending and the potential for cross-market hedging are tested, and common bank lending is concluded to be the most important channel for contagion. Given the huge size and volatility of bank credits, as well as the magnitude of losses by banks during crisis episodes, the common lender argument deserves further investigation.[3]

As for the behavior of mutual funds and hedge funds, some believe that 'contagious selling' of higher-risk assets can be explained by the basic portfolio theory without recourse to market imperfection (Schinasi and Smith, 2000). For example, fund managers will rebalance their portfolios in a large scale when an adverse shock affects some assets' return distribution, when the return on the leveraged portfolio is less than the cost of funding due to liquidity consideration, or just to obey the 'value-at-risk' portfolio management rules when a crisis takes place.

On the other hand, bubbles or investors' irrational behavior is a major source of contagion. Christiansen (2000) argues that the presence of mutual funds might have magnified price fluctuations. Investors tend to withdraw funds from mutual funds in the case of significantly negative returns. This behavior is similar to that described by incomplete information or information cascade arguments. In this situation, risk management techniques can induce investors to treat groups of countries – especially emerging economies – indiscriminately, thus herding occurs across countries.

The role played by rating agencies may exacerbate such situations. Christiansen (2000) reports that the sovereign ratings on the terms on which money can be raised in global financial markets tend to amplify both the upturn and the downturn volatility. Such rating can be a source of overshooting and contagion during bad times. Changes in risk ratings may be, again, based upon perceived similarities of countries, especially the grouping of countries according to regions, macroeconomic similarities or development level.

From the individual investor's point of view, herding can be a rational strategy. Bikhchandani and Sharma (2000) discuss the incentives for different types of herding behavior. The information asymmetry argument assumes that poorly informed traders obtain cost-effective benefit by observing and copying better-informed investors' positions. Reputation-based herding occurs when there is uncertainty regarding the ability of the manager to manage the portfolio. In this case, conformity with other investment professionals would help. When an investor's compensation depends on how his performance compares to other investors' performance, he can end up with an inefficient portfolio, due to the so-called compensation-based herding. But collectively, according to the authors, herding behavior can precipitate a bubble or an irrational result, which in worst cases leads to financial contagion.

In sum, losses in one country spill over to other countries as creditors or investors try to retrench their portfolios, restore their capital-adequacy ratios or meet margin calls. Herding can play a role, too, mainly based upon the argument of perceived grouping of countries.

Information Cascades Models of Contagion

According to Drazen (2000), the best-developed general model of contagion is that of 'information cascades,' or, less formally, information externalities. A cascade is a series of self-reinforcing signals obtained from the direct observation of others (Rizzi, 2008). Individuals perceive these signals as information even though they may be reacting to noise. Information cascade is mainly manifested in the format of herding behavior, which, as previously discussed, can be justified by information costs.[4] Calvo and Mendoza (2000) use a standard mean–variance framework to show that the costs of verifying the validity of market rumors can lead to asset sales unrelated to real fundamentals.

Models of information externalities have been developed on various assumptions. King and Wadhwani (1990) assume that asset prices depend on an idiosyncratic and a common factor. 'Signal extraction' occurs where a shock to the idiosyncratic factor in one market prompts investors to adjust positions in other markets because of uncertainty about the type of shock that has occurred. Other studies have incorporated incomplete information of speculators or investors' assessment of an economy's fundamentals. Morris and Shin (1998) base their model on the assumption that speculators have uniform prior probability distributions over the state of fundamentals that are updated according to the observation of a private signal. Sbracia and Zaghini (2001) further argue that not only the mean of speculators' probability assessment over the fundamentals matters. Uncertainty of the assessment also influences speculative attacks. Therefore crisis is like a 'wake up call' that induces financial markets to reassess other countries' fundamentals. Countries with weak macroeconomic and financial fundamentals can be more vulnerable to contagion effects from a shift in market sentiment or increased risk aversion.

Masson (1998) proposes a model where financial markets are subject to multiple equilibria. When fundamentals are good, there is a unique equilibrium in which the exchange rate is maintained; when fundamentals deteriorate, the currency depreciates; when fundamentals fall in an 'intermediate' range (the 'ripe for attack' zone), either outcome is possible. He views contagion as a jump between equilibria triggered by a crisis elsewhere. As suggested by Masson (1998), only models of this type can produce pure contagion, which involves changes in expectations that are self-fulfilling and sometimes unrelated to economic fundamentals.

The information externality argument may help explain some financial crises that occurred in the 1990s. With uncertainty about policy makers' commitment to defending a fixed exchange rate, the collapse of the exchange rate in one country, say, Thailand, provides information that another country in similar macroeconomic circumstances is also likely to abandon its fixed parity. However, the extent of decline in other countries depends on the informational value attributed by investors, which varies across countries. For example, a negative shock in Thailand may provide more informational value (in the eyes of the investors) about other Southeast Asian nations than a shock in Mexico. Alternatively, investors tend to link the negative shock in Thailand to other emerging markets rather than industrialized countries. This hypothesis is justified by the fact that most episodes of financial crisis are regional. In the Asian episode, many crisis-affected economies are those that applied the so-called 'East Asian model' successfully over the last two decades. Hence we can assume that development patterns and thus macroeconomic circumstances are similar for countries in this region. Therefore, in investors' perceptions, the information conveyed by a crisis that takes place in the ground-zero country is heavily influenced by the relationship and/or similarity between the affected country in question and the originating country.

Membership Contagion and Other Explanations

Drazen (2000) proposes a model of 'membership contagion,' which is inherently political. It emphasizes the relevance of 'membership in a "club," whether explicit or implicit, where the benefits of membership are heavily political and the condition for membership is the maintenance of a fixed exchange rate' (p. 10). In this argument, investors presumably use the membership of a certain 'club,' not just macroeconomic similarity, as a relevant predictor of the probability distribution of a government's intention to devaluate.

Similarly, Hernandez and Valdes (2001) investigate the neighborhood effect on contagion. The relevance of geographic neighborhood is justified by arguing that financial links are due to institutional practices in international financial markets. That is, institutional investors treat all countries from the same region as equal, without accounting for the differences in their fundamentals.

Emerging markets as a group are viewed as a club that is more vulnerable to financial crisis. Ahluwalia (2000) indicates that contagious currency crises usually occur in emerging markets and initiates the concept of 'discriminating contagion,' which suggests that investors' confidence about emerging markets is relatively thin, and thus their behavior more volatile. The implication is that the title of 'emerging market' can be an indicator of investors' perception of the country, although there is no strong evidence in place that all emerging markets bear the same fundamental weaknesses.

The 'discriminating contagion' argument is related to the well-accepted term 'monsoonal effects' used by Masson (1998). As previously indicated, 'monsoonal effects' refers to the fact that a common shock usually affects countries differently due to different macroeconomic fundamentals. While 'discriminating contagion' may amplify the negative impact of 'monsoonal effects' by assuming irrational behavior in explaining the spread of crises, the macroeconomic fundamentals cannot be eliminated in a model of financial contagion, even when the contagion studied is a 'pure' one.

Institutional Factors and Financial Crisis Contagion

Credible institutional arrangements can prevent crises from occurring. Christiansen (2000) finds that the principal triggers of risk clustering and herding behavior on the part of investors fall into two categories: (1) factors making investors perceive that a financial system (including the exchange rate regime of the country) is unable to sustain a massive withdrawal of funds; and (2) factors affecting transparency and, hence, giving rise to uncertainty and information asymmetries. Among a long list of the relevant factors, two institutional variables are more important and easily discernible – exchange rate regime and capital control.

Calvo (2001) asserts that the exchange rate regime is the most important institutional arrangement affecting markets' vulnerability to external turmoil. Edwards (2000) concludes that countries with either a super-fix (through a currency board or dollarization) or a freely floating exchange rate system are less vulnerable to contagion. The reason is that only those two regimes meet the requirement of transparency and credibility. Capital control has attracted a great deal of attention in the literature. The wave of financial liberalization and structural reforms undertaken by emerging countries in recent years attracted large capital inflows to emerging markets. But the excessive degree of capital mobility of the 1990s may have contributed to emerging countries' increasing vulnerability. Some argue that countries with large inflows tend to experience sharp corrections. When the liberalization is more limited and gradual, we may see smaller overshooting of capital inflows than in countries that have more aggressively liberalized the capital account (Bacchetta and Wincoop, 1998). So the degree of openness of the capital account is tested as a contributing factor of financial contagion in this study.

The Concept of Psychic Distance and Financial Crisis Contagion

Monsoonal effects, spillover effects and institutional factors in financial crisis contagion are relatively easily identified. However, the remaining explanations, such as information cascading, membership effects, neighborhood effects and macroeconomic similarities, are interrelated and much harder to isolate. These effects, as manifested by herd behavior, reflect the behavioral aspects of financial crisis contagion. We take a behavioral approach to synthesize these effects by employing a composite variable – psychic distance.

Mishkin (2003) defines financial crisis as 'a disruption to financial markets in which adverse selection and moral hazard problems become much worse, so that financial markets are unable to efficiently channel funds to those who have the most productive investment opportunities' (p. 94). The emphasis on adverse selection and moral hazard implies that the behavioral approach may actually be providing an alternative tool to further explain the herding mentality during times of crisis.

There has been a burgeoning literature on behavioral economics and behavioral finance in recent years. As Shiller (2003) points out, the collaboration between finance and other social sciences that has become known as behavioral finance has led to a profound deepening of our knowledge of financial markets. The basic argument is that a theory of complete rationality and the assumption of utility maximization do not provide sufficient bases for explaining and predicting all economic behaviors. The financial system is far from efficient because human behavior demonstrates only bounded rationality. For example, an individual investor's trading is often driven by irrational, sentimental shocks; institutional investors often exhibit herding behavior (Kim and Wei, 1999). Rizzi (2008) emphasizes the role of sentiment risk, which is based on biases and exists only in a less efficient market. The sentiment can be either optimistic or pessimistic and is time varying. He points out that most risk models ignore sentiment risk. This causes losses when sentiment changes, leading to closed markets and mark-to-market losses, which has threatened the basis of originate-to-distribute model in modern banking.

On the basis of a comprehensive survey of the behavioral finance literature, Shiller (1998) summarizes a dozen behavioral principles. Among them, some provide useful leads for the understanding of the herd mentality from the perspective of human behavior.

One of the major behavioral principles is related to 'mental compartments,' which we view as virtual categories assigned by human beings. According to Shiller (1998), there is 'a human tendency to place particular events into mental compartments based on superficial attributes' (p. 18). Instead of carefully analyzing the full picture of a country's macroeconomic fundamentals, investors may look at individual similarities independently. Therefore 'people may tend to place their investments into arbitrarily separate mental compartments, and react separately to the investments based on which compartment they are in (ibid., p. 18).

As argued by Shiller (1998), mental compartments can result in overconfidence, and/or over- and underreaction due to the 'representativeness heuristic,' when, in making probability estimates, investors overstress the importance of the categorization, neglecting evidence about the underlying probabilities. This may explain a general market overreaction or the excess volatility of speculative asset prices during crises.

'Magical thinking,' as discussed in Shiller (1998), may play a role in deepening a crisis. If people believe the theories, they may then behave in a way that leads things, say market volatility, to move as hypothesized. The consistency of the correlations further reinforces the initial belief.

Another relevant principle is attention anomalies, which highlights the impact of the change of public attention in investment decision making. Shiller (1998) believes that the volatility of speculative asset prices is related to the capriciousness of public attention. Also he indicates that the major crashes in financial markets can be viewed as phenomena of attention, in which 'an inordinate amount of public attention is suddenly focused on the markets' (p. 41), sometimes on the markets in a specific region.

Based on the foregoing discussions of behavioral principles, we envision the following picture of financial contagion from the perspective of human behavior. Investors fit different countries into different mental compartments. When a country is hit by a financial crisis, due to the representativeness heuristic and attention anomalies, other countries perceived to be in the same mental category are subject to an excess volatility in asset prices due to overreaction on the part of investors. 'Magical thinking' reinforces such turmoil. The behavioral principles borrowed from psychology provide a fresh insight into the analysis of contagion, which reveals the role human behavior has played in the process of a financial crisis. Based on these principles, it is well justified to link the herd mentality that takes over in times of crisis with the concept of psychic distance, which can be considered as a continuous measure of mental compartments.

The concept of psychic distance has attracted increasing attention in international business and management literature (Ojala and Tyrvainen, 2009). It was first proposed by Beckerman (1956) and later popularized by Johanson and Wiedersheim-Paul (1975) and Johanson and Vahlne (1977). It is 'the sum of factors preventing the flow of information from and to the market. Examples are differences in language, education, business practices, culture and industrial development' (Johanson and Vahlne, 1977, p. 24).[5] It has been applied in theory and practice in cross-country trade and investment flows and cross-cultural management. Specifically, psychic distance has been used to explain firms' internationalization process (O'Grady and Lane, 1996), export market selection (Dow, 2000), foreign market entry (Ellis, 2008), and FDI (Alves, 2008). Geographic distance, cultural distance (Hofstede, 1980, 1983; Kogut and Singh, 1988) and market similarity (Sethi, 1971) were all used as approximations of psychic distance based on the nature of the research.[6] Other indicators or dimensions include level of economic development, level of education, language and so on (O'Grady and Lane, 1996). Accordingly, as stated by O'Grady and Lane (1996), the definition of psychic distance varies greatly within the literature, depending upon the way in which the concept is operationalized.

Psychic distance has rarely been applied in financial studies. We define it as the perceived degree of similarities in the characteristics of a country that can cause investors to 'group' it alongside other countries exhibiting similar characteristics. This definition is quite similar to Ahluwalia's (2000) 'visible similarities.' We emphasize, however, the role of perceived similarities in determining a country's vulnerability to financial contagions because such mental categorization is not solely based on the true and visible similarities in macroeconomic fundamentals. Psychic distance also captures the interactions among countries that may not be accounted for by Ahluwalia's visible similarities. Based on the literature review above, we incorporate the following dimensions to operationalize psychic distance in this study: economic development level, cultural distance, common membership and geographical distance.[7]

EMPIRICAL STRATEGY AND DATA

The Empirical Model

In their study of financial crisis contagion arising from the Mexican peso crisis in 1994, Sachs et al. (1996) adopt an empirical model that combines three explanatory factors in one linear regression – real exchange rate overvaluation, weakness in the banking system and low international reserves (relative to broad money). We extend their study in three respects – data sample, variable selection and empirical framework.

First, we expand the data coverage to include the five major episodes of financial crises between 1994 and 2002, namely the financial crises that occurred in Mexico (1994–95), Thailand (1997), Russia (1998), Brazil (1999) and Argentina (2000–01). The first three episodes are generally considered as triggers of contagion to other nations. We also include the Brazilian and Argentina episodes since they occurred in relatively larger economies although there is no clear evidence that they are directly connected to other later crises (Taylor, 2007).

Second, we set up our empirical model with the same dependent variable as that of the STV model – the crisis index – but employ four sets of independent variables that are derived from the literature reviewed in the previous section, which are specified as follows: (1) monsoonal effects, which refer to each country's weaknesses in macroeconomic fundamentals and thus its vulnerability to a common shock originated from somewhere else in the world; (2) spillover effects due to financial and trade interdependence between two countries; (3) psychic distance, a variable measuring the perceived similarity across countries and composed of various dimensions including geographic distance, cultural distance, development level and membership and/or neighborhood effects; and (4) institutional factors, including exchange regime and capital control arrangements. The inclusion of the psychic distance variable in our analysis represents novelty in the study of contagion. It is designated to account for the occurrence of so-called true or pure contagion, presumably due to changes in expectations that are not related to a country's macroeconomic fundamentals.

Third, we adopt the gravity model approach in synthesizing our empirical framework. Newton's theory of gravitation has been used for a long time in social sciences because it provides an empirically tractable framework.[8] The gravity model has two pillars: (1) the product of the masses of two celestial bodies; and (2) the distance between the two bodies. For any pair of particles the force is directly proportional to the product of the masses (the pull factor) and inversely proportional to the square of the distance between them (the push factor). The simplest form of the gravity model for international trade posits that the volume of trade between any two trading partners is an increasing function of their national incomes, and a decreasing function of the distance between them (Wall, 1999). The gravity model has also been used to study international capital flows (see Rosati and Secola, 2006 for a study of cross-border interbank payments). We believe the gravity model also provides a coherent framework for the study of financial contagion, which in essence is an interaction among countries when a financial crisis occurs. While spillover effects caused by trade and financial linkages among countries can be viewed as the pull factor, psychic distance represents the push factor in our model, when monsoonal effects and institutional factors are controlled for.

Based on our foregoing discussions, we set up our multiple regression equation as follows:

$$CIND_i = \alpha + \beta_1 MonsoonalControls_i + \beta_2 Spillover_{ij} + \beta_3 PsychicDistance_{ij} + \beta_4 InstitutionalControls_i + \mu_i \quad (7.1)$$

where *CIND* is the crisis index and the right-hand side variables correspond to the four categories of explanation. A higher value of *CIND* indicates a higher degree of severity in financial crisis. Here, country *i* is a country subject to contagion and *j* a 'ground-zero' country, the country that triggers the wave of crisis in each episode or the country of interest (i.e. Brazil and Argentina in the last two episodes examined in the sample). For country *i*, the severity of crisis is a function of its own fundamentals (the monsoonal effects), its linkages with country *j* (the spillover effects), its psychic distance to country *j* and its own domestic institutional factors. The direction and magnitude of β_3 will be of key interest as they are indications of the presence and severity of pure contagion. β_3 is important also because it is the only behavioral predictor in the model. Our hypothesis is that the severity of the contagion effect is in direct proportion to the trade and financial linkages and inversely proportional to the psychic distance between the originating country and the country affected, when macroeconomic fundamentals and institutional factors are controlled for.

In addition to the five episodes of financial crises that took place in the eight-year period between 1994 and 2002, we construct a sixth data sample by stacking up all the observations over five episodes to see if there is coherence and consistency across all the crisis episodes. In our samples, we include all the countries in the world as listed in

International Financial Statistics (*IFS*), published by the International Monetary Fund (IMF). However, due to data availability, the actual number of observations used in each empirical test varies across data samples and is reported in the empirical results tables. Our data are mostly retrieved from the *IFS* database, unless otherwise specified in the ensuing discussion.

The Dependent Variable

In the STV model, the crisis index, $CIND_i$, is a weighted average of the percentage depreciation of country *i*'s exchange rate (*EXD*) and percentage loss in the country's international reserves (*RLOS*) over a certain time interval. To capture the overall volatility of the two indicators over the crisis period, we modify the construction of this variable by combining the averages of monthly percentage depreciation in the exchange rate and percentage loss in international reserves over a specific time interval. For each episode, a certain interval is selected as the period of crisis. According to common practice in the literature (see Ahluwalia, 2000), the starting point of each episode of interest is as follows: December 1994 for the Mexican crisis, July 1997 for the Asian crisis, August 1998 for the Russian crisis, January 1999 for the Brazilian crisis and November 2001 for the Argentine crisis. The crisis index is constructed using the intervals 1994M11 (November 1994; same interpretation throughout)–1995M4, 1997M5–1997M10, 1998M7–1998M10, 1998M12–1999M2, and 2001M11–2002M2 for the five crises respectively.[9] Following Ahluwalia (2000) and Caramazza et al. (2000), to equalize the conditional variance of the two components, we weigh each component by the inverse of its variance divided by the sum of the inverses of the variances of the two components:

$$CIND = \left[((1/\sigma^2_{EXD})/((1/\sigma^2_{EXD}) + (1/\sigma^2_{RLOS})))*EXD\right] + \left[((1/\sigma^2_{RLOS})/((1/\sigma^2_{EXD}) + (1/\sigma^2_{RLOS})))*RLOS\right] \quad (7.2)$$

The exchange rate used is the end-of-period monthly exchange rate versus the US dollar. The international reserves are defined as 'total reserves minus gold' in the *IFS*. The variances used for the equalization process, that is, σ^2_{EXD} and σ^2_{RLOS} in expression (7.2), are calculated from the monthly percentage changes in the exchange rate and reserves over the 36 months prior to the occurrence of each crisis episode.

Monsoonal Effects

To account for the fundamental vulnerability to external financial shocks, we follow the conventional wisdom as well as making reference to the study by Ahluwalia (2000) in selecting the following measures into the set of macroeconomic control variables denoted as $MonsoonalControls_i$: (1) real effective exchange rate appreciation (*REER*); (2) ratio of broad money relative to international reserves (*M2_RES*); (3) percentage change in the ratio of domestic claims to GDP (*CLM*); and (4) current account balance as a percentage of GDP (*CA_GDP*).

A real exchange rate appreciation (*REER*) indicates a loss of international price competitiveness. More importantly, it may also imply an exchange rate misalignment, which may be an indicator, perceived by the investors, of the pressure a government faces to adjust the nominal exchange rate. This variable is constructed as the ratio of the average real effective exchange rate 12 months before the crisis over the average in the previous three years.

Ratio of broad money relative to international reserves (*M2_RES*) is an indicator of the vulnerability of a country's financial system to a run by investors. The level of international reserves ('total reserves minus gold' from the *IFS*, as described above) over M2 (the sum of 'money and quasi money' in the *IFS*) in December of the year prior to the crisis are used to construct this variable.

Variable *CLM* measures the percentage change in the ratio of domestic credits to gross domestic product (GDP) over a two-year period ending in December of the year preceding the crisis year. Domestic lending boom would increase the vulnerability of the banks' portfolios to economic contractions. If a large proportion of the domestic banks' liabilities are denominated in the domestic currency, the government will be more willing to devaluate rather than bail out domestic banks. The data source is termed as 'claims on the private sector at current prices' in the *IFS*.

The fourth measure, *CA_GDP*, is current account balance as a percentage of GDP during the calendar year prior to crisis time. For one thing, the size of the current account deficit measures the extent to which the capital inflow is needed to cover the deficit. Alternatively, the current account balance in part determines a country's ability to repay foreign-denominated debt. Hence it is an essential determinant of foreign investors' confidence in an economy. For another, a government is more likely to devalue its currency in the hope of boosting exports when there is a huge current account deficit, especially for emerging markets that appreciate export-led growth. The current account deficit can be viewed as an indicator of the adjustment in the real exchange rate needed to restore external balance.

Spillover Effects

For the spillover effects, we use measures for both trade and financial linkages. We adopt the indicator of trade competition in third markets ($TCOMP_{ij}$) used by Glick and Rose (1999), and build a measure of direct trade ($DTRD_{ij}$) to account for trade interdependence between the ground-zero country, j, and the affected country, i. These variables are constructed as follows:

$$TCOMP_{ij} = \sum_k \left[(x_{jk} + x_{ik})/(x_j + x_i) \right] \left[1 - |(x_{jk}/x_j) - (x_{ik}/x_i)|/((x_{jk}/x_j) + (x_{ik}/x_i)) \right] \tag{7.3}$$

$$DTRD_{ij} = (m_{ij} + x_{ij})/(m_i + x_i) \tag{7.4}$$

In Equation (7.3), k represents the most important trade partners for the ground-zero countries in different crises episodes. Table 7.1 provides a list of top exporting markets included as components of k for each originating country j in the calculations. x_{ik} denotes aggregate exports from country i to k and x_i is the aggregate exports from country i. $TCOMP_{ij}$ reaches its highest value if country i has a similar exporting market structure

Table 7.1 Top exporting markets of each ground-zero country in the five episodes[a]

Mexico (1993)		Thailand (1996)		Russia (1997)		Brazil (1998)		Argentina (2001)	
Partner	Share (%)[b]	Partner	Share (%)[b]	Partner	Share (%)[b]	Partner	Share (%)[b]	Partner	Share (%)[b]
USA	83.3 (83.3)	USA	18.0 (18.0)	Ukraine	8.5 (8.5)	USA	19.4 (19.4)	Brazil	23.3 (23.3)
		Japan	16.8 (34.8)	Germany	7.7 (16.2)	Argentina	13.2 (32.6)	USA	10.9 (34.2)
		Singapore	12.1 (46.9)	USA	5.8 (22.0)	Germany	5.9 (38.5)	Chile	10.7 (44.9)
		Hong Kong	5.8 (52.7)	Belarus	5.4 (27.4)	Netherlands	5.4 (43.9)	China	4.2 (49.1)
		Malaysia	3.6 (56.3)	Netherlands	5.4 (32.8)	Japan	4.3 (48.2)	Spain	4.1 (53.2)
		China	3.4 (59.7)	China	5.4 (38.2)	Belgium–Luxembourg n.s.[c]	4.3 (52.5)	Italy	3.2 (56.4)
		UK	3.3 (63.0)	Switzerland	4.7 (42.9)	Italy	3.8 (56.3)	Netherlands	3.1 (59.5)
		Netherlands	3.2 (66.2)	Italy	4.4 (47.3)	UK	2.6 (58.9)	Uruguay	2.8 (62.3)
		Germany	2.9 (69.1)	Japan	4.2 (51.5)	France	2.5 (61.4)	Paraguay	1.9 (64.2)
		Korea	1.8 (70.9)	UK	3.4 (54.9)	Paraguay	2.4 (63.8)	Mexico	1.8 (66.0)

Notes:

[a] We include top ten export markets for each ground-zero country in the calculation of *TCOMP* except for Mexico, whose exports to the USA accounted for 83% of its total exports in 1993. Only the USA is included in the calculation for the Mexican episode.

[b] Cumulative shares in parentheses.

[c] Data refer to the Belgium–Luxembourg Economic Union. 'n.s.' means 'not specified' in the database. For the years that a country reports trade seperately from Belgium and Luxembourg, it is assumed that the reported trade with Belgium–Luxembourg n.s. refers to the combined trade with Belgium and Luxembourg.

Data source: Direction of Trade Statistics, IMF.

Table 7.2 Top bank lenders for each ground-zero country in the five episodes

Mexico (1993)		Thailand (1996)		Russia (1997)		Brazil (1998)		Argentina (2001)	
Lender	Share (%)[a]	Lender	Share (%)[a]	Lender	Share (%)[a]	Lender	Share (%)[a]	Lender	Share (%)[a]
USA	34.3 (34.3)	Japan	54.41 (54.41)	Germany	41.30 (41.30)	USA	17.4 (17.4)	USA	28.3 (28.3)
UK	15.5 (49.8)					Germany	15.4 (32.8)	Spain	24.5 (52.8)

Note: [a] Cumulative shares in parentheses.

Data source: Statistical annex of 'The BIS Consolidated International Banking Statistics' (formerly known as 'The Maturity, Sectoral and Nationality Distribution of International Bank Lending'), BIS, various issues.

as that of country *j*, where crisis initiated/occured. Thus $TCOMP_{ij}$ is a measure of trade competition in third markets between a ground-zero country *j* and an individual country (country *i*) that might be affected.[10]

Expression (7.4) measures bilateral trade linkage between two countries. m_{ij} (x_{ij}) stands for country *i*'s imports (exports) from (to) country *j* and m_i (x_i) is the total imports (exports) of country *i*. $DTRD_{ij}$ measures the importance of country *j* as a bilateral trade partner for country *i*. All the bilateral trade data are obtained from IMF's *Direction of Trade Statistics (DOTS)* database.

To account for the common bank lender argument for contagion, we adopt a variable measuring competition for funding from the same bank lenders ($BCOMP_{ij}$) used by Rijckeghem and Weder (2000):

$$BCOMP_{ij} = \sum_c \left[(b_{jc} + b_{ic})/(b_j + b_i) \right] \left[1 - |(b_{jc}/b_j) - (b_{ic}/b_i)|/((b_{jc}/b_j) + (b_{ic}/b_i)) \right] \quad (7.5)$$

Parallel to $TCOMP_{ij}$, $BCOMP_{ij}$ measures (debtor) country *i*'s similarity in borrowing patterns to that of country *j* in terms of shares in total borrowing. In Equation (7.5), *c* stands for the country of common lender, and b_{ic} represents bank lending from a country *c* to country *i*. The first component of the equation is a measure of the overall importance of the common lender for countries *i* and *j*. The second component captures the extent to which shares of borrowing from the same creditors are different. The most important common lenders included in the calculations are the US and UK banks in the case of the Mexican crisis, the Japanese banks during the Asian crisis, the German banks during the Russian episode, the US and German banks in the Brazilian episode, and banks from the USA and Spain in the case of Argentina (see Table 7.2). As in Rijckeghem and Weder (2000), data for this variable are obtained from the Bank for International Settlements (BIS) semi-annual consolidated database covering banking systems in 18 industrialized countries.

Psychic Distance

Psychic distance is one of the most commonly cited, yet vaguely measured, constructs in international business research (Dow and Karunaratna, 2006). Our construct for the psychic distance variable $PDIST_{ij}$ is a single ordinal scale that combines some single indicators used in the literature. The essential building blocks for the scale are the standardized values for four sub-factors, including geographic distance, common language, development level and common membership. The weight for each dimension is equal. All the sub-factors are objective measures.

Geographic distance ($GDIST_{ij}$) is approximated by the great circle distance between the capital cities of two countries of interest.[11] We use physical distance to reflect the perception that geographically adjacent countries are more likely to share similarities than others. Having a common border and being in the common continental region may increase perceived closeness.

Cultural differences or similarities play a major role in determining psychological distance. However, until recently, economists have been reluctant to rely on culture as a possible determinant of economic phenomena (Guiso et al., 2006). Much of this reluctance stems from the definitional ambiguity of culture and testability of hypotheses in the relationship between culture and economic performance (see Reuter, 2009 for an overwhelming diversity of approaches in the way culture is conceptualized and operationalized).[12] Nonetheless, it is obvious that language is an essential indicator of culture. We use whether or not countries have a common language as a proxy for cultural distance. $COML_{ij}$ is set to be one if country *i* and ground-zero country *j* share a same official or primarily spoken language. Otherwise, it is zero.

It is a stylized fact that most crisis-affected countries in our test period are less developed countries (LDCs) and/or emerging markets. LDCs with a demonstrated potential for economic expansion are typically entitled as 'emerging.' It is arguable whether the term 'less developed countries (LDCs)' or 'emerging market' connotes bad macroeconomic fundamentals that need to be developed. However, according to the 'discriminating contagion' argument, the term 'emerging market' itself can increase volatility simply by the negative information it conveys (Ahluwalia, 2000), as the term 'emerging' implies a status of being in transition, increasing in size, activity or level of sophistication. All the five ground-zero countries in our sample – Mexico, Thailand, Russia, Brazil and Argentina – are generally considered as leading emerging markets. Investments in emerging markets have the potential to generate high returns in a relatively short period of time. Meanwhile, however, there is a higher level of risk involved in these investments as they are subject to various macroeconomic weaknesses as well as unexpected political and economic turmoil. In investors' perception, upheaval in one emerging market can serve as a 'wake-up call' for other emerging markets as well as other LDCs. Per capita income is the most important indicator to measure a country's development level.[13] We use the difference of GDP per capita in dollars between two countries immediately before the respective crises to measure the development level aspect of psychic distance, denoted as $DDIST_{ij}$.

'Membership effect' distinguishes the role played by political and economic integration at regional or global level. We have seen a prevailing trend toward regional integration on the economic perspective. We incorporate the common regional bloc

Table 7.3 Countries with the smallest psychic distance from the ground-zero nations[a]

Mexico	Thailand	Russia	Brazil	Argentina
Costa Rica	Malaysia	Kazakhstan	Cape Verde	Uruguay
El Salvador	Philippines	Kyrgyz Republic	Paraguay	Chile
Colombia	Lao PDR	Tajikistan	Colombia	Paraguay
Panama	Cambodia	Latvia	Venezuela, RB	Peru
Guatemala	Vietnam	Lithuania	Chile	Colombia
Venezuela, RB	Indonesia	Belarus	Angola	Bolivia
Honduras	Sri Lanka	Estonia	Peru	Venezuela
Dominican Republic	Bangladesh	Ukraine	Bolivia	Ecuador
Chile	India	Moldova	Ecuador	Brazil
Ecuador	Korea, Rep.	Armenia	Argentina	Nicaragua

Note: [a] Psychic distance is calculated based on the following equation:

$$PDIST_{ij} = GDIST_{ij} - COML_{ij} + DDIST_{ij} - COMM_{ij}$$

where $GDIST_{ij}$ = geographic distance between country *i* and ground-zero country *j*;
$COML_{ij}$ = 1 if there is common language between country *i* and ground-zero country *j*, otherwise 0;
$DDIST_{ij}$ = difference in GDP per capita between country *i* and ground-zero country *j*;
$COMM_{ij}$ = country *i*'s number of common regional bloc membership with ground-zero country *j*.
$GDIST_{ij}$~$N(0,1)$, $COML_{ij}$~$N(0,1)$, $DDIST_{ij}$~$N(0,1)$, $COMM_{ij}$~$N(0,1)$.

Sources:
Data for *GDIST* are obtained from John A. Byers, Swedish University of Agricultural Sciences at Alnarp at the following website: http://www.vsv.slu.se/johnb/java/lat-ong.htm.
Data for *COML* are from the following website: http://www.infoplease.com/ipa/A0855611.html.
Data for *COMM* are calculated from GDP per capita, PPP (purchasing power parity current international dollar) based from the World Bank's *World Development Indicators* database. We use the 1994 data for the Mexican episode, the 1996 data for the Asian crisis, the 1997 data for the Russian crisis, and the 1998 data for the Brazilian episode.
Information on *COMM* is available at the *World Development Indicators* by the World Bank.

membership with the ground-zero countries as a sub-factor ($COMM_{ij}$) of psychic distance, since such common membership may induce coordinated efforts or common reaction on the part of the governments to maintain 'integration,' and thus increase the perceived similarity between two countries. $COMM_{ij}$ is set to be one if country *i* and ground-zero country *j* have at least one common membership at the regional or global level.

Before adding up the sub-factors, we transform the data into a standardized value with a mean of zero and a unit standard deviation:

$$PDIST_{ij} = GDIST_{ij} - COML_{ij} + DDIST_{ij} - COMM_{ij} \quad (7.6)$$

where $GDIST_{ij}$~N(0, 1), $COML_{ij}$~N(0, 1), $DDIST_{ij}$~N(0, 1), $COMM_{ij}$~N(0, 1). Table 7.3 lists countries that are psychologically closest to each crisis-triggering country, according to our calculation.

Institutional Factors

Information on exchange rate regime and capital control is obtained from the IMF *Annual Report on Exchange Arrangements and Exchange Restrictions.* We include two dummy variables for the exchange rate regime factor to see if a rigidly fixed or a freely floating exchange rate system would affect the chance of being affected by a crisis. *EXRFX* is set as one if the exchange rate for a country was pegged to another currency (or other currencies) as of the year-end before each episode. *EXEFL* has a value of one if exchange regime for a country is free floating. Intermediate arrangements, such as pegged-but-adjustable and managed floating and (narrow) bands, are not accounted for by the above two variables. For foreign exchange restrictions, *CACON* takes the value of one if a country was restricting payments for current transactions. Dummy variable *KACON* is set to be one if a country imposed restrictions on capital account transactions, including those on capital market securities and money market instruments, at the end of the year before a certain episode.

EMPIRICAL RESULTS

Table 7.4 lists the countries with the highest values of *CIND* (the 'crisis index') in each episode. As a commonly used measure, the ordinal index *CIND* captures the exchange rate depreciation and loss in international reserves during the crisis time.[14] To see how this index correlates with the proposed explanatory variables, we obtain the Pearson correlation coefficients for all the six samples, which are presented in Table 7.5. Correlations between the crisis index and most of the explanatory variables are statistically significant at the 90 percent level or better. Among the monsoonal effects variables, the change of real effective exchange rate (*REER*) shows statistical significance in four of the five crisis episodes (the Mexican, Russian, Brazilian and Argentine crises). The correlations are positive, as expected. Ratio of broad money over international reserves (*M2_RES*), domestic lending boom variable (*CLM*) and current account balance over GDP (*CA_GDP*) are significantly correlated with *CIND* in at least one of the five episodes. The signs of these correlations are consistent with rational expectations.

For variables that account for the spillover effects, we find significant and positive correlation coefficients for 'direct trade linkage' (*DTRD*) for the Asian and Russian samples. For 'trade competition in third markets' variable (*TCOMP*), the coefficient for the Asian crisis is statistically significant and positive, as expected. The correlation coefficients for the 'competition for funding from the common bank lender' variable (*BCOMP*) for the Mexican, Asian and Argentine samples are all positive at 90 percent confidence level at least.

Among the institutional factors, fixed exchange rate regime (*EXRFX*) is found to be significantly and negatively associated with the crisis index in all the episodes except the Russian and Argentine. On the contrary, floating exchange rate (*EXRFL*) is positively related with *CIND* in the Mexican and Asian samples. Meanwhile, current account constraints (*CACON*) and capital account constraints (*KACON*) do not show any statistical significance in any individual episode. The psychic distance variable (*PDIST*) shows statistically significant and negative correlation with the severity of crisis in all

Table 7.4 Countries with the highest value of crisis index in each crisis episode[a]

	Mexican crisis[b]	Asian crisis[b]	Russian crisis[b]	Brazilian crisis[b]	Argentine crisis[b]
1	Mexico (0.080)[c]	Lao People's Dem.Rep (0.093)	Russia (0.238)[c]	Brazil (0.215)[c]	Argentina (0.206)[c]
2	Brazil (0.048)	Thailand (0.079)[c]	Ukraine (0.133)	Suriname (0.147)	Libya (0.172)
3	Sudan (0.035)	Indonesia (0.077)	Belarus (0.076)	Ecuador (0.124)	Venezuela (0.101)
4	Congo, Dem. Rep. Of (0.034)	Malaysia (0.058)	Ecuador (0.074)	Georgia (0.121)	Angola (0.071)
5	Chad (0.027)	Philippines (0.052)	Kyrgyz Republic (0.071)	Romania (0.073)	Liberia (0.070)
6	Suriname (0.024)	Sudan (0.047)	Lao PDR (0.049)	Croatia (0.057)	South Africa (0.029)
7	Uruguay (0.018)	Turkey (0.038)	Israel (0.046)	Turkey (0.049)	Israel (0.029)
8	Hungary (0.018)	Cambodia (0.038)	Romania (0.045)	Russia (0.040)	Egypt (0.027)
9	Philippines (0.018)	Kenya (0.032)	Burundi (0.043)	Peru (0.038)	Belarus (0.026)
10	Ghana (0.017)	Colombia (0.025)	Colombia (0.041)	Ukraine (0.037)	Uruguay (0.026)

Notes:

[a] Due to data availability, not all the countries in the table are included in the regression analysis.

[b] Crisis indices of ground-zero countries are presented in the table but are not included in the regression analysis, since we are interested only in the severity of crisis in the contagion-affected countries.

[c] Calculated values of crisis index in parentheses.

five episodes. The correlation is the strongest for the Asian sample, whose correlation coefficient is a negative 66 percent at the 99.9 percent confidence level. For the pooled sample, significant relationship is detected for two of the macroeconomic factors (*REER* and *RES_M2*), two spillover variables (*TCOMP* and *BCOMP*), both exchange rate regime variables, capital account restrictions and the psychic distance variable. All the statistically significant coefficients show the expected signs.

Our correlation analysis provides a basis for selecting variables, among all the possible candidates discussed so far and listed in Table 7.5, to enter into our regression analysis. Variables that are not statistically correlated with the dependent variable are removed in the regressions to reduce the extent of missing data. Some of the explanatory variables are believed to be correlated among themselves. For example, countries in the same region usually trade more with each other, and/or at the same time compete for the same exporting markets as well as for funds from the same creditor, thus leading to high correlations between *TCOMP* and *BCOMP*, the measures for competition for the same trade market and common lender respectively. High correlation between trade and financial linkages is well documented by previous work (e.g. Kaminsky and Reinhart,

Table 7.5 Correlation coefficients between the dependent variable and the explanatory variables

	CIND (Mexican)	*CIND* (Asian)	*CIND* (Russian)	*CIND* (Brazilian)	*CIND* (Argentina)	*CIND* (Pooled)
REER	0.291*	0.146	0.542***	0.505***	0.335**	0.224***
M2_RES	−0.327**	0.063	−0.190	−0.214	0.010	−0.059†
CLM	0.174	0.384**	0.228†	0.167	−0.035	0.039
CA_GDP	−0.138	−0.037	0.002	−0.259†	−0.091	−0.018
DTRD	−0.033	0.389**	0.530***	−0.076	0.025	0.002
TCOMP	0.179	0.444***	0.091	−0.135	0.126	0.193***
BCOMP	0.347**	0.441***	0.179	−0.136	0.263*	0.150***
EXRFX	−0.303**	−0.349**	−0.116	−0.311*	−0.131	−0.086**
EXRFL	0.305**	0.290*	−0.199	−0.166	−0.108	0.074**
CACON	0.082	0.022	0.163	0.153	0.148	.0.054†
KACON	0.028	−0.020	0.047	0.122	0.125	0.061*
PDIST	−0.285*	−0.664***	−0.466**	−0.331**	−0.313**	−0.271***

Notes: ***$p < 0.01$, **$p < 0.05$, *$p < 0.10$, and †$p < 0.20$.

Table 7.6 Correlation matrix of key regression variables (the Mexican crisis)

	CIND	*REER*	*M2_RES*	*BCOMP*	*EXRFX*	*EXRFL*	*PDIST*
CIND	1.000						
REER	0.291*	1.000					
M2_RES	−0.327**	−0.429***	1.000				
BCOMP	0.347**	0.360**	−0.305**	1.000			
EXRFX	−0.303**	−0.240	0.260*	**−0.566***	1.000		
EXRFL	0.305**	.0098	−0.131	0.310**	−0.497***	1.000	
PDIST	−0.285*	−0.205	0.131	**−0.574***	0.181	−0.115	1.000

Note: ***$p < 0.01$, **$p < 0.05$, and *$p < 0.10$. In bold are the coefficients that are higher than 0.500, where multicollinearity may be a concern.

2000). Psychic distance is correlated with these trade or financial interdependence variables probably because *PDIST* has a geographic approximation dimension. To detect multicollinearity, we obtain the correlation matrix of the regression variables for each of the six samples. As shown in Tables 7.6–7.11, statistically significant correlations do exist among the explanatory variables in each sample, particularly among *DTRD*, *TCOMP*, *BCOMP* and *PDIST*, as expected. Some of the correlation coefficients are higher than 50 percent, which suggests that a potential multicollinearity problem needs to be addressed on related variables.

Table 7.12 reports estimates of our empirical model from the OLS (ordinary least squares) regressions for the pooled sample and the five subsamples. Due to data availability, each regression involves different numbers of observations, as reported in the table. First we run the regressions without the psychic distance variable, *PDIST*. Then

Table 7.7 Correlation matrix of key regression variables (the Asian crisis)

	CIND	*CLM*	*DTRD*	*TCOMP*	*BCOMP*	*EXRFX*	*EXRFL*	*PDIST*
CIND	1.000							
CLM	0.384**	1.000						
DTRD	0.389**	0.091	1.000					
TCOMP	0.444***	0.168	**0.573*****	1.000				
BCOMP	0.441***	−0.109	**0.572*****	**0.662*****	1.000			
EXRFX	−0.349**	−0.219	−0.226	0.315*	−0.222	1.000		
EXRFL	0.290*	0.249	−0.071	0.101	0.040	−0.343**	1.000	
PDIST	−0.664***	−0.127	**−0.613*****	**−0.511*****	**−0.525*****	0.143	0.057	1.000

Note: ***$p<.01$, **$p<.05$, and *$p<.10$. In bold are the coefficients that are higher than 0.500, where multicollinearity may be a concern.

Table 7.8 Correlation matrix of key regression variables (the Russian crisis)

	CIND	*REER*	*CLM*	*DTRD*	*PDIST*
CIND	1.000				
REER	0.542***	1.000			
CLM	0.228	0.119	1.000		
DTRD	0.530***	0.258	0.436***	1.000	
PDIST	−0.466***	−0.385**	−0.355**	**−0.675*****	1.000

Notes: *** $p<0.01$, **$p<0.05$, and *$p<0.10$. In bold are the coefficients that are higher than 0.500, where multicollinearity may be a concern.

Table 7.9 Correlation matrix of key regression variables (the Brazilian crisis)

	CIND	*REER*	*CA_GDP*	*EXRFX*	*PDIST*
CIND	1.000				
REER	0.505***	1.000			
CA_GDP	−0.259	−0.325*	1.000		
EXRFX	−0.311*	−0.211	−0.002	1.000	
PDIST	−0.331**	−0.370**	0.300*	0.193	1.000

Note: ***$p<0.01$, **$p<0.05$, and *$p<0.10$.

we add *PDIST* to the regression to see if it increases the explanatory power of the model. Multicollinearity diagnostics are performed in the process by estimating the variance inflation factor (VIF) for all the independent variables. We find that none of the VIF values exceeds three, which is well below the rule of thumb threshold value of ten that is indicative of a multicollinearity problem (Neter et al., 1985). To stay on the safe side, however, we follow another rule of thumb by comparing a variable's VIF with the VIF calculated from the R-square of the model as a whole, i.e. $1/(1 - R^2)$, for the following

Table 7.10 Correlation matrix of key regression variables (the Argentine crisis)

	CIND	*REER*	*BCOMP*	*PDIST*
CIND	1.000			
REER	0.335**	1.000		
BCOMP	0.263*	0.158	1.000	
PDIST	−0.313**	−0.154	**0.831*****	0.193

Note: ***$p<0.01$, **$p<0.05$, and *$p<0.10$. In bold are the coefficients that are higher than 0.500, where multicollinearity may be a concern.

four variables: *DTRD, TCOMP, BCOMP* and *PDIST*, as correlation analysis indicates that multicollinearity is most likely to be existing among these variables.[15] As a result, in the Mexican case, we removed the *BCOMP* variable in our estimation since when *PDIST* is present, the VIF values related to the common lender variable were relatively high and the removal of this variable leads to a higher R-square and lower VIF values in general.

As Table 7.12 shows, our estimation generates a number of interesting results for the control variables, namely monsoonal effects and institutional factors. Among the variables for macroeconomic fundamentals, or the monsoonal effects, the real exchange rate variable *REER* obtains positive and statistically significant coefficients for the Russian, Brazilian, Argentina and the pooled samples, showing that a more overvalued currency does lead to more severe financial crisis. This finding is consistent with that obtained in the STV study. The results for the percentage change in the ratio of domestic credits to gross domestic product *CLM* are less compelling, as the coefficient is positive and statistically significant at the 99 percent level only for the Russian sample. The other two monsoonal effects variables – the ratio of broad money to international reserves (*RES_M2*) and the current account balance as a ratio to GDP (*CA_GDP*) – show little statistical significance in their estimated coefficients, although they bear the expected signs.

For the institutional factors, our estimates present mixed findings. A fixed exchange rate regime seems to have a deterring effect on financial crisis contagion, as the coefficients for the Asian and the pooled samples are negative and statistically significant at the 95 percent level when the psychic distance variable is included in the regressions (see Table 7.12). The findings in general confirm the conclusion by Edwards (2000) that a super-fix exchange rate system is less vulnerable to contagion. The results seem to suggest that as long as the market participants perceive a given fixed exchange rate as appropriate and not yet in the 'ripe for attack' zone, fixing the rate can actually reduce speculative activities that are not related to macroeconomic fundamentals and protect a country from the negative impact brought by the turmoil somewhere else. A case in point is China during the Asian crisis. China was essentially maintaining a fixed exchange rate against the dollar and keeping tight control on capital account transactions, which may otherwise destabilize the target peg, at the same time. Many believe that this combination of foreign exchange policy is one of the main reasons why China survived the crisis. Surprisingly, the capital control variable (*CACON*) in our regression, by itself, does not appear to help explain the occurrence of financial contagion. It is used only in the pooled sample and its coefficient is slightly positive at some statistical significance. This result

Table 7.11 Correlation matrix of key regression variables (the pooled sample)

	CIND	*REER*	*M2_RES*	*TCOMP*	*BCOMP*	*EXRFX*	*EXRFL*	*CACON*	*KACON*	*PDIST*
CIND	1.000									
REER	0.224***	1.000								
M2_RES	−0.059	−0.235***	1.000							
TCOMP	0.193***	0.044	0.031	1.000						
BCOMP	0.150***	0.069	−0.084**	0.333***	1.000					
EXRFX	−0.086**	−0.009	0.122**	0.046	−0.169***	1.000				
EXRFL	−0.074**	−0.114**	−0.042	−0.020	−0.024	−0.450***	1.000			
CACON	0.054	0.169***	−0.009	−0.038	−0.106***	0.180***	−0.089***	1.000		
KACON	0.061*	0.015	−0.004	−0.037	−0.050	0.154***	−0.147***	0.469***	1.000	
PDIST	−0.271***	−0.146***	0.052	−0.321***	0.418***	0.004	0.062*	−0.092**	−0.041	1.000

Notes: ***$p < 0.01$, **$p < 0.05$, and *$p < 0.10$.

Table 7.12 Estimation results for gravity model of contagious financial crisis

	CIND (Pooled)		*CIND (Mexico)*		*CIND (Asia)*		*CIND (Russia)*		*CIND (Brazil)*		*CIND (Argentina)*	
	W/O PDIST	*W/ PDIST*	*W/O PDIST*	*W/ PDIST*	*W/O PDIST*	*W/ PDIST*	*W/O PDIST*	*W/ PDIST*	*W/O PDIST*	*W/ PDIST*	*W/O PDIST*	*W/ PDIST*
Intercept	−0.039***	−0.022*	−0.014	−0.015	0.006	0.013***	−0.105***	−0.085***	−0.075	−0.056	−0.035	−0.124*
	(0.014)	(0.012)	(0.012)	(0.012)	(0.005)	(0.005)	(0.024)	(0.026)	(0.041)	(0.043)	(.039)	(0.065)
REER	0.043***	0.035***	0.013	0.008			0.093***	0.075***	0.087**	0.068†	0.039	0.132**
	(0.013)	(0.000)	(0.011)	(0.011)			(0.023)	(0.024)	(0.040)	(0.042)	(0.040)	(0.065)
M2_RES	−0.000	−0.000	−0.000†	−0.000†								
	(.000)	(0.000)	(0.000)	(0.000)								
CLM					−0.002	0.004	0.038***	0.036**				
					(0.011)	(0.012)	(0.014)	(0.014)				
CA_GDP									0.035	0.053		
									(0.050)	(0.054)		
DTRD					0.096	−0.050	0.223†	0.225†				
					(0.218)	(0.228)	(0.135)	(0.142)				
TCOMP	0.021†	−0.004			0.004	−0.015						
	(0.013)	(0.011)			(0.018)	(0.018)						
BCOMP	0.004	−0.019†	−0.000		0.049**	0.014					0.019†	−0.002
	(0.013)	(0.012)	(0.017)		(0.021)	(0.021)					(0.014)	(0.031)
EXRFX	−0.011***	−0.011***	0.000	0.005	−0.008*	-0.011**			−0.003	−0.003		
	(0.004)	(0.003)	(0.005)	(0.004)	(0.005)	(0.004)			(0.010)	(0.010)		
EXRFL	−0.006†	−0.003	0.006†	0.006†	0.000	0.000						
	(0.004)	(0.003)	(0.005)	(0.004)	(0.005)	(0.005)						
CACON	−0.000	0.001										
	(0.003)	(0.003)										
KACON	0.000	−0.002										
	(0.004)	(0.004)										
PDIST		−0.002***		−0.001***		−0.003***		−0.003**		−0.003†		−0.001
		(0.001)		(0.000)		(0.0001)		(0.002)		(0.002)		(0.001)
F-statistic	4.52***	5.39 ***	1.89†	3.19**	3.11***	4.56***	9.04***	7.44***	1.75†	2.01†	1.74	2.97**
R^2	0.12	0.17	0.17	0.21	0.16	0.28	0.28	0.32	0.09	0.14	0.06	0.12
No. of obs.	267	253	51	66	102	90	75	67	59	56	59	44

Note: Pooled OLS. Standard errors in parentheses. ***$p < 0.01$, **$p < 0.05$, *$p < 0.10$, and †$p < .20$.

is contrary to the belief that when financial liberalization is more limited there is smaller overshooting in capital flows (Bacchetta and Wincoop, 1998). However, the insignificant results we found on the capital controls variables are consistent with those of Caramazza et al. (2000). A floating exchange rate regime appears to be unrelated to the financial crisis contagion since its coefficients in the Mexican and the Asian samples, the only samples that employ the variable, register little statistical significance.

The spillover effects, or the trade and financial linkages variables, represent one of the two important aspects of our empirical framework formulated after the gravity model. However, the evidence to support the hypothesis that closer linkages lead to greater contagion is generally not robust. We do not find statistically significant evidence (on *DTRD*) to show that a currency crisis in one country results in an increased trade deficit and a loss in international reserves on the part of its trading partners. Meanwhile, there is no evidence that third market trade competition *TCOMP* has any impact on financial crisis contagion. We do find some support for the common lender variable *BCOMP* in the Asian sample when the psychic distance variable is not included in the regression. The finding that third market competition for trade and for funds has little or no relevance to financial crisis is contrary to what has been found in previous studies. For example, Rijckeghem and Weder (2001) document that the bank-lending channel had a pronounced effect in contagion during the Asia financial crisis.

It is interesting to note that, for the Asian sample, the variable for the common lender competition, *BCOMP*, loses statistical significance when the psychic distance variable is added to the regression. In other words, with the presence of an instrument that combines the geographic distance, developmental level, language similarity and economic integration, the presumably relevant bank-lending channel no longer plays a role in explaining the spillover effect during the Asian financial crisis. This observation suggests that the behavioral factor – psychic distance – rather than the 'real' economic linkages, as highlighted in other studies, may be the real contributor to financial contagion in some crisis episodes. Therefore financial contagion can be partly attributed to irrational herd behavior of financial agents who assess financial stability on the basis of perceived similarity, rather than financial linkage through a common lender, or trade linkage through competition in the same third market.

The significance of the psychic distance variable is obvious in the pooled sample and the three financial crises initiated in Mexico, Asia and Russia. The coefficients estimated based on the above-mentioned samples are all negative and statistically significant at the 95 percent level. For the Brazilian episode, the coefficient for the psychic distance variable is less robust and significant only at the 85 percent level. The behavioral predictor is not statistically significant based on the Argentine crisis.

The findings based on four of our six samples all provide support for the hypothesis that financial crisis is less contagious with greater psychic distance between countries or, conversely, that countries that are believed to be more psychologically close are prone to financial contagion. Of all the components of the psychic distance variable – cultural distance as measured by common language, common membership, geographical proximity, and the similarity in economic development levels – the importance of the latter two are particularly self-explanatory. As Table 7.4 indicates, Latin American countries were more affected by the Mexican and Brazilian crises, several Southeast Asian countries were hit by the Asian financial crisis initiated in Thailand, and East European countries experienced some turmoil after the occurrence of Russian financial crisis. Those countries that were affected severely were at more or less the same economic development levels – in most cases developing countries or transitional economies are among those most severely affected.

The contribution of the psychic distance variable to our empirical analysis is further evidenced by the increase in the *F*-statistics and the coefficients of determination of our regressions. The global *F*-tests show that when the psychic distance variable is included in our regressions, the significance levels increase in five samples while remaining at the highest level (99 percent) for two. Also, the empirical model can explain more variance by the inclusion of the psychic distance variable in all six samples. This is particularly so in the case of the Asian crisis, where the coefficient of determination of the model increases from 16 percent to 28 percent.

Meanwhile, the role of the behavioral predictor is particularly robust in the earlier stage of our test period, when crises that originated in Mexico, Thailand and Russia spread to other nations through 'contagion.' The gradually weakening impact of psychic distance as detected in the two 'later' episodes in our test period may suggest the weakening and even diminishing effect of true contagion. This is actually consistent with Taylor's (2007) description of the development/progress of the 'mega' turmoil, which he refers to as 'eight-year crisis.' In his summary, there were three episodes of financial crisis contagion during the eight-year period from 1994 to 2002. The tequila effect initiated in Mexico in 1994–95 and spread to Argentina in 1995–96. The Asian crisis contagion started in Thailand in 1997–98 and hit Indonesia, Malaysia and Korea during the same time period. The Russian contagion in 1998 could be connected to crises in Brazil (1998–2002), Romania (1998–99), Ecuador (1998–99) and Argentina (1999–2001). Then there are two seemingly unrelated setbacks in Turkey (2000–01) and Uruguay (2002) afterwards. There have been no major currency crises or contagion of this nature since 2002, except the major financial crisis originated in the debt markets in 2008.

Our result suggests that if there is financial crisis contagion, much of the change in investors' expectations about a particular country is probably related to a 'psychic distance' factor, which is essentially not linked to macroeconomic fundamentals, trade linkages and international banking activities. Perceived 'similarity' leads to the perception of increased risk in 'similar' countries. That is, investors tend to believe that a country 'similar' to the crisis country is equally vulnerable and equally likely to suffer from withdrawals of funds and speculative attacks.

CONCLUDING REMARKS

The objective of this chapter is to investigate the factors that contribute to financial crisis contagion. We synthesize the literature on contagion and add a behavioral dimension by combining all major explanatory variables into an adapted gravity model borrowed from physics. Our hypothesis is that financial crisis contagion is positively related to trade and financial linkages and negatively related to psychic distance between crisis-originating countries and crisis-affected countries, when macroeconomic fundamentals or monsoonal effects and institutional factors are controlled for. The psychic distance variable is of key interest in our study since it has not been employed specifically in prior studies. Our empirical test is carried out using data from the five financial crisis stages in the eight-year period between 1994 and 2002.

Our empirical work yields a number of interesting findings. First, we find that, among all the macroeconomic fundamentals, the real exchange rate has the most significant relevance to contagion. When a country's currency is more overvalued, the country is more likely to be affected by a financial crisis occurring in other countries. Broad money relative to international reserves and domestic credit expansion are also found to contribute to financial crisis contagion, although the statistical significance varies across samples. Second, a fixed exchange rate system shows a negative and significant impact on contagion for the pooled sample, suggesting that such a system has some preventive power over contagion. On the other hand, other institutional variables, such as a floating exchange rate system or capital controls, are found to be insignificant. Third, we find some evidence that competition for common fund lenders, one of designated 'pull' factors in our gravity model, is a contributing factor to contagion in the Asian and the pooled samples. The significance of variables showing direct trade linkage and competition for common trade markets is not robust, though. Finally, the psychic distance variable is found to be the single most significant factor among all the variables, contributing to the overall explanatory power of the model. The role of the behavioral predictor is especially robust in the Mexican, Asian and Russian crises, when financial crisis contagion was believed to have been prevalent. An overall sample pooling data for all the five crisis episodes lends support to the same conclusion. Our study provides evidence that financial crisis contagion is a result of herding behavior among investors who make decisions based on perceived similarities among countries. The finding also shows the importance of the psychological perceptions in investors' behavior that leads to financial contagion. Moreover, the behavioral approach we have adopted in this study may shed new light on the analysis of financial crisis contagion in general, such as the one the world has been going through in 2008–09.

NOTES

1. Some have argued that crises induced by common fundamental weaknesses are not really 'contagious' since a crisis in one country does not cause a crisis in another directly.
2. Some studies (Kaminsky and Reinhart, 1999; Pesenti and Tille, 2000) have viewed currency crises and banking crises as being intertwined. Most, if not all, financial crises are exemplified by banking crises and are coupled with economic downturns. The 2008–09 financial crisis is a case in point.
3. For example, the flow of funds from banks to 29 emerging markets dropped from $120 billion in 1996 to −$29 billion in 1998 (Rijckeghem and Weder, 2001).
4. In this chapter, herding behavior is not defined in its restrictive sense. For example, if A sells off its assets in Mexico, and B obviously follows this action by selling off in Argentina, then B is regarded as herding. We regard this behavior as 'herding across markets.'
5. The definition of psychic distance has changed substantially since its first use in Beckerman's (1956) study on the distribution of international trade. See Evans and Mavondo (2002) for a discussion of such changes.
6. See Reuter (2009) for a survey of the literature on culture and finance.
7. One important dimension of psychic distance is macroeconomic similarity, which may overlap with the macroeconomic weaknesses measured by monsoonal effects. So, in constructing the psychic distance variable, it is not included.
8. See Askari et al. (2003) for a discussion of the application of the gravity model to international trade studies.

9. Alternative selections of intervals to construct the crisis index are available in the literature. Also, there are alternative ways to compute the crisis index. For example, some studies incorporate only currency depreciation in their calculation of the crisis index (Ahluwalia, 2000; Caramazza et al., 2000).
10. The Glick and Rose (1999) paper uses the absolute values of exports in the second component of the expression. Similar to the modification method adopted by Rijckeghem and Weder (2000) in their measurement of 'competition for common lender,' we replace the absolute values with the proportion values, which are the value of exports to a common third market over the total exports from a given country. Compared with the absolute values, the use of share values can measure the relative importance of a third market to a given country on the same scale. So the problem of vastly different export volumes can be eliminated.
11. Great circle distance is the shortest distance between two points on a sphere. It is often used to measure the distance between two locations on the surface of the earth.
12. Based on Hofstede's (1980, 1983) cultural dimensions theory, Kogut and Singh (1988) develop a four-dimensional cultural scale as a measure of cultural distance. However, Hofstede's (1980, 1983) studies provide the cultural scale for only about 50 countries. Data for Russia, one of the ground-zero countries, are not available. It is not possible to calculate the cultural distance between Russian and other countries based on the scale provided by the Hofstede studies. So we use only common language as an indicator of cultural distance due to the data limitation.
13. As a convention, if a country's per capita income does not achieve the World Bank's threshold for a high-income country, this country can be regarded as an emerging market.
14. Although commonly used, *CIND* is not a perfect measure of the severity of financial crisis. For example, in the Mexican episode, the tequila effect triggered a severe banking crisis in Argentina. But Argentina is not on the list probably because the effect of banking crisis is not explicitly captured by the index. Other possible outcomes of a financial crisis, such as a sharp decline in stock market price or other asset market prices, are not incorporated in the index, either. But overall, as shown in Table 7.4, the majority of the obvious victims of each episode appear on the list as expected.
15. The rule is that any variables whose VIF values exceed the model's VIF are more closely related to the other independent variables than they are to the dependent variable. Thus, variables whose VIF values exceed the model's VIF value are likely candidates for suffering from multicollinearity.

REFERENCES

Ahluwalia, P. (2000) 'Discriminating contagion: an alternative explanation of contagious currency crises in emerging markets,' *IMF Working Paper* 00/14, International Monetary Fund, Washington, DC.

Alves, Ricardo Pinheiro (2008), 'Behavioural determinants of foreign direct investment,' Ph.D. thesis.

Askari, H., J. Forrer, H. Teegen and J. Yang (2003), *U.S. Economic Sanctions: Philosophy and Efficacy*, Westport, CT: Praeger.

Bacchetta, P. and E.V. Wincoop (1998) 'Capital flows to emerging markets: liberalization, overshooting, and volatility,' NBER Working Paper 6530, National Bureau of Economic Research, Cambridge, MA.

Beckerman, W. (1956), 'Distance and the pattern of inter-European trade', *Review of Economics and Statistics*, **38** (1), 31–40.

Bikhchandani, S. and S. Sharma (2000), 'Herd behavior in financial markets: a review', IMF Working Paper 00/48, International Monetary Fund, Washington, DC.

Calvo, G.A. (2001), 'Capital markets and the exchange rate with special reference to the dollarization debate in Latin America,' *Journal of Money, Credit and Banking*, **33** (2), 312–34.

Calvo, G.A. and E.G. Mendoza (2000), 'Rational contagion and the globalization of securities markets', *Journal of International Economics*, **51** (1), 79–113.

Caramazza, F., L. Ricci and R. Salgado (2000), 'Trade and financial contagion in currency crises', IMF Working Paper 00/55, International Monetary Fund, Washington, DC.

Christiansen, H. (2000), 'International financial contagion,' *Financial Market Trends*, **76**, 65–108.

Dow, D. (2000), 'A note on psychological distance and export market selection,' *Journal of International Marketing*, **8**(1), 51–64.

Dow, Douglas and Amal Karunaratna (2006), 'Developing a multidimensional instrument to measure psychic distance stimuli,' *Journal of International Business Studies*, **33**, 578–602.

Drazen, A. (2000), 'Political contagion in currency crises,' in P. Krugman (ed.), *Currency Crises*, Chicago, IL: University of Chicago Press, pp. 47–70.

Edwards, S. (2000), 'Interest rates, contagion and capital controls,' NBER Working Paper 7801, National Bureau of Economic Research, Cambridge, MA.

Ellis, Paul D. (2008), 'Does psychic distance moderate the market size–entry sequence relationship?,' *Journal of International Business Studies*, **39**, 351–69.

Evans, Jody and Felix T. Mavondo (2002), 'Psychic distance and organizational performance: an empirical examination of international retailing operations,' *Journal of International Business Studies*, **33**(3), 515–32.

Flood, R. and P. Garber (1984), 'Collapsing exchange rate regimes: some linear examples,' *Journal of International Economics*, **17**, 1–13.

Gilens, M. (1997), 'Teaching notes for introductory statistics (fall 1997),' Department of Statistics, Yale University; see http://www.stat.yale.edu/Courses/1997-98/101/linreg.htm, accessed 18 June 2005.

Glick, R. and A. Rose (1999), 'Contagion and trade: why are currency crises regional?,' *Journal of International Money and Finance*, **18** (4), 603–17.

Guiso, Luigi, Paola Sapienza and Luigi Zingales (2006), 'Does culture affect economic outcomes?,' *Journal of Economic Perspectives*, **20** (2), 23–48.

Hernandez, L.F. and R.O. Valdes (2001), 'What drives contagion: trade, neighborhood, or financial links?,' *International Review of Financial Analysis*, **10** (3), 203–18.

Hofstede, G. (1980), *Cultural Consequences: International Differences in Work Related Values*, Beverly Hills, CA: Sage Publications.

Hofstede, G. (1983), 'The cultural relativity of organizational practices and theories,' *Journal of International Business Studies*, **14** (2), 75–89.

Hufbauer, G.C., K.A. Elliott, T. Cyrus and E. Winston (1997), 'US economic sanctions: their impact on trade, jobs and wages,' Institute for International Economics Working Paper.

Johanson, J. and J. Vahlne (1977), 'On the internationalization process of firms: a critical analysis,' *Journal of International Business Studies*, **8** (1), 23–32.

Johanson, J. and F. Wiedersheim-Paul (1975), 'The internationalization process of the firm: four Swedish cases,' *Journal of Management Studies*, **12** (3), 305–22.

Kaminsky, G.L. and C.M. Reinhart (1999), 'The twice crises: the causes of banking and balance-of-payments problems,' *American Economic Review*, **89** (3), 473–500.

Kaminsky, G.L. and C.M. Reinhart (2000), 'On crises, contagion, and confusion,' *Journal of International Economics*, **51**, 145–68.

Kim, W. and S. Wei (1999), 'Foreign portfolio investors before and during a crisis,' NBER Working Paper 6968, National Bureau of Economic Research, Cambridge, MA.

King, M. and Wadhwani, S. (1990), 'Transmission of volatility between stock markets,' *Review of Financial Studies*, **3** (1), 5–33.

Kogut, B. and H. Singh (1988), 'The effect of national culture on the choice of entry mode,' *Journal of International Business Studies*, **19** (3), 411–32.

Krugman, P. (1979), 'A model of balance-of-payment crises,' *Journal of Money, Credit and Banking*, **11** (3), 311–25.

Krugman, P. (1996), 'Are currency crises self-fulfilling?,' *NBER Macroeconomics Annual*, pp. 345–78.

Masson, P. (1998) 'Contagion. Moosoonal effects, spillovers, and jumps between multiple equilibria,' IMF Working Paper 98/142, International Monetary Fund, Washington, DC.

Mishkin, F.S. (2003), 'Financial policies and the prevention of financial crises in emerging market countries,' in M. Feldstein (ed.), *Economic and Financial Crises in Emerging Market Countries*, Chicago, IL: University of Chicago Press, pp. 93–130.

Morris, S. and H.S. Shin (1998), 'Unique equilibrium in a model of self-fulfilling speculative attacks,' *American Economic Review*, **88** (3), 587–97.

Neter, J., W. Wasserman and M.H. Kutner (1985), *Applied Linear Statistical Models* (2nd edn), Homewood, IL: Irwin.

O'Grady, S. and H.W. Lane (1996), 'The psychic distance paradox,' *Journal of International Business Studies*, **27** (2), 309–33.

Obstfeld, M. (1994), 'Risk-taking, global diversification, and growth,' *American Economic Review*, **84**, 1310–30.

Obstfeld, M. (1997), 'Destabilizing effects of exchange rate escape clauses,' *Journal of International Economics*, **43** (1), 61–77.

Ojala, Arto and Pasi Tyrvainen (2009), 'Impact of psychic distance to the internationalization behavior of knowledge-intensive SMEs,' *European Business Review*, **21** (3), 263–77.

Pesenti, Paolo and Cedric Tille (2000), 'The economics of currency crises and contagion: an introduction,' *Economic Policy Review* (Federal Reserve Bank of New York), **6** (3), 3–16.

Reisen, Helmut (2008), 'The fallout from the financial crisis (1): emerging markets under stress,' *Policy Insights*, No. **83** (December), OECD Development Center.

Reuter, Charles-Henri (2009), 'Culture and finance: a survey of the literature and a synthesis,' Ph.D. dissertation, European School of Management.

Rigobon, R. (2002), 'Contagion: how to measure it?,' in S. Edwards and J. Frankel (eds), *Preventing Currency Crises in Emerging Markets*, Chicago, IL: The University Chicago Press, pp. 269–334.
Rijckeghem, C.V. and B. Weder (2001), 'Sources of contagion: is it finance or trade?,' *Journal of International Economics*, **54** (2), 293–308.
Rizzi, Joseph V. (2008), 'Behavioral basis of the financial crisis,' *Journal of Applied Finance*, Fall/Winter 2008, 84–96.
Rosati, Simonetta and Stefania Secola (2006), 'Explaining cross-border large-value payment flows: evidence from TARGET and EURO1 data,' *Journal of Banking & Finance*, **30**, 1753–82.
Sachs, J., A. Tornell and A. Velasco (1996), 'Financial crises in emerging markets: the lessons from 1995,' *Brookings Papers*, **27** (1), 147–99.
Sbracia, M. and A. Zaghini (2001), 'Expectations and information in second generation currency crises models,' *Economic Modelling*, **18** (2), 203–22.
Schinasi, G.J. and R.T. Smith (2000), 'Portfolio diversification, leverage, and financial contagion,' *IMF Staff Papers*, **47** (2), 159–76.
Sethi, S.P. (1971), 'Comparative cluster analysis for world markets,' *Journal of Marketing Research*, **8**, 348–54.
Shiller, R.J. (1998), 'Human behavior and the efficiency of financial systems,' NBER Working Paper 6375, National Bureau of Economic Research, Cambridge, MA.
Shiller, R.J. (2003), 'From efficient markets theory to behavioral finance,' *Journal of Economic Perspectives*, **17** (1), 83–104.
Taylor, J.B. (2007), 'Lessons of the financial crisis for the design of the new international financial architecture,' Keynote address, Conference on the 2002 Uruguayan Financial Crisis and its Aftermath, http://www.stanford.edu/~johntayl/UruguayKeynote.pdf, accessed 10 September 2009.
Wall, H.J. (1999), 'Using the gravity model to estimate the costs of protection,' *Review of the Federal Reserve Bank of St. Louis*, **81** (1), 33–40.
Wysocki Jr, Bernard (1995), 'Some painful lessons on emerging markets,' *Wall Street Journal*, 18 September.
Yang, J. (1997), 'U.S. interest rate and portfolio investments in Latin American,' *Global Business and Financial Review*, **1**, 37–42.

APPENDIX: SYMBOLIC NOTATIONS USED

CIND	Crisis index
EXD	Exchange-rate depreciation
RLOS	Loss in international reserves
REER	Real effective exchange rate appreciation
RES_M2	Ratio of international reserves relative to broad money
CLM	Percentage change in the ratio of domestic claims to GDP
CA_GDP	Current account balance as a percentage of GDP
TCOMP	Trade competition in third markets
DTRD	Direct bilateral trade linkage
BCOMP	Competition for funding from the same bank lenders
PDIST	Psychic distance
GDIST	Geographic distance
COML	Common language (cultural distance)
DDIST	Difference in development level
COMM	Common membership
EXRFX	Rigidly fixed exchange rate regime
EXEFL	Freely floating exchange rate system
CACON	Current account restriction
KACON	Capital account restriction

PART II

BEHAVIOR IN THE INVESTMENT PROCESS

8 The effects of higher transaction costs on trader behavior

Ryan Garvey and Anthony Murphy

When traders place risky bets in securities markets, they incur transaction costs. Part of the cost of trading is explicit (e.g. broker commission) and the other part is implicit (e.g. dealer bid–ask spread). While implicit costs are frequently analyzed in financial studies, explicit costs receive little attention. This is likely due to researchers being able to estimate implicit costs from publicly available trade and quote data sources (e.g. NYSE TAQ),[1] while explicit costs can only be analyzed by obtaining proprietary data from a brokerage firm. In addition, public data sources do not reveal trader identity, which makes it difficult to examine the influence of (implicit and/or explicit) transaction costs on individual trader behavior.

In our study, we use proprietary data from a US brokerage firm that caters to active traders to examine how differences in explicit costs affect trader behavior. The data provide an ideal setting for isolating the effects of explicit costs on trader behavior. Although the retail and institutional traders in this firm have the same overall objective (to maximize their earnings from intraday trading), they pay very different commissions to the broker. Retail traders, who trade their own capital, pay a standard commission rate per trade. On the other hand, institutional traders, who trade the firm's capital, negotiate their commissions with the firm and pay few (or no) commissions per trade. Our examination of trader behavior shows that active retail traders focus their trading on higher-priced stocks and hold onto their trades much longer, which leads to larger absolute price changes (and profits) per round trip than those of institutional traders. The higher transaction costs paid by retail traders cause them to trade less, but when they do trade, they seem to take on considerably more risk in order to cover their higher cost of trading.

The observed differences in the trading behavior of active retail and institutional traders are a rational (albeit not necessarily optimal) response to the different trading costs they incur. For example, if the retail traders in our sample traded in the same manner as the institutional traders – trading frequently but taking on less risk – they would be highly unprofitable, due to the substantial commissions they would incur. However, if many of the retail traders switched to working for a firm, rather than for themselves, they would be better off. Over time, we expect traders to migrate towards the most cost-effective way to trade.

Our study is related to behavioral studies examining how retail (see, e.g., Odean 1998, 1999) and institutional (see, e.g., Coval and Shumway, 2005; Locke and Mann, 2005) market participants make risky choices in securities markets. However, the data used in previous studies in this area do not generally contain any information on transaction costs, and so researchers tend to omit them from their analyses (or, in some cases, estimate them). The role of transaction costs in traders' decision-making processes is not well understood and there is little research devoted to this topic because of data limitations.

If transaction costs are small and/or non-transparent, traders are probably likely to overlook them in their decisions. For example, Kahneman and Tversky (1979) note that, when confronted with complex risky choices, decision makers will often simplify the problem by reducing their options. Along these lines, Garvey and Wu (2008) find that institutional traders are much more reluctant to realize a gross loss rather than a net loss. However, the institutional traders studied in Garvey and Wu incur minimal costs when they trade, their trading costs are not easily calculable, and their full cost of trading is not precisely known until after execution occurs. In our study, retail traders pay higher commissions, their trading costs are straightforward to calculate, and their cost of trading is known *ex ante*.

The remainder of this study is organized as follows. In the next section, we describe the data. The empirical results, examining the effects of higher transaction costs on trader behavior, are reported in the section after that. The final section provides concluding remarks.

DATA

We obtained our data from a US broker–dealer who provides clients with direct market access (DMA) to the US equity markets. Brokers providing DMA tend to attract more active traders, because they provide sophisticated trading tools and software that allow their clients to choose where and how to execute their orders. Active traders, who trade through DMA brokers, account for a sizeable portion of trading volume in US equity markets. For example, Goldberg and Lupercio (2004) find that active (25+ trades per day) retail and institutional traders, who trade through brokers providing DMA, account for approximately 40 percent of Nasdaq and NYSE trading volume.[2]

The size (trade volume) of the active trader market is somewhat puzzling because research generally suggests that active trading lowers investor performance (e.g. Barber and Odean, 2000). Although many active traders do lose money, research shows that some active traders are able to consistently make money (e.g. Garvey and Murphy, 2005). The principal characteristic that distinguishes an active trader from a long-term investor is their mind-set. Many active traders hold stocks for short periods – minutes or hours, and seldom overnight – closing out positions for small profits. In fact, the brokerage firm used in this study specifically markets its trading system to equity day traders who open and close almost all positions within the same day. It provides training courses in this area. A constant message on the firm's website, and in its trading courses, is that traders should close out all their open stock positions by the end of the day. In the data set, most traders adhere to this trading strategy.

Our data are for the period 8 March through 13 June 2000. During this period, there were 68 trading days and two market holidays. In total, the data relate to 1386 traders (account holders) and 413 399 equity trades.[3] Thus the average trader executed 298 trades in 68 days. The data are in the form of a transaction database that, for each trade, lists the trader identification, the time the order was executed, the order type, the action taken, the volume, the price, the market where the trade was executed, the contra-party on the trade, the number of parties on the other side of the trade, whether margin was used on the trade, the location of the account in the USA (branch office or remote location) or abroad, and most importantly for our study, whether the account was an institutional account (i.e. the trader was trading the capital of the firm) or a retail account (i.e. the trader was trading own capital). There are 49 institutional accounts and 1337 retail accounts in our data set.

We also know the commissions charged on all 303 206 trades made by the 1337 retail account holders. However, only 4 percent of the 110 193 trades originating from the 49 institutional accounts are labeled with a designated commission. Most institutional traders had variable commission plans, in which their commissions were based on the number of trades conducted over a given time period (so their accounts are billed at the end of the month). Therefore the exact commissions are not available for each of these institutional trades. The retail traders did not have this option and they paid a set commission fee of $25 per trade. In addition, they sometimes paid a small fee for accessing certain US equity markets. On average, the retail traders pay $26 per trade.

In our data set, over 87 percent of the institutional trades were generated by 15 proprietary traders, who traded the capital of the trading firm from whom we obtained the data. The trading manager stated that the traders did not pay commissions *per se*.[4] Instead the traders were charged a small fee per trade to cover execution costs as well as other costs associated with running a proprietary trading desk (clearing fees, technology fees etc.). This fee typically ranged from $1.50 to $3.00 per trade. The traders would then receive 50 percent of their trading profits while the firm received the other half.[5]

The trading manager confirmed that traders employed by the firm were, by and large, allowed to trade as they wished, and our observation of these traders confirmed that this was the case. Of course, their trading activities are monitored and, as noted above, their compensation is directly linked to their performance, just as it is for active retail traders. The traders were hired, fired and retained based on their performance. Unprofitable traders did not last long. We can confirm that the traders were employing a variety of strategies, by examining differences in the stocks they traded, frequency of trading, trade size, holding time, order routing method and so on. As a group, their trading strategies were also very different from those of the retail traders.

We do not have the profit or loss on each round-trip transaction in our data set. To determine this, we matched the opening trade for each stock in each trader's account with the subsequent trade of the opposite sign each day. Traders do not always open and close positions with two trades. A trader can lay off part of an open position, or combine a closing transaction with an opening transaction. Regardless of whether the traders opened, closed, or simultaneously opened and closed a position, we searched forward in time each day until the opening position was closed out, keeping track of accumulated inventory and the corresponding prices paid or received. We used these matched trades to calculate the profits of each round trip trade.

We matched the majority of the trades in our data set using this matching algorithm. Over 80 percent of trades were part of a simple sequence of trades – an opening trade matched by a corresponding closing trade for the same amount of shares. For example, a trader buys 2000 shares of Microsoft and then turns around and sells 2000 shares of Microsoft. These two trades would comprise a sequence of trades resulting in one round-trip trade (one opening trade and one closing or round-trip trade). Another 7 percent of trades were part of a sequence of trades where the inventory was not set to zero at the end of the day, although one or more round trip(s) had occurred. For example, suppose a trader makes three trades during the day. First, the trader buys 1000 shares of Microsoft. Second, the trader buys 400 shares of Microsoft. Lastly, the trader sells 1200 shares of Microsoft. The third trade would be the actual round-trip trade. However, 200 shares of inventory (from the second trade) are unaccounted for and not factored into our profitability calculations. These three trades would be an example of the 7 percent of trades where the inventory was not set to zero. Of course, the 200 shares may be sold the following trading day. The 13 percent of unmatched trades (over the full 68-day trading period) are most likely long-term investments.

EMPIRICAL RESULTS

Both the retail and institutional traders in our data set trade with the same overall objective – to generate maximum intraday trading profits. However, despite their common goal, there are significant differences in how they go about achieving this. Figure 8.1 highlights some of the differences. First, the retail traders trade higher-priced stocks, which, in our sample period, tended to experience larger price fluctuations. For example, the top five most heavily traded stocks and their closing stock price on the first day of the sample period for the retail traders are: QCOM ($129.12), CSCO ($132.38), JDSU ($273.00), ORCL ($83.12) and RMBS ($363.00). For the institutional traders they are: WCOM ($44.51), DELL ($46.94), ORCL ($83.12), GBLX ($53.31) and ERICY ($100.00). The average price of the stocks traded by the retail traders is much higher than that traded by the institutional traders ($85 versus $46). The difference in the average prices, along with all of the other mean differences shown in Figures 8.1 and 8.2, is significantly differently from zero at the 1 percent level. Consistent with retail traders' focus on higher-priced stocks is the larger absolute price change per round trip that they experience. For example, the average absolute round-trip change in absolute prices is $1.20 for retail traders, as opposed to $0.15 for institutional traders.

Retail traders trade higher priced stocks, yet they also trade in smaller sizes. The average trade size for retail traders is 540 shares and for institutional traders 978 shares. It is not surprising that institutional traders trade in larger trade sizes.[6] In fact, it is a little surprising that the difference in trade size is not wider still, given that institutional traders have access to the firm's capital whereas retail traders do not. The relatively small difference in trade size may be due to differences in information that the two types of traders have. Financial research suggests that individual investors and traders differ from institutional ones in their level of financial sophistication. Institutional market participants are often considered better informed.[7] Moreover, the stealth trading hypothesis suggests that better-informed traders may trade in medium trade sizes (similar to the average trade size we observe) so as not to reveal their information. Chakravarty (2001) finds evidence of this with institutional trades, using NYSE audit trail data.

The round-trip holding time difference between retail and institutional traders is quite large. On average, institutional traders hold onto their trades for 381 seconds (or about six and a half minutes), while retail hold onto their trades for about 2647 seconds (or about 44 minutes). Both groups of traders suffer from the disposition effect, i.e.

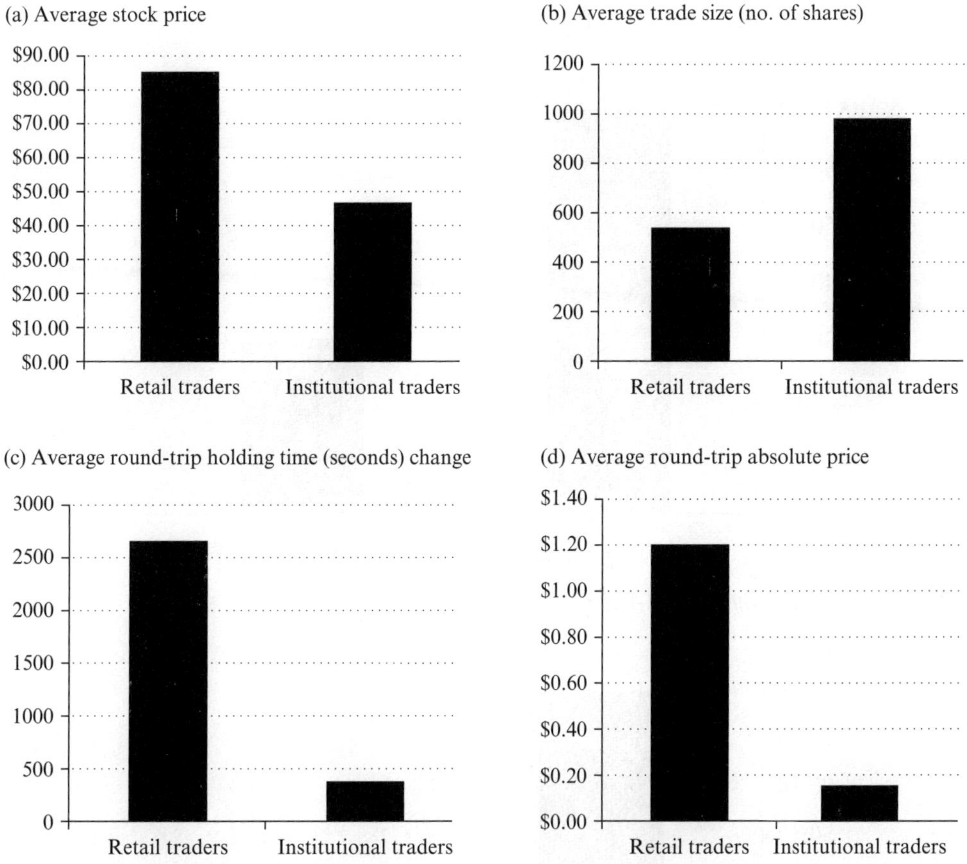

Figure 8.1 Trading differences between retail and institutional traders

the tendency for traders to sell their winning positions at a faster rate than their losing ones. This is consistent with prior research examining the holding-time patterns of retail market participants (e.g. Odean, 1998) and institutional market participants (e.g. Garvey and Murphy, 2004b). In our sample data, the retail traders hold their winning positions for 2543 seconds and their losing positions for 2861 seconds. The institutional traders hold their winners for 348 seconds and their losers for 513 seconds.

If both groups of traders intend to close out their positions by end of the trading day, why then is the difference in the duration of round trips between the two groups so large? We surmise that the difference in trading costs is the main reason. Since retail traders pay much higher commissions, they hold trades longer to experience larger price swings per round trip and offset their higher trading costs. In doing so, they are of course taking on more risk. On average, retail traders experience an absolute price change per round trip eight times larger than that of institutional traders. As a result, they generate larger profits per round trip. Figure 8.2 shows the average difference in profits per round trip between retail traders and institutional traders. The average round-trip (gross) profit for retail traders is $71.26 and for institutional traders $30.93.

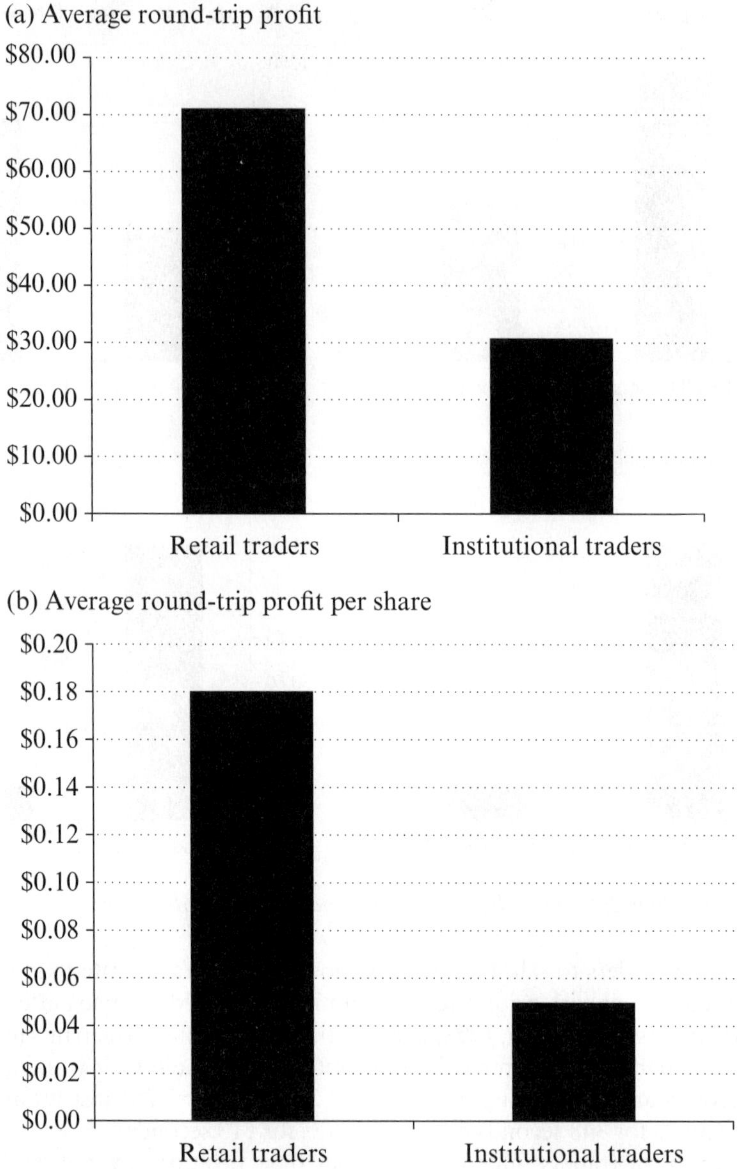

Figure 8.2 Differences in the profitability of retail and institutional traders

On a profit per share basis, the average round trip profit for retail (institutional) traders is \$0.18 (\$0.05).[8]

There are far more retail traders than institutional traders in our data set, and there are differences in how actively the retail traders trade. Because of this, one could argue that our comparison may not be very meaningful, since some of the retail account holders are pretty inactive. Accordingly, in order to check the robustness of our results, we segregate

Table 8.1 Retail trader profitability

Round-trip trading profits before commissions	$9080959
Commissions on round trips	$6453531
Other commissions on long-term trades	$1438088
Round-trip trading profits after all commissions	$1189340
Mean round-trip profit after (net of) commission	$20.62*
Median round-trip profit after commission	$10.00*
Mean profit per share after commission	−$0.001
Median profit per share after commission	$0.02*
Percentage of profitable accounts after commission	49
Percentage of profitable accounts before commission	66
Percentage of profitable round-trip trades after commission	52
Percentage of profitable round-trip trades before commission	57

Note: * Significantly different from zero at the 1% level.

the retail traders based on how actively they trade and examine the behavior of the more active ones. During the 68-day trading period covered by our data, 72 retail traders made more than 999 trades, 95 made between 500 and 999 trades, 167 made between 250 and 499 trades, 277 made between 100 and 249 trades, and 731 made fewer than 100 trades. Despite the differences in trading activity, the results for price, trade, size, holding time, trading profits and price change are consistent across all groups of retail traders.[9]

Retail traders appear to take on more risk than institutional traders in order to cover their higher costs of trading. However, when trading costs are factored in, retail traders are not that profitable. For example, only 52 percent of round trips are profitable after commission. Table 8.1 shows that retail traders generated $9080 959 in gross intraday round-trip trading profits over our sample period, but it cost $6453 531 to achieve those profits. In addition, they paid another $1438 088 in commissions on their long-term trades (those held overnight). These commissions severely reduced their overall profitability. Indeed, the higher trading costs incurred with trading one's own capital will probably eventually force many retail traders to stop trading for themselves. Although 66 percent of the retail accounts and 57 percent of their trades are profitable before commissions, the net profitability figures drop to 49 percent of accounts and 52 percent of trades. Of course, these profitability figures may change somewhat when long-term trades are factored in. However, the more active traders closed out nearly all of their positions by the end of the day (recall more than 80 percent of the trades are matched intraday).

In Table 8.2, we examine the trading behavior and performance of the 15 most active retail and institutional traders. As previously noted, over 87 percent of the institutional trades originated from these 15 proprietary traders. In contrast to retail traders, the proprietary traders are less concerned about their level of trading because they trade the firm's capital and they incur few costs when they do trade. The average price, trade size, holding time, absolute price change and round-trip profit results for the most active retail and institutional traders are similar to the overall group results. It is interesting

Table 8.2 Differences in the trading behavior and profitability of the 15 most active retail and institutional traders

	Institutional traders	Retail traders
Total profitability		
Number of trades	96323	37585
Intraday trading profits before commission	$1431626	$1413083
Commission	$288969*	$1014229
Trading profits after commission	$1142657*	$398854
Trader 'take-home' trading profits	$571329*	$398854
Trading profits before commissions		
Average profit per share	$0.03	$0.19
Average profit per round trip	$24.33	$79.53
Average gain per winning round trip	$85.43	$507.20
Average loss per losing round trip	−$100.46	−$417.53
Frequency of winning round trips	62%	52%
Number of profitable accounts	15	14
Round-trip trading strategies		
Average trade price	$42.43	$81.49
Average trade size (no. of shares)	1010	669
Average holding time (seconds)	197	1563
Average absolute price change	$0.08	$0.93

Notes: * Estimated commissions and net profitability figures assuming the (maximum) $3 commission per trade suggested by the trading manager of the broker–dealer.

The 15 institutional traders trade the capital of the broker–dealer. An interview with the trading manager of the firm revealed that these traders pay a maximum of $3 commission per trade to cover the cost of running the proprietary trading desk. They are then paid half of their trading profits. The commission and after-commission profitability figures for institutional traders are calculated using a figure of $3 commission per trade. Thus the commission and the net profitability figures for institutional traders represent the upper bounds and lower bounds respectively.

that both groups generate approximately the same amount of trading profits, excluding commissions, yet the institutional traders trade three times as much to earn their profits and are able to 'take home' a higher amount. The retail traders generate $1413626 in profits before commissions and pay $1014 229 in commissions. Thus the retail traders 'take home' $398854. The institutional traders generate $1431 626 in profits before commissions and pay an estimated $288969 in commissions (using the $3 upper bound commission figure suggested by the trading manager). Because the proprietary traders' profits are typically split in half with the firm, their estimated take home is $571329.

The differences in trading costs and compensation structures between retail and institutional traders raises the issue of whether the traders are better off self-employed or employed by the firm. We explore this issue in greater depth by examining the profits and commissions of the individual 30 traders. While 11 of the retail traders incur more in commissions than they actually earn, only three of the institutional traders are unable to cover their cost of trading. If the 15 retail traders traded as much as the institutional

Table 8.3 The profitability of the most active 15 retail and institutional traders

15 most active retail traders – by trader			15 most active institutional traders – by trader		
Number of trades	Total commission ($)	Profit after commission ($)	Number of trades	Estimated upper bound for total commission ($)*	Estimated lower bound for profits after commission ($)*
3,577+	95710	23166	14304	42912	263470
3,494+	88973	51030	13039	39117	190225
2,799	71235	123367	11528	34584	80983
2,665	72178	85601	10012	30036	203399
2,513	58419	101943	9211	27633	128108
2,499+	54726	−51284	7849	23547	93286
2,337+	64439	−68729	6511	19533	83928
2,283+	66773	13925	5265	15795	14955
2,239+	61258	−45196	4558	13674	−2901
2,229+	72628	41071	4538	13614	45255
2,220+	59935	−28046	3024	9072	−2490
2,216	54392	118860	2271	6813	−4203
2,197+	69588	26520	1927	5781	25398
2,177+	59778	−38471	1227	3681	22081
2,140+	64198	45097	1059	3177	1161
Totals					
37,585	1014229	398854	96323	288969	1142657

Notes: See Table 8.2. * Estimated based on a (maximum) $3 commission per trade. + The retail trader would be better off working for the broker–dealer rather than trading for themselves.

traders, clearly they would not be profitable because they pay commissions of $26 on average per trade. And if the institutional traders had to pay this $26 per trade commission rate, they would not be profitable either. However, the compensation structure for the two types of traders suggests that 11 of the 15 retail traders would be better off trading for the firm than for themselves. If this pattern persisted over time, then we would naturally expect many of the retail traders to switch to trading for a firm, assuming the barriers to entry for this option remain relatively low. However, this may not be in the best interest of the broker–dealer! Table 8.3 shows that the firm earns a good deal more in commissions from the 15 most active retail traders ($1.014 million) than it does from commissions and its 50 percent share of the trading profits of the 15 most active institutional/proprietary traders ($0.860 million, using an upper-bound commission figure of $3).

CONCLUSION

In this study, we examine the effects of higher commissions on active trader behavior. Our findings are based on a unique data set of retail and institutional US equity traders over a 68-day trading period in the second quarter of 2000. Although both types of traders aim to maximize their earnings from intraday trading, they go about it differently. Retail traders concentrate their trading on higher-priced stocks, hold onto their positions longer, and experience larger absolute price changes on their round trips. Consequently, the round-trip gains and losses of retail traders are much larger than those of institutional traders. The higher transaction costs paid by retail traders force them to trade less, but when they do trade, they appear to take on considerably more risk in order to cover their higher cost of trading, which averages $26 per trade.

Although our findings are based on the behavior of active US stock traders, we suspect that these results can be generalized to other market participants as well. All market participants are confronted with some sort of costs when they trade securities. Our research suggests that the extent of these costs can significantly impact how much people trade, and how much risk they take on. Differences in trading costs also matter when choosing between working for oneself as a retail trader (self-employment) and working as a proprietary trader (employee). For example, we find that many profitable retail traders, who pay a high cost to trade yet keep all of their net profits, would be better off working for a firm, paying low (or no) commissions and receiving a percentage of their trading profits.

If higher trading costs influence traders' risky choices, than our results have important implications for behavioral finance research. Studies show that traders often classify their trades in terms of gains and losses, and they accordingly tend to act differently. For example, the disposition effect, the tendency of traders to realize their gains too early and hold their losses too long, is based on traders classifying trades into winners and losers. Higher trading costs will alter the classification of winning and losing trades, thereby influencing the way different market participants trade. Studying the effect of different trading costs on behavior in other financial markets is an interesting area for future research.

NOTES

1. See Bessembinder (2003) for a discussion on the limitations of using trade and quote data to estimate trading costs.
2. This figure has remained relatively constant over the years. For example, over the previous three years these traders accounted for 35 percent, 35 percent and 32 percent of Nasdaq and NYSE trading volume respectively. Source: Bear Stearns annual report on DMA brokers and the active trader market.
3. A small percentage of trades (8253 or less than 2 percent of all transactions) were executed on options. We exclude these from our analysis.
4. We spent some time at the firm's headquarters in the New York City area observing both retail and institutional traders trade, and talking with the firm's management so that we could better prepare this study.
5. Proprietary trading firms structure their traders' compensation differently. Some firms do not charge their traders per trade, although the traders receive a smaller take-home percentage.
6. The average dollar value traded for retail (institutional) traders is $36 582 ($50 048).
7. Chakravarty (2001) discusses some of the academic literature that emphasizes this point. He finds that

institutional traders account for a majority of the cumulative price impact on medium-sized trades. The trades we observe here, both retail and institutional, are considered medium-sized. Chan and Lakonishok (1995) also find that institutional traders are better informed. They find that a sequence of institutional block trades leads to a significant impact on stock prices.

8. The average gain, before commissions, is $512 for the retail traders and $110 for the institutional traders. The average loss before commissions is −$550 for the retail traders and −$125 for the institutional traders.
9. These results are omitted for brevity, but they are available in Garvey and Murphy (2004a).

REFERENCES

Barber, B.M. and T. Odean (2000), 'Trading is hazardous to your wealth,' *Journal of Finance*, **55** (2), 773–806.

Bessembinder, H. (2003), 'Issues in assessing trade execution costs,' *Journal of Financial Markets*, **6** (3), 233–57.

Chakravarty, S. (2001), 'Stealth trading: which traders' trades move stock prices?,' *Journal of Financial Economics*, **61** (2), 289–307.

Chan, L.K. and J. Lakonishok (1995), 'The behavior of stock prices around institutional trades,' *Journal of Finance*, **50** (4), 1147–74.

Coval J. and T. Shumway (2005), 'Do behavioral biases affect prices?,' *Journal of Finance*, **60** (1), 1–34.

Garvey, R. and A. Murphy (2004a), 'Commissions matter: the trading behavior of individual and institutional active traders,' *Journal of Behavioral Finance*, **5** (4), 214–21.

Garvey, R. and A. Murphy (2004b), 'Are professional traders too slow to realize their losses?,' *Financial Analysts Journal*, **60** (4), 45–53.

Garvey, R. and A. Murphy (2005), 'The profitability of active stock traders,' *Journal of Applied Finance*, **15** (1), 93–100.

Garvey, R. and F. Wu (2008), 'Are trading costs invisible in trading decisions?,' *Journal of Trading*, **2** (3), 23–33.

Goldberg, D. and A. Lupercio (2004), 'Cruising at 30,000, semi-pro numbers level off, but trading volumes rise,' Bear Stearns Company Report, August.

Kahneman, D. and A. Tversky (1979), 'Prospect theory: an analysis of decision under risk,' *Econometrica*, **47** (2), 263–91.

Locke, P. and S. Mann (2005), 'Professional trader discipline and trade disposition,' *Journal of Financial Economics*, **76** (2), 401–44.

Odean, T. (1998), 'Are investors reluctant to realize their losses?,' *Journal of Finance*, **53** (5), 1775–98.

Odean, T. (1999), 'Do investors trade too much?,' *American Economic Review*, **89** (5), 1279–98.

9 *Homo communitatis*: a rigorous foundation for behavioral finance

H. Joel Jeffrey

INTRODUCTION

Behavioral finance, and behavioral economics in general, is based on the insight that the fundamental conceptual model of neoclassical economics, the rational utility-maximizing *homo economicus*, is unrealistic. Just as the model of planets following circular orbits had to be replaced with one based on elliptical orbits, human behavior, including economic behavior and non-economic behavior with economic impacts, is not describable in terms of rational self-interest, even if enhanced by boundedness.

This raises the question of what behavioral factors to include. Barberis and Thaler, for example, note that for guidance on behavioral models economists rely on cognitive psychologists for insight into beliefs and preferences (Barberis and Thaler, 2003, p. 1054). The basic thesis of this chapter is that the range of factors that affect economic actions in general, and financial decisions in particular, is much broader than the subject matter of cognitive psychology, and that therefore both good science and predictive power demand a rigorous framework incorporating as many of these factors as possible.

The question of what factors must be included is inextricably bound up with the fundamental fact that a very wide range of human actions have economic consequences. An example, discussed in more detail below, is the Tongan *fakaafe*, a feast in honor of a visiting Wesleyan minister (Bennardo, 1996, pp. 307–12). These feasts involve a good deal of food gathering and preparation, labor, and consumption of food, and so are quintessentially economic activities. However, they take place when the minister comes to a village, a schedule based solely on social and religious concerns as evaluated by the minister. Because of this fundamental logical connection between economic and non-economic activities, it is impossible to set an *a priori* limit on what behaviorally significant factors must be included in our economic and finance models. In addition, as the range under consideration expands, concerns about how to maintain a mathematically rigorous and empirically justified framework increase.

Work to date has primarily focused on the cognitive aspect of behavior, using concepts and methods of cognitive psychology. Intrinsic motivation and identity have been included to an extent, and incorporation of fairness concerns in the utility function is well known, but efforts have been piecemeal, in the sense that there has been no single systematic framework incorporating cognition, motivation, social values and identity, as well as other relevant aspects of human behavior. Indeed, the discipline in widest use in behavioral economics and finance, cognitive psychology, rejects *in toto* the concept of motivation, and is similarly silent on the concept of identity. Identity illustrates an important additional difficulty in expanding the model while maintaining rigor: how does one rigorously formulate identity, a concept widely discussed but never mathematically formulated in any of the disciplines of psychology?

In previous work we presented the community-practice model, a rigorous framework for creating economic simulations incorporating a much wider range of such behavioral factors (Jeffrey, 2006). This chapter is an expansion of that work, in four ways:

1. The model has been enhanced to incorporate personality characteristics, a formalization of the concept of identity, and a significantly expanded treatment of motivation and value.
2. The simulation algorithm has been enhanced to incorporate the new aspects of the model.
3. The model is used to analyze certain foundational issues in behavioral economics and finance, including use of the concept of mathematical probability, and to develop a new formulation of action under uncertainty.
4. It is further used to develop a new formulation of value as a vector, rather than scalar, quantity.

Less importantly, in recognition of and in deliberate contrast to *homo economicus*, we have renamed the model *homo communitatis*.

Homo communitatis is a rigorous formal model of human behavior, both individually and in groups, that incorporates intrinsic or expressive behavior, identity and all the other aspects of individual behavior that affect decisions and the impact of the group on individual choice: families, professions, firms, work teams, religions, subcultures and so on. Having these factors represented formally enables formal treatment of a much wider range of economic-related and finance-related behavior. This includes significantly more realistic simulations incorporating a much wider range of variables, particularly when the economic facts and quantities of interest are affected by, and affect, other, non-economic, factors.

INCORPORATION OF NON-ECONOMIC CONCEPTS

Every discipline is based on a certain set of concepts central to it – the states, objects, processes and relationships (including quantitative attributes) between them. Work in that discipline is devoted to elaborating those concepts and their logical relationships, and, to one extent or another, empirical study of the applicability and usefulness of the concepts and derivations to the real world. Simulation is based on explicit formal representation of those concepts. Thus, in chemistry, a simulation of the Belouzhov–Zabotinsky chemical reaction involves representing chemical objects, quantities and mathematically stated relationships between them (Thompson and Stewart, 1986). In computer science, a simulation of a computer system uses formal variables to represent parts of the system and the processing of input. In each case, the concepts are elements of the underlying theoretical framework that defines the discipline.

In modeling of economic systems, this logic leads naturally to the conclusion that the objects, facts, processes, conditions and relations among them to be included and formalized are economic ones. In neoclassical economics, the factors included are limited to those involved in calculation of self-interest, limited by bounds on actors' ability to assess it. Because economic systems address facts and issues directly involving human behavior, limiting analysis or simulation to purely economic facts and processes has been subject to two kinds of objections.

First, the disciplines of psychology, sociology and anthropology (to name only three) all address human behavior, and the psychologists, sociologists and anthropologists all tell us that economic factors alone are not sufficient to describe and explain human behavior (Abelson, 1996; Ossorio, 2006, 1981; Putman, 1981; Spradley, 1979). These disciplines tell us that prediction of behavior, the central concern of economists of all kinds, cannot be made based solely on analyzing economic variables. Second, persons observably act in ways that are not in their self-interest and are not seen by themselves as being so. The kinds of facts cited in such objections include the empirical fact that people engage in 'expressive' behaviors (also called 'intrinsic practices' in sociology and psychology), that they are commonly observed to act counter to their economic self-interest due to the influence of identity and group membership, that they commonly engage in actions at considerable cost to themselves due to ethical and moral considerations, and so on. Further, social scientists have long known that the multiplicity of memberships in significant groups in modern societies – individuals holding positions in a family, a culture, a subculture, an organization, a profession, a church, and several other social groups, all with their own coherence and identity – presents the individual with a multitude of influences on behavior, both personal and group-based, many of which may conflict. The psychologists, sociologists and anthropologists note that all of these factors observably affect behaviors with economic consequences, and as a result, solely economic models are incomplete. For example, in his study of the spread of birth control, Chattoe (2003) points out that that, even with all other factors taken into account, the choice to adopt birth-control practices depends critically on non-economic factors such as the potential adopter's religion and the devoutness of their beliefs.

While some economists (and philosophers) take the position that these other factors are explainable in terms of self-interest and economic impact, there seems little doubt that if the goal is accurate prediction of economic variables, these factors need to be included in some form, whether regarded as legitimately separate factors or 'epiphenomenal' summaries of fundamentally economic concepts. Practically speaking, we have little choice but to include these factors in our models, unless we happen to be working in the relatively narrow range of behaviors in which only *prima facie* economic factors are present.

It can be argued that while inclusion of a wider range of factors may be necessary in principle, in practice the net effect on economic or financial outcomes, when averaged over a population, is insignificant. This is possible. However, whether or not behavioral effects outside the economic realm 'wash out' is fundamentally an empirical, not a theoretical, question, to be answered by observation and experiment, and without a rigorous and comprehensive framework incorporating these factors and their relationships, there is no systematic and precise basis for formulating experiments or gathering and analyzing data. For example, we know that racial prejudice can and often does lead a loan officer to assess risk differently for members of certain races, a fact leading to a large number of economic consequences. However, we also know that individuals in an organization are expected to adhere to the principles governing choices in that organization. As a result, a racially biased loan officer in a committed race-neutral lending organization has conflicting influences on his or her decisions. Further, these influences are of more than one kind: cognitive, in that a biased officer may actually judge the risk higher or lower based on race; and motivational, in having motivation to approve or deny a loan in spite of assessed risk level. A comprehensive model incorporating these various factors permits mathematical and/or simulation studies of lending choices and evaluation of results against empirical data. Without such a model, neither step can be done precisely and systematically. The customary way to include other factors in economic models has been to expand the domain of the utility function, but this does not reduce the need for a rigorous and comprehensive model to use in constructing more sophisticated and elaborate functions.

The *fakaafe* example above introduced this phenomenon. A second example illustrates an important characteristic of it: the need to represent the process–subprocess structure of the activities of interest. Consider a computer software maker building a document management system for a large bank. One of the processes generating load on the computing resources is transfer of files from the document repository. The software maker needs to model the design, to find out whether it can handle the load that actual use will impose on the system. To do this, they must find out precisely what the primary users will use the system for. To achieve a useful level of accuracy, the model must include not only the specific commands, but the entire hierarchically structured set of bank work practices in which the file transfer is a step: by transferring files, the bank officer is getting ready to do a site visit to a client company; by doing a site visit the officer is doing due diligence on the customer; due diligence is a step in carrying out the mission (the practice) of the loan division, namely, to invest in low-risk businesses. Load on the document management system from the file-transfer activity is produced when the larger practice of carrying out a site visit takes place. While in principle empirical data on file transfer might exist, in practice what can be accurately estimated is the number of site visits. Thus, having accurate input data relies on having an accurate model of non-economic business practices, that is, practices that may have economic inputs and impacts, but do not themselves involve the overt use and manipulation of economic facts, objects and processes.

In this chapter we use the analysis of human behavior and communities by two psychologists, P.G. Ossorio and A.O. Putman, as the basis of a formal model incorporating a significantly wider range of facts and processes that affect economic behaviors and choices in a single, formally articulated, systematic framework (Ossorio, 2006, Putman, 1981). Descriptions in this framework may be used, directly or indirectly, as the basis for simulations that explicitly represent these several kinds of factors and their relationships.

HOMO COMMUNITATIS

A systematic, comprehensive framework incorporating as wide as possible a range of factors involved in human behavior is, as might be expected, not simple. In the interests of clarity, therefore, we first give a brief summary of its core concepts, without formalism.

Individuals engage in actions intended to bring about some change in their circumstances, and they do this because they value the new circumstance more than the existing one. ('Value,' however, does not mean 'self-interest'; self-interest is one type of value. This is discussed extensively below.)

Engaging in action involves having the necessary facts and concepts and the requisite skills.

The action taken depends in part on the personality characteristics of the actor: attitudes, traits and priorities.

Every person is a member of one or more communities, i.e. coherent groups of persons such as families, businesses, ethnic groups, nations, work teams and so on, and furthermore occupies one or more positions in every community of which they are a member: father (in their family), cousin (in their extended family), investment advisor (in a bank), certified financial analyst (in their profession), citizen (of their country), deacon (in their church) and so on.

Every action a person does is an instance of engaging in a practice of a community, a community of which they are a member.

Communities have priorities, principles governing choices to which members are expected to adhere. For example, Catholics are expected to eschew birth control, Mormons alcohol, Muslims charging interest. The direct effect of a choice principle on actor choice is that it gives the actor motivation to engage or not to engage in a practice.

In the paradigm case, and in the vast majority of actual cases, a person knows what they are doing and chooses to do it, in light of the reasons they have to engage in various alternative actions. (By this we do not imply 'rationality,' any 'decision-making process,' or any episode of deliberation. It is simply a reminder that an action is always selected from one of several perceived alternatives.) Choice is always a choice between alternative actions, i.e. between engaging in practices (or versions of a practice) actually available to the actor (and known to be).

The specific connections to behavioral economics and finance are:

- Some of the actions, i.e. practices engaged in, directly impact economic facts, in that the outcome of the practice is a change in an economic or financial situation. Decisions to invest in a security, and not in others, are of this sort.
- A wide range of actions produce goods or provide services, the focus of economics and, indirectly, finance. Thus economically significant behavior is a subset of behavior in general, and there is no reason to expect, *a priori*, that this subset is simpler than behavior in general.
- Many actions, whether economic or not, require the use of 'resources' quantified in economics – capital, raw materials etc. – and are therefore impacted by economic behaviors.

The *Homo Communitatis* Model in Detail

In more detail, the elements of the *homo communitatis* model are spelt out below.

The central concept of the model is that everything a person does is an instance of engaging in a *social practice* of a *community* of which they are a member. Following customary anthropological use, the social practices of the community are the organized patterns of action recognizable by members of the community as a single, known, repeatable, 'done thing.' (Both of these key concepts are formalized below.)

Everything that happens in such a group – a community – is an instance of engaging in an *instantiated version* of a social practice. A version is a set of other, smaller, practices such that accomplishing all of the set is a case of engaging in the overall practice. Investing in a particular mutual fund, for example, requires engaging in several other, smaller, practices: deciding on criteria on which to base the choice, getting a list of potential funds, gathering data to assess the degree to which each fund meets each criterion, actually making the choice, and buying shares.

The practices of a community are organized hierarchically. Intrinsic practices (following customary usage in psychology) are those practices engaged in simply because the actor occupies the position they do (or, equivalently, has the relationship they do with some other member of the community). Intrinsic practices are at the top of the hierarchy, and are engaged in by engaging in other, smaller, or more limited practices, the *instrumental* ones. This logical structure includes optional subpractices and alternate ways of accomplishing the same component practice. For example, in a city one often has the option of walking, driving or taking a train to a destination.

Each practice itself has a complex structure, incorporating several factors in addition to the practice–subpractice structure. These factors include the knowledge necessary to carry out the practice, the necessary skills, relevant personality characteristics, the logical roles in the practice, and rules governing the eligibility of actual persons and objects to fill those roles.

'Knowledge' includes both what the person takes to be the case and the concepts they must have to carry out the action, i.e. the distinctions they must able to make. The seminal work of Tversky and Kahneman on judgment under uncertainty, for example, deals with what persons take to be the facts, under various conditions (Tversky and Kahneman, 1974). 'What the actor takes to be the case' includes what are informally called perceptions, beliefs, verified fact, and more generally whatever the actor is prepared, to one degree or another, to act on. However, this is not a version of the customary model of beliefs updated by Bayesian rules, correctly or incorrectly. It is not assumed that what the actor takes to be the case is in any way a probabilistic concept, that probabilities must necessarily be associated with an item of knowledge, or that any rules involving probability calculations are appropriate models of what persons actually do. In the 'Applications' section below we discuss this issue in more detail, including when and how the use of probabilities is justified.

In addition to its practices, what makes a community what it is includes the concepts, cultural choice principles and recognizable positions in the community, both official and unofficial. These aspects of a community affect member choices of what practices to engage in and how to do so.

An individual person is a member of several different communities (as illustrated by Chattoe, 2003), and commonly occupies several positions in the same community. For example, a typical academic situation is to be both teacher and researcher in one's department and both spouse and parent in one's family.

Each position occupied by an individual gives him or her motivation to engage in social practices intrinsic to that position. These are the intrinsic practices of the community. Chess players play chess; mountain climbers climb mountains; CEOs devise corporate strategies. Refining the central observation that a person is at all times engaged in a practice of some community, each individual is, at all times, engaged in a practice *intrinsic to some position he or she holds in a community.*

Each individual has a number of relationships with members of the community including those due to their position (e.g. having the position of financial advisor means one has the relationship of financial advisor–client. This can be formalized as follows: having relationship R_i means that one is tautologically motivated to engage in social practices $P_i^1, P_i^2, \ldots, P_i^n$, to degree $d_i^1, \ldots, d_i^n$. More generally, for each relationship R_i and each practice P_j, P_j is consistent with relationship R_i to degree d_i^j, where $-1 \leq d_i^j \leq 1$, where -1 denotes that P_j is the strongest possible violation of R_i and $+1$ denotes that it is the strongest possible affirmation of it. Further, the relationships R_i are not limited to physically definable ones; as is done in mathematical logic, any relationship may be formally incorporated in a model of phenomena of interest by the mathematical device of giving it a formal name, and measuring the values $d_i^1, \ldots, d_i^n$.

In general, motivations $\mu_1, \ldots, \mu_m$, may be of the following four types:

- *Prudential*: what is in the individual's direct self-interest. The *homo economicus* model is a commitment to restricting analyses to this type of motivation.
- *Hedonic*: doing something for the pleasure or 'the fun of it.' Examples include riding a roller coaster, watching a sporting event or reading 'for pleasure.'
- *Ethical*: doing something, or refraining from doing something, for ethical reasons. Ethical motivations are frequently the subject of philosophical argument, with some philosophers and other social scientists arguing that ethical motivations are pre-scientific intuitions or convenient fictions to be replaced with prudential (self-interest) motivations. We regard this philosophical argument as specious, but for the purposes of this chapter it does not matter: analyses, including simulations, must take these factors into account in some fashion, whether or not it is possible in principle to replace them with groups of other motivations.
- *Esthetic*: motivation to do, or not do, something on the basis of:
  - The traditional concept of beauty or esthetic value
  - Appropriateness or 'fittingness' of the action with one's position. An important kind of appropriateness motivation is expressive behavior (intrinsic practices). A chess player playing chess, or a grandfather doting on his granddaughter (Abelson, 1996), is acting appropriately on their status (in the chess and family communities, respectively). Having motivation to engage in a practice due to having a particular relationship is a form of appropriateness motivation: the practice fits the relationship.

  As with ethical motivations, some argue that esthetic motivations ought properly to be replaced with self-interest ones, but for our purposes the point is that these motivations need to be included in a comprehensive model of human behavior in some form.

Noting that an actor may have motivation to engage or not engage in a practice, it is convenient to model motivations mathematically by $-1.0 \leq \mu_i \leq +1.0$, the strongest possible motivation to not engage or engage in a practice. No assumptions are made as to consistency or inconsistency of these values; an actor typically has multiple motivations, of various strengths, to engage in more than one action, including the strongest possible motivation to engage in distinct and conflicting practices.

An individual is always engaging in a version of a practice that is one of the several in which he or she could engage in this situation, knows at least some of those possible practices, and chooses to engage in this one.

The specific practice chosen depends in a complex way on the actor's motivations to engage in each practice, including the following:

- The choice principles of each community of which the individual is a member. Choice principles give a member motivation to engage or not engage in a practice.
- The individual's personal characteristics: attitudes, traits and states.
- The hedonic, prudential, ethical and esthetic value of each practice to the individual, including the case in which a practice is expressive of a status the individual holds.
- The degree to which each of the individual's relationships gives motivation to them to engage or not engage in each practice.
- The degree to which each practice is an expression of a status *S* that the individual has need to affirm. Need may be due to having been treated in a way that will, unless countered, result in loss of the status *S*, or due to having not engaged in any of the practices intrinsic to the status *S* for a period of time. A chess player who has not played chess for some time, for example, will have stronger motivation to play.

The novel aspect of *homo communitatis* is not the various concepts of communities, relationships, motivation or identity; each of these is a routine part of the subject matter of anthropology, psychology, political science and all of the disciplines whose focus is human action, individually or in groups. What is novel is that (1) all of these aspects of group and individual behavior are included and are explicitly formulated, rather than being background intuitions, and (2) the concepts of the model are articulated in a single formal framework that incorporates all of the relationships between them.

Example: an Anniversary Celebration

We illustrate the *homo communitatis* model with a common event: a couple in the USA goes out to dinner to celebrate their wedding anniversary. They are both professionals, and have children, aged 8 and 10. The children want to spend the weekend at the nearby city known for its many water parks. The husband has an opportunity to attend an important professional conference, and the wife has a legal brief due the following week. In addition, their church has a picnic this weekend. Of these practices in these six communities (family, each spouse's company, each spouse's profession, and church), the couple decides to celebrate their anniversary by dining out. They go to a nice restaurant, have wine with their meal, and end with dessert.

'Eating dessert' illustrates the concept of a practice: it is immediately recognizable in the USA as a known, repeatable, 'done thing' – if two people have dessert in separate places on separate occasions, both are instances of the practice 'have dessert.' We see the hierarchical structure of the practices: going out to dinner at a nice restaurant is a practice (a known, repeatable, pattern of action); to do it, one engages in several other, smaller, practices, such as going to the restaurant, dining and paying; dining in turn consists of several other, yet smaller, component practices, often called 'courses' – have salad, have soup, have the main course, and have dessert.

Many of the subpractices involved are optional or may be achieved via alternate practices. The couple must go to the restaurant (or it is not an instance of the practice 'dining out'), but they may walk, take a car, take a train, or take a taxi; salad, soup, dessert and wine are all optional. There are therefore many possible combinations of subpractices that could be ways to dine out, but only some of them are so recognized by the community. For example, if the couple went to the restaurant, ordered a bottle of wine, drank it and had dessert, that would not be counted as an instance of dining out, although it might well be considered an instance of going out for dessert. The combinations of subpractices, including the optional ways of accomplishing some practice, that are recognized by members of the community as ways of doing the practice are the valid *versions* of it.

When the couple actually has a bottle of wine and their meal, specific objects fill the logical roles of 'main course,' 'dessert,' 'the wine' and so forth. Thus, what actually occurs here is that the couple having the dinner is engaging in an instantiated version of the practice of going out to celebrate their anniversary.

Celebrating a wedding anniversary, the largest practice in this example, is a clear example of an 'expressive' or 'intrinsic' practice. A couple celebrates their anniversary as an expression of their relationship, not in order to gain something or avoid some consequence. (A dinner that was actually a step in forming a business partnership, or a means for one of the couple to avoid the other's anger, would not be an anniversary celebration.) This is therefore an example of an intrinsic practice with economic consequences. Conversely, economic facts will play a role in the practice, for the couple's choice of restaurant, and perhaps the food and wine selected, may be affected by their economic resources, a widely recognized phenomenon in the restaurant industry during the recession of 2008–09.

Going out to dinner is only one way to celebrate an anniversary. Two of the better-known alternatives are buying gifts for each other and going on a cruise. These actions bear no resemblance to each other, and yet are all recognizable, by members of US society, as ways of engaging in the practice of celebrating one's anniversary, a fact of considerable importance in the jewelry and travel industries. Following Ossorio (2005), we term these major varieties of a practice its 'paradigms'.

Finally, let us note that the practice of ordering wine with the meal reflects the identity, that is, the community membership, of the individuals. The acceptability of wine as part of dining out is a principle in the community that is modern US society, but a number of communities do not share it. If the individuals dining out are members of one or more of those communities, they are making a choice to act as a member of one community or another. This is the situation that Chattoe describes in his discussion of the choice by a Catholic to adopt birth control (Chattoe, 2003). This is a second form of choice that may be impacted by non-economic facts but with a potentially very large economic impact.

Box 9.1 displays the hierarchical structure of the practice and the sets of subpractices that are counted as actual instances of dining out.

BOX 9.1 THE SOCIAL PRACTICE OF CELEBRATING AN ANNIVERSARY

Couple celebrates their wedding anniversary
- Paradigm 1: Couple buys gifts for each other
- Paradigm 2: Couple dines at a nice restaurant
- Paradigm 3: Couple goes on cruise together

Paradigm 2: Couple dines at a nice restaurant

Stages:

1. Couple goes to restaurant
   a. (Option) By car
   b. (Option) By train
   c. (Option) Walking
2. Couple gets seated
3. (Optional) Couple examines menu
4. (Optional) Couple examines wine menu
5. (Optional) Couple orders wine
6. Couple orders food
7. Couple eats meal together
   a. Husband eats meal
      i. (Optional) Person eats salad
      ii. (Optional) Person eats soup
      iii. Person eats main course
      iv. (Optional) Person eats dessert
      v. (Optional) Person drinks wine
   b. Wife eats meal
      i. (Optional) Person eats salad
      ii. (Optional) Person eats soup
      iii. Person eats main course
      iv. (Optional) Person eats dessert
      v. (Optional) Person drinks wine
   c. Husband and wife converse

   Versions: a, b, c
   Constraint: Stages a and b are concurrent

8. Couple pays
9. Couple departs restaurant

Versions: 1, 2, 3, 4, 5, 6, 7, 8, 9
1, 2, 3, 6, 7, 8, 9
1, 2, 6, 7, 8, 9
1, 2, 3, 4, 6, 7, 8, 9
1, 2, 5, 6, 7, 8, 9

(Although the subpractices of each practice are numbered sequentially for ease of reference, no actual temporal relationships are assumed, whether sequential or parallel. Any such relationships are explicitly represented as formal constraints on the occurrence of subpractices.)

Formalizing *Homo Communitatis*

Homo communitatis analyzes actions in terms of communities and practices of those communities. In this section I formalize those concepts.

A 'community' (Putman) is, formally, a 6-tuple:

$$<M, P, Cp, S, C, W> \tag{9.1}$$

where:
- M = members
- P = practices
- Cp = choice principles
- S = statuses
- C = concepts
- W = world

The 'practices' parameter specifies, by formal name, the social practices of the community of interest. Practices encompass everything that a member of that community can do, *as* a member of that community; whatever they do will be engaging in one or more of the practices of the community.

The 'choice principles' of a community constitute one of the key ways in which it differs from other communities. This is therefore one of the items of information that must be included in a representation of a community whose economics are of interest, because these community-specific values govern choices of members, as well as individual preferences.

The 'statuses' parameter represents the recognizable positions in the community. These are all the positions identifiable by members of that community, both formal an informal. 'President,' 'Senator,' 'husband,' 'child,' 'suicide bomber,' 'respected leader,' 'doctor,' 'farmer' and so on are all names of positions in different communities. Central to the concept of a Status is that each status has associated with it certain practices that are intrinsic to a person in that status, that is, practices done simply because the member has that status. A person in that status will therefore always have motivation to engage in that practice.

The 'concepts' of the community are the distinctions acted on by the members of the community in question – by engaging in the practices. They are specified by formal name and, when further description is necessary, by specifying a formal description D, a list of the major constituents of the item (by formal name) and the (formally named) relationships between them. (A more complete specification of these descriptions may be found in Ossorio, 2005, and a complete mathematical formulation in Jeffrey, 2010.)

W represents the community's 'world'. This is not what it may at first seem, a list of all the items available to members. It is a specification (once again, by formal name) of the major constituents of the community's world and their relationships. In practice, the W parameter represents the most fundamental distinctions found in the practices of the community. In a business, for example, these major constituents are often 'customers,' 'regulators' and 'competitors.'

The observation that each person is a member of several communities, and occupies one or more positions in each, gives us the means of formalizing identity: actor A's identity is the set $\{S \mid S \text{ is a status of } A \text{ in a community of which } A \text{ is a member}\}$.

Practices have an extensive logical structure, because although they have a process aspect, and processes have subprocesses, there is more to a practice than the procedures for doing it. To articulate this structure, each practice is further described by formally specifying, for each major variety of the practice (its paradigms), what is necessary to engage in the practice. This formal description is the social practice canonical form (SPCF) for the practice. Each SPCF thus consists of a set of paradigms Π_i, and the details of paradigm Π_i are specified via the following parametric formulation:

$$\Pi_{i}, = \langle G, S, E, L, C, V, Sk, Kn, PC \rangle \qquad (9.2)$$

where

G = the goal of the practice: a formal name of the goal state of affairs. Actors engage in actions in order to bring about some state of affairs; success of a practice is, by definition, the achievement of this result.

S = stages/options of the practice, the other, smaller, practices necessarily or optionally involved in carrying out this one. Essentially a task analysis, S is specified by a set of formal names.

E = Elements: the logical roles of persons or objects in the practice, each specified by formal name.

L = Eligibilities of individuals for each role, specified by lists of individuals or formal rules.

C = constraints: formal specification of the dependence of the occurrence of combinations of stages/options on either another stage/option or on specified states of affairs being the case.

V = versions: the sets of stages/options that are considered, by members of this community, to be valid instances of this practice.

Sk = skills needed to carry out this practice, that affect the way in which the stages are carried out but are not themselves separate tasks, again specified by formal name.

Kn = Knowledge: item-by-item specification, by formal name, of the facts and concepts required for the practice. These are not 'cognitive structures' or 'mental events,' but are only specifications, by formal identifier, of the distinctions that this behavior is an instance of acting on. For example, the couple celebrating their anniversary is acting on the concept (the distinction) of a wedding anniversary versus other things; a couple carrying out the actions of an anniversary dinner but who had no idea what an anniversary was or could not distinguish it from other forms of celebration would not be considered to be having an anniversary celebration.

PC = personality characteristics: these are identifiable patterns of actions, including attitudes, traits, and values, and specified by giving the formal name of the characteristic. They are not "internal variables," but rather identify consistent patterns in kinds of actions.

Kn and *Sk* acquired are of central importance in modeling the economic impact of training and education, because the outcome of education and training is that individuals have knowledge and skills that enable them to engage in practices, as articulated in the SPCF parameters.

The SPCF is a parametric analysis originally devised by A.O. Putman to extend Ossorio's basic process unit (Ossorio, 2005). This formulation encompasses Putman's SPCF and certain elements of Ossorio's intentional action formulation (Ossorio, 2006). The description formally encodes both the logical structure of the practice and the actual individuals involved in instantiations of it. What actually takes place is an instantiated version of a practice, that is, a specific set of stages/options recognized in the community as a way of engaging in this practice, with an actual individual person or object filling each logical role (element).

Using the SPCF, we can now be precise about what is meant by 'use or manipulation of economic concepts': economic practices are those whose SPCFs involve elements that are economic.

To illustrate this formal structure, Box 9.2 presents a substantial portion of the SPCF for a high-level practice in an actual large software development organization (Jeffrey and Putman, 1983). Although not an economic practice, it is a part of a production process in an economically important industry, and one that is, in one form or another, common to every software development organization.

Several software systems using SPCF descriptions have been built, including the one this example is taken from, a system to coach managers in specifically human-oriented management practices, an automated marketing coach for a major accounting firm, and a system to be used by loan clerks in a major bank system to create signature-ready documents for filing with state and county offices to perfect the bank's claim on loan collateral (Jeffrey et al., 1989). One of the most interesting features of the SPCF is its demonstrated capability for formally representing a range of human behaviors not normally considered capturable in a machine-usable form.

Each of the practices 1–1, 1–2, 1–3, 2, 3, 4–1, 4–2, 4–3, 4–4 and 5 in Box 9.2 have SPCF descriptions that completely specify each of those practices, at that level of detail. This further elaboration continues down to any level of description needed or desired, including persons issuing commands to software and the execution of the command by the software/computer system. The following example illustrates this recursive elaboration capability.

Hierarchical Structure of the *Fakaafe*

A wide variety of practices impact economic facts. Conversely, economic facts, because they deal with degree of availability of fundamental resources, impact non-economic practices. This pair of relationships lies at the heart of the well-known phenomenon of feedback in economic systems. As a result, the usability of the *homo communitatis*

BOX 9.2 SPCF FOR A HIGH-LEVEL PRACTICE IN AN ACTUAL LARGE SOFTWARE DEVELOPMENT ORGANIZATION

Name: [Responsible persons in the Laboratory] find and fix a problem in [a No. 4 Generic]

Stages options:

1. [Responsible persons in the Laboratory] find out about [a problem]
   - Option 1–1: [A person at Indian Hill] discovers a problem and reports it
   - Option 1–2: [A person at Indian Hill] discovers a problem and has [the responsible programmer] file [a Failure Report]
   - Option 1–3: [A person at Indian Hill] discovers a problem and has [the FR coordinator] tell [the responsible programmer] about it
2. [People who keep track of problems] track the course of the problem
3. [The responsible programmer] decides the response to the problem
4. [The responsible programmer] implements the chosen response to the problem
   - Option 4–1: [The responsible programmer] produces the fix for the problem
   - Option 4–2: [The responsible programmer] files a Not-Applicable Correction Report
   - Option 4–3: [The responsible programmer] files a Not-Implemented Correction Report
   - Option 4–4: [The responsible programmer] files a Cancel Correction Report
5. [People in a support group] install the fix for the problem in [a No. 4 Generic].

Elements

1. responsible persons in the Laboratory
2. a problem
3. a person at Indian Hill
4. a Failure Report
5. the responsible program-mer
6. a Not Applicable Correction Report
7. a Not Implemented Correction Report
8. a Cancel Correction Report
9. the FR coordinator

Individuals

0. any person at Indian Hill
1. member of the 4ESAC
2. any technical staff member at Indian Hill
3. 4E5
4. 4E6
5. members of the No. 4 Support Group
6. the FR for the problem
7. the Not Applicable CR for this problem
8. the Not Implemented CR for this problem

10. people who keep track of problems
11. people in a support group
12. a No. 4 Generic

Versions:
(1–1 or 1–2 or 1–3), 2, 3, 4–1, 5
(1–1 or 1–2 or 1–3), 2, 3, (4–2 or 4–3 or 4–4)

9. the Cancel CR for this problem
10. incorrect behavior by a No. 4 machine
11. people in System Test
12. people in a development group
13. people in the Field Support Group
14. Bill Davidson
15. Jane Arment

model is directly dependent on the range of practices to which it can be applied. To illustrate this range, we show the SPCF description of a different kind of practice, a feast in honor of a visiting Wesleyan minister, that regularly takes place in Tongan village society (Bennardo, 1996). Box 9.3 presents a representative portion of the practice–subpractice structure of holding this feast, including planning, gathering resources, transporting the resources, physical processes such as burning wood to prepare the food, and the feast itself. The other parts of the SPCFs of the practices and subpractices (constraints, elements, individuals, eligibilities and versions), which, as the No. 4 ESS example in Box 9.2 shows, play a central role in capturing the nuances and details of actual life involving these practices, are omitted for reasons of space. The full set of practices and subpractices, as derived from Bennardo (1996), and a brief discussion of the mathematical structure of a community's practices, may be found in the Appendix.

Including descriptions down to the level of the burning wood emitting smoke (4.1.3.3) illustrates the capability of incorporating high-level human practices and low-level physical processes in a single formal model. This capability makes possible unified models of behaviors, at any level, and their impact on physical quantities. For example, the practice structure here is the appropriate model to drive a simulation study of resource depletion (wood) and environmental impact (smoke) under various circumstances involving the community, its high-level practices, and relationships among its members. The kind and amount of detail included in a simulation model depend on the kind of information needed from the study, which in turns depends on what the information is to be used for. A study of the environmental impact of *fakaafes* would include information that would typically be of little value to a study of the family dynamics of organizing and holding *fakaafes*.

Formal, not Discursive, Specifications

The examples given may suggest that an SPCF is simply a set of discursive statements, albeit detailed ones, as might be found in an anthropological discussion. Although the hierarchically organized practices and subpractices, and the elements and individuals, are typically stated in ordinary English sentences for the sake of readability (e.g. 'Members of the household giving the *fakaafe* plan it'), these sentences are being used here as formal

BOX 9.3 HIERARCHICAL STRUCTURE OF THE *FAKAAFE*

Name: Tongan Wesleyan villagers hold a *fakaafe*

Stages options:

1. People in the village decide who will give the *fakaafe*
2. Members of the household giving the *fakaafe* plan it
   - 2.1 Household members decide food for *fakaafe*
   - 2.2 Household members decide who shall contribute food for *fakaafe*
   - 2.3 Household members decide who shall contribute utensils and decorations
   - 2.4 Member of family giving *fakaafe* gets *kainga* member to contribute to the *fakaafe*
     - 2.4.1. Family member sends request for help to family member abroad
     - 2.4.2. The *kainga* member asked decides whether to contribute
     - 2.4.3 The *kainga* member asked contributes to the *fakaafe*
   - 2.5 Members of family giving the *fakaafe* decide who will be responsible for which tasks in special circumstances
3. Members of the family giving the *fakaafe* gather the food for the *fakaafe* at the premises of the household giving it
   - 3.1 Tongan village boys capture free-range animals
   - 3.2. Tongan village boys bring captured animals to household where *fakaafe* is to be held
   - 3.3. Tongan village men bring crops from their gardens to household where *fakaafe* is to be held
   - 3.4. Women and children of the family collect shellfish
   - 3.5. Men and women buy food at the market
4. Members of the household prepare the food for the *fakaafe*
   - 4.1. Men of the household prepare the oven
     - 4.1.1. Men of the household fill the oven with wood
     - 4.1.2. Men of the household light the wood
     - 4.1.3. Wood in oven burns
       - 4.1.3.1. Wood in oven oxidizes
       - 4.1.3.2. Wood in oven emits heat
       - 4.1.3.3. Wood in oven emits smoke
   - 4.2. Men and women of the household cook the food
5. Member of family invites church member to *fakaafe*
   - 5.1. Member of family giving *fakaafe* issues invitation to *fakaafe* to church member
   - 5.2. Church member responds to invitation to *fakaafe*
     - Option 1: Church member accepts invitation to *fakaafe*
     - Option 2: Church member declines invitation to *fakaafe*

6. Family members prepare the room for the *fakaafe*
7. Family members and guests take part in the *fakaafe*
    7.1. Family members and *fakaafe* guests sit down for the *fakaafe*
    7.2. Family members and *fakaafe* guests say a brief prayer
    7.3. Head of household gives a speech
    7.4. Visiting minister gives a speech
    7.5. Chief gives a speech
    7.6. Family members and guests at the *fakaafe* have the feast
    7.7. Others who prepared food for the *fakaafe* eat
8. Women of the household distribute remaining food to family and *kainga*
    8.1. Women of the house distribute remaining food to members of family present
    8.2. Women of the house distribute remaining food to other members of the *kainga*

names, much as names of methods and variables in computer programs may be ordinary English phrases (usually with blank spaces omitted), not discursive English statements that 'refer' to physical things. 'Members of the household giving the *fakaafe*' is the name of an element in this practice, instantiated by individuals as articulated in the eligibilities. In the example of the practice of celebrating an anniversary, 'a nice restaurant' is the name of an element, not simply an adjectival phrase 'referring' to a concept that would be essentially impossible to render formally. The SPCF for this social practice includes individuals and eligibility rules that specify what individuals can or must instantiate the element. SPCFs commonly include identifiers of elements, individuals, eligibilities and constraints that can be recognized by members of the community but which cannot be defined physically or algorithmically, such the appraisal of a restaurant as 'nice' (Jeffrey and Putman, 1983; Jeffrey et al., 1989).

A full derivation of the formal *homo communitatis* model is beyond the scope of this chapter; a more complete discussion may be found in (Jeffrey, 2007, 2010). Briefly, referring to the elaboration of the model above, we note that we have used the technique from mathematical logic and mathematical computer science of specifying a 'thing,' its constituent aspects and relationships between those aspects by formal name. An SPCF of a practice is a 9-tuple of formal names, and a community specification a 6-tuple of formal names that identify objects, processes, events, or situations or states of affairs. Further information about any named object, process, event or state of affairs is specified by a description that is itself a set of (formal) names of (1) constituents of the item, and (2) relationships between the constituents. Thus each item is specified by a formal ordered pair (N, D), in which N and D are formal names (or sets of them), and so a specification of a set communities and practices is a complex, but formal, description.

APPLICATIONS TO BEHAVIORAL ECONOMICS AND FINANCE

Simulation

With a formal specification of a community or set of communities of interest, including SPCFs of the communities' practices (as much as possible with the available information), simulation can proceed via mathematical or statistical modeling of the behaviors and phenomena of interest, using the SPCFs to guide the selection of factors to be included. Alternatively, the SPCFs can be used directly as the basis for agent-based simulation (Jeffrey and Nadro, 2007).

To give SPCFs for agent-based simulation, we directly represent the life of the communities of interest, i.e. the daily practices engaged in by members, and measure the economic quantities of interest as the community activities proceed. This is done by simulating individuals engaging in the intrinsic practices of the community, which they do by engaging in instantiated versions of the intrinsic practices. Those practices, in turn, are engaged in by engaging in other, smaller, practices, recursing down to the level at which no further SPCFs are available. In practice, this may be small, detailed actions such as issuing a specific command on a computer or large and broad practices for which no further description is available. At that level, mathematical functions specifying input–output relations, including probabilistic ones, are used. As the simulation proceeds, quantities of interest, whether outcomes or resources or quantities derived from them, whether economic or other, are measured.

In more detail, the algorithm is as follows:

Initialization: the community (or, more commonly, communities) to be simulated are specified, including the community parameters for each, and the initial state of the constituents of the community's world (*W* parameter). Many of these conditions, including attributes of individuals (*PC*s found in SPCFs of the community's practices), initial distribution of members in statuses, initial quantities of individuals and objects, and attributes of objects and processes will be probability distributions. Having specified each community to be simulated, simulation now proceeds as follows:

For each time t_0, $t_0 + \Delta t$, $t_0 + 2\Delta t$, . . ., for each individual *I*:

(a) Identify every practice *I* is eligible to engage in, in all communities of which *I* is a member.
(b) For each practice P_i for which *I* is eligible, assess *I*'s motivations – prudential, hedonic, ethical and esthetic – to engage in P_i, taking into account:
  - choice principles of each community of which *I* is a member.
  - *I*'s personal characteristics: attitudes, traits and states.
  - The hedonic, prudential, ethical and esthetic value of P_i to *I* (including the case in which P_i is intrinsic to a status *I* holds, and the degree to which each of *I*'s relationships give *I* motivation to do or not do P_i).
  - *I*'s certainty that P_i will result in the hedonic, prudential, ethical and esthetic values. (By 'certainty,' we do not mean probability, but rather the degree, on a

scale of −1.0 to +1.0, to which *I* is prepared to act on the assessed values. This is discussed in more detail in the section below, 'Behavioral certainty.')
- The degree to which each of *I*'s relationships gives *I* motivation to do or not do each practice.
- The degree to which each practice is an expression of a status *S* that *I* has need to affirm, due to the need to counter an action that will otherwise result in loss of the status *S*, or due to having not engaged in any of the practices intrinsic to *S* for a period of time.
- Any P_i in which *I* is already engaging, but which is not yet complete.

(c) Identify *I*'s optimally motivated practice, P_M. As discussed in more detail below, because there are four kinds of motivation, motivation is mathematically a four-element vector, not a scalar, and therefore the motivations at any time *t* may not be fully ordered. Nevertheless, persons do make choices among the possible practices whose value to them is this set, and therefore the simulation will contain a function to identify what we call the 'optimally motivated practice.' Perhaps the simplest example of such a function is the maximum want model (Mitchell, 1967), in which the practice chosen is the one with maximum total motivation, i.e. the sum of the hedonic, prudential, ethical and esthetic motivations. Other examples include the vector magnitude of each motivation quadruple, multiplicative models in which the quantity maximized is the product of the four kinds of motivation, and other more complex functions designed to model mathematically the case of possibly conflicting motivations. These include cases of a single overwhelming motivation and multiple, conflicting, overwhelming motivations of various kinds. A choice of optimally motivated practice selection algorithm constitutes a choice of a theory of motivation, for the population being simulated. Many such behavior-selection functions will be based on proposed frequency distributions of relative priorities of motivations in the population. In some communities, for example, practices such as theft are much less frequent due to the priority of ethical motivations among members. As noted earlier, choice principles give members additional motivations: sometimes one does something 'because one is supposed to.' This is a significant factor in many families.

(d) Individual *I* carries out the practice P_M for which there is a version for which *I* is eligible and has the resources – i.e. the individuals necessary to take the places of the elements in that version.

(e) Each stage of the version is itself a practice with an SPCF, and so the stage itself is done by engaging in a version of that practice. This recursion ends when there is no further description of the practice, and engaging that practice is represented by the fact of occurrence (or, probabilistically, failure) of the bottom-level practice.

(f) *I* carries out as much of P_M as can be done in time slice Δt. The list of states of affairs descriptions identifying known facts is then updated. Practices do not always succeed, and this is modeled by probabilities of success for each practice. When a practice is completed, the goal state *G* defines what is to be updated. Partial completion of a practice results in recording that the goal state *G* is partially achieved.

(g) When a practice occurs whose outcome is the creation or change of a social practice, the SPCF for the practice is created or updated.

(h) Each social practice has an associated latency, a time period after completion of the practice during which the reason to engage in it is zero. Latencies vary by individual and practice, and are typically modeled by frequency distributions. They model the empirical fact that although a practice may be intrinsic, it is common to find a delay before the person wants to engage in it again. They also provide the formal mechanism for including biological and physical facts in the simulation, without the need to specify physiological details such as blood sugar or neurotransmitter levels. Examples include eating a meal, having sex, going to a movie, playing chess or taking a vacation.

(i) That I is engaging in practice P_i is a fact, recorded and observable by other members of the community (or, if desired, by a subset of the members).

(j) Non-behavioral events, things that happen in and to the community, are specified in a way that represents how those things occur in the real world, namely by alteration of the specification of the facts representing the world state. In this way events such as crop failure, a bankruptcy or an attack by someone outside the community are included.

EXAMINING THE USE OF PROBABILITY

In this section, we employ the *homo communitatis* model to re-examine some of the foundational work in behavioral economics and show how to reformulate much of that work to derive models not limited by assumptions of unconscious processing or probability calculations, models that potentially have significantly greater predictive power.

Every field's conceptual framework carries with it, usually only implicitly, a methodology, i.e. a set of related methods for using it, assumptions about what constitutes a valid result and an appropriate theoretical interpretation of a result. Applying the fundamental concept of *homo communitatis*, work in the field is a matter of engaging in the practices of it. As formula (9.2) indicates, this means using the concepts of the field. Physicists, for example, engage in the practices of the field of physics – theoretical and/or experimental – using concepts of energy, mass, time and so on.

The (Tversky and Kahneman, 1974) experiment in which subjects were given descriptions of persons and then asked which statement about described persons is more likely to be correct and interpreting the results of the experiment as (incorrect) versions of Bayesian analysis are both instances of practices of the community of cognitive psychology, and the concepts used include the mathematical definition of probability, sample spaces, Bayes's rule, priors, and the more fundamental ones of experimental subject and question and answer.

Behavioral economics and finance are based on the insight that we need to incorporate a wider range of behavioral concepts in models of economic and financial behavior, but to date most of the extensions have come from the relatively narrow sub-field of cognitive psychology, perhaps because only cognitive psychology provides formal models of its concepts. More fundamentally, the fields of economics and finance as traditionally constituted (the *homo economicus* model) are embedded entirely in the mathematical model and methodology of probability, and it has been universally assumed that this is an appropriate model of human actions and decisions in general. Rationality and subjective expected utility, for example, are defined as updating beliefs consistently with Bayes's law, which is a statement about the ratios of mathematical probabilities, and making decisions in accordance with subjective expected utility, which is defined by multiplication of probabilities and utilities, and behavioral economics as understanding the errors in applying mathematical probability theory, such as Bayesian calculations and sampling theory (Barberis and Thaler, 2003).

Behavioral economics rejects *homo economicus* as unrealistic and a poor predictor, but has retained the fundamental assumption that it is appropriate to model actors making decisions in terms of probability as that term is formally defined, i.e. repeated selections from a sample space. This foundational assumption is seen in the methodological assumption of asking subjects questions phrased in the language of probability, and assuming (without verification) that the subjects are 'internally' calculating Bayesian probabilities. Because of the pre-empirical commitment to redescribing empirical observations in terms of 'internal' processes for doing mathematical probability calculations, a great deal of the research program in behavioral economics and finance has focused on developing internal process models of the calculation of probabilities.

If we treat the proposition that experimental subjects use probabilistic models in decision making as a hypothesis, rather than an assumption, in many cases we find no empirical basis for it. Unless they have been trained in mathematical probability and its application, we never observe experimental subjects, or persons in the world at large, identifying a sample space, estimating a probability distribution satisfied by the sample space, determining priors, calculating ratios, or any of the other practices that comprise applying mathematical probability. The exceptions are those cases in which subject are asked questions overtly using the concept of relative frequency, such as, 'If you have 100 securities with this balance sheet and this set of industry facts, how many of them would you expect to see 10 percent growth in stock price over the next year?' In a large number of others, however, we find experimental subjects asked questions such as, 'What is the probability the St Louis Cardinals will win the World Series this year?' and we never observe an instance of subject behavior that resembles constructing a sample space, mentally selecting samples from it and so on. Further, in many such cases it is difficult to see what such a sample space could be. It could be that subjects are mentally constructing a set of 100 baseball teams that all share the characteristics of this year's St Louis Cardinals and sampling that space, but there is no evidence that they do so. Further, using *homo communitatis*, we shall see below that there is strong reason to take it that they do not.

The classic work on judgment under uncertainty (Tversky and Kahneman, 1974), which led to the development of the concept of the representativeness heuristic and the various errors engendered by its use, such as insensitivity to prior probabilities and sample size, clearly illustrates these issues. In this work, subjects were shown brief personality descriptions of several individuals and asked which statement about the person is more likely to be correct. In one experiment, for example, subjects were shown descriptions in terms of personality traits of individuals supposedly sampled at random from a group of lawyers and engineers, and then asked whether it was more likely that the individual was a lawyer or engineer.

Barberis and Thaler (2003, p. 1064) cite an example that highlights the centrality of the mathematical model of probability:

> Linda is 31 years old, single, outspoken, and very bright. She majored in philosophy. As a student, she was deeply concerned with issues of discrimination and social justice, and also participated in anti-nuclear demonstrations.
>
> When asked which of 'Linda is a bank teller' (statement A) and 'Linda is a bank teller and is active in the feminist movement' (statement B) is more likely, subjects typically assign greater probability to B.

They then analyze the errors by subjects in terms of probability theory, including Bayesian probability calculations, noting for example that it is mathematically impossible for statement B to have higher probability than statement A.

In more detail, we can see that the procedure followed was:

1. The experimenter presents a subject with a description of a person's personality.
2. The experimenter asks the subject a question about the person, using the language of probability, such as, 'Which is more likely to be correct?,' or, 'What is the probability that the description is of a lawyer or engineer?'
3. The subject replies.
4. The experimenter redescribes the subject's judgments as the outcome of (internal) cognitive processes. In this specific case, the judgments have the linguistic form of statements of probability.
5. The experimenter compares the subject's answers to the mathematically correct methods and concepts from probability and statistics.
6. The experimenter ascribes deviations from the correct answers to various heuristics for and errors in carrying out the cognitive processes that produce the results.

Incorporating observations from linguistics and psychology (Austin, 1962; Wittgenstein, 1958; Ossorio, 2006), we can note that asking and answering questions are *behaviors*. Applying *homo communitatis*, noting that behaviors are instances of engaging in practices of a community, we see that:

(a) The first three steps above comprise an experimental procedure, i.e. a practice, in the community of experimental psychologists.

(b) Each of the steps is itself a practice, and as formula (9.2) articulates, steps 2 and 3 involve the use of particular concepts, i.e. distinctions.

(c) In Step 2, the experimenter is using the mathematical concept of probability, i.e. relative frequency of selection from a sample space.

(d) In Step 3, the subject replies. However, referring again to formula (9.2), it is appropriate to ask what concepts the subject is using in his/her reply: what do the subjects take the question to be? Are they taking the question to be one of assigning a mathematical probability (the experimenter's concept), or something else? To state it less technically, the subject may or may not have been answering the question the experimenter asked. In the example of Linda, questions the subject may have been answering include at least the following:

> 'Which statement is a better description of Linda?'
> 'Which statement best characterizes what kind of person Linda is?'
> 'Which statement best states what is most important about Linda?'

'Which statement is the most important thing to say about Linda?'
'Which statement is most like what you would say of Linda?'

(I have carried out preliminary, small-*n*, experiments that show that several of these are common. However, sufficient work to allow reliable estimation of the frequency of each interpretation, or others, has not been done.)

(e) The second three steps comprise a second practice, the one customarily referred to as 'interpreting the results.'
(f) In this practice, Tversky and Kahenemann redescribe the subjects' responses as instances of acting on the concepts of mathematical probability. They do not report engaging in the practice of evaluating whether this particular redescription is appropriate.

Item (d) above is essentially a restatement, using *homo communitatis* formulations, of the phenomenon of misunderstanding, but without any assumptions as to the existence, or lack of same, of internal processes, including 'interpretation' processes. Misunderstanding or misinterpretation by members of one community of the language of another community is a universally recognized phenomenon in anthropology, linguistics, communication studies and computer systems analysis. (It is instructive to note that systems analysis and design textbooks caution students to remember that their technical language and concepts are, in the large majority of cases, not shared by the clients, and therefore misunderstandings are extremely common and repeated steps must be taken to ensure that what is asked is what is heard – and answered.)

Members of communities must learn to engage in the practices of the communities. (This not an empirical claim, but merely an acknowledgment that the alternative is to assume instinctive behaviors.) They do this typically in their families, schools, professional training, and in some cases by observation, attempt and correction ('trial and error'). This is the basis for saying there is strong reason to suppose that subjects are not engaging in mathematical probabilistic analysis: it is unlikely that they have had any opportunity to learn these practices – and here we are using 'likely' in the strict, mathematical sense: only a small percentage of persons have a history that would allow them to learn these practices.

As a result, the characterization by Barberis and Thaler that subjects attribute higher probability to statement B, which is the typical characterization elsewhere in the literature as well, is based on the assumption that subjects are assigning probabilities *at all*, an assumption that does not withstand careful examination and whose implications are misleading. Specifically, it misleads Barberis and Thaler, and has misled researchers and practitioners of behavioral economics and finance, to the conclusion that experimental subjects and persons in general are customarily applying the laws of probability but doing it badly, when in fact, using *homo communitatis*, we can see that it is much more likely that subjects are not producing probabilistic judgments at all (and here, by 'likely,' we do not mean 'mathematically probable').

To summarize, when a subject reports, 'Statement B is more likely true of Linda,' or, as in the Tversky and Kahneman work answers the question, 'Is it more likely that Steven is a lawyer or librarian?,' there is no reason to take it that they have an internal model of a sample space of statements and personality descriptions. They *could* have such a model, and cognitive psychology and traditional behavioral economics insist that they must, but they could equally be replying to what they understood the question to be: 'Which of the following is the best description of Linda?' Perhaps most importantly, which of these is the case is properly a matter for empirical investigation, not assumption based on a particular theory in psychology.

IMPLICATIONS FOR PRACTICE

The analysis is more than philosophical or semantic nit-picking. Whether economic actors use the concept of mathematical probability or something else affects both the questions an experimenter asks and the conclusions reached about economic decision making. It also directly affects the professional practices of financial analysts when they are asked questions by clients and make recommendations. Knowing how a question will be interpreted, and careful avoidance of ambiguity of meaning, are crucial to the practice of finance.

Clinical psychologists, ethnographers, journalists, linguists, computer systems analysts and public opinion researchers are all keenly sensitive to the phenomenon that what can be discovered by asking subjects questions depends very strongly on the wording of the questions. Precise identification of the possibilities and careful choice of phrasing in referring to them is central to experimental design and professional practice in all these fields. If, for example, an experimenter or practitioner wants to know whether a subject would say statement A or statement B applies to a situation, they would ask questions such as, 'Do you think A or B is most applicable here?,' 'Would it be correct to say A here? To what extent? How about B?' or 'You seem to be saying [statement A] here. Is that right?' All of these are ways of discovering the applicability, in the subjects' view, of statements about situations described in a certain way.

Applying this analysis to an investment situation, consider an investor seeking an opinion on the future price behavior of a security. They might ask, 'How certain are you that X will be up by *p* percent in one year?', or alternatively, 'If you had 100 securities like this, in this industry, how many of them would you expect to see up by *p* percent in one year?' These two questions are not the same, are not inquiring about the same possible fact, and the careful investor would not be surprised if they yielded different answers.

Further, financial analysts and investors routinely carry out their professional practices in ways that have no observable resemblance to using the concept of mathematical probability. If we first clarify what exactly we mean by 'probably,' i.e. ratio of frequency of outcomes, and then ask analyst subjects whether that is a good model of what they mean when they say, 'Security X will probably do Y in the next *m* months,' the typical response is, 'No, that is not what I do. That's not what I mean.' They commonly state, 'I look at the financial facts about the company and the industry, and sometimes at their management, and based on that I assess what I believe will happen, with as much certainty as I can. But I'm not counting things, in any way.' It is of course possible that a decision maker is, in effect, doing mathematical probability calculations without knowing it, but experimental results consistently show that probability is not a good model of certainty determinations (Tversky and Kahneman 1974; Kahneman and Tversky, 1979).

Knowledge Certainty and Behavioral Certainty

Mathematical probability has been used as a tool to address the need to model formally the fact that actors must often act in the face of uncertainty: uncertainty about what the facts are and uncertainty about whether an action will bring about an intended outcome (the G parameter). The traditional approach has been to treat uncertainty as an attribute of the knowledge, and thus we have language such as 'probability that x is true,' and so forth.

Using *homo communitatis*, we can develop a different approach, which we term the 'behavioral approach.' Knowing and acting are distinct concepts. Individuals are always acting; they can, tautologically, only act on what they take to be the case. This is the relationship between knowledge and action articulated in the SPCF. For an actor, and therefore for those modeling actors, the central question about any particular belief, regardless of the certainty of that belief, is the degree to which they are prepared to act on it. This is the focus of economics and finance: prediction of what actors will *do*.

Thus there are two equally important distinctions: (1) what the actor takes to be the case; and (2) the degree to which the actor is prepared to act on what they take to be the case. Preparedness to act on what they take to be the case is a fact about the actor, not about the knowledge. Traditionally, all uncertainty has been considered a matter of knowledge uncertainty, with various mathematical models: probability, Kahneman and Tversky's $w(p)$, fuzzy set theory and fuzzy logic (Russell and Norvig, 2003) and so on. The behavioral approach is to keep the two distinctions separate, formally model preparedness to act, and incorporate knowledge uncertainty insofar at it is necessary or useful in calculating preparedness to act. What the actor takes to be the case is modeled formally by the Kn parameter; we define the degree to which the actor is prepared to act on x as the *behavioral certainty* of x (to distinguish it from the more common term 'certainty,' which has a long history of interpretation as 'with probability 1'), denoted $\beta(x)$, with $0 < \beta(x) \leq 1$. (The item x may be 'doing P will bring about G.') In some cases, it may be that Bayesian probability or a modification of it such as $w(p)$ accurately models β, or is an input to its calculation, a question to be empirically determined. This allows us to generalize prospect theory without using probability (unless it is appropriate in specific cases): a situation x with value $v(x)$ and behavioral certainty $\beta(x)$ has a 'net' value $\beta(x)v(x)$. When $\beta(x) = w(p)$, this reduces to $w(p)v(x)$, the formulation in prospect theory.

The behavioral approach and behavioral certainty have further implications for practice. It can be expected that experimental protocols based on the concept of behavioral certainty will yield significantly different data from those based on mathematical probability and phrased in that language. Examples of such experiments include:

'How certain are you that X will occur?'
'How certain are you that X is the case?'
'Here are two statements, A and B. Which of the following are you more certain is true?'
'In the following situation, you can do X or Y. Which of these would you do, and how sure are you?'
'On a scale of −1 to +1, −1 meaning you are certain X is not the case and +1 meaning you are certain that it is, how certain are you that X?'
'What would you bet that X is the case?' (This is the method adopted by Ramsey to measure degree of belief, and is attractive for its obvious connection to economic and finance decisions.

Here we use it not to determine an attribute of X such as certainty or probability, but as a technique to discover the degree to which the subject is prepared to act on X.)
'What are you prepared to bet that X will happen?'

Experimental protocols of this type develop the kind of data that are directly of interest in economics and finance: how is the subject prepared to act?

Value as a Vector

Neoclassical economics postulates that individuals act to maximize their utility, more particularly their subjective expected utility (SEU). The well-documented failure of SEU to agree with several cases of actual behavior (Barberis and Thaler, 2003; Kahneman and Tversky, 1979) has led to prospect theory, in which the function maximized is $U = \sum w(p_i) v(x_i)$. However, both models consider 'value' to be a scalar quantity.

Measuring value with a single number conflicts with both common observation and the entire literature of social and clinical psychology, sociology, political science and anthropology. The *homo communitatis* framework incorporates and formalizes the much more inclusive and realistic model of persons as having four kinds of motivation: hedonic, prudential, ethical and esthetic. While some have taken a philosophical position that these motivations are not 'real,' and are aspects of self-interest, for the purposes of creating a comprehensive, realistic, formal framework to serve as the foundation of behavioral economics that discussion is moot: a complete model of human action must include the four kinds of motivations in some form.

To say that something has value to an actor is to say that the actor has motivation to try to bring it about. Accordingly, value is of four kinds: hedonic, prudential, ethical and esthetic. The kinds of value are not interconvertible; they are logically distinct categories. Prudential motivation, for example, is categorically distinct from hedonic, ethical or esthetic. An assignment of prudential value (being in an actor's interest) cannot be replaced with a hedonic, ethical or esthetic value. Further, these types of motivation, i.e. measures of value, may conflict: what is fun (hedonic value) may not be in one's interest (prudential value); what is ethical may be unpleasant, dangerous and ugly; what is appropriate may be onerous and costly; and so on. Because hedonic, prudential, ethical and esthetic values are categorically distinct, specifying the value of a state of affairs requires specification of four quantities, not one: its hedonic value, prudential value, ethical value and esthetic value. This means that mathematically value is a four-dimensional vector (h, r, e, t), not a scalar quantity. (The symbol 'r' is used to avoid notational conflict with the customary use of 'p' to denote probability.)

Mathematically, the value of an action is the four-element vector quantifying the value of the state when the practice is complete. This is the G parameter in the SPCF of the practice or, in the case of intrinsic practices, the state of having engaged in the action, since intrinsic practices are by definition those done in order to be doing it, not to accomplish a result. Each action thus corresponds to an ordered pair $(\overline{v}_{before}, \overline{v}_{after})$. If the value of the outcome is $(h_{after}, r_{after}, e_{after}, t_{after})$, we can define the total value as the vector magnitude $\|\overline{v}\| = \sqrt{h^2_{after} + r^2_{after} + e^2_{after} + t^2_{after}}$, and the change in total value as the difference of the magnitudes $\|\overline{v}_{before}\| - \|\overline{v}_{after}\|$.

Since value is a vector, the axioms that define a preference relation are of course not satisfied, other than in those cases in which $\bar{v}_1 = (h_1, r_1, e_1, t_1)$, $\bar{v}_2 = (h_2, r_2, e_2, t_2)$, $h_1 \leq h_2$ and $p_1 \leq p_2$ and $e_1 \leq e_2$ and $t_1 \leq t_2$, and similarly for the other axioms that define the relationship. Mathematically, the curve $v(x)$, such as in Kahneman and Tversky (1979), for the value function v are projections of four-dimensional value surfaces.

The methods and approach of multi-attribute utility (MAU) may prove useful here, potentially including MAU theory in defining functions to calculate the scalar utility of the vector (h, r, e, t). However, in general the functions $h(x)$, $r(x)$, $e(x)$ and $t(x)$ do not exhibit mutual preferential independence. Consider the following example. An investment firm must choose between investments that offer varying rates of return, but also are more or less inconsistent with the firm's choice principles, e.g. a firm whose choice principles are to invest in low-volatility large cap companies, with an opportunity to invest in subprime mortgage-backed securities. Mutual preferential independence in this case would mean that the firm preferred higher return ($r(x)$) regardless of how inconsistent an investment is with its principles ($e(x)$), and consistency with its principles regardless of the difference in return, conditions obviously not the case in general. As a result, Debreu's theorem (see Debreu, 1960), which in this case would state that the overall value of $x = h(x) + p(x) + r(x) + t(x)$, does not hold. Without this theorem, finding a function to correctly calculate a scalar value from the vector $\bar{v}(x)$ is 'burdensome' (Apostolakis, 2007), but perhaps not as much as in the general case because the components of the value vectors are categorically distinct and the axes of value space are therefore orthogonal, unlike the general case in which many attributes of the same type may be involved.

SEU is the special case of prospect theory in which w is the identity function, i.e. $w(p_i) = p_i$, so using the definition of behavioral certainty we can reformulate and generalize prospect theory and SEU as follows:

Axiom 9.1 An individual always chooses the alternative (of the ones of which they are aware) that maximizes $U = \Sigma\beta(x_i)\bar{v}(x_i)$, *when such a maximum exists.*

The specifics of the function $\bar{v}(G) = (h(G), r(G), e(G), t(G))$ are a matter for empirical investigation. The appropriate mathematical models of hedonic, prudential, ethical and esthetic values may be quite complex, are almost certainly not similar to each other, and are similarly a matter for empirical investigation. Kahneman and Tversky (1979) is an example of one such study, but the range of issues on which empirical data are needed is substantially broader, including at a minimum investigations into the following kinds of cases:

- *'All other things being equal' cases.* These are cases in which a decision (a chosen action) results in no net change in hedonic, ethical or esthetic value, i.e. $h(x_1) = h(x_2)$, $e(x_1) = e(x_2)$, and $t(x_1) = t(x_2)$. The experiments in Kahneman and Tversky (1979) identify the form of the $v(x_i)$ curve, but mathematically they are deriving data about the projection of the vector $\bar{v}(x_i)$ onto the P axis, and reveal nothing about the curve in various regions of the space, i.e. for various ranges of $h(x_i)$, $e(x_i)$, and $t(x_i)$. For example, does the shape of $r(x_i)$ differ if the x_i are equally unpleasant or equally inappropriate?
- *Types of value cases.* Behavioral economics experiments commonly conflate types of value, such as cases in which subjects are asked, 'Which would you prefer,

winning $1000 with probability 1, or $2000 with probability 0.6)?' and, in the same experimental protocol, asked, 'Which would you prefer, a 50 percent chance of winning a three-week tour of England, France and Italy, or a one-week tour of England, with certainty?' (Kahneman and Tversky, 1979). These are two kinds of value, prudential and hedonic. While it may be that on average subjects treat the two equivalently, there are no data to support the *a priori* aggregation of the cases.

- *Real conflict cases.* At the beginning of this section we cited examples of conflicting motivations: what is ethical may be unpleasant, dangerous and ugly, and so on. Such cases are not the exception: human life includes a very large range of cases in which actors are faced with important conflicting motivations: ethical versus hedonic, prudential and esthetic; esthetic versus hedonic and prudential; prudential versus hedonic, ethical versus hedonic, prudential versus ethical; esthetic versus prudential, and so on. The rise of socially conscious mutual funds of various kinds shows that these are factors in both microeconomic analysis and finance. A great deal of research is needed to identify the shape of the choice surface in four-dimensional value space, and there is no *a priori* reason to expect this surface to be simple.

Since it is by no means clear that subjects take questions phrased in the language of probability ('probable,' 'likely,' etc.) as mathematical probability questions, it is quite possible that the behavioral certainty function $\beta(x)$ (including the special case in which $\beta(x)$ is modeled by $w(p)$) may be significantly different if the alternative values involve $h(x_i)$, $e(x_i)$ or $t(x_i)$, rather than only $r(x_i)$, as in previous research.

All investigations in which subjects are asked what they would prefer, or would do, suffer from the problems of self-report data, some of which are discussed in Barberis and Thaler (2003). There are additional problems in self-report investigations of values, including ethical and esthetic values, particularly in cases of conflicting values. Sociologists, for example, know that subjects will frequently lie when asked about something they know is considered dishonest or inappropriate, even when guaranteed privacy.

For this reason we envision simulation as a major tool for investigation into the various choice surfaces in value space. *Homo communitatis* does not incorporate any theory of motivation; as noted in step (b) of the simulation algorithm above, choice of an algorithm to select the particular practice for each individual I at time t from the set of possible practices, based on the four-element vector of motivations for each practice, constitutes a choice of a theory of motivation. The research methodology most in accord with the desire in behavioral finance and economics for rigorous, comprehensive, predictive, models of economic behavior appears to be as follows:

1. Identify the population of interest.
2. Identify the communities of which members of this population are members.
3. Build *homo communitatis* models of each of these communities. The most basic model incorporates the statuses, practices intrinsic to each status, and choice principles. The basic model is complete in the sense of modeling all the practices of

the community, but only at the highest level; all finer-grained specification of the practices – the details of how they are carried out – is omitted.

4. Give SPCF formulations of each of the practices in each of the communities. Two points are important here:
   - Specification of the *Kn* parameter of the practices does not involve theoretical constructs or 'internal' processes or states. The value of this parameter is a set of formal names of the facts and concepts (the distinctions) necessary to carry out the practice. These facts and concepts are discovered, in general, by observing and interviewing members of the community, identifying distinctions they appear to be acting on, and verifying the conjectured distinctions by further interviews. This is essentially the practice of ethnography, a methodology developed for this purpose and used in anthropology, some branches of psychology, and computer systems analysis.
   - Nothing, including the simulation of the communities involved (Step 8 below), depends on having complete specifications of either a community or all of the practices of one or more of them. The impact of greater detail on a simulation is analogous to having more bits in a digitization of a picture: finer resolution. As more details of the practices of a community are added at lower and lower levels of the hierarchy of practices, the resolution of the picture presented by the output of the simulation increases.

   The result of these steps is a purely descriptive model, embodying neither normative nor theoretical commitments as to what actors do or how they do it. This model is a framework for incorporating empirical data and theories about motivation, distribution of characteristics, and any of the ways in which the population of interest may vary.
5. Empirically investigate the functions $\beta(x)$ and $\bar{v}(x)$.
6. Empirically determine the choices of each community's members in selecting practices: maximum value vector magnitude, maximum sum of components, maximum sum of components subject to constraint and so on.
7. Write the optimal-value selector module to model the value-based practice selection employed by each community. The selection of an algorithm to do optimal-value selection in a community constitutes adopting a theory of motivation for that community. The results of the simulation then constitute a test of the predictive value of the theory.
8. Simulate the population, using the simulation algorithm presented above.
9. Compare the results of the simulation to actual data.
10. Revise the *homo communitatis* model of the population to reflect discrepancies between simulated and observed data.

REFERENCES

Abelson, R. (1996), 'The secret existence of expressive behavior,' in Jeffrey Friedman (ed.), *The Rational Choice Controversy*, New Haven, CT: Yale University Press, pp. 25–36.

Apostolakis, G. (2007), 'Multiattribute utility theory', course notes for Engineering Risk Benefit Analysis, Massachusetts Institute of Technology, Spring 2007. http://ocw.mit.edu/NR/rdonlyres/Engineering-Systems-

Division/ESD-72Spring-2007/B89D1F76-8B62-4740-AEA0-1142A84E1AF7/0/da6.pdf, accessed 26 August 2009.

Austin, J.L. (1962), *How to Do Things With Words*, Oxford: Oxford University Press.

Barberis, N. and R. Thaler (2003), 'A survey of behavioral finance,' in G.M. Constantinides, M. Harris and R. Stulz (eds), *Handbook of the Economics of Finance*, Amsterdam: Elsevier Science.

Bennardo, G. (1996), *A Computational Approach to Spatial Cognition: Representing Spatial Relationships in Tongan Language and Culture*, Doctoral Dissertation, University of Illinois at Urbana-Champaign, Urbana, Illinois, pp. 307–12.

Chattoe, E. (2003). 'The role of agent-based modelling in demographic explanation,' in Francesco C. Billari and Alexia Prskawetz (eds), *Agent-Based Computational Demography: Using Simulation to Improve Our Understanding of Demographic Behaviour*, Heidelberg: Physica-Verlag, pp. 41–54.

Debreu, G. (1960), 'Topological methods in cardinal utility theory,' in K.J. Arrow, S. Karlin and P. Suppe (eds), *Mathematical Methods in the Social Sciences*, Stanford, CA: Stanford University Press, pp. 16–26.

Jeffrey, H.J. (2006), 'Expanding the range of behavioral factors in economic simulations,' *The Journal of Behavioral Finance*, **7** (2), 97–106.

Jeffrey, H.J. (2007), 'High-fidelity mathematical models of social systems,' AGENT 2007 Conference on Complex Interaction and Social Emergence, 15–17 November 2007. (Sponsored by Northwestern University and Argonne National Laboratory, in association with the North American Association for Computational Social and Organizational Science.) http://agent2007.anl.gov/2007pdf/Agent%202007%20Proceedings.pdf, accessed 26 August 2009.

Jeffrey, H.J. (2010), 'Structure,' in K.E. Davis (ed.), *Advances in Descriptive Psychology*, vol. IX, Ann Arbor, MI: Descriptive Psychology Press.

Jeffrey, H.J. and J. Nadro (2007), 'Implementing the community-practice model for agent-based simulation,' Fourth Lake Arrowhead Conference on Human Complex Systems, Lake Arrowhead, CA, 22–25 April.

Jeffrey, H.J. and A.O. Putman (1983), 'MENTOR: replicating the functions of an organization,' in K.E. Davis and R.M. Bergner (eds), *Advances in Descriptive Psychology*, vol. III, Greenwich, CT: JAI Press, pp. 243–69.

Jeffrey, H.J., T. Schmid, H.P. Zeiger and A.O. Putman (1989), 'LDS/UCC: intelligent control of the loan documentation process,' *Proceedings of the Second International Conference on Industrial & Engineering Applications of Artificial Intelligence and Expert Systems*, University of Tennessee Space Institute, Tullahoma, TN, June, New York, NY: ACM Press, pp. 573–91.

Kahneman, D. and A. Tversky (1979), 'Prospect theory: an analysis of decision under risk,' *Econometrica*, **47**, 263–91.

Mitchell, T.O. (1967), 'Computer simulation of observational judgment of persons,' unpublished thesis, University of Colorado, reported in P.G. Ossorio, *Meaning and Symbolism*, Ann Arbor, MI: Descriptive Psychology Press, 2009.

Ossorio, P.G. (1981), 'Outline of descriptive psychology for personality theory and clinical applications,' in K.E. Davis (ed.), *Advances in Descriptive Psychology*, vol. I, Greenwich, CT: JAI Press, pp. 57–81.

Ossorio, P.G. (2005), *What Actually Happens*, Ann Arbor, MI: Descriptive Psychology Press. Originally published University of South Carolina Press, Columbia, SC, 1978.

Ossorio, P.G. (2006), *The Behavior of Persons*, Ann Arbor, MI: Descriptive Psychology Press.

Putman, A.O. (1981), 'Communities,' in K.E. Davis (ed.), *Advances in Descriptive Psychology*, vol. I, Greenwich, CT: JAI Press, pp. 194–209.

Ramsey, F.P. (1931), 'Truth and probability,' in R.B. Braithwaite (ed.), *The Foundations of Mathematics and other Logical Essays*, London: Routledge & Kegan Paul, Ch. VII, pp.156–198.

Russell, S.J. and P. Norvig (2003), *Artificial Intelligence: A Modern Approach*, 2nd edn, Upper Saddle River, NJ: Pearson Education.

Spradley, J. P. (1979), *The Ethnographic Interview*, Fort Worth, TX: Harcourt College Publishers.

Thompson, J.M.T. and H.B. Stewart (1986), *Nonlinear Dynamics and Chaos*, Chichester, UK: John Wiley & Sons.

Tversky, A. and D. Kahneman (1974), 'Judgment under uncertainty: heuristics and biases,' *Science*, n.s., **185** (4157), 1124–31.

Wittgenstein, L. (1958), *Philosophical Investigations*, 3rd edn, trans. G.E.M. Anscombe, New York: Macmillan.

APPENDIX: HIERARCHICAL STRUCTURE OF THE *FAKAAFE*

Below are shown the stage option portion of the SPCF of the *fakaafe* and several other, smaller, practices that are parts of it:

- Stages options of practices 3, 4, 5, 7, and 8
- Stages options of practices 2.1, 2.4, 4.1, 7.1, and 8.2
- Stages options of practice 4.1.3

Outline form is used in order to highlight the hierarchical practice–subpractice structure. However, mathematically the structure of a community's practices is considerably more complex than this hierarchical aspect alone indicates. First, it is common for a practice to be part of more than one larger practice. For example, boys capturing free-range animals (3.1 below) is also part of the practice of gathering food for a meal. Physical processes, such as wood burning (4.1.3 below) is part of many practices. Thus the entire set of a community's practices is a directed graph. In addition, the SPCF includes constraints and eligibilities, both of which may reference the occurrence of another practice or a particular stage option within it.

Name of the Practice: Tongan Wesleyan villagers hold a *fakaafe*

Stages options:

1. People in the village decide who will give the *fakaafe*
2. Members of the household giving the *fakaafe* plan it
    - 2.1. Household members decide food for *fakaafe*
        - 2.1.1. Kainga members decide number and size of pigs for the *fakaafe*
        - 2.1.2. Kainga members decide number and size of goats for the *fakaafe*
        - 2.1.3. Kainga members decide number and size of sheep for the *fakaafe*
        - 2.1.4. Kainga members decide number and size of fish for the *fakaafe*
        - 2.1.5. Kainga members decide quantity of shellfish for the *fakaafe*
        - 2.1.6. Kainga members decide number and size of vegetables for the *fakaafe*
        - 2.1.7. Kainga members decide beverages for the *fakaafe*
        - 2.1.8. Kainga members decide desserts
    - 2.2. Household members decide who shall contribute food for *fakaafe*
    - 2.3. Household members decide who shall contribute utensils and decorations
    - 2.4. Member of family giving fakaafe gets *kainga* member to contribute to the *fakaafe*
        - 2.4.1. Family member sends request for help to family member abroad
        - 2.4.2. The *kainga* member asked decides whether to contribute
            - Option 1: The *kainga* member asked agrees to contribute to the *fakaafe*
            - Option 2: The *kainga* member asked refuses to contribute to the *fakaafe*
        - 2.4.3. The *kainga* member asked contributes to the *fakaafe*

   2.5. Members of family giving the fakaafe decide who will be responsible for which tasks in special circumstances
3. Members of the family giving the *fakaafe* gather the food for the *fakaafe* at the premises of the household giving it
   3.1. Tongan village boys capture free-range animals
   3.2. Tongan village boys bring captured animals to household where *fakaafe* is to be held
   3.3. Tongan village men bring crops from their gardens to household where *fakaafe* is to be held
   3.4. Women and children of the family collect shellfish
   3.5. Men and women buy food at the market
4. Members of the household prepare the food for the *fakaafe*
   4.1. Men of the household prepare the oven
      4.1.1. Men of the household fill the oven with wood
      4.1.2. Men of the household light the wood
      4.1.3. Wood in oven burns
         4.1.3.1. Wood in oven oxidizes
         4.1.3.2. Wood in oven emits heat
         4.1.3.3. Wood in oven emits smoke
   4.2. Men and women of the household cook the food
5. Member of family invites church member to *fakaafe*
   5.1. Member of family giving fakaafe issues invitation to *fakaafe* to church member
   5.2. Church member responds to invitation to *fakaafe*
      - Option 1: Church member accepts invitation to *fakaafe*
      - Option 2: Church member declines invitation to *fakaafe*
6. Family members prepare the room for the *fakaafe*
7. Family members and guests take part in the *fakaafe*
   7.1. Family members and *fakaafe* guests sit down for the *fakaafe*
      7.1.1. Chief sits on *mua*
      7.1.2. Visiting Wesleyan minster sits in the place for the visiting minister
      7.1.3. *Ofisa kolo* sits in the place for the *ofisa kolo*
      7.1.4. Other *fakaafe* guest sits down
   7.2. Family members and *fakaafe* guests say a brief prayer
   7.3. Head of household gives a speech
   7.4. Visiting minister gives a speech
   7.5. Chief gives a speech
   7.6. Family members and guests at the *fakaafe* have the feast
      7.6.1. Family members and guests eat the food
      7.6.2. *Fakaafe* guest gives a speech
      7.6.3. Chief signals end of *fakaafe*, leaving the room
      7.6.4. Other family members and *fakaafe* guests leave
   7.7. Others who prepared food for the *fakaafe* eat
8. Women of the household distribute remaining food to family and *kainga*
   8.1. Women of the house distribute remaining food to members of family present

8.2. Women of the house distribute remaining food to other members of the *kainga*
    8.2.1. Women give food for missing family given to child to deliver to missing family
    8.2.2. Child delivers food to missing family

10 Does mutual fund flow reflect investor sentiment?

Daniel C. Indro

Behavioral finance studies routinely challenge the traditional argument that market participants behave rationally (see, e.g., Barber and Odean, 2001; Barberis and Thaler, 2002; Coval and Shumway, 2001; DeBondt and Thaler, 1985; Dreman and Lufkin, 2000; Hirshleifer, 2001; Kahneman and Riepe, 1998; Shefrin and Statman, 1985; Shiller and Pound, 1989; and Shleifer, 2000, among others). In addition, Black (1986) and DeLong et al. (1990) contend that noise traders acting in concert on non-fundamental signals can cause asset prices to deviate from their intrinsic values.

However, Shefrin and Statman (1994) offer an appealing alternative explanation of noise traders. Because noise traders do not all commit the same cognitive errors, cognitive biases cause some to be positive feedback traders, and others to be negative feedback traders. As a result, both momentum and contrarian traders may simultaneously participate in the financial markets.[1]

The mounting evidence that investor trading behavior is driven by behavioral biases has seriously called into question the extent to which arbitrage can eliminate the divergence between prices and fundamental values. Market participants and watchers already seem to believe that sentiment plays a role in the financial markets. A recent *Business Week* article states:

> On March 12, the stock market abruptly switched directions and rose 7% in the following three sessions. The powerful rally may have surprised many investors – but certainly not those who believe in sentiment indicators. In the days leading up to the market's about-face, fans of this contrarian strategy found mounting evidence that investors were overly gloomy . . . Elsewhere, investors continued to yank their money out of equity funds, to the tune of $1.4 billion during the first week of March, marking the seventh straight week of redemptions . . . (Scherreik, 2003, p. 100)

While psychology plays a role in this phenomenon, Scherreik (2003) notes that money is a bigger factor. Rick Bensignor, the chief technical strategist at Morgan Stanley, states, 'Overly gloomy investors hoard cash, which gives them plenty of buying power when their mood returns' (Scherreik, 2003). This perspective is consistent with that of Steven Norwitz, a spokesman at T. Rowe Price, who points out that 'Mutual fund cash flows seem to be the new sentiment indicator . . . Analysts believe that as long as money is pouring into the stock market, it's only logical that stock prices will power higher' (Raghavan, 1994).

Edelen and Warner (2001) and Warther (1995) document a positive relationship between fund flow and subsequent returns. Similarly, Neal and Wheatley (1998) find that fund flow can predict returns. Except for Warther, however, these studies do not formally address the impact of investor sentiment on fund flow.

But why should mutual fund flow reflect investor sentiment? Grossman (1976) and Grossman and Stiglitz (1980) argue that in a market with costly information acquisition and trading, rational investors have an incentive to become informed if the marginal benefits of becoming informed exceed the marginal costs. Mutual fund investors are generally considered to be the least informed investors in the market because they delegate their investment management to fund managers. As a result, Warther (1995, p. 212) asserts, 'mutual fund flows are a logical place to look for indicators of unsophisticated investor sentiment.'

For mutual fund flow to reflect investor sentiment, mutual fund investors must invest or divest in response to bullish or bearish sentiment. Interestingly, by using closed-end fund discounts as a proxy for investor sentiment, Warther (1995) finds they do not affect the net aggregate inflow into equity mutual funds. Given the practitioner view that mutual fund flow is a measure of investor sentiment, Warther (1995) cautions that it is not clear whether closed-end fund discounts or mutual fund flow properly measure investor sentiment.

This study aims to establish a relationship between net aggregate equity fund flow and investor sentiment. Similar to Warther's (1995) study, I examine the behavior of mutual fund investors at the aggregate level, in contrast to other studies done at the individual fund level (Ippolito, 1992; Sirri and Tufano, 1998). However, unlike Warther (1995), who uses closed-end fund discounts as an *indirect* measure of investor sentiment, I use a poll-based measure, which is generally regarded as a *direct* measure of sentiment. The use of these more popular measures from the American Association of Individual Investors and Investor Intelligence permits me to link what investors say with what they do. Also in contrast to the monthly data used by Warther (1995) and Brown and Cliff (2001), I use more recent and weekly data for net aggregate equity fund flow and investor sentiment.

By establishing a relationship between net aggregate equity fund flow and investor sentiment, this chapter answers the following questions: do mutual fund investors react to sentiment when moving money into and out of equity funds? Whose sentiment drives the behavior of mutual fund investors?

Understanding such a relationship is important for two reasons. Because net aggregate equity fund flow is positively related to market returns (Edelen and Warner, 2001; Warther 1995), a significant relationship between net aggregate equity fund flow and investor sentiment would prove that investor sentiment affects market returns. Moreover, because market professionals consider investor sentiment as a measure of crowd psychology (Harding, 1999), and to the extent that such a measure captures non-fundamental signals, a significant relationship between net aggregate equity fund flow and investor sentiment would also imply that investor behavior in equity mutual funds is influenced by factors other than economic fundamentals.

SENTIMENT INDICES

The two most popular direct measures of sentiment are from the American Association of Individual Investors (AAII) and Investor Intelligence (II). The AAII sentiment is based on a survey of randomly selected AAII members who give their stock market expectations over the next six months. It has been conducted since July 1987. Fisher and Statman (2000) find a significant negative relationship between the AAII sentiment level and the S&P 500 returns in the subsequent month, but a significant positive relationship

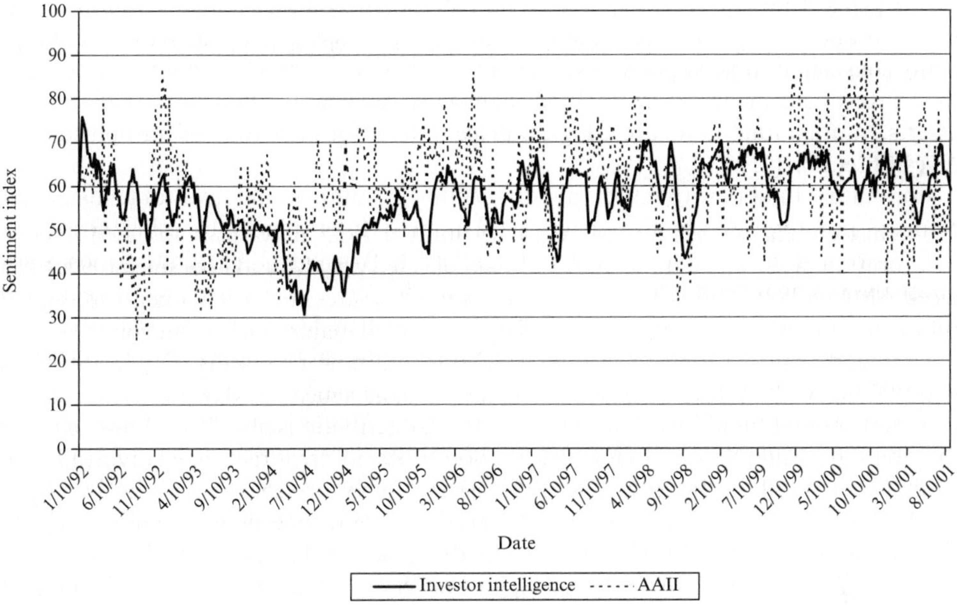

Figure 10.1 *Weekly levels of bullish investor sentiment, 10 January 1992–31 August 2001*

between the monthly change in AAII sentiment and the monthly change in the stock allocations of individual investors. The response from survey participants can be classified as bullish, bearish or neutral. The survey results are reported weekly in *Barron's* and are available at www.aaii.com.

The II sentiment is based on a weekly analysis of about 140 independent investment newsletters. This sentiment indicator is widely recognized as a reliable contrarian indicator of market movements (Siegel, 2002; and Pring, 1991), although Solt and Statman (1988) and Clarke and Statman (1998) argue against using it to predict the direction of the stock market. Each week, the editor of II classifies newsletters as bullish, bearish or expecting a correction. II has compiled its sentiment data since 1963.

Figure 10.1 shows the weekly AAII and II bullish sentiment, defined as the ratio of bullish respondents to the sum of bullish and bearish respondents, from January 1992 to August 2001.

Three features of Figure 10.1 are noteworthy. First, both the AAII and II bullish sentiment indices experience periodic spikes. Siegel (2002) observes that the periodic spikes in the II bullish sentiment coincide with major market events. For example, the 1994 collapse of the bond market and the 1997 Asian financial crisis both caused declines in the index. The index also fell during July–September 1998, as a result of the Russian debt problem and the subsequent fall of Long-Term Capital Management.

Second, although both indices have similar time-series behavior, the AAII index is more volatile, suggesting that individual investors exhibit more diversity in sentiment than newsletter writers. Third, for most of the period from 10 January 1992 to 31 August 2001, both the AAII and II bullish sentiment indices stayed within the 40–70 percent range. Pring (1991) suggests that important buy signals occur when the II indicator falls below 35 percent and then rises. On the other hand, a decline from 80 percent to below 75 percent signals impending trouble.

MUTUAL FUND FLOW

I purchased data on net aggregate equity mutual fund flow from the AMG Data Corporation, www.amgdata.com. AMG has collected weekly fund flow since 1992. Each week AMG collects and verifies data from over 500 sources on 16900 open-end mutual funds. Its weekly reports reflect net fund flows from all major market categories.[2]

For equity mutual funds, the weekly AMG fund flow represents 93 percent of all equity funds with 60 percent of net assets under management. AMG uses two methods to report mutual fund flow: fund flow including distributions and fund flow excluding distributions. Fund flow excluding distributions does not treat reinvested dividends and capital gains as inflow. Because reinvested distributions represent shareholder liability to the IRS (Internal Revenue Service), not incoming assets, fund flow excluding distributions more accurately reflects the actual activity of marginal investors, and is used here.

Figure 10.2 shows the weekly net aggregate equity fund flow as a percentage of aggregate assets of all equity funds from January 1992 to August 2001.[3]

Net aggregate equity fund flow also exhibits periodic spikes. Furthermore, its time-series behavior appears similar to that of the sentiment indices.

SUMMARY STATISTICS

Table 10.1 reports the summary statistics of the weekly levels in bullish sentiment indices and the weekly returns on the Wilshire 5000. The Wilshire 5000 returns are computed as the natural logarithm of the relative price levels in week t and week $t - 1$. Table 10.1 also shows the summary statistics of weekly dollar net aggregate equity mutual fund flow, net aggregate equity mutual fund flow as a percentage of aggregate assets of all equity funds, weekly 90-day Treasury bill yields as a proxy for inflation, and weekly equity risk premium, measured as the difference between the weekly returns of the S&P 500 and the weekly yield of 10-year Treasury bonds.

From 10 January 1992 to 31 August 2001, weekly AAII and II bullish sentiments average 59.6 percent and 56.8 percent, respectively. Confirming the time-series behavior shown in Figure 10.1, the AAII bullish sentiment displays greater variability (a standard deviation of 11.81 percent versus 8.16 percent).[4]

Table 10.1 also shows that the weekly average Wilshire 5000 return is 0.26 percent with a standard deviation of 2.14 percent from 10 January 1992 to 31 August 2001. On average, the 90-day Treasury bill weekly yield is 0.09 percent, while the weekly equity risk premium is 0.08 percent. Over this period, the weekly average net aggregate equity fund flow is \$1.8 billion (0.24 percent) with a standard deviation of \$3.1 billion (0.30 percent).[5]

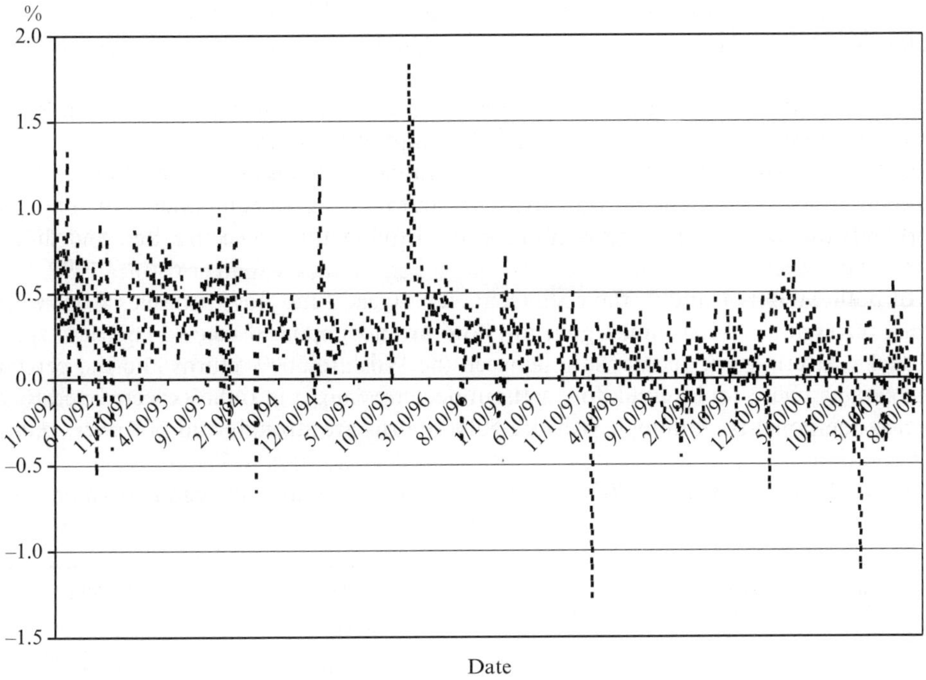

Figure 10.2 *Weekly percentage net aggregate equity fund flow, 10 January 1992–31 August 2001*

Table 10.1 *Weekly summary statistics of net aggregate equity fund flow, bullish investor sentiment and market returns, 10 January 1992–31 August 2001*

Variable	Mean	Median	Std deviation	Minimum	Maximum
AAII bullish sentiment (%)	59.59	60.33	11.81	25.00	88.83
II bullish sentiment (%)	56.79	57.74	8.16	30.70	75.85
Wilshire 5000 return (%)	0.26	0.41	2.14	−12.97	8.23
3-month Treasury bill yields (%)	0.09	0.10	0.02	0.05	0.12
Equity risk premium (%)	0.08	0.20	2.08	−12.91	6.19
Net aggregate equity fund flow ($ million)	1835.93	1839.33	3068.55	−20588.78	15 25.88
Net aggregate equity fund flow (%)	0.24	0.23	0.30	−1.28	1.84

Note: The AAII and II bullish sentiment data are from the American Association of Individual Investors and Investor Intelligence, respectively. The weekly return on Wilshire 5000, obtained from the Wilshire Associates, is computed as the natural logarithm of relative price levels in weeks t and $t-1$. The weekly yield of 3-month Treasury bills, obtained from the Federal Reserve, is used as a proxy for inflation. The equity risk premium is measured as the difference between weekly S&P 500 returns and the weekly yield of 10-year Treasury bonds. The weekly dollar net aggregate equity fund flow and net aggregate equity fund flow as a percentage of aggregate assets of all equity funds are from the AMG Data Corporation.

MUTUAL FUND FLOW AND MARKET RETURNS RELATIONSHIP

To establish the relationship between equity fund flow and market returns, Table 10.2 shows regression analyses of the weekly Wilshire 5000 returns on the percentage net aggregate equity fund flow. Due to the high autocorrelation in the monthly fund flow data, Warther (1995) separates the expected and unexpected components of fund flow and finds that an AR(3) model is appropriate. I follow this procedure, and find that an AR(14) fits weekly data well.

In both Models 1 and 2, the coefficients for lagged fund flow variables from weeks $t - 4$ through $t - 14$ are not significant, and are not reported here to conserve space. Model 1 describes the relationship between the Wilshire 5000 returns and the percentage net aggregate equity fund flow without decomposing it into the expected and unexpected components. Although Wilshire 5000 returns are strongly and positively related

Table 10.2 Regression of Wilshire 5000 returns on percentage net aggregate equity fund flow, 10 January 1992–31 August 2001

Independent variables	Model 1	Model 2
Constant	0.238	0.251
	(1.170)	(0.680)
Fund flow week t	1.537***	
	(3.652)	
Fund flow week $t - 1$	0.742**	
	(2.222)	
Fund flow week $t - 2$	−0.995***	
	(−2.675)	
Fund flow week $t - 3$	−0.410	
	(−0.937)	
Expected fund flow week t		0.121
		(0.084)
Unexpected fund flow week t		1.797***
		(3.859)
Unexpected fund flow week $t - 1$		0.952**
		(2.409)
Unexpected fund flow week $t - 2$		−0.672
		(−1.303)
Unexpected fund flow week $t - 3$		−0.269
		(−0.573)
F-statistics	2.117***	2.257***
Adjusted R^2 (%)	3.312	4.061

Note: The dependent variable is the weekly Wilshire 5000 returns. An AR(14) model was used to decompose net aggregate equity fund flow into expected and unexpected fund flows. Due to their insignificance, the coefficients for lagged fund flow variables from weeks 4 through 14 are not reported to conserve space. Expected fund flow is computed from Model 1, and unexpected fund flow is actual fund flow minus expected fund flow. T-statistics, computed using heteroskedasticity-consistent standard errors, are in parentheses. *, ** and *** denote statistical significance at the 10 percent, 5 percent and 1 percent levels, respectively.

to concurrent net aggregate flow into equity funds, fund flow in the previous two weeks seems to significantly affect the returns as well. Model 2 investigates this relationship further by examining the impact on the Wilshire 5000 returns of expected and unexpected components of fund flow.

Similar to Warther (1995), the concurrent expected fund flow is not significantly related to the Wilshire 5000 returns, while the coefficient for concurrent unexpected fund flow is positive and highly significant (at the 1 percent level). The coefficient for week $t - 1$ unexpected fund flow is also positive and significant at the 5 percent level. Together, the results in Table 10.2 suggest that higher fund flow in the previous and current weeks leads to higher market returns. This finding supports the practitioner claims that higher fund flow will power up the stock market.

Previous studies also suggest that small-firm returns are more sensitive to sentiment than large-firm returns (Lee et al., 1991). To confirm this result, Table 10.3 shows three regression models that relate the weekly returns of two sized-based NYSE–AMEX–Nasdaq decile portfolios. The decile 1 portfolio contains the smallest firms; decile 10 contains the largest. The decile portfolios are value-weighted and constructed on the basis of the market value of equity at the beginning of each year. Returns on decile portfolios come from the Center for Research in Security Prices (CRSP). Model 2 in Table 10.2 is

Table 10.3 Regressions of decile returns and size premium on percentage net aggregate equity fund flow, 10 January 1992–31 August 2001

Independent variables	Decile 1	Decile 10	Decile 1–Decile 10
Constant	0.569	0.263	0.306
	(1.292)	(0.691)	(0.693)
Expected fund flow week t	−1.169	0.072	−1.241
	(−0.689)	(0.048)	(−0.728)
Unexpected fund flow week t	2.560***	1.741***	0.819
	(4.372)	(3.675)	(1.626)
Unexpected fund flow week $t - 1$	2.893***	0.930**	1.963***
	(5.219)	(2.312)	(3.864)
Unexpected fund flow week $t - 2$	1.445**	−0.652	2.097***
	(2.022)	(−1.233)	(2.823)
Unexpected fund flow week $t - 3$	−0.576	−0.245	−0.331
	(−0.758)	(−0.517)	(−0.374)
F-statistics	5.589***	2.069***	2.779**
Adjusted R^2(%)	13.389	3.477	5.653

Note: The dependent variable is weekly returns of the NYSE+AMEX+Nasdaq decile portfolios, obtained from the Center for Research in Security Prices (CRSP). Weekly returns are computed as the natural logarithm of the relative price index in weeks t and $t - 1$. The decile 1 portfolio contains the smallest firms, and decile 10 contains the largest firms. Decile portfolios are value-weighted, and constructed on the basis of the market value of equity at the beginning of each year. An AR(14) model was used to decompose net aggregate equity fund flow into expected and unexpected fund flows. The coefficients for lagged fund flow variables from weeks 4 through 14 are not reported to conserve space. Expected fund flow is computed using Model 1 from Table 10.2, and unexpected fund flow is actual fund flow minus expected fund flow. T-statistics, computed using heteroskedasticity-consistent standard errors, are in parentheses. *, ** and *** denote statistical significance at the 10 percent, 5 percent and 1 percent levels, respectively.

used to examine the relationship between net aggregate equity fund flow and the returns on size-decile portfolios.

Note from Table 10.3 the positive and significant relationship between unexpected fund flow and the returns of both decile 1 and decile 10 portfolios. Concurrent expected fund flow does not affect the returns of these portfolios. More importantly, the coefficients of concurrent unexpected fund flow and unexpected fund flow in the previous two weeks are larger for decile 1 than for decile 10.

To further assess the significance of these coefficients, the last column of Table 10.3 shows a regression of the size premium (returns of decile 1 minus returns of decile 10) on the expected and unexpected fund flow. Concurrent unexpected fund flow is only weakly positively related to size premium (11 percent significance level). On the other hand, there is a strong positive relationship between unexpected fund flow in the previous two weeks and the size premium. This evidence implies that a larger size premium is associated with a higher unexpected fund flow, which confirms the prior findings that small-firm returns are more sensitive to investor sentiment.

INVESTOR SENTIMENT AND MUTUAL FUND FLOW RELATIONSHIP

Table 10.4 shows the results of regression analyses that examine the relationship between the percentage net aggregate equity mutual fund flow and changes in bullish sentiments, defined as the difference between bullish sentiment indicators from week $t - 1$ to t. The regressions also control for the changes in weekly yield of the 90-day Treasury bills as a proxy for changes in inflation, and differences between the weekly S&P 500 returns and weekly 10-year Treasury bond yields as a proxy for the equity risk premium.

The Wilshire 5000 return in the previous week is included in the regressions to examine whether fund investors move money into and out of equity funds in response to recent market movement. The regressions also contain a January dummy variable to capture seasonality in fund flows. Cassidy (2002) notes there is usually a strong net fund flow in January because many employees invest their year-end bonuses at that time. The regressions contain 14-week lagged percentage fund flow variables to control for the persistence of fund flow, but the coefficients are not reported to conserve space.

Model 1 excludes the effect of sentiment on net aggregate equity fund flow. Note the positive and highly significant coefficient for the January dummy. This result supports Cassidy's (2002) claim that net equity inflow is significantly higher in January. Similarly, the coefficient for equity risk premium is positive and highly significant, indicating that mutual fund investors tend to move money into equity funds when the equity risk premium rises.

On the other hand, the coefficient for changes in inflation is not significant, implying that mutual fund investors are not concerned with inflationary changes when moving money. The significance of the coefficient for the Wilshire 5000 return over the previous week suggests positive feedback trading. Equity mutual fund investors seem to respond to recent market performance, in contrast to Warther's (1995) analysis.

Model 2 describes the relationship between net aggregate equity fund flow and changes in the AAII bullish sentiments in weeks $t - 1$, t and $t + 1$. In this model, change

Table 10.4 Regressions of percentage net aggregate equity fund flow on changes in bullish sentiment; full period: 10 January 1992–31 August 2001

Independent variables	Model 1	Model 2	Model 3
Constant	0.023	0.021	0.020
	(1.084)	(0.980)	(0.987)
January dummy	0.203***	0.205***	0.202***
	(4.027)	(3.893)	(3.931)
Change in inflation in week t	−1.542	−1.350	−0.656
	(−0.126)	(−0.113)	(−0.057)
Equity risk premium in week t	0.025***	0.021***	0.015**
	(4.326)	(3.562)	(2.422)
Wilshire 5000 return in week $t-1$	0.012*	0.010	0.003
	(1.859)	(1.544)	(0.368)
Change in AAII bullish sentiment in		0.002*	
week $t-1$		(1.786)	
Change in AAII bullish sentiment in		0.003**	
week t		(2.432)	
Change in AAII bullish sentiment in		0.000	
week $t+1$		(0.021)	
Change in II bullish sentiment in			−0.003
week $t-1$			(−0.533)
Change in II bullish sentiment in			0.013**
week t			(2.220)
Change in II bullish sentiment in			0.021***
week $t+1$			(3.733)
F-statistics	9.418***	8.573***	9.435***
Adjusted R^2 (%)	23.657	24.578	26.632

Note: The dependent variable is weekly net aggregate equity fund flow as a percentage of aggregate assets of all equity funds. The above regressions also include 14-week lagged percentage net aggregate equity fund flows as independent variables. For brevity, their coefficients are not reported. T-statistics, computed using heteroskedasticity-consistent standard errors, are in parentheses. Changes in bullish sentiment are defined as the difference between bullish sentiments in weeks t and $t-1$. Change in bullish sentiment in week t has been made orthogonal to change in bullish sentiment in week $t-1$, and change in bullish sentiment in week $t+1$ has been made orthogonal to changes in bullish sentiment in weeks $t-1$ and t. This procedure was carried out for both AAII and II sentiments. *, ** and *** denote statistical significance at the 10 percent, 5 percent, and 1 percent levels, respectively.

in week t AAII sentiment was made orthogonal to change in week $t-1$ AAII sentiment. Likewise, change in week $t+1$ AAII sentiment was made orthogonal to changes in week t and week $t-1$ AAII sentiments. Orthogonalization captures additional information in week t and $t+1$ changes in sentiment that is not contained in the changes in sentiment over the previous week(s).

Note that the coefficients for changes in AAII bullish sentiment in weeks $t-1$ and t are positive and statistically significant at the 10 percent and 5 percent levels, respectively. In contrast, the coefficient for change in week $t+1$ AAII bullish sentiment is not statistically significant. These findings indicate both a contemporaneous and non-contemporaneous relationship between investor sentiment and net aggregate equity fund flow, contrary to

Warther's (1995) findings. Specifically, there is a higher net fund flow into equity funds in week t, when individual investors became more bullish in the previous and current weeks.

Model 3 describes the relationship between net aggregate equity fund flow and changes in the II bullish sentiments in weeks $t - 1$, t, and $t + 1$. Similar to Model 2, change in week t sentiment was made orthogonal to change in week $t - 1$ sentiment. Likewise, change in week $t + 1$ sentiment was made orthogonal to changes in week t and week $t - 1$ sentiments.

The coefficients for changes in II bullish sentiment in weeks t and $t + 1$ are both positive and statistically significant. However, the coefficient for change in week $t - 1$ is negative and not statistically significant. Again, these findings suggest both a contemporaneous and non-contemporaneous relationship between sentiment and net equity fund flow. In particular, there is a higher net fund flow into equity funds in the current week, when newsletter writers are currently more bullish. Note, however, that the non-contemporaneous relationship between newsletter writer sentiment and net aggregate equity fund flow is different from that between individual investor sentiment and net aggregate equity fund flow in Model 2.

The significant positive coefficient for change in II bullish sentiment in week $t + 1$ in Model 3 implies that a higher net aggregate equity fund flow in week t induces newsletter writers to be more bullish in the subsequent week. This result is consistent with the notion that newsletter writers believe that current inflow into equity funds will subsequently propel the market to a higher level, which therefore makes them more bullish in the following week.[6]

Note from Models 2 and 3 the strong evidence of the January seasonality effect in net aggregate equity fund flow. This is again consistent with Cassidy's (2002) assertion. However, there is no evidence that equity mutual fund investors follow a feedback trading strategy. More importantly, the relationship between net aggregate equity fund flow and changes in sentiment is very strong even after controlling for the effects of risk premium and changes in inflation. This implies that the behavior of equity mutual fund investors is influenced by investor sentiment as well as by economic fundamentals.

The results in Table 10.4 suggest that Warther's (1995) failure to find a significant relationship between closed-end fund discounts and net aggregate equity fund flow is probably due to the use of closed-end fund discounts as a measure of sentiment. Using the daily fund flow of three Fidelity funds, Goetzmann and Massa (2003) also find that bullish sentiment, proxied by market-timing newsletters recommendation, is positively related to fund flow.

ROBUSTNESS TESTS

To examine the robustness of these results, I first reran Models 2 and 3 in Table 10.4 without orthogonalizing changes in the AAII and II sentiments. The results with respect to both measures are qualitatively similar to those first reported in Table 10.4.

Second, I replaced changes in weekly sentiment with the weekly unusual level of bullish sentiment, computed as the difference between the week t sentiment index from its 10-week moving average.[7] Using this alternative measure, I again reran Models 2 and 3. The results indicate a positive and significant (at the 5 percent level) contemporaneous relationship between net aggregate equity fund flow and the unusual level of AAII bullish sentiment, suggesting a higher inflow into equity mutual funds when individual investors are currently unusually bullish.

On the other hand, there is only a non-contemporaneous relationship between net aggregate equity fund flow and the unusual level of II bullish sentiment. Specifically, there is a negative and significant (at the 10 percent level) relationship between net aggregate equity fund flow in week t and the unusual level of bullish sentiment in week $t - 1$. Moreover, I also found a positive and significant (at the 1 percent level) relationship between net aggregate equity fund flow in week t and the unusual level of bullish sentiment in week $t + 1$. These results imply that investors in equity mutual funds act in a contrarian manner in response to the unusual bullishness of the newsletter writers in the previous week. In turn, the newsletter writers become unusually bullish in the subsequent week in response to a higher net aggregate equity fund flow in the current week. Again, these findings highlight the importance of sentiment in explaining the behavior of equity mutual fund investors.

For a third robustness test, I divided the 10 January 1992–31 August 2001 period into two subperiods of equal length. I then ran the same three regression models from Table 10.4. The results are reported in Tables 10.5 and 10.6.

Table 10.5 shows that the January dummy variable has positive and statistically significant coefficients across Models 1–3. The coefficients for equity risk premium and changes in inflation are not statistically significant in all models.

Interestingly, over the 10 January 1992–1 November 1996 subperiod, there is evidence of positive feedback trading. Mutual fund investors tended to move money into equity funds in response to good recent market performance. More importantly, Table 10.5 indicates a positive contemporaneous relationship between the sentiment of individual investors and net aggregate equity fund flow, but a positive non-contemporaneous relationship between the sentiment of newsletter writers and net aggregate equity fund flow. When individual investors are more bullish in the current week, mutual fund investors pour more money into equity funds. An increase in the net aggregate equity fund flow in the current week then leads newsletter writers to be more bullish the subsequent week.

For the 8 November 1996–31 August 2001 subperiod, Table 10.6 reveals highly significant coefficients (at the 1 percent level) for the January dummy variable in Models 1–3. The equity risk premium has positive and highly significant coefficients (at the 1 percent level) in all three models. Changes in inflation and the Wilshire 5000 return in the previous week show no statistical significance. The coefficient for changes in the week $t - 1$ AAII bullish sentiment is positive and statistically significant at the 10 percent level. In addition, the coefficient for changes in the week $t + 1$ II bullish sentiment is positive and statistically significant at the 1 percent level, while changes in weeks t and $t - 1$ are only significant at the 13 percent and 12 percent levels, respectively.

Overall, the relationship between net aggregate equity fund flow and both sentiments is robust with respect to alternative specification of sentiment measures and time periods. The relationship between net aggregate equity fund flow and II sentiment is statistically

Table 10.5 Robustness tests of the regressions of percentage net aggregate equity fund flow on changes in bullish sentiment; subperiod: 10 January 1992–1 November 1996

Independent variables	Model 1	Model 2	Model 3
Constant	0.194***	0.185***	0.187***
	(3.132)	(3.094)	(3.204)
January dummy	0.178**	0.166*	0.179**
	(2.164)	(1.934)	(2.049)
Change in inflation in week *t*	−22.518	−22.857	−21.732
	(−1.030)	(−1.060)	(−1.034)
Equity risk premium in week *t*	0.016	0.006	0.004
	(0.835)	(0.283)	(0.208)
Wilshire 5000 return in week $t-1$	0.058***	0.054***	0.046***
	(3.940)	(3.296)	(2.822)
Change in AAII bullish sentiment in week $t-1$		0.000 (0.180)	
Change in AAII bullish sentiment in week *t*		0.004* (1.683)	
Change in AAII bullish sentiment in week $t+1$		0.001 (0.581)	
Change in II bullish sentiment in week $t-1$			0.000 (0.038)
Change in II bullish sentiment in week *t*			0.009 (1.055)
Change in II bullish sentiment in week $t+1$			0.015* (1.857)
F-statistics	3.263***	2.967***	3.038***
Adjusted R^2 (%)	14.667	14.844	15.298

Note: The dependent variable is weekly net aggregate equity fund flow as a percentage of aggregate assets of all equity funds. The above regressions also include 14-week lagged percentage net aggregate equity fund flows as independent variables. For brevity, their coefficients are not reported. *T*-statistics, computed using heteroskedasticity-consistent standard errors, are in parentheses. Changes in bullish sentiment are defined as the difference between bullish sentiments in weeks *t* and $t-1$. Change in bullish sentiment in week *t* has been made orthogonal to change in bullish sentiment in week $t-1$, and change in bullish sentiment in week $t+1$ has been made orthogonal to changes in bullish sentiment in weeks $t-1$ and *t*. This procedure was carried out for both AAII and II sentiments. *, **, and *** denote statistical significance at the 10 percent, 5 percent, and 1 percent levels, respectively.

stronger than that between net aggregate equity fund flow and AAII sentiment. Tables 10.4–10.6 consistently show that sentiment of individual investors in the current or previous week is positively related to net aggregate equity fund flow in the current week, while the sentiment of newsletter writers in the subsequent week is positively related to net aggregate equity fund flow in the current week.

The main results indicate that mutual fund investors react to the sentiment of individual investors when moving money into and out of equity mutual funds. And this trading behavior subsequently affects the sentiment of newsletter writers.

Table 10.6 Robustness tests of the regressions of percentage net aggregate equity fund flow on changes in bullish sentiment; subperiod: 8 November 1996–31 August 2001

Independent variables	Model 1	Model 2	Model 3
Constant	0.009	0.005	0.004
	(0.317)	(0.168)	(0.135)
January dummy	0.280***	0.288***	0.286***
	(4.185)	(4.096)	(4.367)
Change in inflation in week t	11.082	9.579	10.474
	(0.830)	(0.748)	(0.879)
Equity risk premium in week t	0.026***	0.024***	0.018***
	(4.069)	(3.787)	(2.639)
Wilshire 5000 return in week	0.003	0.002	−0.004
$t-1$	(0.404)	(0.251)	(−0.505)
Change in AAII bullish sentiment in		0.003*	
week $t-1$		(1.820)	
Change in AAII bullish sentiment in		0.002	
week t		(1.162)	
Change in AAII bullish sentiment in		0.000	
week $t+1$		(0.218)	
Change in II bullish sentiment in			−0.009
week $t-1$			(−1.558)
Change in II bullish sentiment in			0.011
week t			(1.595)
Change in II bullish sentiment in			0.022***
week $t+1$			(2.994)
F-statistics	3.740***	3.492***	4.246***
Adjusted R^2 (%)	16.424	17.309	21.425

Note: The dependent variable is weekly net aggregate equity fund flow as a percentage of aggregate assets of all equity funds. The above regressions also include 14-week lagged percentage net aggregate equity fund flows as independent variables. For brevity, their coefficients are not reported. T-statistics, computed using heteroskedasticity-consistent standard errors, are in parentheses. Changes in bullish sentiment are defined as the difference between bullish sentiments in weeks t and $t-1$. Change in bullish sentiment in week t has been made orthogonal to change in bullish sentiment in week $t-1$, and change in bullish sentiment in week $t+1$ has been made orthogonal to changes in bullish sentiment in weeks $t-1$ and t. This procedure was carried out for both AAII and II sentiments. *, ** and *** denote statistical significance at the 10 percent, 5 percent and 1 percent levels, respectively.

CONCLUSION

By examining the relationship between the poll-based investor sentiment measures and net aggregate equity fund flow, this study links what investors say with what they do. The results reconcile the differences between the practitioner view and empirical evidence regarding the impact of investor sentiment on the behavior of equity mutual fund investors.

Using weekly data, I find that the sentiment of both individual investors and newsletter writers is related to net aggregate equity fund flow. Fund investors pour money into equity funds in the current week when individual investors were more bullish in the current and previous weeks. In addition, newsletter writers subsequently become more bullish when fund investors put more money into equity mutual funds in the current week.

This relationship between investor sentiment and net aggregate equity fund flow is strong even after accounting for the effect of equity risk premium and changes in inflation. Furthermore, there is a strong January seasonality effect in net aggregate equity fund flow, but mixed evidence that equity fund investors are positive feedback traders. Overall, the evidence supports the notion that the behavior of equity fund investors is influenced not only by economic fundamentals, but also by investor sentiment.

ACKNOWLEDGMENT

Financial support from Penn State University–Great Valley is gratefully acknowledged. The author also thanks seminar participants at Penn State University–Great Valley, and an anonymous referee for helpful comments and suggestions. This chapter is a version of an article that appeared in *The Journal of Behavioral Finance*, **5** (2), 105–15 (2004).

NOTES

1. Indeed, Grinblatt and Keloharju (2000) find the presence of both momentum and contrarian traders in the Finnish market, while Kumar and Dhar (2002) document the presence of both types of traders in the US market. Gompers and Metrick (2001) show that momentum trading by mutual funds is offset by contrarian trading by other institutions. For further evidence of momentum and contrarian trading by individual and institutional traders, see Badrinath and Wahal (2002), Fisher and Statman (2000, 2003), and Nofsinger and Sias (1999).
2. It would have been ideal to examine the impact of investor sentiment on equity and bond fund flow as well as on fund flow in different categories of equity and bond funds. Budgetary constraints, unfortunately, prevented me from doing such an analysis.
3. As an alternative measure, I computed the weekly net aggregate equity fund flow as a percentage of the total value series of the CRSP's stock indices or as a percentage of the entire stock market (NYSE+AMEX+NASDAQ). The results based on this alternative measure are virtually identical to those reported in the tables.
4. Because the sentiment indices are highly autocorrelated, subsequent analysis uses changes in the sentiment indices.
5. To alleviate concern about non-stationarity of the series reported in Table 10.1, I ran Phillips–Perron unit root tests for each series. The null hypothesis of unit root was strongly rejected for all series except for the 3-month Treasury bill yields. First-differencing the Treasury bill yields results in a stationary series. As a result, subsequent analysis uses the first difference in 3-month Treasury bill yields as a proxy for changes in inflation.
6. To test whether the sentiment of individual investors is more important than the sentiment of newsletter writers in explaining the variation in net aggregate equity fund flow, I included weeks $t-1$, t and $t+1$ changes in AAII and II sentiments in one regression. Multicollinearity is not a problem. The coefficients of the sentiment variables remained significant and had the same signs as in Table 10.3. This result confirms the importance of both groups' sentiments in explaining the variation. To conserve space, this result is not reported.
7. The choice of 10-week period to compute the moving average was motivated by Pring (1991), who suggests using a 10-week period to smooth out the fluctuations in the sentiment index. The results do not change

if the average of the AAII and II sentiment indices reported in Table 10.1 is used to compute the weekly unusual level of bullish sentiments.

REFERENCES

Badrinath, S.G. and S. Wahal (2002), 'Momentum trading by institutions,' *Journal of Finance*, **57**, 2449–78.

Barber, B.M. and T. Odean (2001), 'Boys will be boys: gender, overconfidence, and common stock investment,' *Quarterly Journal of Economics*, **116**, 261–92.

Barberis, N. and R. Thaler (2002), 'A survey of behavioral finance,' National Bureau of Economic Research (NBER) Working Paper.

Black, F. (1986), 'Noise,' *Journal of Finance*, **41**, 529–43.

Brown, G.W. and M.T. Cliff (2001), 'Investor sentiment and the near-term stock market,' Working Paper, University of North Carolina, Chapel Hill.

Cassidy, Donald L. (2002), *Trading on Volume: The Key to Identifying and Profiting from Stock Price Reversals*, New York: McGraw-Hill.

Clarke, R.G. and M. Statman (1998), 'Bullish or bearish?,' *Financial Analysts Journal*, **54**, 63–72.

Coval, J.D. and T. Shumway (2001), 'Do behavioral biases affect prices?,' Working Paper, University of Michigan, Ann Arbor.

DeBondt, W.F.M. and R. Thaler (1985), 'Does the stock market overreact?', *Journal of Finance*, **40**, 793–808.

DeLong, J.B., A. Shleifer, L.H. Summers and R.J. Waldman (1990), 'Noise trader risk in financial markets,' *Journal of Political Economy*, **98**, 703–38.

Dreman, D.N. and E.A Lufkin (2000), 'Investor overreaction: evidence that its basis is psychological,' *Journal of Psychology and Financial Markets*, **1**, 61–75.

Edelen, R.M. and J.B. Warner (2001), 'Aggregate price effects of institutional trading: a study of mutual fund flow and market returns,' *Journal of Financial Economics*, **59**, 195–220.

Fisher, K.L. and M. Statman (2000), 'Investor sentiment and stock returns', *Financial Analysts Journal*, **56**, 16–23.

Fisher, K.L. and M. Statman (2003), 'Sentiment, value and market timing', Working Paper, Santa Clara University.

Goetzmann, W.N. and M. Massa (2003), 'Index funds and stock market growth,' *Journal of Business*, **76**, 1–28.

Gompers, P.A. and A. Metrick (2001), 'Institutional investors and equity prices,' *Quarterly Journal of Economics*, **116**, 229–59.

Grinblatt, M. and M. Keloharju (2000), 'The investment behavior and performance of various investor types: a study of Finland's unique data set,' *Journal of Financial Economics*, **55**, 43–67.

Grossman, S. (1976), 'On the efficiency of competitive stock markets when traders have diverse information,' *Journal of Finance*, **31**, 573–85.

Grossman, S. and J. Stiglitz (1980), 'On the impossibility of informationally efficient markets,' *American Economic Review*, **70**, 393–408.

Harding, Sy (1999), *Riding the Bear: How to Prosper in the Coming Bear Market*, Avondale, MA: Adams Media Corporation.

Hirshleifer, D. (2001), 'Investor psychology and asset pricing,' *Journal of Finance*, **56**, 1533–98.

Ippolito, R.A. (1992), 'Consumer reaction to measures of poor quality: evidence from the mutual fund industry,' *Journal of Law and Economics*, **35**, 45–70.

Kahneman, D. and M. Riepe (1998), 'Aspects of investor psychology,' *Journal of Portfolio Management*, **24**, 52–65.

Kumar, A. and R. Dhar (2002), 'A non-random walk down the main street: impact of price trends on trading decisions of individual investors,' Working Paper, Yale University.

Lee, C.M.C., A. Shleifer and R.H. Thaler (1991), 'Investor sentiment and the closed-end fund puzzle,' *Journal of Finance*, **46**, 75–109.

Neal, R. and S.M. Wheatley (1998), 'Do measures of investor sentiment predict returns?', *Journal of Financial and Quantitative Analysis*, **33**, 523–47.

Nofsinger, J.R. and R.W. Sias (1999), 'Herding and feedback trading by institutional and individual investors,' *Journal of Finance*, **54**, 2263–95.

Pring, M.J. (1991), *Technical Analysis Explained: The Successful Investor's Guide to Spotting Investment Trends and Turning Points*, New York: McGraw-Hill.

Raghavan, A. (1994), 'Growing investor bearishness is a good sign, some say,' *The Wall Street Journal*, 14 March, C1.

Scherreik, S. (2003), 'Break away – and cash in,' *Business Week*, 31 March, 100–101.
Shefrin, H. and M. Statman (1985), 'The disposition to sell winners too early and ride losers too long,' *Journal of Finance*, **40**, 777–90.
Shefrin, H. and M. Statman (1994), 'Behavioral capital asset pricing theory,' *Journal of Financial and Quantitative Analysis*, **29**, 323–49.
Shiller, R.J. and J. Pound (1989), 'Survey evidence on diffusion of interest and information among investors,' *Journal of Economic Behavior and Organization*, **12**, 47–66.
Shleifer, A. (2000), *Inefficient Markets*, Oxford: Oxford University Press.
Siegel, J.J. (2002), *Stocks for the Long Run*. 3rd edn, New York: McGraw-Hill.
Sirri, E. and P. Tufano (1998), 'Costly search and mutual fund flows,' *Journal of Finance*, **53**, 1589–622.
Solt, M.E. and M. Statman (1988), 'How useful is the sentiment index?,' *Financial Analysts Journal*, **44**, 45–55.
Warther, V.A. (1995), 'Aggregate mutual fund flow and security returns,' *Journal of Financial Economics*, **39**, 209–35.

11 The impact of motivational and cognitive factors on optimistic earnings forecasts

Anna M. Cianci and Satoris S. Culbertson

INTRODUCTION

Prior research indicates that sell-side analysts' (SSAs') earnings forecasts are optimistic (e.g. DeChow et al., 2000; Easterwood and Nutt, 1999; Rajan and Servaes, 1997; Stickel, 1992; Abarbanell, 1991; Ali et al., 1992; Kang et al., 1994; Das et al., 1998; Bathke et al., 1991; Dreman and Berry, 1995; Dugar and Nathan, 1995; Fried and Givoly, 1982; Klein, 1990; O'Brien, 1988; Brav and Lehavy, 2003; Gu and Wu, 2003; Bradshaw et al., 2006; Herrmann et al., 2007). Only one study (Willis, 2001), however, has found that buy-side analysts (BSAs) are also optimistic. Motivational explanations hold that SSAs (but not BSAs) are optimistic in response to incentives to foster management relations, encourage investment banking and underwriting activities, and promote trading commissions (Francis and Philbrick, 1993; Lin and McNichols, 1998; Dugar and Nathan, 1995; Hayes, 1998; Mest and Plummer, 2003). Cognitive explanations, on the other hand, suggest that information processing biases such as under- and overreaction (DeBondt and Thaler, 1990; Easterwood and Nutt, 1999), imaginary thinking (Sedor, 2002) and information processing biases involving base rate neglect and missing information inferences (White and Koehler, 2004; Braun and Yaniv, 1992; Kahneman and Tversky, 1973; Kalish, 2001) may contribute to optimism.

Almost all of the research on analysts' optimism is market-based research using archival data, while only a few take an experimental approach (e.g. Ashton and Cianci, 2007; Sedor, 2002; Affleck-Graves et al., 1990; Whitecotton, 1996). Of the experimental studies, none has examined how motivational and cognitive factors jointly influence the forecast optimism of individuals.[1] This is the focus of the current chapter. Specifically, regarding motivational factors, we examine how the presence or absence of institutional incentives contributes to optimistic forecasts. As for the cognitive factors, we examine whether the valence of earnings trends (positive, negative) and the task characteristic of information completeness (complete, incomplete) contribute to optimism. In addition, we examine the relation between attention to base rate information and optimism.

We sought to determine how assigned incentives (motivational factor) and information completeness, earnings trend and base rate attention (cognitive factors) independently and jointly contribute to forecast optimism. We conducted an experiment in which 132 MBA students were assigned either a directional or accuracy goal and predicted earnings per share (EPS) for current-year, one-year-ahead and two-year-ahead horizons for eight fictitious companies. For each of the companies, a six-year prior EPS series was manipulated to create differing increasing or decreasing trends.

The results indicated that motivational and cognitive factors interact to determine optimism. Consistent with expectations, earnings trend interacted with incentives and information completeness to determine earnings forecasts and the presence (versus absence) of incentives differentially impacted the evaluation of base rate information. Specifically, (1) individuals with institutional incentives (compared to those without such incentives) made more favorable forecasts in response to negatively trended earnings but not in response to positively trended earnings; and (2) individuals made less favorable forecasts when information was framed as less (compared to more) complete for negatively trended earnings but not for positively trended earnings. Also, individuals with incentives (compared to those without incentives) rated industry data as less relevant to their forecasts. Finally, attention to base rates was inversely related to the favorableness in forecasts. These findings are consistent with prior research that suggests that SSAs' institutional incentives encourage them to make optimistic forecasts, that optimism is more prevalent in response to negative information, and that judgments are often unduly influenced by irrelevant factors (such as whether information is framed as more or less complete) and inadequately influenced by relevant ones (such as base rates).

The study presented within this chapter makes three important contributions. First, it provides experimental information on the joint effects on forecasts of institutional incentives (a motivational factor) and information completeness, earnings trend and base rate attention (cognitive factors). Such information is not provided by the existing evidence. A notable exception is Ashton and Cianci (2007). However, while these authors examined SSAs' and BSAs' forecasts in response to negatively and positively trended earnings series, they did not consider the interaction of the presence (or absence) of institutional incentives (in the form of explicitly imposed goals) and the cognitive factors considered here. On the contrary, we explicitly manipulate participants' goals or incentives that have been proposed to underlie the optimism phenomenon; in Ashton and Cianci (2007), the authors assume that such goals or incentives are embedded in their analyst participants. We believe that we more purely (by controlling the actual goal imposed and providing a controlled experimental setting) test the interactive impact of goals and various cognitive factors. Second, it has been suggested that 'informationally irrelevant variations in the presentation of financial data can influence (investor) decision-making' (Koonce and Mercer, 2005, pp. 194–5). Along these lines, we provide evidence that individuals are influenced by how information is framed (i.e. less complete or more complete), thus suggesting that a psychological approach is appropriate for understanding forecasting behavior. Third, research on analysts' optimism is very important since optimistic forecasts are statistically and economically significant (e.g. Darrough and Russell, 2002; Duru and Reeb, 2002). Indeed, optimistic forecasts are potentially costly to investors who, according to prior research (e.g. Abarbanell and Bernard, 1992; Rajan and Servaes, 1997; Thomas, 1999; Dechow et al., 2000; Khurana et al., 2003; Bradshaw et al., 2006; Herrmann et al., 2007), do not fully unravel analysts' optimistic earnings forecasts. In addition, the experimental approach used in this study differs from most studies examining optimism, and offers the advantages of (dis)confirming the results of capital markets research and providing new hypotheses for archival researchers to investigate.

The chapter is organized as follows. The next section reviews research on analysts' optimism, describes the conceptual model upon which the hypotheses are based, and then presents the hypotheses. The section after that describes the experimental design and method, followed by the presentation of the results. Finally, conclusions are discussed and future research directions are offered.

THEORETICAL BACKGROUND AND HYPOTHESES DEVELOPMENT

Figure 11.1 shows a conceptual model of the proposed cognitive and motivational determinants of forecast optimism along with the hypothesized relations that we explain in more detail in the following paragraphs. As an overview, we propose that institutional incentives (versus the lack of such incentives) will lead to more favorable earnings forecasts (Hypothesis 1). Additionally, we propose that earnings trends and information completeness will each independently predict forecast optimism (Hypothesis 2 and Hypothesis 4, respectively). We further propose that the presence or absence of incentives will interact with positively or negatively trended past earnings to determine earnings forecasts (Hypothesis 3). Additionally, we suggest that institutional incentives may contribute to more favorable earnings forecasts for companies with less complete information than for companies with more complete information (Hypothesis 5). Furthermore, we suggest that earnings trend will interact with information that is framed as more or less complete to determine earnings forecasts (Hypothesis 6). Finally, we suggest that individuals with incentives will attend less to base rate information than will those with accuracy goals (Hypothesis 7) and that this base rate attention will be inversely associated with optimism (Hypothesis 8).

As noted, in this chapter we examine how motivational and cognitive factors independently and jointly contribute to optimistic forecasts. The specific motivational factor we examine is the presence or absence of institutional incentives, while the cognitive factors we examine include earnings trend, information completeness and base rate attention. Each of these factors is described in greater detail in the following sections, along with the supporting theory and rationale for the hypotheses we summarized in the preceding paragraph regarding how the different motivational and cognitive factors independently and jointly relate to optimism.

Motivational Determinants of Optimism

Individuals can be motivated both intrinsically, such as through personal interest, and extrinsically, such as through the use of incentives (Deci and Ryan, 1985). Research suggests that SSAs' optimism may be due to motivational determinants such as incentives. For example, various archival studies (e.g. Dugar and Nathan, 1995; Francis and Philbrick, 1993; Lin and McNichols, 1998) and one experimental study (Hunton and McEwen, 1997) provide evidence that SSAs may have incentives to make optimistic earnings forecasts. Specifically, SSAs may be optimistic about increasing their performance evaluation and compensation (Dorfman, 1991; Francis and Philbrick, 1993). Furthermore, prior research has found that SSAs are frequently motivated to be optimistic about fostering business relationships (Francis and Philbrick, 1993; Dugar and Nathan, 1995; Lin and McNichols, 1998; Das et al., 1998; Dechow et al., 2000), please firm management and address career (reputation) concerns (Richardson et al., 2004; Lim, 2001), increase firm revenue via trading commissions and underwriting support (Dugar and Nathan, 1995; Dechow et al., 2000; Lin and McNichols, 1998; Hayes, 1998; Michaely and Womack, 1999; Jackson, 2005). Even financial press reports suggest that analysts who resist optimistic forecasts suffer negative professional consequences (e.g.

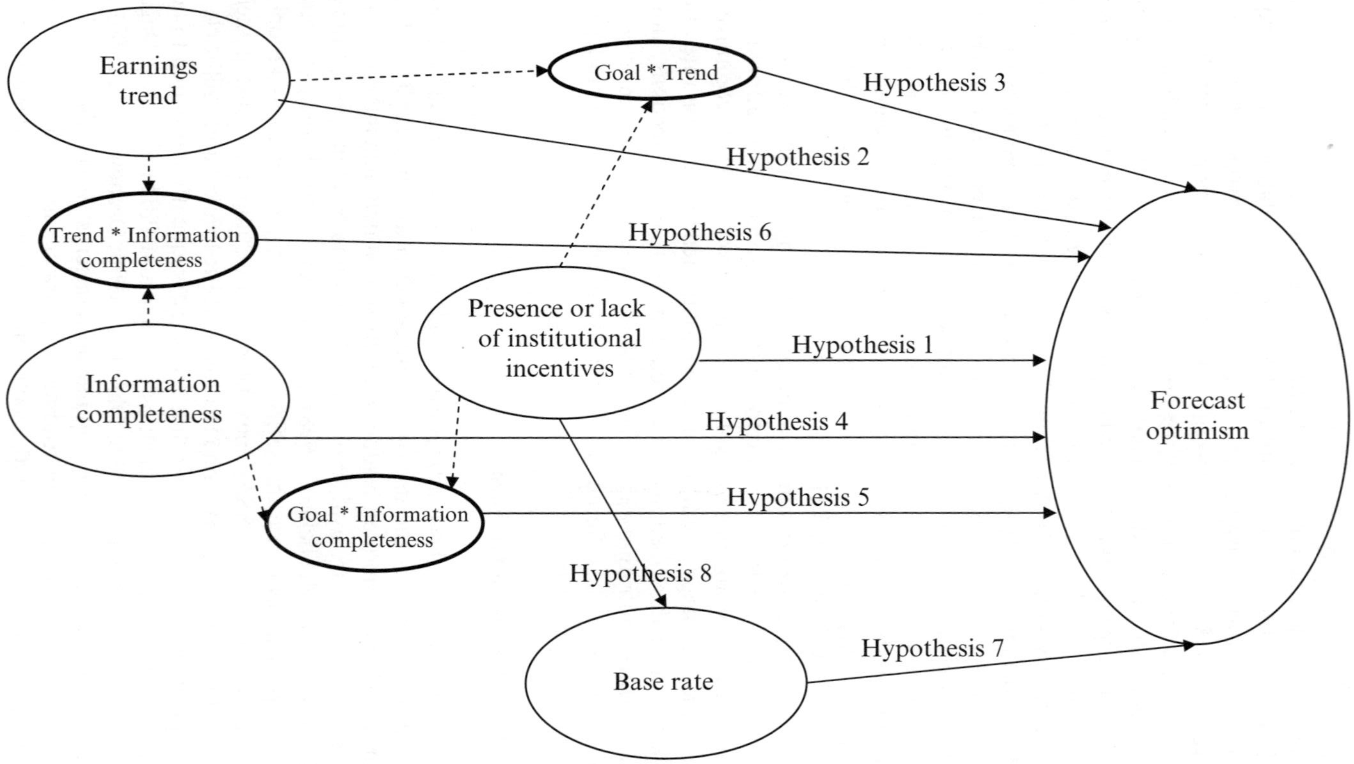

Figure 11.1 *Conceptual model of the proposed cognitive and motivational determinants of forecast optimism*

Cole, 2001; Hansell, 2001) and anecdotal evidence suggests that analysts prefer supporting investment-banking aspects of brokerages rather than providing unbiased forecasts (Boni and Womack, 2002). Thus it appears that there are clear incentives for SSAs to be optimistic in their forecasts.

Despite these incentives to be optimistic, SSAs also have reason to be accurate since their forecasts are publicly disclosed, and therefore may reveal potential inaccuracies on their part. Consistent with this dual-incentive notion, Dugar and Nathan (1995) found that SSAs can be accurate even if they are optimistic. In addition, one study (Willis, 2001) found that BSAs are also optimistic, and SSAs' optimism may be transferred to BSAs by the latter's use of SSAs' optimistic forecasts in developing their own forecasts (Schipper, 1991; Williams et al., 1996). Despite these findings that BSAs may be optimistic at times, Ashton and Cianci (2007) provided experimental evidence that SSAs are more optimistic in their earnings forecasts than BSAs. Thus it appears that SSAs, who have institutional incentives, are relatively more optimistic than analysts without such incentives (e.g. BSAs). Correspondingly, we make the following directional hypothesis:

H_1: Individuals with institutional incentives will make more favorable earnings forecasts than those without such incentives.

Cognitive Determinants of Optimism

Some research suggests that analysts may not issue intentionally optimistic earnings forecasts (Eames and Glover, 2003; Irvine, 2004). Other research provides evidence consistent with the notion that forecast optimism may be driven by something other than motivational factors or institutional incentives. For instance, in addition to financial analysts (Darrough and Russell, 2002), other individuals – analysts employed by independent research firms (Jacob et al., 2003) and students (Affleck-Graves et al., 1990) – also make optimistic earnings forecasts. Thus optimism may not be explained by motivational factors.

Research in accounting and finance has proposed cognitive determinants of SSAs' optimism, or those related to perception, memory, judgment or reasoning. For example, prior research has shown that analysts often discount negative earnings news and overreact to changes in recent earnings (e.g. Easterwood and Nutt, 1999; Abarbanell and Bernard, 1992; DeBondt and Thaler, 1990; Klein, 1990; Daniel et al., 1998; for a review see Brown, 1993). Research provides evidence that while a time-series model of earnings tends not to demonstrate optimism (Affleck-Graves et al., 1990), both SSAs and student subjects do tend to be optimistic, with SSAs being more optimistic than students (Whitecotton, 1996). Additionally, it appears that optimism increases when the information analysts receive is structured in a way that encourages the envisioning of positive future earnings outcomes (Sedor, 2002). Furthermore, research in psychology has documented a positive association between extremity of predictions and neglect of base rates and inferences made in response to missing information (e.g. White and Koehler, 2004; Braun and Yaniv, 1992; Kahneman and Tversky, 1973; Kalish, 2001). Thus there are certainly factors that are cognitive in nature (related to perception, judgment and reasoning) that contribute to optimistic forecasts.

In the following sections, we present three cognitive factors that are likely to interact with institutional incentives (a motivational factor) to determine forecast optimism. Specifically, based on research and theory, described earlier, we propose that earnings trends will lead to information-processing biases (changes in cognition), which will influence optimism. Additionally, we suggest that the task characteristic of information completeness is likely to produce uncertainty (a cognitive factor), which will also influence optimism. Finally, we propose that the extent to which individuals cognitively attend to base-rate information influences SSAs' optimism. We now describe each of these relations in more detail.

Earnings trend

Prior research (e.g. Lobo and Nair, 1990, 1991; Beaver, 1981; Conroy and Harris, 1987) suggests that the prior year's earnings are a good starting point in forecasting future earnings. Specifically, earnings have been shown on average to follow a process that can be approximated by a 'random walk' or 'random walk with drift' (see Foster, 1978 for a discussion of the literature). The random walk model for earnings – one that predicts next year's earnings will be equal to last year's earnings – implies that the best estimate about future earnings is current earnings. The model assumes that past shocks to earnings persist forever, but that future shocks are random or unpredictable. Thus this model suggests that past earnings are useful in predicting future earnings. Consistent with the notion that a simple random walk forecast is useful in predicting future earnings, O'Brien (1988) documents that financial analysts' year-ahead forecasts are only 22 percent more accurate, on average, than a simple random walk forecast.

As for the 'random walk with drift,' this model includes a drift term that allows earnings to grow (or decline) by a constant amount or at a constant rate each period. In this chapter, we conceptualize drift as earnings trend. Thus, based on the aforementioned research, we contend that although analysts have a rich information environment that includes more than past earnings, they will use past earnings and earnings trends to predict future earnings (e.g. Givoly, 1985). Given this, and assuming all other information is constant, when presented with an increasing earnings trend (i.e. a positive drift), analysts will make more favorable forecasts than when presented with a decreasing earnings trend (i.e. a negative drift). Thus we present the following hypothesis:

H_2: The earnings forecasts for companies with an increasing earnings trend will be more favorable than those for companies with a decreasing earnings trend.

Goals × earnings trend interaction

Jointly examining motivational and cognitive factors associated with optimism provides information on their potential interaction. We suggest that SSAs' institutional incentives to be optimistic may increase any cognitive tendency toward optimism. Thus we hypothesize interactions between the motivational and cognitive factors that we study.

Research in psychology has shown that individuals tend to predict more desirable than undesirable events (Babad and Katz, 1991; Babad et al., 1992; Budescu and Bruderman, 1995; Byram, 1997) and require less information to do so (Morlock, 1967). In line with these findings, archival research in accounting has shown that SSAs are more optimistic when making negative forecast revisions than when making positive forecast revisions (Amir and Ganzach, 1998) and following poor earnings or price performance (Dreman and Berry 1995; Easterwood and Nutt, 1999; Butler and Saraoglu, 1999; Ali et al., 1992; Amir and Ganzach, 1998; Bauman and Dowen, 1994; Elgers and Lo, 1994; Klein, 1990; Moses, 1990). Moreover, research has demonstrated that SSAs generally overestimate (underestimate) earnings in response to negative (positive) securities returns (Abarbanell, 1991; Klein, 1990) and underreact to prior losses and overreact to prior profits (Easterwood and Nutt, 1999; Nutt et al., 1999).

Consistent with this research, we suggest that individuals' goals will interact with their evaluation of negative information to contribute to their optimism. We operationalize negative information as decreasing earnings trends over the prior six years consistent with prior research that defines poor past earnings performance as negative information (Ali et al., 1992; Abarbanell and Bernard, 1992; Daniel et al., 1998). Specifically, consistent with research documenting a positive relation between negative information and optimism, we propose that the presence of institutional incentives will contribute to more favorable earnings forecasts than the absence of institutional incentives, especially for companies with decreasing earnings trends. Thus we hypothesize the following:

H_3: The difference between the earnings forecasts of individuals with directional goals and those with accuracy goals will be greater for companies with decreasing earnings trends than for companies with increasing earnings trends.

Information completeness and uncertainty

Another cognitive factor that we propose relates to forecast optimism involves the task characteristic of information completeness, which is likely to produce uncertainty. Regarding the role of uncertainty in optimism, uncertainty and extremity in predictions and uncertainty and judgments of desirable outcomes are positively related (e.g. Peterson and Pitz, 1986; Harvey, 1995; Sears, 1983; Weinstein, 1980). Regarding optimistic earnings forecasts in particular, SSAs' optimism and uncertainty are positively related where uncertainty has been defined in terms of variability of earnings, earnings forecasts and forecast errors (Ackert and Athanassakos, 1997, 2003; Maines and Hand, 1996; Huberts and Fuller, 1995; Diether et al., 2002); forecast horizon (Ackert and Athanassakos, 1997; Ali et al., 1992; Hussain, 1996); and information unavailability defined as low earnings predictability (Das et al., 1998) and less information disclosure (Higgins, 1998) and proxied by small company size, low SSA coverage and small brokerage firm size (Lim, 2001).

One task characteristic that is likely to lead to uncertainty is how complete (or incomplete) information is that an analyst receives. Although there may be situations in which too much information could lead to uncertainty (e.g. information overload), knowing there is missing information that may be relevant to one's decision is more likely to lead to uncertainty. Indeed, consistent with research documenting a positive relation between optimism and uncertainty, consumer research has documented 'omission neglect' – that is, a positive relation between missing information and extremity of predictions. Omission neglect or insensitivity to missing or unmentioned options, attributes or issues occurs when consumers form inappropriately extreme evaluations on the basis of weak evidence (Sanbonmatsu et al., 1991, 1992, 1997, 2003). For example, products described by a small amount of information are often evaluated as extremely and confidently as products described by a large amount of information. This occurs because consumers overestimate the diagnosticity or information value of the presented evidence when the limitations of the evidence are overlooked. Even a little evidence seems like a lot when omissions are not apparent. Consistent with this prior research, Kardes et al. (2006) find that when consumers are insensitive to important missing information, overly extreme product evaluations are formed; however, when consumers are sensitive to important missing information, they form more moderate and appropriate evaluations.

In apparent contradiction to this positive relation between uncertainty and optimism, evidence from consumer behavior research suggests that decision makers tend to devalue alternatives with missing information or infer discounted values for the missing information (Jagacinski, 1991; Ford and Smith, 1987; Huber and McCann, 1982; Johnson and Levin, 1985; Meyer, 1981; Stone and Stone, 1987; Yamagishi and Hill, 1981; Yates et al., 1978; Jaccard and Wood, 1988; Highhouse and Hause, 1995). That is, individuals tend to give lower mean level ratings of attributes for incompletely versus completely described alternatives, suggesting that missing information is perceived negatively (Levin et al., 1991). Specifically, research suggests that missing information has a negative impact on evaluations of job candidates (Jagacinski, 1991; Johnson, 1988; Stone and Stone, 1987), clinical competence (Levin et al., 1991), university courses (Yates et al., 1978), potential purchases (Johnson and Levin, 1985; Meyer, 1981) and security valuation decisions (Lewis et al., 1992). The extent of devaluation is positively related to the perceived importance of the missing information (Johnson, 1988) and negatively related to the availability of a plausible reason for its omission (Lewis et al., 1992). In addition, this 'incomplete information bias' (Johnson, 1987) has also been found with experts (e.g. business professors) (Loke and Tan, 1992), who are more likely to detect relevant missing information (Sanbonmatsu et al., 1992).

Based on the findings from the different research streams described above, we present the following hypothesis:

H_4: The earnings forecasts for companies with more complete information will be more favorable than those for companies with less complete information.

Goals × information completeness interaction

Based on prior research documenting a positive relation between optimism and uncertainty, we conceptualize uncertainty in terms of information completeness and suggest that information framed as less complete will increase the uncertainty in forecasting earnings. We hypothesize that this uncertainty offers an opportunity for individuals with institutional incentives to give in to their incentives to be optimistic and, in so doing, make more favorable forecasts than individuals without institutional incentives. In this way, institutional incentives may diminish the incomplete information bias, while the lack of such incentives may exacerbate it. That is, incentives may contribute to more favorable earnings forecasts for companies with less complete information than for companies with more complete information. Thus we hypothesize the following:

H_5: The difference between the earnings forecasts of individuals with institutional incentives and those without institutional incentives will be greater for companies with less complete information than for companies with more complete information.

Earnings trend × information completeness interaction

Recall that evidence from consumer behavior research suggests that decision makers tend to devalue alternatives with missing information or infer discounted values for the missing information (Ford and Smith, 1987; Huber and McCann, 1982; Johnson and Levin, 1985; Meyer, 1981; Stone and Stone, 1987; Yates et al., 1978). That is, individuals tend to give lower ratings of attributes for incompletely versus completely described alternatives, suggesting that missing information is perceived negatively (Levin et al., 1991). We suggest that this 'incomplete information bias' (Johnson, 1987) will interact with the trend of the earnings series such that individuals given information framed as less complete will infer more negative earnings when presented with negatively (compared to positively) trended earnings. In this way, the difference between the earnings forecasts of individuals given information framed as more complete and those given information framed as less complete will be greater when individuals are presented with negatively (compared to positively) trended past earnings.

H_6: The difference between the earnings forecasts of individuals given information framed as more complete and those given information framed as less complete will be greater when individuals are presented with negatively (compared to positively) trended past earnings.

Base rate information

Numerous studies have documented base-rate neglect (e.g. Krosnick et al., 1990; Lynch and Ofir, 1989; Gluck and Bower, 1988; Bar-Hillel, 1980; Bar-Hillel and Fischhoff, 1981; Borgida and Brekke, 1981; Fischhoff and Beyth-Marom, 1983; Sherman and Corty, 1984; Tversky and Kahneman, 1982; see Koehler, 1996 for a review).[2] Across a broad range of Bayesian probability judgment experiments, it has been found that base-rate information is usually ignored or grossly underweighted relative to the prescriptions of the normative Bayesian model (Bar-Hillel, 1980; Hammerton, 1973; Kahneman and Tversky, 1973; Lyon and Slovic, 1976). Similarly, in causal attribution and social judgment, neglect or underuse of base-rate information is typical (e.g. Nisbett and Borgida, 1975; Nisbett et al., 1976).

The underutilization of base-rate information and the excessive reliance on case-specific information may result in more extreme forecasts than statistical theory would support (Braun and Yaniv, 1992; Kalish, 2001; Ganzach and Krantz, 1990; Kahneman and Tversky, 1973; Martin, 1985; Shanteau, 1989; Kahneman and Lovallo, 1993; Klar et al., 1996). Kahneman and Lovallo (1993) relate individuals' inattention to base rates to an inside (as opposed to an outside) view of forecasting. They suggest that decision makers are prone to adopt an inside view of problems that results in optimistic forecasts. Similarly, Klar et al. (1996) provide evidence that a singular judgmental perspective, which is characterized by a focus on available individuating information and a neglect of base-rate information, leads to an optimistic bias in favor of concrete and familiar rather than generalized targets.

A number of studies of this neglect of base-rate information and this dominance of case information implicate Kahneman and Tversky's (1972) representativeness heuristic. In an early demonstration of representativeness, Kahneman and Tversky (1973) evaluated the use of base rates and similarity rating in making a prediction. Participants were divided into three groups. One group estimated the base rates of students belonging to nine academic majors while the other two groups were given a bogus personality sketch of a graduate student designed to fit the stereotype of an engineer. One of the two groups given a personality sketch was asked how similar the graduate student was to the typical student in each of the nine majors. The third group was asked to predict the major of the graduate student from the personality sketch. Kahneman and Tversky (1973) showed that the predictions correlated highly with the similarity ranking, and that there was a negative correlation between base rates and prediction. They pointed out that this violated Bayes's theorem, which states that the prior probabilities (base rates) should directly affect the predictions.

Based on this research and the suggestion that a key construct affecting the use of base-rate information is its perceived relevance (Bar-Hillel, 1980; Ginossar and Trope, 1980), we propose the following hypothesis:

H_7: Individuals' relevance ratings of base-rate information will be inversely related to the favorableness of their forecasts.

In Hypothesis 1, we hypothesized that individuals with institutional incentives will make more favorable forecasts than those without such incentives. Given the association between optimism and base-rate neglect documented by prior research and discussed above, we contend that institutional incentives may underlie individuals' optimism. Thus we predict that institutional incentives will exacerbate the tendency for individuals to neglect base-rate information. Therefore, based on the prior research discussed above that indicates that the neglect of base-rate information is associated with more extreme and optimistic forecasts and predictions, we hypothesize the following:

H_8: Individuals with institutional incentives will rate base-rate information as less relevant to their forecasts than those without institutional incentives.

METHOD

The hypotheses were tested in an experiment involving a $2 \times 2 \times 2$ design with incentives (presence versus absence) and information completeness (less complete, more complete) as the between-subjects variables and past earnings trend (increasing, decreasing) as a within-subject variable.[3] The dependent variables were EPS forecasts for the current year and base-rate relevance ratings.[4]

Participants

The study was administered (in class) to 69 first-year and 63 second-year MBA students. All students had some exposure to financial accounting, and second-year students were currently taking intermediate accounting. Forecasts of first- and second-year MBA students did not differ significantly. Therefore data for first- and second-year students are combined for the analyses. Students in both goal conditions had limited general and industry-specific (chemical industry) experience. Both the professor of the class and one of the experimenters asked the students to participate and stressed the importance of the study. Students were given as long as they wanted to complete the questionnaire, although most students took approximately 40 minutes to complete, and all questionnaires were completed within 60 minutes.

Experimental Materials and Procedures

All participants read instructions containing background information about the chemical industry in which the fictitious companies used within the current study were located based on a review of composite industry data for basic, diversified and specialty chemicals. Additionally, the instructions contained summary information about 14 companies that participants were told had been randomly selected, with half having decreasing earnings trends and half having increasing earnings trends over the most recent six-year period. The summary information also indicated that each company was of moderate size, had assets and annual gross sales between $100 and $250 million, and had a low stock beta.[5] The only company-specific information that was provided was six years of EPS for each of the 14 companies.

In the task instructions, participants were given either a directional goal or an accuracy goal. Directional goals are defined here as the presence of institutional incentives that increase the incentives to issue optimistic forecasts, while accuracy goals are defined as the absence of such incentives. The directional goal manipulation read as follows:

> Imagine that you are a financial analyst who is forecasting earnings for companies that are clients of the brokerage firm in which you work. Also assume that your firm has agreed to underwrite a very sizable share offering for each of these companies. Favorable earnings forecasts and recommendations may positively affect your firm's revenues and, in turn, your compensation. Client relations are important for accessibility to information sources that are needed for your work and to support the revenue-producing part of your firm. Such relations may be threatened by unfavorable earnings forecasts and recommendations.

The accuracy goal manipulation read as follows:

> Imagine that you are a financial analyst who is forecasting earnings for companies that have no connection with your employer. Your firm has no current or future plans to underwrite share offerings or provide other similar services for any of these companies. There are no benefits associated with providing favorable earnings forecasts and recommendations. You are rewarded for accuracy in your forecasts and recommendations above all else.

We also manipulated information completeness. Although all participants received the same background information regarding the chemical industry and summary information for the companies, participants in the less complete information condition were told that they did not receive information provided in a conference call with company management, whereas those in the more complete information condition were not told they missed a conference call. Specifically, information completeness was manipulated by including the following paragraph in the less complete information condition: 'More specific information on recent industry and company developments was discussed during a conference call with management. However, you were unable to participate in the conference call due to transmission problems and a tape recording of the call was not made.' In the more complete information condition, this additional paragraph was not presented.

A six-year EPS series for each of the 14 fictitious companies and the average industry EPS for all companies in the chemical industry were presented to the participants. The average industry EPS constituted the base-rate information. Participants were asked to predict EPS for the current year and for each of the two following years. The six-year EPS series was manipulated to create eight of the 14 fictitious companies. The remaining six companies were not actually used for analyses, but were included to make it less obvious which variables were being manipulated. For the eight manipulated companies, earnings trend was manipulated by giving participants EPS series with increasing/decreasing trends. The increase and decrease patterns of both series were similar, with the sixth-year EPS approximately 225 percent of the first-year EPS for the increasing earnings trend condition and the first-year EPS approximately 225 percent of the sixth-year EPS in the decreasing earnings trend condition. For the dependent variables, we took participants' earnings forecasts for the four negatively trended companies and averaged them. This is the dependent variable in the negative earnings trend condition. Likewise, for the dependent variable in the positive earnings trend condition, we took participants' earnings forecasts for the four positively trended companies and averaged them. This is the dependent variable in the positive earnings trend condition.

Finally, participants answered the post-experimental questionnaire containing the goal manipulation check and questions about their general financial analysis experience and their specific experience, if any, in the chemical industry. In addition, participants rated the relevance of industry data (base-rate relevance) to their forecasts by responding to the question, 'How relevant was the industry data to your EPS forecasts?' using a seven-point scale anchored by 'not at all' (1) and 'very' (7). Finally, participants indicated their level of experience in financial analysis in general and in the chemical industry in particular. The specific wording and response options for each of these measures are provided in the note to Table 11.1.

RESULTS

Manipulation Check

A manipulation check was included to test whether the directional and accuracy goal manipulation was effective. Participants were asked to indicate how important it was to them to make accurate and favorable forecasts. As expected, students with directional goals, relative to those with accuracy goals, felt that it was more important to make favorable forecasts ($t = -4.13$, $p < 0.001$; means = 3.49 and 2.29, respectively). As reported in Table 11.1 and consistent with this finding, the importance of favorable forecasts was positively correlated with forecasts ($r = 0.22$, $p < 0.05$). In addition, subjects felt it was equally important to be accurate in their forecasts, regardless of goal condition, suggesting that directional and accuracy goals are not mutually exclusive and that even individuals with incentives to be optimistic are concerned with accuracy.

Table 11.1 Pearson correlations among post-experimental questionnaire responses and forecasts[a]

	Importance of accurate forecast[c]	Importance of favorable forecast[d]	Relevance of industry data for forecasts[e]	Chemical industry experience[f]	Financial analysis experience[g]	Current year forecasts[h]
Industry trend[b]	0.08	0.11	0.14	0.03	–0.04	0.20**
Importance of accurate forecast	–	0.40***	0.25***	0.16*	0.13	0.09
Importance of favorable forecast	–	–	0.07	0.12	0.09	0.22**
Base-rate relevance for forecasts	–	–	–	0.083	0.26***	–0.187**
Chemical experience	–	–	–	–	0.38***	0.03
Financial analysis experience[j]	–	–	–	–	–	–0.08

Notes: *Significant at $p < 0.10$ (two-tailed test); ** Significant at $p < 0.05$ (two-tailed test); *** Significant at $p < 0.01$ (two-tailed test).

[a] $n = 126$ to 132; differences in n result from the fact that some participants did not provide responses to some questions.

[b] Participants responded to the question: 'Was the trend in average annual EPS for all companies in the industry generally decreasing, generally flat, or generally increasing?' They indicated their answer on a scale of 1 to 7, where 1 means 'generally decreasing trend', 4 means 'generally flat trend' (i.e. neither increasing nor decreasing), and 7 means 'generally increasing trend'.

[c] Participants responded to the question: 'How important was it to you to make accurate forecasts?' Participants indicated their response using a seven-point scale anchored by 'not at all' (1) and 'very' (7).

[d] Participants responded to the question: 'How important was it to you to make favorable forecasts?' Participants indicated their response using a seven-point scale anchored by 'not at all' (1) and 'very' (7).

[e] Participants responded to the question: 'How relevant was the industry data to your EPS forecasts?' Participants indicated their response using a seven-point scale anchored by 'not at all' (1) and 'very' (7).

[f] Participants responded to the question: 'How experienced in financial analysis are you with companies in the chemical industry?' Participants indicated their response using a seven-point scale anchored by 'not at all' (1) and 'very' (7).

[g] Participants responded to the question: 'How experienced are you in financial analysis of any kind?' Participants indicated their response using a seven-point scale anchored by 'not at all' (1) and 'very' (7).

[h] Participants made earnings forecasts.

Test of Hypotheses

Table 11.2 presents the means (standard deviations) of the current-year forecasts of individuals with directional and accuracy goals in each experimental condition (earnings trend, information completeness) and averaged over all eight companies. The participants' earnings forecasts associated with those companies that had an increasing trend and those forecasts associated with those companies that had a decreasing

Table 11.2 Descriptive statistics for the experimental conditions (current-year forecasts)

	More complete information condition			Less complete information condition			Total across information conditions		
	AG	*DG*	*All*	*AG*	*DG*	*All*	*AG*	*DG*	*All*
Decreasing earnings trend									
Mean	2.01	2.29	2.16	1.93	2.04	1.99	1.97	2.17	2.07
SD	0.45	0.56	0.53	0.38	0.49	0.44	0.42	0.54	0.494
N	31	34	65	32	32	64	63	66	129
Increasing earnings trend									
Mean	3.52	3.26	3.38	3.48	3.58	3.53	3.50	3.42	3.46
SD	0.62	0.70	0.67	0.46	0.48	0.47	0.54	0.62	0.579
N	31	34	65	32	32	64	63	66	130
Total data									
Mean	2.76	2.78	2.77	2.70	2.81	2.76	2.73	2.79	2.76
SD	0.359	0.364	0.359	0.303	0.322	0.315	0.330	0.342	0.337
N	31	34	65	32	32	64	63	66	129

Key: AG = accuracy goal; DG = directional goal.

Table 11.3 Repeated measures ANOVA (results of hypothesis tests on current-year forecasts)

Source of variance	SS	df	*F*-statistic	Sig.
Incentive (H_1)	0.258	1	1.13	0.145*
Information completeness (H_4)	0.009	1	0.038	0.424*
Earnings trend (H_2)	124.64	1	376.61	< 0.001*
Incentive × information completeness (H_5)	0.141	1	0.618	0.217*
Incentive × earnings trend (H_3)	1.20	1	3.62	0.03*
Information completeness × earnings trend (H_6)	1.50	1	4.54	0.02*
Incentive × information completeness × earnings trend	1.16	1	3.51	0.064
Error (trend)	41.369	125		

Note: *One-tailed.

trend constituted the dependent variables used in the ANOVAs shown in Table 11.3. The hypotheses are tested using the ANOVAs shown in Table 11.3 and the correlations shown in Table 11.1.[6]

Hypothesis 1 maintains that individuals with institutional incentives (operationalized as those with directional goals) will make more favorable earnings forecasts than those without such incentives (operationalized as those with accuracy goals). As shown in Table 11.3, the forecasts of individuals with directional goals did not differ from those with accuracy goals. Thus Hypothesis 1 is not supported.

Hypothesis 2 predicts that earnings forecasts for companies with an increasing earnings trend will be more favorable than those for companies with a decreasing earnings trend. Consistent with expectations, as shown in Table 11.3, the main effect of earnings trend was significant ($F = 376.61$, $p < 0.001$ one-tailed). As reported in Table 11.2, the mean forecasts for companies with an increasing earnings trend was 3.46 (0.579) compared to 2.07 (0.494) for companies with a decreasing earnings trend. Thus Hypothesis 2 is supported.

Hypothesis 3 predicts an interaction between incentives and earnings trend for earnings forecasts. Specifically, it is predicted that the difference between the earnings forecasts of individuals with institutional incentives (directional goals) and those without such incentives (accuracy goals) will be greater for companies with decreasing earnings trends than for companies with increasing earnings trends. Repeated measures ANOVA results presented in Table 11.3 indicate a significant interaction between goals and earnings trend for forecasts ($F = 3.62$, $p = 0.03$ one-tailed). To further examine the interaction between incentives and earnings trend, contrasts were conducted. Contrast results indicate that individuals with directional (compared to accuracy) goals made significantly more favorable forecasts in response to a negatively trended earnings series ($F = 5.71$, $p = 0.018$) but made equally favorable forecasts in response to a positively trended earnings series. Consistent with expectations, and as shown in Table 11.2, the mean (SD) forecasts of individuals with directional and accuracy goals in response to a negatively trended earnings series were 2.17 (0.54) and 1.97 (0.42), respectively. Thus Hypothesis 3 is supported.

Hypothesis 4 maintains that the earnings forecasts for companies with more complete information will be more favorable than those for companies with less complete information. As shown in Table 11.3, the forecasts of individuals who received more complete information did not differ from those who received less complete information. Thus Hypothesis 4 is not supported.

Hypothesis 5 predicts an interaction between incentives and information completeness for earnings forecasts. Specifically, it is predicted that, in the less complete information condition, the forecasts for individuals with institutional incentives (directional goals) compared to those without such incentives (accuracy goals) will be more favorable but they will not differ in the more complete information condition. Repeated measures ANOVA results presented in Table 11.3 indicate a non-significant interaction between goals and information completeness for forecasts. Therefore Hypothesis 5 is not supported.

Hypothesis 6 predicts an interaction between information completeness and earnings trend for earnings forecasts. Specifically, it is predicted that the difference between the earnings forecasts of individuals given information framed as more complete and those given information framed as less complete will be greater when individuals are presented with negatively (compared to positively) trended past earnings. Repeated-measures ANOVA results presented in Table 11.3 indicate a significant interaction between information completeness and earnings trend ($F = 4.54$, $p = 0.02$ one-tailed). To further examine the interaction between goals and earnings trend, contrasts were conducted. Contrast results indicate that forecasts were significantly more favorable in response to a negatively trended earnings series when information was framed as more complete than less complete ($F = 3.95$, $p = 0.049$). However, forecasts were equally favorable in response to a positively trended earnings series when information was framed as more or less complete. Consistent with expectations and as shown in Table 11.2, the mean (SD) forecasts in response to a negatively trended earnings series were 2.16 (0.53) for information framed as more complete information and 1.99 (0.44) for information framed as less complete. Therefore Hypothesis 6 is supported.

Hypothesis 7 maintains that individuals' relevance ratings of base-rate information will be inversely related to the favorableness of their forecasts. As reported in Table 11.1, the correlation between individuals' relevance ratings of base rate information to their current year forecasts was significant ($r = -0.187$, $p = 0.035$). This suggests that the relevance of base-rate information is inversely related to the favorableness in forecasts. Thus Hypothesis 7 is supported.[7]

Hypothesis 8 maintains that individuals with institutional incentives (directional goals) will rate base-rate information as less relevant to their forecasts than those without institutional incentives (those with accuracy goals). Consistent with expectations, t-test results indicate that individuals with directional goals rated the relevance of base-rate information to their forecasts lower ($t = 2.42$, $p = 0.017$). Thus Hypothesis 8 is supported.

DISCUSSION

In this chapter, we have described a study that provides experimental evidence on motivational and cognitive factors contributing to earnings forecast optimism. Consistent with prior research documenting the importance of SSAs' institutional incentives and certain cognitive factors to optimism, this study provides evidence that incentives and cognitive factors (earnings trend, information completeness and base-rate attention) contribute to optimism.

The study described herein has three main findings. First, consistent with expectations, earnings trend interacted with incentives and information completeness to determine earnings forecasts. Specifically, (1) individuals with institutional incentives (compared to those without such incentives) made more favorable forecasts in response to negatively trended earnings but not in response to positively trended earnings; and (2) individuals made less favorable forecasts when information was framed as less (compared to more) complete for negatively trended earnings but not for positively trended earnings. Second, incentives differentially impacted the evaluation of base-rate information. Specifically, individuals with incentives (compared to those without incentives) rated industry data as less relevant to their forecasts. Third, attention to base rates was inversely related to the favorableness in forecasts. These findings are consistent with prior research that suggests that SSAs' institutional incentives encourage them to make optimistic forecasts and that optimism is more prevalent in response to negative information, and that judgments are often unduly influenced by irrelevant factors (such as whether information is framed as more or less complete) and inadequately influenced by relevant ones (such as base rates).

In that the current results help elucidate the determinants of optimism, they may be useful in debiasing the extent of optimism by altering individuals' views of their incentives or their processing of base-rate or negatively trended information. For instance, Whitecotton et al. (1998) provide evidence that the biased judgment caused by base-rate neglect is diminished when a decision model is used, and Elgers et al. (1995) provide evidence of mechanical debiasing of forecasts using statistical methods. It may be that training and/or modifying analysts' institutional incentives and altering the way they evaluate base-rate and negative information may reduce or eliminate optimism in analysts' forecasts. On the other hand, prior research has found that debiasing efforts may be ineffective (Fischhoff, 1982). However, understanding what produces optimism is an important initial step to determining debiasing remedies.

The current findings also clarify prior research. While prior research indicates that motivational features (Francis and Philbrick, 1993; Lin and McNichols, 1998) or cognitive features (Affleck-Graves et al., 1990; DeBondt and Thaler, 1990; Whitecotton, 1996) may lead to optimism, the results presented here reveal that both motivational and cognitive factors contribute to optimism. Therefore both factors must be considered to obtain a more complete understanding of optimism.

In addition, from a theoretical perspective, the findings suggest that non-economic factors – specifically, variations in the presentation framing (less complete, more complete) of information – influence judgments. These results are in line with prior research on the influence of irrelevant factors such as framing effects (for review, see Levin et al., 1998) and disproportionate influence of negative information (Tversky and Kahneman,

1981; Brown and Harlow, 1988). This sheds additional light on the ability of non-economic factors to influence individuals and raises the need for future research to examine ways to distinguish and mitigate the effect of irrelevant factors.

As with most studies, the current study is not without limitations. First, the information provided to the participants is only a subset of the firm, industry and management information actually used to forecast earnings. However, a limited amount of information was provided in order to obtain subject participation and to isolate the effects of interest in this study.

A second limitation concerns the use of students as proxies for professional analysts. Although MBA students have been used for similar tasks by other researchers (e.g. Eames et al., 2006; Maines and McDaniel, 2000), and some researchers have provided evidence that practicing stock analysts have biases similar to those of students (e.g. Eames et al., 2002), generalizing findings to professional analysts should be done with caution. That is, our findings might have differed had professional analysts been used rather than students. For example, our measure of analyst experience concerned a self-rating of experience (as opposed to years of experience) and did not explicitly define what was (and was not) included as experience. Given the ambiguity in the definition of experience, students could have considered classroom experience to be relevant. Thus the use of students with inadequate experience combined with the paucity of information inherent in the task could have influenced the results. Despite this, Whitecotton (1996) provides evidence that while both SSAs and student subjects are optimistic, SSAs are even more optimistic than student subjects. Thus the results found with student participants in the current study may be even greater with professional analysts. This issue is for future research.

Another limitation is that the data for this study were collected in 2000. Since then, two events may have altered the current market conditions compared to the conditions during the data collection period of this paper. First, Regulation FD in 2000 prohibits US public companies from making selective, non-public disclosures to particular investment professionals such as analysts. This regulation reduced the information asymmetry between non-professional and professional market participants. This change may have altered analysts' optimism, although analysts' optimism does exist post-Regulation FD (Kwag and Small, 2007). Second, corporate scandals and bankruptcy (including Enron and WorldCom) increased the market's skepticism and catalyzed new regulations, including the Sarbanes–Oxley Act of 2002, which imposed additional requirements on corporate management and the auditors in an effort to better protect the public from fraudulent financial reporting. This regulation may also have changed analysts' propensity to be optimistic. Thus, although our results shed light on the factors that may contribute to forecast optimism, additional research is needed to ensure that the results are robust to current market and regulatory changes that have occurred since our data collection.

The results suggest several directions for future research. First, in line with a suggestion made by Ashton and Cianci (2007), we note the need to disentangle the independent impact of the typical motivational explanations for analysts' optimism. Although the current results support the notion that SSAs' institutional incentives encourage optimism when making forecasts in response to negatively (compared to positively) trended earnings information, our design does not permit us to distinguish among the various motivational explanations. Future researchers could investigate independent and joint effects of the different institutional incentives that analysts face.

Second, the characteristics of other aspects of the information disclosed to sophisticated and less sophisticated market participants should be investigated. In the current study, participants were presented with a six-year series of past earnings, and were influenced by their goals and earnings trend. However, the characteristics of the series other than earnings trend may interact to influence earnings forecasts. For example, would an analyst make more (less) favorable forecasts for a firm that has an extended earnings series of small positive (negative) information or infrequent larger positive (negative) information? In addition, the effects of such information characteristics and others may extend beyond forecasts and may affect the value of the firm and investors' perceptions of management's credibility, as shown in Mercer (2005). Future research could also examine the effects information (ir)relevance and timeliness (current or prior) on forecasts. That is, what is the impact on analysts' forecasts of irrelevant information that is announced along with relevant news, and negative news that is disclosed along with previously announced positive information? Are analysts distracted by irrelevant news and/or positive news that is not new?

Third, future research could examine whether negative nonfinancial statement information – such as management discussion and analysis (MD&A) – might lead to greater optimism than the financial information (i.e. earnings series) used in the current study. The SEC (2003), AICPA (1994) and FASB (2001) emphasize the importance of such information to financial reporting, and prior research documents its importance to financial analysts (Williams et al., 1996) and to the prediction of future earnings (see Cole and Jones, 2005 for review of this research). However, this information may be more susceptible to institutional pressures because it is not as easily verifiable and is produced by management or conversations with management. Forecasts based on such information may thereby be more biased or optimistic.

Fourth, in addition to the motivational and cognitive factors examined here, other factors could be examined to determine their effects on forecasts and other investment-related judgments. For instance, future research could examine the relations between optimistic forecasts and dispositional optimism (Carver and Scheier, 2001; Scheier et al., 2001). Additionally, investor status may lead to different outcomes based on incentives in that current investors may have incentives to protect their investment whereas prospective investors may have incentives to make an investment. These different incentives may lead to different investment-related judgments, as shown in Cianci and Falsetta (2008).

Finally, while the current study provides evidence of differential forecasts by individuals with and without institutional incentives and in response to earning information with different trends, future research should examine how these judgments map into other investment-related decisions such as firm valuation and risk judgments. In addition, researchers should investigate factors other than incentives, such as how analysts' prior forecasting successes or failures impact their sensitivity to information disclosed. It may be that analysts adjust their subsequent forecasts and sensitivity to different information in response to positive or negative forecast feedback.

In conclusion, the current study suggests that both motivational and cognitive determinants impact forecasts. SSAs' institutional incentives (a motivational factor), negative prior earnings trends and information completeness (cognitive factors) interactively contributed to optimism. Specifically, incentives, negatively trended earnings and low relevance ratings of base rates were related to optimism; incentives differentially impacted the evaluation of negative and base-rate information; and information completeness and earnings trend interacted to affect forecasts. Further research is warranted to better understand when such factors will influence forecasting and other investment-related judgments and the nature of their interactive effects. This, in turn, will help to illuminate underlying causes of anomalous market behavior and contribute to a more comprehensive understanding of forecast judgments.

NOTES

1. Ashton and Cianci (2007) examined SSAs' and BSAs' forecasts in response to negatively and positively trended earnings series and did not find an interaction between analyst type and earning trend.
2. Other studies reveal that base-rate information can have substantial impact when the base rate is derived from a representative sample (Wells and Harvey, 1977); when the individuating information lacks credibility (Schwarz et al., 1991) or diagnosticity (Ginossar and Trope, 1980); when the base rate has strong causal implications (Ajzen, 1997; Bar-Hillel, 1980; Tversky and Kahneman, 1980; Locksley and Strangor, 1984); when people bring a scientific orientation to a problem (Zukier and Pepitone, 1984); when inferential rules suggesting the use of base rates have been activated (Ginossar and Trope, 1987); when base rates are varied within subject (Fischhoff and Bar-Hillel, 1984; Fischhoff et al., 1979; Birnbaum and Mellers, 1983); when the problem is framed as repetitive rather than unique (Kahneman and Tversky, 1973); when the individuating information lacks when participants bring a scientific orientation to the problem (Zukier and Pepitone, 1984; Schwarz et al., 1991); when the base rate is presented after the individuating information (Krosnick et al., 1990); when the problem is reframed into frequency instead of probability (Gigerenzer and Hoffrage, 1995); when participants are shown the random sampling process (Gigerenzer et al., 1988); or when a decision model is used (Whitecotton et al., 1998).
3. Two other cognitive factors – recency and variability – were considered in our original design. The results reported here are substantively the same as when recency and variability are included in the model. We do not include details related to these variables because they are not the focus of our study.
4. EPS forecasts for one- and two-year-ahead horizons and stock recommendations for the current year were also examined. Several participants indicated that they did not have enough information to make forecasts for subsequent forecast horizons or stock recommendations. Thus the results for these variables are not reported.
5. A low stock beta indicates that the stock is relatively insensitive to market movements.
6. It should be noted that the number of participants varies across analyses due to missing data from some participants. In particular, two participants missed a few dependent variable questions towards the end of the forecasting part of the questionnaire (i.e. did not make an earnings forecast for a few years). To see if dropping these participants would make a difference, we re-ran analyses without them and found that dropping them did not change the results. Therefore these participants were retained for all analyses and results are reported based on available responses.
7. Although the correlation matrix allows one to know what is correlated, it does not explain its overall impact within the context of the experiment. The current study was a first step in exploring this issue but future researchers may wish to explore this issue in greater depth.

REFERENCES

Abarbanell, J.S. (1991), 'Do analysts' forecasts incorporate information in prior stock price changes?,' *Journal of Accounting and Economics*, 14 (June), 147–65.

Abarbanell, J.S. and V.L. Bernard (1992), 'Tests of analysts' overreaction/underreaction to earnings information as an explanation for anomalous stock price behavior,' *The Journal of Finance*, **47** (July), 1181–207.

Ackert, L.F. and G. Athanassakos (1997), 'Prior uncertainty, analyst bias, and subsequent abnormal returns,' *The Journal of Financial Research*, **20** (Summer), 263–73.

Ackert, L.F. and G. Athanassakos (2003), 'A simultaneous equations analysis of analysts' forecast bias, analyst following, and institutional ownership,' *Journal of Business, Finance & Accounting*, **30** (7), 1017–41.
Affleck-Graves, J., L.R. Davis and R.R. Mendenhall (1990), 'Forecasts of earnings per share: possible sources of analyst superiority and bias,' *Contemporary Accounting Research*, **6** (Spring), 502–17.
Ajzen, I. (1997), 'Intuitive theories of events and the effects of base-rate information on prediction,' *Journal of Personality and Social Psychology*, **35** (5), 303–14.
Ali, A., A. Klein and J. Rosenfeld (1992), 'Analysts' use of information about permanent and transitory earnings components in forecasting annual EPS,' *The Accounting Review*, **67** (January), 183–98.
American Institute of Certified Public Accountants (AICPA) (1994), *Special Committee on Financial Reporting*. AICPA Professional Standards. New York: AICPA.
Amir, E. and Y. Ganzach (1998), 'Overreaction and underreaction in analysts' forecasts,' *Journal of Economic Behavior and Organization*, **37** (November), 333–47.
Ashton, R.H. and A.M. Cianci (2007), 'Motivational and cognitive determinants of buy-side and sell-side analysts' earnings forecasts: an experimental study,' *Journal of Behavioral Finance*, **8** (1), 9–19.
Babad, E. and Y. Katz (1991), 'Wishful thinking – against all odds,' *Journal of Applied Social Psychology*, **21** (December), 1921–38.
Babad, E., M. Hills and M. O'Driscoll (1992), 'Factors influencing wishful thinking and predictions of election outcomes,' *Basic and Applied Social Psychology*, **13** (December), 461–76.
Bar-Hillel, M. (1980), 'The base-rate fallacy in probability judgments,' *Acta Psychologica*, **44**, 211–33.
Bar-Hillel, M. and B. Fischhoff (1981), 'When do base-rates affect predictions?,' *Journal of Personality and Social Psychology*, **41** (4), 671–80.
Bathke, A.W. Jr, J.M. Hassell and J.M. Lukawitz (1991), 'Relative accuracy of quarterly earnings forecast announcements,' *Advances in Accounting*, **9**, 19–33.
Bauman, W.S., and R.J. Dowen (1994), 'Security analyst forecasts and the earnings yield anomaly,' *Journal of Business Finance & Accounting*, **21** (March), 283–91.
Beaver, W.H. (1981), *Financial Reporting: An Accounting Revolution*, Englewood Cliffs, NY: Prentice-Hall.
Birnbaum, M. and B.A. Mellers (1983), 'Bayesian inference: combining base rates with opinions of sources who vary in credibility,' *Journal of Personality and Social Psychology*, **45**, 792–804.
Boni, L. and K. Womack (2002), 'Wall Street's credibility problem: misaligned incentives and dubious fixes?,' *Brookings–Wharton Papers on Financial Services*, 93–128.
Borgida, E. and N. Brekke (1981), 'The base-rate fallacy in attribution and prediction,' in J.H. Harvey, W.J. Ickes and R.F. Kidd (eds), *New Directions in Attribution Research*, Hillside, NJ: Erlbaum, pp. 63–95.
Bradshaw, M.T., S.A. Richardson and R.G. Sloan (2006), 'The relation between corporate financing activities, analysts' forecasts and stock returns,' *Journal of Accounting and Economics*, **42** (1–2), 53–85.
Braun, P.A. and I. Yaniv (1992), 'A case study of expert judgment: economists' probabilities versus base-rate model forecasts,' *Journal of Behavioral Decision Making*, **5** (3), 217–31.
Brav, A. and R. Lehavy (2003), 'An empirical analysis of analysts' target prices: short term informativeness and long term dynamics,' *Journal of Finance*, **58**, 1933–68.
Brown, K.C. and W.V. Harlow (1988), 'Market overreaction: magnitude and intensity,' *Journal of Portfolio Management*, **14** (2), 6–13.
Brown, L.D. (1993), 'Earnings forecasting research: its implications for capital markets research,' *International Journal of Forecasting*, **9** (November), 295–320.
Brown, L.D. (1997), 'Analyst forecasting errors: additional evidence,' *Financial Analysts Journal*, **53** (November/December), 81–8.
Budescu, D.V. and M. Bruderman (1995), 'The relationship between the illusion of control and the desirability bias,' *Journal of Behavioral Decision Making*, **8** (June), 109–25.
Butler, K.C. and H. Saraoglu (1999), 'Improving analysts' negative earnings forecasts,' *Financial Analysts Journal*, (May/June), 48–56.
Byram, S.J. (1997), 'Cognitive and motivational factors influencing time prediction,' *Journal of Experimental Psychology: Applied*, **3** (September), 216–39.
Carver, C.S. and M.F. Scheier (2001), 'Optimism, pessimism, and self-regulation,' in E.C. Chang (ed), *Optimism and Pessimism: Implications for Theory, Research, and Practice*, Washington, DC: American Psychological Association, pp. 31–51.
Cianci, A.M. and D. Falsetta (2008), 'Impact of investors' status on their evaluation of positive and negative, and past and future information,' *Accounting & Finance*, **48**, 719–39.
Cole, B.M. (2001), *The Pied Pipers of Wall Street: How Analysts Sell You Down the River*, Princeton, NJ: Bloomberg Press.
Cole, C.J. and C.L. Jones (2005), 'Management discussion and analysis: a review and implications for future research,' *Journal of Accounting Literature*, **24**, 135–74.
Conroy, R. and R. Harris (1987), 'Consensus forecasts of corporate earnings: analysts' forecasts and time series methods,' *Management Science*, **33** (6), 725–38.

Daniel, K., D. Hirshleifer and A. Subrahmanyam (1998), 'Investor psychology and security market under- and overreactions,' *Journal of Finance*, **53**, 1839–85.

Darrough, M.N. and T. Russell (2002), 'A positive model of earnings forecasts: top down versus bottom up,' *Journal of Business*, **75** (1), 127–52.

Das, S., C.B. Levine and K. Sivaramakrishnan (1998), 'Earnings predictability and bias in analysts' earnings forecasts,' *The Accounting Review*, **73** (April), 277–94.

DeBondt, F.M. and R. Thaler (1990), 'Do security analysts overreact?,' *American Economic Review Papers and Proceedings*, **80** (May), 52–7.

Dechow, P.M., A.P. Hutton and R.G. Sloan (2000), 'The relation between analysts' forecasts of long-term earnings growth and stock price performance following equity offerings,' *Contemporary Accounting Research*, **17** (Spring), 1–33.

Deci, E.L. and R.M. Ryan (1985), *Intrinsic Motivation and Self-determination in Human Behavior*, New York: Plenum.

Diether, K.B., C.J. Malloy and A. Scherbina (2002), 'Differences of opinion and the cross-section of stock returns,' *The Journal of Finance*, **57**, 2113–41.

Dorfman, J.R. (1991), 'Analysts devote more time to selling as firms keep scorecard on performance,' *The Wall Street Journal*, 29 October, C1–2.

Dreman, D. and M. Berry (1995), 'Overreaction, underreaction, and the low-P/E effect,' *Financial Analysts Journal*, **51** (July–August), 21–30.

Dugar, A. and S. Nathan (1995), 'The effect of investment banking relationships on financial analysts' earnings forecasts and investment recommendations,' *Contemporary Accounting Research*, **12** (Fall), 131–60.

Duru, A. and D.M. Reeb (2002), 'International diversification and analysts' forecast accuracy and bias,' *The Accounting Review*, **77** (2), 415–33.

Eames, M.J. and S.M. Glover (2003), 'Earnings predictability and the direction of analysts' earnings forecast errors,' *Accounting Review*, **78** (July), 707–24.

Eames, M.J., S.M. Glover and J.J. Kennedy (2002), 'The association between trading recommendations and broker–analysts' earnings forecasts,' *Journal of Accounting Research*, **40** (March), 85–104.

Eames, M.J., S.M. Glover and J.J. Kennedy (2006), 'Stock recommendations as a source of bias in earnings forecasts,' *Behavioral Research in Accounting*, **18**, 37–51.

Easterwood, J. C. and S.R. Nutt (1999), 'Inefficiency in analysts' earnings forecasts: systematic misreaction or systematic optimism?,' *The Journal of Finance*, **54** (October), 1777–97.

Elgers, P.T. and M.H. Lo (1994), 'Reductions in analysts' annual earnings forecast errors using information in prior earnings and security returns,' *Journal of Accounting Research*, **32** (Autumn), 290–303.

Elgers, P.T., M.H. Lo and D. Murray (1995), 'Note on adjustments to analysts' earnings forecasts based upon systematic cross-sectional components of prior-period errors,' *Management Science*, **41** (8), 1392–6.

Financial Accounting Standards Board (FASB) (2001), *Improving Business Reporting: Insights Into Enhanced Voluntary Disclosure*, Norwalk, CT: FASB.

Fischhoff, B. (1982), 'Debiasing,' in D. Kahneman, P. Slovic and A. Tversky (eds), *Judgment and Uncertainty: Heuristics and Biases*, New York: Cambridge University Press, pp. 422–44.

Fischhoff, B. and M. Bar-Hillel (1984), 'Diagnosticity and the base-rate effect,' *Memory & Cognition* (July), 402–10.

Fischhoff, B. and R. Beyth-Marom (1983), 'Hypothesis evaluation from a Bayesian perspective,' *Psychological Review*, **90**, 239–60.

Fischhoff, B., P. Slovic and S. Lichtenstein (1979), 'Subjective sensitivity analysis,' *Organizational Behavior and Human Decision Processes*, **23**, 339–59.

Ford, G.T. and R.A. Smith (1987), 'Inferential beliefs in consumer evaluations: an assessment of alternative processing strategies,' *Journal of Consumer Research*, **14** (3), 363–71.

Foster, G. (1978), *Financial Statement Analysis*, Englewood Cliffs, NJ: Prentice Hall.

Francis, J. and D. Philbrick (1993), 'Analysts' decisions as products of a multi-task environment,' *Journal of Accounting Research*, **31** (Autumn), 216–30.

Fried, D. and D. Givoly (1982), 'Financial analysts' forecasts of earnings: a better surrogate for earnings expectations,' *Journal of Accounting and Economics*, **4** (October), 85–107.

Ganzach, Y. and D.H. Krantz (1990), 'The psychology of moderate prediction: experience with multiple determination,' *Organizational Behavior and Human Decision Processes*, **47** (2), 177–204.

Gigerenzer, G. and U. Hoffrage (1995), 'How to improve Bayesian resorting without instruction: frequency format,' *Psychological Review*, **102** (4), 684–704.

Gigerenzer, G., W. Hell and H. Blank (1988), 'Presentation and content: the use of base rates as a continuous variable,' *Journal of Experimental Psychology: Human Perception and Performance*, **14**, 513–25.

Ginossar, Z. and Y. Trope (1980), 'The effects of base rates and individuating information on judgments about another person,' *Journal of Experimental Social Psychology*, **16**, 228–42.

Ginossar, Z. and Y. Trope (1987), 'Problem solving in judgment under uncertainty,' *Journal of Personality and Social Psychology*, **52**, 464–74.
Givoly, D. (1985), 'The formation of earnings expectations,' *The Accounting Review*, **LX** (3), 372–86.
Gluck, M.A. and G.H. Bower (1988), 'From conditioning to category learning: an adaptive network model,' *Journal of Experimental Psychology: General*, **117**, 227–47.
Gu, Z. and J. Wu (2003), 'Earnings skewness and analyst forecast bias,' *Journal of Accounting and Economics*, **35**, 5–29.
Hammerton, M. (1973), 'A case of radical probability estimation,' *Journal of Experimental Psychology*, **101**, 242–54.
Hansell, S. (2001), 'As tech stocks fall, some analysts prosper,' *New York Times*, online edition, 4 March.
Harvey, N. (1995), 'Why are judgments less consistent in less predictable task situations?,' *Organizational Behavior and Human Decision Processes*, **63** (September), 247–63.
Hayes, R.M. (1998), 'The impact of trading commission incentives on analysts' stock coverage decisions and earnings forecasts,' *Journal of Accounting Research*, **36** (Autumn), 299–321.
Herrmann, D. and W.B. Thomas (2000), 'An analysis of segment disclosures under SFAS No. 131 and SFAS No. 14,' *Accounting Horizons*, **14** (3), 287–302.
Herrmann, D., T. Inoue and W.B. Thomas (2007), 'The effect of changes in Japanese consolidation policy on analyst forecast error,' *Journal of Accounting & Public Policy*, **26** (January), 39–61.
Higgins, H.N. (1998), 'Analyst forecasting performance in seven countries,' *Financial Analysts Journal*, **54** (May–June), 58–62.
Highhouse, S. and E.L. Hause (1995), 'Missing information in selection: an application of Einhorn–Hogart ambiguity model,' *Journal of Applied Psychology*, **80** (1), 86–93.
Huber, J. and J. McCann (1982), 'The impact of inferential beliefs of product evaluations,' *Journal of Marketing Research* (August), 324–33.
Huberts, L.C. and R.J. Fuller (1995), 'Predictability bias in the U.S. equity market,' *Financial Analysts Journal*, **51** (March–April), 12–28.
Hunton, J.E. and R.A. McEwen (1997), 'An assessment of the relation between analysts' earnings forecast accuracy, motivational incentives and cognitive information search strategy,' *The Accounting Review*, **72** (October), 497–515.
Hussain, S. (1996), 'Over-reaction by security market analysts: the impact of broker status and firm size,' *Journal of Business Finance & Accounting*, **23** (December), 1223–44.
Irvine, P.J. (2004), 'Analysts' forecasts and brokerage-firm trading,' *The Accounting Review*, **79** (1), 125–49.
Jaccard, J. and G. Wood (1988), 'The effects of incomplete information on the formation of attitudes toward behavioral alternatives,' *Journal of Personality and Social Psychology*, **54** (4), 580–98.
Jackson, A.R. (2005), 'Trade generation, reputation, and sell-side analysts,' *The Journal of Finance*, **60** (2), 673–717.
Jacob, J., S. Rock and D.P. Weber (2003), 'Do analysts at independent research firms make better earnings forecasts?,' Working Paper, University of Colorado at Boulder.
Jagacinski, C.M. (1991), 'Personnel decision making: the impact of missing information,' *Journal of Applied Psychology*, **76**, 19–30.
Johnson, R.D. (1987), 'Making judgments when information is missing: inferences, biases, and framing effects,' *Acta Psychologica*, **66** (1), 69–82.
Johnson, R.D. (1988), 'Making decisions with incomplete information: the first complete test of the inference model,' *Advances in Consumer Research*, **16**, 522–8.
Johnson, R.D. and I.P. Levin (1985), 'More than meets the eye: the effect of missing information on purchase evaluations,' *Journal of Consumer Research*, **12**, 169–77.
Kahneman, D. and D. Lovallo (1993), 'Timid choices and bold forecasts: a cognitive perspective on risk taking,' *Management Science*, **39** (1), 17–31.
Kahneman, D. and A. Tversky (1972), 'Subjective probability: a judgment of representativeness,' *Cognitive Psychology*, **3**, 430–54.
Kahneman, D. and A. Tversky (1973), 'On the psychology of prediction,' *Psychological Review*, **80**, 237–51.
Kalish, M.L. (2001), 'An inverse base rate effect with continuously valued stimuli,' *Memory & Cognition*, **29** (4), 587–97.
Kang, S., J. O'Brien and K. Sivaramakrishnan (1994), 'Analysts' interim earnings forecasts: evidence on the forecasting process,' *Journal of Accounting Research*, **32**, 103–12.
Kardes, F.R., S.S. Posavac, D. Silvera, M.L. Cronley, D.M. Sanbonmatsu, S. Schertzer, F. Miller, P.M. Herr and M. Chandrashekaran (2006), 'Debiasing omission neglect,' *Journal of Business Research*, **59**, 786–92.
Khurana, I.K., R. Pereira and K.K. Raman (2003), 'Does analyst behavior explain market mispricing of foreign earnings for U.S. multinational firms?,' *Journal of Accounting, Auditing and Finance*, **18** (4), 453–78.
Klar, Y., A. Medding and D. Sarel (1996), 'Nonunique invulnerability: singular versus distributional prob-

abilities and unrealistic optimism in comparative risk judgments,' *Organizational Behavior and Human Decision Processes*, **67** (2), 229–45.
Klein, A. (1990), 'A direct-test of the cognitive bias theory of share price reversals,' *Journal of Accounting and Economics*, **13** (July), 155–66.
Koehler, J.J. (1996), 'The base rate fallacy reconsidered: descriptive, normative and methodological challenges,' *Behavioral & Brain Sciences*, **19**, 1–53.
Koonce, L. and M. Mercer (2005), 'Using psychology theories in archival financial accounting research,' *Journal of Accounting Literature*, **24**, 175–215.
Krosnick, J.A., F. Li and D.R. Lehman (1990), 'Conversational conventions, order of information acquisition, and the effect of base rates and individuating information on social judgments,' *Journal of Personality and Social Psychology*, **59** (6), 1140–52.
Kwag, S. and K. Small (2007), 'The impact of Regulation Fair Disclosure on earnings management and analyst forecast bias,' *Journal of Economics and Finance*, **31** (1), 87–98.
Levin, I.P., R.D. Johnson and D.P. Chapman (1991), 'Individual differences in dealing with incomplete information: judging clinical competence,' *Bulletin of the Psychonomic Society*, **29** (5), 451–54.
Levin, I.P., S.L. Schneider and G.J. Gaeth (1998), 'Not all frames are created equal: a typology and critical analysis of framing effects,' *Organizational Behavior and Human Decision Processes*, **76** (2), 149–89.
Lewis, B.L., K. Schipper and M. Zmijewski (1992), 'The effect of missing information on security valuation,' Working Paper, University of Colorado, Duke University and University of Chicago.
Lim, T. (2001), 'Rationality and analysts' forecast bias', *The Journal of Finance*, **56** (1), 369–85.
Lin, H.W. and M. McNichols (1998), 'Underwriting relationships, analysts' earnings forecasts and investment recommendations,' *Journal of Accounting and Economics*, **25** (February), 101–27.
Lobo, G.J. and R.D. Nair (1990), 'Combining judgmental and statistical forecasts: an application to earnings forecasts,' *Decision Sciences*, **21** (2), 446–60.
Lobo, G.J. and R.D. Nair (1991), 'Analysts' utilization of historical earnings information,' *Managerial and Decision Economics*, **12** (5), 383–93.
Locksley, A. and C. Strangor (1984), 'Why versus how often: causal reasoning and the incidence of judgmental bias,' *Journal of Experimental Social Psychology*, **20**, 470–83.
Loke, W.H. and K.F. Tan (1992), 'Effects of framing and missing information in expert and novice judgment,' *Bulletin of the Psychonomic Society*, **30** (3), 187–90.
Lynch, J.G. and C. Ofir (1989), 'Effects of cue consistency and value on base-rate utilization,' *Journal of Personality and Social Psychology*, **56** (2), 170–81.
Lyon, D. and P. Slovic (1976), 'Dominance of accuracy information and neglect of base rates in probability estimation,' *Acta Psychologica*, **40**, 287–98.
Maines, L.A. and J.R.M. Hand (1996), 'Individuals' perceptions and misperceptions of time series properties of quarterly earnings,' *The Accounting Review*, **71** (July), 317–37.
Maines, L.A. and L.S. McDaniel (2000), 'Effects of comprehensive-income characteristics on nonprofessional investors' judgments: the role of financial-statement presentation format,' *The Accounting Review*, **75** (April), 179–207.
Martin, L.M. (1985), 'Uncertain? How do you spell relief?,' *The Journal of Portfolio Management*, **11** (3), 5–8.
Mercer, M. (2005), 'The fleeting effects of disclosure forthcomingness on management's reporting credibility,' *The Accounting Review*, **80** (2), 723–44.
Mest, D.P. and E. Plummer (2003), 'Analysts' rationality and forecast bias: evidence from sales forecasts,' *Review of Quantitative Finance and Accounting*, **21**, 103–22.
Meyer, R.J. (1981), 'A model of multiattribute judgments under attribute uncertainty and informational constraints,' *Journal of Marketing Research*, **18**, 428–41.
Michaely, R. and K. Womack (1999), 'Conflict of interest and the credibility of underwriter analyst recommendations,' *Review of Financial Studies*, **12**, 653–86.
Morlock, H. (1967), 'The effect of outcome desirability on information required for decisions,' *Behavioral Science*, **12** (July), 296–300.
Moses, O.D. (1990), 'On analysts' earnings forecasts for failing firms,' *Journal of Business Finance & Accounting*, **17** (Spring), 101–18.
Nisbett, R.E. and E. Borgida (1975), 'Attribution and the psychology of prediction,' *Journal of Personality and Social Psychology*, **32** (5), 932–43.
Nisbett, R.E., E. Borgida, R. Crandall and H. Reed (1976), 'Popular induction: information is not necessarily informative,' in J.S. Carrol and J.W. Payne (eds), *Cognitive and Social Behavior*, Hillsdale, NJ: Erlbaum, pp. 113–33.
Nutt, S.R., J.C. Easterwood and C.M. Easterwood (1999), 'New evidence on serial correlation in analyst forecast errors,' *Financial Management*, **28** (4), 106–17.
O'Brien, P. (1988), 'Analysts' forecasts as earnings expectations,' *Journal of Accounting and Economics* (January), 53–83.

Peterson, D.K. and G.F. Pitz (1986), 'Effects of amount of information on predictions of uncertain quantities,' *Acta Psychologica*, **61** (April), 229–41.
Rajan, R. and H. Servaes (1997), 'Analyst following of initial public offerings,' *The Journal of Finance*, **52** (2), 507–29.
Richardson, S., S. Teoh and P. Wysocki (2004), 'The walk-down to beatable analysts' forecasts: the role of equity issuance and inside trading incentives,' *Contemporary Accounting Research*, **21** (4), 885–24.
Sanbonmatsu, D.M., F.R. Kardes and P.M. Herr (1992), 'The role of prior knowledge and missing information in multiattribute evaluation,' *Organizational Behavior and Human Decision Processes*, **51**, 76–91.
Sanbonmatsu, D.M., F.R. Kardes and C. Sansone (1991), 'Remembering less and inferring more: the effects of the timing of judgment on inferences about unknown attributes,' *Journal of Personality and Social Psychology*, **61**, 546–54.
Sanbonmatsu, D.M., F.R. Kardes, S.S. Posavac and D.C. Houghton (1997), 'Contextual influences on judgment based on limited information,' *Organizational Behavior and Human Decision Processes*, **69**, 251–64.
Sanbonmatsu, D.M., F.R. Kardes, D.C. Houghton, E.A. Ho and S.S. Posavac (2003), 'Overestimating the importance of the given information in multiattribute consumer judgment,' *Journal of Consumer Psychology*, **13**, 289–300.
Sarbanes–Oxley Act (SOX) (2002), Public Law No. 107–204, Washington, DC: Government Printing Office.
Scheier, M.F., C.S. Carver and M.W. Bridges (2001), 'Optimism, pessimism, and psychological well-being,' in E.C. Chang (ed.), *Optimism and Pessimism: Implications for Theory, Research, and Practice*, Washington, DC: American Psychological Association, pp. 189–216.
Schipper, K. (1991), 'Analysts' forecasts,' *Accounting Horizons*, **5** (December), 105–21.
Schwarz, N., F. Strack, D. Hilton and G. Naderer (1991), 'Base rates, representativeness, and the logic of conversation: the contextual relevance of "irrelevant" information,' *Social Cognition*, **9**, 67–83.
Sears, D.O. (1983), 'The person-positivity bias,' *Journal of Personality and Social Psychology*, **44** (February), 233–50.
Securities and Exchange Commission (SEC) (2003), *Commission Guidance Regarding Management's Discussion and Analysis of Financial Condition and Results of Operations*, Release No. 33–8350; FR No. 72. Washington, DC: SEC.
Sedor, L.M. (2002), 'An explanation for unintentional optimism in analysts' earnings forecasts,' *The Accounting Review*, **77** (October), 731–53.
Shanteau, J. (1989), 'Cognitive heuristics and biases in behavioral auditing: review, comments and observations,' *Accounting, Organizations and Society*, **14** (1/2), 165–77.
Sherman, S.J. and E. Corty (1984), 'Cognitive heuristics,' in R.S. Wyer and T.K. Srull (eds), *Handbook of Social Cognition*, Hillsdale, NJ: Erlbaum, pp. 189–286.
Stickel, S.E. (1992), 'Reputation and performance among security analysts,' *Journal of Finance*, **47** (December), 1811–36.
Stone, D.L. and E.F. Stone (1987), 'Effects of missing application-blank information on personnel selection decisions: do privacy protection strategies bias the outcome?,' *Journal of Applied Psychology*, **72**, 452–6.
Thomas, W.B. (1999), 'A test of the market's mispricing of domestic and foreign earnings,' *Journal of Accounting and Economics*, **28** (December), 243–67.
Tversky, A. and D. Kahneman (1980), 'Causal schemata in judgment under uncertainty,' in M. Fishbein (ed.), *Progress of Social Psychology*, Hillsdale, NJ: Erlbaum, pp. 153–260.
Tversky, A. and D. Kahneman (1981), 'The framing of decisions and psychology of choice,' *Science*, **211** (4481), 453–8.
Tversky, A. and D. Kahneman (1982), 'Evidential impact on base rates,' in D. Kahneman, P. Slovic and A. Tversky (eds), *Judgment under Uncertainty: Heuristics and Biases*, Cambridge: Cambridge University Press, pp. 49–72.
Weinstein, N.D. (1980), 'Unrealistic optimism about future life events,' *Journal of Personality and Social Psychology*, **39** (November), 806–20.
Wells, G.L. and J.H. Harvey (1977), 'Do people use consensus information in making causal attributions?,' *Journal of Personality and Social Psychology*, **35**, 279–93.
White, M.W. and D.J. Koehler (2004), 'Missing information in multiple-cue probability learning,' *Memory & Cognition*, **32** (6), 1007–18.
Whitecotton, S.M. (1996), 'The effects of experience and a decision aid on the slope, scatter, and bias of earnings forecasts,' *Organizational Behavior and Human Decision Processes*, **66** (April), 111–21.
Whitecotton, S.M., D.E. Sanders and K.B. Norris (1998), 'Improving predictive accuracy with a combination of human intuition and mechanical decision aids,' *Organizational Behavior and Human Decision Processes*, **76** (3), 325–48.
Williams, P.A., G.D. Moyes and K. Park (1996), 'Factors affecting earnings forecast revisions for the buy-side and sell-side analyst,' *Accounting Horizons*, **10** (September), 112–21.

Willis, R.H. (2001), 'Mutual fund manager forecasting behavior,' *Journal of Accounting Research*, **39** (December), 707–25.
Yamagishi, T. and C.T. Hill (1981), 'Initial impression versus missing information as explanations of the set-size effect,' *Journal of Personality and Social Psychology*, **44** (5), 942–51.
Yates, J.F., C.M. Jagacinski and M.D. Faber (1978), 'Evaluation of partially described multiattribute options,' *Organizational Behavior and Human Performance*, **21** (April), 240–51.
Zukier, H. and A. Pepitone (1984), 'Social roles and strategies in prediction: some determinants of the use of base-rate information,' *Journal of Personality and Social Psychology*, **47**, 349–60.

12 Overconfidence and active management

Christoph Gort and Mei Wang

INTRODUCTION

One area of today's behavioral finance literature deals with the phenomenon of overconfidence, which has its roots in psychology but lends itself very well to describe behavioral patterns on financial markets. This chapter reveals that investors represented by a sample of decision makers of Swiss pension funds are on average miscalibrated and prone to the better than average effect, which are both typical facets of overconfidence.[1] Miscalibration generally refers to the fact that people provide very narrow confidence intervals in various estimation tasks and by doing so they overestimate the precision of their knowledge and potentially underestimate risks of being wrong. The better than average effect describes the evidence that most people believe they achieve above average performances in various fields despite lack of indication or validation for it. Both miscalibration and the better than average effect influence the decision making on financial markets as well as the managing style of financial assets. Miscalibration can affect asset allocation decisions of investors and lead to overly risky portfolios or unintentionally high exposures to risky assets because of an underestimation of financial risks. The better than average effect, on the other hand, influences the style of managing assets and can lead to a high reliance on expected benefits of very active trading strategies and an underestimation of the inevitable difficulties of maintaining a competitive edge over the market and over peers.

The basic goal of this chapter is to document the surprisingly high level of confidence in the domain of return estimation of financial assets and judgment of one's own return potential relative to peers. In particular, we investigate professional pension fund managers in Switzerland. We then relate those findings to the way financial assets are managed today. The reliance on traditional active management relative to benchmark indices across institutional investors represented in this chapter, despite the lack of success on average, might be rooted in the degree of overconfidence of the decision makers. As previous academic and practical research shows, overconfidence can lead to reduced returns, increased risks and suboptimal financial decision making, so it seems very important to address those issues in order to help investors to manage their assets more efficiently.

It is beyond the scope of this chapter to take a general view on the advantages and disadvantages of active management compared to indexing. Successful active management depends on an array of factors such as skills, resources, information, processes, risk aversion and investment constraints. So it is difficult to argue for an optimal degree of active management in general because there is too much heterogeneity across investors with respect to those different circumstances. Indeed, we find several samples of highly successful active managers, for example, in the hedge-fund industry. However, we also find clear evidence of failure among less successful hedge funds, mutual funds, pension funds and private investors. One may argue that the degree of an investor's overconfidence is related to his investment behavior and success.

Looking deeper into our results on overconfidence, we note that the degree of overconfidence seems to vary across individuals and across different domains of questions. We also show that those differences are related to individual characteristics. For example, younger people with a degree from university and more experience in finance are significantly less overconfident than older participants with less education and less experience.

The remainder of the chapter is organized as follows. The first section reviews related research on overconfidence in general and in the domain of financial markets. The second section describes the data and the methods to measure two of the major aspects of overconfidence – miscalibration and the better than average effect – and the third section introduces the applied linear regression model to relate individual characteristics to the degree of overconfidence. The fourth section summarizes all results and the last section discusses and concludes.

RELATED RESEARCH ON OVERCONFIDENCE

Overconfidence is a complex phenomenon with various facets, including miscalibration and the so-called better than average effect. In this section we discuss first the literature in psychology on miscalibration and the better than average effect. Then we address effects of these traits on the potential success on financial markets.

People tend to overestimate the precision of their knowledge. As a result, they are miscalibrated in estimating and forecasting by providing too narrow confidence intervals (Lichtenstein et al., 1982). Instead of providing reasonably large confidence intervals to increase the probability of including the correct result, they often provide very narrow ranges. It has been observed that task difficulty and blurred feedback lead to higher degree of overconfidence (Lichtenstein et al., 1982; Griffin and Tversky, 1992). Odean (1998) argues that forecasting and estimating returns on financial markets are not easy tasks and the available feedback is blurred as the market prices of assets are affected by noise. So the chances to observe overconfident behaviour in the domain of financial markets are high.

Current psychological research debates whether miscalibration is a stable human trait or only a statistical illusion (see Gigerenzer et al., 1991; Griffin and Tversky, 1992; Erev et al., 1994; Brenner et al., 1996; Klayman et al., 1999). As Soll and Klayman (2004) point out, the type of questions matters, and tasks that involve estimations of confidence intervals typically lead to higher measures for miscalibration. Although there exists a broad range of estimation tasks and many different measures of miscalibration, in this chapter we focus on estimating historical returns and forecasting future asset returns on financial markets, which are similar to tasks the decision makers of pension plans frequently face in their jobs and which might affect their performance.

In line with the results presented in this chapter, several empirical studies show that professionals in the financial industry are subject to miscalibration. Russo and Schoemaker (1992) report that money managers tend to formulate too narrow 90 percent confidence intervals in a questionnaire about meta-knowledge. The participants' subjective confidence intervals in their sample contain the correct solutions only in about half of the cases, instead of 90 percent as required. Graham and Harvey (2003) analyze economic forecasts on the equity risk premium from CFOs in the USA over different time horizons and conclude that the size of the average confidence interval is very narrow compared to the volatility of equity markets. Deaves et al. (2005) and Glaser et al. (2007) present similar evidence in the domain of financial markets as the confidence intervals of the participants in their samples of professionals capture significantly fewer realized returns for economic forecasts than required. They also notice that the individual degree of overconfidence is stable across different tasks. This result indicates that people are in general overconfident in the domain of financial markets and not just within particular asset classes or particular tasks. It is also in line with the finding of Alpert and Raiffa (1982), who argue that people tend to respond similarly to the same types of questions.

The better than average effect was first observed in psychological research, too. The perception of oneself as above average is deeply rooted in human nature and can be observed in many different domains. Svenson (1981) notes that more than 80 percent of the participants in a survey believe themselves to be above average with respect to their driving skills. Studies in psychology show that people tend to have the illusion that they are capable of delivering above-average performances in various tasks despite having neither evidence nor any adequate means to compare them with a representative average (Taylor and Brown, 1988). People in the asset management industry offer a good example as they are typically very confident about their market knowledge, their forecasting accuracy and their abilities to beat market index returns. Broad market indices represent the investable universe of assets on financial markets and typically gain (or lose) the average across all investors' gains and losses on a market. Most active asset managers usually claim to outperform market indices in the future, that is generating higher returns than the market index for a particular asset class. In contrast to other domains, an adequate measure of the average performance is easily available on financial markets thanks to freely accessible data about various broad market indices for investors. The evidence is clear: beating the average represented by a broad market index is difficult. As Sharpe (1991) demonstrates based on simplifying assumptions, active management is a zero-sum game because every dollar an investor gains above the average return must correspond to another investor's loss below the average return. Most academic studies report that only a minor percentage of investors can realize an outperformance over market indices in the long run after costs (Carhart, 1997, Malkiel, 2007). Nevertheless the lure of potential outperformance ensures that active management remains very popular across investors who express surprisingly high confidence in relation to beating to beat their peers in the future. Such optimistic expectations are puzzling when academic evidence on the rather disappointing past performance of several types of market participants is taken into account, even though there are a few very interesting exceptions of well-known successful active managers (Siegel et al., 2001). On the other hand, in a more recent paper, Taylor and Brown (1994) confirm that being overly optimistic usually increases the well-being of an individual. So from a psychological point of view, being prone to the better than average effect can be seen as rather healthy and definitely non-pathological, but in the domain of financial markets it can lead to overoptimistically biased expectations about one's own abilities and own performance in the future.

Graham et al. (2006) and Glaser et al. (2005) report that the level of overconfidence in the domain of financial markets is different across individuals. Although it is observed that individual characteristics affect overconfidence, the evidence about stable relationships is ambiguous. Glaser et al. (2007) find that professionals are more overconfident than students about their trend recognition abilities although they do not provide more accurate estimations. In contrast, Russo and Schoemaker (1992) report that professionals are generally miscalibrated, but to a lesser degree than lay people. In a model from Odean and Gervais (2001), more experience can reduce overconfidence. Inexperienced but successful investors are most prone to overconfidence since they tend to attribute their success solely to their own abilities. Over time more experience will help them to better evaluate their true abilities. Locke and Mann (2001) confirm this theory in an empirical study and find no indication of miscalibration among highly experienced traders on the Chicago Mercantile Exchange. In light of those results, we present evidence that individual characteristics, such as education or experience, influence the degree of overconfidence in the domain of financial markets. In particular, consistent with the previous studies, we find that more experience and higher education are associated with lower degree of overconfidence.

Potential impacts of overconfidence for investors are reduced returns, increased risks and selection of inefficient portfolios. In a theoretical model, DeLong et al. (1991) show that overconfident investors can survive on financial markets but tend to take more risk and gain less expected utility than rational investors. Kyle and Wang (1997) show with their model that employing overconfident managers can be the best strategy, in the context of game theory, as both participants face a prisoner's dilemma. However, the choice of an overconfident manager does not lead to an efficient outcome for both players. It is acknowledged that these models are applied directly to investors and not to decision makers who have the choice of delegating the portfolio management to an external asset manager. However, the point is to show that overconfident market participants can theoretically survive on financial markets but do not achieve the best risk-adjusted performance. Lakonishok et al. (1992) argue that overconfidence can lead to a preference for active management in a pension plan despite the fact that it might deliver returns below a market index. They point out that overconfidence about selection skills used to identify good active managers can explain the high percentage of active management within US pension plans. Camerer and Lovallo (1999) present evidence from an experimental market that roughly 70 percent of the participants in their sample are prone to the better than average effect in a market entry game when relying on the subjective perception of own skills relative to the competitors in the game. They further report that the participants on average lose money due to their propensity to the better than average effect and their overestimation of their own skills; this results in financial decisions that lower their wealth.

In addition to experimental evidence, empirical research using real trading data also suggests harmful effects of overconfidence on investments and portfolio management. In a large sample of private investors dealing on a brokerage account in the USA, Odean and Barber (2001) show that overconfidence leads to a higher trading volume and reduces returns. Guiso and Jappelli (2006) use a sample of Italian bank clients in which the clients – whom the authors suppose to be more overconfident (people with a lower education but a higher self-declared knowledge) – hold portfolios with lower Sharpe ratios than other clients.

However, in this chapter we do not evaluate the portfolios and the trading activities at the individual level, and we cannot postulate any causal relationships between the degree of overconfidence of our participants and their pension funds' investments and returns. Some evidence of individual overconfidence and returns on financial markets is presented by Menkhoff and Schmidt (2005), who describe how overconfidence is related to investment strategies of mutual fund managers.

DATA AND METHODS

The results discussed in this chapter are based on the authors' questionnaires which were applied to address miscalibration and the better than average effect (Gort et al., 2008 and Gort, 2009). In total, 584 questionnaires have been distributed among decision makers of Swiss pension plans, that is managers and members of investment committees, and 132 have been returned for a response rate of 22.6 percent. Twenty-four questionnaires contained no confidence intervals and therefore have been excluded from the analysis, leading to 108 participants in the sample, which we refer to as the professional sample. Of those, only six participants are female. Fifty-eight persons have a university degree, 36 of them in finance, and 65 attended education courses in finance for practitioners. Experience in finance and in pension plans is symmetrically distributed between less than two years and more than 25 years, and the respondents are between 25 and 80 years old.

A lay people sample is based on people working for the City of Zurich in several departments not related to financial markets or pension plans but with a self-declared interest in financial topics. In total 104 persons, 19 women and 85 men, returned a complete questionnaire. Among the lay people sample, 25 of them have a degree from university but only 16 in finance or economics, and 32 have attended courses in finance for practitioners. Two-thirds have no experience in working in financial areas but two-thirds frequently read newspapers related to financial topics. The participants in the lay people sample are between 20 and 65 years old.

The questionnaire for the participants in both the professional and lay people sample consists of three parts, where the first two parts are related to miscalibration and the last to the better than average effect.[2] Additionally the respondents provided data about individual characteristics such as age, education and job experience. In the part that measures miscalibration, the participants were asked to formulate two sorts of 90 percent confidence intervals. The first was 90 percent confidence intervals for historical annual returns for six different asset classes over the years 1972–2005 to estimate the participants' degree of miscalibration. Those questions have been worded as follows:

> In this task you have to provide an upper and a lower boundary for the annual returns of asset class x over the last 34 years. Please choose the boundaries in such a way that 90 percent of the realized single annual returns of asset class *x* are within your boundaries.

The second sort was 90 percent confidence intervals for return forecasts for six different asset classes for the year 2006 to assess how confident the participants are about their forecasting abilities given their confidence intervals. The following wording is used:

In this task you have to provide an upper and a lower boundary for the return of asset class x in the year 2006. Please choose the boundaries in such a way that the realized return of asset class x in 2006 will be within your boundaries with a probability of 90 percent.

Two different methods to judge the participants' confidence intervals, that is their level of miscalibration, are applied. First, following an idea of Hilton (2001), the participants' subjective confidence intervals for annual returns are compared with the distribution of historical annual returns over the years 1972–2005. More concretely, the number of annual returns over these 34 years that are included within the participants' 90 percent confidence intervals are counted. For each asset class realized historical annual returns between 1972 and 2005 were collected and the two highest and lowest returns were cut off to approximate a 90 percent (precisely 88.9 percent) interval of the annual returns in each asset class. In other words, 90 percent of the annual returns over these 34 years are included in those intervals and this corresponds to 32 annual returns. A miscalibrated participant will provide too narrow 90 percent confidence intervals and thus capture fewer than 32 of these 34 annual returns.[3]

Second, the implied volatility of the participants' confidence intervals is analyzed, where a relationship described by Pearson and Tukey (1965) has been used. The term implied volatility refers to a relationship between the 95 percent and 5 percent return quantile (which corresponds to a 90 percent interval) and the standard deviation. The standard deviation is equal to the difference between the 95 percent quantile and the 5 percent quantile divided by 3.25. As in the first approach, the participants' responses are compared with historical data, that is the participants' implied volatilities in their confidence intervals with the historically implied volatility of each asset class based on the annual returns over those 34 years. Volatility is a popular way to express uncertainty about future returns of an asset class, and the higher the volatility, the broader is the spectrum in which the realization of the future return will fall with a certain probability. If a participant formulates confidence intervals with very low implied volatilities, we interpreted it as an indication that he is miscalibrated. The historically implied volatilities, of the annual returns therefore serve as guidelines to judge the size of the participants' implied volatilities.

To measure the better than average effect in the third part of the questionnaire, the participants were asked to provide a self-evaluation of the accuracy of their own responses given in the first two parts versus those of the other participants. Additionally they were asked about their expectations with respect to their own pension plans' future success relative to the other participants in the sample. More concretely, the questions asked about:

- the chances of their pension plan to find above-average active managers in the future;
- the likelihood that their pension plan would achieve an above-average risk-adjusted return in the future; and
- the chances that their internal and external managers would outperform the other active managers of Swiss pension plans in the sample in the future.

To answer the questions in the third part, the participants always had to tick a box on a Likert scale from one (clearly below average) to seven (clearly above average). The possibility of four (average) is included as many participants probably would choose this option. The participants were well informed about their competitors in this sample, as explicitly stated in the questionnaire.

To analyze the relationships between overconfidence and the participants' individual characteristics, a linear regression model with four predictive variables is applied. It differentiates between three sorts of education: a degree from university; practical financial education, and no such education. It is specified with two dummy variables. Further predictive variables for experience, for example an aggregation of experience in finance and in pension plans, and age are used. Those four predictors are positively correlated but never above a level of 0.6. Gender is not included in the regression model as the number of females in the sample is too low. In the analysis of confidence intervals across all participants, median values are presented as there are a few outliers that have big impacts on the mean. In the application of the linear regressions analysis, the logarithm of the confidence intervals is used and the corresponding boundaries to mitigate such outlier effects. However, the results do not substantially change if the non-transformed data are analyzed. To aggregate confidence intervals of different asset classes, the data are normalized by calculating the *z*-scores of the participants' log intervals. R^2 provides information about the amount of variance the regressions explain. For the self-evaluation the participants' aggregated scores from the responses from one to seven are used. No significant interaction effects have been identified within the predictive variables for the regression model, so no interaction variables are included. Cooks distance values indicate no significant effects of outliers in the data.

It is important to note that the term active management refers in this chapter to the implementation of a strategic asset allocation with long-only active managers instead of indexers across our sample of Swiss pension plans. Active managers try to achieve higher returns than market indices by implementing active trading strategies, whereas indexers try to replicate the return of a market index. The availability of market indices and replicating instruments today gives the decision makers of Swiss pension plans a true choice between active managers and indexers when implementing the strategic asset allocation for traditional asset classes like equities or bonds. In contrast, the selection of a strategic asset allocation and dynamic shifts in the asset allocation can also be regarded as active management as the board of trustees of a pension plan has to take active decisions. But for the strategic asset allocation of a Swiss pension plan there is no market index that could be used as a default portfolio, so there is no true choice between active managers and indexers. Therefore our focus is only on the performance of pension plans within asset classes and not across total pension plan portfolios. Market-timing skills of pension plans will be excluded from the analysis in this chapter because meaningful data are not available. On the other hand, there are enough data supporting the hypothesis that pension funds favor active management. A report by Lusenti (2003) indicates that most of the Swiss pension plan assets in various different asset classes are managed actively. Out of 110 plan managers who answered that question, two-thirds of them apply indexing on less than 10 percent of their total assets and only 14 report applying indexing at least on 50 percent of their assets. For a comparison, Ennis (1997) reports that around 35 percent of the assets of US pension plans rely on indexing, and that the trend is increasing.

In order to have enough observations and a true choice between active management and indexing, the chapter analyzes the performances in only three of the most common asset classes for Swiss pension funds. Those are domestic and international equities, as well as CHF (Swiss francs) bonds. The pension plans' average and median performances in those asset classes is compared to well-established market indices. For domestic equities the Swiss Performance Index (SPI) is applied as a benchmark; for international equities the MSCI World Index is used; and for CHF bonds the Swiss Bond Index (SBI). Because Swiss pension plans are tax exempt, the loss due to taxes on dividends is in most of the cases marginal, and so a total return index is a fair comparison. Data about the absolute and relative performance of Swiss pension plans within asset classes are based on two different types of empirical surveys: annual studies from Lusenti Partners (Lusenti, 2005, 2006, 2007), based on a sample of 123, 123 and 130 Swiss pension plans respectively; and on the performance data from the ASIP Performance Comparison across 60 to 73 Swiss pension plans over different annual periods (ASIP, 2000–2006). None of those surveys is singularly representative for Swiss pension plans because both include only a part of all pension plans in Switzerland. However, in terms of assets under management, the samples from Lusenti include roughly CHF 200 billion in each year while the samples in ASIP contain assets of roughly CHF 80 billion in 2000 to CHF 160 billion in 2006 (there is some overlap in the samples). This reflects roughly one third and one quarter respectively of total assets under management. A size bias cannot be ruled out as larger pension plans tend to participate more often. There could be also a selection bias because there is no obligation to participate in the surveys and it cannot be excluded that only successful and above-average pension plans participate. Both of these biases put the presented results on the conservative side, as larger pension plans tend to index more assets than smaller funds, according to Lusenti (2003), and the performance of participants might be higher than that of non-participants.

RESULTS

In this section the results on miscalibration and the better than average effect are presented. The miscalibration part contains one section about estimation of historical returns and one section about forecasting accuracy. The part about the better than average effect addresses first the past performances of active management in the sample of Swiss pension funds and then the results based on the participants' responses in the questionnaire related to the better than average effect. Additionally a correlation analysis of both aspects is made. Finally, a linear regression model is presented that links the participants' personal characteristics to their degree of overconfidence based on their responses in the questionnaire. Note that neither the historical returns of asset classes nor the performance of pension funds in the sample contain the performances of the years 2006, 2007 or 2008 because these data were not available when the research was conducted. The heavily negative returns in 2008 in particular would increase the intervals containing 90 percent of the past returns and the implied volatilities of asset classes, so the results presented in this chapter tend to underestimate the overconfidence of participants. Also, one can argue that the experience of losing roughly 40 percent with Swiss and international equities in the year 2008 might have had an impact on the way participants provide confidence intervals to estimate past returns and to forecast future returns.

Estimation of Historical Returns

The median 90 percent confidence intervals of professionals only capture around 60 percent to about 80 percent of the past annual returns in each asset class.[4] This is evidence that professionals in the sample are miscalibrated in the median because their confidence intervals were meant to contain 90 percent of the annual returns from 1972 to 2005 (the time series for oil starts in 1982). The lay people sample provides even narrower boundaries for almost all asset classes, so lay people are more miscalibrated than professionals. A Mann–Whitney test, however, reveals that the differences between the confidence interval sizes are not significant except for two asset classes. The bars in Figure 12.1 show the median lower and the median upper boundaries for the confidence intervals in the professional and the lay people sample for historical return estimates in all six different asset classes. Those are Swiss and world equities, CHF bonds, gold, oil and the CHF–US$ exchange rate. The bars with light shading represent the distribution of 90 percent of all annual returns between 1972 and 2005 for those six asset classes and serve as a guideline to judge the size of the participants' confidence intervals. It can be seen that in the median the professionals and the lay people underestimate the downside risk but also the upside potential in almost all asset classes. That explains why medians

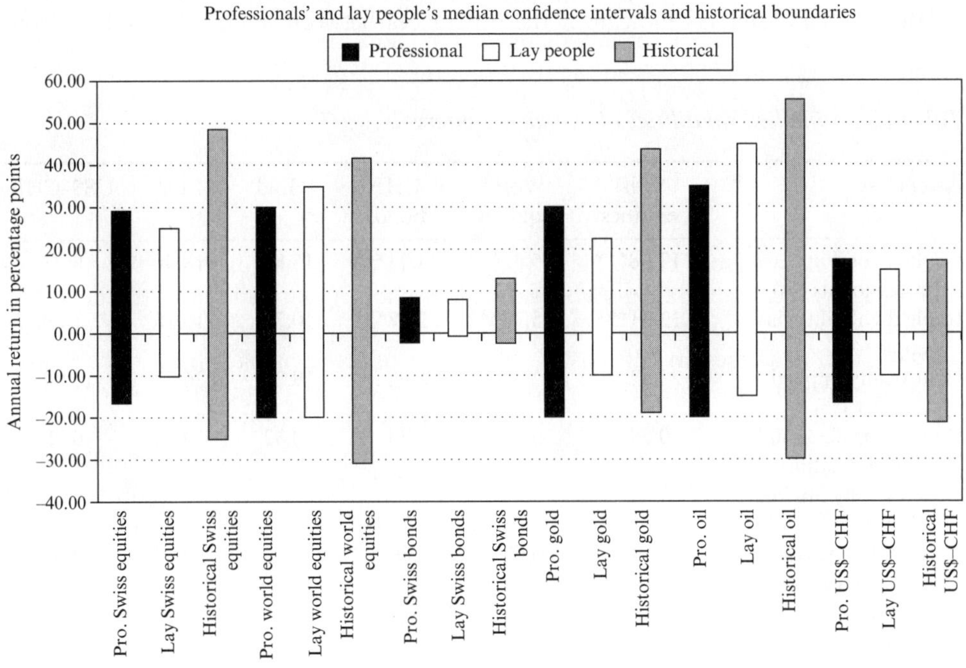

Source: Based on Gort et al. (2008).

Figure 12.1 Confidence intervals for historical returns

for 90 percent confidence intervals from both samples are narrower than the historical 90 percent intervals for annual returns over those 34 years. It is acknowledged that an analysis of only the size of the participants' confidence intervals does not provide any information about the accuracy, which is how much the lower and upper boundaries of a subjective confidence interval deviate from the historical intervals. Mann–Whitney tests show that the professional sample provides significantly more accurate boundaries for every asset class than the lay people. So the professionals might be not significantly less miscalibrated than lay people, but at least more knowledgeable than them.

Figure 12.1 shows the median lower and the median upper boundaries for the confidence intervals in the professional and the lay people sample for historical return estimates of six different asset classes as well as the upper and lower boundaries of the realized return of those asset classes over the 34 years from 1972 to 2005.

Further indication of miscalibration is given by a comparison of the implied volatilities embedded in the confidence intervals and the implied volatility of historical returns. Table 12.1 shows the implied volatilities of the confidence intervals from the professionals and the lay people respectively for historical returns for each asset class. Apparently the implied volatilities in both samples are lower than the historically implied volatilities in all asset classes, and the difference is highly significant for equities and bonds.

Table 12.1 shows the implied volatilities of the confidence intervals from the professionals and the lay people respectively for historical returns for each asset class. It also contains the historically implied volatility in each asset class over 34 years from 1972 to 2005 and the ratio of the participants' implied volatilities and historically implied volatilities. The asterisks indicate if the differences between implied volatilities from

Table 12.1 Implied volatilities of confidence intervals

Asset class	Swiss equities	World equities	CHF bonds	Gold	Oil	US$–CHF
Implied volatility, professionals (%)	13.08***	15.38***	3.23***	15.85	18.46	9.23
Implied volatility, lay people (%)	12.31***	15.38***	2.77***	10.77	15.38	7.69
Historically implied volatility (%)	22.62	22.30	4.62	19.26	26.22	11.84
Ratio of professionals' implied volatility vs historically implied volatility	0.58	0.69	0.70	0.82	0.70	0.78
Ratio of lay people's implied volatility vs historically implied volatility	0.54	0.69	0.60	0.56	0.59	0.65

Note: * significant at 10% level; ** significant at 5% level; *** significant at 1% level.

Source: Based on Gort et al. (2008).

participants' confidence intervals are significantly different than the historically implied intervals in each asset class.

An unexpected but interesting result is the fact that the professionals as well as the lay people seem to have a good feeling for the relative risk of each asset class. The ratios between the historical intervals and the subjective confidence intervals vary between 0.54 and 0.82, but are more often than not in a pretty narrow range, as the last two lines in Table 12.1 show. Those ratios are calculated by dividing the historically implied volatility by the median implied volatility of the participants' confidence intervals. Across all asset classes the average of the professional sample is 0.72 and 0.61 for the lay people. So both professionals and lay people are well informed about the relative risk of each asset class. This result indicates that people are generally miscalibrated across the historical returns of different asset classes, but further evidence is necessary to prove that point.

Return Forecasts

The participants were asked to provide 90 percent confidence intervals for return forecasts in Swiss equities, CHF bonds, their own pension plan, and the average Swiss pension plan. The implied volatilities of the professional sample for Swiss equities (3.1 percent), CHF bonds (1.2 percent) and the two types of pension plan returns (1.5 percent for each forecast) are difficult to compare against reasonable benchmarks, but are strikingly narrow relative to the historical implied volatilities (see Table 12.1). The participants express a high conviction about their own forecasting abilities because they choose very narrow upper and lower boundaries in their forecasting intervals.[5] Similar to the estimation of historical returns, lay people provide even narrower confidence intervals than professionals and, this time, in the forecasting task, a Mann–Whitney test confirms that the confidence interval sizes are significantly different. So the professionals express less confidence in their own forecast precision than the lay people, and on average they expect a higher downside risk, which is larger potential losses, but a comparable upside potential.

Performance with Active Management

In the annual surveys from Lusenti for the years 2004 to 2006 and ASIP from 2000 to 2006 there is no indication that Swiss pension plans perform better than market indices on average. Table 12.2 provides an overview of the median performances of Swiss pension plans in different asset classes according to those two surveys. The median was favored over the mean to mitigate outlier effects. The first three rows show the median annual returns according to the Lusenti and the ASIP survey, as well as the return of the Swiss Bond Index (SBI) domestic. Rows 4–6 and 7–10 contain the median annual returns for Swiss and international equities of the pension plans and for the market indices. Except for the median returns in the ASIP sample for CHF bonds in 2000 and 2003, Swiss equities in 2001 and foreign equities in 2001 and 2006, Swiss pension plans have on average never outperformed the corresponding market index neither net of fees (Lusenti) nor gross of fees (ASIP).

In Table 12.2, for each asset class the top rows show the sample median returns of the Lusenti Partners survey and the second rows the sample median returns for the ASIP

Table 12.2 Past performance of Swiss pension plans (%)

Year	Median annual returns from Lusenti and ASIP surveys and market indices						
	2000	2001	2002	2003	2004	2005	2006
Sample size for Lusenti/ASIP	na/50	na/63	na/65	na/70	123*/71	123**/73	130***/72
Aum for Lusenti/ASIP in CHF bn	na/80	na/80	na/75	na/100	215/145	190/145	212/161
CHF bonds							
Lusenti medium	na	na	na	na	3.4	2.7	0.3
ASIP medium	3.7	3.9	9.9	1.6	3.6	2.7	0.0
Swiss Bond Index (SBI) TR domestic†	3.4	4.4	10.8	1.5	4.6	3.6	−0.3
Swiss equities							
Lusenti median	na	na	na	na	5.9	34.0	20.0
ASIP median	11.4	−21.5	−26.9	21.7	6.3	35.2	20.1
Swiss Performance Index (SPI) TR	11.9	−22.0	−25.9	22.1	6.9	35.6	20.7
World equities							
Lusenti median	na	na	na	na	5.5	27.0	13.0
ASIP median	−11.1	−16.3	−33.6	19.1	5.4	27.0	11.2
MSCI world index in CHF TR	−11.9	−14.5	−33.0	19.6	6.0	27.5	11.8
MSCI world index ex Switzerland in CHF TR	−12.4	−14.3	−33.3	19.6	6.0	27.3	11.5

Notes: † The SBI domestic index covers only CHF bonds from Swiss companies whereas the SBI general reflects the whole universe of the CHF denominated bonds. Most of the Swiss pension plans use the SBI domestic as benchmark.

* Only 123 out of 174 in the Swiss pension plans in the sample provided an answer to this question.
** Only 123 out of 162 in the Swiss pension plans in the sample provided an answer to this question.
*** Only 130 out of 172 in the Swiss pension plans in the sample provided an answer to this question.

Source: Based on Gort (2009).

Performance Comparison. The last rows each present the returns of market indices for the asset classes. The last two rows in the table present the returns of the MSCI World Index in CHF inclusive of Switzerland and exclusive of Switzerland. The reason to show both indices is that the treatment of Swiss equities in a world equity index is different across Swiss pension plans and also across the surveys from Lusenti Partners and ASIP. Some plans include Swiss equities within the universe of world equities and others do not.

To defend the pension funds' performance, one might argue that the pension plans in the samples from ASIP manage the asset classes with a lower volatility than the market indices and therefore achieve better risk-adjusted returns. However, available data reveal that this is not the case as the Sharpe ratios of market indices are higher than the sample annual averages per asset class. Therefore our analyses of historical data do not support the belief that average Swiss pension funds are superior to market performance, so it is curious to observe that large reliance on traditional active management in reality. The next section offers the better than average effect as one explanation.

Better than Average Effect

To report the susceptibility to the better than average effect, we first analyze the participants' expectations concerning their current manager's chances for future success, their own manager selection skills and their pension plan's chances of outperforming those of other participants in the sample. In the questionnaire the participants were invited to tick a corresponding box on a Likert scale between one (clearly below average) to seven (clearly above average) including four (average) to express their opinion.

Each column in Table 12.3 contains the mean, the *t*-statistic, the median and the standard deviation (rows 3–6) for each of those questions. The sample mean is above four (average) for all questions and one-sample *t*-tests reveal significant differences between the sample means and the answering option 'average' at the 1 percent level for all questions except for the question on the chance of finding above average active managers in the future, which is significant only at the 10 per cent level. This is evidence that the professionals are on average prone to the better than average effect in the domain of judging their own and their managers' abilities on financial markets. Rows 8–14 in Table 12.3 contain the percentage of chosen responses by the participants in the questionnaire. The options "average" and "slightly above average" are chosen more often than all three options below average, and this is again evidence of the better than average effect. More than 93 percent of the participants believe in having at least average internal and external managers and in performing at least on an average level compared to the other pension plans in the sample. The first two rows in Table 12.3 show the sample size and the number of missing participants. A participant's answer is missing either because she refused to answer or because he does not apply internal or external management. The latter case applies in most cases.

Each column in Table 12.3 lists the summary statistics of the participants' responses from the questionnaire. The participants were invited to tick a box with values from one (clearly below average) to seven (clearly above average) to indicate how they perceive the chances of their own pension plan compared to the other participants' pension plans in the sample. A value of four indicates average. Rows 8–14 list the percentage of participants who ticked the different answering boxes. Missing values occur either because a participant did not answer the question or because a participants' pension plan does not work with internal or external managers. The latter case occurs much more often.

In a second step we check whether our sample is also prone to the better than average effect when forecasting returns of different asset classes. The six columns in Table 12.4 each represent an asset class for which the participants had to judge the accuracy of their own return forecast relative to the other participants in the survey. The same Likert scale from one to seven is applied. The means for all asset classes in Table 12.4 are above 4 but

Table 12.3 Perceived chances of active management in the participants' own pension plan

	Own pension plan's chances to find above average active managers	Current internal active managers' chances to outperform the other internal managers in the sample	Current external active managers' chances to outperform the other external managers in the sample	Own pension plan's chances to outperform the other pension plans in the sample
Valid	104	74	91	105
Missing	4	34	17	3
Mean	4.17*	4.55***	4.37***	4.57***
T-value	1.69	5.74	5.26	6.53
Median	4	5	4	5
Std dev.	1.05	0.83	0.68	0.90
Percentages of answers				
% clearly below average	1.92	0.00	0.00	0.95
% below average	3.85	1.35	1.35	0.00
% slightly below average	14.42	5.41	5.41	4.76
% average	43.27	39.19	39.19	43.81
% slightly above average	28.85	47.30	47.30	39.05
% above average	6.73	4.05	4.05	8.57
% clearly above average	0.96	2.70	2.70	2.86

Note: * 10% significance level; ** 5% significance level; *** 1% significance level.

Source: Based on Gort (2009).

one-sample *t*-statistics provide evidence that the differences are not significantly different from 4 (row 4). In other words, our participants do not generally think they can provide superior forecasts. Exceptions are equities and their own pension plan returns, as the participants judge their own forecasts to be significantly above average. Unsurprisingly, the option 'average' is by far the most chosen in the questionnaire. The option 'slightly above average' is more popular than the option 'rather below average', but the differences are much smaller in the forecasting task than in the tasks about a pension plans' chances of future success.

Each column in Table 12.4 lists the summary statistics of the participants' responses from the questionnaire. The participants were invited to tick a box with values from one (clearly below average) to seven (clearly above average) to indicate how they judge the accuracy of their own forecasts in each asset class compared to the other participants in the sample. A value of four indicates average. Rows 8–14 list the percentage of participants who ticked the different answering boxes. Missing values occur because participants did not answer the questions.

This section can be concluded by saying that decision makers of Swiss pension plans

Table 12.4 Better than average effect in the task of forecasting returns

Asset class	Swiss Equities in General	Pension Plan Swiss Equities	CHF Bonds in General	Pension Plan CHF Bonds	Own Pension Plan	Average Pension Plan
Valid	90	86	88	84	90	86
Missing	18	22	20	24	18	22
Mean	4.12*	4.10	4.08	4.10	4.26***	4.07
T-value	1.69	1.38	1.12	1.18	3.20	0.90
Median	4.00	4.00	4.00	4.00	4.00	4.00
Std dev.	0.68	0.70	0.66	0.74	0.76	0.72
Percentages of answers						
% clearly below average	0.00	0.00	0.00	0.00	0.00	0.00
% below average	0.00	1.16	1.14	1.19	0.00	1.16
% rather below average	13.33	12.79	12.50	14.29	11.11	13.95
% average	65.56	63.95	65.91	63.10	60.00	66.28
% rather above average	16.67	18.60	18.18	16.67	21.11	13.95
% above average	4.44	3.49	2.27	4.76	7.78	4.65
% clearly above average	0.00	0.00	0.00	0.00	0.00	0.00

Note: * 10% significance level; ** 5% significance level; *** 1% significance level.

Source: Based on Gort (2009).

are significantly prone to the better than average effect when evaluating the chances of future success for their current managers and their own pension plans. But they do not believe that they can personally forecast future returns of different asset classes significantly better than their colleagues from other Swiss pension plans.

Correlations Within and Between the Different Tasks

In line with the observation of Alpert and Raiffa (1982) and the results in the previous subsections, the participants in both samples express very stable answering patterns within both types of tasks, providing confidence intervals and evaluating the accuracy of their intervals relative to peers. Across all asset classes in both tasks, not only are correlations very high, but also Cronbach's alphas (Cronbach, 1951) are very high, indicating the consistency of the answering patterns across the tasks in both samples. For the professionals' (lay people's) forecast intervals, Cronbach's alphas are at 0.88 (0.86) and for the historical intervals at 0.84 (0.84), clearly exceeding the standard threshold for applicability of 0.7. The correlation in the professional sample (lay people sample) for forecast intervals are all significant at the 1 percent level, with two exceptions, and range from 0.72 to 0.92 (0.47 to 0.89). For the historical intervals the range lies between 0.33 and 0.92 (0.44 and 0.77). Even the correlations between forecast intervals and historical intervals are always positively correlated, with an average of 0.32 (0.18). With respect to self-evaluation task, Spearman rank correlations indicate a high level of general proneness to the better than average effect because correlations across the participants' responses for each asset class are significant at the 1 percent level and range from 0.31 to 0.54. So providing narrow confidence intervals and being prone to the better than average effect seems to be a stable trait across individuals regardless of the asset class and the type of questions. That allows for an aggregation of the confidence intervals and the self-evaluations of the different asset classes in each task to define the dependent variables in our linear regression models in the next section. On the other hand, we find no significant relationship between both tasks, that is, participants' confidence intervals and their scores on the self-evaluation tasks. In other words, there is no indication that the more miscalibrated participants are also more prone to the better than average effect.

LINEAR REGRESSIONS

This section relates personal characteristics of the participants in both the professional and the lay people sample to their degree of miscalibration and better than average effect to see if there are particular personal traits that increase a person's level of overconfidence. The dependent variables for miscalibration are the normalized log values of the participants' 90 percent confidence intervals for forecasts and historical returns divided into professional and lay people samples. For the better than average effect the dependent variables are the participants' responses ranging from one to seven in the questionnaire. Two predictive variables capture different types of education, that is holding a degree from university or experience of practical financial education, and are specified as dummy variables. Participants with both a university degree and a practical finance education were considered as people with university degree to avoid double counting. Two additional predictive variables reflect a participant's experience in finance or pension plans and his age. Both variables can take values from one (no experience / below 25 years) to seven (more than 25 years of experience / above 65 years). Table 12.5 summarizes the results of the linear regression, the upper panel for the confidence intervals and the lower panel for the self-evaluation relative to peers based on the score from one to seven on the Likert scale. The last two rows in both parts of Table 12.5 each contain the R^2 of the regression models for each type of confidence interval together with its F-value.

Table 12.5 shows in panel (a) the standardized beta and T-statistics of the predictors in the linear regression models for professionals' and lay people's forecast intervals and historical estimation intervals as well as R^2 and F-values for the four different linear regression models. In panel (b), the same parameters are listed for professionals and lay people with respect to their self-evaluation about the accuracy of their own forecasts and historical estimations.

In the tasks of confidence intervals, the four predictive variables of the regression model explain 13.9 percent of the variance in the forecast intervals and 32.9 percent of the variance in the historical intervals for the professional sample based on R^2 measures. They also explain 19 percent of the variation in the confidence intervals for laypeople's forecasts but fail to explain the variation of confidence intervals for historical returns in the lay people sample with 3.1 percent. Having a degree from university is significantly related to broader confidence intervals in all asset classes and is also related to a lower self-evaluation relative to peers. In contrast, practical financial education is not

Table 12.5 Linear regression models on confidence interval sizes and self-evaluation

(a)

Dependent variable	Professionals' aggregated forecast interval size	Lay people's aggregated forecast interval size	Professionals' aggregated historical interval size	Lay people's aggregated historical interval size
Predictors	Standardized beta coefficients and *T*-values for 90% confidence interval sizes			
University degree	0.344	0.316	0.432	0.125
	2.600**	3.427***	2.641**	0.741
Practical finance education	0.160	0.050	0.235	−0.057
	1.210	0.530	1.460	−0.324
Experience	0.209	0.143	0.360	−0.028
	1.953*	1.401	2.845***	−0.142
Age	−0.226	−0.334	−0.465	−0.077
	−2.111***	−3.360***	−3.641***	−0.418
R^2	0.139	0.190	0.329	0.031
F-values	3.234**	5.642***	5.754***	0.285

Note: * significant at 10% level; ** significant at 5% level; *** significant at 1% level.

Source: Based on Gort et al. (2008) and Gort (2009).

(b)

Dependent variables	Professionals' aggregated own evaluation of forecasts vs peers' forecasts	Lay people's aggregated own evaluation of forecasts vs peers' forecasts	Professionals' aggregated own evaluation of history vs peers' forecasts	Lay people's aggregated own evaluation of history vs peers' forecasts
Predictors	Standardized Beta Coefficients and T values for 90% confidence interval sizes			
University Degree	−0.131	−0.288	−0.355	−0.205
	−0.109	−0.132	−0.264*	−0.088
Practical finance education	−0.352	−0.085	−0.699	−0.121
	−0.268**	−0.041	−0.500***	−0.054
Experience	0.071	0.020	0.054	0.105
	0.186*	0.039	0.128	0.198
Age	−0.097	0.258	−0.001	−0.045
	0.152	0.260**	−0.001	−0.043
R^2	0.111	0.094	0.147	0.043
F-values	2.470*	2.485**	3.015**	0.803

Note: * significant at 10% level; ** significant at 5% level; *** significant at 1% level.

Source: Based on Gort et al. (2008) and Gort (2009).

significantly related to the interval sizes, and participants judge their own forecasts and historical estimates no better compared to peers. In line with the model from Odean and Gervais (2001), the variable for experience tends to reduce miscalibration as professionals with more financial or pension plan experience provide significantly broader confidence intervals. Age is related to narrower confidence intervals as older people provide significantly narrower confidence intervals.

In the domain of self-evaluation, the predictive variables in the model are significant at the 10 percent level for the professional sample and explain 11.1 percent and 14.7 percent of the variance in the responses of the participants. For the lay people sample, the results are significant when evaluating own forecasts but not the estimates of historical returns. The professionals with a financial education and to a less significant extent a degree from university demonstrate a lower proneness to the better than average effect. Their education probably has taught them that beating the forecasts of peers is very difficult on financial markets. On the other hand, more experience tends to be linked to a slightly higher self-evaluation, but the effect is not significant in any sample and the evidence on the relationship between age and the better than average effect is mixed but never significant.

To summarize, the regression analysis indicates that older people without a degree from university and with little experience in finance or pension plans provide significantly narrower confidence intervals for returns on financial markets than younger people with a degree from university and more experience. Additionally a better education leads to a lower level of proneness to the better than average effect.

DISCUSSION

This chapter provides evidence that decision makers of Swiss pension plans as well as lay people are overconfident in the domain of financial markets. They are miscalibrated and prone to the better than average effect, but there are significant differences between individuals, which can be attributed partly to individual characteristics such as education, experience and age. In this section we emphasize some practical issues related to our results that might apply to all types of investors, and we list some open areas for further research.

First, miscalibrated expectations of returns and risks for a volatile asset class such as equities could increase its perceived attractiveness because of an underestimation of risks. This might result in an overweight of that asset class and expose a pension plan's portfolio to higher downside risks, which is dangerous if the decision makers are not aware of those. A practical example is the global equity market losses of around 40 percent in 2008, which reduced the funding ratio of many pension funds dramatically (see Swisscanto, 2009 for a survey across Swiss pension funds) and some pension funds might not be able to digest those losses and now need government support. On the theoretical side, the model of DeLong et al. (1990) indicates that noise traders with erroneous stochastic beliefs, for example due to miscalibration of proneness to the better than average effect, take excessive risk and gain less expected utility than rational investors. Further research is needed to study the relationship between overconfidence and asset allocations. A related research question is to see whether the level of overconfidence has changed during the recent experience of massive losses in equities and commodities in 2008 during the global financial crisis. One might argue that people should have learnt their lesson in 2008 and might not underestimate risks anymore. Given that people tend to overweight the recent history and their recent experiences, they might even overestimate risks on financial markets in the following years and under-allocate to risky assets such as equities.

Second, overconfidence influences trading decisions and the management style of investors. Overconfident investors overestimate their skills in beating the market or market indices, and have the illusion of adding value by frequent trading or by letting external managers trade frequently. According to Odean (1999), overconfidence is detrimental to performance because of higher transaction costs from an increased trading volume. Tactical trading always generates additional transaction costs that have to be compensated by higher returns, but so far academic research rejects the claim that tactical trading, often referred to as timing, pays off in general. Daniel et al. (1997) report no systematic timing success for mutual funds, and Blake et al. (1999) report that UK pension plans have on average no timing skills. Furthermore Daniel et al. (1998) argue that investors misperceive the true probabilities of market situations and then over- or underreact on the market based on their flawed information, which also leads to reduced returns. In a simplified form we must accept that beating market indices is possible only at the expense of other investors, as shown in Sharpe (1991). Thorley (1999) compares the competition to generate above-average returns on financial markets to a basketball freethrow shooting contest. Every participant can choose between throwing freethrows himself or not throwing and just getting the average score. The throwing corresponds to active management and the latter to indexing. It only makes sense to shoot the freethrows for participants who believe they are above-average freethrow shooters compared to all the other contestants in the game. So it seems important to have a fair and unbiased estimate about one's own skills relative to competition on financial markets.

Third, the reported performance of the pension funds in our sample does not imply that active management can generally not add value, but it shows how difficult are the selection and the maintenance of successful active managers. It is puzzling that most of the decision makers of Swiss pension funds are highly convinced about the abilities of their current managers, their own manager selection skills and the chances for future success of their pension plan despite the observable track record and the ease of observing the performance of market indices. Some further research should shed light on that puzzle, but some preliminary thoughts are listed next.

At first glance one might argue that the pension plans in our sample are not aware of their below-indices performances and therefore express overconfident views. However, this seems unlikely because the pension plans in our sample participate voluntarily in surveys across Swiss pension plans and therefore are presumably interested in those issues. Another explanation could be that decision makers of Swiss pension plans continue to believe in their managers and their own selection skills in the very long run despite the underperformance relative to market indices so far. Indeed, it takes a great deal of time and data to be able to correctly differentiate between a manager's level of skill and pure luck, as Waring and Siegel (2003) explain. If that is the case, the participants in our sample apparently do not put much weight on their recent performance but more on their perception about their chances of future performance. Camerer and Lovallo (1999) offer the so-called reference group neglect as an explanation for why people might seem to be prone to the better than average effect. It might be the case that decision makers in the professional sample are more concerned with being above average in the Swiss pension plan universe than with the relative performance versus a market index (this is the case for UK pension plans, according to a study by Blake et al., 2002). However, this argument is no excuse for the poor relative performance versus market indices, because the goal of active management in traditional asset classes such as equities and bonds is usually to outperform market indices and not pension plan peer groups. Incidentally, on average investing in market indices would have been a better way to outperform peers in the past.

Lakonishok et al. (1992) present two further incentives for pension plan managers to apply active management despite a lack of success in the past – job security and 'schmoozing'. Job security relates to the fact that active management requires the decision makers to select active managers, which is a more complex, time-consuming and interesting process compared to the selection of indexers. So decision makers have incentives to demonstrate confidence about their active managers and their own manager selection skills, and ignore disappointing performance relative to market indices in the past to defend their employment. Another reason is schmoozing, which describes the colorful manner in which asset managers sometimes explain their stock decisions, hold hands with their clients and explain their absolute and relative performance *ex post*. With successful schmoozing, active managers might be able to convince decision makers at Swiss pension plans about their skills in spite of an unsuccessful track record. In line with this thinking, an additional incentive for pension plans not to replace unsuccessful active managers can be seen in the linkage of other corporate services that some captive active managers provide. The decision makers at the sponsor organization have incentives to retain active managers for the pension fund who also provide other valuable services to the company. Further research is needed to analyze the incentives on a personal level, and the effects of the regulatory framework with respect to the separation of the pension plan and the sponsor group.

Fourth, overconfidence is present in financial markets, but more in-depth research is needed to model the relationship between individual characteristics and overconfidence. The more we know about it, the better we can judge if a person is the right choice of financial decision maker. One thesis to explain why people tend not to be homogenously overconfident is perceived task difficulty. Task difficulty cannot be measured in our questionnaire on an absolute basis. However, it might be the case that older people with less education and less experience find it more difficult to come up with appropriate confidence intervals for asset returns on financial markets than younger people with a better education and more financial experience. According to Lichtenstein et al. (1982), a higher level of task difficulty is linked to a higher level of miscalibration, and this is in line with our observations. However, the unexplained variance in our model indicates that other factors or a differently specified model are necessary to explain individual differences in overconfidence in the domain of financial markets, which needs further exploration.

To put the results and the implications in this chapter into perspective, Yaniv and Foster (1997) argue that there is a trade-off between accuracy and informativeness when providing confidence intervals. Narrow confidence intervals usually provide more information than large but accurate intervals. It cannot be ruled out that the participants in the samples want to provide very informative confidence intervals, especially in the forecasting task, knowing that those might not be totally accurate. This might also explain why they expressed overconfident views when evaluating themselves relative to peers. Cesarini et al. (2006) argue that many people, especially investment professionals, use narrow confidence intervals and a high self-evaluation as a signal to demonstrate knowledge.

Nevertheless we must not forget that the reliance on very narrow confidence intervals, especially in the domain of forecasting returns of asset classes, and the belief in having above-average skills can lead to disappointing investment results on financial markets.

NOTES

1. Some of the results in this chapter are based on the authors' work in that field (Gort et al., 2008 and Gort, 2009). Financial support by the National Centre of Competence in Research 'Financial Valuation and Risk Management' (NCCR FINRISK), Project 3, 'Evolution and Foundations of Financial Markets,' and by the University Research Priority Program 'Finance and Financial Markets' of the University of Zurich is gratefully acknowledged.
2. The period for handing in the questionnaire was from May 2006 until the beginning of August 2006. The returns of the different asset classes were volatile over that time period so maybe the 90 percent confidence intervals may have been affected. A *t*-statistic reveals that there are no differences between the means for 90 percent confidence intervals from people who handed in their questionnaires before or after mid of June 2006, so there is no need to split samples.
3. This approach cannot be used in the return forecasting task because an *ex post* comparison between a subject's forecast interval for the return of an asset class in the coming year and the accuracy of his answer might be biased and unreliable. This is because the measurement is heavily dependent on the future outcome that is the realized return in that particular future year 2006. One single annual return represents only one single observation, which is not necessarily representative of the participant's true level of overconfidence. A return close to historical means will lead to the conclusion that few participants are miscalibrated, whereas an extremely positive or negative return would probably fall out of almost everybody's confidence intervals. For example, the losses experienced in equity and commodity markets during the financial crisis in 2008 would have fallen out of almost every 90 percent confidence interval provided.
4. In the analysis of confidence intervals for historical returns, only participants who provided negative lower boundaries in the confidence intervals for the asset class world equities are included. This is so as not to bias the study with respondents who might have misunderstood the question (i.e. provided a 90 percent confidence interval for the annualized mean return over the whole 34 years instead of a 90 percent confidence interval for all annual returns in that period). In total, 56 participants from the professional sample are included. If the confidence intervals from all the participants were included, miscalibration would appear to be much higher, but arguably may be spurious. In the analysis of confidence intervals for return forecasts, we include all participants.
5. It is acknowledged that the participants provided their responses between May 2006 and August 2006, and it might be the case that they used the available information for the year 2006. But even then the upper and lower boundaries are on average very close to each other.

REFERENCES

Alpert, M. and H. Raiffa (1982), 'A Progress Report on the Training of Probability Assessors,' in D. Kahnemann, P. Slovic and A. Tversky (eds), *Judgement under Uncertainty: Heuristics and Biases*, Cambridge and New York: Cambridge University Press, pp. 294–305.

ASIP (2000–2006), *ASIP Performance Comparison*, Zurich: ASIP.

Blake, D., B. Lehman and A. Timmermann (1999), 'Asset allocation dynamics and pension fund performance,' *The Journal of Business*, **72**, 429–61.

Blake, D., B. Lehman and A. Timmermann (2002), 'Performance clustering and incentives in the UK pension fund industry,' *Journal of Asset Management*, **3**, 173–94.

Brenner, L., V. Liberman and A. Tversky (1996), 'Overconfidence in probability and frequency judgements: a critical examination,' *Organizational Behaviour and Human Decision Processes*, **65**, 212–19.
Camerer, C. and D. Lovallo (1999), 'Overconfidence and excess entry: an experimental approach,' *American Economic Review*, **89**, 306–18.
Carhart, M.M. (1997), 'On persistence in mutual fund performance,' *The Journal of Finance*, **52**, 57–82.
Cesarini, D., O. Sandewall and M. Johannesson (2006), 'Confidence interval estimation tasks and the economics of overconfidence,' *Journal of Economic Behavior & Organization*, **61**, 453–70.
Cronbach, L. (1951), 'Coefficient alpha and the internal structure of tests,' *Psychometrika*, **16**, 297–334.
Daniel, K., M. Grinblatt, S. Titman and R. Wermers (1997), 'Measuring mutual fund performance with characteristic benchmarks,' *Journal of Finance*, **52**, 1035–58.
Daniel, K., D. Hirshleifer and A. Subrahmanyam (1998), 'Investor psychology and security market under- and overreaction,' *Journal of Finance*, **53**, 1839–85.
DeLong, J.B., A. Shleifer, L. Summers and R. Waldman (1990), 'Noise trader risk in financial markets,' *Journal of Political Economy*, 703–38.
DeLong, J.B., A. Shleifer, L. Summers and R. Waldman (1991), 'The survival of noise traders in financial markets,' *The Journal of Business*, **64**, 1–19.
Deaves, R., E. Lueders and M. Schroeder (2005), 'The dynamics of overconfidence: evidence from stock market forecasters,' ZEW Discussion Paper, No. 05–83.
Ennis, R. (1997), 'The structure of the investment management industry: revisiting the new paradigm,' *Financial Analysts Journal*, **53**, 6–13.
Erev, I., T. Wallsten and D. Budescu (1994), 'Simultaneous over- and underconfidence: the role of error in judgement process,' *Psychological Review*, **101**, 519–27.
Gigerenzer, G., U. Hoffrage and H. Kleinbölting (1991), 'Probabilistic mental models. A Brunswikian theory of confidence,' *Psychological Review*, **98**, 506–28.
Glaser, M., M. Weber and T. Langer (2005), 'Overconfidence of professionals and lay men: individual differences within and between tasks,' *Sonderforschungsbereich*, 504.
Glaser, M., M. Weber and T. Langer (2007), 'On the trend recognition and forecasting ability of professional traders,' *Decision Analyses*, **4**, 176–93.
Gort, C. (2009), 'Overconfidence and active management: an empirical study across Swiss pension plans,' *The Journal of Behavioral Finance*, **10**, 69–80.
Gort, C., M. Wang and M. Siegrist (2008), 'Are pension fund managers overconfident?,' *The Journal of Behavioral Finance*, **9**, 163–70.
Graham, J.R. and C.R. Harvey (2003), 'Expectations of equity risk premia, volatility and asymmetry,' Working Paper, Fuqua School of Business, Duke University.
Graham, J.R., C.R. Harvey and H. Huang (2006), 'Investor competence, trading frequency and home bias,' National Bureau of Economic Research (NBER) Working Paper 11426.
Griffin, D. and A. Tversky (1992), 'The weighing of evidence and the determinants of confidence,' *Cognitive Psychology*, **24**, 411–35.
Guiso, L. and T. Jappelli (2006), 'Information acquisition and portfolio performance,' CSEF Working Papers 167, Centre for Studies in Economics and Finance (CSEF), University of Naples, Italy.
Hilton, D. (2001), 'The psychology of financial decision-making: applications to trading, dealing and investment analysis,' *The Journal of Psychology and Financial Markets*, **2**, 37–53.
Klayman, J., J. Soll, C. Gonzales-Vallejo and S. Barlas (1999), 'Overconfidence: it depends on how, what and whom you ask,' *Organizational Behaviour and Human Decision Processes*, **79**, 216–47.
Kyle, A. and A. Wang (1997), 'Speculation duopoly with agreement to disagree: can overconfidence survive the market test?,' *Journal of Finance*, **5**, 2073–90.
Lakonishok, J., A. Shleifer and R. Vishny (1992), 'The structure and performance of the money management industry,' *Brookings Papers on Economic Activity. Microeconomics*, 339–91.
Lichtenstein, S., B. Fischhoff and L. Philips (1982), 'Calibration of Probabilities,' in Daniel Kahnemann, Amos Tversky and D. Slovic (eds) *Judgement under Uncertainty: Heuristics and Biases*, Cambridge: Cambridge University Press, pp. 306–34.
Locke, P. and S. Mann (2001), 'House money and overconfidence on the trading floor,' *AFA 2002*, Atlanta Meetings.
Lusenti Partners (2003), *Anlagen Schweizer Institutioneller Investoren: Umfrageergebnisse*, Nyon: Lusenti Partners.
Lusenti Partners (2005), *Swiss Institutional Survey: Umfrageergebnisse 31.12.2004*, Nyon: Lusenti Partners.
Lusenti Partners (2006), *Swiss Institutional Survey: Umfrageergebnisse 31.12.2005*, Nyon: Lusenti Partners.
Lusenti Partners (2007), *Swiss Institutional Survey: Umfrageergebnisse 31.12.2006*, Nyon: Lusenti Partners.
Malkiel, B. (2007), *A Random Walk Down Wall Street*, New York: W.W. Norton & Company; Revised and updated edn.

Menkhoff, L. and U. Schmidt (2005), 'The use of trading strategies by fund managers: some first survey evidence,' *Applied Economics*, **37**, 1719–30.
Odean, T. (1998), 'Volume, volatility, price and profit when all traders are above average,' *The Journal of Finance*, **53**, 1887–34.
Odean, T. (1999), 'Do investors trade too much?,' *The American Economic Review*, **89**, 1279–98.
Odean, T. and B. Barber (2001), 'Boys will be boys: gender, overconfidence and common stock investment,' *The Quarterly Journal of Economics*, **116**, 261–92.
Odean, T. and S. Gervais (2001), 'Learning to be overconfident,' *The Review of Financial Studies*, **14**, 1–27.
Pearson, E. and J. Tukey (1965), 'Approximate means and standard deviations based on distances between percentage points and frequency curves,' *Biometrika*, **52**, 533–46.
Russo, E. and P. Schoemaker (1992), 'Managing overconfidence,' *Sloan Management Review*, **33**, 7–17.
Sharpe, W. (1991), 'The arithmetic of active management,' *Financial Analysts' Journal*, **47**, 7–9.
Siegel, L., K. Kroner and S. Clifford (2001), 'The greatest return stories ever told,' *The Journal of Investing*, Summer, 91–102.
Soll, J. and J. Klayman (2004), 'Overconfidence in interval estimates,' *Journal of Experimental Psychology*, **30**, 299–314.
Svenson, O. (1981), 'Are we all less risky and more skillful than our fellow drivers?,' *Acta Psychologica*, **47**, 143–8.
Swisscanto (2009), *Schweizer Pensionskassen 2008*, Zurich: Swisscanto.
Taylor, S. and J. Brown (1988), 'Illusion and well-being: a social psychological perspective on mental health,' *Psychological Bulletin*, **103**, 193–210.
Taylor, S. and J. Brown (1994), 'Positive illusions and well-being revisited – separating fact from fiction,' *Psychological Bulletin*, **116**, 21–7.
Thorley, S. (1999), 'The inefficient markets argument for passive investing,' Marriot School at BYU Working Paper.
Waring, B. and L. Siegel (2003), 'The dimensions of active management,' *Journal of Portfolio Management*, **29**, 35–51.
Yaniv, I. and D. Foster (1997), 'Precision and accuracy in judgemental estimation,' *Journal of Behavioral Decision Making*, **10**, 21–32.

13 Availability heuristic and observed bias in growth forecasts: evidence from an analysis of multiple business cycles

Byunghwan Lee, John O'Brien and K. Sivaramakrishnan

INTRODUCTION

A conclusion emerging from recent advances in behavioral finance research is that the trading crowd in real-world markets is boundedly rational. A direct implication of this research, especially relevant to social and computer scientists, is that the efficacy of extant decision rules and trading heuristics can be improved upon. In fact, recent evidence demonstrates that algorithmic trading can take advantage of a human trading crowd. This reinforces the fact that the human trading crowd is boundedly rational, which is currently raising serious regulatory, ethical and economic questions in relation to the integrity of the financial markets.[1] In a recent paper that appeared in the *Journal of Behavioral Finance*, Lee, O'Brien and Sivaramakrishnan (2008) (hereafter LOS), we examined these issues by formally testing two contrasting theoretical approaches, rational versus boundedly rational, to understanding the growth forecasting behavior of financial analysts as well as related decision making by managers. By drawing upon the work of Sargent (2001), we were able to exploit hypothesized drivers of the boundedly rational behavior to identify the nature of the bounded rationality as well as to construct a forecast rule that improves upon growth forecasts issued by analysts. Given the central importance of growth forecasts to the financial markets, this result reinforces current observed trends. In this chapter, we extend the original results to one additional completed business cycle to provide a more robust *ex ante* test of the original results.

In LOS, we show that the availability heuristic of Tversky and Kahneman (1973), and not rational expectations, is more descriptive of the behavior of agents in the economy making long-term growth forecasts. In particular, because the boundedly rational approach applies to human behavior in general, it should apply equally to both analysts and managers interested in long-term growth prospects of firms. Therefore we examine both the behavior of analysts in making long-term growth forecasts and managers in making real decisions that translate to realized growth, when both groups lack knowledge about the underlying laws of motion that govern the economy. The absence of this knowledge is in essence the driver of boundedly rational behavior (Sargent, 2001). In LOS, we hypothesized that this boundedly rational behavior is reflected in the use of the availability heuristic in making long-term growth forecasts. This is because a growth forecast requires assessing both the current and the future states of the economy. The current state is observable; assessing the future state requires knowledge of the underlying laws of motion that govern the economy. Under the availability heuristic, agents forecasting long-term growth prospects would overweight current economic conditions (i.e. current state of the business cycle and current firm performance) and underweight economic conditions that are expected to prevail at the end of the growth forecast horizon.

The sample period of 1982 to 1998 used in LOS encompasses an expansion period of 92 months between November 1982 and July 1990, one contraction period of eight months from July 1990 to March 1991, followed by a portion of another expansion period of 120 months that ended eventually in March 2001. Since the LOS study, therefore, long-term growth forecasts and realized growth data have become available for one additional complete expansion period from 1991 to 2001, and one more contraction period from 2001 to 2003. Given the predictive nature of the hypothesized associations between the prevailing economic conditions and subsequent forecast errors in LOS, the availability of data for two complete business cycles permits stronger tests of these associations and helps in examining whether these associations are robust beyond one business cycle.

The chapter proceeds as follows. In the next section, we revisit the theoretical framework and the hypotheses presented in LOS; readers familiar with LOS may skip this section. We describe our data in the third section. In the fourth section we present our analysis and results, followed by conclusions and discussion in the last section.

THEORY AND HYPOTHESES (A REVIEW OF LOS)

Background

Rational expectations and bounded rationality offer two alternate approaches to understanding forecasting and decision-making behavior of agents when faced with uncertainty. Financial economists often start from the premise that the human trading crowd and financial analysts form rational expectations when forecasting (Grossman, 1976, 1978). In contrast, social scientists/computer scientists often start with the premise that they are boundedly rational and look for heuristics that best describe their decision-making behavior. One major advantage of the boundedly rational approach over the fully rational approach is that researchers can address the question regarding how to improve the forecasting and decision-making behavior of agents in the economy. In LOS, we test the premise that financial analysts are boundedly rational by appealing to two major approaches to bounded rationality espoused by Simon and Sargent (Sent, 1997) to develop testable implications in the context of long-term growth forecasts.

There is now a preponderance of evidence that long-term growth forecasts are, on average, optimistically biased. That is, the hypothesis of rational expectations has been rejected (e.g. Chan et al., 2003). Some empirical evidence suggests that the bias is more pronounced when there is an incentive to influence a boundedly rational trading crowd. For example, Lin and McNichols (1998) and Dechow et al. (2000) provide evidence that analysts affiliated with brokerage firms issue more optimistic growth forecasts around equity offerings in order to attract and retain underwriting business. Rajan and Servaes (1997) document that optimism in analysts' long-term growth forecasts is more pronounced for initial public offerings (IPOs) and find that the firms with the highest projected growth experience the greatest post-IPO underperformance. Bradshaw et al. (2006) find that overoptimism in analysts' long-term growth forecasts is most pronounced for firms issuing equity and debt and least for firms repurchasing equity and debt. Chan et al. (2003) report that analysts' growth estimates are overly optimistic, on average.

Despite the observed overoptimism in analysts' long-term growth forecasts, there is evidence that the trading crowd is indeed influenced by these forecasts. First, every major financial site on the web provides consensus analyst growth forecasts. In the academic literature, Frankel and Lee (1998) document that value estimates derived from analysts' forecasts account for more than 70 percent of variation in stock prices. Yet Chan et al. (2003) show that analysts' growth estimates add little by way of predicting realized growth. Combined, these results support the premise that both the analysts and the trading crowd are boundedly rational.

In this chapter, as in LOS, we extend the set of testable hypotheses that link the existing empirical evidence to bounded rationality by appealing to Simon (1982) and Sargent (2001).[2] First, Sargent identifies the possible driver of boundedly rational behavior. That is, rational expectations impose assumptions on human behavior that are too strong for an econometrician. Indeed, it appears eminently reasonable to ask that if econometricians do not know the laws of motion governing the economy, then it does not appear plausible to assume the human trading crowd does. Simon's approach to bounded rationality focuses upon the decision maker's heuristics or rules of thumb that drive the information-gathering and forecasting behavior of analysts. As a result, by combining Sargent and Simon we look for the presence of heuristics in the context of forecasting and or decision-making behavior that requires knowledge of the laws of motion that govern business cycles. In this chapter we formalize testable hypotheses that relate existing empirical growth evidence to the influence of the availability heuristic (Tversky and Kahneman, 1973).

Hypotheses

The availability heuristic focuses on the notion of recency or ease of recall. Under this precept, humans are not good 'Bayesians' because they assess probabilities by overweighting current or easily recalled information as opposed to processing all relevant information. Since information regarding the current state of the economy is presumably readily available, we exploit properties of business cycles to predict the nature of the bias in analysts' growth forecasts.

Growth forecasts provide a nice context in which to test the availability heuristic because both current and future states must be assessed in order to make a growth forecast. As Sargent observed, rational expectations imply that analysts possess precise knowledge about the laws of motion for the economy that an econometrician does not have. In the context of growth forecasts, assessing the relationship between current and future states correctly requires knowledge of such laws. Absence of this knowledge leads naturally to the use of a heuristic, such as the availability heuristic, to forecast growth.

Of relevance to us are two classes of economic agents – analysts and managers – both of whom should be predisposed to the same behavioral heuristic that captures an important aspect of human cognitive processing. If both ignore information about the business cycle in favor of availability heuristic approach, then both analysts and managers will overestimate (underestimate) growth in good (bad) states of the economy. Overestimating growth by managers (either directly or via analyst forecasts) will cause excessive investment relative to the 'first-best' allocation or investment decision predicted under rational expectations. Assuming that most technologies exhibit decreasing marginal returns to investment, excess investment in turn implies a lower realized return, and lower realized growth rates, relative to the first best. The lower realized growth rates and analysts' overestimates of growth, taken together, will result in an optimistic bias *ex post*. In a similar vein, a manager underestimating growth will result in underinvestment and higher realized growth rates relative to the first best, resulting in a pessimistic (less optimistic) bias *ex post*.[3] In other words, business cycles are consistent with the presence of some form of boundedly rational behavior in the economy.[4]

In the first hypothesis we relate implications from the availability heuristic (via analysts' growth forecasts) to the business cycle.

Hypothesis 1: The bias in analysts' growth forecasts is systematically related to the business cycle. In particular, long-term growth forecasts will be relatively optimistic when the economy is expanding and relatively pessimistic when the economy is contracting.

Our next objective is to derive more specific hypotheses by exploiting the feedback loop implied when moving from individual behavior to aggregate economic effects. Under the assumption that the availability heuristic influences forecasting behavior, a rich simultaneity problem exists between the investment decision given assessed growth and the realized growth given the actual investment decision. This simultaneity problem generates an interesting set of testable implications. To tease out these implications, we consider the analysts and the managers separately.

Consider the analysts' perspective first. The availability heuristic implies a systematic relationship between current performance (e.g. earnings per share, return on assets) and analysts' growth forecast errors in the following way. When current conditions are strong (i.e. high return on assets), analysts will overweight current conditions when forecasting growth. When current conditions are weak, analysts will overweight the weakness of the current conditions. As a result, if we measure forecast error as realized growth minus forecasted growth, then all else equal, strong current conditions imply a more negative error and weak current conditions imply a more positive error. No such relationship is predicted under rational expectations. These arguments lead us to the following refutable hypothesis:

Hypothesis 2: If the availability heuristic is a driver of analysts' long-term growth forecasts, current performance should bear a negative association with forecast errors (realized growth minus forecasted growth).

If the behavioral heuristic truly captures a significant aspect of human behavior in general, then it should apply equally to analysts and managers. Therefore, consider next the manager's perspective. When the current state of the economy is expanding and/or the current performance is strong, a boundedly rational manager will overinvest. That is, the availability heuristic will generate excess investment relative to what is predicted under rational expectations. Similarly, when the current state of the economy is contracting and/or the current performance is weak, a boundedly rational manager will underinvest.

Overinvestment implies lower realized growth subsequently because of decreasing returns beyond the first-best investment level. Underinvestment implies a higher realized growth on the investments undertaken because the marginal returns on investment will exceed the marginal cost of investment below the first-best investment level. Therefore overinvestment (underinvestment) implies lower (higher) realized growth, implying a negative relationship between current performance and realized growth. Notice no such relationship will obtain under the assumption of rational expectations because there is no a priori reason to expect any systematic association between investment opportunity set and current performance. Thus we can state the following hypothesis:

Hypothesis 2A: If the availability heuristic is a driver of management's investment decisions, then the current performance should bear a negative association with realized long-term growth.

Together, Hypotheses 2 and 2A provide a test of internal consistency across different classes of economic agents.[5]

Another implication of the availability heuristic is that the forecaster will behave in an adaptive manner by relying (to some extent) on past growth to predict the future. Such a behavior can be Bayesian if growth rates persist over time. However, as Chan et al. (2003) and others have documented, growth rates do not persist over time. Using past growth rates to predict future growth can lead analysts to make potentially systematic errors if they do not take this lack of persistence fully into account. In particular, if the availability heuristic is descriptive of the forecasting behavior, analysts will overweight past growth in their forecasting rule. Notice that under the null hypothesis of rational expectations, analysts will fully factor in past growth and the realized forecast error should be unrelated to past growth. Accordingly we have the following hypothesis:

Hypotheses 3: If the availability heuristic is descriptive of analysts' long-term forecasting behavior, then future realized forecast errors should bear a systematic association with past growth realizations.

Next, we draw on the availability heuristic to test what bounded rationality models can provide that rational expectations models cannot. First, we note that the set of arbitrage-free prices is much larger than the set of rational expectations prices and therefore a boundedly rational market does not necessarily conflict with traditional financial market theory, which assumes that prices are arbitrage free.[6] The set of rational expectations prices is a strict subset because of the strong informational assumptions underlying rational expectations. That is, fully rational investors process information with the precise knowledge of how the economy works in aggregate and thus implicitly have much more knowledge than, for example, an econometrician. A weaker information requirement is to impose the restriction of arbitrage-free prices relative to the knowledge possessed by an econometrician.[7] With this line of reasoning, the next question is whether incorporating the drivers of the forecast bias into the forecasting model augments its predictive ability.

Although the question has not been directly addressed in the previous growth literature, the inferable evidence is mixed. For example, Chan et al. (2003) conclude that analysts' growth estimates add little by way of predicting realized growth. However, La Porta (1996) suggests that the market exhibits the same bias as the analysts because investment strategies designed to exploit errors in analysts' forecasts earn superior returns. Claus and Thomas (2001) adjust for optimism in the analysts' five-year growth forecasts to estimate the recent equity premium behavior. We state the testable hypothesis as follows:

Hypotheses 4: Including any driver of the forecast bias identified by the availability heuristic (along with analysts' growth forecasts) improves the ability to predict growth.

DATA

We analyze forecasts of long-term earnings per share (EPS) growth provided by I/B/E/S, generally acknowledged to cover a five-year horizon (I/B/E/S, 2004). We also use the actual long-term EPS growth provided by I/B/E/S in its actuals data file. I/B/E/S computes the actual long-term EPS growth from the slope of a least square curve fit to the logarithm of the reported EPS over the last five years. We refer to the actual EPS growth over the forecasting horizon as the realized EPS growth. For example, we define the actual long-term EPS growth of April 1997 as the realized long-term EPS growth corresponding to the long-term forecast issued in April 1992. We restrict our sample to firm–month observations that have forecasts (or, a forecast) of long-term growth and realized long-term growth to the corresponding forecast. Following Bradshaw et al. (2006) and Dechow et al. (2000), we compute forecast error as realized EPS growth minus forecasted EPS growth.[8]

We use all available growth forecasts in the I/B/E/S summary statistics file in the period between 1982 and 2003. Given a five-year forecast horizon, we are only able to compute forecast errors corresponding to forecasts issued in or before 2003 using the 2008 I/B/E/S data files. Following LOS and other studies in this area, we exclude firms with fiscal year ending in any month other than December. I/B/E/S supplies a growth forecast once every month in its summary file. However, because the growth forecast does not typically change on a month-to-month basis, we retain only the April growth forecast for each firm in every year.[9] Since we are focusing only on December fiscal year-end firms, we assume that the April growth forecast will reflect all relevant information in the previous year's financial statements. Finally, we also eliminate loss firms from our sample because it is difficult to interpret growth for these firms.

In addition to the forecast and actual EPS growth data, we obtain the number of analysts who forecast EPS growth and earnings stability from I/B/E/S. I/B/E/S calculates earnings stability as the mean absolute difference between actual reported EPS and a five-year historical EPS growth trend line, as a percentage of trend line EPS. Therefore the lower the number, the greater is earnings stability. Earnings stability is an indicator of EPS growth consistency over the past five years.

We access accounting data from a merged COMPUSTAT annual industrial file, including PST, full coverage and research files. We exclude ADRs and restrict our sample to US domicile firms which are listed in NYSE, AMEX and Nasdaq National List. In order to eliminate the effect of the small size or penny stock companies on our test, we exclude firms from our sample if the firms' total assets (AT) are less than \$100 million, or if the firms' last year-end stock price (PRCC_C) is less than \$1/share. We winsorize the top 1 percent and bottom 1 percent of all the variables to eliminate the influence of outliers. Our final sample has 15431 firm–year observations.

We access information about business cycles from the website of the National Bureau of Economic Research (www.nber.org/cycles.html). According to this website, our sample period of 1982 to 2003 encompasses two business cycles of expansion and two business cycles of contraction. Specifically, the first business expansion cycle in our sample period spans 92 months from November 1982 to July 1990, followed by a contraction period of eight months from July 1990 to March 1991 and the next expansion period of 120 months beginning March 1991. The second contraction period in our sample period is between 2001 and 2003. The NBER Business Cycle Dating Committee uses a number of indicators including gross domestic product, personal income excluding transfer payments, volume of sales of the manufacturing and wholesale sectors, payroll employment and industrial production as measure of economic activity (see NBER, 2003).

Figure 13.1 presents a graph of some of the leading indicators of business cycles over our sample period. We obtain data for this graph from BEA (US Department of Commerce, Bureau of Economic Analysis), and FRB (Federal Reserve Bank). As this figure indicates, the gross domestic product (GDP) reveals a sharp drop in the mid-1980s (1985, 1986), but stabilizes in the late 1980s. Although federal fund rate is not included in the graph, the GDP trend seems to lead federal fund rate, as would be expected. While the official contraction period only lasted for eight months in the early 1990s, an examination of GDP reveals that there is relatively low (real) GDP from 1990 to 1993, but then it sharply increases in 1994. GDP also reveals that there is relatively low (real) GDP from 2001 to 2003. The NBER Business Cycle Dating Committee makes a *post facto* determination of peaks and troughs for the economy. For example, the November 2001 trough was announced on 17 July 2003, the March 1991 trough was announced 22 December 1992 and so on. In this chapter we are more interested in testing predictions based upon the current inferable state of the economy as opposed to the precise post facto determination of a peak or a trough. For our purposes, therefore, we consider four distinct sub-sample periods of the business cycle (BC) – 1982 to 1989 (BC1), 1990 to 1993 (BC2), 1994 to 2000 (BC3) and 2001 to 2003 (BC4) – to analyze the impact of the business cycle on growth forecasts, with the period between 1990 to 1993 and the period between 2001 to 2003 encompassing the contraction (as defined by NBER).

Table 13.1 shows the descriptive statistics by sub-components of the business cycle that correspond to states of the economy in terms of contractionary versus expansionary states. Referring to Table 13.1, earnings appear most unstable during the contractionary phases (BC2, BC4), which is consistent with conventional wisdom that uncertainty is more pronounced in periods of economic hardship. Notice that the earnings-to-price ratio decreases steadily from BC1 to BC3, while the market-to-book ratio increases gradually from BC1 to BC3. Given the overall market expansion that has taken place since the 1980s until the year of 2000, which is right before the second contraction cycles in our sample period, this decrease (increase) in earnings-to-price ratio (market-to-book) over time appears to be largely the result of the disproportionate change in market prices relative to EPS. Turning to short-term performance metrics, both return

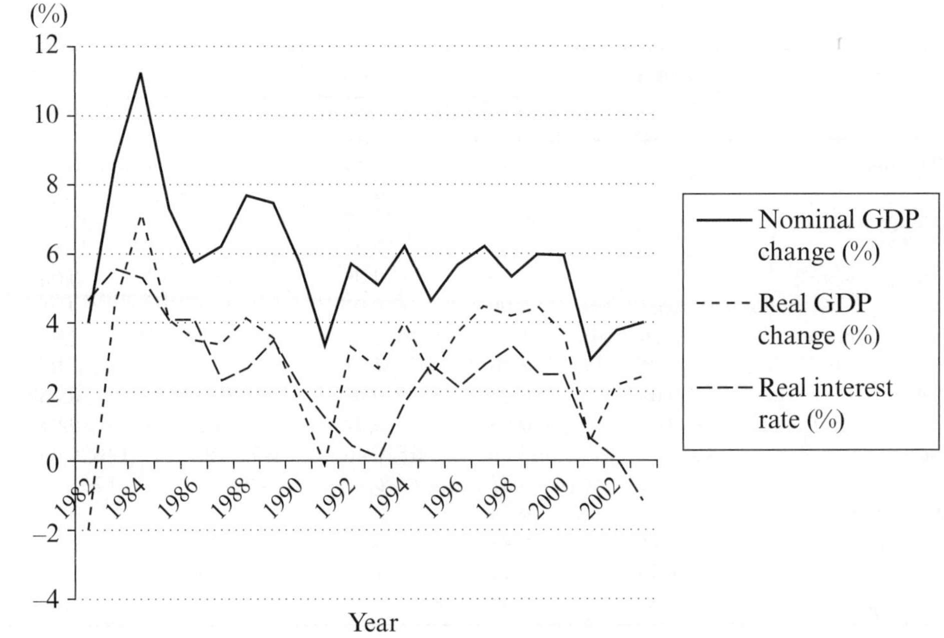

Source for nominal and real GDP data: US Department of Commerce, Bureau of Economic Analysis (BEA). Web address (all following websites were available as of September 2009): http://www.bea.gov/national/index.htm (and click Current-dollar and 'real' GDP).
We calculate the real interest rate using the Fisher's formula. The nominal interest rate is a money charge for the use of borrowed money or the return someone receives for lending out money as a percentage of the amount borrowed or lent. The real interest rate adjusts the nominal interest rate for changes in inflation over the time period, and thus measures the purchasing power (in terms of goods and services) of the loan.
Source: Federal Reserve Bank (FRB), Cleveland, O.H. Web address: http://www.clevelandfed.org/Research/Glossary/nomvreal.htm.
Source for nominal interest rate: Three-month treasury constant maturity rate from Federal Reserve Bank, St Louis. Web address: http://research.stlouisfed.org/fred2/series/GS3M/downloaddata.
Source of inflation rate: Consumer price index for all urban consumers – all items, from Federal Reserve Bank, St Louis. Web address: http://research.stlouisfed.org/fred2/series/CPIAUCSL/downloaddata.

Figure 13.1 Macroeconomic indices (1982–2003)

on assets (ROA) and earnings per share (EPS) do not appear to exhibit an appreciable trend across the business phases. Keep in mind, however, that the EPS is stated without adjusting for the changing value of the dollar. It is interesting to note that the debt-to-equity ratio, which is widely regarded as a proxy for financial risk, is higher during the contractionary periods (BC2, BC4) compared to the preceding expansionary periods (BC1, BC3).

ANALYSIS

In this section, we present our main results. We begin our analysis by focusing on the nature and the extent of bias in growth forecasts. Specifically, using the behavioral

Table 13.1 Descriptive statistics by state of the economy

Firm characteristics	Overall	Business cycle[a]			
		1	2	3	4
Following[b]	6.71	7.43	7.12	6.45	5.80
	5	*6*	*6*	*5*	*5*
Earnings stability	36.08	30.39	42.67	35.75	38.74
	21.82	*17.63*	*27.4*	*22.41*	*23.68*
Earnings-to-price	0.08	0.10	0.08	0.06	0.06
	0.07	*0.09*	*0.07*	*0.06*	*0.06*
Market-to-book	2.56	1.72	2.27	3.14	2.90
	1.86	*1.40*	*1.73*	*2.26*	*2.07*
ROA	0.06	0.06	0.06	0.06	0.06
	0.05	*0.05*	*0.04*	*0.05*	*0.04*
Assets	8033.87	5165.58	6816.46	8723.60	12026.90
	1574.50	*1480.31*	*1670.78*	*1498.7*	*1762.70*
Debt-to-equity	0.74	0.64	0.76	0.76	0.84
	0.48	*0.42*	*0.51*	*0.49*	*0.55*
EPS	1.28	1.21	1.18	1.29	1.44
	1.02	*0.88*	*0.95*	*1.06*	*1.22*

Notes:

[a] Business cycle (state of the economy) definition: BC1 is years 1982 to 1989. BC2 is years 1990 to 1993. BC3 is years 1994 to 2000. BC4 is years 2001 to 2003.

[b] Variable definitions: following is number of analysts contributing to the I/B/E/S data set for a firm. All I/B/E/S information pertains to the month of April. Earnings stability is reported in I/B/E/S. I/B/E/S calculates earnings stability as the mean absolute difference between actual reported EPS and a five-year historical EPS growth trend line, as a percentage of trend line EPS. Therefore, the lower the number, the greater the earnings stability. Earnings-to-price is income before extraordinary items (COMPUSTAT Annual Item #18) divided by market value of equity (MVE = price of the share (#24) multiplied by common shares outstanding (#25)), for the year prior to the year of the forecast. Market-to-book is market value of equity (MVE = price of the share (#24) multiplied by common shares outstanding (#25)) divided by book value equity (#60), for the year prior to the year of the forecast. Debt-to-equity is long-term debt (#9) divided by book value equity (#60), for the year prior to the year of the forecast. ROA is income before extraordinary items (#18) divided by total assets (#6) averaged the beginning and ending of the fiscal year (year prior to the year of the forecast). Assets is total assets (#6) for the year prior to the year of the forecast. EPS is the most recent annual earnings per share known to the analyst at the time of issuing the growth forecast, as reported in I/B/E/S actual data file.

[c] We access accounting data from a merged COMPUSTAT annual industrial file, including PST, full coverage, and research files. We exclude ADRs and restrict our sample to US domicile firms listed in NYSE, AMEX and Nasdaq National List. In order to eliminate the effect of the small size or penny stock companies on our test, we exclude firms from our sample if the firms' total assets (AT) are less than \$100 million, or if the firms' last year-end stock price (PRCC_C) is less than \$1/share.

[d] We winsorize all variables at the 1 percent and 99 percent level to mitigate the outlier effect.

The italicized numbers represent median values.

theoretical framework of the previous sections, we investigate the effects of key firm-specific characteristics in relation to the business cycle on forecast bias. We then use the insight from these analyses to examine the predictive ability of growth forecasts using a cross-sectional regression framework similar to that in Chan et al. (2003).

Primary Results

Consistent with the literature on forecast bias, we use an *ex post* forecast error as a measure of forecast bias. As mentioned before, we define forecast error as the realized growth less the corresponding forecast. Thus a negative (average) forecast error indicates optimism. The null hypothesis of rational expectations posits that the average forecast error should be zero.

Panel (a) of Table 13.2 presents the statistics on growth forecasts, corresponding realizations, and forecast errors for the overall sample and for the business cycles. Because these are growth rates, we report these values in percentage terms. Referring to the panel, the null hypothesis that the mean (median) forecast error is zero for the overall sample is rejected at conventional level of significance. In particular, consistent with prior literature, the negative mean (median) forecast error of −5.89 (−3.9) indicates that growth forecasts are reliably optimistic over the entire sample period of 1982–2003.

Turning our attention to the behavior of forecast errors for different BCs, we can see that over optimism prevails in BC1 and BC3. Because these BCs belong to expansion cycles in the economy, growth forecasts are overly optimistic in expansion phases of the economy. Growth forecasts appear not to be significantly optimistic in BC2 and BC4 which encompasses contraction periods. The mean/*median* forecast error of BC2 (BC4) is −0.67/*−0.36* (−1.02/*−1.84*). Furthermore, tests of differences in means and medians reveal that the forecast errors in BC2, BC4, the contractionary periods, are significantly less negative than the forecast errors in BC1, BC3, the expansionary periods. We present the mean and median forecast errors year by year in panel (b). Notice that the mean and median forecast errors are reliably negative in all years except 1991 to 1993 (years in BC2) and 2002 to 2003 (two years out of three years in BC4). In these periods, the mean and median forecast errors are not significantly different from zero, except for the median forecast of the year of 2003.

It is well documented that contraction periods are much shorter than expansion periods. Most contractions fall well within the horizon of five years over which growth forecasts are issued. While a rational forecaster would presumably take this into account in issuing growth forecasts, evidence seems to suggest otherwise. The relatively lower optimism in BC2 and BC4 draws attention to the possibility that analysts typically underemphasize the likely duration (and perhaps even the amplitude) of the contraction period. Taken together, this evidence supports Hypothesis 1 that the availability heuristic is more descriptive of analysts' forecasting behavior than the Bayesian rule. Further, recency bias induces analysts toward greater overoptimism in expansionary relative to contractionary periods.

Hypothesis 2 provides us with a basis for investigating this recency effect further. It predicts a negative relationship between performance and forecast errors when assessing future growth. There should be no such relationship under the rational expectations equilibrium. We test this hypothesis using a simple regression in which we use the forecast error corresponding to the growth forecast at time t as the dependent variable, and the actual EPS of the year (obtained from I/B/E/S) immediately prior to the forecast year as a measure of the current performance as the independent variable.[10]

Panel (c) of Table 13.2 presents these results. In model 1, EPS is the sole independent variable. The coefficient of this variable is negative (−3.33) and statistically significant

Table 13.2 Forecast versus actual long-term EPS growth

Source: I/B/E/S EPS forecast summary and actual data files. All I/B/E/S information pertains to the month of April.

Notes:

[a] Variable definitions: Forecast is long-term (usually five years) EPS growth forecasted by financial analysts. Realized is actual long-term growth as reported in the I/B/E/S data files, over the five years corresponding to forecasting horizon. For example, we define the actual long-term EPS growth of April 1997 as realized long-term EPS growth of April 1992, in order to match it to the corresponding long-term forecast which analysts forecasted in April 1992. I/B/E/S computes the actual growth from the slope of a least square curve fit to the logarithm of the reported EPS over the last five years. Past is actual long-term growth over the previous five years at the time analysts issue growth forecasts, as reported in the I/B/E/S data files and measured as the slope of a least square curve fit to the logarithm of the reported EPS over the last five years. Forecast error is realized EPS growth minus Forecasted EPS growth. BC1, BC2 BC3 are dummy variables that take on a value of one if the observation belongs to business cycle 1, 2 and 3 respectively; zero otherwise. EPS is the most recent annual earnings per share known to the analyst at the time of issuing the growth forecast, as reported in I/B/E/S actual data file.
We winsorize all variables at the 1 percent and 99 percent level to mitigate the outlier effect.
The italicized numbers represent median values.

[b] The numbers in parentheses represent *t*-values.

(a) Forecast versus actual long-term EPS growth by business cycle

Variables[a]	Overall	Business cycle			
		1	2	3	4
Realized	7.18	3.58	10.94	5.11	13.18
	7.56	*4.44*	*10.02*	*6.84*	*11.44*
Forecast	13.03	11.67	11.57	14.16	14.14
	12	*11.64*	*11*	*13*	*13*
Forecast error	−5.89	−8.13	−0.67^	−9.09	−1.02^
	−3.9	*−5.82*	*−0.36**	*−5.62*	*−1.84*
Past	13.52	9.79	9.52	18.53	12.48
	10.29	*8.38*	*7.25*	*13.54*	*9.6*
Number of observations	15431	4123	2716	5805	2787

Notes

^ Mean is not significantly different from zero at the 1 percent level;

* Median is not significantly different from zero using nonparametric test at the 1 percent level, otherwise all are significant at this level (two-tailed test).

(b) Forecast versus actual long-term EPS growth by year

Year	No. of observations	Long-term EPS growth			
		Realized	Forecast	Forecast error	Past
1982	454	3.60	12.67	−9.05	12.59
		4.88	*12.8*	*−5.17*	*11.75*
1983	435	4.56	11.74	−7.23	7.56
		4.98	*12*	*−4.62*	*7.89*
1984	479	5.53	12.13	−6.65	5.21
		6.17	*12*	*−5.02*	*5.61*

Table 13.2 *(continued)*

Year	No. of observations	Long-term EPS growth			
		Realized	Forecast	Forecast error	Past
1985	514	7.93	11.70	−3.77	6.26
		6.84	*12*	*−3.04*	*6.26*
1986	514	5.89	11.50	−5.67	9.32
		5.52	*11.5*	*−5.07*	*8.8*
1987	530	1.90	11.21	−9.40	9.73
		2.66	*11*	*−6.94*	*7.71*
1988	574	−1.41^	11.28	−12.74	12.48
		*0.88**	*11*	*−8.49*	*9.39*
1989	623	1.91^	11.39	−9.55	13.68
		3.19	*11*	*−6.87*	*9.85*
1990	669	7.63	11.50	−3.92	13.20
		6.41	*11*	*−3.09*	*9.95*
1991	684	11.75	11.26	0.44^	10.08
		10.01	*10.1*	*0.11**	*8.42*
1992	675	11.91	11.49	0.40^	7.27
		10.48	*11*	*0.34**	*6.43*
1993	688	12.39	12.01	0.33^	7.58
		11.48	*11.75*	*0.5**	*5.06*
1994	711	9.45	12.63	−3.17	12.25
		9.68	*12*	*−1.19*	*7.84*
1995	755	7.71	12.83	−5.20	16.33
		8.45	*12*	*−2.55*	*11.64*
1996	746	7.21	13.28	−6.15	21.22
		8.11	*12*	*−3.46*	*14.27*
1997	795	4.25	14.11	−9.88	21.92
		5.84	*13*	*−6.64*	*15.5*
1998	892	2.68	15.19	−12.57	22.52
		4.68	*14*	*−8.8*	*16.02*
1999	923	1.78	14.93	−13.18	18.36
		4.12	*13.5*	*−9.26*	*14.29*
2000	983	4.40	15.34	−10.95	16.54
		6.27	*14*	*−7.62*	*12.6*
2001	963	11.54	15.37	−3.96	15.84
		10.48	*14*	*−2.83*	*11.43*
2002	887	15.27	14.03	1.18^	11.66
		12.32	*13*	*−0.94**	*9.25*
2003	937	12.91	12.97	−0.08^	9.80
		11.34	*12*	*−1.64*	*7.91*
	15431				

Notes:

^ Mean is not significantly different from zero at the 1 percent level;

* Median is not significantly different from zero using nonparametric test at the 1 percent level, otherwise all are significant at this level (two-tailed test).

Table 13.2 (continued)

(c) Firm performance versus forecasted long-term EPS growth (dependent variable: forecast error)

Variable[a]	Model 1	Model 2	Model 3
Intercept	−1.64	−1.02	4.24
	(−6.82)[b]	(−2.77)	(6.81)
EPS	−3.33		−3.66
	(−23.20)		(−10.36)
BC1		−7.11	−7.93
		(−14.93)	(−10.59)
BC2		0.35+	−0.47+
		(0.66)	(−0.56)
BC3		−8.07	−9.66
		(−18.03)	(−13.02)
EPS*BC1			−0.01+
			(−0.02)
EPS*BC2			−0.12+
			(−0.25)
EPS*BC3			0.82+
			(1.91)
R^2 (adjusted)	0.034	0.036	0.072
Observations	15431	15431	15431

(d) Firm performance versus actual long-term EPS growth (dependent variable: realized growth)

Variable[a]	Model 1	Model 2	Model 3
Intercept	13.48	13.18	21.47
	(59.21)[b]	(37.08)	(36.60)
EPS	−4.92		−5.75
	(−36.36)		(−17.32)
BC1		−9.60	−12.15
		(−20.86)	(−17.25)
BC2		−2.25	−4.33
		(−4.44)	(−5.51)
BC3		−8.08	−9.80
		(−18.67)	(−14.04)
EPS*BC1			1.03
			(2.58)
EPS*BC2			0.49+
			(1.03)
EPS*BC3			0.68+
			(1.69)
R^2 (adjusted)	0.079	0.038	0.122
Observations	15431	15431	15431

Table 13.2 (continued)

Note:
+ Not significantly different from zero at the 1 percent level, otherwise all are significant at this level (two-tailed test).
^ Mean is not significantly different from zero at the 1 percent level;
* Median is not significantly different from zero using nonparametric test at the 1 percent level, otherwise all are significant at this level (two-tailed test).

(t-statistic = −23.20, $p < 0.01$). In model 3, we allow the intercept and the slope coefficients to vary across the four BC periods. In this model the coefficient for years 1982 to 1989 (BC1) can be computed from the main EPS effect and the interaction between EPS and the indicator variable BC1, which equals one for the period 1982 to 1989 and zero otherwise. As a result, the regression coefficient for the period 1982 to 1989 (BC1) equals −3.66 + (−0.01) = −3.67. Similarly, it follows that for the period 1990 to 1993 (BC2) the coefficient equals −3.66 − 0.12 = −3.78, and the period 1994 to 2000 (BC3) −3.66 + 0.82 = −2.84. Similarly, the coefficient of EPS that covers 2001 to 2003 (BC4) is negative (−3.66). That is, each period's coefficient is negative, which is consistent with Hypothesis 2.

Hypothesis 2A predicts that if the availability heuristic is a driver of management's investment decisions, we should see an inverse relationship between current performance and realized growth. There should be no such systematic relationship under the rational expectations equilibrium. To test this hypothesis, we regress the realized growth on EPS. Panel (d) of Table 13.2 presents these results. Referring to model 1, the coefficient of EPS is negative (−4.92) and significant (t-statistic = −36.36, $p < 0.01$). In model 3, we allow the intercept and the slope coefficients to vary across the four BC periods. The coefficient of EPS, which corresponds to the period 2001 to 2003 (BC4), is again negative (−5.75) and significant (t-statistic = −17.32, $p < 0.01$). In addition, the net coefficients for BC1 (−5.75 + 1.03 = −4.72), BC2 (−5.75 + 0.49 = −5.26) and BC3 (−5.75 + 0.68 = −5.07) are also negative and significant. Overall, these results support Hypothesis 2A.

Referring to model 2 of panel (d), the intercept estimate indicates that the average growth rate following BC4 is 13.18. The negative coefficients of −9.60 for BC1 and −8.08 for BC3 imply that the average growth rates following BC1 and BC3 are 3.58 and 5.10 respectively. It is interesting to note that the coefficient of BC2 is −2.25 (t-statistic = −4.44, $p < 0.01$), indicating that the growth rate following BC2, 10.93, is significantly higher (lower) than that following BC1, BC3 (BC4). In summary, realized growth rate following BC2, BC4, the contractionary periods, are higher than that following BC1, BC3, the expansionary periods. This is consistent with the predictions from the availability heuristic of under- (over)investment relative to rational expectations equilibrium when the current state of the economy is contracting (expanding). That is, the realized growth following a contraction period is significantly higher than the realized growth following expansion periods.

Overall, these results are consistent with the predictions of the availability heuristic regarding how current performance influences forecasting and investment behavior. Further analysis reveals that these results are not sensitive to the use of replication of the ROA and ROE as alternate measures of current performance (not reported here).

Table 13.3 Forecast errors and past long-term growth: impact of mean reversion on long-term growth forecasts (dependent variable = forecast error)

Variable[a]	Model 1	Model 2	Model 3	Model 4	Model 5
Intercept	−3.46	1.10	0.93	5.64	5.60
	(−19.27)[b]	(2.97)	(2.26)[+]	(12.62)	(12.21)
Past	−0.18	−0.17	−0.16	−0.15	−0.15
	(−27.13)	(−25.61)	(−9.93)	(−9.54)	(−6.43)
BC1		−7.57	−7.27	−8.05	−8.05
		(−16.22)	(−13.85)	(−15.60)	(−15.60)
BC2		−0.16[+]	0.16[+]	−0.67[+]	−0.68[+]
		(−0.30)	(0.28)	(−1.20)	(−1.21)
BC3		−7.04	−6.97	−7.23	−7.20
		(−16.00)	(−13.59)	(−14.35)	(−14.16)
Past*BC1			−0.03[+]	−0.02[+]	−0.02[+]
			(−1.29)	(−1.05)	(−1.02)
Past*BC2			−0.03[+]	−0.03[+]	−0.03[+]
			(−1.22)	(−1.34)	(−1.31)
Past*BC3			−0.01[+]	−0.02[+]	−0.02[+]
			(−0.44)	(−1.31)	(−1.35)
EPS				−3.35	−3.34
				(−24.24)	(−23.91)
Past*GD					0.01[+]
					(0.39)
R^2 (adjusted)	0.046	0.076	0.076	0.109	0.109
Observations	15431	15431	15431	15431	15431

Notes:

[+] The coefficient is not significantly different from zero at the 1 percent level; otherwise all are significant at this level (two-tailed test).

[a] Variable definitions: GD is dummy variable that takes a value of one if the observation has above median past EPS growth; zero otherwise. For other variable definitions, see notes to Tables 13.1 and 13.2. We winsorize all variables at the 1 percent and 99 percent level to mitigate the outlier effect.

[b] The numbers in parentheses represent *t*-values.

Growth Forecasts and Past Growth

In Hypothesis 3, we posit a relationship between future realized forecast errors and past growth realizations. Any such association would indicate that analysts do not efficiently process information contained in past growth in issuing growth forecasts. We test this association using a simple regression framework with the realized forecast error as the dependent variable and past growth as the independent variable. Table 13.3 presents the results.

Referring to the results corresponding to the estimation of model 1 in Table 13.3, the coefficient of past growth is negative (−0.18, *t*-statistic = −27.13, $p < 0.01$) and statistically significant, as predicted. In models 2 and 3, we allow the intercept and the slope coefficients to vary across business cycles. Referring to model 3, the coefficient of past growth is reliably negative in all four periods. In model 4, we additionally control for the impact of current performance (EPS) on behavior, and obtain the same qualitative inference.[11] Finally, in model 5, we allow the coefficient of past growth to be different for high and low past growth firms based on a median split (GD equals one for high past growth firms, zero otherwise). In this specification, the coefficient of past growth captures the association between realized forecast errors and past growth for firms in the low past growth portfolio and the coefficient of the interaction variable Past*GD captures any incremental association for high growth firms. Because the coefficient of this variable is not significantly different from zero, we are unable to detect any asymmetry in the way analysts respond to firms with high versus low past growth. Thus this evidence is consistent with the prescriptions of the availability heuristic as in Hypothesis 3.

Predicting Growth

In this section we provide some descriptive statistics in relation to the firm-specific effects. Evidence on analyst optimism relating to forecasts over shorter horizons indicates that firm-specific characteristics such as analyst following, earnings stability, accounting performance, earnings-to-price and market-to-book ratios, size and leverage influence the distribution of forecast errors. Accordingly, we investigate whether these variables, which are also part of analysts' information sets at the time of forecasting, are useful in understanding the properties of growth forecast errors in addition to current performance and past growth that we have examined thus far. We classify sample observations into 'high' and 'low' portfolios along each of these dimensions and perform a test for differences in mean and median forecast errors between these two portfolios. Table 13.4 presents these results.

There is not much difference in the degree of optimism between the firms followed by a smaller number of analysts and the firms followed by a greater number of analysts. High-stability firms (do not) show a higher level of optimism in growth forecasts in terms of mean (median) value. Earnings-to-price ratio (EP) is a measure that is widely used by the investment community to evaluate stocks. A lower EP ratio is often interpreted as indicative of greater earnings (growth) persistence. Both the mean and median tests indicate that low EP ratio firms exhibit a significantly higher level of analyst optimism. Thus analysts appear to be more optimistic with respect to firms with greater perceived earnings (growth) persistence.

The literature in accounting and finance has often employed the market-to-book ratio as a measure of future growth opportunities. It is common to refer to high market-to-book stocks as 'glamour' stocks, and low market-to-book stocks as 'value' stocks. In keeping with these views, Table 13.4 indicates that optimism is significantly more pronounced for glamour stocks relative to value stocks. Because glamour stocks are typically in the news and high-growth stocks, portfolios based on forecasted EPS growth (not reported here) as well as market-to-book ratios yield consistent results in terms of the degree of optimism, as we would expect.

Return on assets (ROA) and earnings per share (EPS) are widely used measures of short-term performance. Table 13.4 suggests that high ROA (high EPS) firms exhibit a higher degree of optimism in growth forecasts than low ROA (low EPS) firms. This result confirms the earlier results in panel (c) of Table 13.2. In a large sample, a split

Table 13.4 Forecasted versus actual long-term EPS growth by firm characteristics

Firm characteristics		Long-term EPS growth			
		Realized	Forecast	Forecast Error	Past
Following[a]	Big	6.90	12.63	−5.76	13.16
	Small	7.47	13.44	−6.03	13.87
	Difference	−0.57^*	−0.81	0.27^*	−0.71^*
Earnings Stability	High	6.09	12.86	−6.80	14.80
	Low	8.28	13.20	−4.99	12.24
	Difference	−2.19*	−0.34^*	−1.80*	2.56
Earnings-to-Price	High	5.29	10.66	−5.42	13.55
	Low	9.09	15.41	−6.37	13.48
	Difference	−3.80	−4.75	0.95	0.07^
Market-to-Book	High	6.93	15.32	−8.41	18.28
	Low	7.42	10.74	−3.39	8.89
	Difference	−0.49^	4.58	−5.02	9.39
ROA	High	5.59	14.64	−9.11	19.75
	Low	8.79	11.42	−2.67	7.27
	Difference	−3.20	3.22	−6.43	12.49
Assets	Big	6.70	10.92	−4.26	10.22
	Small	7.67	15.15	−7.53	16.82
	Difference	−0.97*	−4.23	3.27	−6.59
Debt-to-Equity	High	6.40	11.36	−4.99	10.55
	Low	7.94	14.72	−6.84	16.62
	Difference	−1.54	−3.36	1.85*	−6.08
EPS	High	1.98	10.83	−8.88	12.63
	Low	12.41	15.24	−2.89	14.41
	Difference	−10.43	−4.41	−5.99	−1.77

Notes:

^ Not significantly different between the means of the two different groups at the 1 percent level; * not significantly different between the medians of the two different groups using nonparametric test at the 1 percent level, otherwise all are significant at this level (two-tailed test).

[a] Variable definitions: see notes to Tables 13.1 and 13.2 for variable descriptions.
High (low) in earnings stability means high (low) stable earnings growth.
We winsorize all variables at the 1 percent and 99 percent level to mitigate the outlier effect.

based on EPS (ROA) may well be delineating 'good' firms (i.e. well-managed firms with higher performance) from 'bad' firms. Thus one could view the higher degree of optimism for high EPS (ROA) firms as being consistent with the results with respect to the market-to-book ratio.

Size appears to be a factor as well. Portfolios based on total assets indicate that the growth estimates appear to be more optimistic for small firms than for large firms. Finally, the debt-to-equity ratio is a commonly used measure of financial risk. Table 13.4 indicates that high debt-to-equity firms are associated with less optimism than low debt-to-equity firms (median p-value = 0.015, mean p-value < 0.01). That is, analysts appear to be less enamored by firms that are highly leveraged.

Our results thus far indicate that analysts are influenced by a behavioral bias when predicting future growth. This has the immediate implication that incorporating drivers of this behavioral bias explicitly should improve the ability to predict growth. Stated differently, the question is whether we can construct an expectation model that improves the prediction of earnings growth using the insights we have gained from examining the properties of growth forecasts thus far.

The study by Chan et al. (2003) provides some precedent in this respect. The authors examine the predictive ability of growth forecasts in a cross-sectional multiple-regression framework in which realized growth is regressed on forecasted growth and a set of financial statement and market-related variables. Interestingly, they find that the coefficient of forecasted long-term growth is not statistically significant. While our results indicate that growth forecasts are inefficient, we would still expect analysts' growth forecasts to possess predictive content because we expect the behavioral bias to impact general investment behavior, implying underinvestment during a contractionary period and overinvestment during an expansionary period.

Table 13.5 presents results from our multiple-regression models of realized long-term growth (the dependent variable).

In model 1, the sole independent variable is the forecasted growth. Under the null hypothesis of rational expectations, the forecasted growth should efficiently incorporate all information in the analysts' information set, and any forecast error should be just white noise. In this case, the coefficient of the forecasted growth in this model should not be significantly different from one. However, consistent with the evidence that growth forecasts are biased and inefficient, this coefficient is 0.13 (0.34) for expansion periods (the contraction period), and is significantly different from zero (t-statistic = 4.48, $p <$ 0.01 for expansion periods; t-statistic = 7.94, $p < 0.01$ for the contraction period).[12] The adjusted R^2 for this simple specification is 0.2 percent for expansion periods and 1.1 percent for the contraction period.

Recall that past growth and current EPS were systematically related to forecast errors in our earlier analysis. In model 2, we control for the inefficiency of the growth forecasts with respect to these variables by including them on the right-hand side. We include additional firm-specific variables that we examined in Table 13.4 as control variables. The coefficient of past growth is negative and statistically significant for both expansion and contraction periods. The sign of this coefficient is consistent with our earlier analysis, and confirms in general the presence of mean reversion in long-term EPS growth, as reported by Chan et al. (2003). The coefficient of current EPS levels is also negative and statistically significant for both expansion and contraction periods, which is again consistent with our earlier findings in relation to the validity of the availability heuristic.

Model 2 shows that the coefficient of analysts' growth forecast is positive (0.24) and statistically significant (t-statistic = 4.88, $p < 0.01$) for the contraction period. Interestingly, it is negative (−0.03) and not significant for the expansion period (t-statistic = −0.72, $p = 0.47$). Untabulated results show that growth forecast does (not) have explanatory power on realized growth when forecasts are issued in contraction (expansion) periods with the additional inclusion of only EPS and past growth in the explanatory variables. This finding indicates that analysts' growth forecasts contribute significantly to growth prediction in the contraction periods only but not in the expansion periods, over and beyond variables in the analysts' information set that we have exogenously included

Table 13.5 Predicting long-term growth

	Dependent variable = Realized Growth			
Variable[a]	Expansion periods (BC1, BC3)		Contraction periods (BC2, BC4)	
	Model 1	Model 2	Model 1	Model 2
Intercept	2.78	12.23	7.73	14.88
	(6.58)[b]	(14.88)	(12.74)	(13.31)
Forecast	0.13	−0.03*	0.34	0.24
	(4.48)	(−0.72)	(7.94)	(4.88)
Past		−0.04		−0.05
		(−4.75)		(−4.22)
EPS		−4.87		−4.53
		(−28.50)		(−17.00)
Following		0.14		0.18
		(3.91)		(3.40)
Earnings Stability		0.01*		0.05
		(1.43)		(8.91)
Earnings-to-Price		−18.33		−18.12⁺
		(−3.87)		(−2.42)
Market-to-Book		−0.33		−0.55
		(−3.57)		(−4.21)
Debt-to-Equity		0.62		−0.01*
		(3.39)		(−0.04)
R^2 (adjusted)	0.002	0.096	0.011	0.103
Observations	9928	9837	5503	5408

Notes:

* Not significantly different from zero at the 10 percent level; ⁺ not significantly different from zero at the 1 percent level, otherwise all are significant at the 1 percent level (two-tailed test).

[a] Variable definitions: see notes to Tables 13.1 and 13.2.
We winsorize all variables at the 1 percent and 99 percent level to mitigate the outlier effect.

[b] The numbers in parentheses represent *t*-values.

in the prediction model. This finding represents perhaps the most noticeable departure from the finding in LOS, where analysts' growth forecasts contribute significantly to growth prediction in both the contraction and the expansion periods.

Turning our attention to the other variables, the coefficient of analyst following is positive and significant in both expansion and contraction periods. The coefficient of earnings stability is significant in contraction periods, but not so in expansion periods. Earnings-to-price ratio has a marginal explanatory power in contraction periods (t-statistic = −2.42, p = 0.015), but has a negative and significant coefficient in expansion periods. Market-to-book ratio also has significant explanatory power in both expansion and contraction periods, with negative and significant coefficients. Coefficient of debt-to-equity ratio is positive and significant only in expansion periods.

More importantly, the predictive power of the regression improves greatly in both expansion and contraction periods with the inclusion of EPS and past growth – variables identified by the availability heuristic as driving forecasting and investment behavior. In particular, the adjusted R^2 in expansion periods (contraction period) improves from 0.2 percent (1.1 percent) for the regression involving just the forecasted growth to 9.6 percent (10.3 percent) for the more detailed specification.[13] Untabulated results show that the adjusted R^2 in expansion periods (contraction period) improves from 0.2 percent (1.1 percent) for the regression involving just the forecasted growth to 9.3 percent (8.6 percent) for the model with the additional inclusion of only EPS and past growth. These results provide support to Hypothesis 4 that the drivers of the forecast bias that we have identified using the availability heuristic (i.e. EPS and past growth) improves the ability to predict growth.

DISCUSSION AND CONCLUSIONS

In this chapter, we revisit the analysis presented in LOS by augmenting their sample period to include two complete business cycles. In LOS, we provide evidence that analysts and managers form expectations in a boundedly rational manner. In particular, that the availability heuristic, and not rational expectations, is more descriptive of the behavior of both the financial analysts in predicting long-term growth and managers when making the firm's investment decisions. Growth forecasts have a significant impact upon the allocation of scarce resources in the economy. This is because all of the most widely used models for assessing intrinsic value, the free cash flow to equity model, the residual income valuation model, and the abnormal earnings growth model, rely heavily on consensus of analyst growth forecasts. Furthermore, as reviewed in the literature review section of this chapter, stock market prices respond accordingly. Given this importance of growth forecasts, our objective in this chapter is to present stronger tests of boundedly rational behavior of analysts and managers by analyzing data from two complete business cycles. Indeed, we show that the results of LOS are not specific to the sample period examined therein, but are robust across business cycles.

The confirming nature of the results of this chapter reinforces the conclusions in LOS that the observed boundedly rational behavior of analysts and managers in forecasting growth is consistent with the premise that they lack complete knowledge of the relationship between expectations and investment decisions that produces the business cycle. That is, our evidence provides additional support for Sargent's assumption.

The collective findings of LOS and this chapter also suggest that growth forecasts can be improved upon by incorporating specific pieces of information that are already in the forecasters' information sets. Whether or not this implies that artificial intelligence/econometric techniques can be used to improve forecasts is a topic for future research. But casual empiricism strongly suggests that the answer is yes, and the likely drivers of boundedly rational behavior further strengthen this conclusion. This is because these results are consistent with the observed Wall Street trend that has resulted in a current explosion of investment activity directed at the problem of using computers to augment algorithms used by traders (Kelly, 2007), including high-frequency trading. Furthermore, the evidence from Wall Street is pointing towards increasing gains being made from this approach (ibid., p. 37):

> A third of all U.S. stock trades in 2006 were driven by automatic programs, or algorithms, according to Boston-based consulting firm Aite Group LLC. By 2010, that figure will reach 50 percent, according to Aite.

The results from this chapter would further suggest that these implications are independent of the business cycle because we disaggregated the business cycle to look at expansions and downturns separately. Again, the force of recent evidence from Wall Street in relation to the success of computer and algorithmic trading provides 'economic proof' that the human trading crowd is boundedly rational. For example, in the *New York Times* article cited earlier (note 1), it was observed that the significant success that Wall Street firms were having even in the current economic downturn raises concerns that already the boundedly rational human trading crowd is being too badly beaten. In other words, what happened to the world of world championship chess is now starting to happen to the world of boundedly rational trading crowds! This raises many sensitive regulatory, ethical and economic issues that immediately follow from the body of evidence being generated from behavioral finance studies.

NOTES

1. In a *New York Times* article (23 July 2009), Charles Duhigg quotes Andrew M. Brooks, head of United States equity trading at T. Rowe Price (a mutual fund and investment company that often competes with and uses high-frequency techniques) as saying: 'You want to encourage innovation, and you want to reward companies that have invested in technology and ideas that make the markets more efficient. . . 'But we're moving toward a two-tiered marketplace of the high-frequency arbitrage guys, and everyone else. People want to know they have a legitimate shot at getting a fair deal. Otherwise, the markets lose their integrity.'
2. Sargent (2001) notes that existing rational expectations models impute greater knowledge to agents in the economy than the knowledge an econometrician, facing the same inference problem, possesses.
3. With underinvestment, capacity will be in short supply and the marginal return to a dollar of investment will be higher than the first-best level, assuming decreasing marginal returns to investment.
4. Even in the rational expectations literature on business cycles, boundedly rational behavior at some level becomes an important driver. In the Lucas rational expectations theory of the business cycle, bounded rationality supports the assumed confusion between the drivers of aggregate price levels and relative price levels by producers and workers required to produce economy-wide fluctuations. That is, it relies upon boundedly rational behavior on the part of producers and workers when forecasting profit opportunities given time constraints (Lucas, 1977).
5. In a very different context when Smith et al. (1988) studied bubbles and crashes in laboratory markets, they observed that in markets with bubbles, forecast errors were inversely related to the forecasting objective. That is, their observations are consistent with the influence of the availability heuristic upon human (subject) expectations in turn influencing actual investment behavior.
6. For example, Shefrin and Statman (1994) construct an equilibrium with endogenous noise and some boundedly rational traders.
7. This applies the arguments of Sargent (2001, p. 3) to a financial market setting. This also characterizes standard tests of the efficient markets hypothesis.
8. Notice that growth forecasts and realized growth are already annualized and expressed in percentage terms. Therefore, following Bradshaw et al. (2006) and Dechow et al. (2000), we do not scale the growth forecast error further.
9. We note that this procedure reduces the number of observations per firm in each of the business cycles utmost to number of years in the business cycle. However, given the nature of our hypotheses we are able to rely on cross-sectional tests. Thus, to the extent that there are enough firm–year observations in each business cycle, sample size is not an issue.
10. One could argue that this specification is subject to a potentially spurious positive correlation between the growth forecast error (dependent variable) and current EPS (independent variable) if analysts use current EPS as the basis for predicting growth, i.e. the denominator effect. To see this, notice that COV(Growth

forecast error, EPS) = COV(Realized Growth – Forecasted Growth, EPS) = COV(Realized Growth, EPS) – COV(Forecasted Growth, EPS). Recall from our data section that I/B/E/S computes realized growth as the slope of a least square curve fit to the logarithm of the reported EPS over the last five years. Therefore the denominator effect minimally influences the first term, COV(Realized Growth, EPS). On the other hand, if analysts predict the geometric mean of the growth forecast over time, the denominator effect will result in the term COV(Forecasted Growth, EPS) being negative, and therefore the term COV(Growth forecast error, EPS) being positive. This positive association biases our tests against rejecting the null (Hypothesis 2). Nevertheless, we use ROA and ROE as alternate measures of current performance to check the robustness of our results.

11. We get similar results when we use ROA and allow the coefficient of ROA to be different across the four periods (not reported here).
12. Under the null hypothesis of rational expectations, these coefficients should be one. Thus these estimates indicate a rejection of rational expectations.
13. Chan et al. (2003) use annualized growth rate (over five years) in income before extraordinary items available to common equity from the COMPUSTAT as dependent variable and analysts' long-term forecasts as an independent variable – its coefficient is not significantly different from zero (Table X, panel C). They include other independent variables such as past sales growth (instead of past EPS growth), EP ratio, R&D expenses scaled by sales, a dummy variable for the technology sector firms, the firm stock's prior six-month compound rate of return; the coefficient of each of these variables is significant at conventional levels. The coefficients of the remaining independent variables such as book-to-market ratio, dividend-per-share ratio are not significantly different from zero, and the adjusted R^2 is 3.13 percent. When they use annualized growth rate, over the five years after the forecast year, of operating income before depreciations from the COMPUSTAT as an alternate dependent variable, the aforementioned coefficients show qualitatively the same significance at conventional levels, except that dividend-per-share ratio (EP ratio) is (not) significantly different from zero; the adjusted R^2 is 3.67 percent.

REFERENCES

Bradshaw, M., S. Richardson and R. Sloan (2006), 'The relation between corporate financing activities, analysts' forecasts and stock returns,' *Journal of Accounting and Economics*, **42**, 53–85.

Chan, L., J. Karceski and J. Lakonishok (2003), 'The level and persistence of growth rates,' *Journal of Finance*, **58**, 643–84.

Claus, J. and J. Thomas. (2001), 'Equity premia as low as three percent? Evidence from analysts' earnings forecasts for domestic and international stock markets,' *Journal of Finance*, **56**, 1629–66.

Dechow, P., A. Hutton and R. Sloan (2000), 'The relation between analysts' forecasts of long-term earnings and stock price performance following equity offerings,' *Contemporary Accounting Research*, **17**, 1–32.

Frankel, R. and C. Lee (1998), 'Accounting valuation, market expectation, and cross-sectional stock returns,' *Journal of Accounting and Economics*, **25**, 283–319.

Grossman, S. (1976), 'On the efficiency of competitive stock markets where trades have diverse information,' *Journal of Finance*, **31**, 573–85.

Grossman, S. (1978), 'Further results on the informational efficiency of competitive stock markets,' *Journal of Economic Theory*, **18**, 81–101.

I/B/E/S (2004), *The I/B/E/S Glossary: A Guide to Understanding I/B/E/S Terms and Conventions*, I/B/E/S International Inc.

Kelly, J. (2007), 'The ultimate money machine,' *Bloomberg Markets*, June, 36–43.

La Porta, R. (1996), 'Expectations and the cross-section of stock returns,' *Journal of Finance*, **51**, 1715–42.

Lee, B., J. O'Brien and K. Sivaramakrishnan (2008), 'An analysis of financial analysts' optimism in long-term growth forecasts,' *Journal of Behavioral Finance*, **9**, 171–84.

Lin, H. and M. McNichols (1998), 'Understanding relationships, analysts' earnings forecasts and investment recommendations,' *Journal of Accounting and Economics*, **25**, 101–28.

Lucas, R. (1977), 'Understanding Business Cycles,' in K. Brunner and A. Meltzer (eds), *Stabilization of the Domestic and International Economy*, Carnegie-Rochester Conference Series in Public Policy.

NBER Business Cycle Dating Committee (2003), *Announcement of Business Cycle Trough/End of Last Recession*, NBER, 17 July.

Rajan, R. and H. Servaes (1997), 'Analyst following of initial public offerings,' *Journal of Finance*, **52**, 507–29.

Sargent, T. (2001), *Bounded Rationality in Macroeconomics*, Oxford: Oxford University Press.

Sent, E. (1997), 'Sargent versus Simon: bounded rationality unbound,' *Journal of Economics*, **21**, 323–38.

Shefrin, H. and M. Statman (1994), 'Behavioral capital asset pricing theory,' *Journal of Financial and Quantitative Analysis*, **29**, 323–49.
Simon, H. (1982), *Models of Bounded Rationality*, Vols 1&2, Cambridge, MA: MIT Press.
Smith V., G. Suchanek and A. Williams (1988), 'Bubbles, crashes, and endogenous expectations in experimental spot asset markets,' *Econometrica*, **56**, 1119–51.
Tversky, A. and D. Kahneman (1973), 'Availability: a heuristic for judging frequency and probability,' *Cognitive Psychology*, **5**, 207–32.

14 Weak and strong individual forecasts: additional experimental evidence

Lucy F. Ackert, Bryan K. Church and Kirsten Ely

INTRODUCTION

Much research recognizes the importance of individual biases in market settings. Although finance theory traditionally assumes that market prices reflect available information, behavioral finance researchers have documented that individual psychology, including biased expectations, has an important role in understanding observed outcomes (Hirshleifer, 2001). Any bias in forecasts has the potential for significant impact on outcomes given the nature of forecasts as generated by individuals and their widespread use in capital markets. Individuals use forecasted information in making personal decisions and forecasts are critical inputs that direct the decisions of corporations. Professional financial analysts, in particular, are important intermediaries who provide information to investors and corporations. But, do analysts' forecasts reflect their private information in an unbiased manner?

In Trueman's (1994) model, individual forecasts can rationally reflect forecaster bias. Ackert et al. (2008) provide evidence supportive of Trueman's hypotheses in an experimental setting for one form of earnings distribution. However, earnings distributions vary widely across industries, between firms in the same industry and over time. One goal of the current study is to examine the robustness of the Ackert et al. (2008) (hereafter ACE) findings to a less disperse distribution, because companies have incentives to smooth earnings (e.g. Trueman and Titman, 1988; Arya et al., 2003). A second goal of the current study is to assess the usefulness of Trueman's (1994) model as a guide to individual behavior when decisions are made in an alternative environment. While ACE's findings are consistent with Trueman's hypotheses, the current study investigates the consistency of the findings in a different, less variable earnings setting.

The findings in ACE, consistent with Trueman (1994), suggest that analysts who are 'weak' engage in herd behavior, while analysts who are 'strong' forecast based on their private information. Forecast ability (weak versus strong) is defined by the accuracy of the signal each experimental participant receives. The import of Trueman's model is that releasing forecasts that do not reflect one's private information in an unbiased manner can be rational. In Trueman's model, earnings are high or low and negative or positive. Extreme earnings of either sign are uncommon. Analysts know the prior distribution of earnings and can gauge the sign with certainty. However, analysts can gauge only the likelihood that the level is high or low.

The two situations addressed by Trueman's model and examined in ACE are the behavior of analysts when all analysts forecast concurrently as compared to sequentially. Using Bayes's rule, Trueman shows that it can be rational for weak analysts to make forecasts that are not unbiased reflections of private signals in both circumstances.

In his model, the signal indicates whether earnings are high or low. When analysts forecast simultaneously, it is rational for weak analysts to be less inclined to predict high earnings regardless of their signal. When analysts forecast sequentially, it is rational for weak analysts to update the probability that their signal is correct based on the forecasts released by other analysts. This leads to herd behavior because weak analysts' forecasts are influenced by the forecasts they see rather than being unbiased reflections of their own private information. The experimental evidence in ACE supports these conclusions.

Several assumptions provide the foundation for Trueman's model. Analysts know their own ability to forecast earnings levels correctly, and there are two types of analysts (strong and weak). Strong analysts receive an information signal that has a higher likelihood of correctly forecasting the level of earnings. All weak analysts receive the same signal and all strong analysts receive the same signal. Others infer analyst ability by observing forecast accuracy relative to that of other forecasters. And analysts have the incentive to forecast so as to maximize the probability that they are considered strong analysts. Given these assumptions, Trueman shows that in the simultaneous setting, on average, a weak analyst gains more than a strong analyst by reporting low earnings even when the private signal is high.[1] In the sequential setting, a weak analyst gains more by mimicking the forecast of a strong analyst who has released first because the weak analyst updates the probability of the earnings level using both his/her own signal and the forecast of the strong analyst. Because the probability of high earnings is lower in Trueman's model than that of low earnings, it is only when the weak analyst's private information indicates high earnings that a low forecast by a strong analyst will induce mimicking behavior. The behavior of strong analysts, on the other hand, is not affected since they receive no useful information from the forecast of weak analysts.

The experimental results of ACE support these conclusions for an earnings probability distribution in which negative and positive earnings are equally likely, but high positive (or negative) earnings are less likely than low positive (or negative) earnings (20 percent for high compared to 30 percent for low). However, earnings distributions vary substantially across industries, between firms within an industry and over time. Therefore the current experiment looks at issues similar to those examined in ACE (2008) to assess the robustness of the results to a different, less disperse distribution (10 percent for high compared to 40 percent for low outcomes). With this distribution we first examine whether weak and strong analysts report forecasts that reflect their private information. Then we consider whether weak and strong analysts are affected by the forecasts previously announced by others. Before presenting the results, we describe the experimental method.

RESEARCH METHOD

Participants

We conduct six experimental sessions, administered to participants in cohorts of four, which means that 24 individuals take part. Three sessions include simultaneous forecast release and three include sequential forecast release. Participants are recruited from third- and fourth-year undergraduate and fifth-year post-baccalaureate students in business and economics at a medium-sized Canadian university. Participants include 16 males and eight females, with an average age of 22.3 years. Students earn from $14.50 to $29.75, with an average of $21.17, for participating for approximately 70 minutes.

Procedures

The procedures are similar to those used by ACE. Each session consists of 48 periods in which participants forecast earnings level. Participants are informed of the following earnings distribution.

Earnings level	Sign	Magnitude	Probability
1	negative	high	0.10
2	negative	low	0.40
3	positive	low	0.40
4	positive	high	0.10

As mentioned earlier, the earnings distribution is less disperse than that used by ACE.

At the beginning of each period, participants privately receive an earnings signal. The signal indicates the sign of the earnings with certainty and the magnitude of earnings with error. Participants' signal accuracy is constant over the entirety of the experiment. Strong analysts have a signal accuracy of 80 percent and weak analysts 55 percent. Participants know their own signal accuracy, but not that of others. Participants also know that signal accuracy can vary among analysts. By design, two participants are strong analysts and two are weak each session.

We manipulate the timing of forecasting decisions and announcements. In one half of the sessions, all participants make a forecast and announce their forecasts simultaneously. In the other half, a sequential procedure is used, with one participant going first. A designated participant makes a forecast of earnings and publicly announces it. The others then make individual forecasts and announce their forecasts concurrently. We rotate the order in which a participant goes first such that each participant goes first every four periods. Because we have 48 periods, each participant goes first 12 times.

After all participants have announced a forecast of earnings (in the simultaneous and sequential settings), the experimenter reveals the earnings realization: that is, whether earnings are high or low. Each time a participant's forecast matches the realized earnings, the participant accumulates 50 points. Upon completion, points are converted to dollars. Strong and weak analysts have different conversion rates in an effort to equalize experimental earnings. At the end of the session, participants complete a post-experiment questionnaire to collect demographic information. Lastly, participants are paid and dismissed.

RESULTS

Are Forecasts Consistent with Private Information?

ACE find that participants' forecasts are not always consistent with their private information, where such behavior is much more pronounced for weak analysts than for strong analysts. We examine whether such behavior holds when the distribution of earnings is less dispersed (i.e. the magnitudes are more concentrated around low earnings). In this case, strong analysts potentially may ignore high earnings signals.

Weak Analysts with Simultaneous Forecasts

First we examine the behavior of weak analysts in the simultaneous setting. Table 14.1 shows the frequency of earnings forecasts conditioned on the signal received over the 48 periods and then splitting the data into halves. For periods 1–48, weak forecasts do not match the earnings signal 34 percent of the time (97 of 288 periods, which represents the sum of the off-diagonal cells).[2] The percentage is close to the 36.5 percent reported in ACE, with the difference in percentages between the two studies being insignificant ($\chi^2 = 0.49$, $p = 0.485$). Looking at the first and second half of the current experiment separately, the percentages are quite similar.

Further inspection of the data indicates that weak analysts ignore high earnings signals more often than low earnings signals, as suggested by Bayesian updating. With a high earnings signal, the Bayesian posterior that the earnings realization does not match the signal is 76.6 percent. With a low earnings signal, the Bayesian posterior is 17.0 percent. We find that when the earnings signal is high, weak forecasts differ from the signal 68.5 percent of the time (74 of 108). In contrast, when the earnings signal is low, weak forecasts differ from the signal only 12.8 percent of the time (23 of 180). A chi-square test indicates that the difference is statistically significant ($\chi^2 = 14.88$, $p < 0.001$). The observed difference in percentages (68.5 versus 12.8 percent) is more pronounced than the difference (48.3 versus 28.0 percent) reported in ACE. This finding may be attributed to the fact that the earnings distribution is very concentrated around low earnings in the current study (i.e. the distribution is less disperse in the current study). We also note that the results are similar, separating the data into halves.

Next, we formally assess whether weak analysts' behavior is consistent with Bayesian updating. If forecasters behave as Bayesians, they may reasonably ignore private information. We test whether

$$P(F \neq S) = P(E \neq S|S),$$

where F is the forecast, S is the signal and E is the earnings realization. The left-hand-side probability is the observed frequency that the forecast differs from the earnings signal. The right-hand-side probability is the updated Bayesian posterior – the earnings realization differs from the earnings signal, conditioned on the signal. We perform a binomial test for high and low earnings signals separately using the normal approximation to the binomial distribution (Mendenhall et al., 1981). We perform tests on data from periods 1–48, 1–24 and 25–48.

Table 14.1 Forecasts conditioned on earnings signal for weak analysts in simultaneous setting

(a) Periods 1–48

Forecast	Signal				Total
	1	2	3	4	
1	13	12	–	–	25
2	47	72	–	1	119
3	–	–	85	26	111
4	–	–	11	21	33
Total	60	84	96	48	288

(b) Periods 1–24

Forecast	Signal				Total
	1	2	3	4	
1	7	10	–	–	17
2	23	26	–	1	50
3	–	–	45	14	59
4	–	–	3	15	18
Total	30	36	48	30	144

(c) Periods 25–48

Forecast	Signal				Total
	1	2	3	4	
1	6	2	–	–	23
2	24	46	–	–	55
3	–	–	40	12	36
4	–	–	8	6	30
Total	30	48	48	18	144

Note: The cell entries indicate the frequency with which earnings forecast by earnings signal combinations are observed in the simultaneous setting for weak analysts.

As shown in Table 14.2, we reject the null hypothesis that the observed frequency equals the Bayesian posterior in three of six comparisons. In all instances, the weak forecast differs from the earnings signal less often than the Bayesian posterior. Weak analysts do not ignore earnings signals to the extent suggested by the Bayesian posterior. Our findings are directionally consistent with the results reported in ACE, although we find stronger evidence of significant differences (i.e. observed frequencies that differ significantly from the Bayesian posterior).

Table 14.2 Comparing observed frequencies with Bayesian posteriors for weak analysts in the simultaneous setting

Signal (S)	Periods	$P(F \neq S)$	$P(E \neq S \mid S)$	z-statistic
S = 2, 3 (Low)	1–48	0.128	0.170	−1.508
	1–24	0.155		−0.372
	25–48	0.104		−1.717**
S = 1, 4 (High)	1–48	0.685	0.766	−1.988*
	1–24	0.633		−2.433*
	25–48	0.750		−0.262

Notes: S is the signal, F is the forecast, and E is the earnings realization. The column headed $P(F \neq S)$ is the observed frequency that the earnings forecast does not match the signal. The column headed $P(E \neq S \mid S)$ is the probability that the earnings realization does not match the signal, conditioned on the signal. It is the Bayesian posterior, which incorporates the forecaster's ability (i.e. the weak analyst's signal is accurate 55 percent of the time). For each row, we conduct a binomial test using the normal approximation to determine whether $P(F \neq S) = P(E \neq S \mid S)$. One and two asterisks denote that the null hypothesis can be rejected at the 5 and 10 percent level (two-tailed test), respectively.

Strong Analysts with Simultaneous Forecasts

We perform similar analyses looking at strong analysts in the simultaneous setting. Table 14.3 shows the frequency of earnings forecasts conditioned on the signal received over periods 1–48, 1–24 and 25–48. For periods 1–48, strong forecasts do not match the earnings signal 13.9 percent of the time (40 of 288 periods, which represents the sum of the off-diagonal cells). The percentage is slightly less than the 18.8 percent reported in ACE, although the difference is insignificant ($\chi^2 = 2.49$, $p = 0.114$). Looking at the first and second half of the experiment separately, we note that the percentage is slightly higher over the second half than the first half: 17.4 percent (periods 25–48) versus 10.4 percent (periods 1–24).

The data suggest that strong analysts are more likely to ignore a high earnings signal than a low one. With a high signal, the Bayesian posterior that the earnings realization does not match the signal is 50.0 percent. With a low signal, the Bayesian posterior is 5.9 percent. We find that strong forecasts differ from the earnings signal 36.9 percent of the time (31 of 84) when the signal is high. In contrast, strong forecasts differ from the earnings signal only 4.4 percent of the time (9 of 204) when the signal is low. A chi-square test indicates that the difference is statistically significant ($\chi^2 = 121.29$, $p < 0.001$). The difference in percentages (36.9 versus 4.4 percent) is more noticeable than that (27.5 versus 12.5 percent) reported in ACE. Again, the finding can be attributed to the less disperse earnings distribution used in the current study: that is, a lower likelihood of a high earnings realization. Separating the data into halves, we find that inferences are unaffected.

We test whether strong analysts' behavior is consistent with Bayesian updating. As before, we perform binomial tests to compare the observed frequencies with the Bayesian posteriors, conditioned on the earnings signal (high or low). The results are presented in Table 14.4. As can be seen, we reject the null hypothesis in two of six comparisons. In

Table 14.3 Forecasts conditioned on earnings signal for strong analysts in the simultaneous setting

(a) Periods 1–48

Forecast	Signal				Total
	1	2	3	4	
1	30	4	–	–	34
2	18	91	2	1	112
3	–	1	104	12	117
4	–	–	2	23	25
Total	48	96	108	36	288

(b) Periods 1–24

Forecast	Signal				Total
	1	2	3	4	
1	9	3	–	–	12
2	3	51	1	1	56
3	–	–	52	6	58
4	–	–	1	17	18
Total	12	54	54	24	144

(c) Periods 25–48

Forecast	Signal				Total
	1	2	3	4	
1	21	1	–	–	22
2	15	40	1	–	56
3	–	1	52	6	59
4	–	–	1	6	7
Total	36	42	54	12	144

Note: The cell entries indicate the frequency that earnings forecast by earnings signal combinations are observed in the simultaneous setting for strong analysts.

both cases, the strong forecast is less likely to deviate from a high earnings signal than the Bayesian posterior. Overall, the directional differences for strong analysts (comparing observed frequencies with Bayesian posteriors) are similar to those for weak analysts. But strong analysts are less likely to disregard private information than weak analysts, which is similar to the conclusion in ACE.

Table 14.4 Comparing observed frequencies with Bayesian posteriors for strong analysts in the simultaneous setting

Signal (S)	Periods	$P(F \neq S)$	$P(E \neq S \mid S)$	z-statistic
$S = 2, 3$ (Low)	1–48	0.044	0.059	−1.047
	1–24	0.046		−0.573
	25–48	0.042		−0.707
$S = 1, 4$ (High)	1–48	0.369	0.500	−2.401*
	1–24	0.278		−2.664*
	25–48	0.438		−0.859

Notes: S is the signal, F is the forecast, and E is the earnings realization. The column headed $P(F \neq S)$ is the observed frequency that the earnings forecast does not match the signal. The column headed $P(E \neq S|S)$ is the probability that the earnings realization does not match the signal, conditioned on the signal. It is the Bayesian posterior, which incorporates the forecaster's ability (i.e. the strong analyst's signal is accurate 80 percent of the time). For each row, we conduct a binomial test using the normal approximation to determine whether $P(F \neq S) = P(E \neq S|S)$. One and two asterisks denote that the null hypothesis can be rejected at the 5 and 10 percent level (two-tailed test), respectively.

Do Second Analysts Follow the Forecasts of Others?

At this point we turn to the sequential forecast setting. ACE provide evidence that weak second analysts follow the reporting behavior of strong first analysts. By comparison, strong second analysts do not follow the behavior of others. We examine whether this result replicates using a less disperse earnings distribution. As before, we present data for weak (second) analysts and then strong (second) analysts.

Weak Analysts with Sequential Forecasts

We investigate whether weak second analysts follow the reporting behavior of the first analyst. We use additional notation (subscripts) to denote analyst ability (w for weak and s for strong) and forecast order (1 for first and 2 for second). When no subscript appears, ability does not need to be differentiated (i.e. it does not matter for the issue at hand). We are interested in cases in which $F_{2w} = F_1$: that is, the weak second forecast (F_{2w}) matches the first announced forecast (F_1).

One difficulty arises with the data. If $F_{2w} = F_1$, the weak second forecast may reflect the first forecast or it may reflect private information. Accordingly, we separate the data by whether the weak second analyst's earnings signal (S_{2w}) matches the first announced forecast (F_1). Table 14.5 summarizes the frequency of weak second forecasts, partitioned by whether the earnings signal matches the second announced forecast ($S_{2w} = F_1$ or $S_{2w} \neq F_1$) and whether the first and second forecasts are the same ($F_{2w} = F_1$ or $F_{2w} \neq F_1$). The data are presented for periods 1–48, 1–24 and 25–48. Over periods 1–48, the first and second forecasts match 89.6 percent of the time (138 of 154 periods) when $S_{2w} = F_1$. This percentage is close to the 93.6 percent reported by ACE, with the difference being insignificant ($\chi^2 = 1.64$, $p = 0.200$). The first and second forecasts match 71.0 percent of the time (44 of 62 periods) when $S_{2w} \neq F_1$. Again, the percentage is close to the 59.3 percent

Table 14.5 Weak second analysts partitioned by signal match and first forecast in the sequential setting

(a) Periods 1–48

First forecast	$S_{2w} = F_1$		$S_{2w} \neq F_1$	
	$F_{2w} = F_1$	$F_{2w} \neq F_1$	$F_{2w} = F_1$	$F_{2w} \neq F_1$
1	12	5	5	3
2	54	2	15	5
3	56	6	16	6
4	16	3	8	4
Total	138	16	44	18

(b) Periods 1–24

First forecast	$S_{2w} = F_1$		$S_{2w} \neq F_1$	
	$F_{2w} = F_1$	$F_{2w} \neq F_1$	$F_{2w} = F_1$	$F_{2w} \neq F_1$
1	7	1	1	1
2	21	2	10	5
3	29	5	6	4
4	10	3	2	1
Total	67	11	19	11

(c) Periods 25–48

First forecast	$S_{2w} = F_1$		$S_{2w} \neq F_1$	
	$F_{2w} = F_1$	$F_{2w} \neq F_1$	$F_{2w} = F_1$	$F_{2w} \neq F_1$
1	5	4	4	2
2	33	0	5	0
3	27	1	10	2
4	6	0	6	3
Total	71	5	25	7

Notes: F_1 is the first announced forecast, S_{2w} is the weak second analyst's signal, and F_{2w} is the weak second forecast. The cell entries indicate the frequency of weak second forecasts, partitioned by whether the second analyst's earnings signal matches the first announced forecast (i.e. $S_{2w} = F_1$ or $S_{2w} \neq F_1$) and whether the second analyst follows the first analyst ($F_{2w} = F_1$ or $F_{2w} \neq F_1$). The cell frequencies are those observed in the sequential setting.

reported by ACE, with the difference being insignificant ($\chi^2 = 1.22$, $p = 0.270$). The findings suggest that weak second analysts are inclined to follow the reporting behavior of others. Breaking the data into halves, we observe that the percentages increase from the first to second half of the experiment: the percentage goes from 85.9 percent to 93.4 percent when $S_{2w} = F_1$ and from 63.3 percent to 78.1 percent when $S_{2w} \neq F_1$.

To formally test whether weak second analysts follow the reporting behavior of others,

Table 14.6 Tests to determine whether weak second analysts follow others

Periods	$P(F_{2w} = F_1 \| S_{2w} \neq F_1)$	$P(F_{1w} \neq S_{1w})$	z-statistic
1–48	0.710	0.244	8.630*
1–24	0.633	0.339	3.489*
25–48	0.781	0.294	6.088*

Notes: F_{2w} is the weak second forecast, F_1 is the first forecast, S_{2w} is the weak second analyst's earnings signal, F_{1w} is the weak first forecast, and S_{1w} is the weak first analyst's earnings signal. The column headed $P(F_{2w} = F_1 | S_{2w} \neq F_1)$ is the probability that the second analyst follows the first forecast and disregards private information. The column headed $P(F_{1w} \neq S_{1w})$ is the probability that the weak forecast differs from private information when the weak analyst goes first (i.e. the weak first analyst disregards his or her earnings signal absent any other information). For each row, we conduct a binomial test using the normal approximation to determine whether $P(F_{2w} = F_1 | S_{2w} \neq F_1) > P(F_{1w} \neq S_{1w})$, which is indicative of weak second analysts following the reporting behavior of the first analyst. One asterisk denotes that the null hypothesis can be rejected at the 1 percent level (one-tailed test).

we compare $P(F_{2w} = F_1 | S_{2w} \neq F_1)$ with $P(F_{1w} \neq S_{1w})$. The first probability represents the frequency with which weak second forecasts match the first forecast, conditioned on the second earnings signal being different from the first forecast. The second probability represents the frequency that weak first forecasts differ from the private earnings signal. If weak second analysts follow the reporting behavior of others, then the first probability will be greater than the second probability.

We perform binomial tests to determine whether $P(F_{2w} = F_1 | S_{2w} \neq F_1) > P(F_{1w} \neq S_{1w})$. The second probability represents the benchmark basis of comparison. To obtain a reliable estimate of the second probability, we use the observed frequency of all weak first analysts, including those in the simultaneous setting and those going first in the sequential setting. We conduct tests using data from periods 1–48, 1–24 and 25–48. The results are presented in Table 14.6. For all three comparisons, the conditional probability (i.e. the probability that the weak second analysts follow others) is significantly greater than the unconditional probability (i.e. the probability that weak analysts ignore private information) at $p < 0.01$ (one-tailed test). The results indicate that weak analysts follow the reporting behavior of others, which is consistent with those reported by ACE.

Strong Analysts with Sequential Forecasts

We assess whether strong second analysts follow the reporting behavior of others. We examine cases where $F_{2s} = F_1$: that is, the strong second forecast (F_{2w}) matches the first announced forecast (F_1). As before, we separate the data by whether the strong second analyst's earnings signal (S_{2s}) matches the first announced forecast (F_1). Table 14.7 shows the frequency of strong second forecasts, partitioned by whether the earnings signal matches the second announced forecast ($S_{2s} = F_1$ or $S_{2s} \neq F_1$) and whether the first and second forecasts are the same ($F_{2s} = F_1$ or $F_{2s} \neq F_1$), including periods 1–48, 1–24 and 25–48.

We find that over periods 1–48, the first and second forecasts are the same 93.7 percent of the time (164 of 175 periods) when $S_{2s} = F_1$. The percentage is slightly less than the 98.9 percent reported by ACE, with the difference being significant ($\chi^2 = 6.42, p = 0.011$).

Table 14.7 Strong second analysts partitioned by signal match and first forecast in the sequential setting

(a) Periods 1–48

First forecast	$S_{2s} = F_1$		$S_{2s} \neq F_1$	
	$F_{2s} = F_1$	$F_{2s} \neq F_1$	$F_{2s} = F_1$	$F_{2s} \neq F_1$
1	19	4	0	7
2	60	3	5	13
3	70	3	2	6
4	15	1	1	7
Total	164	11	8	33

(b) Periods 1–24

First forecast	$S_{2s} = F_1$		$S_{2s} \neq F_1$	
	$F_{2s} = F_1$	$F_{2s} \neq F_1$	$F_{2s} = F_1$	$F_{2s} \neq F_1$
1	6	1	0	3
2	33	3	1	1
3	32	3	2	6
4	9	1	1	6
Total	80	8	4	16

(c) Periods 25–48

First forecast	$S_{2s} = F_1$		$S_{2s} \neq F_1$	
	$F_{2s} = F_1$	$F_{2s} \neq F_1$	$F_{2s} = F_1$	$F_{2s} \neq F_1$
1	13	3	0	4
2	27	0	4	12
3	38	0	0	0
4	6	0	0	1
Total	84	3	4	17

Notes: F_1 is the first announced forecast, S_{2s} is the strong second analyst's signal, and F_{2s} is the strong second forecast. The cell entries indicate the frequency of strong second analysts, partitioned by whether the second analyst's earnings signal matches the first announced forecast (i.e. $S_{2s} = F_1$ or $S_{2s} \neq F_1$) and whether the second analyst follows the first analyst ($F_{2s} = F_1$ or $F_{2s} \neq F_1$). The cell frequencies are those observed in the sequential setting.

The first and second forecasts match only 19.5 percent of the time (8 of 41 periods) when $S_{2s} \neq F_1$. The percentage is more than the 4.8 percent reported in ACE, again with the difference being significant ($\chi^2 = 4.26, p = 0.039$). Our findings suggest that strong second analysts are not inclined to follow the behavior of others, although the results are not as marked as those in ACE. Partitioning the data into halves, the findings are comparable.

We perform binomial tests to formally assess whether strong second analysts follow the

Table 14.8 Tests to determine whether strong second analysts follow others

Periods	$P(F_{2w} = F_1 \mid S_{2w} \neq F_1)$	$P(F_{1w} \neq S_{1w})$	z-statistic
1–48	0.195	0.125	1.355
1–24	0.200	0.111	1.268
25–48	0.190	0.138	0.759

Notes: F_{2s} is the strong second forecast, F_1 is the first forecast, S_{2s} is the strong second analyst's earnings signal, F_{1s} is the strong first forecast, and S_{1s} is the strong first analyst's earnings signal. The column headed $P(F_{2w} = F_1 \mid S_{2w} \neq F_1)$ is the probability that the second analyst follows the first analyst and disregards private information. The column headed $P(F_{1w} \neq S_{1w})$ is the probability that the strong forecast differs from private information when the strong analyst goes first (i.e. the strong first analyst disregards his or her earnings signal absent any other information). For each row, we conduct a binomial test using the normal approximation to determine whether $P(F_{2w} = F_1 \mid S_{2w} \neq F_1) > P(F_{1w} \neq S_{1w})$, which is indicative of strong second analysts following the reporting behavior of the first analyst. In no case is the z-statistic statistically significant at the 5 percent level (one-tailed test).

reporting behavior of others. As before, we look at cases in which $F_{1s} \neq S_{1s}$ and compare $P(F_{2s} = F_1 \mid S_{2s} \neq F_1)$ with $P(F_{1s} \neq S_{1s})$. For the benchmark (second) probability, we use the observed frequency of all strong first analysts, including those in the simultaneous setting and those going first in the sequential setting. If strong second analysts are followers, the conditional probability will be greater than the unconditional probability.

As shown in Table 14.8, the conditional and unconditional probabilities are not significantly different for any of the comparisons at the 5 percent level (one-tailed test). Thus strong second analysts do not follow the first analyst. This result is entirely consistent with ACE.

CONCLUDING REMARKS

This chapter reports the results of an experiment designed to investigate individual forecasting behavior in settings with simultaneous and sequential forecast release. In each session, four individuals are given private information and asked to predict the earnings of a hypothetical firm. The two strong analysts are given more accurate information signals than the two weak analysts. When all four group members release forecasts simultaneously, we expect that weak analysts will not always release forecasts that are consistent with their private information. In contrast, we expect that strong analysts will release forecasts that reflect their private information. When forecasts are released sequentially, we expect that weak second analysts follow the reporting behavior of the first analyst. However, we expect that strong second analysts do not engage in herd behavior.

In the simultaneous forecast setting, individuals' forecasts are not always unbiased reflections of their private information. Though stronger for weak analysts, both weak and strong analysts release forecasts that are not consistent with private information. These inconsistent forecasts are observed more frequently when private information indicates that the earnings level is extreme (i.e. individuals tend to report low earnings when their private information indicates high earnings). In the sequential forecast setting, weak second analysts follow the reporting behavior of the first analyst but strong analysts are not inclined toward herd behavior. Across experimental sessions, the results are largely consistent with Trueman's theoretical predictions as well as the experimental results of ACE.

Our results have important implications for observers, participants and regulators of markets. Research shows that financial analysts sometimes ignore private information and issue forecasts that are too optimistic. Some argue that analysts have incentives to issue optimistic forecasts because they generate trading activity for their firm by releasing optimistic forecasts, which indirectly impacts their compensation (Schipper, 1991). But our experimental participants ignore private information even though they are not subject to the same incentives faced by professional financial analysts. In addition, our participants felt the forces of the herd. Additional research might investigate the conditions under which people follow the herd. Some suggest that people follow the behavior of others because their actions reflect private information, to positively affect ability assessments or to avoid being viewed as a contrarian (e.g. Banerjee, 1992; Trueman, 1994, Scharfstein and Stein, 1990). However, analysts are not always afraid to stand out in the crowd (Ackert and Athanassakos, 1997). Accordingly, additional research on situational and behavioral motivations is called for.

ACKNOWLEDGMENTS

The views expressed here are those of the authors and not necessarily those of the Federal Reserve Bank of Atlanta or the Federal Reserve System. The authors gratefully acknowledge the financial support of the Federal Reserve Bank of Atlanta and the Certified General Accountants of Canada and the research assistance of Karen Butler, Dan Li, Betty Soares and Shawna White.

NOTES

1. Refer to observations 1 and 2 in Trueman (1994, p. 105). According to proposition 2 (p. 106), the probability that a weak analyst reports low earnings when the information signal indicates high earnings is strictly positive as long as the analysts' ability is less than twice the probability of low earnings. This restriction holds in our experimental setup.
2. In a small number of instances, participants announce forecasts that are not plausible (once for weak analysts and four times for strong analysts in the simultaneous forecast setting). Forecasts are not plausible when the forecast errs in predicting whether earnings are positive or negative. Inferences are not affected if these observations are excluded from the data analyses.

REFERENCES

Ackert, L.F. and G. Athanassakos (1997), 'Prior uncertainty, analyst bias, and subsequent abnormal returns,' *Journal of Financial Research*, **20** (2), 263–73.

Ackert, L.F., B.K. Church and K. Ely (2008), 'Biases in individual forecasts: experimental evidence,' *Journal of Behavioral Finance*, **9** (2), 53–61.

Arya, A., J. Glover and S. Sunder (2003), 'Are unmanaged earnings always better for shareholders?,' *Accounting Horizons*, **17** (Supplement), 111–16.

Banerjee, A.V. (1992), 'A simple model of herd hehavior,' *Quarterly Journal of Economics*, **107** (3), 797–817.

Hirshleifer, D. (2001), 'Investor psychology and asset pricing,' *The Journal of Finance*, **51** (4), 1533–97.
Mendenhall, W., R.L. Scheaffer and D.D. Wackerly (1981), *Mathematical Statistics with Applications*, 2nd edn, Boston, MA: Duxbury Press.
Scharfstein, D.S. and J.C. Stein (1990), 'Herd behavior and investment,' *American Economic Review*, **80** (3), 465–79.
Schipper, K. (1991), 'Commentary on analysts' forecasts,' *Accounting Horizons*, **3** (4), 106–21.
Trueman, B. (1994), 'Analyst forecasts and herding behavior,' *Review of Financial Studies*, **7** (1), 97–124.
Trueman, B. and S. Titman (1988), 'An explanation for accounting income smoothing,' *Journal of Accounting Research*, **26** (Supplement), 127–39.

15 Behavioral finance and investment advice

Kremena Bachmann and Thorsten Hens

INTRODUCTION

Behavioral finance studies the psychological factors that influence financial behavior both at the level of the individual as well as at the level of the market. So far these results have been used mainly to explain the existence of patterns in asset prices and to develop investment strategies that exploit them.[1] While these applications of behavioral finance aim to understand the market, this chapter focuses on the individual investors and asks how to help them to make optimal investment decisions.

To give advice, one first needs to make a clear distinction between behavioral biases and behavioral preferences. Biases are deviations from rational behavior, while preferences are personal variants of rational behavior. As a rational benchmark we use expected utility and state-dominance. Measured against this benchmark, psychologically driven decisions are not always irrational. Moreover, they can be helpful in building realistic images of investors' preferences, which is particularly important for decisions related to the optimal allocation of wealth. This chapter shows how to solve the asset allocation problems of investors without imposing restrictions on the distribution of asset returns while using realistic images of investors' preferences. Within the suggested framework the attractive features of mean–variance analysis of Markowitz (1952) appear as a special case. Finally, this chapter analyzes the optimal investment behavior of investors over time and discusses the suitability of some well-known rules of thumb for investors with different preferences.

While this chapter is based on recent results of our research group, which includes Enrico De Giorgi, János Mayer, Marc-Oliver Rieger and Mei Wang, we should mention that we draw on the fundamental insights provided by Amos Tversky, Daniel Kahneman, Hersh Shefrin, Meir Statman, Nick Barberis and Richard Thaler.[2] To put our approach into perspective, it is important to distinguish it from the approaches of Kahneman and Riepe (1998) and that of Pompian (2006).

Kahneman and Riepe (1998) are the first scholars challenging financial advisors to examine their practice from a behavioral standpoint. They leverage the decision theory work of Raiffa (1968) by categorizing behavioral biases on three grounds: (1) 'biases on judgment,' (2) 'errors of preferences' and (3) 'biases associated with living with the consequences of decisions'. Biases of judgments include overconfidence, hindsight, optimism and overreaction to chance events. Errors of preferences include nonlinear weighting of probabilities, the tendency to value changes and not levels of payoffs, the use of a purchase price as a reference point, narrow framing, and the adoption of short versus long views. Living with the consequences of decisions is connected to regret of omission and regret of commission, and also to the relationship between regret and risk taking. Among a description of the biases including test questions, Kahneman and Riepe provide practical recommendations that should help advisors deal with the biases. For example, their recommendation to advisors with loss-averse clients is to avoid investing in very risky assets because 'the clients will accept such investments only if they optimistically underestimate the risks.' As compared to Kahneman and Riepe (1998), the approach taken here is more analytical since it is based on a model distinguishing between behavioral risk preferences including an investor's loss aversion and behavioral biases driving an over- or underestimation of investment risks.

More recently, Pompian (2006) published a book that explains various behavioral biases and offers ideas that should help overcome them. In his prescriptive analysis, Pompian considers all decisions that are driven by psychological, cognitive or emotional factors as biased, that is, irrational decisions. To derive optimal portfolios that account for behavioral biases, the author distinguishes between emotional and cognitive biases. Emotional biases include the endowment effect, loss aversion and self-control. Cognitive biases include heuristics, availability, representativeness biases, ambiguity aversion, self-attribution and conservatism. According to Pompian, it is better to adapt to emotional biases because they result from intuition, which is difficult to rectify. Therefore a moderation of emotional biases is needed only for investors with low levels of wealth. Cognitive biases should be moderated unless the investor is very wealthy. In terms of the optimal asset allocation of behavioral clients, Pompian concludes that 'to override the mean–variance optimizer is to depart from the strictly rational portfolio' and that 'a behavioural adjusted allocation should not stray more than 20 per cent from the mean–variance optimized allocation' (Pompian, 2006, p. 45). As compared to Pompian (2006), the approach taken here does not adopt the mean–variance outcome as the best because mean–variance-based decisions may violate some basic principles of rationality. Therefore advisors cannot be sure that a recommendation based on the mean–variance analysis is more rational than any other one.

In our prescriptive analysis we follow the long tradition in discussions of decision making that distinguishes between preferences and beliefs. In the first step we point out that psychologically or cognitively driven decisions are not always irrational. Then we use the rational aspects of psychologically driven decisions to build realistic images of investors' preferences. We distinguish between risk preferences, risk awareness and risk ability to find an optimal asset allocation that is consistent with an investor's preferences and restrictions but that is free from biases that motivate him to take risks without acknowledging them and experience outcomes that he did not anticipate.

This chapter is structured as follows. The next section reviews two paradigms of traditional finance: expected utility theory and mean–variance analysis. It shows that the broadly used mean–variance analysis is not always consistent with the concept of rationality as defined by the expected utility theory. The section after that offers a brief overview of the main insights of behavioral finance and shows which aspects of an investor's behaviour should be accepted as part of his preferences and which aspects should be corrected because they can motivate irrational decisions. The fourth section uses the investor's preferences within a specific risk–reward framework to solve the asset allocation problem of investors without imposing unrealistic assumptions on their preferences as well as on the distribution of asset returns. The fifth section analyzes the optimal investment behavior of investors over time and discusses the suitability of some well-known rules of thumb for investors with different preferences.

TRADITIONAL FINANCE: A RATIONAL BENCHMARK OF INVESTMENT DECISION MAKING?

Traditional finance has at least two paradigms that are important for financial advisors: expected utility theory and mean–variance analysis. Expected utility theory defines benchmarks for rational decision making. The mean–variance analysis is the best-known investment decision framework used in practice. This section provides a short description of the two paradigms and discusses why for modern investment opportunities the mean–variance analysis does not serve well as a rational benchmark for investment decision making.

By now expected utility theory has been generally accepted as a normative model of decision making. One of the advantages of a normative model is that it provides a valuable guide for action. In particular, if one accepts the criteria of expected utility theory defining rational decisions, then one can use the theory as a guide in the decision process. The criteria for a rational choice are defined as axioms. In the expected utility theory decisions are rational if the decision-maker's preferences are complete, transitive, continuous, and if they satisfy the independence axiom.[3] An additional, even more fundamental criterion for rationality is state-dominance, which says that a lottery that in each state of the world (in the sense of Savage, 1954) pays off at least as much as another lottery (and something more in at least one state) is preferable.[4] For the purpose of judging investment decisions in terms of rationality, this chapter adopts the view that decision makers with preferences satisfying the four axioms of expected utility and state-dominance make rational decisions.

While expected utility is based on theoretical reasoning, mean–variance analysis originates from practical problems such as the question of whether or not to hold wealth in cash or to buy risky assets in the financial market. When comparing alternatives only in terms of their average returns, it is unclear why long-term investors should hold anything else but equities. The mean–variance theory of Harry Markowitz (1952) was the first portfolio theory adding a risk dimension to the problem of selecting among different assets. The theory made it clear that risk-averse investors may not necessarily invest all their wealth in the assets with the highest mean returns, as the variance of asset returns (risk) increases with the mean (reward). Moreover, the mean–variance theory suggested how to use the principle of diversification to form efficient portfolios, i.e. portfolios with minimum variance for different levels of mean return.

Within this mean–variance analysis, the optimal asset allocation for an investor can be determined by following the two-fund-separation theorem of Tobin (1958). The theorem says that, according to their risk aversion, investors should combine the risk-free asset (e.g. cash) and a single optimal portfolio of risky assets (also called tangent portfolio). Investors with higher (lower) risk aversion should invest more (less) of their wealth in the tangent portfolio. The structure of the tangent portfolio remains the same for all investors. The heterogeneity of investors is reduced to a single dimension: the mix of the risk-free asset and the tangent portfolio. It is, however, well known that advisors do not follow the two-fund-separation theorem. The so-called asset allocation puzzle (see Canner et al., 1997) describes the finding that professional advisors adjust the recommended mix of risky assets according to the risk preferences of their clients. The question that arises then is whether practitioners do something wrong.

To answer this question one needs first to examine whether mean–variance should be accepted and applied as a rational benchmark for asset allocation decisions. There are many papers discussing the relationship between the expected utility theory and mean–variance analysis.[5] The main finding is that portfolio selection based on the maximization of a mean–variance utility function maximizes expected utility if assets' rates of return are normally distributed or if the utility is quadratic. In general, the mean–variance criterion might however violate the independence axiom since variance-based preferences are not linear in probabilities, and linearity in probabilities is a direct consequence of the independence axiom. Another well-known problem of the mean–variance analysis is the mean–variance paradox, which points to a lack of state-dominance in mean–variance analysis. It is most easily illustrated in a simple lottery, in which, with probability $p > 0$, one can get a payoff $x > 0$. In the rest of the cases, the payoff is zero. Since one cannot lose in this lottery, any agent satisfying state-dominance would prefer it to a constant payoff of 0. This is, however, not clear for a mean–variance decision maker. If the probability p converges to zero while the payoff x increases so that the expected value of the lottery is constant, the variance of the lottery $\sigma^2 = p(x - \mu)^2 + (1 - p)(-\mu)^2 = \mu x - \mu^2$ tends to infinity. Any variance-averse investor will eventually prefer to get nothing rather than to play the lottery.

To summarize, even though in special cases the mean–variance criterion is consistent with expected utility, it generally fails to deliver rational decisions since it might fail to satisfy the state-dominance axiom. In this case, mean–variance decision makers may eventually prefer to get nothing than to play a lottery where they cannot lose anything.

The following section provides a short overview on the main achievements of behavioral finance and shows that psychologically motivated decisions are not always irrational. Moreover, it shows that psychology can help build more realistic images of an investor's preferences.

BEHAVIORAL FINANCE LESSONS FOR INVESTMENT ADVISORS

Behavioral finance, commonly defined as 'the application of psychology to finance,' studies the human side of financial decision making. From the very beginning, behavioral finance has benefited mainly from experimental research questioning the existence of the rational economic man. But also the field of cognitive psychology contributed a great deal to the development of behavioral finance and in particular to the development of prospect theory, which can be seen as the foundation of behavioral finance.

This section provides a selective summary of the main insights of behavioral finance that should help advisors guide clients in making decisions that best serve their interest. Following the tradition in discussion of decision making, this section distinguishes between psychologically or cognitively motivated preferences and beliefs. Since psychologically motivated preferences do not necessarily violate the axioms of rationality, they may not lead to irrational decisions. However, systematical errors occur because of wrong beliefs driven by mistakes that people make in assigning probabilities to future outcomes or from improper combination of probabilities and values. These mistakes are also known as behavioral biases. Investors prone to behavioral biases take risks that they are not aware of, may experience outcomes that they did not anticipate when making the particular decision, and may engage in unjustified trading.

An Overview of Prospect Theory

Prospect theory is the best-known theory describing the manner in which real people actually make decisions under risk. It is founded on the observation that when individuals evaluate different alternatives, they (1) treat gains differently to losses and (2) overweight outcomes received with small probability relative to more certain outcomes.[6] Based on these observations, Kahneman and Tversky (1979) and Tversky and Kahneman (1992) offer a theory, prospect theory, that can predict individual choice even in cases where expected utility is violated. In prospect theory, the utility function is replaced by a value function and the objective probabilities are substituted by psychological probability weights.

The value function has three important properties. First, it is defined over gains and losses with respect to some reference point. Second, the function is steeper for payoffs x below the reference point (losses) than for payoffs above the reference point (gains). Third, the value function is concave in gains and convex for losses.

Tversky and Kahneman (1992) suggest the following piecewise power function with these properties.

$$v(\Delta x) = \begin{cases} \Delta x^{\alpha} & \text{for } \Delta x \geq 0 \\ -\beta(-\Delta x)^{\alpha} & \text{for } \Delta x < 0 \end{cases}$$

where $\Delta x = x - RP$ is a gain or a loss associated with the payoff x relative to the reference point RP. The parameter β reflects the steepness of the value function over losses or the individual's loss aversion. The parameter α reflects the concavity (convexity) of the function. The preferences of the median individual as observed by Tversky and Kahneman (1992) are given by the parameters $\alpha = 0.88$ and $\beta = 2.25$.

Note that the properties of the value function do not induce irrational decisions. As Friedman and Savage (1948) have already argued long ago, expected utility is consistent with S-shaped utility functions and these utility functions, being non-standard in finance,[7] are actually quite good at describing observed behavior. Note, however, that irrationality might result from reference-point-based value functions if over time the reference point shifts. We discuss this issue in more details in a later section where we analyse multi-period investment decisions.

The psychological probability weights are determined analytically by a probability weighting function $w(p)$ with a parameter γ capturing the bias in the perception of probabilities.

$$w(p) = \frac{p^{\gamma}}{(p^{\gamma} + (1 - p)^{\gamma})^{1/\gamma}}$$

Tversky and Kahneman (1992) find in their experiment that the parameter γ is approximately equal to 0.65.

Combining the value and the probability weighting part of prospect theory in a simple model with a finite number of states, the prospect theory criterion to evaluate a lottery is then:

$$PT(x) = \sum_{s=1}^{S} w(p_s)v(\Delta x_s)$$

While decisions motivated by loss aversion and non-constant risk aversion are consistent with rationality, the observation that very rare events are overweighted is irrational since it violates the linearity of probabilities and hence the independence axiom. Moreover, overweighting small probabilities can lead to a violation of state-dominance.[8] Subsequently, some adjustments of prospect theory have been suggested. Tversky and Kahneman (1992) proposed cumulative prospect theory, in which the cumulative distribution is modified by decision weights, and Karmakar (1978, 1979) and Rieger and Wang (2008) suggested normalized prospect theory, in which each prospect probability is divided by the sum of all prospect probabilities. This chapter will not deal further with probability weighting since for the purpose of advising investors optimally any sort of probability weights can be considered as irrational. Other psychological factors leading to irrational decisions are summarized in the following section.

Irrational Decisions Driven by Behavioral Biases

It is far beyond the purpose of this section to provide a description of all biases that can lead to irrational decisions. Emphasis is put on the relevance of biases that affect the choice of an asset allocation (or investment strategy) and the adjustment of the asset allocation over time. The aim of this summary, presented in Table 15.1, is to help advisors to recognize situations in which errors might occur and provide timely warnings to their clients about the pitfalls of intuitive decisions.

A combination of these biases may lead to some severe mistakes that could be avoided if investors followed a proper strategy. Without a strategy guiding future investment decisions, investors influenced by the representativeness bias may develop the belief that perfect market timing is possible. With the recent past as an anchor and certain degree of overconfidence, they may forget that in the course of investing, events may happen that could not have been anticipated. This initial underreaction can turn into an overreaction, in particular under the influence of the availability bias, which makes recent surprising events appear more severe as they are seen from a long-term perspective. Over time, investors may underreact to some events and overreact to others, so that perfect market timing is not always possible. To avoid being swept away by hectic market movements, one should follow a strategy of future investments that has already been proven to achieve the characteristics that suits one's preferences and restrictions. The following section provides a framework for solving such investment problems.

Table 15.1 Behavioral biases driving irrational investment decisions: description, relevance, evidence and strategies for overcoming the biases

Short description of biases	Relevance for investor's decisions	Evidence	Recommendations
Availability bias When individuals estimate probabilities and judge the attractiveness of alternatives, they decide in favor of the alternative that comes easily to their minds (e.g. because they have experienced it) or that is easy to imagine (e.g. because it is easy to construct an instance).	Investors will probably choose investments by relying too strongly on easily available information (e.g. headlines in newspapers or recent experience such as a market crash). When selecting assets, investors are likely to choose assets that match their narrow range of experience, such as the industry they work in. Only by chance can this choice turn out well.	Barber and Odean (2005) show that individuals manage the problem of selecting among various stocks by focusing on those that catch their attention (stocks in the news, with high abnormal trading volume or with extreme one-day returns). However, attention-grabbing stocks do not outperform the market.	Look at long-term results before making decisions based on the current hot stories in the newspapers. Consider examples of glamor stories that have failed. Bad events (such as accidents or market crashes) can make decisions appear riskier than they are from a long-term perspective.
Representativeness bias Individuals (1) tend to estimate probabilities depending on their pre-existing beliefs even if the conclusions are statistically invalid, i.e. rely on stereotypes and (2) tend to believe that even small samples represent entire populations.	(1) Investors believe that well-performing firms with a good reputation are also good investments; believe that there are investment managers with a 'hot hand.' (2) Investors believe that after a relatively short sequence of good returns the prospect of returns has changed for the better.	Shefrin and Statman (1995) show that survey respondents believe that the shares of companies that do well in the annual *Fortune* magazine survey of corporate reputation will prove to be good investments. The empirical evidence is that such companies actually tend to be poor long-term investments. Sirri and Tufano (1998) indicate increased inflows into mutual funds	When data appear to show some pattern, employ statistical methods to verify your opinion. Before making an active decision, consider the possibility that the decision is driven by factors that are random. Assess the predictability of the market and define a strategy

Table 15.1 (continued)

Short description of biases	Relevance for investor's decisions	Evidence	Recommendations
		with exceptional but statistically short-lived past performance. Jegadeesh and Titman (2001) find a stock return continuation on horizons between 6 and 12 months with historically earned profits of about 1% per month over the following 12 months. After some time investors realize that there is overreaction on the market and stock returns reverse. Investment strategies buying the losers and selling the winners of the last three years for a horizon of three to five years become profitable (De Bondt and Thaler, 1985).	that is also consistent with the client's risk preferences and restrictions.
Framing Individuals give different and conflicting answers to the same question asked in two different ways. Alternative description of a decision problem may give rise to different preferences.	The optimistic or pessimistic manner in which an investment or a recommendation is framed can affect investor's willingness or lack of willingness to invest. Even long-term investors can change their attitude to risk when they are confronted with short-term price fluctuations (e.g. by	Benartzi and Thaler (1999) observe that investors who receive one-year distribution as information choose to allocate 41%, on average, of their retirement to stocks. Investors that examined 30 years' return distributions choose to invest 82% of their savings in stocks. Benartzi and Thaler (2001) observe that employees aiming to hold on average 60% in stocks and 40% in bonds by investing in mutual funds	Search for an alternative representation of the problem and check whether it would change the decision. Adopt as broad a frame as possible. Design statements that pay less attention to the last quarter but more to what happened over the lifetime of the account. Present the results of decisions in a frame that is suitable for the

	re-analysing long-term investments on a daily basis).	decide differently in favor of the category that is presented in more detail.	client (e.g. for clients with a retirement goal, level of wealth can be presented as income per year or per month that can be expected after retirement).
Anchoring Individuals tend to be overly influenced in their assessment by arbitrary values mentioned in the statement of the problem, even when these values are clearly not informative.	The present is a very strong anchor. Investors may fail to anticipate the possibility of dramatic changes. If investors receive information about the possible earnings of a firm under the best economic conditions, they will probably have difficulties in estimating the earnings of the firm under real conditions.	Tversky and Kahneman (1974) asked subjects to estimate various quantities, stated in percentages. For each quantity, a number between 0 and 100 was determined by spinning a wheel of fortune in the subjects' presence. These arbitrary numbers had a marked effect on estimates.	Update expectations by focusing on some relevant scenarios that reflect the changes in fundamentals. Do not stick to last estimates. Broaden your perspective by using different frames.
Overconfidence Unwarranted faith in one's intuitive reasoning, judgments and cognitive abilities. The intervals that investors assign to their investment predictions are too narrow.	Overconfident investors overestimate the precision of information signals. As a consequence they take more risks than they can actually afford. Overconfident investors trade excessively as a result of their belief that they possess special knowledge.	Stotz and Nitzsch (2005) asked analysts at major investment banks how many of their rivals were more accurate and less accurate than themselves with respect to earnings forecasts and target prices. The average overconfidence with regard to earnings was 68.44% and 61.49% with respect to target prices. Barber and Odean (2001) find that individuals turn over their common stock investements about 70% annually because of overconfidence.	Explain to clients that other investors also try to outsmart them. Only investors that find the right balance between their skills and investment style perform the best. As an advisor, keep a list of recommendations that were not successful, as people are more likely to remember successful decisions.

Table 15.1 (continued)

Short description of biases	Relevance for investor's decisions	Evidence	Recommendations
		Huber (2007) finds in an experiment controling the information level of individuals that the best-informed individuals clearly make the highest returns but the medium-informed individuals do worst because they have tried to exploit the least-informed individuals on the market. However, as the least-informed individuals knew that they were worst off from the outset, they did not engage in trading.	
Time-inconsistent preferences Individuals face a conflict between the optimal plan from today's perspective and the optimal decision from tomorrow's perspective. This conflict can be explained by the notion that individuals discount the future depending on the decision point of time.	Investors save much less than they should given the private incentives they face.	Thaler (1981) shows that the average discount rate individuals apply is decreasing over time. Ainslie and Haslam (1992) observe that a majority of subjects would prefer 'to have a prize of $100 certified check available immediately over a $200 certified check that could not be cashed before 2 years; the same people do not prefer a $100 certified check that could be cashed in 6 years to a $200 certified check that could be cashed in 8 years.'	Consider the advantages of commitment strategies such as contracts requiring constant instead of flexible payments and high penalties for an early termination of the contract.

USING PROSPECT THEORY TO SOLVE INDIVIDUAL ASSET ALLOCATION PROBLEMS

An individual asset allocation is a mix of assets that is optimal for an investor given his risk preferences and risk ability and the risk–return trade-off offered by the market. Essential for building an image of the investor's preferences is the choice of a utility function. Recalling the extensive experimental literature on individual decision making under uncertainty, a common criterion for the utility function is that it is psychologically sound. This means that the individual's behavior resulting from maximizing this utility function is in consensus with the risk in the way the investor wants to avoid it. Furthermore, the asset allocation resulting from solving the optimization problem has to be robust to small changes in the parameters of the functional form describing the preferences.

Having found such a utility function, the next step toward an optimal asset allocation is the choice of a framework describing the trade-offs offered by the market. Ideally, the chosen framework is consistent with the investor's understanding of reward and risk and does not restrict investors from choosing among assets with normally distributed returns.

Modeling Preferences of Behavioral Investors

The first idea of how to solve the asset allocation problem of a behavioral investor is to use the piecewise power function suggested by Tversky and Kahneman (1992) within the mean–variance analysis of Markowitz (1952). This is possible under the assumption that asset returns are normally distributed, since any utility integrated over normally distributed returns is a mean–variance utility. However, using the piecewise power value function within the mean–variance analysis is not robust to small changes in the parameters, so that the mix of riskless and risky assets may change abruptly when the parameters change.[9] To solve this problem, De Giorgi et al. (2004) suggest the use of a piecewise exponential function. With this function, the indifference curves are shaped in a way that gives robust solutions to the optimization problem applied on the efficient frontier or on the capital market line. Specifically, the higher the loss aversion, the steeper is the indifference curve, and consequently the less risky the assets the loss-averse investor would hold. The effect is similar if the reference point increases.

Unfortunately, many assets (and even asset classes) do not have normally distributed returns. To make the choice of the behavioral investor compatible with an analysis of assets with any return distribution, one can use a piecewise quadratic value function with the following form (see also Figure 15.1).

$$v(\Delta x) = \begin{cases} \Delta x - \dfrac{\alpha^+}{2}(\Delta x)^2 & \text{if } \Delta x \geq 0 \\ \beta\left(\Delta x - \dfrac{\alpha^-}{2}(\Delta x)^2\right) & \text{if } \Delta x < 0 \end{cases}$$

where Δx is defined as the portfolio return R relative to the investor's reference point RP. Note that for $\alpha^+ > 0$ and $\alpha^- < 0$ the function is S-shaped, i.e. concave for $\Delta x \geq 0$ and

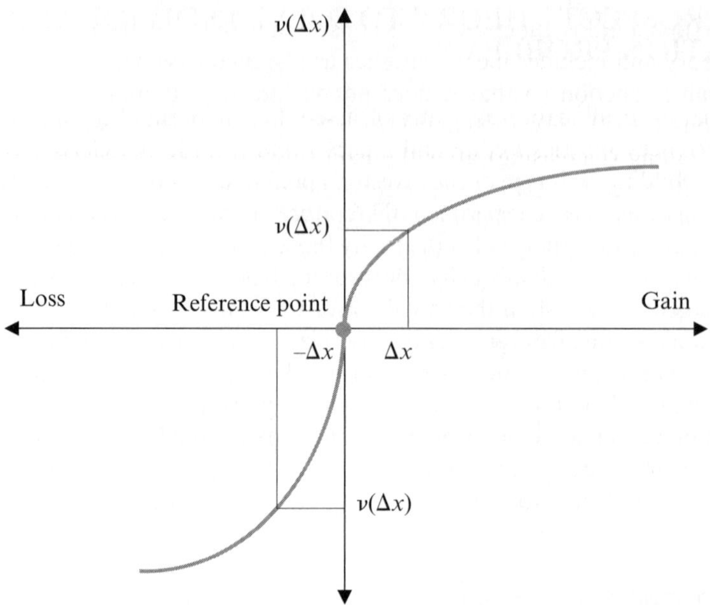

Figure 15.1 Prospect theory value function

convex for $\Delta x < 0$ as the piecewise power function of Tversky and Kahneman (1992). The parameter $\beta > 1$ indicates the degree of loss aversion.

An important property of the piecewise quadratic value function is that for $\beta = 1$, $\alpha^+ = \alpha^-$, and a reference point $RP = \mu$ where μ is the expected return of the investor's portfolio,[10] one gets $v(\Delta x) + RP = \mu - \frac{\alpha}{2}\sigma^2$. Thus the optimal asset allocations of an investor with a quadratic utility function, as in the standard mean–variance analysis, will be equivalent to the asset allocation of a specific behavioural investor maximizing the piecewise quadratic function suggested above.

Tversky and Kahneman (1992) find that the median risk aversion over gains and losses is equal to 0.88 and the median loss aversion is equal to 2.25. These parameters are specific for the piecewise power function used by Tversky and Kahneman to represent the preferences of behavioral investors. If one wants to describe the median investor in the experiments of Tversky and Kahneman with the piecewise quadratic function, one needs to find the parameters $\alpha^+, \alpha^-, \beta, \gamma^+, \gamma^-$ that govern individuals' behavior as observed in the experiments of Tversky and Kahneman. In other words, we look for the set of parameters that motivates individuals to give the same answers (as certainty equivalents) as the answers to the lottery questions used by Tversky and Kahneman.

For payoffs between 0 and 400 the median investor of Tversky and Kahneman with piecewise quadratic value function has preferences described by $\alpha^+ = 0.00215$ and $\alpha^- = -0.00185$. The loss aversion parameter is still $\beta = 2.25$. If the payoffs are in the form of returns between 10 percent and 380 percent (respectively between −10 percent and −380 per cent), the parameters are $\alpha^+ = 0.21512$, $\alpha^- = -0.18469$. For low payoffs, i.e. between 1 percent and 38 percent (respectively between −1 percent and −38 percent), the parameters of the piecewise quadratic function are $\alpha^+ = 2.15114$, $\alpha^- = -1.84688$ and so forth.

Finally, to find a utility function that is consistent with rational choice, has features of prospect theory and includes mean–variance as a special case, we modify the piecewise quadratic value function so that it does not violate state-dominance, by introducing the restrictions $(1/\alpha^+) > \Delta x \geq 0$ and $(1/\alpha^-) < \Delta x < 0$. These restrictions prevent the utility from falling (increasing) after the gain (loss) reaches the levels $1/\alpha^+$ and $1/\alpha^-$ respectively. Beyond this gain (loss), we assume a constant utility of $v(\Delta x) = 1/2\alpha^+$, respectively $v(\Delta x) = 1/2\alpha^-$. Taking into account these considerations, the piecewise quadratic value function takes the form:

$$v(\Delta x) = \begin{cases} \dfrac{1}{2\alpha^+} & \text{if } \Delta x \geq \dfrac{1}{\alpha^+} \\ \Delta x - \dfrac{\alpha^+}{2}(\Delta x)^2 & \text{if } \dfrac{1}{\alpha^+} > \Delta x \geq 0 \\ \beta\left(\Delta x - \dfrac{\alpha^-}{2}(\Delta x)^2\right) & \text{if } \dfrac{1}{\alpha^-} < \Delta x < 0 \\ \dfrac{1}{2\alpha^-} & \text{if } \Delta x \leq \dfrac{1}{\alpha^-} \end{cases}$$

In this way we can ensure rational decisions, i.e. decisions compatible with both expected utility and state-dominance. However, by ensuring state-dominance, the compatibility with mean–variance gets lost. Since we believe that the most attractive feature of mean–variance is the reward–risk principle, which does not need to be specified as a mean–variance trade-off, we prefer to keep compatibility with state-dominance and to find other reward–risk measures that are compatible with prospect theory.

The following example shows how to compute the parameters of the piecewise quadratic utility function from elementary lottery questions. The first lottery question determines the risk aversion parameter over gains α^+.

Question 1: What would you be willing to pay (as a percentage of your investment) to have a 50 percent chance of gaining 10 percent on your investment, while otherwise you break even?

Suppose the investor answers '4 percent.' Then the equation to determine α^+ is:

$$0.5\left(10 - \frac{\alpha^+}{2}100\right) = 4 - \frac{\alpha^+}{2}16, \text{ which yields } \alpha^+ = 1/17.$$

The second lottery question determines the risk aversion parameter over losses α^-.

Question 2: Suppose you follow a strategy that can either have a loss of 10 percent or can break even with equal probability. Which sure loss would you consider to be equivalent to the strategy?

Suppose the investor again answers '4 percent.' Then the equation to determine α^- is:

$$0.5\beta\left(-10-\frac{\alpha^-}{2}100\right)=\beta\left(-4-\frac{\alpha^-}{2}16\right),\text{ which yields }\alpha^-=-1/17.$$

The third lottery question determines investors' loss aversion β.

Question 3: Suppose you follow a strategy that can lose 4 percent with a 50 percent chance. What is the minimum gain that you find acceptable in the other 50 percent cases so that the strategy is acceptable?

Suppose the investor answers '10 percent.' Then the equation to determine β is:

$$0.5\left(10-\frac{\alpha^+}{2}100\right)+0.5\beta\left(-4-\frac{\alpha^-}{2}16\right)=0,\text{ which yields }\beta=2.$$

The final lottery question determines whether probabilities are perceived in a biased way as captured by the parameter γ:

Question 4: What percentage of your investment would you consider to be equivalent to a strategy that with 1 percent chance achieves an 8 percent gain and otherwise breaks even?

Suppose the investor answers '0.6 percent.' Then the equation to determine γ is:

$$\frac{0.01^\gamma}{(0.01^\gamma+0.99^\gamma)^{1/\gamma}}\left(8-\frac{1}{34}64\right)=\left(0.6+\frac{0.6}{34}\right),\text{ which yields }\gamma=0.44.$$

Using Risk Profiles in Client Advisory

To judge whether a client is like the median investor of Tversky and Kahneman, advisors need to elicit the parameters of the utility function suggested above. Together with information about the financial ability of the client to take risks (risk ability) and his awareness of the risks he takes (risk awareness), the client's risk preferences are the critical determinant of his risk profile and ultimately of his optimal asset allocation.

Risk ability represents a constraint on the maximization of the client's utility. In general, one would like to find an asset allocation that maximizes the client's utility while ensuring that he is able to finance his liabilities in almost all circumstances. In this respect, a prioritization of liabilities can be helpful so that one can achieve the risk ability constraint by employing different classes of risky assets for different priorities of liabilities, e.g. using bonds for hard liabilities like education of children and stocks for soft liabilities like plans and wishes. Alternatively, concepts like the 'value at risk' (VaR) or the 'conditional value at risk' (CVaR) can be applied as a restriction on the optimization problem in order to ensure the risk ability constraint.

The risk preferences of the client are described by his risk and loss aversion. The client's risk aversion describes his attitude to uncertainty. A risk-averse (risk-loving) client prefers a sure payment that is lower (higher) than the average payment of a lottery, that is, he is ready to pay less (more) than the average return of a lottery in order to play it. The client's loss aversion is reflected in the asymmetry that he puts on gains and losses. Facing a lottery with a potential loss in one scenario, investors usually require at least twice as much in the other scenario in order to play it. The utility function mentioned in the previous section models these aspects of preferences.

The risk awareness of the client can be captured by his tendency to overweight small-probability events and underweight events that are more likely. Also some behavioural biases such as the availability bias or the representativeness bias can have a negative impact on an investor's risk awareness.

Assessing the client's risk preferences, risk ability and risk awareness in a systematic way has several advantages for institutions with many advisors. First, it ensures that they deliver the highest-quality advice based on the results of well-established research. Second, they can improve the conformability of their services with the requirements of the European 'Markets in Financial Instruments Directive' (MiFID). Third, following a systematic approach, they can make sure that the advice given by all their advisors is more dependent on the client than on the advisor. Besides using modern theories to assure this, it is essential to separate two aspects of advice: the understanding of the client and the understanding of the market. While the first should be done by the advisor, the second is better outsourced to an investment committee so that all advisors of the institution base their advice on the common view of the institution.

Having evaluated the client's risk preferences, risk ability and risk awareness, we want to re-establish a risk–reward methodology since it is very useful in communication with clients. Nowadays every professional advisor uses a risk–reward diagram in communication with clients since it links to ideas like good and bad which have been burned into the clients' thinking since early childhood. Note that it is very important that the clients understand their portfolio since otherwise they might disrupt the investment strategy, for example when times become difficult, which is a commonly observed mistake.

Risk–Reward Perspective on Prospect Theory

Within the mean–variance analysis, the risk–reward trade-off is implemented using the idea that investors who wish to increase the expected return of their investments must accept returns that deviate more strongly from the mean. De Giorgi et al. (2006) suggest a different perspective on implementing the risk–reward principle. From the investor's point of view, the reward of an investment is not its expected return as in the mean–variance analysis, but the expected return over his reference point, or its average utility gain. It is defined as the sum of all portfolio returns over the investor's reference point, weighted with the corresponding probabilities as perceived by the investors. More precisely, the average gain is defined as

$$pt^{+} = \sum_{\substack{s=1 \\ \Delta s>0}}^{S} w(p_s)v(R_s - RP)$$

where R_s is the return of the portfolio in state s.

Respectively, the risk of the investment is not the deviation from the expected return as in the mean–variance analysis, but the expected portfolio return below the investor's reference point. This is the portfolio's average utility loss, i.e.

$$pt^{-} = -\frac{1}{\beta}\sum_{\substack{s=1 \\ \Delta s<0}}^{S} w(p_s)\,v(RP_s - R_s)$$

where β is the investor's loss aversion. Therefore the utility over the average gains and losses is $PT = pt^{+} - \beta pt^{-}$.

Similar to mean–variance, the average utility gain/loss diagram has a risk–reward dimension, leading to an efficient frontier and a straight line (like the capital market line does in mean–variance analysis) that selects the optimal portfolio. This visual coincidence does not imply that prospect theory portfolios are very similar to mean–variance portfolios. For example, prospect theory will satisfy two-fund separation only in special cases. One such case is the piecewise power value function of Tversky and Kahneman with the risk-free rate being the reference point, as De Giorgi et al. (2006) have shown. Since this value function does not function well due to the non-robustness of the asset allocations, as mentioned above, other value functions like the piecewise quadratic need to be applied and then two-fund separation does not hold. This gives a behavioral explanation of the asset allocation puzzle.

Whether this prospect theory approach in particular makes a difference relative to the industry standard, the mean–variance approach, is a matter of how far actual preferences depart from mean–variance preferences. De Giorgi and Hens (2009) evaluate the risk profiles of 792 clients of a private bank and compare their optimal prospect utility relative to the highest prospect utility restricted to the mean–variance efficient portfolios. They find that on average a client gains utility equivalent to 11 basis points measure in certainty equivalents (i.e. the risk-free rate). Since the average wealth of the clients of that

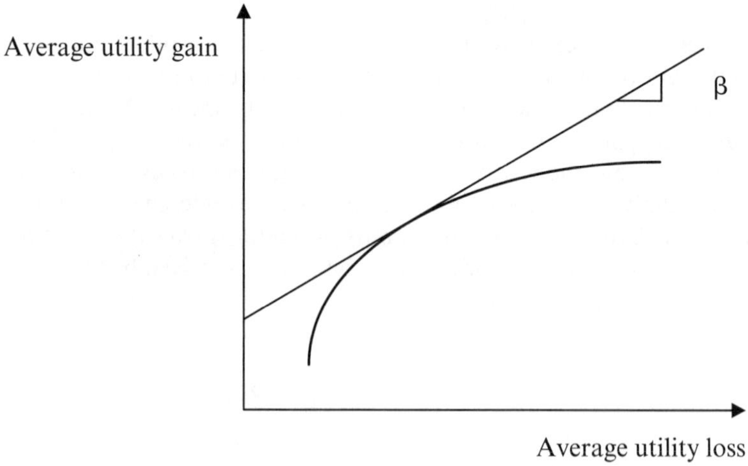

Figure 15.2 A risk–reward perspective on prospect theory

bank is about US$1million, these basis points cumulate a total gain of US$876753 over five years that the bank can share with its clients.[11]

ADVISING CLIENTS OPTIMALLY OVER TIME

This section addresses two questions: (1) how should a behavioral investor adjust his asset allocation over time and (2) should a behavioral investor hold more risky assets when his investment horizon is long rather than short? Note that expected utility restricted to constant relative risk aversion (CRRA) has a simple answer to both questions, as Samuelson (1969) and Merton (1969) showed some long time ago. If markets are efficient so that past returns are not indicative of future returns, then a CRRA investor should hold the same asset allocation independently of the ups and downs of the market and independently of his investment horizon.

The optimal behavior of a rational investor with prospect theory preferences is different. Consider first the second question, which is actually easier to answer. Note that a prospect theory investor is typically loss-averse, i.e. he suffers more from losses than from volatility of returns. Since investments in risky assets are typically rewarded with on average higher returns than investments in the risk-free asset, the probability of making a loss with the risky investment decreases over time. Thus, as Benartzi and Thaler (1995) first observed, a loss-averse investor will hold more risky assets when he has a longer investment horizon, a common feature of advice in practise.[12]

Coming back to the first question, it is instructive to consider two extreme cases. A prospect theory investor who is loss-averse but is neither averse to volatility in gains nor in losses would take more (fewer) risks after a gain (loss), as after a gain (loss) the danger (hope) of ending in the loss (gain) area is smaller. That is to say, this prospect theory investor invests pro-cyclical. As Thaler and Johnson (1990) have described it, every gain is a cushion for later losses and considered to be 'house money' that one is more likely to risk on the market. In the other extreme case, when the investor is not loss-averse but very sensitive to volatility in gains and in losses, then after a gain (loss) the investor finds himself in a more concave (convex) region of his value function so that he reduces (increases) the risk of his portfolio. This is the reasoning of Shefrin and Statman (1985) when they explain the disposition effect, i.e. the observation that investors have a tendency to realize gains more than losses.[13]

Before we close this section, we need to give some warnings. First, it may well be that a behavioral investor changes his reference point over time. Typically after a short period of good returns the investor is no longer satisfied with the risk-free rate. Thus his reference point may change with his risk awareness. This induces time-inconsistent behavior that is irrational. The hope is that the advisor can help the client to focus on moderate reference points independently from the current market phase. Second, one should realize that with gains and losses the risk ability of the client changes over time, implying that after a good period of returns the client can take more risk since his assets now exceed his liabilities to a greater extent than before. The asset allocation then results from the combination of all three aspects of risk: risk awareness, risk preference and risk ability. While risk preferences are relatively stable over time, risk awareness and risk ability might change considerably. Hence optimal dynamic asset allocations are not easy to determine and to convince the client about, so that simple rules like rebalancing fixed proportions of wealth or buying-and-holding of broad diversified indices might after all still be good approximations to solutions of an otherwise intricate decision problem. Thus we argue that advice should rather focus on the static asset allocation problem described above and make sure that the clients really get an asset allocation that suits them well so that they can hold it through the ups and downs of the market. In the course of events over time, the advisor can then refer back to the reasons why the asset allocation is best for the client, even though temporarily it looks suboptimal.

CONCLUSION

This chapter argued that behavioral finance not only gives a theoretical foundation for financial advising, but also has highly practical relevance. To support this claim, this chapter reviewed the main paradigms of traditional finance, expected utility theory and mean–variance analysis, and showed that mean–variance analysis does not serve well as a rational benchmark for investment decision making. Then the chapter gave a short overview on the main insights of behavioral finance and showed which aspects of the observed investor's behavior should be accepted as part of his preferences and which should be corrected because they lead to irrational decisions. The summary of selected behavioral biases and the suggested recommendations should help advisors recognize situations in which one is likely to make mistakes, and provide timely warnings about the pitfalls of intuitive decisions. The aspects of observed investor's behaviour that can be considered as rational are used to build realistic images of investor's preferences. This is important for finding an asset allocation that is optimal for the client because it matches his risk preferences, risk ability and risk awareness, and does not restrict the client to choose among assets with normally distributed returns. A match with investor's risk preferences, restrictions and risk awareness helps the client to identify himself with the recommended asset allocation and hold to the strategy even in turbulent markets.

Further research in behavioral finance and investment advice is currently being conducted to optimize the methods of evaluating clients' risk profiles in laboratory experiments. In those experiments the effect of evaluating the risk profiles in a treatment group can be measured relative to a control group. Moreover, in this chapter we assumed that the advisor is benevolent, i.e. tries to elicit the client's preferences and then suggest a portfolio that is best for the client. An interesting question is how to align the incentives of the advisor with those of the clients when the clients are not totally rational and might want portfolios that are suboptimal for them. In such cases the advisor needs to have the better arguments than his competitors, who might decide to cater to the biases of the client. To this end one can improve the advisory process by introducing diagnostic tools showing the client his biases and by introducing a training module that helps the client to understand the market trade-offs. These tools are currently being introduced, in addition to risk profilers, in the Swiss market – one of the most advanced markets for investment advising and wealth management.

NOTES

1. See Montier (2007) for a through account of this application of behavioral finance.
2. Excellent surveys of general results on the relevance of individual decision making for finance are, e.g., Barberis and Thaler (2002) and Ritter (2003).
3. A preference is complete if it can rank all alternatives (including indifference as a possibility). It is transitive if a ranking of one alternative is better than another while the latter is still better than a third alternative implies that the first alternative is also better than the third alternative. A preference is continuous if it is robust to small changes in the characteristics of the alternatives. Finally, the independence axiom holds if in the comparison of any two alternatives one can reduce the decision to those aspects in which the alternatives differ.
4. Anyone who prefers more to less (i.e. anyone who has monotonic preferences) would prefer a state-dominant lottery.
5. For a sampling of such works see, e.g., Ormiston and Quiggin (1993).
6. Actually, prospect theory has two phases: an editing phase in which the given situation is coded as a choice between lotteries, and an evaluation phase in which the value function and the probability weighting function are applied to the lotteries. In this section we only refer to the valuation phase.
7. Finance mostly uses utility functions with constant relative or constant absolute risk aversion since they are easier to apply in continuous time or continuous state-space models.
8. A lottery with 10 different payoffs from 99 to 99.9 with a 10 percent probability each has a higher prospect utility than the certain payoff of 100.
9. The non-robustness of prospect theory asset allocations based on the piecewise power value function can most easily be seen in the case of a finite state space. Note that excess asset returns are linear in portfolio weights and that by the budget constraint the portfolio weight of the risk-free asset can be expressed by a factor that is one minus the sum of the risky assets' portfolio weights. Hence, e.g., if the reference point is the risk-free rate, this term factors out from the prospect theory criterion, leading to a bang-bang solution of the asset allocation problem. See De Giorgi and Hens (2006) for details.
10. $E(v(R) + RP) = E(v(R)) - \frac{\alpha}{2}E(R - RP)^2 = \mu(R) - \frac{\alpha}{2}\sigma^2(R)$ where $RP = \mu$. For general reference points we still get compatibility with some mean–variance utility – however, not with such a simple one (see Hens and Bachmann, 2008).
11. If the comparison of the optimal prospect theory utility were to a mean–variance portfolio that is based on a mean–variance view of the investor's preferences and not to the highest prospect theory on the mean–variance efficient frontier, then the differences would be even higher.
12. Practical advice uses simple rules like the so-called 'age rule': the proportion of risky assets in the portfolio should be 100 minus the age of the investor, which is clearly in violation of CRRA and efficient markets, but might be acceptable for specific prospect theory parameters.
13. Hens and Vlcek (2009) show, however, that parameter constellations leading to the disposition effect imply that the investment would not have been made in the first place. They then argue that backward-looking behavior in which utility is derived from realizations of gains and losses can explain the disposition effect and, indeed, recently Barberis and Xiong (2008) showed that this idea can be made rigorous.

REFERENCES

Ainslie, G. and G. Haslam (1992), 'Hyperbolic discounting,' in G. Loewenstein and J. Elster (eds), *Choice over Time*, New York: Russell Sage Foundation, pp. 57–92.

Barber, B.M. and T. Odean (2001), 'Boys will be boys: gender, overconfidence and common stock investment,' *Quarterly Journal of Economics*, **116**, 261–92.

Barber, B. and T. Odean (2005), 'All that glitters: the effect of attention and news on the buying behavior of individual and institutional investors,' mimeo, Haas School of Business, Berkeley University, CA.

Barberis, N. and R. Thaler (2002), 'A survey of behavioral finance,' in G.M. Constantinides, M. Harris and R.M. Stulz (eds), *Handbook of the Economics of Finance*, Amsterdam: Elsevier, pp. 1054–116.

Barberis, N. and W. Xiong (2008), 'Realization utility,' Working Paper, Yale University and Princeton University.

Benartzi, S. and R.H. Thaler (1995), 'Myopic loss aversion and the equity premium puzzle,' *Quarterly Journal of Economics*, **110**, 73–92.

Benartzi, S. and R.H. Thaler (1999), 'Risk aversion or myopia? Choices in repeated gambles and retirement investments,' *Management Science*, **45**, 364–81.

Benartzi, S. and R.H. Thaler (2001), 'Naive diversification strategies in defined contribution saving plans,' *American Economic Review*, **91**, 79–98.
Canner, N.N., G. Mankiw and D.N. Weil (1997), 'An asset allocation puzzle,' *American Economic Review*, **87**, 181–91.
De Bondt, W.F.M. and R.H. Thaler (1985), 'Does the stock market overreact?,' *Journal of Finance*, **40**, 793–808.
De Giorgi, E. and T. Hens (2006), 'Making prospect theory fit for finance,' *Financial Markets and Portfolio Management*, **20**, 339–60.
De Giorgi, E. and T. Hens (2009), 'Prospect theory and mean–variance analysis: does it make a difference in wealth management?,' *Investment Management and Financial Innovations*, **6**, 122–9.
De Giorgi, E., T. Hens and H. Levy (2004), 'Prospect theory and the CAPM: a contradiction or a coexistence?,' NCCR Working Paper 85, University of Zurich.
De Giorgi, E., T. Hens and J. Mayer (2006), 'A behavioural foundation of reward–risk porfolio selection and the asset allocation puzzle,' NCCR Working Paper 286, University of Zurich.
Friedman, M. and L.J. Savage (1948), 'The utility analysis of choices involving risk,' *The Journal of Political Economy*, **56**, 279–304.
Hens, T. and K. Bachmann (2008), *Behavioural Finance for Private Banking*, New York: John Wiley & Sons.
Hens, T. and M. Vlcek (2009), 'Does prospect theory explain the disposition effect?,' *Journal of Behavioral Finance*, forthcoming.
Huber, J. (2007), 'J-shaped returns to timing advantage in access to information – experimental evidence and a tentative explanation,' *Journal of Economic Dynamics and Control*, **31**, 2536–72.
Jegadeesh, N. and S. Titman (2001), 'Profitability of momentum strategies: an evaluation of alternative expectations,' *Journal of Finance*, **54**, 699–720.
Kahneman, D. and M.W. Riepe (1998), 'Aspects of investor psychology: beliefs, preferences, and biases investment advisors should know about,' *Journal of Portfolio Management*, **24**, 52–65.
Kahneman, D. and A. Tversky (1979), 'Prospect theory: an analysis of decision under risk,' *Econometrica*, **47**, 263–91.
Karmakar, U.S. (1978), 'Subjective weighted utility and the Allais paradox,' *Organizational Behavior and Human Performance*, **24**, 67–72.
Karmakar, U.S. (1979), 'Subjective weighted utility: a descriptive extension of the expected utility model,' *Organizational Behavior and Human Performance*, **21**, 61–72.
Markowitz, H. (1952), 'Portfolio selection,' *Journal of Finance*, **7**, 77–91.
Merton, R.C. (1969), 'Lifetime portfolio selection under uncertainty: the continuous-time case,' *Review of Economics and Statistics*, **51**, 247–57.
Montier, J. (2007), *Behavioural Investing: A Practitioner's Guide to Applying Behavioural Finance*, New York: John Wiley & Sons.
Ormiston, M. and J. Quiggin (1993), 'Two-parameter decision models and rank-dependent expected utility,' *Journal of Risk and Uncertainty*, **7**, 273–82.
Pompian, M.M. (2006), *Behavioural Finance and Wealth Management: Building Optimal Portfolios that Account for Investor Biases*, New York: John Wiley & Sons.
Raiffa, H. (1968), *Decision Analysis: Introductory Lectures on Choice under Uncertainty*, Reading, MA: Addison-Wesley.
Rieger, M.O. and M. Wang (2008), 'Prospect theory for continuous distributions,' *Journal of Risk and Uncertainty*, **36**, 83–102.
Ritter, J.R. (2003), 'Behavioral finance,' *Pacific-Basin Finance Journal*, **11**, 429–37.
Samuelson, P. (1969), 'Lifetime portfolio selection by dynamic stochastic programming,' *Review of Economics and Statistics*, **51**, 239–46.
Savage, L.J. (1954), *The Foundations of Statistics*, New York: John Wiley & Sons.
Shefrin, H. and M. Statman (1985), 'The disposition to sell winners too early and ride losers too long: theory and evidence,' *Journal of Finance*, **40**, 777–90.
Shefrin, H. and S. Statman (1995), 'Making sense of beta, size, and book-to-market,' *Journal of Portfolio Management*, **21**, 26–34.
Sirri, E.R. and P. Tufano (1998), 'Costly search and mutual funds flow,' *Journal of Finance*, **53**, 1589–622.
Stotz, O. and R. von Nitzsch (2005), 'The perception of control and the levels of overconfidence – evidence from analysts' earnings estimates and prices targets,' *Journal of Behavioral Finance*, **6**, 121–8.
Thaler, R.H. (1981), 'Some empirical evidence on dynamic inconsistency,' *Economics Letters*, **8**, 201–7.
Thaler, R. and E.J. Johnson (1990), 'Gambling with the house money and trying to break even: the effects of prior outcomes on risky choice,' *Management Science*, **36**, 643–60.
Tobin, J. (1958), 'Liquidity preference as behavior towards risk,' *Review of Economic Studies*, **25**, 65–86.
Tversky, A. and D. Kahneman (1974), 'Judgment under uncertainty: heuristics and biases,' *Science*, **185**, 1124–31.

Tversky, A. and D. Kahneman (1981), 'The framing of decisions and the rationality of choice,' *Science*, **211**, 455–8.
Tversky, A. and D. Kahneman (1992), 'Advances in prospect theory: cumulative representation of uncertainty,' *Journal of Risk and Uncertainty*, **5**, 297–323.

PART III

GLOBAL BEHAVIOR

16 Measuring the impact of behavioral traders in the market for closed-end country funds from 2002 to 2009

Hugh Kelley and Tom Evans

A diverse body of empirical evidence demonstrates deviations of market prices from their fundamental values (see Froot and Thaler, 1990; Hirshleifer, 2001; Barberis and Thaler, 2003, and Pesendorfer, 2006 for introductions to, or surveys of, behavioral finance research and examples of the many field anomalies). Smith et al. (1988) is an early study that documents these bubbles in experimental markets. One anomaly that has received a substantial amount of attention but remains largely unexplained is the large and variable discount observed between closed-end country fund prices and their exchange-rate-adjusted net asset values (NAV); see Lee et al. (1991) and Kelley (2004).

To account for this and other field anomalies, theorists have attempted to inject more reality into asset pricing models. One strain of the literature has attempted to model the institutional environment within which agents trade by including realistic features such as: market incompleteness, forms of market segmentation, unknown risk features, asymmetric private information, transaction costs and price stickiness, all of which produce some type of limits to arbitrage and therefore inefficient prices. Increased theoretical reality may also be beneficial for specifying the expectations formation traits of economic agents.

Some of the earliest extensions to the rational expectations utility-maximizing agent included state-invariant features such as risk aversion and discounting of future utility. More recent theories postulate the presence of state-dependent irrational biases on the part of agents. See Basov (2005) for a comparative study of static versus dynamic/state-dependent bounded rationality approaches. In these theories the information state of the environment, referring to the amount and characteristics of the public financial news, can influence traders' expectations formation abilities. In subsequent tests of these behavioral theories, the magnitude of price deviations from fundamental value can be shown to be a function of the severity of agents' state-dependent boundedly rational beliefs, and the timing is related to the timing of bias trigger states.

Unfortunately, in many of the early behavioral models the irrational traders incorporated into theory were hypothesized, rather than being based upon direct experimental evidence. The natural criticism of such an approach, well described in Daniel et al. (2000), is that the potential universe of conceivable cognitive bias is unbounded. As a result, almost any in-sample pricing behavior can be reproduced with enough cognitive biases.

To address this problem, many authors argue that the goal of the behavioral literature should be to find the one top bias describing all anomalous economic behavior. Unfortunately, such an approach operates on the assumption that there are in fact a small number of non-rational behaviors that produce all these observed anomalies, which is strongly rejected by experimental data. However, another way to reduce this universe is to use experimental evidence as a basis for one's assumptions about traders' expectations formation behavior. This allows more rigorous specifications of the non-rational agents, while avoiding the pitfalls of identifying a likely non-existent all-encompassing bias.

The primary purpose of this behavioral research is to determine whether a model incorporating one rational and two experimentally based behavioral traders can provide additional insight into the timing and magnitude of NYSE closed-end country fund discount movements. The study provides several methodological extensions relative to earlier research. First, to provide a more rigorous basis for the new behavioral traders, the state-dependent over- and underreaction biases incorporated into theory have direct experimental support from financially oriented forecasting experiments. Second, the information that defines the financial news states are obtained from a newly updated news data set from transcripts of Lou Dobbs CNN *Moneyline* and its later incarnations. Third, empirical tests of the model's out-of-sample predictive ability utilizes a recent sample of weekly data for a large number of country funds.

The general result of the behavioral model is a predicted relationship between the timing and magnitude of country fund discount changes and experimentally based behavioral variables constructed to quantify particular event states. These behavioral variables interact with indicator variables summarizing the variance/noise in the predictor variable or the volume of relevant CNN news with information describing the sign of the rationally expected NAV revision. Out-of-sample tests with field country fund data indicate that a significant amount of unexplained price movements relative to fundamental information can be explained by these behavioral variables.

RELATED BEHAVIORAL LITERATURE

Empirical Literature

The empirical literature that motivates this study describes anomalous closed-end country fund price movements relative to their underlying stocks' overall NAVs, i.e. the weighted average of the prices of the underlying stocks of the fund (see Lee et al., 1991). Like most closed-end funds, these country funds trade at persistent and variable discounts relative to their NAVs. And some of the most dramatic deviations of price from NAV occur after prominent news events about the funds' host country, or following previous episodes of NAV volatility.

Country fund data provide a particularly useful data set for exploring behavioral hypotheses because: (1) they have a well-defined measure of fundamental value, the NAVs; (2) there is substantial evidence of anomalous fund price movements relative to NAV; and (3) these and other asset prices have been shown to be influenced by news events (see Ramchander et al., 2008; Fuertes and Thomas, 2006; Mullainathan and Shleifer, 2005; Clark et al., 2004).

The presence and variability of country fund discounts themselves represent a pricing anomaly. The value-additivity principal predicts that, in an efficient market, the price of the funds should match their NAV. Two branches of literature have developed to explain these price anomalies, one focusing on institutional incompleteness or market frictions, and the other focusing on the potential bounded rationality of individual or groups of traders (see Bosner-Neal et al., 1990 for an application of the former theories to the country fund literature, and Heaton and Korajczyk, 2002 for a more general review).

In subsequent tests of these theories, the magnitude and to some extent the timing of price deviations from fundamental value can be related to specific institutional features. However, market institutions are fairly slow to evolve, so this approach doesn't fully explain the timing of price discount movements, which occur at a much higher frequency than institutional changes. The competing theories postulate that closed-end fund discounts are more generally a result of the interaction among boundedly rational and rational market participants.

Behavioral Theory

The theoretical behavioral literature that motivates this study considers hypothetical asset markets with traders who form heterogeneous expectations about the distribution of revisions to a risky asset. Typically these distributional uncertainty theories include both: (1) rational agents, who can correctly identify the mean and variance of this distribution; and (2) behavioral agents, whose beliefs about this distribution may be biased and mistaken.

The most directly comparable theoretical paper is DeLong et al. (1990) (henceforth DSSW90), which combines rational expectations traders with Black's (1986) 'noise' traders, whose expectations about asset returns are randomly distributed around the true mean. An extension by Klibanoff et al. (1998) (KLW98) includes behavioral traders who display state-dependent inertia in their expectations updating. The states in KLW98's model refer to periods with larger or smaller amounts of *New York Times* front-page financial news coverage. They argue that in usual states, traders display inertia; that is, their expectations of the random walk mean return is a weighted average of many lagged returns. But in event states, that is, periods with a large amount of financial news, this inertia evaporates and traders' expectations of the mean return is based simply upon last-period returns, which should be the case for a random walk variable.

Their model provides predictions about the timing of country fund discount movements and suggests that these movements should be related to the salience of *New York Times* news. They successfully test their model's predictions regarding the timing of discount movements with NYSE country fund data and *New York Times* news information.

Odean (1998) examined the effects of including behavioral traders who show overconfidence toward privately available information. This overconfidence intuitively takes the form of overreaction to information signals due to their perceived high salience. Varian (1989) and Harris and Raviv (1993) also postulate that traders have different expectations about the mean of the returns distribution due to differences in their processing of public information. In Varian, traders use the same Bayesian processing methodology but have different priors; and in Harris and Raviv, agents are assumed to use heterogeneous information processing methods with similar information.

Kandel and Pearson (1995) include behavioral traders whose perceptions of the mean and the variance of the returns distribution differs from the rational traders' beliefs. In all these models traders' heterogeneous expectations lead to irrational demands for assets, and therefore distorted equilibrium prices.

Shefrin and Statman (1994) provide another relevant model with: (1) rational traders who use Bayes's rule for forming expectations about a stochastic asset's mean returns, and (2) behavioral traders who display two types of cognitive errors. Based on earlier experimental evidence, they postulate that one behavioral trader overweights recent information while neglecting priors, that is displays 'base rate neglect' (see Gluck and Bower, 1988). The second is susceptible to 'gambler's fallacy,' and expects short-run probabilities to mimic long-run probabilities more than is justified (see Camerer, 1995). Shefrin and Statman's (1994) model shows that in the presence of only rational traders, the market has a 'single driver' property, and prices are based only on rational Bayesian processing of fundamental information. Alternatively, in the presence of behavioral traders, the market has a 'multiple drivers' characteristic, and prices depend on both fundamental information and traders' irrational beliefs.

Importantly, a key feature of these distributional uncertainty models is the assumption that there are some institutional or other limits to rational traders' ability to arbitrage away country fund price differentials from fundamental value. In the absence of such segmentation and under sufficient conditions, boundedly rational traders may be competed out of the market, resulting in rational prices (Sandroni, 2005). In the presence of an incomplete market, however, behavioral biases can potentially persist and affect prices (Blume and Easley, 2006).

Remaining consistent with the latter literature, this study assumes that some segmentation exists between the country fund and NAV markets. This assumption can be justified for country fund data because international markets have at least limited market segmentation, and by the fact that the funds considered are closed-end. A crucial point is that this market segmentation is not the sole source of anomalous price movements. Instead, it simply allows individual behavior to be incompletely arbitraged out of the market. As a result, market incompleteness is only an indirect cause of anomalous price behavior.

In summary, these empirical and theoretical studies demonstrate that additional insights into the behavior of asset prices can be provided by multi-agent models that allow investor bounded rationality. Theoretically, price deviations from fundamental value can be shown to be a function of traders' misperceptions. Empirically, the timing of states that trigger these biases can be shown to significantly predict the timing of anomalous price movements.

The next section presents the experimental evidence for the forms of bounded rationality we consider. The third section presents a general model that combines rational traders and traders displaying state-dependent over- and underreaction. The last section tests model predictions about the timing and magnitude of discount variations using NYSE asset prices for active funds and CNN *Moneyline* transcript data spanning 2002–09. Previous work (Kelley, 2004) conducts similar tests for a 1998–2002 sample. A new sample is used in current work to provide a generalization test of model predictions.

EXPERIMENTAL EVIDENCE OF COGNITIVE BIAS

The Relevance of Experimental Results for Behavioral Theory

A key aspect of this study is the use of experimental evidence as a basis for the theoretical assumptions about traders' potentially boundedly rational behavior. Although some notable studies link their assumptions about non-rational behavior to experimental evidence (see in particular Shefrin and Statman, 1994; Laibson, 1997; and Odean, 1998; Henker and Owen, 2008), many others simply assume the presence of some bias. These latter studies certainly extend our knowledge of financial markets by demonstrating how prices will behave if traders of the postulated type are present. However, experimental evidence provides even more insights into market price movements by incorporating agent types actually observed in financially oriented forecasting experiments.

The Experimental Evidence

A large body of experimental economics and psychology evidence demonstrates that humans display a variety of cognitive errors when forming expectations and making decisions. Evidence of cognitive bias described as systematic over- or underreaction to information has been observed in experimental studies by Estes (1954), Dudycha and Naylor (1966), and later by Griffin and Tversky (1992); more recent articles include Friedman and Massaro (1997), Kitzis et al. (1998), Gillette et al. (1999), and Brunnermeier and Parker (2005). This evidence suggests that over- and underreaction biases are a generally permanent characteristic of some subset of subjects.

Other experimental research has begun to investigate if humans' forecasting biases are in fact triggered by some feature or state of the experimental information environment. If we can show that traders' bias is triggered by specific information state, we could theoretically provide out-of-sample predictions about when country fund price discounts will have the multiple driver feature described by Shefrin and Statman (1994).

Kelley and Friedman (2002, 2008) investigate the state-dependency of bias with a financially oriented individual-choice experiment. In this experiment subjects are asked to provide a forecast f of a continuous and stochastic target price change p. The target is dependent upon two observed stochastic stimuli realizations $x = [x_1, x_2]$ and the indirectly observed stochastic term $\varepsilon \sim U(0, \sigma_\varepsilon^2)$ via the functional relationship $p = a \cdot x + \varepsilon$. The authors presented several treatment states to subjects designed to mimic variable field forecasting conditions. The primary manipulation of interest was motivated by the financial market regularity, heteroskedasticity.

The simplification studied in these experiments postulates the presence of two forecasted-price variance states, a low- and high-noise/variance state. We note that most subjects attempting to forecast in the high-noise state overreacted or overweighted the importance of all current information.

Other experimental work by Edgell et al. (1996) and Kelley and Busemeyer (2008) asked subjects to forecast a probabilistic price change p that was dependent upon a larger number of predictors x_j. The functional relationship among prices and predictors was identical to the earlier experiment except that $j > 2$. This high-information manipulation was designed to determine if the field regularity, variable news levels, influences subjects'

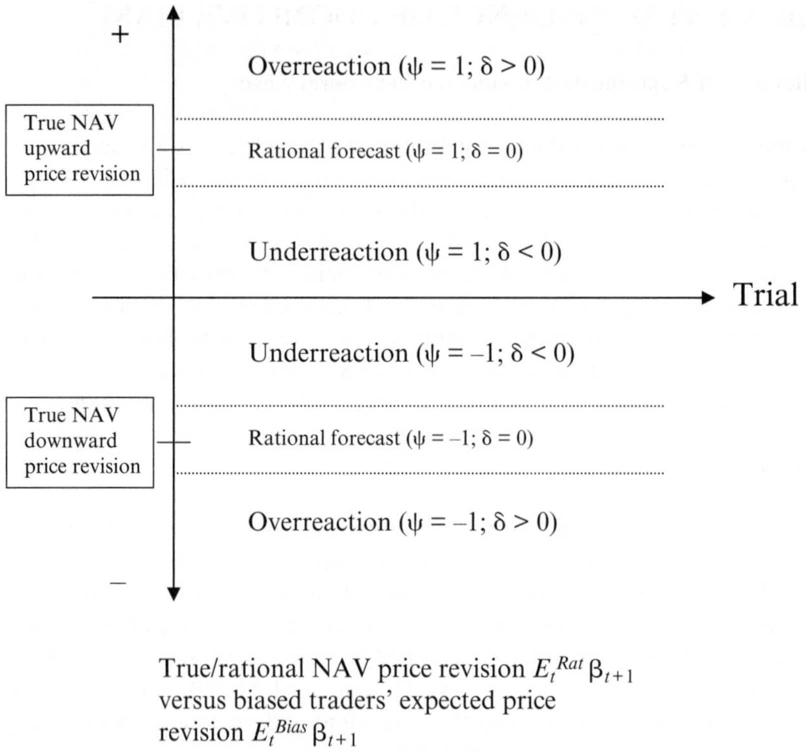

Note: This figure represents the forecasting bias patterns observed in the experimental data; and it represents how the model's rational and the over- and underreaction traders' NAV price forecasts would be related to the true NAV price change, for two possible NAV price revisions. Expected prices are denoted $E(n_{t+1}|\beta_t) = n_t + E_t\beta_{t+1} + \psi \cdot \delta$. The rational forecast is indicated by the confidence interval around the true price change. ($\psi = 1$) refers to rationally expected NAV appreciation, while ($\psi = -1$) refers to a rationally expected depreciation. Overreaction, ($\delta > 0$), corresponds to the outer regions where traders overweight fundamental information and jump too high or too low in the expectations. Underreaction, ($\delta < 0$), corresponds to the inner regions where traders do not jump far enough upward or downwards in their expectations.

Figure 16.1 Experimentally observed forecasting patterns for over- or underreaction given two potential NAV price changes

ability to form expectations. Here discrete news events are considered analogous to the number of experimental price predictors. A low number of news events would be equivalent to the $j = 2$ experiments, while many news events can be proxied by the $j > 2$ manipulation. As expected, cognitive errors emerged in the high-information state as subjects became overwhelmed with information. But surprisingly, these errors proved to be systematic: across all trials, individuals underreacted to all current information.

Figure 16.1 is a graphic representation of over- and underreaction forecasting patterns. Both are measured relative to what would be the rational expectations response to NAV change information. From the figure one can see that overreaction can correspond to jumping too high or too low relative to what fundamental information rationally predicts. Similarly, underreaction means a subject did not jump far enough upwards or downwards in response to fundamental information. To test for such behavior with field data one needs: (1) to know the sign of the rationally expected NAV revision, $\psi = 1$ or -1, that is an appreciation or depreciation of the NAV; and (2) to have an indicator of the presence and severity of the event state, that is δ describing the level of variance of NAV or amount of news in the environment.

The Information State

The institutional and informational settings of these individual-choice experiments are very similar to the context of the model in the third section. As a result, we can draw a connection between information states in these two settings. In theory, one can simply postulate the existence of unique market states, and hypothesize that some traders alter their behavior during these states.

To provide empirical content to these information states, however, we need to be more specific. The information states that trigger over- and underreaction behaviors in the individual-choice experiments were either: (1) the presence of high noise, that is high variance of the forecasted price, or (2) the presence of a large amount of predictor information. The empirical counterpart of these states for the field country fund data are either: (1) high sample variance of the country funds' NAVs, or (2) a large amount of CNN *Moneyline* financial news. We provide details for constructing the behavioral variables corresponding to the field data in Section IV.

Cognitive Bias in Field Financial Markets

Why are we likely to observe these individual trader biases in field markets? In addition to ubiquitous experimental evidence, there is a large amount of field evidence that prices seem to over- or underreact relative to the change predicted by fundamental information. Examples are provided by many authors, particularly Shiller (1981) and Hong and Stein (1999).

A second reason concerns the complexity of the field forecasting setting relative to the experimental environment. In many experimental settings, subjects face a favorable information environment that should facilitate accurate forecasts. They are usually aware that the forecasted target is largely dependent upon only a few observed predictors, and they receive quick and clear feedback about their forecasting accuracy. Also, there are no endogenous aspects of price determinations *vis-à-vis* their own or others' past decisions. Yet, despite the simplicity of the financial market, subjects still display persistent expectations biases. We can then reasonably expect that actual traders in the field setting might display similar behavior, if only because of the increased complexity of the field markets. A final reason why bias may influence field financial markets is that traders may attend to media information that does not necessarily embody relevant fundamental value information and instead is more geared toward entertainment (Clark et al., 2004).

A common counter-argument to this assertion, though, is that there may be insufficient financial motivations for the experimental subjects to provide accurate forecasts. Field traders have much more to gain or lose, so their forecasts are forced to be efficient through Darwinian profit forces. This criticism cannot be avoided, but it could be applied to any experimental study. However, Holt and Laury (2002) find that behavior remains fairly consistent over relatively large ranges of payments, so this is most likely not the major source of the biased behavior.

Finally, it is possible that experimental subjects make systematic errors because they are relatively inexperienced in a particular forecasting task. Alternatively, some argue that in field financial markets, successful traders that have not succumbed to Darwinian profit forces have more experience, and will therefore not display bias. However, some financial research suggests that the experienced traders may actually display more bias than novice traders due to overconfidence in perceived successful theories and models (see DeBondt and Thaler, 1990; Gervais and Odean, 2001).

In general, these experimental results extend our knowledge of financial markets by offering direct evidence about asset price forecasting behavior. First, as we noted earlier, the evidence suggests that overreaction to information may be triggered by high-noise states. Second, underreaction toward information may be triggered by high-information states. Most importantly, these results indicate that the over- and underreaction biases are state-dependent, i.e. dependent upon the previous measurable information state of the environment. The next step is to describe an analytical model that aggregates both rational and behavioral traders' expectations into an equilibrium price.

THE EXPERIMENTALLY BASED BEHAVIORAL MODEL

The model used to aggregate traders' expectations and asset demands into an equilibrium price is an overlapping-generations distributional-uncertainty approach. It is based on the work of DSSW90 and KLW98, but it is unique in that the characteristics of the behavioral trader class are based on evidence from related asset price forecasting experiments. The purpose of the model is to analytically quantify the influences of both fundamental information and behavioral traders' biased expectations on the equilibrium price of a country fund asset.

The key aspects of this model are that:

1. There are two markets of interest, the home market with rational and behavioral traders, and the foreign market with only rational traders.[1]
2. There are two states of the world, usual states, which trigger no biased behavior, and event states, which cause some fraction of agents in the home market to display biases in their expectations about risky asset price changes.
3. The home market is assumed to contain riskless (known return) and risky (probabilistic return) assets. The riskless asset earns the rate of return $1 + r$, is elastically supplied, and has price p_t normalized to one unit of a consumable good. In an optimally balanced portfolio, a domestic investor should be just indifferent between investing in the riskless asset and the domestically traded country fund. Thus this riskless asset price is representative of the rationally expected return to the country fund. The risky asset, which represents the net asset value (NAV) or the weighted average of the security prices underlying the country fund, has supply normalized to 1 and has price n_t.
4. Traders are assumed to live for two periods.

Traders in the home market receive an endowment which they invest at the end of period t. They then consume the proceeds of their investment at the end of period $t + 1$, and they leave no bequests. These investors are assumed to have constant absolute risk aversion utility functions incorporating the proceeds from investments in risky and riskless assets. The goal of each agent is to maximize the expected value of their portfolio in the second period given expected revisions to the foreign asset n underlying p.

Each period the investors receive a public signal β describing the actual revision to the price of the risky assets n; that is $n_{t+1} = n_t + \beta_{t+1}$. This signal could be interpreted as information describing the dividend payments or retained earnings of the productive assets within the country fund's NAV. Further, the efficient markets hypothesis (EMH) suggests that all relevant information needed to predict the revisions to n should already be incorporated into its market price. As a result, any new relevant information should arrive randomly, so the NAV revision process should objectively follow a random walk.

The key distinction between rational and behavioral traders, then, hinges on the expectations they form about the revision process for the risky NAV asset n. Since the EMH states that asset prices should evolve randomly, the rationally expected revision β to the risky asset n has the objective distribution:

$$E_t\beta_{t+1} \sim N(\beta_t(1 + r), \sigma_\beta^2) \tag{16.1}$$

That is, the time t rational expectation of next period revision $E_t\beta_{t+1}$ is simply the interest-rate-adjusted revision observed last period, that is $E_t\beta_{t+1} = \beta_t(1 + r)$.

However, it is also assumed that some fraction of all investors in the home market are behavioral and display state-dependent bias in their expectations regarding the revision to the risky asset. These behavioral traders' expectations are described by:

$$E^B_t\beta_{t+1} \sim N((\beta_t + \pi_t)(1 + r), \sigma_\beta^2) \tag{16.2}$$

The superscript B refers to behavioral traders' expectations, which include some state-dependent over- or underreaction bias π_t in the perceived mean of the NAV revisions distribution. This bias equals zero during usual states, but is non-zero in event states.

Since the country fund is composed of the NAV asset, its price p should reflect investors' expectations regarding revisions to the NAV n (Tsai et al., 2007). Thus domestic country fund price will have the multiple driver characteristic and reflect both fundamental NAV information and the biased expectations of behavioral traders if: (1) there are some behavioral trades present, and (2) they over- or underreact in their expectations of NAV revisions following event states. We can obtain closed-form expressions that quantify this multiple driver property of country fund prices by assuming that the conditional variance of the country fund asset σ_p^2 is constant through time, and can be related to the variance of the true revision process σ_β^2.

A key aspect of this multi-state pricing model is that there will be two equilibrium expressions for country fund prices, one for usual states and one for event states. The differences in the expressions define the event state impact of bias on the country fund price. The usual state equilibrium price for the country fund is

$$p_{t+1,u} = a_u{\cdot}n_{t+1} - A_u{\cdot}\sigma^2_\beta + B_u{\cdot}\pi_t - C_u{\cdot}\sigma^2_\pi \tag{16.3}$$

while the event state price is given as

$$p_{t+1,e} = a_u{\cdot}n_{t+1} - A_e{\cdot}\sigma^2_\beta + B_e{\cdot}\pi_t - C_e{\cdot}\sigma^2_\pi \tag{16.4}$$

In both these expressions a_u represents the usual level of market sentiment, that is bullish versus bearish expectations, which are assumed not to change across states. n represents the NAV price of the stocks underlying the country fund price p. σ^2_β represents the variance of the NAV revision process, π_t represents any state-dependent bias in traders' NAV revision expectations, and σ^2_π represents the variance of these biased expectations. It can be shown that $A_u = A_e$ and $C_u = C_e$, but $B_u \neq B_e$ (see Kelley, 2004 for more details regarding this derivation).

It is useful to construct the following variable to represent the deviation of the country fund p from its fundamental or NAV n:

$$D_{t+1} = (n_{t+1} / p_{t+1}) - 1 \tag{16.5}$$

These deviations can represent a discount $D_{t+1} > 0$ or a premium $D_{t+1} < 0$.

Price Effects of Behavioral Traders

Equations (16.3) and (16.4) summarize the model predictions about the drivers that may cause the fund's price to deviate from its NAV. The first two and the fourth terms represent conflicting state-invariant influences on the equilibrium price. In both expressions any bearish market sentiment, $a_u < 1$, and the 'create space' or risk adjustment terms, σ^2_β and σ^2_π, tend to imply state-invariant market-price discounts relative to their NAVs. Any bullish sentiment, $a_u > 1$, would imply state-invariant price premia.

Finally, if some traders do display bias in their expectations following event states, the two pricing equations will differ since $B_e \neq B_u$. The state-dependent prediction of the model is summarized by the difference $p_{t+1,e} - p_{t,u}$, equation (16.4) minus lagged (16.3).

$$p_{t+1,e} - p_{t,u} = a_u{\cdot}(n_{t+1} - n_t) - E{\cdot}\pi_t \tag{16.6}$$

$E = B_e - B_u > 0$ for all parameter values. This expression describes the change in the observed fund price when moving from a time t usual state to a $t + 1$ event state. The difference $n_{t+1} - n_t$ represents the change in the country fund price attributable to changes in the fund's NAV, that is its fundamental value after adjusting for market sentiment. The last right-hand-side term represents the state-dependent effect that biased traders have on the country fund prices. Rearranging (16.6) gives:

$$a_u\Delta n_{t+1} - \Delta p_{t+1} = E{\cdot}\pi_t \tag{16.7}$$

where $\Delta n_{t+1} = n_{t+1} - n_t$, $\Delta p_{t+1} = p_{t+1} - p_t$. Intuitively, the timing of country fund price deviations from NAV should correspond to the event states that create expectations bias, and the magnitude of the deviation reflects the severity of the event state.

Defining State-dependant Expectations Bias

Equation (16.7) indicates that market prices will deviate from NAV based upon the extent of the behavioral traders' bias π. For this variable to mimic the expectations biases observed in the experimental results it needs to be a function of the sign of the rationally expected NAV revision ψ, and of an event state indicator δ.

Let the indicator variable ψ represent the sign of the expected NAV revision:

$$\psi_t = \begin{matrix} 1 & \text{if} & E_t\beta_{t+1} > 0 \\ 0 & \text{if} & E_t\beta_{t+1} = 0 \\ -1 & \text{if} & E_t\beta_{t+1} < 0 \end{matrix} \tag{16.8}$$

Next, let the indicator variable δ identify the type and severity of an event state. $\delta > 0$ describes an overreaction trigger state, $\delta < 0$ describes an underreaction state, and $\delta = 0$ describes a usual state. The specific data used to relate these indicator variables to measurable data are described in equations (16.11) and (16.12). δ will characterize either the level of NAV variance or the level of financial news.

This then allows us to define the behavioral bias term as

$$\pi_t = \psi_t \cdot \delta_t \tag{16.9}$$

Figure 16.1 graphically represents the expectations bias patterns observed in the forecasting experiments, and the forecasting patterns associated with the behavioral variable $\pi = f(\psi, \delta)$. Overreaction means jumping too far up or down in expectation of price change. Underreaction means not jumping far enough in either direction. Intuitively, we observe that a bias variable with the properties of (16.9) can generate the expectations bias patterns described in Figure 16.1. Then, combining the solution to the behavioral pricing model (16.7) with the definition of the bias term (16.9), we obtain four predictions regarding possible discount movements (see Figure 16.2).

If there is overreaction (underreaction) and a rationally expected NAV appreciation, then $\delta > 0$ ($\delta < 0$) and $\psi = 1$; so the sign of the bias term will be $\pi > 0$ ($\pi < 0$) and with (16.7) this predicts an increase (decrease) in the discount following event states.[2]

If there is overreaction (underreaction) and a rationally expected NAV depreciation, then $\delta > 0$ ($\delta < 0$) and $\psi = -1$; so the sign of the bias term will be $\pi < 0$ ($\pi > 0$) and with (16.7) this predicts a decrease (increase) in the discount after event states.

Testable Hypotheses

These predictions suggest two testable propositions regarding changes in the country fund discount and traders' state dependent expectations biases π:

Proposition 1: If agents overreact to price signals in high-noise event states, the discount should increase if there is a rationally expected NAV appreciation and decrease if there is an expected depreciation.

Proposition 2: If agents underreact to price signals in high-information event states,

> the discount should decrease if there is an expected NAV appreciation and increase if there is an expected depreciation.

If one defines $\delta > 0$ for both event trigger states and $\delta = 0$ for usual states, the estimated sign of θ from equation (16.10) will allow us to distinguish whether over- or underreaction is influencing prices for a particular event state i.

$$\Delta D_{t+1} = \theta_i \pi_{i,t} + e_t \tag{16.10}$$

Overreaction would be described by $\theta > 0$, while $\theta < 0$ would signify underreaction. The significance of these coefficients describes the extent to which the timing of discount movements can be related to the timing of event trigger states. The absolute size of the coefficient describes the magnitude of the behavioral driver's influence on country fund prices.

The next section defines the specific behavioral terms and tests the validity of the two propositions for a sample of field country fund data.

DATA

Country Fund Summary Statistics

The sample of country fund data used to test the model propositions includes 34 active single and multi-country funds spanning January 2002 to August 2009 on a weekly basis (the appendix gives more details). The data cover 29 countries, and are obtained from

Rationally expected NAV change at t	Forecasting bias at t	Overreaction $\delta > 0$	Underreaction $\delta < 0$
	Appreciation of fundamental value $\psi = 1$	Discount increases at $t + 1$	Discount decreases at $t + 1$
	Depreciation of fundamental value $\psi = -1$	Discount decreases at $t + 1$	Discount increases at $t + 1$

Figure 16.2 Possible discount movements predicted by the behavioral model equations (16.7)–(16.9)

Datastream and the funds themselves, and represent the approximately synchronous Friday closing values for the country fund and NAV prices.[3] The NAVs are reported by the funds themselves and converted into dollars with the most recent spot exchange rate. There are 397 observations for each fund for a total of 13498 observations.

Table 16.1 provides summary statistics describing each country fund's NAV and market-price changes. Several stylized facts stand out. First, both average NAV and market-price changes lie within 1 standard deviation of zero. This suggests that we cannot reject the hypothesis that these price revisions evolve as a random walk at the 1 percent significance level; and this is consistent with our modeling assumptions.

Second, comparing the standard deviations for the NAVs (column 4) and market prices (column 6) indicates that 26 of 34 funds' prices are more variable than would be expected from variations in their fundamental or net asset values. To illustrate this effect, column 7 provides an indicator variable with a value of 1 if the fund price standard deviation exceeds fundamental NAV standard deviation. This result is consistent with Shiller's (1981) observation that market prices seem to display 'excess volatility' with respect to fundamental information.

Table 16.2 provides summary statistics demonstrating the central anomaly of the study, the average and volatile country fund discount. We first observe that 12 of 34 funds have statistically significant average discounts during this sample period, that is discounts 2 or more standard deviations from zero, implying significance at the 5 percent level (see column 7, which reports an indicator variable with a value of 1 for funds with significant discounts).

Second, many more funds have large episodic deviations, as illustrated by the maximal and minimal discount values. Discounts are as large as 171 percent, for the Thailand fund, compared to a maximum premium of −52 percent for the Cornerstone Total Return fund. Together these facts suggest that something other than fundamental information is influencing price changes, and investors' biased expectations is one possibility.

State-dependent Bias in the Country Fund Market

To construct the behavioral variable π we must define the event state indicator variable δ as well as the expected sign of the revision ψ. In the experimental data, an event state was represented by either high forecasted variable variance, or large amounts of predictor information. For the country fund market, an event state is defined by either the NAV variance or by the volume of relevant investing news. Furthermore, since we observe in Table 16.1 that the NAV prices evolve as a random walk, the sign of the expected revision is simply the sign of the previous revision, that is $\psi_t = (sign(\beta_{t-1}))$ (see section III).

Next, let the indicator for the high forecasted variable variance, that is an overreaction event state, take the general form $\delta_{HN} = \sigma_n^2$. The high-noise behavioral variable, $\pi_{1,t,}$ is:

$$\pi_{1,t} = \psi_t \cdot \sigma_{n,t}^2 \tag{16.11}$$

In other words, the overreaction bias displayed by traders is a function of the sign of the rationally expected revision ψ times the NAV variance from the week preceding the current time *t* Friday.

Next, let the indicator for the high-information state δ_{NEWS} take the general form

Table 16.1 Country fund NAV (n) and country fund price (p) summary statistics

Fund	Nobs	$n_{t+1} - n_t$ mean	Std dev. σ_n	$p_{t+1} - p_t$ mean	Std dev. σ_p	Excess volatility? $(\sigma_n > \sigma_p) = 1$
APB	396	0.00	0.78	0.00	0.80	1
CH	396	0.02	0.58	0.02	0.73	1
CHN	396	0.02	1.15	0.03	1.62	1
CRF	396	−0.07	0.46	−0.05	1.23	1
GCH	396	0.01	1.03	0.01	1.18	1
GF	396	0.01	0.46	0.01	0.44	0
GRR	396	0.02	0.60	0.03	0.71	1
IAF	396	0.01	0.36	0.01	0.51	1
IFN	396	0.04	1.49	0.05	2.05	1
IIF	396	0.02	1.53	0.03	1.81	1
IRL	396	−0.02	0.70	−0.01	0.87	1
ISL	396	0.00	0.49	0.00	0.62	1
JEQ	396	0.00	0.18	0.00	0.26	1
JFC	396	0.01	0.73	0.02	0.81	1
JOF	396	0.01	0.29	0.00	0.51	1
KEF	396	0.01	0.36	0.01	0.36	0
KF	396	−0.35	13.52	−0.28	13.27	0
LAQ	396	0.05	1.59	0.05	1.53	0
LDF	396	0.01	1.09	0.01	1.11	1
MSF	396	0.00	0.86	0.01	0.88	1
MXE	396	0.00	0.91	−0.01	1.17	1
MXF	396	0.01	1.14	0.01	1.07	0
SGF	396	0.02	0.39	0.02	0.43	1
SNF	396	0.00	0.29	−0.01	0.42	1
SWZ	396	0.00	0.40	0.00	0.41	1
TKF	396	0.01	0.76	0.01	0.85	1
TTF	396	0.02	0.32	0.01	0.50	1
EWZ	396	0.12	2.39	0.12	2.38	0
EEA	396	0.00	0.31	0.00	0.30	0
IF	396	0.02	0.34	0.02	0.50	1
MAY	396	0.01	0.20	0.01	0.27	1
TFC	396	0.00	0.19	0.00	0.21	1
TDF	396	0.05	0.72	0.05	0.88	1
TF	396	0.02	0.30	0.02	0.49	1

$\delta_{NEWS} = news_t$, where news refers to the quantity of news events regarding a particular investing area. The high-news behavioral variable, $\pi_{2,t}$ is then:

$$\pi_{2,t} = \psi_t \cdot news_t \tag{16.12}$$

These news data are obtained from historical transcripts of *Lou Dobb's Moneyline*, as reported by Nexus UK. We use this program because it provides a historical sequence of transcripts, reported in a digital format, for the seven years of the sample.

Table 16.2 Country fund discount summary statistics: equation (16.5) $D_{t+1} = ((n_{t+1} / p_{t+1}) - 1)$

Fund	Nobs	Average discount % Percent	Std dev. σ_D	Minimum discount (premium)	Maximum discount	Significant discount? (yes = 1) $\lvert ave(D) \rvert - 2*\sigma_D > 0$
APB	396	9.96	4.53	−4.82	24.89	1
CH	396	7.83	9.28	−22.66	33.17	0
CHN	396	2.90	13.89	−39.54	29.47	0
CRF	396	−21.06	20.14	−51.62	34.69	0
GCH	396	9.66	7.58	−22.17	26.46	0
GF	396	18.57	7.06	5.77	42.84	1
GRR	396	8.28	4.98	−11.44	30.00	0
IAF	396	3.57	8.97	−16.32	24.96	0
IFN	396	3.24	12.66	−26.89	29.79	0
IIF	396	4.41	11.47	−18.00	28.60	0
IRL	396	15.54	7.64	−7.23	44.31	1
ISL	396	13.38	9.82	−18.84	39.88	0
JEQ	396	2.76	8.76	−22.90	22.76	0
JFC	396	11.41	6.81	−25.17	24.65	0
JOF	396	−3.31	9.28	−25.65	23.05	0
KEF	396	11.45	5.75	−6.16	26.00	1
KF	396	11.26	6.49	0.71	31.47	0
LAQ	396	14.97	4.29	6.23	32.00	1
LDF	396	12.71	5.67	0.03	24.85	1
MSF	396	12.24	4.42	0.24	24.52	1
MXE	396	11.60	6.52	−15.69	26.90	0
MXF	396	13.54	3.43	5.07	24.87	1
SGF	396	16.03	6.02	−2.84	34.15	1
SNF	396	−7.54	12.49	−35.74	41.04	0
SWZ	396	17.75	4.64	6.36	42.80	1
TKF	396	−0.69	11.00	−26.53	43.63	0
TTF	396	−2.97	11.25	−22.25	27.38	0
EWZ	396	0.00	1.23	−5.62	11.33	0
EEA	396	12.74	3.86	2.02	27.33	1
IF	396	4.95	14.13	−34.25	48.11	0
MAY	396	9.72	8.10	−8.87	33.06	0
TFC	396	11.19	4.24	0.61	29.41	1
TDF	396	11.54	6.05	−8.65	32.66	0
TF	396	16.00	33.64	−16.98	171.35	0

The $news_t$ variable tallies the number of specific keywords representing relevant investment areas on *Moneyline* in the trading week preceding the Friday at t. For all funds, key words for country name, country fund name and ticker symbol, and the company names of the top ten underlying foreign constituents, were included for each country.

Employing both market-wide and asset-specific information is similar to the approach of Fuertes and Thomas (2006). The search was case-sensitive and included spaces after defined keywords so as to avoid picking up unrelated similar words. For obvious reasons the ticker symbols for the Indonesia Fund (IF) and Malaysia Fund (MAY) were excluded. Transcript and keyword spot checking of the series demonstrates that the search method accurately identifies relevant news events.

RESULTS

This work investigates whether traders' state-dependent expectations biases can account for anomalous country fund price movements for a seven-year period spanning the 2007–08 banking crises. We provide a multiple agent asset pricing model that includes both rational traders and traders who display biases in expectations formation following market states with large amounts of fundamental value variance or CNN financial news. Importantly, traders' biased behavior is based on evidence of state-dependent over- or underreaction biases observed in asset price forecasting experiments. Closed-form solutions from the multi-agent pricing model predict a multiple driver property of fund prices. Empirical tests for these drivers' influence in field data finds that a significant amount of out-of-sample country fund discount variance can be explained by dummies representing the occurrence of behavioral bias trigger states.

The goal of the empirical analysis is to quantify the extent to which state-dependent trader bias π can explain country funds' discount movements ΔD. Equation (16.10) summarizes the model predictions about this relationship, and is estimated for each country fund individually.[4]

Table 16.3 reports the model fits of equation (16.10) for π_1 and π_2 simultaneously, including a constant term to capture other unexplained variation. Columns (3) and (5) provide the estimates for θ_i, columns (4) and (6) give *t*-ratios, and (7) and (8) give *p*-values. If all agents forecast rationally, we should observe $\theta_i = 0$, which implies one cannot reject the null that the discount simply evolves as a random walk. If agents display consistent state-dependent forecasting bias, we should observe $\theta_i \neq 0$. Specifically, $\theta_i > 0$ implies that agents' overreaction to information is influencing the country fund discount following event state *i*, while $\theta_i < 0$ implies that agents' underreaction is influencing the discount after event state *i*.

Table 16.3 shows that the parameter θ_1 for the high-noise bias variable is positive and significant for 19 (22) of the 34 funds at the 10 percent (15 percent) level. Of the 19, 15 are consistent with the experimental results and indicate failure to reject the hypothesis that the timing and magnitude of country fund discounts changes can be related to traders' overreaction to information following high NAV variance states.

For the high-information bias variable the results are less significant. The experimental result predicting underreaction to high information suggests that these coefficients would be significantly negative. One observes that only seven (nine) of the 34 coefficients for the high-information variable θ_2 were significant at the 10 percent (15 percent) level. Five of the seven coefficients were significantly negative, failing to reject the hypothesis that the timing of country fund discounts movements can be related to traders' underreaction to information following high news information states. This result is consistent

Table 16.3 Country fund discount model fits – multivariate OLS: Equation (16.10)'
$\Delta D_{t+1} = C + \theta_1 \pi_{1,t} + \theta_2 \pi_{2,t} + e_t$

Fund	Nobs	High variance ($\pi_{1,t}$)		High news ($\pi_{2,t}$)		Pr value > |*t*|	
		θ_1	*t*-ratio	θ_2	*t*-ratio	θ_1	θ_2
APB	397	0.17**	2.47	0.07**	4.22	0.01	<0.0001
CH	397	1.00**	3.92	−0.27*	−1.53	0.00	0.13
CHN	397	0.00	−0.01	0.00	−0.53	0.99	0.59
CRF	397	2.94**	3.50	−0.01**	−1.92	0.00	0.06
EEA	397	2.28**	2.08	−0.01	−0.60	0.04	0.55
EWZ	397	−0.02**	−1.71	0.05	0.66	0.09	0.51
GCH	397	−0.09**	−1.70	0.00	0.54	0.09	0.59
GF	397	2.19**	6.54	−0.02	−1.23	<0.0001	0.22
GRR	397	−0.67**	−2.46	−0.01	−0.46	0.01	0.64
IAF	397	4.64**	9.54	−0.10	−1.21	<0.0001	0.23
IF	397	2.77*	1.60	−0.05	−0.57	0.11	0.57
IFN	397	0.00	−0.09	0.01	0.60	0.93	0.55
IIF	397	−0.03	−0.93	0.01	0.46	0.35	0.65
IRL	397	−0.25*	−1.47	−0.01	−0.87	0.14	0.38
ISL	397	1.27**	2.85	0.00	−0.07	0.00	0.94
JEQ	397	7.30**	1.88	0.00	−0.01	0.06	0.99
JFC	397	−0.07	−0.41	0.00	0.26	0.68	0.80
JOF	397	−2.51**	−2.81	0.00	0.06	0.01	0.95
KEF	397	−3.20**	−3.80	0.00	0.06	0.00	0.95
KF	397	0.00	0.37	−0.01	−0.45	0.71	0.65
LAQ	397	0.17**	6.72	−0.01*	−1.61	<0.0001	0.11
LDF	397	0.37**	5.70	−0.01	−1.41	<0.0001	0.16
MAY	397	1.78**	1.92	−0.05	−0.81	0.06	0.42
MSF	397	0.05	0.86	0.01**	1.69	0.39	0.09
MXE	397	0.32**	4.55	−0.02**	−2.11	<0.0001	0.04
MXF	397	0.17**	4.03	−0.02**	−2.91	<0.0001	0.00
SGF	397	−1.02*	−1.46	−0.06	−1.06	0.15	0.29
SNF	397	2.16**	2.14	−0.06**	−2.62	0.03	0.01
SWZ	397	2.39**	3.76	−0.02	−1.39	0.00	0.17
TDF	397	−0.12	−0.61	0.00	0.52	0.54	0.60
TF	397	−3.58	−0.87	−0.29**	−1.82	0.38	0.07
TFC	397	0.40	0.45	−0.01	−1.05	0.65	0.30
TKF	397	−0.94**	−3.49	−0.03	−0.62	0.00	0.54
TTF	397	−0.68	−0.54	0.05	0.77	0.59	0.44

Note: Significance Levels – **(10%), *(15%).

with the evidence from the forecasting experiments. However, two of the significant estimates are positive, which suggests that traders' overreaction influences discounts. This is contrary to the experimental results and implies that overreaction is triggered by high news states.

DISCUSSION

This study investigates whether traders' state-dependent expectations biases can account for anomalous country fund discount movements. A distributional uncertainty model is provided that includes both rational and two types of behavioral traders. The characteristics assumed for the behavioral traders are based on the biased behaviors observed in financially oriented forecasting experiments. In particular, overreaction to current information was observed to be triggered by states with high forecasted price variance. And underreaction to current information was observed to be triggered by states characterized by a large amount of predictor information.

The closed-form equilibrium price solutions of the model demonstrate a multiple driver property of fund prices. We see that country fund prices are a function of their fundamental NAVs and risk adjustment terms, as well as of behavioral variables that identify the timing and severity of bias-triggering event states.

Some caveats are necessary, however. First, this study does not argue that all discount variance should be accounted for with these two biases. There is substantial evidence of many more forms of bias in individual forecasting ability. As noted in Hogarth and Reder (1987), the motivation for considering these two biases is the fact that they obtain in an experimental setting directly comparable to the analytical model.

Second, several empirical studies have identified a variety of other discount predictors that are not included in this model and are significant predictors of discount movements. Since these drivers are not an aspect of the analytical model, they are absent.

The model suggests two key testable propositions regarding the timing of country fund discount movements:

1. If agents overreact to current information following high-forecast–price-variance states, the discount should increase if there is an expected NAV appreciation and decrease if there is an expected depreciation.
2. If agents underreact to current information following event states with large amounts of predictor information, the discount should decrease if there is an expected NAV appreciation and increase if there is an expected depreciation.

The empirical results are moderately consistent with these two propositions. A simple regression comparing changes in the discounts to the high-variance overreaction bias variable finds that these terms can predict the timing and direction of discount movements for 19 of 34 funds at the 10 percent significance level. The second result is less significant and finds that underreaction, triggered by high CNN news levels, can predict the timing and direction of discount movements for 9 of 34 funds, but only at the 15 percent level.

NOTES

The analysis described herein utilized SAS and Matlab for data organization and analysis.

1. The assumption that only rational traders are present in the home market is based on research describing the observed characteristics of traders in country fund versus foreign markets, see Lee et al. (1991).

2. This is the case since the values for δ and ψ with (16.7) imply that $\Delta n_{t+1} > 0$, $\Delta p_{t+1} > 0$, and $\Delta n_{t+1} - \Delta p_{t+1} > 0$. As a result, the NAV increases more than the country fund price, so the discount increases or the premium decreases.
3. These include: Australia, Brazil, Chile, China, France, Germany, Hong Kong, India, Indonesia, Ireland, Israel, Italy, Japan, Luxembourg, Malaysia, Mexico, New Zealand, Philippines, Russia, Singapore, South Korea, Spain, Sweden, Switzerland, Taiwan, Thailand, Turkey, the UK, and the USA.
4. Equation (16.10) is estimated for each fund individually with a constant term to capture sentiment or other unobserved variation. This is motivated by earlier fixed-effects analyses of fund returns rejecting the hypothesis of fund homogeneity, implying that a pooled analysis would not be appropriate.

REFERENCES

Barberis, N. and R. Thaler (2003), 'A survey of behavioral finance,' in George M. Constantinides, Milton Harris and Rene M. Stulz (eds), *Handbook of the Economics of Finance*, Amsterdam: Elsevier, pp. 1053–128.

Basov, S. (2005), 'Bounded rationality: static versus dynamic approaches,' *Economic Theory*, **25** (4), 871–85.

Black, F. (1986), 'Noise,' *Journal of Finance*, **41**, 529–44.

Blume, L. and D. Easley (2006), 'If you're so smart why aren't you rich? Brief selection in complete and incomplete markets,' *Econometrica*, **74** (4), 929–66.

Bosner-Neal, C., G. Brauer, R. Neal and S. Wheatley (1990), 'International investment restrictions and closed-end country fund prices,' *Journal of Finance*, **45**, 523–47.

Brunnermeier, M. and J. Parker (2005), 'Optimal expectations,' *American Economic Review*, **95** (4), 1092–118.

Camerer, C. (1995), 'Individual decision-making,' in John H. Kagel and Alvin Roth (eds), *The Handbook of Experimental Economics*, Princeton, NJ: Princeton University Press, pp. 587–703.

Clark, G., N. Thrift and A. Tickell (2004), 'Performing finance: the industry, the media and its image,' *Review of International Political Economy*, **11** (2), 289–310.

Daniel, K., D. Hirshleifer and A. Subrahmanyam (2000), 'Covariance risk, mispricing, and the cross section of security returns,' Working Paper 7615, NBER.

DeBondt, W. and R. Thaler (1990), 'Do security analysts overreact?: in stock market volatility,' *The American Economic Review*, **80** (2); Papers and Proceedings of the 102nd Annual Meeting of the American Economic Association, pp. 52–7.

DeLong, J.B., A. Shleifer, L. Summers and R.J Waldmann (1990), 'Noise traders and risk in financial markets,' *Journal of Political Economy*, **98** (4), 703–38.

Dudycha, L.W. and J.C. Naylor (1966), 'Characteristics of the human inference process,' *Organizational Behavior and Human Performance*, **1**, 110–28.

Edgell, S., N.J Castellan, R. Roe, J. Barnes, N. Pak, R. Bright and L. Ford (1996), 'Irrelevant information in probabilistic categorization,' *Journal of Experimental Psychology*, **22** (6), 1463–81.

Estes, W.K. (1954), 'Individual behavior in uncertain situations: an interpretation in terms of statistical association theory,' in R.M. Thrall, C.H. Coombs and R.L. Davis (eds), *Decision Processes*, New York: John Wiley & Sons, pp. 127–36.

Friedman, D. and D. Massaro (1997), 'Understanding variability in binary and continuous choice,' *Psychonomic Bulletin & Review*, **3**, 370–89.

Froot, K. and R. Thaler (1990), 'Anomalies: foreign exchange,' *Journal of Economic Perspectives*, **4** (3), 179–92.

Fuertes, A. and D. Thomas (2006), 'Large market shocks and abnormal closed-end fund price behavior,' *Journal of Banking and Finance*, **30** (9), 2517–35.

Gervais, S. and T. Odean (2001), 'Learning to be overconfident,' *Review of Financial Studies*, **14** (1), 1–27.

Gillette, A., D. Stevens, S. Watts and A. Williams (1999), 'Price and volume reactions to public information releases: an experimental approach incorporating traders' subjective belief,' *Contemporary Accounting Research*, **16** (3), 437–79.

Gluck, M. and G. Bower (1988), 'From conditioning to category learning: an adaptive network model,' *Journal of Experimental Psychology General*, **117**, 225–44.

Griffin, D. and A. Tversky (1992), 'The weighing of evidence and the determinants of confidence,' *Cognitive Psychology*, **24** (3), 411–35.

Harris, M. and A. Raviv (1993), 'Differences of opinion make a horse race,' *Review of Financial Studies*, **6**, 473–506.

Heaton, J. and R. Korajczyk (2002), 'Introduction to *Review of Financial Studies* Conference on Market Frictions and Behavioral Finance,' *Review of Financial Studies*, **15** (2), 353–61.

Henker, J. and S. Owen (2008), 'Bursting bubbles: linking experimental finance market results to field market data,' *Journal of Behavioral Finance*, **9** (1), 5–14.
Hirshleifer, D. (2001), 'Investor psychology and asset pricing,' *Journal of Finance*, **56** (4), 1533–97.
Hogarth, R. and M. Reder (eds) (1987), *Rational Choice: The Contrast Between Economics and Psychology*, Chicago, IL: The University of Chicago Press.
Holt, C. and S. Laury (2002), 'Risk aversion and incentive effect,' *American Economic Review*, **92** (5), 1644–55.
Hong, H. and J. Stein (1999), 'A unified theory of under-reaction, momentum trading, and over-reaction in asset markets,' *Journal of Finance*, **54** (6), 2143–84.
Kandel, E. and N. Pearson (1995), 'Differential interpretation of public signals and trade in speculative markets,' *Journal of Political Economy*, **103**, 831–72.
Kelley, H. (2004), 'Measuring the impact of behavioral traders on the market for closed-end country funds,' *Journal of Behavioral Finance*, **5** (4), 201–13.
Kelley, H. and J. Busemeyer (2008), 'A comparison of models for learning how to dynamically integrate multiple cues in order to forecast continuous criteria,' *Journal of Mathematical Psychology*, **52** (4), 218–40.
Kelley, H. and D. Friedman (2002), 'Learning to forecast price,' *Economic Inquiry*, **40** (4), 556–73.
Kelley, H. and D. Friedman (2008), 'Learning to forecast rationally,' in Charles R. Plott and Vernon L. Smith (eds), *Handbook of Experimental Economics Results*, Amsterdam: Elsevier, pp. 303–10.
Kitzis S., H. Kelley, E. Berg, D. Massaro and D. Friedman (1998), 'Broadening the tests of learning models,' *Journal of Mathematical Psychology*, **42**, 327–55.
Klibanoff, P., O. Lamont and T. Wizman (1998), 'Investor reaction to salient news in closed-end country funds,' *Journal of Finance*, **53** (2), 673–99.
Laibson, D. (1997), 'Golden eggs and hyperbolic discounting,' *Quarterly Journal of Economics*, **62**, 443–77.
Lee, C., A. Shleifer and R. Thaler (1991), 'Investor sentiment and the closed-end fund puzzle,' *Journal of Finance*, **46**, 75–109.
Mullainathan, S. and A. Shleifer (2005), 'The market for news,' *American Economic Review*, **95** (4), 1031–53.
Odean, T. (1998), 'Volume, volatility, price, and profit when all traders are above average,' *Journal of Finance*, **53** (6), 1887–934.
Pesendorfer, W. (2006), 'Behavioral economics comes of age: a review essay on *Advances in Behavioral Economics*,' *Journal of Economic Literature*, **44** (3), 712–21.
Ramchander, S., M. Simpson and H. Thiewes (2008), 'The effect of macroeconomic news on German closed-end funds,' *Quarterly Review of Economics and Finance*, **48** (4), 708–24.
Sandroni, A. (2005), 'The efficient markets and Bayes' rule,' *Economic Theory*, **26** (4), 741–64.
Shefrin, H. and M. Statman (1994), 'Behavioral capital asset pricing theory,' *Journal of Financial and Quantitative Analysis*, **29**, 323–49.
Shiller, R. (1981), 'Do stock prices move too much to be justified by subsequent changes in dividends?,' *American Economic Review*, **71**, 421–36.
Smith, V., G. Suchanek and A. Williams (1988), 'Bubbles, crashes, and endogenous expectations in experimental spot asset markets,' *Econometrica*, **56** (5), 1119–51.
Tsai, P., P. Swanson and S. Sarkar (2007), 'Mean and volatility linkages for closed-end funds,' *Quarterly Review of Economics and Finance*, **47** (4), 550–75.
Varian, H. (1989), 'Differences in opinion in financial markets,' in Courtenay C. Stone (ed.), *Financial Risk: Theory, Evidence and Implications*, Boston, MA: Kluwer Academic Publishers, pp. 3–37.

APPENDIX TICKER SYMBOLS AND NAMES OF ACTIVE COUNTRY FUNDS ANALYZED

APB	Asia Pacific Fund Inc
EWZ	iShares MSCI Brazil Index
CH	Chile Fund Inc.
CHN	China Fund Inc.
CRF	Cornerstone Total Return Fund Inc.
GCH	Greater China Fund Inc.
EEA	European Equity Fund
GF	New Germany Fund

GRR	Asia Tigers Fund Inc.
IF	Indonesia Fund
IAF	Aberdeen Australia Equity Fund Inc.
IFN	India Fund
IIF	Morgan Stanley Indian Investment Fund
IRL	New Ireland Fund
ISL	First Israel Fund
JEQ	Japan Equity Fund Inc.
JFC	JF China Region Fund Inc.
JOF	Japan Smaller Capitalization Fund Inc.
KEF	Korea Equity Fund
KF	Korea Fund
LAQ	Latin America Equity Fund Inc.
LDF	Latin America Discovery Fund Inc.
MAY	Malaysia Fund Inc.
MSF	Morgan Stanley Emerging Markets Fund Inc.
MXE	Mexico Equity and Income Fund Inc.
MXF	Mexico Fund Inc.
SGF	Singapore Fund Inc.
SNF	Spain Fund Inc.
SWZ	Swiss Helvetia Fund Inc.
TDF	Templeton Dragon Fund
TF	Thai Capital Fund
TFC	Taiwan Greater China Fund
TKF	Turkish Investment Fund Inc.
TTF	Thai Fund Inc.

17 Holding on to the losers: Finnish evidence

Mirjam Lehenkari and Jukka Perttunen

It is widely acknowledged that investor behavior is often at odds with traditional finance theory. More importantly, the recent literature abounds with examples in which investors systematically deviate from the tenets of such theories as rationality. One of the currently debated behavioral patterns arising from this line of research is the tendency of investors to hold losing investments too long and sell winning investments too soon. Shefrin and Statman (1985) have dubbed this phenomenon the 'disposition effect.'[1]

The disposition effect is commonly interpreted as a consequence of human behavioral theories, most notably prospect theory. Kahneman and Tversky (1979) developed this descriptive theory of decision under risk as an alternative to expected utility theory.[2] They formalized an S-shaped value function with three essential properties. First, instead of being defined over levels of wealth, the value function is defined in terms of gains and losses relative to a reference point. Second, the value function is concave above the reference point and convex below it, that is, the marginal value of both gains and losses diminishes with their magnitude. Third, the slope of the value function is steeper for losses than for gains, which implies greater detriment from a loss than utility from an equal gain.

Jointly, these three properties cause risk aversion in the domain of gains and risk-seeking in the domain of losses. Consequently, an investor with preferences described by the prospect theory value function is inclined to sell an asset that has gained value and to hold an asset that has lost value. There may be behavioral reasons why investors prefer selling winners to selling losers. It is also conceivable that investors expect that prices will be mean-reverting, that is, current losers will be future winners and vice versa.[3]

Yet other factors, such as liquidity reasons, life-cycle considerations, or purely speculative motives, may also contribute to investor behavior. After a large price increase, investors may seek to restore diversification to their portfolios by selling a portion of the appreciated stock (Lakonishok and Smidt, 1986). Moreover, because trading costs are often higher for low-priced stocks, and losing stocks are more likely than winning stocks to be priced lower, investors' unwillingness to realize losses may simply be due to the higher trading costs associated with lower stock prices (Harris, 1988).

However, from the viewpoint of optimal tax planning, investors' tendency to realize gains rather than losses is anomalous. Tax considerations should induce investors to defer capital gains and realize capital losses. Constantinides (1984) considers optimal tax trading policies in various scenarios with different assumptions on tax rates and transaction costs. He finds that the optimal tax trading strategy, with annual taxation, transaction costs, and without the distinction between short- and long-term tax rates, is to increase tax loss selling gradually as the year progresses. Dyl (1977) and others provide empirical evidence that investors realize proportionately more losses than gains in December.

We participate in the ongoing debate to explain this tendency by examining it above and beyond what is implied by pure rationales. We use highly extensive and detailed data on the Finnish stock market to analyze the stock holdings and market transactions of all individual investors in a stock market. Existing empirical research has heretofore focused predominantly on analyzing only investors in a single securities firm, or only a small subset of investors in a stock market. The only comprehensive work we are aware of that analyzes the trading behavior of all market participants – both institutions and individual investors – is Grinblatt and Keloharju (2001), which also focused on the Finnish market.

We make several other contributions to the existing literature. First, given that prospect theory deals with individual decision making, using individual investor data seems to be the most appropriate way to test the theory. Also, our methodological approach is entirely different from those found in previous studies.

Finally, we believe our investigation is made even more interesting by the fact that during our sample period the Finnish stock market was on a steep downward trend. It is very likely that part of the selling occurred because of rational motives such as liquidity reasons. In these cases, it should not matter whether the stock is a winner or a loser. In a downturn, investors will tend to sell disproportionately more losers than winners because they will have more losing stocks in their portfolios. Consequently, we expect to find weaker evidence of the disposition effect in a downward-moving market.[4] In fact, finding evidence of the disposition effect in these data would suggest that behavioral motives additionally and independently contribute to investor behavior.

Overall, our results show that the propensity of investors to sell decreases with capital losses, which is consistent with existing evidence. There is, however, no opposite effect identifiable for capital gains. So, although the investors in our sample tend to hold losing stocks, they are not necessarily selling their winning stocks. Moreover, the negative association between losses and the selling propensity of investors persists after controlling for several investor- and stock-specific factors affecting trading behavior.

Finally, our results suggest that historical returns on stocks, both positive and negative, significantly reinforce the decreasing selling propensity of investors with respect to capital losses.

The remainder of the chapter is organized as follows. The next section briefly reviews the relevant literature on the disposition effect. The third section describes the data, and then we outline our research design. We present the results in the section after that, and conclude with a discussion in the sixth section.

PREVIOUS RESEARCH

Most of the early research on the disposition effect focused on the relationship between aggregate trading volume and stock prices. Lakonishok and Smidt (1986) study the turnover rates of US stocks that have risen or fallen in price. They find higher abnormal volume for winners. Ferris et al. (1988) use price and volume data for 30 small-cap US stocks to examine the relationship between current trading volume and historic trading volume at differential prices. Consistent with the disposition effect, current volume was negatively (positively) correlated with volume on those days when the stock price was higher (lower) than the current price. This line of empirical research is not, however, particularly relevant to our study, which aims to explore the behavior of individuals – not investors in aggregate.

Shefrin and Statman (1985) develop a positive theory of capital gain and loss realization in which investors tend to sell winners too early and hold losers too long relative to the prescriptions of Constantinides's (1984) normative theory. Their framework includes five major elements – prospect theory, mental accounting, regret aversion, self-control and tax considerations.

1. Prospect theory predicts a propensity to sell winners and hold losers when the proceeds realized will be held as opposed to being rolled over into another gamble.
2. Mental accounting places the prospect theoretic treatment into a broader framework by clarifying conditions under which the disposition effect holds when realization proceeds are reinvested in a 'tax-motivated swap.'
3. Aversion to regret is an important reason why investors may have difficulty realizing gains as well as losses.
4. Self-control is used to explain the rationale for methods that investors use to force themselves to realize losses.
5. Tax considerations may also be important, especially the potential gain from exploiting Constantinides's (1984) strategy and its interaction with the other four elements.

After introducing their theoretical framework, Shefrin and Statman (1985) consider empirical evidence. They use data from two sources, panel data on individual investor trading history from 1964 to 1970, and aggregate data on mutual fund trades from 1961 to 1981. Shefrin and Statman show that the disposition effect exists in real-world financial markets. Specifically, they find that tax considerations alone do not explain the observed patterns of loss and gain realization, which are consistent with a combined effect of tax considerations and the other four elements.

Weber and Camerer (1998) present an experimental investigation of the disposition effect.[5] The subjects of their experiment bought and sold shares in six risky assets. Asset prices fluctuated in each period. Weber and Camerer show that the subjects were inclined to sell fewer shares when the price fell than when it rose. They also sold fewer when the price was below the purchase price than when it was above it. The presence of both effects suggests that multiple reference points – both purchase prices and previous prices – affect choices. These findings are thus consistent with both a prospect-theory-based explanation, and subjects' expectation that prices will mean-revert.

Odean (1998) tests the disposition effect by analyzing trading records from 1987 through 1993 for 10000 accounts at a large discount brokerage house. He finds that, overall, investors prefer selling winners to selling losers. Even after controlling for rebalancing and share price, the disposition effect still exists. His analysis also indicates that many investors exercise tax-motivated selling, especially in December. Furthermore, over the following year, the average market-adjusted return for the winners investors chose to sell is 3.4 percent higher than for the unsold losers. In other words, if investors choose what to sell because they expect mean reversion in the future, they are most often incorrect.

Ranguelova (2001) analyzes daily trading records of 78000 clients of a US brokerage house over a six-year period, and reports that the disposition effect increases with the market capitalization of the underlying stocks. Trades in stocks at the bottom 40 percent of the market capitalization distribution display a reverse disposition effect: investors sell losers rather than winners. The author suggests that investors may be conscious of the strong short-term price persistence of small-cap stocks.[6]

The paper closest to this study in terms of data set is Grinblatt and Keloharju (2001), who analyze the transactions of both individuals and institutions in the Finnish stock market. With a highly comprehensive data set, the authors identified the determinants of buying and selling activity over a two-year period, 1 January 1995 through 10 January 1997. With a variety of tests and control variables, they show that past returns, reference price effects, holding period return, tax loss selling, and the smoothing of consumption over the life cycle all affect trading.

Specifically, the disposition effect and tax loss selling were the major determinants of the propensity to sell. For both individual investors and institutions, the propensity to hold losers strengthened as losses exceeded 30 percent. The authors further show that the propensity to sell a stock is positively related to past returns, and that the disposition effect interacts with these past returns. The effect of past returns on the decision to sell appears to be much more important for positive market-adjusted returns than for negative market-adjusted returns.

The disposition effect is neither a solely US phenomenon nor is it characteristic of just small individual stock traders. Bremer and Kato (1996) report evidence on the disposition effect in Tokyo Stock Exchange, Grinblatt and Keloharju (2001) find it among participants in the Finnish stock market, and Shapira and Venezia (2001) document it for Israeli investors. Furthermore, evidence of the disposition effect has been found among professional futures traders (Locke and Mann, 1999), and in the behavior of home buyers and sellers (Case and Shiller, 1988; Genesove and Mayer, 2001).

DATA DESCRIPTION

We use an extensive database consisting of all shareholdings registered in the Finnish paperless system of stock ownership called the book-entry system. The data are provided by the Finnish Central Securities Depository (FCSD); by the end of our sample period it covered more than 99.99 percent of the market capitalization of stocks on the Helsinki Exchanges (HEX). The data comprise the initial positions in the shareownership records of FCSD on 5 January 1995, and the daily changes in these records up to 29 September 2000. The data consist of information on investor identity,[7] date, stock (e.g. security code, share class), transaction (e.g. trade type, price, volume), and investor attributes such as ownership type, investor category, gender and birth year. To be included in our analysis, each observation was required to have a full set of information available.

We further restrict our sample size in a number of ways. First, because we are interested in the sell versus hold choices of investors, we exclude all the buy transactions. Second, although the data include the shareholdings of both institutional and individual investors, our focus here is on the individual investors. Third, our sample period is 6 March 2000 through 29 September 2000. On the first day of the period, the HEX

Portfolio Index[8] reached a new all-time high, after which it decreased by 25 percent during our 30-week time span.

The motivation for our sample period selection stems from the intuition that in a downward-moving market, one would expect the disposition effect to be less evident. This follows from the fact that in a downturn, investors will have disproportionately more losing investments in their portfolios, and may thus display a tendency toward realizing losses as well as gains. It will be most interesting to find out if the phenomenon can be detected under these circumstances.

We aggregate daily observations into weekly cumulative totals to reduce the burden on computing resources and avoid misspecification of the trading dates. The latter is a problem in a daily analysis, since a maximum three-day clearing lag means that the booking date of a transaction and its actual trading day do not always coincide. We further justify our choice of time unit by arguing that weekly rather than daily analyses generate more meaningful results for our purposes and widen our understanding of investor behavior.

The current database does not cover indirect ownership records. Investors may thus hold shares that are not part of the data set. For example, an investment through a mutual fund has an identification number that belongs to the fund itself, and is not traceable to an individual investor. Although mutual fund investments are currently gaining popularity among Finnish investors, they are far less common in Finland than in the USA. Furthermore, considering the aim of this study, it is unlikely that the exclusion of indirect investments will bias our results.

The 1991 Act on the Book-Entry System made shareholding registration obligatory for Finnish investors, but voluntary for foreign investors, who may register their shares in a specific book-entry account administered by a nominee registration custodian. In such cases, the name and other details of the custodian will appear on the account records instead of the identification number of the individual investor. Since the majority of foreign investors have used this right, we lack adequately detailed data on this investor class. Consequently, we concentrate on domestic investors. Furthermore, due to the small number of observations in the lowest and highest ends of the investor age distribution, we restrict our sample to investors between the ages of 20 and 80.

To conduct our analysis, we need information on the purchase price of each shareholding. Investors may own shares bought before 5 January 1995, for which this information is not available. We therefore exclude the initial positions from the analysis and focus on sales and shareholdings to which we can attach a known purchase price. For the same reason, we are unable to analyze the sales and holdings of shares acquired by some way other than ordinary stock trade or share issue.[9] Finally, we omit the shares of telephone companies from the analysis.

After these adjustments, our final sample consists of 70 204 individual investors who make 258 547 weekly sell or hold decisions in 151 stocks. Similar data sets are uncommon in the literature, except, as we mentioned earlier, that of Grinblatt and Keloharju (2001). However, our database is more recent.

There is a natural explanation for the paucity of such detailed data in the research. The current database is extremely large, yet the Finnish stock market is relatively small worldwide. Consequently, it would be computationally infeasible to conduct a conclusive test on the disposition effect using real market data from, say, the major US exchanges.

While the HEX certainly has its own distinct features, for the purposes of our study, it is improbable that it differs from larger exchanges in any critical respect.

We obtain additional price data from the HEX to supplement our database. We also use this data source to make proper adjustments for splits and dividends. Furthermore, we need data on subscription prices of share issues. We gather this information from company press releases and stock exchange announcements.

METHODOLOGY

Our primary aim is to investigate whether Finnish investors display a tendency to sell winning stocks while holding losing stocks. Obviously, talking about winners and losers is only meaningful with an explicit reference point. As Odean (1998) notes, any test of the disposition effect is a joint test of the hypothesis that investors sell their winners more easily than their losers, and of the specification of the reference point from which gains and losses are evaluated.

The concept of reference point is most commonly related to Kahneman and Tversky's (1979) prospect theory. Although the theory specifies the shape of the value function around the reference point, it is silent about where people set their reference points. Both experimental and empirical research has typically presumed that the reference point is the status quo, that is, the purchase price of the stock. However, it is also possible that investors have other reference points and that reference points adapt over time.[10]

Consensus on a 'true' reference point is lacking, and we do not attempt to disentangle the issue here. To maintain comparability with previous empirical work, we measure gains and losses in relation to the purchase price.

The majority of recent studies testing the disposition effect have replicated the method developed by Odean (1998). In this method, two ratios are calculated: the proportion of gains realized of all gains at hand (PGR), and the proportion of losses realized of all losses at hand (PLR). A large difference between these two ratios reveals that investors tend to realize disproportionately more gains or losses. Specifically, a significantly higher PGR is evidence of the disposition effect. For the most part, studies using Odean's (1998) approach support the hypothesis that investors realize their gains at a much higher rate than their losses. These studies, however, generally cannot discriminate between the various motivations for such behavior.

Grinblatt and Keloharju (2001) introduce an alternative approach, which enables an analysis of the various factors potentially affecting investor behavior. They estimate logit regressions to examine the determinants of the propensity to sell versus hold. The dependent variable is a dummy variable with the value of one when an investor sells a stock. Each sell is then matched with all stocks in the investor's portfolio that are not sold on the same day. For these unsold stocks, the dependent variable takes the value of zero.

Independent variables include an exhaustive set of control variables expected to influence investors' sell versus hold decisions. The disposition effect is captured by two dummy variables representing moderate and extreme capital losses. Grinblatt and Keloharju's (2001) results are consistent with Odean (1998) and many others: capital losses significantly reduce the selling propensity of investors. Moreover, the disposition effect is strong even after controlling for the effect of past returns and tax loss selling.

Using a somewhat different measure of investor selling propensity, we also allow for various motivations investors may have when selling their stocks. Our methodological approach, however, is new. We also control for the overall selling propensity due to stock-specific factors. But our method allows us to cope with the large sample size while avoiding the problems inherent in this type of data. We proceed as follows.

Over all stocks, weeks and investors, we first calculate the return distribution of the shareholdings with respect to their weighted average purchase price. We then divide this distribution into separate deciles for gains and losses. This gives us the reference values for ten winner and loser classes, that is, 20 return categories to be used in the subsequent analysis.

In the next phase, within each return category, we form separate portfolios for men and women in six different age categories (in ten-year intervals ranging from 20 to 80 years). Week by week and separately for each stock we then assign each investor into one of the resulting 240 portfolios. Our data points are thus portfolios of investors, who have either sold shares of a certain stock in a particular week, or kept their holdings intact. For each individual portfolio, we calculate the proportion of investors who have been selling their shares. We term this ratio the selling propensity (*SELLPR*), and use it as our dependent variable in the subsequent analysis.

The main explanatory variable of interest is the return on a stock as defined above. Obviously, whether a stock is a winner or a loser is only one factor possibly affecting an investor's selling propensity. One potentially important set of variables includes other investor-specific factors. Barber and Odean (2001) analyze the common stock investments of US households and find that, in general, men trade more than women. To control for potential gender differences, we include a gender dummy coded as male = 1 and female = 0.

The traditional life-cycle hypothesis (see, e.g., Ando and Modigliani, 1963 and Modigliani, 1986) posits a relationship between age and investments: individuals invest during their working years and disinvest during their retirement years. To adjust for life-cycle effects, we include investor age as a categorial variable. As in the portfolio formation, we include investor age as a categorical variable. As in the portfolio formation, we measure age in ten-year intervals ranging from 20 to 80 years, with the 70- to 80-year category as the omitted reference category. For each portfolio we also calculate investors' average holding period length (*HPL*) in years, and their average selling activity (*ACT*). The selling activity of each individual investor is measured by calculating the number of the weeks the investor has sold any shares between the beginning of 2000 and the end of our sample period. The number of these active weeks is then divided by the total number of weeks in that period.

Because there are separate portfolios for each stock, we can further assign several other measurements to each portfolio. For each stock, we calculate the market value of equity (*MVAL*) and the book-to-market ratio (*BTOM*), both measured at the end of 1999 in billions of euros, as well as the one-month historical return preceding each sample week. These are all variables found in the existing literature to affect the trading behavior of investors. Specifically, we are interested in the potential interactions of these variables with the loss and gain variables. Finally, to account for the individual effects of the stock-specific factors, we enter separate dummies for each stock.

Panel (a) of Table 17.1 shows the mean values of selected variables calculated over the stock- and week-specific portfolios in the different return categories. The first column reports the number of each return category, and the second reports the mean return of the portfolios assigned into each category. The relatively high returns in the most profitable portfolios stand out here. These are probably due to the significant holdings of Nokia's shares, and shares acquired via numerous initial public offerings at the end of the 1990s.[11]

The selling propensities reported in the third column appear to be quite stable, with the winner portfolios somewhat being sold more actively. There is also a sudden increase in selling propensity as one moves from the smallest loss category to the lowest gain category. The fourth column shows the average number of stocks (*STOCKS*), and the fifth column shows the average number of investors (*INV*) included in the portfolios in each return category.

The average age of investors is given in the sixth column, and the average proportion of male portfolios in each return category is given in the seventh column. Both variables appear rather constant across return categories, with the average age around 50 and slightly more men than women in all return categories.

The average selling activity of investors is reported in the eighth column, and the average holding period length in the ninth column. Generally, the most active sellers are found in the loss categories. This is somewhat surprising, because the selling propensities for the loser portfolios are lower than those for the winner portfolios. The average holding period length, on the other hand, is shortest in the smallest loss and lowest gain categories, as would be expected.

The remaining four columns give the means of the stock-specific variables. Column 10 shows that the highest market values are in the highest gain categories, and the lowest ones in the smallest loss categories. There is no systematic pattern identifiable with respect to the average book-to-market ratio reported in the next column. However, the stocks with the lowest book-to-market ratios, that is, the growth stocks, seem to dominate the highest gain categories.

The last two columns give the average one-month historical returns of the stocks in the different return categories. Positive (*PRET*) and negative (*NRET*) lagged returns are considered separately. Overall, the positive lagged returns are smaller in their absolute magnitude than the negative ones. This is due to our sample period, which relates to a time when the Finnish stock market experienced a steep decline. Panel (b) of Table 17.1 reports the respective standard deviations.

We use the generalized least squares (GLS) method to examine whether Finnish investors sell winning stocks and hold losing stocks. We choose the GLS because it allows for the specific nature of panel data by controlling for autocorrelation among the time-series errors and heteroskedasticity of cross-sectional errors. Litzenberger and Ramaswamy (1979) demonstrate that when the periodic estimators are serially uncorrelated, the regression coefficients can be estimated by pooling the time-independent periodic estimates obtained from cross-sectional regressions. In each week, we regress our dependent variable on different sets of explanatory variables. The pooled GLS estimator of each regression coefficient γ_k can be obtained by pooling the periodic estimates $\hat{\gamma}_{k1}, \hat{\gamma}_{k2}, \ldots, \hat{\gamma}_{kT}$,

Table 17.1 Descriptive statistics

(a) Means

Return category	*RETURN*	*SELLPR*	*STOCKS*	*INV*	*AGE*	*MALE*	*ACT*	*HPL*	*MVAL*	*BTOM*	*PRET*	*NRET*
1	−0.6862	0.0129	40.43	65.91	49.07	0.53	0.0978	1.2012	6.82	1.01	0.0332	−0.0980
2	−0.4814	0.0176	58.57	39.74	49.38	0.55	0.0960	1.2848	5.62	1.16	0.0268	−0.0912
3	−0.3682	0.0129	74.37	33.64	49.32	0.54	0.0903	1.1742	4.73	1.03	0.0268	−0.0836
4	−0.2931	0.0131	85.40	29.28	49.15	0.55	0.0958	1.0809	4.28	0.94	0.0267	−0.0780
5	−0.2422	0.0148	88.83	30.08	49.03	0.57	0.1001	0.9985	3.86	0.92	0.0256	−0.0756
6	−0.1980	0.0149	99.37	23.47	49.03	0.56	0.1039	0.9420	3.67	0.97	0.0276	−0.0705
7	−0.1503	0.0137	108.23	21.95	49.09	0.56	0.1042	0.8851	3.49	1.00	0.0281	−0.0653
8	−0.1042	0.0137	114.10	21.90	48.93	0.56	0.1075	0.8048	3.56	1.03	0.0292	−0.0611
9	−0.0612	0.0154	118.17	21.09	48.84	0.56	0.1108	0.7264	3.58	1.05	0.0298	−0.0572
10	−0.0206	0.0182	119.47	19.15	48.82	0.56	0.1129	0.6773	3.70	1.05	0.0310	−0.0544
11	0.0239	0.0287	119.40	19.27	48.88	0.56	0.1119	0.7282	3.88	1.05	0.0346	−0.0533
12	0.0844	0.0290	113.87	21.61	49.05	0.56	0.0965	0.9422	4.00	1.00	0.0383	−0.0533
13	0.1729	0.0244	106.97	23.52	49.26	0.55	0.0842	1.1827	4.25	0.95	0.0413	−0.0542
14	0.3095	0.0196	98.40	23.22	49.64	0.55	0.0697	1.5370	4.86	0.80	0.0432	−0.0585
15	0.5331	0.0156	86.39	24.91	49.69	0.55	0.0574	1.9409	5.50	0.65	0.0459	−0.0609
16	0.7816	0.0125	71.14	18.81	49.60	0.57	0.0523	2.0856	7.52	0.53	0.0500	−0.0629
17	1.0618	0.0132	64.97	28.52	49.53	0.57	0.0503	2.2537	8.12	0.50	0.0500	−0.0661
18	1.5390	0.0127	55.43	62.54	49.86	0.56	0.0508	2.3400	9.15	0.50	0.0502	−0.0721
19	3.0080	0.0227	39.13	52.47	50.32	0.56	0.0417	2.6868	10.35	0.56	0.0557	−0.0754
20	9.0136	0.0204	18.83	191.40	50.03	0.54	0.0382	2.6060	19.47	0.26	0.0539	−0.0872

(b) Standard deviations

Return category	*RETURN*	*SELLPR*	*STOCKS*	*INV*	*AGE*	*MALE*	*ACT*	*HPL*	*MVAL*	*BTOM*	*PRET*	*NRET*
1	0.0607	0.0084	2.73	11.40	0.27	0.01	0.0149	0.2014	2.94	0.26	0.0322	0.0660
2	0.0640	0.0154	5.36	8.93	0.22	0.01	0.0085	0.1116	2.06	0.23	0.0210	0.0584
3	0.0563	0.0102	6.61	7.24	0.23	0.01	0.0085	0.1100	1.52	0.20	0.0195	0.0531
4	0.0436	0.0095	8.46	11.51	0.24	0.02	0.0121	0.1336	1.39	0.20	0.0186	0.0449
5	0.0312	0.0096	8.00	9.72	0.28	0.03	0.0137	0.1091	1.06	0.18	0.0183	0.0410
6	0.0262	0.0103	5.67	6.97	0.28	0.02	0.0135	0.1046	0.93	0.14	0.0180	0.0400
7	0.0239	0.0086	5.23	5.13	0.19	0.01	0.0136	0.1101	0.85	0.12	0.0177	0.0345
8	0.0181	0.0075	4.93	5.37	0.17	0.01	0.0125	0.1077	0.79	0.10	0.0177	0.0313
9	0.0126	0.0075	5.78	4.65	0.20	0.01	0.0123	0.1218	0.65	0.08	0.0178	0.0278
10	0.0056	0.0072	6.68	4.53	0.15	0.01	0.0085	0.1112	0.59	0.07	0.0170	0.0264
11	0.0069	0.0114	7.29	2.85	0.24	0.01	0.0126	0.1278	0.45	0.07	0.0185	0.0275
12	0.0223	0.0107	6.85	2.10	0.22	0.01	0.0126	0.1400	0.26	0.09	0.0211	0.0288
13	0.0416	0.0096	6.97	2.58	0.27	0.01	0.0104	0.1829	0.38	0.08	0.0240	0.0306
14	0.0722	0.0095	10.94	6.21	0.22	0.01	0.0103	0.2366	0.89	0.10	0.0265	0.0340
15	0.1640	0.0093	7.63	9.03	0.24	0.01	0.0066	0.1581	0.86	0.11	0.0296	0.0380
16	0.3445	0.0093	9.91	12.81	0.40	0.03	0.0055	0.1755	2.35	0.10	0.0369	0.0471
17	0.4906	0.0105	11.87	16.30	0.63	0.02	0.0092	0.3294	2.68	0.06	0.0366	0.0457
18	0.4618	0.0137	12.10	29.87	0.39	0.02	0.0114	0.4651	3.59	0.08	0.0382	0.0520
19	0.5055	0.0192	6.65	15.35	0.45	0.01	0.0077	0.2419	1.35	0.09	0.0447	0.0573
20	1.7191	0.0315	3.35	38.89	0.35	0.01	0.0087	0.2946	2.77	0.07	0.0545	0.0713

obtained from cross-sectional regressions in periods 1, 2,. . ., *T*. Specifically, our pooled GLS estimator of γ_k is determined as the weighted mean of the weekly estimates, where the weights are inversely proportional to the variances of these estimates:

$$\hat{\gamma}_k = \sum_{t=1}^{T} Z_{kt}\hat{\gamma}_{kt} \tag{17.1}$$

and

$$\text{var}(\hat{\gamma}_k) = \sum_{t=1}^{T} Z_{kt}^2 \text{var}(\hat{\gamma}_{kt}) \tag{17.2}$$

where

$$Z_{kt} = \frac{[\text{var}(\hat{\gamma}_{kt})]^{-1}}{\sum_t [\text{var}(\hat{\gamma}_{kt})]^{-1}} \tag{17.3}$$

This procedure also allows us to evaluate the statistical significance of the regression coefficients within a reasonable number of observations. Our original portfolio data include approximately 15 000 observations to be used in each weekly cross-sectional regression. Of course, having a sample this large can virtually assure statistically significant results. We consider our approach more conservative in this sense. Indeed, we estimate the original regression coefficients as weekly cross-sections with a huge number of observations. Our test of statistical significance evaluates whether the weekly coefficients are different from zero within 30 weekly observations. 'Everything' is not necessarily statistically significant anymore.

EMPIRICAL RESULTS

Table 17.2 shows the pooled GLS estimates from four alternative specifications of equations (17.1)–(17.3). Before we discuss the results, note that each weekly cross-sectional regression is run with individual dummies fitted for each stock. The coefficient estimates for the stock dummies are not reported. We leave these coefficients unanalyzed partly for brevity, but also to avoid misleading interpretations, as it is rather ambiguous whether they make sense. We would like to learn from the coefficients how each stock deviates from some meaningful norm; what we actually see, however, is how each stock differs from an arbitrarily chosen reference stock.

In the first column of Table 17.2, we regress the selling propensity of investors on the loss and gain variables as well and on a set of investor characteristics. Note that capital losses reduce the selling propensity of investors, as evidenced by the negative and statistically significant coefficient on the loss variable.[12] On the other hand, the statistically significant and positive coefficient on the loss squared suggests that this effect is moderated by sufficiently large losses. There is no statistically significant association between capital gains and the selling propensity of investors. The coefficient on the gain squared, by contrast, is statistically significant and positive. Although the effect of this variable appears only marginal, this finding implies that large enough gains induce investors to sell.

Table 17.2 Determinants of selling propensity

	(1)	(2)	(3)	(4)
LOSS	−0.0457	−0.0547	−0.0534	−0.0444
	(−5.4306)***	(−4.0806)***	(−3.9286)***	(−3.1304)**
LOSS^2	0.0494	0.0491	0.0496	0.0531
	(3.5578)**	(3.5346)**	(3.5674)**	(3.7698)***
GAIN	−0.0020	−0.0028	−0.0028	−0.0018
	(−1.6182)	(−1.3398)	(−1.3304)	(−0.7741)
GAIN^2	0.0001	0.0001	0.0001	0.0001
	(2.9919)**	(2.9126)**	(2.2632)*	(1.0887)
AGE 20–30	0.0082	0.0101	0.0100	0.0099
	(4.2248)***	(4.2317)***	(4.1962)***	(4.1627)***
AGE 30–40	0.0069	0.0084	0.0083	0.0082
	(3.6660)***	(3.8473)***	(3.8115)***	(3.7771)***
AGE 40–50	0.0041	0.0052	0.0051	0.0051
	(2.1999)*	(2.5529)*	(2.5187)*	(2.4781)*
AGE 50–60	0.0017	0.0024	0.0024	0.0023
	(0.9015)	(1.2508)	(1.2243)	(1.1892)
AGE 60–70	0.0001	0.0005	0.0005	0.0004
	(0.0497)	(0.2587)	(0.2379)	(0.2163)
MALE	0.0020	0.0031	0.0030	0.0031
	(1.9002)	(2.2134)*	(2.1715)*	(2.1847)*
ACT	0.1050	0.1049	0.1048	0.1049
	(24.2278)***	(24.1841)***	(24.1550)***	(24.1800)***
HPL	−0.0015	−0.0015	−0.0015	−0.0016
	(−2.4662)*	(−2.4310)*	(−2.3656)*	(−2.5203)*
AGE × *LOSS*		0.0003	0.0003	0.0002
		(1.3206)	(1.2686)	(1.2307)
AGE × *GAIN*		0.0000	0.0000	0.0000
		(0.6018)	(0.6189)	(0.6278)
MALE × *LOSS*		−0.0075	−0.0072	−0.0074
		(−1.1954)	(−1.1416)	(−1.1801)
MALE × *GAIN*		−0.0006	−0.0006	−0.0006
		(−0.5650)	(−0.5793)	(−0.5884)
MVAL × *LOSS*			0.0028	0.0025
			(1.7031)	(1.4867)
MVAL × *GAIN*			−0.0000	−0.0001
			(−0.0495)	(−0.2683)
BTOM × *LOSS*			0.0019	0.0011
			(1.0224)	(0.5530)
BTOM × *GAIN*			0.0000	0.0001
			(0.0575)	(0.0781)
PRET × *LOSS*				−0.1289
				(−3.2097)**
PRET × *GAIN*				−0.0155
				(−2.6680)*
NRET × *LOSS*				−0.0837
				(−2.4788)*
NRET × *GAIN*				0.0014
				(0.2481)

Notes: *t*-values are given in parentheses, ***, **, and * indicate statistical significance at 0.1, 1, and 5 percent, respectively.

To sum up, our results only partially support existing evidence that investors hold losers and sell winners. They do show, however, that investors are loss averse, the fundamental assumption of prospect theory.

Column 1 also reveals that, other things being equal, selling propensity is related to age, consistently decreasing at least up to the 40- to 50-year category. After that, the coefficients, while still of the same sign, are no longer statistically significant. This finding is in contrast to the life-cycle hypothesis, which posits a hump-shaped association between age and investment. Regarding the coefficient on the male dummy, there appears to be no identifiable effect of gender on investor selling propensity. Not surprisingly, both the selling activity and holding period length play an important role in explaining investor selling propensity. The coefficients on both variables are statistically significant, positive for the former and negative for the latter.

Column 2 is similar to column 1, except that we interact the age and male dummies with the loss and gain variables. The results indicate that none of the interaction coefficients is significant, so neither the age nor gender of an investor influences the negative association between selling propensity and capital losses. With the inclusion of the interaction terms, however, the positive coefficient on the male dummy becomes statistically significant, which is in line with Barber and Odean (2001). All other inferences are unchanged, with the coefficient on the loss variable remaining negative and statistically significant and actually increasing slightly in absolute magnitude.

Column 3, which includes four additional interaction terms, reveals results similar to column 2. At this stage, we interact the market value and the book-to-market ratio with the loss and gain variables. As in the previous specification, there is no evidence of a significant association between any of the interaction terms and the selling propensity of investors. The statistically insignificant coefficient on the interaction term ($BTOM \times LOSS$) suggests that whether a stock is growth or value does not affect the decreasing selling propensity of investors with respect to capital losses. Moreover, the positive and statistically insignificant coefficient on the interaction term ($MVAL \times LOSS$) is inconsistent with Ranguelova (2001), who finds that the tendency of investors to hold their losing stocks is concentrated primarily in large-cap stocks. Note here that although both the market value and the book-to-market ratio of a firm have been found to affect investor trading behavior, they should not play any role in a prospect theory context. In other words, an investor with a prospect theory value function would hold on to a losing stock and sell a winning stock regardless of firm characteristics. This is just what the last two findings suggest – behavioral motives, over and above other motives, play a significant part in explaining investor selling propensity.

In column 4, we introduce four more interaction terms, the one-month historical returns with the loss and gain variables. For the most part, the results discussed in the previous paragraph continue to hold, except for the coefficient on the gain squared, which is now insignificant.

In column 4 it is interesting and somewhat peculiar that the lagged returns, both positive and negative, significantly reinforce the negative association between the selling propensity of investors and capital losses. When the stock market has turned bearish and there is no sign of a near recovery, one would expect investors to cut their losses. However, investors actually keep holding their losing stocks, even when the prices of these stocks continue to decline. The coefficient on the interaction term (*PRET* × *GAIN*) is also statistically significant and negative, so whether a stock is a winner or a loser, positive lagged returns significantly reduce the selling propensity of investors. Finally, the coefficient on the interaction term (*NRET* × *GAIN*) turns out to be statistically insignificant.

DISCUSSION

Our aim here was to examine whether individual investors in the Finnish stock market exhibit the disposition effect, the tendency to hold losing stocks and sell winning stocks. Overall, our results suggest that capital losses reduce the selling propensity of investors. There is, however, no opposite effect identifiable with respect to capital gains. While these results offer no direct support for the disposition effect, they do suggest that investors are loss averse.

People are hardly fully rational; nor do investors always behave in accordance with traditional finance theory. But why does it matter if investors are loss averse? The answer is twofold.

First, there is the matter of scientific relevance and overall economic consequences. The tendency of investors to hold losing stocks may have an effect on prices, in which case our results may have important implications for market efficiency and asset pricing. Until now, relatively little has been written about the impact of investor behavior on asset prices. Grinblatt and Han (2001) provide preliminary evidence that the disposition effect may account for the so-called momentum effect, the tendency of past winners to subsequently outperform past losers. But further research on this area is clearly needed.

An equally interesting issue is: what are the practical consequences of investor behavior? Loss aversion may be a common feature of investor behavior, but it generally produces bad decision making and directly affects investor wealth (see, e.g., Odean, 1998). For example, consider pension investors. A large and steadily increasing pot of pension money is being managed by investors who, for the most part, have only little investing ability or knowledge. Since the errors in their decisions are likely to seriously impact their pension incomes and qualities of life, research in this area is of increasing importance.

Given our results, a logical next step would be an examination of whether investor behavior is harmful to portfolio performance. And, over which gains and losses is this harm detectable? We have shown that capital losses on individual stocks reduce the selling propensity of investors. It could be worthwhile to investigate whether this phenomenon holds when gains and losses are defined more broadly, for example at the portfolio level.

Finally, we have used the purchase price of a stock as a reference point against which investors evaluate their gains and losses. As was noted earlier, it is possible that investors have other reference points instead of or in addition to the status quo. Consequently, it would be informative to repeat this study with different reference prices.

ACKNOWLEDGMENTS

This research was financially supported by the Research Foundation of the OKO Bank Group and the University of Oulu Foundation, which is gratefully acknowledged. We also thank the Finnish Central Securities Depository for provision of the data.

NOTES

1. Throughout this chapter, winning and losing investments are determined from the point of view of individual investors. This being the case, a stock that has increased in market value is not necessarily considered a winner by an individual investor. Correspondingly, a stock that has decreased in market value may not necessarily be considered a loser.
2. More recently, these authors have continued to elaborate on this early work to show how prospect theory is applied to certainty situations (prospect theory under certainty, Tversky and Kahneman, 1991) and to prospects with more than two outcomes (cumulative prospect theory, Tversky and Kahneman, 1992).
3. Psychological research shows that people often see patterns in random processes and expect trends to revert (e.g. Tversky and Kahneman, 1971; Andreassen, 1987; 1988). Just as in a series of coin flips, where people easily exaggerate the likelihood of a tail after a sequence of heads, investors may believe that a price increase is more likely following a price decline.
4. The disposition effect in upward-moving markets is well documented in the literature. For example, Grinblatt and Keloharju (2001) find a strong disposition effect in the Finnish stock market during the period 1995–96 using a similar database to the current one.
5. For further evidence on the disposition effect in experimental markets, see Kogut and Phillips (1994), Heilmann et al. (2000) and Chui (2001).
6. Jegadeesh and Titman (1993), among others, demonstrate that trading strategies, which buy past winners and sell past losers, yield significantly positive returns over three- to 12-month holding periods. Hong et al. (2000) establish further that once one moves past the very smallest-capitalization stocks, the profitability of momentum strategies sharply declines.
7. Individual investors are initially identified by their social security number. In our data, for security reasons, a specific running number is assigned to each original identification number.
8. The Portfolio Index includes all stocks listed in the HEX main list. It differs from the All-Share Index in terms of a weight limitation: if a company's market capitalization exceeds a limit of 10 percent, its weight in the index is limited to exactly 10 percent.
9. These include gifts, inheritances, wills, distributions of matrimonial assets, forced auctions, forfeitures of shares, redemptions, mergers, subscription rights, share series conversions, shares subscribed with options or convertible bonds, and miscellaneous activities relating to the maintenance of the register.
10. For example, Heath et al. (1999) consider several potential reference points and find that the maximum stock price reached over the previous year has the strongest effect on investors' decision to exercise stock options. Gneezy (2000) examines the trading behavior of investors in an experimental setting, and finds the maximum stock price to be a significant reference point. Grinblatt and Keloharju (2001) report that monthly highs and lows affect investors' propensity to sell a stock. Reference price dynamics is considered in, e.g., Grinblatt and Han (2001).
11. To check the robustness of our results, we also run the subsequent models without the three most profitable portfolios, as well as excluding the Nokia shares. In both cases, the results remain substantially the same as those reported in Table 17.2.
12. When interpreting the signs of the coefficient estimates, note that both losses and gains are measured in absolute terms.

REFERENCES

Ando, A. and F. Modigliani (1963), 'The "life cycle" hypothesis of saving: aggregate implications and tests,' *American Economic Review*, **53**, 55–84.

Andreassen, P. (1987), 'On the social psychology of the stock market: aggregate attributional effects and the regressiveness of prediction,' *Journal of Personality and Social Psychology*, **53**, 490–96.

Andreassen, P. (1988), 'Explaining the price–volume relationship: the difference between price changes and changing prices,' *Organizational Behavior and Human Decision Processes*, **41**, 371–89.
Barber, B.M. and T. Odean (2001), 'Boys will be boys: gender, overconfidence, and common stock investment,' *Quarterly Journal of Economics*, **116**, 261–92.
Bremer, M. and K. Kato (1996), 'Trading volume for winners and losers on the Tokyo Stock Exchange,' *Journal of Financial and Quantitative Analysis*, **31**, 127–41.
Case, K. and R. Shiller (1988), 'The behavior of home buyers in boom and post-boom markets,' *New England Economic Review*, **80**, 29–46.
Chui, P.M.W. (2001), 'An experimental study of the disposition effect: evidence from Macau,' *Journal of Psychology and Financial Markets*, **2**, 216–22.
Constantinides, G.M. (1984), 'Optimal stock trading with personal taxes: implications for prices and the abnormal January returns,' *Journal of Financial Economics*, **13**, 65–90.
Dyl, E. (1977), 'Capital gains taxation and the year-end stock market behavior,' *Journal of Finance*, **32**, 165–75.
Ferris, S.P., R.A. Haugen and A.K. Makhija (1988), 'Predicting contemporary volume with historic volume at differential price levels: evidence supporting the disposition effect,' *Journal of Finance*, **43**, 677–97.
Genesove, D. and C. Mayer (2001), 'Loss aversion and seller behavior: evidence from the housing market,' Working Paper, University of Pennsylvania.
Gneezy, U. (2000), 'Updating the reference level: experimental evidence,' Working Paper, University of Haifa.
Grinblatt, M. and B. Han (2001), 'The disposition effect and momentum,' Working Paper, UCLA.
Grinblatt, M. and M. Keloharju (2001), 'What makes investors trade?,' *Journal of Finance*, **56**, 589–616.
Harris, L. (1988), 'Predicting contemporary volume with historic volume at differential price levels: evidence supporting the disposition effect: discussion,' *Journal of Finance*, **43**, 698–9.
Heath, C., S. Huddard and M. Lang (1999), 'Psychological factors and stock option exercise,' *Quarterly Journal of Economics*, **114**, 601–28.
Heilmann, K., V. Lager and A. Oehler (2000), 'The disposition effect – evidence about the investors aversion to realize losses: a contribution to behavioral finance through the use of experimental call markets,' Working Paper, University of Bamberg.
Hong, H., T. Lim and J.C. Stein (2000), 'Bad news travels slowly: size, analyst coverage, and the profitability of momentum strategies,' *Journal of Finance*, **55**, 265–95.
Jegadeesh, N. and S. Titman (1993), 'Returns to buying winners and selling losers: implications for stock market efficiency,' *Journal of Finance*, **48**, 65–91.
Kahneman, D. and A. Tversky (1979), 'Prospect theory: an analysis of decision under risk,' *Econometrica*, **47**, 263–91.
Kogut, C.A. and O.R. Phillips (1994), 'Individual decision making in an investment setting,' *Journal of Economic Behavior and Organization*, **25**, 459–71.
Lakonishok, J. and S. Smidt (1986), 'Volume for winners and losers: taxation and other motives for stock trading,' *Journal of Finance*, **41**, 951–74.
Litzenberger, R.H. and K. Ramaswamy (1979), 'The effect of personal taxes and dividends on capital asset prices: theory and empirical evidence,' *Journal of Financial Economics*, **7**, 163–95.
Locke, P.R. and S.C. Mann (1999), 'Do professional traders exhibit loss realization aversion?,' Working Paper, Texas Christian University.
Modigliani, F. (1986), 'Life cycle, individual thrift, and the wealth of nations,' *American Economic Review*, **76**, 297–312.
Odean, T. (1998), 'Are investors reluctant to realize their losses?,' *Journal of Finance*, **53**, 1775–98.
Ranguelova, E. (2001), 'Disposition effect and firm size: new evidence on individual investor trading activity,' Working Paper, Harvard University.
Shapira, Z. and I. Venezia (2001), 'Patterns of behavior of professionally managed and independent investors,' *Journal of Banking and Finance*, **25**, 1573–87.
Shefrin, H. and M. Statman (1985), 'The disposition to sell winners too early and ride losers too long: theory and evidence,' *Journal of Finance*, **40**, 777–90.
Tversky, A. and D. Kahneman (1971), 'Belief in the law of small numbers,' *Psychological Bulletin*, **47**, 105–10.
Tversky, A. and D. Kahneman (1991), 'Loss-aversion in riskless choice: a reference-dependent model,' *Quarterly Journal of Economics*, **106**, 1039–61.
Tversky, A. and D. Kahneman (1992), 'Advances in prospect theory: cumulative representation of uncertainty,' *Journal of Risk and Uncertainty*, **5**, 297–323.
Weber, M. and C. Camerer (1998), 'The disposition effect in securities trading: an experimental analysis,' *Journal of Economic Behavior and Organization*, **33**, 167–84.

18 The impact of business and consumer sentiment on stock market returns: evidence from Brazil

Pablo Calafiore, Gökçe Soydemir and Rahul Verma

INTRODUCTION

In recent years there has been a lively debate on the possible linkages between the behavioral aspects of investors and stock returns. Researchers such as Black (1986), Trueman (1988), DeLong et al. (DSSW) (1990, 1991), Shleifer and Summers (1990), Lakonishok et al. (1992), Campbell and Kyle (1993), Shefrin and Statman (1994), Palomino (1996), Barberis et al. (1998), Daniel et al. (1998) and Hong and Stein (1999) provide the theoretical framework describing the role of investor sentiment in determining stock prices. An implication of these studies is that noise traders, acting as a group of investors who do not make investment decisions based on a company's fundamentals, are capable of affecting stock prices by way of unpredictable changes in their responses.

Several empirical studies examine the influence of sentiments on stock returns based on the 'noise trader model' of DSSW (1990) (Brown and Cliff, 2004, 2005; Lee et al., 2002; Fisher and Statman, 2000; Clarke and Statman, 1998; Solt and Statman 1988; De Bondt, 1993). In general, these studies provide evidence for the existence of strong comovements between individual and institutional investor sentiment and stock market returns.

The previous literature on investor sentiment and stock prices provides inconclusive results on whether causal effects are attributable to rational risk factors, or noise or some combination of both. These studies simply infer that sentiment is fully irrational; however, no empirical test is conducted to investigate the extent to which sentiment may be rational or irrational (e.g. Brown and Cliff, 2004, 2005; Lee et al., 2002). Moreover, any cross-variable dynamics that may exist between consumer and business sentiments are ignored.

In a recent study, Verma et al. (2008) examine the role of sentiments of both individual and institutional investors on US stock market returns, analyzing their simultaneous impact. They find that rational sentiment has a larger impact than irrational sentiment on stock market returns.

Using the framework provided by Verma et al. (2008), in this study we employ a monthly database of consumer sentiment at the individual level, the Brazilian Consumer Confidence Index compiled by the Fundaçao Getulio Vargas. This index is modeled after the University of Michigan consumer sentiment survey. In addition, we analyze the impact of business sentiments on stock market returns using monthly data from the survey of Brazilian leading manufacturers.

We make the following contributions to the existing literature: first, unlike previous studies that treat sentiment as fully irrational, we focus on both consumer and business rational and irrational sentiments, and explore how fundamental and noise trading may affect stock market returns. Second, we examine the impact of rational and irrational sentiment of individual consumers and businesses in an emerging market such as Brazil.

Third, following Verma et al. (2008), we investigate the effects of the consumer and business confidence indexes on the stock market returns simultaneously in one model to differentiate between the two types of sentiment.

Fourth, unlike previous studies that examine the unidirectional relationship between sentiment and stock returns, we examine bidirectional causality to investigate the role of past stock performance in the formation of rational and irrational business and consumer sentiments. Lastly, we examine not only the anticipated adjustments in sentiment but also the unanticipated component of sentiments in stock returns in line with rational expectations theory.

The results of the generalized impulses generated from a vector auto regression (VAR) model reveal the following empirical results. First, the effect of a once-for-all increase in rational business and consumer sentiments on Bovespa (see below) index returns is positive and significant during the first month and insignificant thereafter. Second, in terms of magnitude, rational business and consumer sentiments have a much greater impact than irrational business and consumer sentiments. Third, the finding of positive and significant rational business sentiment impact on Bovespa index returns is also consistent with the earlier findings from rational consumer sentiments that a one-time positive shock to rational (irrational) sentiments leads to an increase (decrease) in stock market returns around the time of the first period. Fourth, the response of Bovespa index returns to consumer irrational sentiments is insignificant. Lastly, the response of Bovespa index returns to irrational business sentiments is negative and significant during the first month, becoming insignificant immediately thereafter. This immediate negative effect of irrational business sentiments, unlike the findings from irrational consumer sentiments, is consistent with the view that irrational sentiments do have the potential to influence stock market returns.

These results have important practical implications for investors and policy makers. We find that business and consumer sentiment measures may be related to both rational as well as irrational behavior. Previous studies treat consumer and business sentiments fully as irrational behavior; however, our results further support the economic-fundamentals-based arguments of stock market returns. Since we find evidence in favor of both types of sentiments, our results are consistent with the view that sentiments are mostly a manifestation of the rational risk factors driving expected returns of stocks, with irrational factors also having an impact on stock returns. Therefore investors could improve their portfolio performance by considering both rational as well as irrational sentiments as determinants of stock returns.

The remainder of this chapter is organized as follows: the second section reviews the existing literature on sentiments and stock prices, and the third section presents the model. The fourth section presents the data and descriptive statistics, and the fifth describes the econometric methodology. The section after that reports the empirical findings, and the final section concludes.

RELATED LITERATURE

Black (1986) is one of the first authors to consider the role of investor sentiments and noise trading in the financial markets. He argues that 'noise' makes trading in financial markets possible, but also makes them imperfect. In his basic model of financial markets, Black contrasts noise with information and suggests that people sometimes trade on noise as if it were information. Trueman (1988) extends Black's assertion that noise trading must be an important factor in securities markets and explains why anyone would rationally want to trade on noise.

DSSW (1990), building upon Black's (1986) noise trader framework, present a model where noise traders acting as a group can influence stock prices in equilibrium. In this model the deviations in price from fundamental value, created by changes in investor sentiment, introduce a systematic risk that is priced. DSSW shows that risk created by the unpredictability of investor sentiment reduces the attractiveness of information traders to carry out arbitrage.

DSSW (1991) present a model of portfolio allocation by noise traders and show that noise traders as a group can earn expected returns higher than rational investors, and can survive in terms of wealth gain in the long run, due to unpredictability in their sentiments. Campbell and Kyle (1993) present a model where stock prices are influenced by competitive interaction between noise traders and rational investors. Noise traders affect stock prices because they do not maximize utility but instead trade exogenously while the rational investors have constant absolute risk aversion.

Shleifer and Summers (1990) present an alternative to the efficient markets paradigm that stresses the role of investor sentiment and limited arbitrage in determining stock prices. They show that the assumption of limited arbitrage is more plausible as a description of risky asset markets than the assumption of complete arbitrage on which the market efficiency hypothesis is based. This implies that changes in sentiments are not fully countered by arbitrageurs and therefore may affect stock returns.

Shefrin and Statman (1994) present the behavioral capital asset pricing theory where noise traders interact with information traders. They show that the effect of noise traders in the market depends on specific cognitive errors committed. In contrast to information, noise traders' sentiment may act as a driver moving the market away from efficiency.

A study by Lakonishok et al. (1992) suggests that institutional investors influence prices in small markets (stocks with small market capitalization). Palomino (1996) extends the DSSW (1990) model for an imperfectly competitive market. Palomino (1996) shows that in an imperfectly competitive market with risk-averse investors, noise traders may earn higher returns and obtain higher expected utility than rational investors. This implies that if relative success breeds imitation, then noise traders will likely survive in the long run.

Wang (2001) argues that the DSSW (1990) model is static in nature and inadequate to capture noise traders' long-run survival aspects. Wang examines the dynamics of non-rational investors by modeling the wealth accumulation process as it emerges from the market competition between the two groups of rational and non-rational investors. The model shows that bullish sentiment can survive while bearish sentiment cannot survive in the long run.

Overall, these models suggest that the unpredictability in investor sentiment of noise traders acting as a group can introduce a systematic risk that is priced in markets. Following these predictions, several empirical studies have examined the role of sentiment in stock pricing. These studies have used either indirect measures or direct measures of investor sentiment.

Studies using indirect measures include the following proxies: close-ended funds discount (Gemmill and Thomas, 2002; Baker and Wurgler, 2006; Sias et al., 2001; Neal and Wheatley, 1998; Swaminathan, 1996; Elton et al., 1998; Chan et al., 1993; Lee et al., 1991); market-performance-based measures (Brown and Cliff, 2004); trading-activity-based measures (Brown and Cliff, 2004; Neal and Wheatley, 1998); derivative variables (Brown and Cliff, 2004); dividend premium (Baker and Wurgler, 2006); and IPOs-related measures (Baker and Wurgler, 2006; Brown and Cliff, 2004). Overall, these studies do not provide a consensus on whether the proxies chosen are appropriate measures of investor sentiment; in addition, these studies show mixed results in their debate on the linkages between sentiment and stock returns.

Studies using direct measures employ sentiment surveys data that indicate the expectations of market participants. Research related to individual investor sentiment find strong comovements with stock market returns (Brown and Cliff, 2004; De Bondt, 1993) and mixed results regarding its role in short-term predictability of stock prices (Brown and Cliff, 2004; Fisher and Statman, 2000). Similarly, studies examining institutional sentiment find strong comovements with stock market returns (Brown and Cliff, 2004) and mixed results regarding its short-run implications on stock prices (Brown and Cliff, 2004; Lee et al., 2002; Clarke and Statman, 1998; Solt and Statman, 1988). Also, Brown and Cliff (2005) examine the long-run implications of institutional investor sentiment and find strong relationships with long-horizon stock returns. Overall, these studies provide powerful and consistent empirical support for the hypothesis that stock prices are affected by individual and institutional investor sentiments.

One major drawback in these studies is that they do not differentiate between sentiment-induced noise trading and sentiment-induced fundamental trading. Specifically, they do not explain whether the effect of sentiment on stock returns can be attributed entirely to investor exuberance or to fully rational expectations or a combination of both. A recent study by Verma et al. (2008) examines the role of sentiment of both individual and institutional investors on US stock market returns analyzing their simultaneous impact. They find that rational sentiments have a larger impact than irrational sentiments on stock market returns.

As mentioned earlier, our study contributes to the existing literature in several different ways. We now describe the model in detail.

MODEL

Given that sentiments partially contain rational expectations-based risk factors (Brown and Cliff, 2005; Shleifer and Summers, 1990), it is very likely that stock returns are affected by both fundamental and noise sentiments. Hirshleifer's (2001) model relates expected returns to both risks and investor misvaluation. When an investor is bullish or bearish, then this could be a rational reflection of the future period's expectation or irrational enthusiasm or a combination of both. Hence, first we decompose investor sentiment into two sentiments: (i) rational sentiment based on the market fundamentals and (ii) irrational sentiment based on noise.

We formulate equations (18.1) and (18.2) and model the rational and irrational effects of fundamentals and noise, respectively, on consumer and business sentiments:

$$Sentt_{1t} = \gamma_0 + \sum_{j=1}^{J} \gamma_j Fund_{jt} + \xi_t \tag{18.1}$$

$$Sentt_{2t} = \theta_0 + \sum_{j=1}^{J} \theta_j Fund_{jt} + \vartheta_t \tag{18.2}$$

where γ_0 and θ_0 are constants, γ_1 and θ_j are the parameters to be estimated; ξ_t and ϑ_t are the random error terms. $Sentt_{1t}$ and $Sentt_{2t}$ represent the shifts in sentiments of consumer and businesses respectively at time t. $Fund_{jt}$ is the set of fundamentals representing rational expectations based on risk factors that have been shown to carry non-redundant information in conditional asset pricing literature. The fitted values of equations (18.1) and (18.2) capture the rational sentiment of sentiments (e.g. $Sent\hat{t}_{1t}$ and $Sent\hat{t}_{2t}$). On the other hand, the residual of equations (18.1) and (18.2) capture the irrational sentiment of sentiments (e.g. ξ_t and ϑ_t).

In order to avoid misspecification, we model jointly the sentiments of consumers and businesses. In particular, shocks originating from sentiments of one class of respondents not considered might mistakenly be seen as a disturbance originating from sentiments of another class of respondents included in the analysis.

Next, we analyze the extent to which the stock returns are affected by consumer and business sentiments. Sentiments may be irrational or rational. Accordingly, the sentiment variables are decomposed into the rational and irrational sentiments based on equations (18.1) and (18.2) and included in the return generating process as:

$$R_t = \alpha_0 + \alpha_1 Sent\hat{t}_{1t} + \alpha_2 Sent\hat{t}_{2t} + \alpha_3 \xi_t + \alpha_4 \vartheta_t + \rho_t \tag{18.3}$$

where α_0 is a constant while α_1, α_2, α_3 and α_4 are the parameters to be estimated; ρ_t is the random error term. Specifically the parameters α_1 and α_2 capture the effects of sentiments induced by fundamental trading on the part of consumers and business respectively; while α_3 and α_4 capture the effects of sentiments induced noise trading by consumer and business respectively.

DATA AND DESCRIPTIVE STATISTICS

The data are in monthly intervals and cover the period from March 1995 to May 2008. All data are from DataStream Advance. To measure consumer and business sentiment we employ survey data similar to those used in the literature. As a proxy for consumer sentiment we use the monthly Brazilian Consumer Confidence Index compiled by the Fundaçao Getulio Vargas. This index is created using a questionnaire based on the University of Michigan consumer sentiment survey. Moreover, we analyze the impact of business sentiments on stock market returns using monthly data from the survey of Brazilian leading manufacturers.

We employ the Bovespa index to characterize the overall performance of the Brazilian stock market. This trade-weighted index is the main indicator of the Brazilian stock market's average performance and reflects the variation of Bovespa's most traded stocks. The index comprises a theoretical stock portfolio and its components are adjusted every four months. The Bovespa index reflects not only the variation of the stock prices but also the impact of the distribution of benefits, and is considered an indicator that evaluates the total return of its components stocks. We use the continuously compounded returns for Bovespa estimated by DataStream.

We include the following variables as fundamentals that have been shown to carry non-redundant information in the asset pricing literature: (i) economic growth (*IIP*): given the absence of GDP monthly series for Brazil, we use the monthly changes in the Brazilian industrial production index (*IIP*) as a proxy for economic growth; (ii) short-term interest rates (*BT_Bill*): measured as the effective yield on Letras do Tesouro Nacional issued by the Brazilian Central Bank (BCB) of 31 days or longer, calculated from the discount. The yield is that of the last issue of the month; (iii) business conditions (*Selic_FFR*): measured as the average rate on loans between commercial banks. The Special Settlement and Custody System (SELIC) overnight rate is a weighted average rate on loans between financial institutions involving firm sales of or repurchase agreements based on federal securities in the SELIC. The rate is weighted by loan amounts; (iv) country risk premia (*EMBI*): measured as the value of JPMorgan Emerging Markets Bond Index Plus (EMBI + Brazil), which evaluates the risk spread of the Brazilian sovereign external debt over a general risk-free bond, in this case the US Treasury; it tracks total returns for actively traded external debt instruments in Brazil, including US-dollar-denominated Brady bonds, Eurobonds and traded loans issued by sovereign entities; (v) currency fluctuation (*ExchRate*): measured as the changes in the Brazilian real to US dollar exchange rate index; (vi) dividend yield (*Div*): measured as the dividend yield for firms trading at the São Paulo stock exchange over the past 12 months calculated by Datastream as Bovespa does not currently calculate this data type; (vii) inflation (*CPI*): measured as the monthly changes in the broad Brazilian consumer price index or IPCA; (viii) terms of trade (*BRTOT*) for Brazil: measured as the monthly ratio between the export price index and the import price index. Export price index measures the changes in the prices of exports of merchandise from a country. The import price index measures the changes in the prices of imports of merchandise into a country. The index numbers for each reference period relate to prices of imports landed into the country during the period.

Table 18.1 reports the descriptive statistics of the variables previously described. The mean of $Sentt_1$ and $Sentt_2$ are approximately 23 percent and 10 percent respectively. This suggests that both consumers and businesses have been bullish during most of the sample period. Interestingly, individual investors have been more bullish than institutional investors.

The two sentiments have higher standard deviations than those of stock market indexes, suggesting that sentiments have been highly volatile during the sample period. The mean return of Bovespa is approximately 1.53 percent, with a standard deviation of 0.1007.

Table 18.1 Descriptive statistics

	Mean	Median	Maximum	Minimum	Std dev.	Skewness	Kurtosis
$Sentt_1$	0.2327	0.3000	19.2000	−20.8000	5.8250	−0.1573	4.3637
$Sentt_2$	0.1023	0.0978	2.3748	−3.8947	0.9397	−1.1528	6.8481
Bovespa	0.0153	0.0179	0.2761	−0.4090	0.1007	−0.4486	4.4783
IIP	0.0026	0.0032	0.0662	−0.1189	0.0199	−1.0106	10.8667
BT_Bill	22.6074	20.1200	84.5700	10.5000	10.4510	2.4425	11.6049
Selic_FFR	24.3507	19.0600	121.9600	11.1800	14.6838	2.8058	14.5708
EMBI	600.0298	592.7090	1936.4620	141.4420	322.4903	1.0610	4.8116
ExchRate	1.9406	1.9217	3.7463	0.8420	0.7475	0.2701	2.2116
Div	3.7498	3.6300	36.1700	0.6900	2.9094	8.1433	91.4306
CPI	0.7087	0.5100	6.8400	−0.5100	0.7658	3.7013	26.3024
BRTOT	99.2854	98.0000	113.2000	89.0000	5.7886	0.4384	2.2544

Notes: the variables are consumer sentiment ($Sentt_1$), business sentiment ($Sentt_2$), monthly returns on Bovespa index (*Bovespa*), Brazilian economic growth (*IIP*), short-term interest rate (*BT_Bill*), business conditions (*Selic_FFR*), country risk premia (*EMBI*), Brazilian Real versus US dollar exchange rate (*ExchRate*), inflation (*CPI*), terms of trade (*BRTOT*).

Table 18.2 reports the cross-correlation between stock market returns, sentiment variables and the fundamentals. The correlations between the two sentiments variables is approximately 0.14. The low contemporaneous correlations between the Bovespa index and consumer and business sentiment measures may indicate an absence of feedback effects between the two. In addition, the low correlations among the fundamentals suggest that each variable represents the unique risk that is independent of the other, with the exception of the Brazilian Central Bank short-term bill rate which, as expected, appears to be highly correlated to the short-term SELIC rate.

ECONOMETRIC METHODOLOGY

Studies such as Brown and Cliff (2004, 2005), Lee et al. (2002), and Verma et al. (2008) suggest that stock market returns and consumer and business sentiments may act as a system. Consequently, to examine the postulated relationships we choose the VAR model by Sims (1980) as an appropriate econometric approach.

In addition, we take into consideration the following issues before the estimation stage. In an efficient financial market, stock market prices will react only to unanticipated events reflected in innovations to explanatory variables. Elton and Gruber (1991) argue that all the variables in a multi-index model need to be surprises or innovations and therefore should not be predicted from their past values. Asset pricing models such as arbitrage pricing theory (APT) use the unanticipated component (innovations) of explanatory variables. Since the formulated models are multi-index models, direct estimation in its present form would give only the relationships between the anticipated components. Such estimation would mean ignoring the effect of changes in the unanticipated components of sentiments and stock market returns, and therefore could be misleading. In order to overcome potential misspecification problems, we use impulse

Table 18.2 Cross-correlations

	$Sentt_1$	$Sentt_2$	*BovespA*	*IIP_ PCT_CH*	*BT_Bill*	*Selic_FFR*	*BT90_BT30*	*EMBI*	*Exch-Rate*	*Div*	*CPI*	*BRTOT*
$Sentt_1$	1.00											
$Sentt_2$	0.14	1.00										
Bovespa	0.16	0.29	1.00									
IIP_PCT_CH	0.05	0.25	0.06	1.00								
BT_Bill	−0.06	−0.27	−0.13	−0.14	1.00							
Selic_FFR	−0.07	−0.22	0.01	−0.09	0.90	1.00						
BT90_BT30	−0.16	−0.20	−0.23	−0.08	0.58	0.42	1.00					
EMBI	−0.03	−0.07	−0.27	−0.02	0.71	0.59	0.69	1.00				
ExchRate	−0.01	0.02	−0.01	−0.03	0.66	0.69	0.38	0.66	1.00			
Div	−0.13	−0.07	−0.17	−0.03	0.69	0.69	0.42	0.62	0.85	1.00		
CPI	0.12	0.11	0.07	−0.14	0.46	0.35	0.35	0.57	0.51	0.26	1.00	
BRTOT	0.01	0.05	0.05	0.09	−0.77	−0.77	−0.46	−0.62	−0.75	−0.70	−0.36	1.00

Notes: the variables are consumer sentiment ($Sentt_1$), business sentiment ($Sentt_2$), monthly returns on Bovespa index (*Bovespa*), Brazilian economic growth (*IIP*), short-term interest rate (*BT_Bill*), business conditions (*Selic_FFR*), economic risk premia (*BT90_BT30*), Country risk premia (*EMBI*), inflation (*CPI*), terms of trade (*BRTOT*).

response functions (predicted pattern of surprise changes or innovations) generated from the VAR model. Additionally, several studies show that prediction performance of VAR models has been better than that of structural models (Litterman and Supel, 1983; Hakkio and Morris, 1984; Litterman, 1984; Lupoletti and Webb, 1986; Webb, 1999).

The transmission of information contained in the stock returns may not always be contemporaneous due to the time delays in the generation and dissemination of information concerning both the noise and rational factors, especially macroeconomic variables. Reporting delays may create lags between the observation of data concerning such variables and the incorporation of this information to stock prices. For this reason, a model in which all variables are measured at time t would imply an unrealistic assumption of only contemporaneous association. We use the Akaike information criterion (AIC) and the Schwarz information criterion (SIC) to help in identifying the appropriate lag lengths. The lags in the VAR model capture the dynamic feedback effects in a relatively unconstrained way and it is a good approximation to the true data-generating process. We express the VAR model as:

$$Z(t) = C + \sum_{s=1}^{m} A(s)Z(t - m) + \varepsilon(t) \tag{18.4}$$

where, $Z(t)$ is a column vector of variables under consideration, C is the deterministic sentiment comprised of a constant, $A(s)$ is a matrix of coefficients, m is the lag length and $\varepsilon(t)$ is a vector of random error terms.

The VAR specification allows researchers to integrate Monte Carlo simulations and obtain confidence bands around the point estimates (Doan, 1988; Genberg et al. 1987; Hamilton, 1994). The probable response of one variable to a one-time unit shock in another variable can be captured by impulse response functions. The impulse response functions represent the behavior of the series in response to pure shocks while keeping the effect of other variables constant. Given that impulse responses tend to be non-linear functions of the estimated parameters, we build confidence bands around the mean response. When the upper and lower bands carry the same sign, impulse responses are considered statistically significant at the 95 percent confidence level.

Traditional orthogonalized forecast error variance decomposition results based on Choleski factorization of VAR innovations may be sensitive to variable ordering (Pesaran and Shin, 1996; Koop et al., 1996; Pesaran and Shin, 1998). In order to alleviate potential problems of misspecifications, we use the generalized impulses technique described by Pesaran and Shin (1998) in which an orthogonal set of innovations does not depend on the variable ordering.

ESTIMATION RESULTS

We check the time-series properties of each variable by performing unit root tests before proceeding to the main results. Table 18.3 reports the results of unit root tests using the augmented Dickey–Fuller (ADF) test (Dickey and Fuller, 1979, 1981). Considering the loss in degrees of freedom and based on the AIC and SIC criteria (Diebold, 2003), the appropriate number of lags is determined to be two. In the case

Table 18.3 Unit root tests

	ADF	Lag length	KPSS (4)
Levels			
$Sentt_1$	−3.684	2	0.523***
$Sentt_2$	−3.818**	2	0.152***
IIP	−1.801	2	0.625***
BT_Bill	−2.983	2	0.169**
Selic_FFR	−3.649	2	0.361***
EMBI	−2.773	2	0.373***
ExchRate	−1.415	2	0.673***
Div	−5.831	2	0.187**
CPI_Chge	−4.361	2	0.284***
Bovespa	−1.764	2	0.653***
SP500	−0.854	2	0.435***
BRTOT	−1.252	2	0.450***
UST_Bill	−1.723	2	0.316***
First difference			
$Sentt_1$	−9.051***	2	0.030
$Sentt_2$	−9.701***	2	0.105
IIP	−7.886***	2	0.173
BT_Bill	−11.611***	2	0.039
Selic_FFR	−10.867***	2	0.417*
EMBI	−7.185***	2	0.041
ExchRate	6.616***	2	0.184
Div	−12.463***	2	0.020
CPI_Chge	−10.720***	2	0.323
Bovespa	−5.762***	2	0.163
SP500	−5.450***	2	0.438*
BRTOT	−5.745***	2	0.142
UST_Bill	−4.236***	2	0.151

Notes: ***, ** and * denote rejection of the null hypothesis of unit roots for the augmented Dickey–Fuller (ADF) tests at the 1%, 5% and 10% significance levels respectively.
***, ** and * denote rejection of the null hypothesis of stationarity for the Kwiatkowski, Phillips, Schmidt and Shin (KPSS) tests at the 1%, 5% and 10% significance levels.
Unit root tests were run with linear trend and intercept at levels, and intercept only at first differences.
Lag lengths were chosen using the Akaike Information Criterion (AIC) and the obtained residuals are white noise.

of the ADF test, the null hypothesis of non-stationarity is rejected. These results do not change if we include drift or trend terms in the ADF test equations (Dolado et al., 1990).

Next we decompose the sentiment variables into rational and irrational components based on fitted and residuals of equations (18.1) and (18.2). Specifically, we estimate two separate ordinary least squares regressions based on equations (18.1) and (18.2). The low correlations among variables related to fundamentals, as presented in Table 18.2, suggests that multicollinearity is not a problem in this analysis.

Table 18.4 Effects of fundamentals on consumer sentiments (dependent variable: $Sentt_1$)

Variable	Coefficient	SE	*t*-statistic	Prob.
IIP	1.09	0.11	10.25	0.00
BT_Bill	−0.14	0.25	−0.56	0.58
Selic_FFR	0.41	0.23	1.78	0.08
EMBI	−0.01	0.00	−3.02	0.00
CPI	2.21	1.72	1.29	0.20
ExchRate	−1.18	2.01	−0.59	0.56
Div	−0.08	0.26	−0.32	0.75
BRTOT	−0.11	0.21	−0.50	0.61
C	17.00	24.25	0.70	0.48
R^2	0.69			
AIC	7.28			
SC	7.46			
Sum squared resid.	12268.77			
Log likelihood	−577.29			
F-statistic	41.71			
Prob(*F*-statistic)	0.00			

Notes: the variables are consumer sentiment ($Sentt_1$), Brazilian economic growth (*IIP*), short-term interest rate (*BT_Bill*), business conditions (*Selic_FFR*), country risk premia (*EMBI*), Brazilian real versus US dollar exchange rate (*ExchRate*), inflation (*CPI*), Bovespa dividend yield (*Div*), terms of trade (*BRTOT*).

$$Sentt_{1t} = \gamma_0 + \sum_{j=1}^{J} \gamma_j Fund_{jt} + \xi_t$$

Table 18.4 reports that consumer sentiment is significantly related to industrial production, business conditions (as measured by the *Selic* rate), and country risk premia (as measured by *EMBI*). In the same way, Table 18.5 presents that business sentiments are significantly related to industrial production, business conditions (as measured by the *Selic* rate), country risk premia (as measured by *EMBI*), changes in inflation (as measured by *CPI*), and changes in the dollar–real exchange rate (*ExchRate*). These results are consistent with the argument of Brown and Cliff (2005) that consumer and business sentiments may contain a combination of both rational and irrational components and not necessarily only noise. We generate the fitted values and residuals for the regression to compute the rational and irrational components of consumer and business sentiments.

To analyze the relative effects of rational and irrational consumer and business sentiments on stock market returns as depicted in equation (18.3), we estimate a five-variable VAR model with two lags. The variables included in this second VAR model are: Bovespa index returns, rational sentiments of consumers and businesses, and irrational sentiments of consumers and businesses. For example, in addition to the returns on the market index, we include the four new variables derived from equations (18.2) and (18.3) related to rational and irrational sentiments of consumers and businesses.[1]

Autoregressive systems are difficult to describe concisely (Sims, 1980). It is difficult to

Table 18.5 Effects of fundamentals on business sentiments (dependent variable: $Sentt_2$)

Variable	Coefficient	SE	*t*-statistic	Prob.
IIP	0.15	0.03	5.67	0.00
BT_Bill	0.11	0.08	1.27	0.21
Selic_FFR	−0.17	0.07	−2.39	0.02
EMBI	0.00	0.00	−3.13	0.00
CPI	2.10	0.37	5.61	0.00
ExchRate	−1.04	0.44	−2.35	0.02
Div	−0.11	0.06	−1.91	0.06
BRTOT	−0.09	0.05	−1.89	0.06
C	97.90	5.28	18.55	0.00
R^2	0.64			
AIC	4.21			
SC	4.38			
Sum squared resid.	551.89			
Log likelihood	−321.46			
F-statistic	32.20			
Prob(*F*-statistic)	0.00			

Notes: the variables are business sentiment ($Sentt_2$), Brazilian economic growth (*IIP*), short-term interest rate (*BT_Bill*), business conditions (*Selic_FFR*), country risk premia (*EMBI*), Brazilian real versus US dollar exchange rate (*ExchRate*), inflation (*CPI*), Bovespa dividend yield (*Div*), terms of trade (*BRTOT*).

$$Sentt_{2t} = \theta_0 + \sum_{j=1}^{J} \theta_j Fund_{jt} + \vartheta_t$$

make sense of them by examining the coefficients in the regression equations themselves. Likewise, Sims (1980) and Enders (2003) show that the *t*-tests on individual coefficients are not very reliable guides and therefore do not uncover the important interrelationships among the variables. Sims (1980) recommends focusing on the system's impulse response functions (IRFs) to typical random shocks. We analyze the relevant IRFs and provide the VAR estimation results in the appendix.

The generalized impulse responses from the VAR model trace the response of one variable to a one-standard-deviation shock to another variable in the system. We utilize Monte Carlo methods to construct confidence bands around the mean response (Doan and Litterman, 1986). When the upper and lower bounds carry the same sign, the responses become statistically significant at the 95 percent confidence level.

Figures 18.1(a) and 18.1(b) plot the impulse responses of Bovespa index returns to one-time standard deviation increase in the rational and irrational sentiments of consumers respectively. The effect of a once-for-all increase in rational sentiments on Bovespa index returns is positive and significant during the first month and insignificant thereafter. However, the response of Bovespa index returns to irrational sentiments is insignificant. In terms of magnitude, the rational sentiments have a much greater impact than the irrational sentiments. These findings provide further empirical support for both rational and irrational sentiments where consumer irrational sentiment does not lead

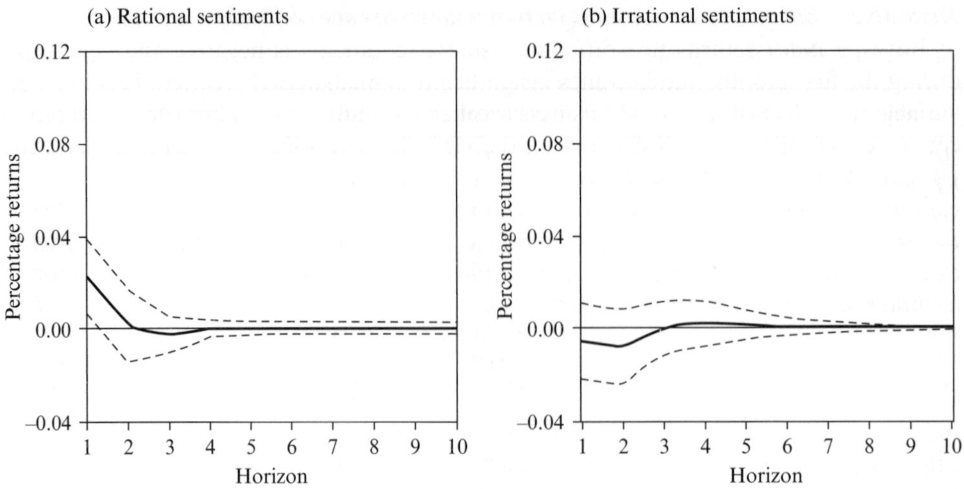

Note: The dashed lines on each graph represent the upper and lower 95% confidence bands. When the upper and lower bounds carry the same sign the response becomes statistically significant.

Figure 18.1 Response of Bovespa to the rational and irrational sentiments of consumers

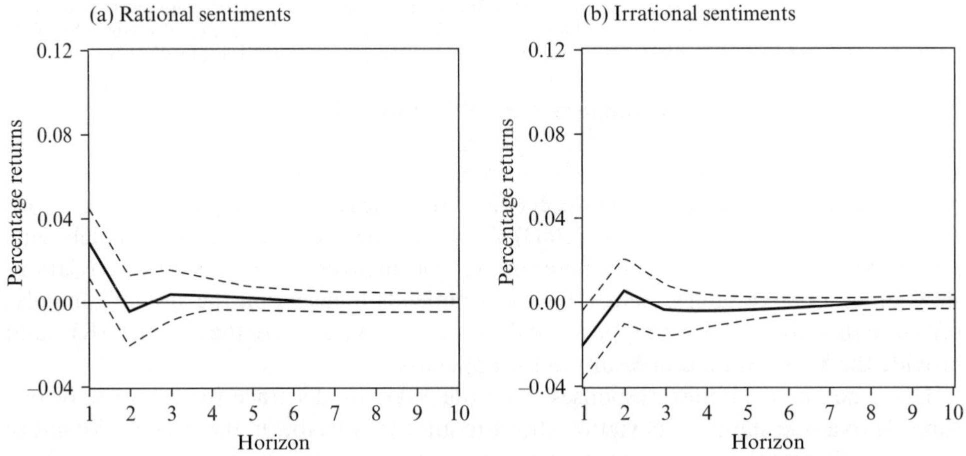

Note: As for Figure 18.1.

Figure 18.2 Response of Bovespa to the rational and irrational sentiments of business

to a statistically significant response of Bovespa index returns while a one-time positive shock to rational (irrational) consumer sentiment leads to an increase (decrease) in stock market returns around the time of the second month.

Figures 18.2(a) and 18.2(b) plot the impulse responses of the Bovespa index to rational and irrational business sentiments. The results are similar to those obtained for consumer sentiments. The effect of the rational business sentiment on Bovespa index returns is positive and significant, becoming insignificant after the second period. The response of Bovespa index returns to irrational business sentiments is negative and significant during the first month, and becomes insignificant immediately thereafter. This immediate negative effect of irrational business sentiments, unlike the findings from irrational consumer sentiments, is consistent with the view that irrational sentiments do have the potential to influence stock market returns. Further, the finding of positive and significant rational business sentiment impact on Bovespa index returns is also consistent with the earlier findings from rational consumer sentiments that a one-time positive shock to rational (irrational) sentiments leads to an increase (decrease) in stock market returns around the time of the first period.

CONCLUSION

In this study, we investigate the relative effects of business and consumer rational and irrational sentiments on Bovespa index returns. Unlike previous studies that conjecture sentiments as fully irrational, we find that business and consumer sentiments are driven by both rational and irrational factors. Overall, we find the following results after estimating a five-variable VAR model. First, the effect of a once-for-all increase in rational business and consumer sentiments on Bovespa index returns is positive and significant during the first month and insignificant thereafter. However, the response of Bovespa index returns to consumer irrational sentiments is insignificant. The impact of rational sentiments is greater than that of irrational sentiments for both business and consumers on stock market returns. Second, in terms of magnitude, rational sentiments have a much greater impact than irrational sentiments. Third, the response of Bovespa index returns to irrational business sentiments is negative and significant during the first month, becoming insignificant immediately thereafter, which implies that irrational sentiments do have the potential to influence stock market returns. Lastly, rational business and consumer sentiments have a more profound effect than irrational sentiments on Bovespa returns.

Previous studies treat consumer and business sentiments as irrational behavior; however, our results further support the economic-fundamentals-based arguments of stock market returns. Since we find evidence in favor of both types of sentiments, our results are consistent with the view that sentiments are mostly a manifestation of the rational risk factors driving expected returns of stocks, with irrational business sentiments also having an impact on stock returns. Therefore investors could improve their portfolio performance by considering both rational as well as irrational sentiments as determinants of stock returns.

First, the effect of a once-for-all increase in rational business and consumer sentiments on Bovespa index returns is positive and significant during the first month and insignificant thereafter. Second, in terms of magnitude, the rational business and consumer sentiments have a much greater impact than irrational sentiments. Third, the finding of a positive and significant rational business sentiment impact on Bovespa index return is also consistent with the earlier findings from rational consumer sentiments that a one-time positive shock to rational (irrational) sentiments leads to an increase (decrease) in stock market returns around the time of the first period. Fourth, the response of Bovespa index returns to consumer irrational sentiments is insignificant. Lastly, the response of Bovespa index returns to irrational business sentiments is negative and significant during the first month, becoming insignificant immediately thereafter. This immediate negative effect of irrational business sentiments, unlike the findings from the irrational consumer sentiment, is consistent with the view that irrational sentiments do have the potential to influence stock market returns.

NOTE

1. The results of the VAR estimates are available in the appendix.

REFERENCES

Baker, M and J. Wurgler (2006), 'Investor sentiment and the cross-section of stock returns,' *Journal of Finance*, **61** (4), 1645–80.

Barberis, N., A. Shleifer and R. Vishny (1998), 'A model of investor sentiment,' *Journal of Financial Economics*, **49** (3), 307–43.

Black, F. (1986), 'Noise,' *Journal of Finance*, **41** (3), 529–43.

Brown, G. and M. Cliff (2004), 'Investor sentiment and the near-term stock market,' *Journal of Empirical Finance*, **11** (1), 1–27.

Brown, G. and M. Cliff (2005), 'Investor sentiment and asset valuation,' *Journal of Business*, **78** (2), 405–40.

Campbell, J. and A. Kyle (1993), 'Smart money, noise trading, and stock price behavior,' *Review of Economic Studies*, **60** (202), 1–34.

Chan, N., R. Kan and M. Miller (1993), 'Are the discounts on closed-end funds a sentiment index?,' *Journal of Finance*, **48** (2), 795–800.

Clarke, R. and M. Statman (1998), 'Bullish or bearish?,' *Financial Analysts Journal*, **54** (3), 63–72.

Daniel, K., D. Hirshleifer and A. Subrahmanyam (1998), 'Investor psychology and security market under- and overreactions,' *Journal of Finance*, **53** (6), 1839–86.

DeBondt, W. (1993), 'Betting on trends: intuitive forecasts of financial risk and return,' *International Journal of Forecasting*, **9** (3), 355–71.

DeLong, B., J. Shleifer, A. Summers and R. Waldmann (1990), 'Noise trader risk in financial markets,' *Journal of Political Economy*, **98** (4), 703–38.

DeLong, B., J. Shleifer, A. Summers and R. Waldmann (1991), 'The survival of noise traders in financial markets,' *Journal of Business*, **64** (1), 1–19.

Dickey, D. and W. Fuller (1979), 'Distribution of the estimators for autoregressive time series with a unit root,' *Journal of the American Statistical Association*, **74** (366), 427–31.

Dickey, D. and W. Fuller (1981), 'Likelihood ratio statistics for autoregressive time series with a unit root,' *Econometrica*, **49** (4), 1057–72.

Diebold, Francis X. (2003), *Elements of Forecasting*, Mason, OH: South Western College Publishing.

Doan, Thomas A. (1988), *RATS User's Manual*, Evanston, IL: VAR Econometrics.

Doan, Thomas A. and Robert Litterman (1986), *Use's Manual RATS: Version 2.0*, Evanston, IL: VAR Econometrics.

Dolado, J., T. Jenkinson and S. Sosvilla-Rivero (1990), 'Cointegration and unit roots,' *Journal of Economic Surveys*, **4** (3), 249–73.

Elton, Edwin and Martin Gruber (1991), *Modern Portfolio Theory and Investment Analysis*, New York: John Wiley & Sons.

Elton, E., M. Gruber and J. Busse (1998), 'Do investors care about sentiment?,' *Journal of Business*, **71** (4), 477–500.

Enders, Walter (2003), *Applied Econometrics Time Series*, New York: John Wiley & Sons.

Fisher, K. and M. Statman (2000), 'Investor sentiment and stock returns,' *Financial Analysts Journal*, **56** (2), 16–23.

Gemmill, G. and C. Thomas (2002), 'Noise trading, costly arbitrage, and asset prices: evidence from closed-end funds,' *Journal of Finance*, **57** (6), 2571–94.

Genberg, H., M. Salemi and A. Swoboda (1987), 'The relative importance of foreign and domestic disturbances for aggregate fluctuations in open economy: Switzerland,' *Journal of Monetary Economics*, **19** (1), 45–67.
Hakkio, C. and C. Morris (1984), 'Autoregressions: a user's guide,' Research Working Paper, Federal Reserve Bank of Kansas City (84-10).
Hamilton, James D. (1994), *Time Series Analysis*, Princeton, NJ: Princeton University Press.
Hirshleifer, D. (2001), 'Investor psychology and asset pricing,' *Journal of Finance*, **56**, 1533–97.
Hong, H. and J. Stein (1999), 'A unified theory of underreaction, momentum trading and overreaction in asset markets,' *Journal of Finance*, **54** (6), 2143–84.
Koop, G., M. Pesaran and S. Potter (1996), 'Impulse response analysis in non linear multivariate models,' *Journal of Econometrics*, **74** (1), 119–47.
Lakonishok, J., A. Shleifer and R. Vishny (1992), 'The impact of institutional trading on stock prices,' *Journal of Financial Economics*, **32** (1), 23–43.
Lee, C., A. Shleifer and R. Thaler (1991), 'Investor sentiment and the closed-end fund puzzle,' *Journal of Finance*, **46** (1), 75–109.
Lee, W., C. Jiang and D. Indro (2002), 'Stock market volatility, excess returns, and the role of investor sentiment,' *Journal of Banking & Finance*, **26** (12), 2277–99.
Litterman, R.B. (1984), 'Forecasting with Bayesian vector autoregressions – five years of experience,' Staff Report, Federal Reserve Bank of Minneapolis, 95.
Litterman, R. and T. Supel (1983), 'Using vector autoregressions to measure the uncertainty in Minnesota's revenue forecasts,' *Quarterly Review Federal Reserve Bank of Minneapolis*, **7** (2), 10–22.
Lupoletti, W. and R. Webb (1986), 'Defining and improving the accuracy of macroeconomic forecasts: contributions from a VAR model,' *Journal of Business*, **59** (2), 263–85.
Neal, R. and S. Wheatley (1998), 'Do measures of investor sentiment predict stock returns?,' *Journal of Financial and Quantitative Analysis*, **34** (4), 523–47.
Palomino, F. (1996), 'Noise trading in small markets,' *Journal of Finance*, **51** (4), 1537–50.
Pesaran, M. and Y. Shin (1996), 'Cointegration and speed of convergence to equilibrium,' *Journal of Econometrics*, **71** (1–2), 117–43.
Pesaran, M. and Y. Shin (1998), 'Generalized impulse response analysis in linear multivariate models,' *Economics Letters*, **58** (1), 17–29.
Shefrin, H. and M. Statman (1994), 'Behavioral capital asset pricing theory,' *The Journal of Financial and Quantitative Analysis*, **29** (3), 323–49.
Shleifer, A. and L. Summers (1990), 'The noise trader approach to finance,' *Journal of Economic Perspectives*, **4** (2), 19–33.
Sias, R., L. Starks and S. Tinic (2001), 'Is noise trader risk priced?,' *The Journal of Financial Research*, **24** (3), 311–29.
Sims, C. (1980), 'Macroeconomic and reality,' *Econometrica*, **48** (1), 1–49.
Solt, M. and M. Statman (1988), 'How useful is the sentiment index?,' *Financial Analysts Journal*, **44** (5), 45–55.
Swaminathan, B. (1996), 'Time-varying expected small firm returns and closed-end fund discounts,' *Review of Financial Studies*, **9** (3), 845–87.
Trueman, B. (1988), 'A theory of noise trading in securities markets,' *Journal of Finance*, **43** (1), 83–95.
Verma, R., H. Baklaci and G. Soydemir (2008), 'The impact of rational and irrational sentiment of individual and institutional investors on DJIA and S&P500 index returns,' *Applied Financial Economics*, **18** (16–18), 1303–17.
Wang, F. (2001), 'Overconfidence, investor sentiment, and evolution,' *Journal of Financial Intermediation*, **10** (2), 138–70.
Webb, R. (1999), 'Two approaches to macroeconomic forecasting,' *Economic Quarterly, Federal Reserve Bank of Richmond*, **85** (3), 23–40.

APPENDIX VECTOR AUTOREGRESSION ESTIMATES

	SENTT1	SENTT1IR	SENTT2	SENTT2IR	BOVESPA
SENTT1(-1)	0.82***	0.09	−0.05	0.06	0.01
	(0.10)	(0.25)	(0.05)	(0.04)	(0.04)
SENTT1(-2)	0.21**	−0.16	0.12**	−0.14***	−0.01
	(0.11)	(0.26)	(0.05)	(0.05)	(0.04)
SENTT1IR(-1)	−0.06	0.98***	−0.03	0.03	−0.01
	(0.03)	(0.08)	(0.02)	(0.01)	(0.01)
SENTT1IR(-2)	0.10***	−0.30***	0.03**	−0.04**	0.00
	(0.03)	(0.08)	(0.02)	(0.01)	(0.01)
SENTT2(-1)	0.27	0.42	0.98***	0.54***	−0.01
	(0.28)	(0.70)	(0.13)	(0.12)	(0.01)
SENTT2(-2)	−0.46	0.11	−0.43**	−0.10	0.00
	(0.32)	(0.79)	(0.15)	(0.14)	(0.01)
SENTT2IR(-1)	0.93***	−0.14	0.44**	1.04***	0.01
	(0.23)	(0.58)	(0.11)	(0.10)	(0.01)
SENTT2IR(-2)	−0.86***	0.40	−0.31***	−0.33***	−0.01
	(0.21)	(0.51)	(0.10)	(0.09)	(0.01)
BOVESPA(-1)	−0.63	4.12	0.17	0.15	−0.06
	(2.01)	(4.97)	(0.94)	(0.86)	(0.09)
BOVESPA(-2)	−1.98	4.12	−0.53	−0.10	−0.09
	(1.87)	(4.62)	(0.87)	(0.80)	(0.08)
C	14.96	−44.16	37.22***	35.89***	0.08
	(15.04)	(37.24)	(7.04)	(6.42)	(0.65)
R^2	0.97	0.63	0.84	0.74	0.05
Sum sq. resids	710.46	4351.02	155.43	129.31	1.34
S.E. equation	2.22	5.50	1.04	0.95	0.10
F-statistic	529.19	24.48	72.90	40.05	0.79
Log likelihood	−337.93	−478.38	−220.15	−205.89	148.46
Akaike AIC	4.50	6.31	2.98	2.80	−1.77
Schwarz SC	4.72	6.53	3.20	3.01	−1.56
Mean dependent	114.53	−0.17	99.86	−0.07	0.02
S.D. dependent	13.20	8.73	2.47	1.78	0.10

Notes: the variables are rational sentiments of consumers ($Sentt_1$), irrational sentiments of consumers (*Sentt*1IR), rational sentiments of businesses (Sentt2)and irrational sentiments of businesses (Sentt2IR), and returns on Bovespa (*Bovespa*).
* ** and *** denote significance levels at the 10, 5 and 1% respectively. SEs are in parentheses.

19 The information-adjusted noise model: theory and evidence from the Australian stock market

Sinclair Davidson and Vikash Ramiah

Eugene Fama (1998) has set the benchmark for comparing the efficient market hypothesis (EMH) and behavioural finance theories. He indicates that many alternatives to the EMH are vague and unspecified. Quite rightly, he argues that alternatives to the efficient market hypothesis need to be well specified and testable. In particular, he suggests that much of the evidence against markets being informationally efficient is, in fact, consistent with market efficiency – this is especially so if anomalies are split evenly between underreaction and overreaction. We show, using daily data from the Australian Stock Exchange (ASX), that the underreaction and overreaction anomalies do not split evenly and that, contrary to EMH-type arguments, information traders do not necessarily correct pricing errors introduced into the market by noise traders. Consistent with the market being behaviourally efficient (Shefrin and Statman, 1994), however, this does not translate into supernormal profit opportunities.

Our model describes the interaction between information traders and noise traders. Unlike much of the behavioural finance literature, we do not assume that information traders necessarily return markets to fundamental values. Information traders trade on the basis of information, but may well make errors in interpreting that information. Noise traders trade in the absence of information. Information traders may well correct the pricing errors introduced by noise traders – this is just one of the outcomes we describe. On the other hand, information traders may undercorrect, or overcorrect, noise errors. This gives rise to either underreaction or overreaction. In this respect we do not rise to Fama's challenge of specifying the cause of errors or explaining why the same investors underreact to some information while overreacting to other information. We simply point out that markets are populated by mere fallible humans. Furthermore, information traders may make similar errors to noise traders and add to pricing errors on the market, and not reduce those errors. The interaction between information traders and noise traders is not likely to be one of information traders mechanistically correcting pricing errors; our information-adjusted noise model (IANM) captures those subtleties.

The Australian Stock Exchange provides an ideal testing ground for our model. The ASX has a continuous disclosure regime where firms are required to immediately disclose any price-relevant information to the market. Our model requires us to 'predict' when information traders are likely to be active on the market. We make the assumption that noise traders are continually active in the market, but information traders trade only when information comes to the market. By observing firms making information disclosure we can determine when information traders are likely to be trading. We present evidence that the ASX is often informationally inefficient. Over our sample period we find that the EMH is violated on 62.98 per cent of days. The most common violation occurs where information traders add to pricing errors. The second most common violation of information efficiency is underreaction.

THE INFORMATION-ADJUSTED NOISE MODEL

Following our discussion in Ramiah and Davidson (2007), this section sets out the information-adjusted noise model, and an empirical analogue of the model. We also provide a brief differentiation between the modern finance theory or traditional efficient market hypothesis and the behavioural finance efficient market hypothesis.

We define information traders as those individuals who form expectations on the basis of information, and then trade on those expectations. We do not assume that information traders are omniscient, or that they always form the 'correct' expectations. Our definition of information trader is broader than the Shefrin and Statman (1994) definition as someone whose subjective beliefs coincide with objective probabilities. To our minds this definition is *ex post*, and is more likely to occur by chance than by design. It is unlikely that any empirical test could ever specify objective probabilities with any accuracy. We suggest that information traders base their expectations on information, but do not always interpret that information correctly; information traders can make mistakes. Noise traders do not employ information to form their expectations, and may trade for any number of reasons. Information traders trade in a particular stock only when value-relevant information has been released to the market. Noise traders, however, can and will trade in any stock on any day. Imagine that on any given day, t, information may be released to the market or not. On those days when no new information comes to the market, noise traders will trade among themselves. On days when information is released to the market, an information event (IE) occurs, and both noise traders and information traders trade. On days when information is not released to the market, only noise traders trade – information traders do not enter the market.

The traditional EMH states that there should be no behavioural errors on the market. The expected value of any behavioural error, given the information set, should be zero, $E(BE_t|\Omega_t) = 0$. The expected change in the behavioural error, given a change in the information set, is a random forecast error, $E(\Delta BE_t|\Delta\Omega_t) = \varepsilon$. In terms of behavioural finance, a market is behaviourally efficient when $E(BE_t|\Omega_t) \neq 0$, but $\Sigma_{i=1}^{\infty} BE_{it} = 0$. This follows from Shefrin and Statman's (1994) definition of a market being behaviourally efficient if and only if behavioural errors average to zero and are uncorrelated to wealth. The IANM models the 'random forecast error' as follows:

$$\Delta BE_{it} = \alpha + \beta IE_{it} + \varepsilon_{it} \tag{19.1}$$

Where ΔBE_{it} is the change in the behavioural error for stock i on day t. IE is an information event, i.e. the arrival of news. We treat this variable as a dummy with value 1 on those days when information is released to the market, and 0 when no information is released to the market. We do not differentiate between 'good' or 'bad' news. α is the mean change in the behavioural error attributable to noise traders. β is the proportion of the mean change in behavioural error attributable to information traders. We assume $\beta \neq 0$.

The IANM has the advantage over other noise trader type models by being able to isolate the impact of noise traders and information traders. In particular, a variable mu ($\mu = \alpha + \beta$) reflects the mean changes in behavioural error caused by noise traders and information traders. If the modern finance theory EMH is 'true', then $\alpha + \beta = \mu = 0$ and $\Delta BE_{it} = \varepsilon$. If we relax the assumption that the modern finance theory EMH is 'true', then $\alpha + \beta = \mu \neq 0$. We exploit this relationship in order to differentiate between different types of potential market inefficiencies. In an efficient market, information traders would quickly correct noise traders' pricing errors. This contrarian investment strategy implies that $\alpha = -\beta$.

On non-information release days, $IE_{it} = 0$, the IANM will take the form $\Delta BE_{it} = \alpha + \varepsilon_{it}$. If alpha is zero, then market efficiency does not change. To the extent that alpha is not zero the market becomes behaviourally inefficient. We define a positive alpha as 'pure noise': noise traders are increasing stock market inefficiency and distorting prices. This argument is consistent with the large literature supporting the notion that noise traders may drive prices away from fundamental values. A negative alpha could be interpreted as a 'Friedman effect': noise traders are trading 'as if' they were information traders, reducing the *BE* and returning the market to fundamental values.

On the days when information is released, $IE_{it} = 1$, the model will take the form of equation (19.1). A significant beta indicates that noise traders and information traders have differential impacts on the market. Beta shows the impact of information traders on the change in behavioural errors and it will show whether information traders increase or reduce the changes in behavioural errors. The interaction of noise traders and information traders will determine the change in *BE* on any particular day. Traditional finance theory suggests that information traders will follow contrarian strategies to noise traders. To the extent that this does in fact occur, $\alpha + \beta = 0$.

INEFFICIENT MARKETS

Underreaction

Underreaction can be explained by conservatism (Edwards, 1968). This suggests that individuals slowly adjust their beliefs in respect to new information. There is a large literature that demonstrates underreaction (see, e.g., Andreassen, 1987; Jegadeesh and Titman, 1993; Rouwenhorst, 1998; Chan et al., 1996). Our model explains underreaction as follows: the market does not clear all errors. Information comes to the market and information traders realize that the market is trading at noisy levels, and trade to reduce these errors. The information traders trade in the 'correct' direction, but fail to completely eliminate the errors. This underreaction can be differentiated into two components, positive underreaction U (+) and negative underreaction U (−).

The first type of underreaction is positive underreaction, i.e. U (+), and it will occur when alpha is positive and mu is positive as well. There is an error alpha caused by noise traders, and information traders trade to reduce this error. They fail, however, to eliminate the error, and $\alpha + \beta = \mu > 0$.

When alpha is negative (i.e. $\alpha < 0$, a Friedman effect), information traders will reduce this error by a positive beta amount. To the extent that information traders fail to eliminate the error, a negative mu will remain.

The conditions that are required for U (+) to prevail on the market can be written as μ, $\alpha > 0$ and $\beta < 0$. The conditions for U (−) can be written as μ, $\alpha < 0$ and $\beta > 0$.

Overreaction

Frank (1935), Griffin and Tversky (1992), DeLong et al. (1990) and Odean (1998) suggest that traders are overconfident, leading to overreaction. In our model, overreaction will occur when information traders adopt a contrarian investment strategy and, while trading in the 'correct' direction, overestimate the magnitude of the errors. Information traders will move prices away from fundamental values. This overreaction can be differentiated into two components, positive overreaction O (+) and negative overreaction O (−).

Negative overreaction occurs when noise traders are increasing noise levels ($\alpha > 0$) and while information traders following a contrarian strategy overestimate the magnitude of the errors. Initially the errors are at alpha level and are reduced by beta (which is a greater amount than the initial noise), leading to a negative mu ($\alpha + \beta = \mu > 0$). Positive overreaction is the converse situation where the alpha is negative and information traders overcompensate, leading to a positive mu ($\alpha + \beta = \mu > 0$).

The conditions for negative overreaction can be written as $\alpha > 0$, $\mu < 0$ and $\beta < 0$. On the other hand, positive overreaction will prevail if $\alpha < 0$, $\mu > 0$ and $\beta > 0$.

Information Pricing Error

A serious market error occurs when information traders fail to adopt a contrarian strategy and so increase the noise level in the market. Under these conditions both alpha and beta will have the same sign. We refer to this type of error as an 'information pricing error' (IPE). Similarly to overreaction and underreaction, there can be two types of IPE, which will depend on the sign of alpha. IPE will occur when information traders copy noise traders' trading technique. They behave as noise traders, and add to the existing errors.

Positive IPE, IPE (+), occurs when both alpha and beta are positive. As alpha and beta are of the same sign, information traders have failed to adopt a contrarian strategy. Consequently, the noise level in the market is increased ($\alpha + \beta > 0$). negative information pricing error, IPE (−), occurs where alpha is negative and information traders fail to adopt a contrarian strategy ($\alpha + \beta < 0$).

For IPE (+) to occur, α and $\beta > 0$, and for IPE (−) α and $\beta < 0$.

Summary

Studying the component parts of equation (19.1), it is possible to identify various market effects. For the market to be behaviourally efficient, mu should not be statistically significantly different from zero. On those days when it is significantly different from zero it is possible to identify the various effects we have described. This framework develops a method of testing whether the market is behaviourally efficient or not. If mu is not

Table 19.1 Summary of market effects

Effects		α	β	μ
Underreaction	U(+)	> 0	< 0	> 0
	U(−)	< 0	> 0	< 0
IPE	IPE (+)	> 0	> 0	
	IPE (−)	< 0	< 0	
Overreaction	O (+)	< 0	> 0	> 0
	O (−)	> 0	< 0	< 0

Source: Ramiah and Davidson (2007).

statistically different from zero, we can conclude that the market is free from errors and informationally efficient in the traditional sense. When mu is statistically different from zero, this will give rise to either one of the following effects, underreaction [U (+) or U (−)] or overreaction [O (+) or O (−)] or an information pricing error [IPE (+) or IPE (−)]. Table 19.1 summarizes all the different conditions that are required for any of the above effects to hold.

CALCULATING BEHAVIOURAL ERRORS

The major challenge in testing the IANM is in deriving the behavioural error, and the subsequent changes in behavioural error. Shefrin and Statman (1994) argue that a behavioural asset pricing model (BAPM) should use a different proxy for the 'true' market portfolio in a CAPM (capital asset pricing model) context. This 'behavioural' proxy should capture the noise traders' investment universe and be composed of stocks they prefer. Another way of looking at this is to say that the BAPM is a model based on 'sentiment'.

As the CAPM does not allow for noise traders, it will generate biased estimates. According to Shefrin and Statman (1994), the CAPM beta will have a noise trader risk component and an 'efficient' beta (i.e. the behavioural beta). Equation (19.2) shows the excess return CAPM.

$$\tilde{r}_{it} - \tilde{r}_{ft} = \varphi_i + \beta_i^c[\tilde{r}_{mt} - \tilde{r}_{ft}] + \tilde{\varepsilon}_{it} \tag{19.2}$$

where

$\tilde{r}_{it}$ = the asset *i*'s return at time *t*
$\tilde{r}_{ft}$ = the risk-free return at time *t*
$\tilde{r}_{mt}$ = the return on the market proxy at time *t*
$\tilde{\varepsilon}_{it}$ = the error term
φ_i = the intercept of the regression equation ($E(\varphi_i) = 0$)
β_i^c = the CAPM beta

Equation 19.3 decomposes the CAPM beta into two components, namely the efficient beta (β_i^B) and the Behavioural Error (BE_i):

$$\beta_i^C = (\beta_i^B + BE_i) \tag{19.3}$$

where

BE_i = the behavioural error, and is expected to be highly correlated with noise trader risk
β_i^B = the efficient beta, i.e. free from noise trader risk

The behavioural error can be defined as the difference between the CAPM beta and the BAPM beta, $BE_i = \beta_i^C - \beta_i^B$. Substituting (19.3) into (19.2) generates the BAPM.

Details of the estimation of equations (19.2) and (19.3) are set out in Ramiah and Davidson (2007). The behavioural market proxy was taken to be the so-called Mums and Dads Index first developed by Commonwealth Securities. As described in Ramiah and Davidson (2007), the process for calculating behavioural errors and then relating that to information releases is very data intensive and time consuming, resulting in an analysis of only 46 firms being undertaken. Data are daily and include the period 22 June 1998 to 31 December 2002 (the first 18 months are used for estimation).

Evidence of Behavioural Errors

Table 19.2 shows the mean alpha, mean beta and mean mu across the different firms. Standard errors were adjusted for independence in the computation of the *t*-statistic. The results show that alpha is positive and significantly different from zero, implying that noise traders were active in the market. Furthermore, mu, the measure of noise trader risk, is positive and significant. This indicates that information traders have not been able to eliminate all behavioural errors introduced by noise traders. A significant mu can represent either an overreaction or underreaction, or IPE.

We then turn our attention to the types of behavioural error that could occur. Over the entire period 2000–02 there were 12273 information days for the 46 companies that were investigated. This study analyses every single day and checks if the market is efficient, or whether there is some underreaction, IPE or overreaction. Those different effects are then broken down into two parts, namely positive or negative. Table 19.3 reports the number of O (+), O (−), IPE (+), IPE (−), U (+), U (−) and EMH that have been occurring on the information days. The table also shows the results in the different sub-periods.

Overall, the traditional EMH is supported by the data just under 40 per cent of the time. Of 12273 information days, 4544 days are consistent with the EMH being 'true' over the period 2000–02. Noise traders appear to be present in the market 60 per cent of the time. That 60 per cent can be split into 5 per cent overreaction, 25 per cent underreaction and around 35 per cent of IPE.

Any effect that is around 5 per cent could be argued to be simply a Type I error, and consequently a test of proportion was carried out to see if the proportion is statistically greater than 5 per cent (Type I error). Table 19.3 shows that the *Z*-statistics for all the different effects and across the different periods. The *Z*-statistics reject the hypothesis that our results are due to a Type I error.

To provide some greater clarity, we produce some graphical results. Figure 19.1 shows

Table 19.2 Descriptive statistics for mean alpha, mean beta and mean mu

	α	β	μ
Mean	0.22505	0.00321	0.22624
T-stat. (mean = 0)	20.45791	0.92625	19.55772
Observations	46	46	46

Note: The computation of the standard error and T-statistics were adjusted for interdependence.

Source: Ramiah and Davidson (2007), Table 4.

Table 19.3 Overreaction, information pricing error and underreaction across the 46 firms on the information days

	Occurrence (%)	Positive (%)	Negative (%)
Overreaction	5.12	3.65	1.47
Underreaction	24.36	23.16	1.20
Information pricing error	33.50	32.00	1.50
Total inefficient days	62.98		
EMH	37.02		

Note: * Significant at 1% level of confidence testing if the proportion is greater than 5% (Z-statistics)

Source: Rumiah and Davidson (2007), Table 6.

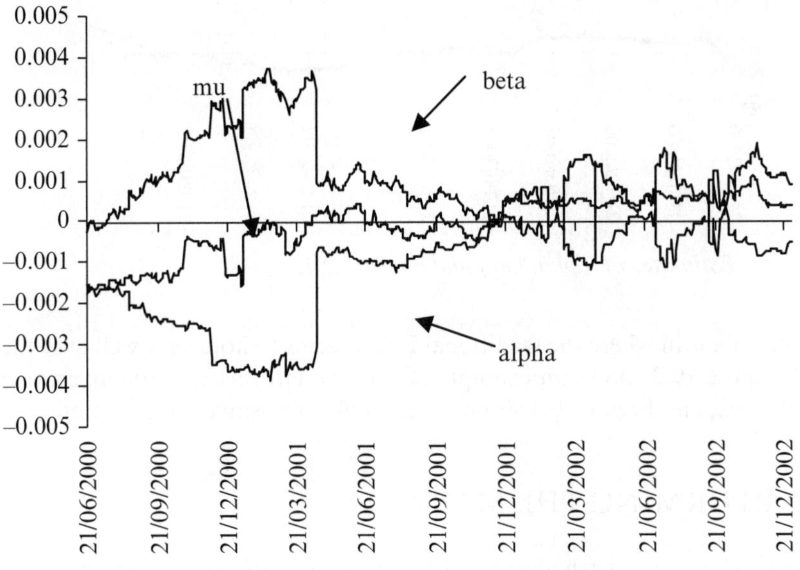

Figure 19.1 Estimates of alpha, beta and mu for BHP-Billiton

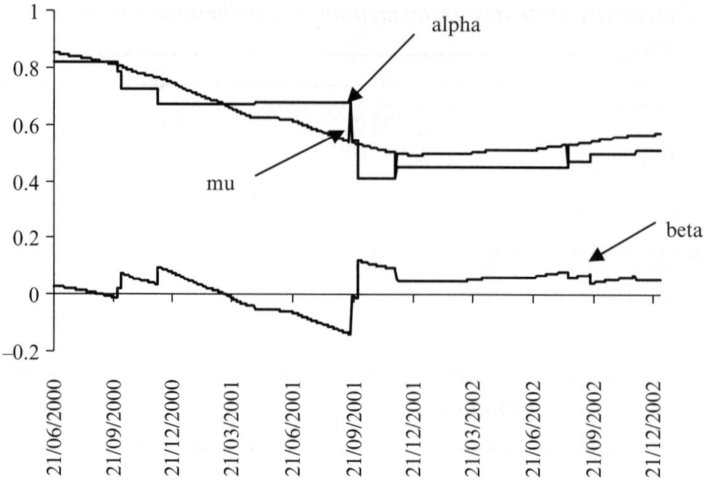

Figure 19.2 Estimates of alpha, beta and mu for Rio-Tinto

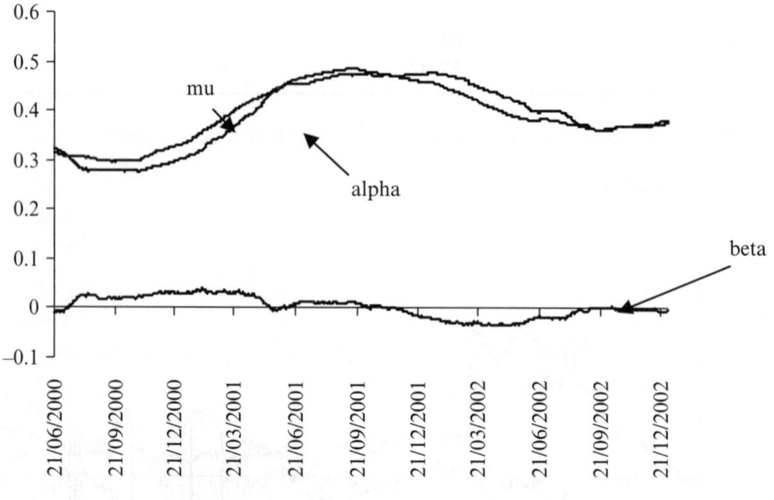

Figure 19.3 Estimates of alpha, beta and mu for CSL

an example of a firm where the traditional EMH seems to hold very well over the period 2000–02. Figure 19.2 shows an example of positive information pricing error over the period 2000–02, and Figure 19.3 shows an example of positive underraction.

OUTPERFORMING THE MARKET

A question of interest is whether the IANM can identify profit opportunities in the market. This represents the difference between statistical significance and economic

Table 19.4 Relationship between stock returns and proxies for noise trader pricing errors

		$\tilde{r}_{it} = \phi_{1,i} + \phi_{2,i}\Delta BE_{t-1} + \tilde{\varepsilon}_{it}$	$\tilde{r}_{it} = \phi_{1,i} + \phi_{2,i}\mu_{t-1} + \tilde{\varepsilon}_{it}$
Intercept	Significant	5	10
	Not significant	41	36
Slope	Significant	6	8
	Not significant	40	38

significance. The model can determine when pricing errors are occurring, but the real interest is in whether those pricing errors can be recognized and incorporated into trading behaviour. There are three possible relationships between stock returns and the change in the behaviour error. First, it is likely that no relationship exists between the two. In this instance, while behavioural errors exist, it is not possible to earn abnormal returns given knowledge of the errors. This is consistent with Shefrin and Statman's (1994) definition of a behaviourally efficient market.

A second possibility is that a positive relationship exists between stock returns and the change in behavioural error. This we call a systematic noise effect. This indicates that noise traders add systematic risk to the market. It is also be consistent with the DeLong et al. (1990) argument that noise traders earn more than information traders by increasing their risk exposure.

The third possibility is a negative relationship between stock returns and changes in behavioural error. This we call the cash noise effect. This suggests that information traders could earn profits by undertaking contrarian investment strategies relative to the noise traders.

In order to test the relationships between stock market returns and our estimates of noise trader behaviour, we estimate two sets of regressions using OLS (ordinary least squares). The lagged change in the behavioural error and the lagged mu are regressed onto individual daily stock returns for each of the 46 stocks in our sample. We report the number of significant intercept and slope terms in Table 19.4.

The evidence in Table 19.4 is consistent with the ASX being behaviourally efficient. There are six instances of a statistically significant relationship between lagged changes in behavioural error and stock returns. Of these four are positive and two are negative, suggesting that information traders could have profited from the existence of noise traders in 4.3 per cent (2/46 = 0.043) instances. In the case of the lagged mu there are eight instances of a significant relationship with stock returns. Of these six are negative, consistent with a cash noise effect, and two are positive, consistent with a systematic noise effect. This suggests that information traders are able to profit from the existence of errors introduced by noise traders.

Overall the results of this exercise tend to support market efficiency – either in the traditional sense or in a behavioural sense.

CONCLUSION

We set out a model that describes the interaction between information traders and noise traders. Unlike most papers in the literature, this chapter does not assume that information traders return the market to fundamental value. Rather, that is one possible outcome in a range of outcomes.

The results contradict the traditional finance school of thought on the EMH but are consistent with behavioural theories, and especially Shefrin and Statman (1994). Noise traders are present in the market and they do introduce behavioural errors into the market. Information traders do not always eliminate those errors and can contribute to pricing errors. It is not clear, however, that easily identifiable arbitrage opportunities exist on the market. For investors, the difference between a traditionally efficient market and a behaviourally efficient market may seem small. There are differences, however. For example, in modern finance theory more information is considered to lead to better market pricing, while in the behavioural finance approach we have demonstrated that this is not always the case: information traders can contribute to pricing errors.

Another conclusion that can be drawn from this study is that the Australian traders tend to underreact rather than overreact, implying that the market displays slow adjustments to new information rather than overconfidence.

ACKNOWLEDGEMENT

We thank Pravna Appadoo and Marie-Anne Cam for their research assistance. A previous version of this paper was published as Vikash Ramiah and Sinclair Davidson (2007), 'An information-adjusted noise model: evidence of inefficiency on the Australian Stock Market', *Journal of Behavioral Finance*, **8**(4), 209–24.

REFERENCES

Andreassen, P. (1987), 'On the social psychology of the stock market: aggregate attributional effects and the repressiveness of prediction', *Journal of Personality and Social Psychology*, **53**, 490–96.

Chan, L., N. Jegadeesh and J. Lakonishok (1996), 'Momentum strategies', *The Journal of Finance*, **51**, 1681–713.

DeLong, J.B., A. Shleifer, L. Summers and J.R.Waldmann (1990), 'Noise trader risks in financial markets', *Journal of Political Economy*, **4**, 703–38.

Edwards, W. (1968), 'Conservatism in human information processing', in B. Kleinmutz (ed.), *Formal Representation of Human Judgment*, New York: John Wiley & Sons, pp. 17–52.

Fama, E.F. (1998), 'Market efficiency, long-term returns, and behavioural finance', *Journal of Financial Economics*, **49**, 283–306.

Frank, J.D. (1935), 'Some psychological determinants of the level of aspiration', *American Journal of Psychology*, **47**, 285–93.

Griffin D. and A. Tversky (1992), 'The weighting of evidence and determinants of confidence', *Cognitive Psychology*, **24**, 411–35.

Jegadeesh, N. and S. Titman (1993), 'Returns to buying winners and selling losers: implications for stock market efficiency', *The Journal of Finance*, **48**, 65–91.

Odean, T. (1998), 'Volume, volatility, price, and profit when all traders are above average', *The Journal of Finance*, **53**, 1887–934.

Ramiah, V. and S. Davidson (2007), 'An information-adjusted noise model: evidence of inefficiency on the Australian Stock Market', *Journal of Behavioural Finance*, **8** (4), 209–24.
Rouwenhorst, K.G. (1998), 'International momentum strategies', *The Journal of Finance*, **53**, 267–84.
Shefrin, H., and M. Statman (1994), 'Behavioural capital asset pricing theory', *Journal of Financial and Quantitative Analysis*, **29**, 323–49.

20 Ambiguity aversion and illusion of control in an emerging market: are individuals subject to behavioral biases?

Benjamin Miranda Tabak and Dimas Mateus Fazio

INTRODUCTION

The traditional financial theory considers individuals as rational, in the sense that they identify and use relevant information and are also able to make optimal decisions. As maintained by Benartzi and Thaler (2002), the definition of rationality is related to the following facts: first, when they receive new information, individuals update their beliefs accordingly; second, considering their beliefs, individuals make decisions that are considered acceptable (consistent with Savage's expected utility theory; Savage, 1953).

Behavioral finance theory proposes that we must consider models in which the agents are not completely rational in order to better understand some financial phenomena. In other words, this theory analyzes what happens when we relax one or both premises of the classical financial theory. With this in mind, Tomer (2007) illustrates behavioral economics by asserting that it is less narrow, rigid, intolerant, mechanical, separate and individualistic than mainstream economics.

Besides, Thaler (1994) also recognizes the influence of behavioral effects on decision making. The author affirms that the completely rational and the almost-rational are only two possible profiles for investors in the financial market. Even though the latter attempt to make good investment decisions, in fact they make predictable mistakes owing to the imperfection in the rational process.

According to Thaler and Mullainathan (2001), behavioral finance studies in which way economic, sociological and psychological concepts combine so as to explain events in the real economy, where the actions of individuals are not fully rational. In traditional financial theory, on the other hand, economic agents are supposed to possess the capacity to operate with unlimited reason, which enables them to make decisions that are compatible with the expected utility theory, forming unbiased expectations about future events.

Behavioral finance analyzes the influence of psychology on human behavior in financial markets and also its consequences. It admits the existence of decision biases and considers that most of them can and should be eliminated. The basic idea, however, is not to become an alternative to the traditional or modern finances by rejecting all their premises, but to improve the financial models through the incorporation of behavioral tendencies, such as cognitive and emotional factors, identified in the economic agents. Thus behavioral finance assists the economic theory to clarify why and in which way financial markets might be inefficient.

This chapter extends the analysis of Grou and Tabak (2008) on illusion of control and ambiguity aversion, at the same time as it presents new experiments about these two important topics for behavioral finance. First a brief review of the behavioral finance literature is developed. After that, the results of ten experiments, five on control illusion and five on ambiguity aversion, will be presented and discussed. In total, 196 people participated, drawn from students of economy and administration in two universities in Brasília, the Catholic University and the University of Brasilia.

The experiments offered the possibility to test what are the effects of relevant information and, above all, how agents behave in risk situations that offer multiple choices. Through systematic and controlled changes of the studied variables, our experiments revealed the choice biases. In addition, financial incentives were offered to the participants to create a realistic investment scenario.

The rest of the chapter is divided as follows. The first section presents a review of the literature on behavioral finance. The third section presents the experiments that were performed and discusses the results. The fourth section concludes.

LITERATURE REVIEW

The classical financial literature is based on the expected utility theory (Savage, 1953). The psychological cognitive paradigm opposes this theory and explains the decision as an interactive process, on which non-trivial factors such as perceptions, convictions and mental models of the decision taker have an influence. As a matter of fact, intrinsic reasons such as emotions, states of mind, tendencies and psychological attitudes when it comes to relating one event with another, peculiar to each decision taker, can influence a decision as much as external incentives. Moreover, the memory of prior decisions and their consequences represents a critical cognitive function that also influences present decisions. Due to this complex vision, it is widely accepted that human behavior is conditioned to the context and the observed conditions in each situation faced by agents.

Tversky (1972) stated that individuals normally use different strategies of analysis when they are faced with several alternatives and when they have to decide in a limited time. Agents do not analyze all the attributes and all the available options. Individuals use an elimination process to narrow down the options to just one attribute. Tversky and Kahneman (1974) observed that many individuals used mental shortcuts that generally limited or distorted their capacity to take rational decisions. They demonstrated that people tend to use a limited number of mental shortcuts, which reduces the complex chores of calculating events and predicting values. The biggest problem of mental shortcuts is that they eventually lead to grave systemic errors.[1]

Countless behavioral effects are documented in the investment decision-making process. Some important effects are loss risk aversion, overconfidence, illusion of control and ambiguity aversion, among others. This chapter will focus on the last two effects.

Ambiguity Aversion

Savage (1953) identifies three different interpretations of mathematical probability concepts: (i) the objectivist, which interprets probability as observed repetitions of an event; (ii) the personalist, which interprets probability as a measure of the trust level of an individual in the truth of a particular proposition; and (iii) the necessary or logical, which defines probability as a measure of the extension in which a set of propositions confirms the truth about another, by simple logical necessity, without regard to opinions.

For Savage, the decision problem, for which the solution supposes that rational individuals are capable of proceeding to probabilistic calculations, is one of choice under any uncertainty scenario.

The most general definition of ambiguity has been offered by Knight (1921), who distinguishes risk from uncertainty, the first being quantifiable in terms of probability, while the latter is not. Knight assumes that in situations of uncertainty, the use of probabilities is inappropriate. Uncertainty situations, consequently, are all those in which decision makers don't know the chances of specific events happening, or when they are unable to make preliminary calculations of their probability of occurrence. Thus, according to Pulford and Colman (2007), game theory is powerless to elucidate the actions of rational agents in these uncertainty situations.

Several experiments were performed by Ellsberg (1961) with the purpose of contesting the axioms of Savage (1953), showing that people have a preference for investing in or betting on situations in which the probability of ocurrence may be represented by a known distribution – in other words, situations in which it is possible to predict the results by calculation of probabilities. Ellsberg's classical experiment consisted in asking individuals to choose between black and red, and then they were asked to extract a ball from one of two closed boxes. Box I presented an unknown distribution with 100 black and red balls. In addition, box II presented a known distribution with 50 black balls and 50 red balls. It was confirmed that the participants had a preference for betting on the known distribution, i.e. the majority withdrew the ball from box II. This result contradicts some of the axioms of Savage's utility theory. For example, suppose that, betting on the color red, the individual preferred to withdraw the ball from box II, bet red_{II}. Applying the basic Ramsey–Savage rule, we conclude that option red_{II} has a bigger probability than option red_{I}. Considering that it is not possible to define which option, red_{II} or $red_{I,}$ is the most likely, we can conclude that the choice was not made through probability. Therefore, since in this case it is impossible to make a probability inference in the choice of option, some of the Savage axioms were violated.

The results of Ellsberg's experiment suggest that individuals do not like situations in which they do not know the distributions of probability of a certain game. Such ambiguity situations generate discomfort, since, as noted Ellsberg, information is imprecise, indicating ambiguity aversion. Savage's theory does not take into consideration that the decision maker may lack the necessary information about an event. The term 'ambiguity aversion' means that people prefer to assume risks based on known probabilities, instead of unknown probabilities. In other words, their personal knowledge, regarding the subject to be decided, has decisive importance.[2]

Another important work on uncertainty and risk differentiated between judged probability, which is the balance of evidence in favor of a supposition, and the weight of evidence supporting that balance (see Keynes, 1921). People tend to choose the option with the higher evidence supporting it. In Ellsberg's dilemma, for example, Keynes would have said that box II was preferred because the weight of evidence is greater in this box than in box I, where the proportions of red and black balls are unknown (see also Pech and Milan, 2009).

An intriguing neuro-economic analysis by Huettel et al. (2006) found that the individual's preference for risk and ambiguity triggers a brain activation associated with decision making. People's choices in risk and ambiguous situations were examined while they were scanned by functional magnetic resonance imaging (fMRI). Since the activated areas of the brain in each situation appear to be different, Huettel et al. reach the conclusion that risk and ambiguity are two distinct definitions, contradicting all those who affirm that the latter is only a more complex case of the former in decision making.

Shackle (1955) proposed an example for the analysis of uncertainty considering an extreme case of the Knight theory. Shackle not only rejects numerical probabilities as a representation of uncertainty, but he also maintains the affirmation that in situations in which all the probabilities of response can occur, given that they do not violate some imposed restriction causing surprise, it is impossible to estimate the final result.

Fox and Tversky (1995) introduced the notion of a comparative ignorance hypothesis, according to which ambiguity aversion is produced in the comparison between ambiguous events and more familiar events or with more knowledgeable individuals (evidencing the notion of competence). This hypothesis has support in the results of experimental studies performed by them, which confirmed the existence of ambiguity aversion when the participants evaluated a circumstance with an unclear context and, at the same time, another with a clear and objective context. On the contrary, in the experiments where the situations mentioned above were also presented, but separately, ambiguity aversion was not observed, because there was no comparison between these two contexts.

The comparative ignorance hypothesis is extended by Fox and Weber (2002), who test individuals' reactions to different situations than those mentioned above in order to evaluate their influence on decision making. First, they prove that people's choices under uncertainty are deeply influenced by the presentation of different situations with which the individual may be more or less familiar. Second, Fox and Weber find that the order in which the options are presented has an effect on the player's willingness to bet. Third, if relevant information is presented to the decision makers, and these cannot understand them completely, their willingness to choose will be diminished. For example, a patient may be less disposed to undergo surgery if he/she is provided with detailed technical medical information about the procedure.

When individuals are paired into dyads, ambiguity aversion still persists at approximately the same level as it does when they are alone. It was Keller et al. (2007) who found these results by analyzing pairs' willingness to pay in risk and ambiguity scenarios. However, the authors expected that these pairs would be less ambiguity averse since they could have better rationalized the problem and, in addition, individual blame or regret would had been moderated in this case.

Heath and Tversky (1991) conducted experiments to determine whether the preference for decisions is restricted to situations of choice involving events with or without the knowledge of probability of success, or whether it was determined by the existence of personal beliefs based on the knowledge of the world. Contrary to the concept of ambiguity aversion, the authors observed that the individuals preferred to bet using their beliefs instead of known probabilities. Thus the result was opposite to the hypotheses of ambiguity aversion. This occurred because the theme that was evaluated in the experiments was the specialty of the participants, and therefore they felt competent and confident. In contrast, when the subject of the experiments was not their specialty, people betted on the option with the known probability. Thus Heath and Tversky show that when people's level of confidence is taken into consideration, the effect of ambiguity aversion disappears entirely.

Additionally, Mukerji (2000) complements Ellsberg's analysis by stating that an ambiguity-averse decision maker adjusts his/her decision cautiously depending on his/her knowledge of the probability distribution of an event. In this same paper, Mukerji analyzes the implications of ambiguity aversion in three economic areas: bilateral economic contracts, trade in financial contracts and financial markets, and strategic decision making of auctions.

Moore and Eckel (2003) introduce a new instrument for measuring ambiguity aversion. They propose to make known the probability distributions over the unknown parameter of the decision. In addition, ambiguity is included in each aspect of the gambling experiment: the probability, the outcome and both simultaneously. The authors find that individuals are ambiguity averse and that this aversion differs depending on whether the bet involves losses or gains. In the former case, ambiguity aversion is directly proportional to the location of this ambiguity, while in the latter it is rather the size of the ambiguity that is positively correlated with the aversion.

Ambiguity aversion is also of extreme importance in criminal processes. Segal and Stein (2006) affirm that the probability of defendant's conviction in a jury trial is ambiguous, and since the defendant is ambiguity averse, he/she will be exploited by the prosecution (who knows about this aversion), and be forced into a plea bargain, that is, an agreement in which the defendant pleads guilty in order to reduce the penalty. According to the authors, this bargain is both unfair and inefficient.

Illusion of Control

According to Taylor and Brown (1988), the illusion of control is defined as an unreal perception of a specific event. In their work they analyzed different forms of illusion, classifying them as unreal self-evaluation, exaggerated perceptions of control and unreal optimism. They reach the conclusion that the illusion of control is a false mental image or notion that can come from flawed analysis of something real or even something imagined by the individual.

A traditional concept of mental health states that the human being possesses conscience, accepting both the positive and negative aspects associated with their personal characteristics. However, empirical evidence suggests that the majority of the individuals have a positive self-evaluation (Greenwald, 1980), thus contradicting this traditional concept. When asked to indicate which are the positive and the negative aspects of their personality, the participants showed a lack of self-criticism by strongly believing that their positive aspects outweighed by far the negative ones. Additionally, Kuiper and MacDonald (1982) state that the majority of individuals assume that the positive information related to their personalities is efficiently processed and or more easily remembered, while the negative information is not as efficiently processed and not as easily remembered.

Empirical evidence presented by Lewinsohn et al. (1980) also confirms the existence of this personal overvaluation. In an experiment, high-school students had to elaborate a ranking including each student from the group and themselves with adjectives that represented their personalities (e.g. friendly, caring, kind, dedicated etc.). The results showed that the self-evaluations were almost always higher than the evaluations of colleagues. The authors concluded that individuals consider themselves better than the rest of the group.

A second type of illusion appears when the majority of individuals believe that they possess more control than they actually have, if they possess any at all, over random events.[3] For example, in familiar tasks, decision makers often feel overconfident that they can control the outcomes, even though this may not be the case.

The expression 'illusion of control' was employed by Langer and Roth (1975a, 1975b) in order to demonstrate, after performing a series of experiments, that people overestimate their capabilities in influencing events and simultaneously underestimate the role of probability when options are given to them. Langer and Roth (1975a, 1975b) define illusion of control as expected probability of personal success that is higher than the real probability of the event, this latter being determined by chance (luck). The authors show some of the motives that increase this sense of control in individuals, such as choice, familiarity with the tasks, competition and active involvement. For instance, agents believe that choosing their own numbers on a lottery ticket gives them a higher probability of winning than tickets with numbers already specified. After this initial study, other researchers also confirmed this tendency in which agents on average sense more control over a specific situation than they actually possess, making casual connections where none really exists.

Therefore 'illusion of control' is a term that refers to the belief that it is possible to manipulate outcomes of random events – in other words that people behave as if they can control an event when, in reality, they cannot. Examples of this are gamblers that offer an *ágio* for tickets with their preferred numbers, or the greater tendency to bet on 'heads or tails' when the coin has not been tossed, based on the equivocate idea that they can manipulate the result of an event that has not yet taken place (Thaler, 1992). Goffman (1967) demonstrates by an experiment that participants behave as if the outcomes of proposed situations are determined by their abilities and, therefore, that they have a certain control.

Fellner (2004) deliberates about illusion of control in individual portfolio allocations. The results show that many agents concentrate their portfolios on a few stocks, especially those whose outcome they think to they can control. However, another finding suggests that this effect of illusion of control seems to vanish with experience.

Presson and Benassi (1996) performed 53 illusions of control experiments and made a distinction between illusion of control and illusion of prediction. They found better results, in other words, a higher identification of the phenomenon in experiments that measured participants' perception concerning their ability to predict events than in experiments that measured their ability to control events. The authors pointed out: 'few experiments really measured illusion of control in the sense that the choices offered to the participants influenced and affected the results' (ibid., p. 496). However, a preference for control over events has also been observed. For example, there are some who believe that they would have more control if they threw the dice in a certain game than they would if someone else threw it.

Regarding young people, Moore and Ohtsuka (1998) show that the majority of them fantasized, incorrectly, that they could influence outcomes in gambling. One of the main motivators for young people to gamble is that they believe that it will provide the money they need, making them more vulnerable to these irrational beliefs.

The purpose of this work consists in testing both hypotheses of ambiguity aversion and illusion of control in a group of Brazilian students through experiments that simulate real decision-making situations under uncertainty. The experiments suggested in Charness and Gneezy (2003) were employed in order to test these two hypotheses, and the outcomes were compared with those found in the USA. Given the various cultural differences between Brazil and the USA, it is necessary to investigate whether the results will turn out to be similar. The next section gives details of the experiments that were run and the results that were obtained.

EXPERIMENTS AND EMPIRICAL RESULTS

Ambiguity Aversion

The ambiguity aversion experiments were performed in classes of the Catholic University of Brasília and of the University of Brasília. A total of 119 students participated in the sessions, each student participated only once in each experiment.

The students were asked not to contact each other so as not to bias the results. In each experiment, a sheet of paper was first given to each individual containing the instructions and a space in which to indicate their decisions/choices. The scenario forced students to take risk decisions. Thus they had to decide how much of their initial assets they would invest and how much they would keep for themselves. The risk investment presented a 50 percent chance of success, with a return of 2.5 percent over the investment. They were also informed that 10 percent of the participants would be chosen at random to receive payment in cash, according to the results of the investment.

The instructions of the five experiments related to the theme of ambiguity aversion are described briefly as follows:

- Experiment 1: two boxes containing 20 balls each were presented to the participants. Box A presented a known distribution (ten red balls and ten black balls) while box B presented an unknown distribution. The students were asked to choose a winning color (black or red), the percentage to be bet and the box from which the ball was to be extracted, without having to pay any cost for their choices.
- Experiment 2: only one box containing 20 balls (ten red balls and ten black balls) was presented to the participants. They had to choose a winning color (black or red), the percentage to be invested in the risk investment and, finally, they had to withdraw a ball.
- Experiment 3: only the box with unknown distribution was presented to the participants.
- Experiment 4: both boxes of experiment 1 were presented. However, the students had to pay 5 percent of their initial assets if they chose to withdraw the ball from the box that presented the known distribution.
- Experiment 5: students were asked whether they would prefer box A (known distribution) or box B (unknown distribution), and if they chose the box with a known

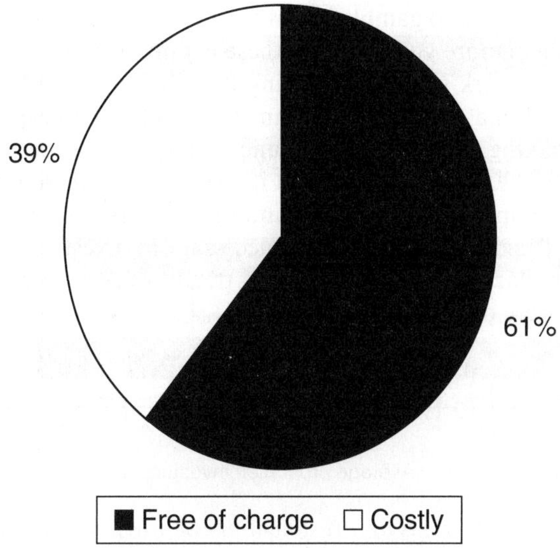

Figure 20.1 Ambiguity aversion: proportion of participants that chose box A in experiments 1 (free of charge) and 4 (costly)

distribution, they were asked to state the maximum amount they would be willing to pay to be allowed to do so.

In experiment 1, 17 out of 28 students chose box A, which corresponds 60.71 percent of the total. The binomial test of proportions which compares this proportion with the expected value of 50 percent is equal to 1.13, with a p-value of 0.13. In experiment 4, we verified that only nine out of 33 students, approximately one-third, of them, chose box A, which means that the majority was not willing to pay the price for a known distribution. The binomial test of randomness is equal to 2.61, with p-value of 0.0001, rejecting the hypotheses with a level of significance of 1 percent. Figure 20.1 presents the proportions of the participants who chose box A in experiments 1 and 4.

The binomial test of equal proportions between experiments 1 and 4 is equal to 2.63, with p-value of 0.004. Thus we reject the hypothesis in which the proportion of students that chooses box A is equal in both experiments. Thus the logical conclusion is that if the participants are averse to ambiguity, judging by experiment 1, they are not willing to pay a price to reduce the ambiguity in their risk decisions.

Figure 20.2 shows the proportions of assets invested in experiments 1, 2, 3 and 4 (80.71 percent, 77.00 percent, 53.55 percent and 66.34 percent, respectively). The comparison between experiments 1 and 4 suggests that the average proportions differ significantly (Wilcoxon–Mann–Whitney equal to 2.74, significant at the 1 percent level). There is no difference between experiments 1 and 2 (Wilcoxon–Mann–Whitney equal to 0.46). However, the difference between experiments 2 (known distribution – box A) and 3 (unknown distribution – box B) is significant (Wilcoxon–Mann–Whitney equal to 2.60, with p-value of 0.0091). This reduction was expected, since the invested proportions are significantly higher in the known distribution, indicating ambiguity aversion.

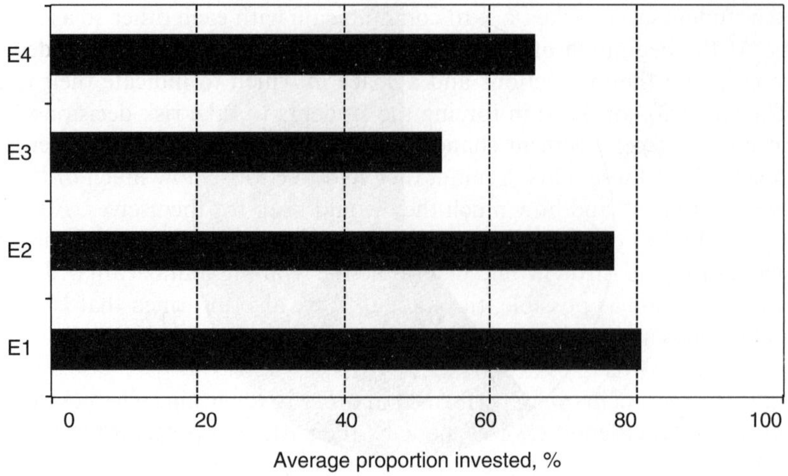

Figure 20.2 Average proportions of investment in risk investments 1, 2, 3 and 4

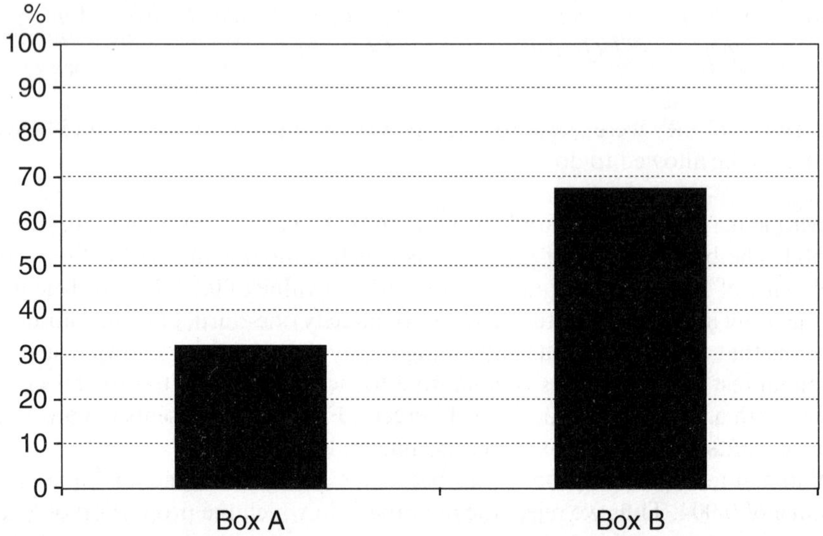

Figure 20.3 Proportion of participants that chose either box A or box B

Figure 20.3 shows the proportion of individuals that chose either box A or B in experiment 5. The results suggest that the majority of the students prefer box B compared with box A, indicating that many do not want to pay to avoid ambiguity.

Illusion of Control

The conditions for these are indicated to those of the ambiguity aversion experiment. A total of 129 students participated in the sessions, one student participating only once in each experiment.

Again the students were asked not to communicate with each other so as not to bias the results. At the beginning of each experiment, each individual was handed a sheet of paper containing the instructions and a space in which to indicate their decisions/choices. The scenario consisted in forcing the students to take risk decisions. The risk investment presented a 50 percent chance of success, with a return of 2.5 percent over the investment. With these odds in mind, they had to choose how much of their initial assets they would invest and how much they would keep for themselves. Additionally, the participants had to opt for three numbers out of six possible ones (numbers 1 to 6 on a dice) and only one throw would determine the winning number. In order to make the scenario as realistic as possible, the students were also informed that 10 percent of them would be chosen at random to receive payment in cash, according to the results of the investment.

Five different experiments were performed in order to determine whether there is illusion of control in the different choices made by the participants according to the different situations they faced. The instructions of these experiments are described briefly as follows:

- Experiment 6: the participants had to choose three numbers on a dice out of six possible numbers, the percentage to be invested in the risk investment and, finally, who would throw the dice, they or the instructor, without having to pay any cost for their choices.
- Experiment 7: as for experiment 6, but in this experiment the participants were forced to throw the dice.
- Experiment 8: as for experiment 6, except that in this experiment the instructor was to throw the dice.
- Experiment 9: besides the three winning numbers on a dice and the percentage to be invested, the participants also had to choose who would throw the dice, they or the instructor. However, in this case they had to pay 5 percent of their initial assets if they chose to throw the dice themselves.
- Experiment 10: this experiment is very similar with the last one. However, if respondents prefer to roll the dice themselves, then we asked the maximum amount they would be willing to pay to be allowed to do so.

It is possible to compare to what extent individuals are willing to exercise control by analyzing experiments 6 and 9, since in the former they can choose it freely and in the latter, they had to pay a charge for choosing to throw the dice themselves. In Figure 20.4 we present the percentage of participants who chose to throw the dice in both cases.

When participants may choose freely whether they prefer to throw the dice, that is, to exercise the preference for control, 14 out of 21, or 66.67 percent of the individuals, chose it. If they were indifferent, it was expected that 50 percent would opt to exercise the preference for control. The binomial test of proportion of students who chose to throw the dice is equal to 1.53, with a p-value of 0.06, suggesting that the null hypothesis that states that the proportion of participants that chooses to throw the dice is random can be rejected. On the other hand, when 5 percent of the initial assets is charged, the proportion of participants that chose to throw the dice fell drastically to four out of 34, which corresponds to 11.76 percent. In this case the binomial test is equal to –4.46, and the null

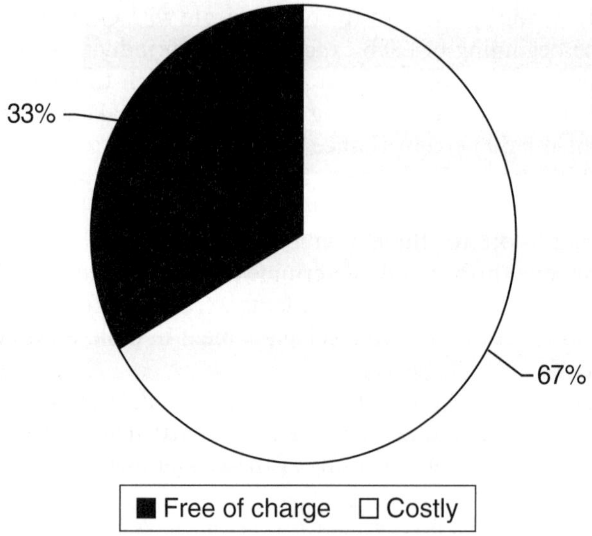

Figure 20.4 Preference for control: proportion of participants that chose to throw the dice themselves in experiments 6 and 9

hypotheses that states that the proportion is equal to 50 per cent can be rejected with a significance of 1 percent. Thus we can draw the conclusion that participants certainly have an illusion of control, but are not willing to pay a price to exercise that control as in the free-of-charge situation. The binomial test of equal proportions for experiments 6 and 9 is equal to 4.21, with a *p*-value of 0.0000, supporting this analysis.

In the test of equal mediums (Wilcoxon–Mann–Whitney), in the comparison of experiments 6 and 9, the statistic is equal to 1.424807, with *p*-value of 0.1542. Therefore the null hypothesis cannot be rejected, since participants appear to invest similar proportions in both experiments.

The first four experiments on illusion control are compared. Figure 20.5 shows the invested proportion in the risk investment of these tests.

As seen in Figure 20.5, there is considerable variation in the average proportion invested in the risk investment between the four experiments. For experiments 6 (free choice), 7 (investor throws dice), 8 (instructor throws dice) and 9 (choice with charge) the average proportions were equal to 76.43 percent, 68.38 percent, 57.86 percent and 87.95 percent, respectively.

Comparing experiment 7 (investor throws dice) with experiment 8 (instructor throws dice), we find that the null hypothesis in which the invested proportions in each experiment are statistically equal cannot be rejected (Mann–Whitney statistic is equal to 1.444367, with *p*-value of 0.1486). We had expected, however, that the proportion invested in the risk investment would be higher when individuals exercised control (in experiment 7).

In addition, the average invested proportions in experiments 8 and 9 are found to be statistically different (Wilcoxon–Mann–Whitney test equal to 3.73, with *p*-value equal to 0.0002).

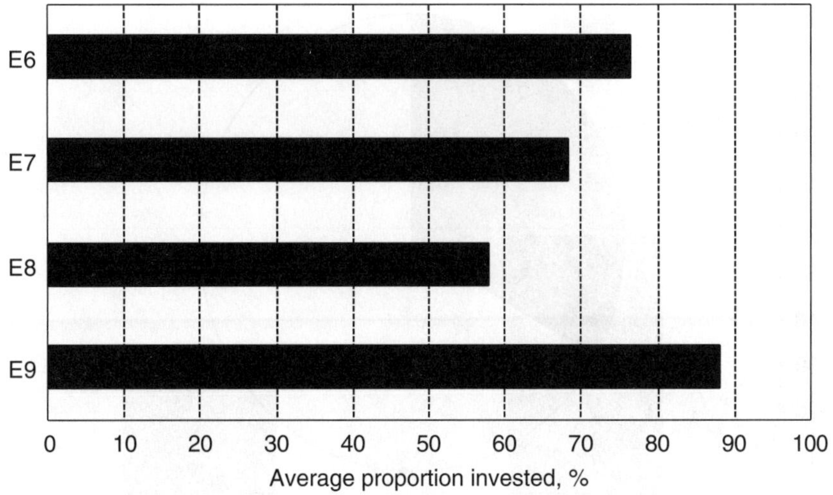

Figure 20.5 *Average invested proportions in experiments 6, 7, 8 and 9*

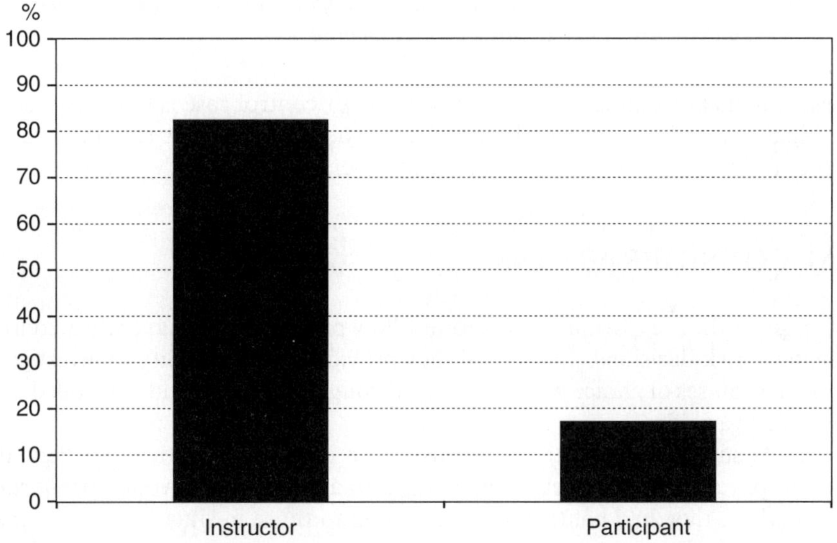

Figure 20.6 *Proportion of participants that prefer to roll the dice themselves or otherwise in experiment 10*

Lastly, in experiment 10, as seen in Figure 20.6, more than 80 percent of the participants preferred to let the instructor roll the dice, which means that they seem to be unwilling to pay a price to exercise control. In addition, although only a few people want to have control by rolling the dice, the maximum amount they are willing to pay is high (58, 75).

In the ambiguity aversion case, respondents are willing to sacrifice at most 27, 78 to be able to choose the box that has a known distribution. Therefore the maximum amount

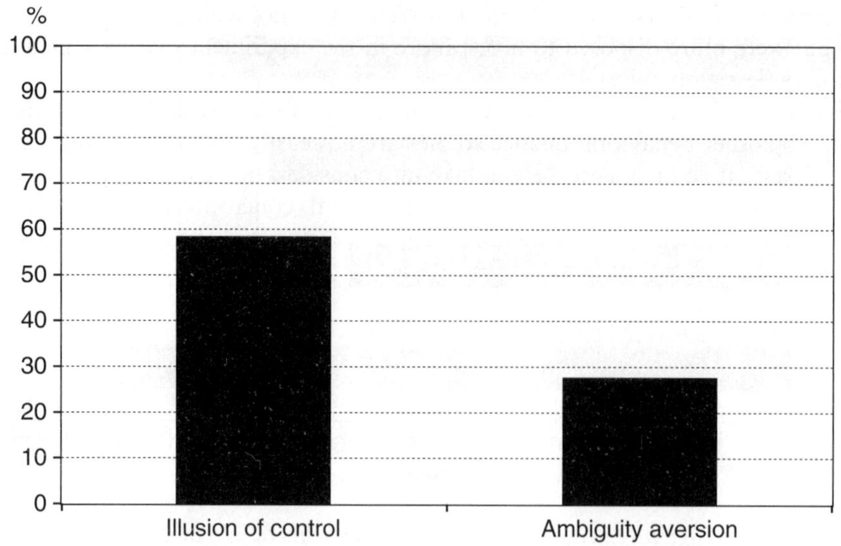

Figure 20.7 Average maximum amounts that participants are willing to pay to exercise control and to avoid ambiguity, respectively

that respondents are willing to pay in the illusion of control case is twice as much as in the ambiguity aversion case (see Figure 20.7). This suggests that respondents have a preference for control as opposed to ambiguity aversion.

FINAL CONSIDERATIONS

The purpose of these experiments was to test how participants behave when confronted with financial risk decisions, and indeed they provided the possibility to investigate this behavior. The biases of choice were identified through systematic and controlled changes of the studied variables.

The results suggest that participants possess an illusion of control, but they are not disposed to pay a price to exercise that control. In addition, the invested proportions in situations where they had control were compared to those in situations where they did not have control. The outcome contradicted the expectation, since it was found that the invested proportions were statistically equal in both situations.

By analogy, the participants were found to be ambiguity averse, but few were willing to pay a price to reduce or eliminate the ambiguity. However, as expected, the proportion invested was found to be higher when the probability of success was known.

It is worth noting that the individuals are willing to pay more for exercising control than for reducing ambiguity. A suggestion for future research is to investigate the causes of this preference.

Two behavioral differences were found in comparison to the study performed by Charness and Gneezy (2003): the students of the University of Chicago were willing to pay for less ambiguity; however, they invested equal proportions in situations with or without ambiguity. In contrast, Brazilian students were not willing to pay for less ambiguity, but were more disposed to invest more in the experiment that presented known probability (less ambiguity).

This chapter makes a contribution to the financial literature by showing that the results obtained by other behavioral finance studies are not easily obtained in other countries such as Brazil. It is, then, necessary to take into consideration cultural and social status differences, among others, before drawing general conclusions from experimental evidence. Future research should try to investigate the origins of such differences.

ACKNOWLEDGEMENTS

Benjamin M. Tabak gratefully acknowledges financial support from CNPQ Foundation. The opinions expressed in this chapter are those of the authors, and do not necessarily reflect those of the Banco Central do Brasil.

NOTES

1. The heuristic processes are formed by rules that are based on individual past experience or in the usual sense of a specific collectivity. They diverge from the methods based on the algorithmic search that result in optimum solutions after combining the problem with all the possible solutions for it (Sternberg et al., 2000).
2. According to Tversky and Kahneman (1974), people evaluate wrongly the probabilities of occurrence of uncertain events. The perception of conviction about an event may be easily manipulated, generating what the authors called pseudo-certainty (when individuals believe that a specific event has 10 percent or 0 percent chance of occurring). The effects of certainty and pseudo-certainty lead to inconsistencies of judgment. However, according to the theory of perspective, individuals attribute higher value to the perceived certainty or to the pseudo-certainty.
3. Several theories, including those of social psychology and psychoanalysis, propose that the sense of perception of control is directly related to self-esteem and overconfidence of individuals. Empirical evidence suggests that individuals' beliefs in personal control are normally greater than warranted.

REFERENCES

Benartzi, S. and R.H. Thaler (2002), 'How much is investor autonomy worth?,' *The Journal of Finance*, **57**, 1593–616.

Charness, C. and U. Gneezy (2003), 'Portfolio choice and risk attitudes: an experiment,' University of California at Santa Barbara, Economics Working Paper Series 1167.

Ellsberg, D. (1961), 'Risk, ambiguity and the Savage axioms,' *Quarterly Journal of Economics*, **75**, 643–69.

Fellner, G. (2004), 'Illusion of control as a source of poor diversification: an experimental approach,' Max Planck Institute of Economics, Strategic Interaction Group, Discussion Paper 28.

Fox, C. and A. Tversky (1995), 'Ambiguity aversion and comparative ignorance,' *Quarterly Journal of Economics*, **110**, 585–603.

Fox, C. and M. Weber (2002), 'Ambiguity aversion, comparative ignorance, and decision context,' *Organizational Behavior and Human Decision Processes*, **88**, 476–98.

Goffman, E. (1967), *Interaction Ritual: Essays on Face-to-Face interaction*, Oxford: Aldine.

Greenwald, B. (1980), 'Admissible rate bases and fair rates of return,' *Journal of Finance*, **35**, 359–68.

Grou, B. and B.M. Tabak (2008), 'Ambiguity aversion and illusion of control: experimental evidence in an emerging market,' *The Journal of Behavioral Finance*, **9** (1), 22–9.

Heath, C. and A. Tversky (1991), 'Preferences and belief: ambiguity and competence in choice under uncertainty,' *Journal of Risk and Uncertainty*, **4**, 5–28.

Huettel, S.A., C.J. Stowe, E.M. Gordon, B.T. Warner and M.L. Platt (2006), 'Neural signatures of economic preferences for risk and ambiguity,' *Neuron*, **49**, 765–75.

Keller, L. Robin, Rakesh K. Sarin and Jayavel Sounderpandian (2007), 'An examination of ambiguity aversion: are two heads better than one?,' *Judgment and Decision Making,* **2** (6), 390–97.

Keynes, J.M. (1921), *A Treatise on Probability*, London: Macmillan.

Knight, F. (1921), *Risk, Uncertainty and Profit*, Boston, MA: Houghton Mifflin.

Kuiper, N.A. and M.R. MacDonald (1982), 'Self and other perception in mild depressives,' *Social Cognition*, **1**, 233–39.

Langer, E.J. and J. Roth (1975a), 'The illusion of control,' *Journal of Personality and Social Psychology*, **32**, 311–28.

Langer, E.J. and J. Roth (1975b), 'Heads I win, tails it's chance: the illusion of control as a function of the sequence of outcomes,' *Journal of Personality and Social Psychology*, **32**, 951–5.

Lewinsohn, P.M., W. Mischel, W. Chaplin and B. Russell (1980), 'Social competence and depression: the role of illusory self-perceptions,' *Journal of Abnormal Psychology*, **89**, 203–12.

Moore, E. and C. Eckel (2003), 'Measuring ambiguity aversion,' AUM School of Business Working Paper 03-22.

Moore, S.M. and K. Ohtsuka (1998), 'Beliefs about control over gambling among young people, and their relation to problem gambling,' *Psychology of Addictive Behaviors*, **13**, 339–47.

Mukerji, S. (2000), 'A survey of some applications of the idea of ambiguity aversion in economics,' *International Journal of Approximate Reasoning*, **24**, 221–34.

Pech, W. and M. Milan (2009), 'Behavioral economics and the economics of Keynes,' *The Journal of Socio-Economics*, **38**, 891–902.

Presson, P. and V. Benassi (1996), 'Illusion of control: a meta-analytic review,' *Journal of Social Behavior and Personality*, **3**, 493–510.

Pulford, B.D. and A.M. Colman (2007), 'Ambiguous games: evidence for strategic ambiguity aversion,' *The Quarterly Journal of Experimental Psychology*, **60** (8), 1083–100.

Savage L. (1953), *The Foundations of Statistics*, New York: John Wiley & Sons.

Segal, U. and A. Stein (2006), 'Ambiguity aversion and the criminal process,' Cardozo Legal Studies Research Paper No. 142.

Shackle, G.L.S. (1955), *Uncertainty in Economics and Other Reflections*, Cambridge: Cambridge University Press.

Sternberg, R. J., G.B. Forsythe, J. Hedlund, J.A. Horvath, R.K. Wagner, W.M. Williams, S. Snook and E.L. Grigorenko (2000), *Practical intelligence in everyday life*, New York: Cambridge University Press.

Taylor, S.E. and J.D. Brown (1988), 'Illusion and well-being: a social psychological perspective on mental health,' *Psychological Bulletin*, **103**, 193–210.

Thaler, R. (1992), *The Winner's Curse: Paradoxes and Anomalies of Economic Life*, New York: Princeton University Press.

Thaler, R. (1994), *Quasi-Rational Economics*, New York: Russell Sage Foundation.

Thaler, R.H. and S. Mullainathan (2001) 'Behavioral economics,' *International Encyclopedia of Social Sciences*, New York: Pergamon Press, 1094–100.

Tomer, J.F. (2007), 'What is behavioral economics?,' *The Journal of Socio-Economics*, **36**, 463–79.

Tversky, A. (1972), 'Elimination by aspects: a theory of choice,' *Psychological Review*, **79**, 281–9.

Tversky, A. and D. Kahneman (1974), 'Judgment under uncertainty: heuristics and biases,' *Science*, **185**, 1124–31.

21 Behavioral finance in Malaysia

Ming-Ming Lai, Lee-Lee Chong and Siow-Hooi Tan

INTRODUCTION

This chapter describes and discusses past and future challenges in behavioral finance in Malaysia. The Malaysian stock market is not considered fully developed, as the investors can easily overreact to market rumors, economic development, and speculative political issues. Hence it is interesting to discover how Malaysian investors make investment decisions. Malaysia, an eminent market force, has drawn global attention and debate, particularly on the measures taken to counteract the 1997 Southeast Asian financial crisis and stock market crash. Back in 1997, *Business Times* (1997) described Kuala Lumpur Stock Exchange (currently known as Bursa Malaysia) as driven by rumor and strong herd mentality rules. Stock players herded together and acted the assumption that they needed to cut their losses and get out fast, just like everyone else. Ironically, facts and statistics were irrelevant. Toh (1997) described the Malaysian stock market scenario in 1997 as one in which both retail and institutional market players are not always rational. Investors are mainly guided by sentiment. Do investors improve their rationality over time? This chapter provides empirical evidence of investor behavior from various perspectives, ranging from investment practices to overreaction.

The background of the Malaysian stock market will be discussed next. Following this is an examination of the past empirical research on investment practices, investor behavior and the overreaction hypothesis, an application of the contrarian investment strategy of buying past loser stocks and selling past winners. We conclude with general remarks and challenges as well as future research opportunities.

BACKGROUND OF THE MALAYSIAN STOCK MARKET

The Stock Exchange of Malaysia was formed in 1964. Then, in 1965, with the secession of Singapore from Malaysia, this common stock exchange continued to function but as the Stock Exchange of Malaysia and Singapore (SEMS). With the termination of currency interchangeability between Malaysia and Singapore in 1973, the SEMS was separated into the Kuala Lumpur Stock Exchange Berhad (KLSEB) and the Singapore Stock Exchange (SSE). Malaysian companies continued to be listed on the SES and vice versa. The Kuala Lumpur Stock Exchange (KLSE) was set up in 1976 to take over the functions of the KLSEB, which was established on 2 July 1973 (KLSE, 1998).

From 1 January 1990, no Malaysian incorporated companies were allowed to be traded on the SSE and vice versa. At the same time, all Singapore incorporated companies were delisted from the KLSE. The KLSEB was incorporated under the Security Industry Act (SIA) enacted in 1973, which had been replaced by SIA (1983) in order to provide better supervision and control of the industry. From 1 March 1993, the

Securities Commission (SC) 'was mooted to problems of fragmented regulation of the capital market. The body is essentially an independent one-stop agency that has two main functions – as an approving body and as a policing body. It will be responsible for promoting Kuala Lumpur as a key financial centre in the region and to encourage the development of securities and financial futures markets in the country and to ensure orderly development of these markets' (Salleh, 1993, pp. 7–8).

In addition, the KLSE is also a self-regulatory organization with its own Memorandum and Articles of Association. Its own sets of rules govern the behavior of its members in securities dealings. It is responsible for the surveillance of the marketplace, and the enforcement of requirements with regard to the criteria for listing, disclosure requirements, and standards to be maintained by the listed companies. In 2006, KLSE had been listed as a public listed company from the demutualization process. To clarify the development of Bursa Malaysia, Table 21.1 presents selected statistics of total firms listed in the main and second board on the bourse, as well as their market capitalization from 1987 to 2008.

In 1993, four years before the financial crisis, the Malaysian stock market was experiencing bullish conditions and stock-chasing behavior. The extreme market performance can be seen from the percentage price changes gained in the sectors in the Malaysian stock market in 1993. Mansor (1994) reported that the top average returns gained in 1993 in the KLSE were in the mining sector (680 percent), followed by stockbroking companies within the finance sector (592 percent), plantation sector (442 percent), and trusts sector (373 percent). Some stocks had even experienced a gain of more than 1000 percent, which indicated that the prices had jumped by more than ten times over the year. Some stocks had exhibited capital gains of less than 10 percent, however. As a whole, only one stock experienced a capital loss. On the other hand, investors threw caution to the wind, although investment managers expressed concerns over investors' fanatical level of activity; they also continued that the continuing upward trend might be based on speculation and rumors (Phoon, 1993). True enough, in 1994, the bullish conditions dissipated.

BEHAVIORAL FINANCE: A REVIEW

A few studies had been conducted to find out more about the investment practices of investors in general in Malaysia prior to the 1997 financial crisis. Osman (1988) had conducted a survey of 477 Malaysian investors on investment behaviour via personal interviews with them at stockbroking companies. The results showed that almost 70 percent of investors were Chinese, followed by 24 percent of Malays and 7 percent of Indians. A majority of investors started their investments with RM10 000 (or US$2850) and increased the amount of investments over time. Investors searched for information and used several methods of analysis before making investment decisions.

Mansor and Lim (1995) conducted a survey in Kuala Lumpur and Petaling Jaya areas in Malaysia, with a total of 192 questionnaires collected on investors' behavior and investment practices. Male respondents accounted for 72.8 percent; female respondents for 27.2 percent. Consistent with earlier results of Osman (1988), Chinese investors made up 75 percent of the respondents, followed by Malays (19 percent) and

Table 21.1 Selected statistics of Bursa Malaysia from 1987 to 2008

Year	Kuala Lumpur Composite Index	Total firms listed on the KLSE			Market capitalization) (RM billion)	Total[a] turnover (million units)	Turnover (daily average)[a] million units	Total[a] Turnover (RM million)
		Main board	Second board	Total firms				
1987	261.19	291	–	291	75.27	5286	22	10077
1988	357.38	295	–	295	98.72	4005	16	6760
1989	562.28	305	2	307	155.87	10162	42	18535
1990	505.92	271	14	285	131.02	13138	54	29522
1991	556.22	292	32	324	161.30	12348	50	30097
1992	643.96	317	52	369	245.78	19265	78	51469
1993	1275.32	329	84	413	619.60	107756	433	387276
1994	971.21	347	131	478	508.90	60143	243	328057
1995	995.17	369	160	529	565.60	33979	140	178859
1996	1237.96	413	208	621	786.90	66461	268	463265
1997	594.44	444	264	708	376.16	72799	294	408558
1998	586.13	454	282	736	374.52	58287	237	115181
1999	812.33	474	283	757	503.17	85157	343	185250
2000	679.64	498	297	795	444.35	75409	280	244054
2001	696.09	520	292	812	464.98	49663	204	85012
2002	646.32	562	294	856	481.62	55630	224	116951
2003	793.94	598	276	874	640.28	112183	456	183886
2004	907.43	622	278	900	722.04	107610	437	215623
2005	899.79	646	268	914	695.27	102338	414	177321
2006	1096.24	649	250	899	848.70	197509	803	250641
2007	1445.03	636	227	863	1106.15	360370	1548	540173
2008	876.75	634	221	855	663.80	141005	630	289250

Note:
[a] Since 1995, includes turnover of call warrants.
RM = Malaysian ringgit.

Source: Kuala Lumpur Stock Exchange (2000), http://www.klse.com.my/website/listing/totallc.htm (klse), access 26 December 2000.
Bank Negara Malaysia (2009) 'Bank Negara Quarterly Statistical Bulletin 2009', http://www.bursamalaysia.com/website/bm/listed_companies/ipos/listing_statistics.html, accessed 7 July 2009.

Indians (6 percent). The Chinese appeared dominant and active in stock market investments. The results indicated that 73 percent of investors speculated and were profit-taking in the bullish market. During this time they traded shares based on tips, rumors, or just picked stocks at random. About 32 percent of respondents used fundamental analysis but only 16 percent adopted technical analysis. Some investors used more than one method of analysis. Interestingly, the investors behaved slightly different in the bear market. About 52 percent of these investors would resort to fundamental analysis in bearish periods and look for long-term profits. Similarly, the use of technical analysis had increased from 16 percent to 26 percent during the bearish period. The dividend appeared to be the more important factor in investment decision in the bearish period than in the bullish period.

Lai et al. (2001) sent the questionnaires in May 1999 to the investment or research manager of companies that had professional dealings with stock market investments. Their study examined the investor behavior during bullish and bearish periods, as well as investors' reactions toward important events in Malaysia from 1998 to 1999. About 77 completed questionnaires were used; the actual response rate for the study was 13.75 percent (77/560). Personal interviews with some respondents were conducted to gain more insight into the reasons behind their financial decisions. The respondents consisted of 18 chief executive officers or general managers, 15 investment or research managers, four research analysts, three corporate dealers, and 36 with positions such as director, corporate treasurer, corporate finance manager, and executives in managerial positions.

Table 21.2 reports the mean and standard deviation of the importance of external factors in making investment decisions during both bullish and bearish markets. No clear differences in terms of importance of external market factors in investment decisions during the bullish and bearish markets were observed. The results showed that interest rate movements and growth rate of GDP are the two most important factors overall. The rationale behind this is that stock prices and interest rates were found to have a negative relationship; hence they move inversely. The respondents, like other investors, have shown concern over the increase (decrease) of interest rates which may cause stock prices to drop (rise). On the other hand, political news such as the 1999 national election, the annual meeting of the Barisan Nasional party, the current ruling party in the country, ranked third with a mean of 3.77. The institutional investors indicated that politics in Malaysia is an important factor, as well as the ringgit peg issue. Malaysia implemented capital control measures on 1 September 1998 to curb the financial and currency crisis that was triggered in mid-July 1997 (RM3.80). The ringgit was pegged with US$1.00 as one of the capital control measures (Yap, 1999; Lai et al., 2001).

Although the Malaysian stock market is perceived as rumor-driven, rumor factors reported a mean score of 3.05 and 2.82, ranking lowest among the external market factors during bullish and bearish markets, respectively. Malaysian institutional investors demonstrate their rationale in that they disregard rumors in their investment decision making despite being surrounded by rumors in the stock market (Lai et al., 2001).

Table 21.2 also presents the mean and standard deviation evaluations of the world stock market performance of institutional investors in making investment decisions. The Dow Jones Industrial Average performance seems to have the most impact on Malaysian stock markets for both bullish and bearish markets. It reflects that when Wall Street sneezes, the Malaysian stock market catches a cold. Surprisingly, respondents are

Table 21.2 The importance of factors in the fundamental analysis during both bullish and bearish markets

External Factors	Mean* (bullish)	Std dev.* (bullish)	Mean* (bearish)	Std dev.* (bearish)
Interest rate movement	4.0130	1.0698	4.3117	1.0420
Growth rate of GDP	3.8961	0.9540	4.0519	0.9445
Political news	3.7662	0.8720	3.8052	0.9324
Inflation rate	3.6447	0.9758	3.7662	0.9583
Foreign reserve fund	3.6316	0.8921	3.7662	0.9854
Trade surplus/deficit	3.5455	0.9535	3.6753	0.9520
Exchange rate	3.4675	0.9812	3.6623	1.0464
Unemployment rate	3.3117	0.9070	3.5195	0.9121
Gut feeling	3.0779	1.0484	2.8312	1.1169
Rumors	3.0519	1.0748	2.8182	1.0970
World stock market performance				
Dow Jones	3.8052	0.9464	3.8571	0.9278
Hong Kong Stock Exchange	3.3987	0.8282	3.3766	0.8742
Singapore Stock Exchange	3.2597	0.8176	3.3247	0.8802
Tokyo Stock Exchange	3.2468	0.8608	3.3158	0.8976
London Stock Exchange	3.0130	0.7863	3.0649	0.8325

Note: * Respondents evaluated the importance of the above factors in investment decision making on a scale of 1 (strongly disagree) to 5 (strongly agree).

Source: Lai et al. (2001), p. 212.

indifferent to the London Stock Exchange performance, despite the fact that Malaysia was a British colony (Lai et al., 2001).

Lai et al. (2001) showed that 88.31 per cent and 94.81 percent respondents of the survey used fundamental analysis during bullish and bearish markets, respectively. On the other hand, 67.53 percent and 57.14 percent respondents employed technical analysis during bullish and bearish markets, respectively. Fundamental analysis appears to be the most popular type used among all analyses.

Lai et al. (2001) concluded that investors in Malaysia were much more rational than previously believed. This rationality can also be seen from the survey results in which respondents were asked to indicate the importance on a five-point scale and their reactions to the imprisonment of Anwar Ibrahim, former deputy prime minister of Malaysia, in their survey conducted in 1999. The survey results indicated a mean value of 2.87 for its importance and minimal change in the investors' holdings pertaining to the imprisonment of Anwar Ibrahim in 1999, despite several street demonstrations that were held. Malaysian prime minister at that time, Datuk Seri Mahathir Mohamed, who was also first finance minister, stated that the majority of market players were aware of the situation in which the investors knew and understood the government ability to deal with the imprisonment. No investors sold shares as a result of this political turmoil (*Business Times*, 1998).

The street demonstrations in Kuala Lumpur over the six-year jail term for Anwar

Ibrahim might have caused a short-term pause, but would not have much impact on the medium- or long-term portfolio flows to the country (*Business Times*, 1999). Likewise, Tam (1999) indicated that the KLSE rose another 31.31 points in the week when the six-year jail term announced. The factors that triggered revival in the KLSE was Bank Negara Malaysia's cuts in the intervention rate and favourable comments received from Standard & Poor's and Morgan Stanley on the Malaysian economy. On 8 August 2000, Anwar Ibrahim was sentenced for a further nine years for other criminal activities in which a brokerage house dealer commented that the verdict of Anwar's trial had been discounted by the market. The Malaysian stock market closed lower in a very thin trade on that day. There was little impact of the verdict by which it could possibly have an impact on the market (*AFX-Asia*, 2000).

About a decade later, Ibrahim was charged with sodomy (*South China Morning Post*, 2009). On 28 August 2008, he rejoined Parliament after a decade's absence. He was appointed as opposition leader and the leader of the Pakatan Rakyat, taking over the position from Datuk Wan Azizah, his wife (Wikipedia, 2009). The Pakatan Rakyat was established on 1 April 2008 and currently has 82 of the 222 seats in Parliament as from the last general election on 8 March 2008. Since then, political stability in Malaysia has deteriorated significantly. The foreign fund managers expressed concerns and were hesitant to invest in Malaysia because of political uncertainties since the election. Foreign fund managers continued to underweight and cut their exposure in Malaysia. The local political uncertainties have now become one of the main risks that hinder foreign investment or investors, in particular (*New Straits Times*, 2008, *The Irish Times*, 2008).

The earlier results of Lai et al. (2001) had indicated that institutional investors appeared to be rational despite being surrounded by rumors. So, did Malaysian investors overreact?[1] Can contrarian investment strategies be used successfully? Several past studies conducted on the Malaysian stock market may provide some insights.

Zamri and Hussain (2001) had conducted a study of long-run overreaction and seasonal effects on the Malaysian stock market for the period 1986–1996. They found that price reversal patterns of Malaysian stocks and two and three years of contrarian investment strategies were recommended.

Lai et al. (2003a, 2003b) had examined short- and long-term overreaction in the Malaysian stock market from January 1987 to December 1999. They also examined both the short- and long-term overreaction hypothesis, an application of the contrarian investment strategy during both bullish (January to December 1993) and bearish (July 1997 to June 1999) periods.

Lai et al. (2003a) conducted a comprehensive examination of investors' long-run overreaction by integrating firm size, time-varying risks and source of profits on the monthly returns of all stocks listed in the main board of the Malaysian stock market from January 1987 to December 1999. They found long-run overreaction in both models with and without controlling for firm size. The results suggest the one- to two-year contrarian strategy of buying loser stocks and selling winner stocks. The evidence also indicates that the contrarian profits gained are mainly due to the overreaction factor rather than firm size effect and time-varying risk. Nonetheless, the overreaction of the loser portfolios was more apparent in smaller firms than in larger firms after controlling for firm size.

Lai et al. (2003b) further examined the short-term overreaction with and without controlling for firm size in the KLSE from January 1987 to December 1999. They tested

Table 21.3 The summary of CARs of short- and long-run contrarian investment

Stock market performance	(Rank period) portfolio formation	Test period 3-month (average)	Test period 6-month (average)	Test period 12-month (average)	Test period 24-month (average)
Bullish period					
Loser portfolio	−ve	+ve	+ve	+ve	+ve
Winner portfolio	+ve	+ve	+ve	+ve	+ve
Loser-winner portfolio	−ve	+/(−)ve*	+/(−)ve*	+/(−)ve*	+/(−)ve*
Normal period**					
Loser portfolio	−ve	+ve	+ve	+ve	+ve
Winner portfolio	+ve	−ve	−ve	−ve	−ve
Loser-winner portfolio	−ve	+ve	+ve	+ve	+ve
Bearish period					
Loser portfolio	−ve	−ve	−ve	−ve	−ve
Winner portfolio	+ve	−ve	−ve	−ve	−ve
Loser-winner portfolio	−ve	+/(−)ve*	+/(−)ve*	+/(−)ve*	+/(−)ve*

Notes:
* Two possibilities of CARs earned in test periods.
The value depends on the magnitude of CARs earned by loser portfolio versus winner portfolio, respectively.
The arbitrage portfolio (loser–winner portfolio) implies selling winner portfolio and buying loser portfolio.
** Normal period means a normal market condition, which is not a bullish or bearish period.
+ve denotes positive CARs, −ve denotes negative CARs.

Source: Lai et al. (2003b), p. 84.

3-, 6-, and 12-month contrarian investment strategies besides a 24-month contrarian investment strategy (see Table 21.3). The findings indicate evidence in favor of the contrarian investment strategy, with significant return reversal patterns for both winner and loser portfolios during normal market periods. However, during the bullish and bearish periods, the results indicate evidence of price continuation and contraction respectively for both winner and loser portfolios.

The finding that the contrarian investment strategy did not work well during both bullish and bearish periods raises more questions. Why was there an anomaly among anomalies? What is the cause of this phenomenon? A review and thorough examination of the Malaysian investment environment and investor psychology during both the bullish and bearish periods may provide plausible explanations and offer new insights into the value of contrarian investment. Table 21.3 presents a summary of the findings of cumulative average abnormal returns (CARs) of short-run contrarian investment during the bullish, bearish and normal periods in the Malaysian stock market.

High investor confidence and strong buying sentiment pushing the prices of all stocks to the next high are usually the scenario of a bullish period. Investors tend to be more confident, and this makes them more eager to take more risks and aim for higher capital gains. The bullish market stimulates investors' egos and consequently investors tend to disregard the fundamentals of the stocks as well as any cautions that stock prices may be overvalued or overbought. They also overreact to the bullish information and believe that the upward trend of stock prices will persist. In other words, winner (loser) stocks will persist in being winner (loser) stocks. Hence the contrarian investment strategy involving selling past winner stocks and buying past loser stocks would be fairly difficult to implement (Lai et al., 2003b).

Jomo (1998) indicated that the Asian financial crisis was partly due to herd behavior. Being in a herd can help investors to share the blame for their mistakes. Investors follow others in their actions, including investment decisions. A contrarian investment strategy would be difficult to implement in a herding environment.

Generally, weak market performances and adverse news surrounding the stock market tends to drive stock prices down. The fear of losing money makes investors sell stocks. Hence heavy selling pressure pushes down prices of stocks, including winner stocks. If investors implement a contrarian investment strategy by selling past winner stocks and buying past loser stocks in a bullish market, this would be questioned by friends and colleagues. This is because such an investor is missing profit opportunities by selling winner stocks early when their prices are on the way up. On the other hand, an investor would look even more foolish if he/she sold past winner stocks and bought past loser stocks in a bearish market. How can loser stocks reverse and perform well in a declining market? Hence herd behavior and social comparison may explain why a contrarian investment strategy may not work during bullish and bearish periods (Cassidy, 1999; Lai et al., 2003b).

FUTURE CHALLENGES AND CONCLUSION

Overall, even though investors in Malaysia showed a high level of overconfidence, they acquired good self-control and were not driven by herd behavior as they always referred to both fundamental and portfolio analysis before making investment decisions. This suggests that Malaysian institutional investors behave more rationally no matter under what the market conditions. Malaysian institutional investors also disregarded rumors and analyzed the market before investing.

In a nutshell, our reviews imply a rational behavior of Malaysian investors in the investment decision-making process. Our understanding of investor behavior and the decision process, however, remains incomplete. A challenge that remains is to examine the effect of each behavioral trait on the investment decision process and investment returns. Research could also be done on the connections between behavioral characteristics, for example, the interrelations of overconfidence and herd behavior, to gain a better understanding of investor behavior as the interactions of these behavior traits may produce effects of different magnitude and/or direction on rational behavior in the decision-making process. Besides, future research of investor behavior in Malaysia could also examine other personality profiles and institutional characteristics of investors.

ACKNOWLEDGEMENT

The authors are grateful for financial support received from the Multimedia University.

NOTE

1. De Bondt and Thaler (1985) examined the monthly returns of stocks listed on the NYSE from January 1926 to December 1982. Winner–loser anomaly (overreaction hypothesis) refers to the strategy of purchasing past loser stocks that performed badly and selling winner stocks that had performed well. Investors overreact to the information in the stock market by overweighting the most recent information and underweighting earlier information. In subsequent periods, the prices of winner (loser) stocks will be corrected down (up) to their fundamental values when the investors realize that they have overreacted to recent information. By buying losers and selling winners, investors will able to earn above-average profits. This is because the past losers will become future winners and current winners will become future losers. The results documented that the loser portfolio tended to outperform the past winner portfolio after 36 months of portfolio formation. The returns earned by the loser portfolio were 25 percent higher than those of the winner portfolio. This reflected the overreaction phenomenon in the stock market, where price reversal patterns were found. In addition, the reversal patterns occurred during the second and the third year of the test period. It should be noted that the overreaction effect was asymmetric, in that the loser portfolio on average yielded 19.6 percent higher than the winner portfolio with −5 percent on average. De Bondt and Thaler (1987) provided further evidence of this overreaction by examining the firm size and risk factors in explaining the overreaction hypothesis. The results provided evidence in favor of the overreaction hypothesis.

REFERENCES

AFX-Asia (2000), 'Kuala Lumpur shares close lower in thin trade; no leads to spur market,' 9 August.

Bank Negara Malaysia (2009) 'Bank Negara Quarterly Statistical Bulletin 2009,' http://www.bursamalaysia.com/website/bm/listed_companies/ipos/listing_statistics.html, accessed 7 July 2009.

Business Times (Malaysia) (1997), 'Discarding the herd mentality,' 21 November, p. 4.

Business Times (1998), 'Anwar's actions will not affect economy: Mahathir,' 23 September, p. 1.

Business Times (1999), 'UK, Singapore players: foreign funds returning to KL,' 15 April, p. 2.

Cassidy, D.L. (1999), *When the Dow Breaks*, New York: McGraw-Hill.

DeBondt, W.F.M. and R.H. Thaler (1985), 'Does the stock market overreact?,' *Journal of Finance*, **40** (3), 793–805.

DeBondt, W.F.M. and R.H. Thaler (1987), 'Further evidence on investor overreaction and stock market seasonality,' *Journal of Finance*, **42** (3), 557–82.

The Irish Times (2008), 'Anwar pleads not guilty to "malicious" sodomy charge,' 8 August, p. 11.

Jomo, Kwame Sundaram (ed.) (1998), *Tigers in Trouble: Financial Governance, Liberalisation and Crises in East Asia*, Hong Kong: Hong Kong University Press. http://www.klse.com.my/website/trdgstlm/howtotrd.htm, accessed 8 Nov 2000.

KLSE (Kuala Lumpur Stock Exchange) (1998), *Information Book*, Kuala Lumpur: Kuala Lumpur Stock Exchange.

Lai, M.M., K.L.T. Low and M.L. Lai (2001), 'Are Malaysian investors rational?,' *Journal of Psychology and Financial Markets*, **2** (4), 210–15.

Lai, M.M., K.G. Balachandher and M.N. Fauzias (2003a), 'Do Malaysian investors overreact?,' *The Journal of American Academy of Business*, **2** (2), 602–9.

Lai, M.M., K.G. Balachandher and M.N. Fauzias (2003b), 'Investor psychology and contrarian investment: a Malaysian perspective,' *Multimedia Cyberscape Journal*, **1**, 183–215.

Mansor, M.I. (1994), '1993 top rated sectors,' *Investors Digest*, April, pp. 10–11.

Mansor, M.I. and C.F. Lim (1995), 'Profile of individual investors in the Klang area,' *Capital Market Review*, **3**, 1–15.

New Straits Times (2008), 'Malaysia 'attractive' but fund managers wary,' 5 August, p. 37.

Osman, M.Z. (1988), 'The study of the extent of knowledge and usage of investment technique on the KLSE individual investors (translated),' *Jurnal Pengurusan*, **6 & 7**, 21–34.

Phoon, Z. (1993), 'Tread warily in the market,' *Investors Digest*, May, p. 49.

Salleh, M. (1993), 'The Malaysian capital market – new rules of the game,' *Capital Market Review*, **1** (1), 1–21.

South China Morning Post (2009), 'Malaysia's reputation at risk as new sodomy trial looms,' 7 July, p. 9.

Tam, F. (1999), 'Composite index likely to test 621 level next week,' *New Straits Times*, 17 April, p. 6.

Toh, E. (1997), 'Will stock market players give DR a break?,' *Business Times* (Singapore), 19 May, p. 21.

Wikipedia (2009), 'Pakatan rakyat,' http://en.wikipedia.org/wiki/Pakatan_Rakyat, accessed 5 August 2009.
Yap, L.K. (1999), 'Ringgit controls,' *The Star*, September.
Zamri, A. and S. Hussain (2001), 'KLSE long run overreaction and the Chinese New-Year effect,' *Journal of Business Finance and Accounting*, **28** (1–2), 63−105.

Index